THE

CATHOLIC

TRADITION

THE CHURCH

—— in the ——

TWENTIETH CENTURY

THE CATHOLIC TRADITION

THE CHURCH —— in the —— TWENTIETH CENTURY

REVISED and EXPANDED
SECOND EDITION

TIMOTHY G. McCARTHY

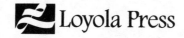 Loyola Press

 Loyola Press

3441 North Ashland Avenue
Chicago, Illinois 60657

Library of Congress Cataloging-in-Publications Data
McCarthy, Timothy G., 1929-
    The Catholic tradition: the church in the twentieth century/Timothy
G. McCarthy.—Rev. and expanded 2nd ed.
        p.   cm.
    Includes bibliographical references and index.
    ISBN 0-8294-0971-8
    1. Catholic Church—History—20th century. 2. Vatican Council (2nd:
1962-1965) 3. Modernism—Catholic Church. 4. Catholic Church—Doctrines—History—20th century. I. Title.
BX1389.M38 1998
282'.09'04—dc21   97-36980
                                                            CIP

99 00 01 / 10 9 8 7 6 5 4 3 2

Table of Contents

Abbreviations

Throughout this book, letters abbreviated in parentheses identify the sixteen documents of Vatican II by their abbreviated Latin title and paragraph number.

AA   *Apostolicam actuositatem:* Decree on the Apostolate of the Laity

AG   *Ad gentes:* Decree on the Church's Missionary Activity

CD   *Christus Dominus:* Decree on the Bishops' Pastoral Office in the Church

DH   *Dignitatis humanae:* Declaration on Religious Freedom

DV   *Dei verbum:* Dogmatic Constitution on Divine Revelation

GE   *Gravissimum educationis:* Declaration on Christian Education

GS   *Gaudium et spes:* Pastoral Constitution on the Church in the Modern World

IM   *Inter mirifica:* Decree on the Instruments of Social Communication

LG   *Lumen gentium:* Dogmatic Constitution on the Church

NA   *Nostra aetate:* Declaration on the Relationship of the Church to the Non-Christian Religions

OE   *Orientalium ecclesiarum:* Decree on Eastern Catholic Churches

OT   *Optatam totius:* Decree on Priestly Formation

PC   *Perfectae caritatis:* Decree on the Appropriate Renewal of Religious Life

PO   *Presbyterorum ordinis:* Decree on the Ministry and Life of Priests

SC   *Sacrosanctum concilium:* Constitution on the Sacred Liturgy

UR   *Unitatis redintegratio:* Decree on Ecumenism

OTHER ABBREVIATIONS

Acts	*Acts of the Apostles*
AIDS	Acquired Immune Deficiency Syndrome
BEM	*Baptism, Eucharist and Ministry*
CCC	*Catechism of the Catholic Church*
CDF	Congregation for the Doctrine of the Faith
CDWS	Congregation for Divine Worship and the Sacraments
CFFC	Catholics for a Free Choice
CTSA	Catholic Theological Society of America
HIV	Human Immunodeficiency Virus
LCWR	Leadership Conference of Women Religious
NARW	National Assembly of Religious Women
NCC	National Council of Churches
NOW	National Organization of Women
PBC	Pontifical Biblical Commission
RCIA	Rite of Christian Initiation of Adults
SCRIS	Sacred Congregation for Religious and Secular Institutes
USSR	Union of Soviet Socialist Republics
WCC	World Council of Churches
WATER	Women's Alliance for Theology, Ethics and Ritual
WOC	Women's Ordination Conference

Preface to the First Edition

Several years ago the religious studies faculty at St. Mary's College of California reorganized its course offerings. We instituted a four-course sequence which offered our students a coherent, chronological and ecumenical understanding of "the one and only church of Christ" (UR 24) from Jesus to the present. I took on the fourth course, The Twentieth Century Church and the Challenge of Modernity.

There were no books that covered this history in a way in which the students could appreciate it and as I understood it. After using chapters of books and magazine articles for several semesters, I decided to write my own text. The present book was used in manuscript form by 180 students during the spring semesters of 1991, 1992, and 1993. I am grateful to the students for their patience and interest; their challenging questions helped me to rewrite each edition.

This book could be used in a classroom setting. Nonetheless, I hope it will reach a wider audience of adult Christians. The book does not have a textbook format. Since it has an ecumenical perspective, I believe it can be helpful to all Christians, especially those interested in the institutional, intellectual, and devotional developments within the Catholic community.

Vatican II is the pivotal point of the history of the Catholic church in the twentieth century. I cite the conciliar documents extensively, using a text edited in 1966 by Walter M. Abbott, a Jesuit scholar. This text does not use inclusive language. Nevertheless, I retain this edition because it captures the style and ethos of the conciliar period. Readers who prefer inclusive language should make their own adjustments as they read along.

In addition to my students' responses, I received help and encouragement from many colleagues and friends, much too many to name. However, I would be remiss if I did not acknowledge the special insights and encouragement of Margaret Duffner, Odile Dwyer, and Honey O'Leary. John C. Dwyer, theologian, author, a former colleague, and true friend, provided invaluable theological and technical assistance with the organization and production of the manuscript.

I am most grateful to the staff of Loyola Press for their gracious assistance: to Joseph F. Downey, Jesuit priest, historian, and editorial director for taking on this project; to Jeremy Langford, editor, who, with his associates, gave the manuscript a meticulous review and proposed many positive changes.

The most help came from my wife, Virginia. This book could not have been written without her support, patience, and love. With deep affection and gratitude, I dedicate this book to Virginia.

Introduction to the First Edition

The twentieth-century Catholic church has undergone startling shifts and developments in theology, spirituality, and demography. Concerning the latter, for example, approximately 77 percent of Catholics lived in Europe and North America in 1900, and 23 percent in what is now known as the third world. In 1990, 70 percent of Catholics were in the third world and 30 percent in Europe and North America. This book is a thematic history of the major events, issues, and concerns that shaped, and often defined the church and the Catholic tradition before and after Vatican II.

There are several ways to write institutional, intellectual, and devotional history. This book focuses on significant events such as the rise of modernity and the loss of the Papal States, and important personalities, particularly the popes, bishops, and theologians. The popes and bishops, called the hierarchical magisterium, are the official teachers in the church; the theologians, called the scholarly magisterium, seek to understand, interpret, and teach the faith. The popes and bishops lead the theologians; sometimes the popes and bishops learn from the theologians as they aid in explaining, correcting, and refining their teachings. Often both sets of teachers are in tension, even serious disagreement and distrust. Nonetheless, both work toward a common goal: to foster, under the inspiration of the Spirit, the faith, hope, and love of the disciples of Christ in the concrete conditions of their daily lives. This is called spirituality.

This study begins with the pontificate of Leo XIII (1878–1903) and traces his influence and that of his eight successors on the church and society. Vatican II (1962–65), the decisive ecclesial event of the century, is the pivotal point of the story. There were theologies and spiritualities before and during the council—and since. I report on these, but occasionally I go beyond reporting to personally evaluate and challenge some of them.

In the first three chapters, I introduce the popes, explain the concept of modernity, and report on Vatican II. These chapters form the background for the remaining eight chapters which investigate the issues that received the greatest attention at Vatican II: the identity and mission of the church, authority, ecumenism, interreligious dialogue, liturgy, social justice, sexual morality, and Mary. There are no chapters about such important topics as christology, feminist theology, atheism, religious orders, and religious education because these did not receive sustained attention during the council. Nevertheless, throughout this book I frequently refer to these important topics, especially feminist issues.

Introduction to the Second Edition

The first edition had eleven chapters, most of which included feminist themes. This edition includes an additional chapter: Women in the Postconciliar Church. The first edition ended with the visit of John Paul II to the Baltic States in September 1993, his sixty-first overseas pilgrimage. This edition ends on September 5, 1997 (see p. 42). During this four year period several important events took place within the church that have had an impact on its identity and mission: there was an international synod of bishops on consecrated life, the pope issued two encyclicals, one on ecumenism and the other on morality, the Vatican promulgated a firmly-worded instruction banning the priestly ordination of women, Tissa Balasuriya, a seventy-two-year-old Sri Lankan priest-theologian, was formally excommunicated, and John Paul made eighteen overseas visits. In June 1997 he made a ten-day tour of his native Poland. This was his seventy-eighth international visit and his seventh to his native country as pope. In August 1997, John Paul spent four days in Paris at the World Youth Days. This was the twelfth edition of one of his treasured innovations. He joined one million people in their spiritual quest by preaching, baptizing ten young adults, and celebrating the Eucharist.

In the first edition I quote more than 125 passages from the documents of Vatican II as edited in 1966 by Walter Abbott, Jesuit scholar. His text does not use gender-inclusive language. In this revised edition I cite the conciliar documents from a 1996 translation edited by Austin Flannery, a Dominican scholar. His text employs "to a very large extent, inclusive language," that is, it uses inclusive language for people but not for God. Although I quote the Vatican documents extensively, readers are encouraged to read all or some of the sixteen documents, especially since many readers may have been born well after the council. October 11, 1997 marked the thirty-fifth anniversary of the opening of the council. Furthermore, it should be noted that Flannery does not capitalize such words as council, scripture, and church. To maintain consistency throughout the whole book, I do not capitalize these words either.

Many thanks are due to Ruth McGugan, senior editor, and Margaret Hammerot, proofreader, for the professional way in which they brought my expanded manuscript to production.

I rededicate this book to my wife, Virginia. Her steadfast love and interest are a source of constant support and energy.

The Popes of the Twentieth Century

Baron Friedrich von Hügel (1852–1925), the son of an Austrian father and a Scottish mother, was a prominent English theologian who made his home in London. Due to poor health, he never received a formal university training. He studied with tutors, especially in philosophy, Hebrew, biblical criticism, mysticism, and the philosophy of religion. He developed a personalist philosophy that called for the full development and harmonization of each person's volitional, intellectual, and emotional powers. His religious studies led him to propose in an influential book (1908) on mysticism and the saintly Catherine of Genoa (1448–1510) that a religion is as strong as the individual strengths and interrelationships of its three principal elements: the institutional, the intellectual, and the devotional (or mystical). He viewed the institutional, intellectual, and devotional dimensions of religion as analogous to the volitional, intellectual, and emotional elements in a person, and, consequently, proposed that the history of any religion is the story of the shifting relationships and tensions among all three elements. David Tracy, priest-theologian at the University of Chicago Divinity School, suggests that Von Hügel's thesis might be "the most fruitful hypothesis for understanding the Roman Catholic tradition" (Tracy 1989b, 548).[1]

In the Roman Catholic church the institutional comprises such factors as the papacy, bishops, parishes, canon (church) law, and the Roman curia (the central administration of the church); the intellectual includes theologians, church historians, biblical scholars, religious educators, philosophers, and other thinkers; the devotional (or mystical) includes the sacramental, scriptural, and prayer life of the church, as well as the involvement of Christians in social justice and works of mercy. In order for Catholicism to flourish, the three elements, embodiments of the Spirit, should be in balance. Finding this harmony, however, is not easy. Although all three elements are indispensable, complementary, and have their own distinct contribution to make, they are often in tension, and more often than not, in conflict. Like three spirited horses in a troika, they clash because each is totalitarian in tendency inasmuch as each has

1

its own particular contribution to make. The three elements also have limitations. The temptation in the realm of devotion is superstition, in the intellectual realm, rationalism (the separation of reason from faith), and in the institutional realm, power for power's sake (and not for the sake of service of the common good). Consequently, these three elements must work together in order to offset one another's weaknesses and provide a healthy equilibrium.

This book uses Von Hügel's triad (or troika) and begins by highlighting the popes and their roles in shaping the church. After all, the papacy is distinctive of the Catholic tradition and as Raymond Brown, Sulpician priest and biblical scholar, has suggested, it has been "a strong cohesive force (perhaps the single most powerful force holding us Catholics together)" (1975a, 80). Peter Hebblethwaite (1930–94), theologian and renowned Vatican affairs writer, has also described the importance of the papacy: "The papacy is not a static institution, frozen once for all in its present form. And popes are not just a mass-produced series of figures in white who appear on distant balconies and mouth interchangeable platitudes. It matters very much who is pope. Each pope makes his own distinctive contribution" (1978a, 195).

Today there is a movement in historical writing to avoid such a conventional, top-down approach that features great public events and great figures. Instead, historians now often begin from the bottom. They write "people history," in which "All human behavior, the actions and thoughts of peoples from all cultures and all segments of all societies within these cultures come within its purview" (Greene 1975).

Jay P. Dolan (1975, 1978a, 1985) and other church historians have written histories from the perspective of the people. However, sometimes the "new social historians" are too dismissive of general histories of the church. For example, Dolan, in his negative review of Thomas Bokenkotter's *A Concise History of the Catholic Church* (1977) maintains that a history of the church limited to the actions of popes and bishops will not truly tell the history because the church is primarily the people of God. Dolan acknowledges that the biblical image "people of God" does not exclude the role of the hierarchy, "but neither does it permit the history of the church to be reduced to a narrative of hierarchical and administrative activities. He then adds, "Popes die and councils come to a close, but the pilgrimage of the people of God never ends" (1978b).

It seems to me that to make his point, Dolan dismisses too easily the far-reaching and long-lasting effects of the papal and episcopal actions and teachings on the very pilgrimage of the people of God he wants to underscore. Is not the pilgrim church still crossing rocky terrain in some places because of the papal condemnations of modernity in the early part of the century? Has Vatican II "come to a close" or are we not hoping against hope that the pilgrim church will catch up to the council's vision of the

Catholic tradition at least by the early part of the twenty-first century? The thesis of this book is that the pilgrimage moves along in part due to the interplay among the faithful, the theologians, and the hierarchy.

The Twentieth Century: Its Beginning

For over one thousand years the popes exercised sovereignty over a vast area of Italy called the Papal States. It has been suggested that "The twentieth century began for the papacy in 1870, when Rome was occupied by the new Italian State, and papal fortunes fell to their lowest ebb since the Reformation" (Rhodes 1983, 9). The term *risorgimento* (literally, resurgence) denotes the period of cultural nationalism that led to the political unification of Italy. Beginning around 1750, this movement created a united Italy from a quilt of separate little kingdoms, republics, and territories occupied by foreign powers. It reached its climax in 1870 when the Italian armies occupied Rome after Napoleon III withdrew his troops defending the last remains of the Papal States so that he could defend Paris in the final stages of the Franco-Prussian War.

The Papal States comprised some sixteen thousand square miles through north-central Italy. According to tradition and some more-than-dubious documentation dating back to Constantine (288–337), Pepin, king of the Franks, bestowed the land on Pope Stephen II (752–57) in 754. In 1870 when the Italian armies occupied Rome, they also confiscated the Papal States. The pope, Pius IX (1846–78), declared himself a "prisoner of the Vatican" and the occupation a "profanation." "Barrels of holy water," he declared, "would be needed to wash away the profanation of the Quirinal," which was once the summer residence of the popes where King Victor Emmanuel II (1820–78) had installed himself. The conflict between the Vatican and Italy that began in 1870 became known as the "Roman question."

The loss of the Papal States meant a major loss of political and financial power for the church. It was difficult for Pius IX and many Catholics to imagine that the papacy could carry on both its apostolic mission and its international role without the trappings of regal power and while confined to Vatican City, a mere 108 acres. It took Rome a long time to realize that the loss of the Papal States not only provided the popes with the opportunity of enhancing their religious and moral authority, but it also freed the church for its real mission in Italy and around the world. Nonetheless, the unresolved Roman question hobbled the activities of the popes until 1929, almost sixty years.

The following sections briefly review the life of each of the nine popes of the twentieth century from his birth to his election. Included is also a brief review of some significant events that affected either each pope personally or the society in which he lived during his pontificate.

Leo XIII (1878–1903)

Gioacchino Pecci was born on March 2, 1810, in Carpineto, a town just south of Rome. He was a brilliant, hard-working student who eventually studied at the Academy of Noble Ecclesiastics (1832–37), the school for papal diplomats. Ordained a priest in 1837, he joined the papal service and was made governor in the Papal States, first of Benevento (1838–41) and then of Perugia (1841–43). He gained a reputation as a firm and capable administrator. At the age of thirty-three and only six years after his priestly ordination, he was made by Gregory XVI (1830–46) an archbishop and nuncio to Belgium (1843–46). A nuncio is a diplomat who represents the Vatican in a foreign capital. He was next appointed bishop of Perugia, where he stayed for thirty-two years, the entire pontificate of Pius IX. As bishop he modernized the curriculum of his seminary, promoted a revival of Thomism, and wrote pastoral letters calling for a reconciliation between Catholicism and contemporary culture. He was made a cardinal in 1853 and attended Vatican Council I (1869–70).

Upon the death of Pius IX, he was elected the 256th pope on February 20, 1878. Because Cardinal Pecci had a frail physique and was in fragile health, it seems his election may have been no more than a stopgap measure after the thirty-two-year reign of Pius IX. When pressed by the cardinals to take the papal throne, the sixty-seven-year-old Pecci warned, "My pontificate will be short. The conclave [a closed meeting of the College of Cardinals, ordinarily held at the Vatican to elect a new pope] will soon have to be held again. My pontificate will be like that of Marcellus II" (Rhodes 1983, 70). Marcellus was pope for twenty-one days in April 1555. Leo's pontificate, however, lasted twenty-five years. Toward the end of Leo's long life, one wit is supposed to have remarked, "We elected a holy Father, not an eternal Father."

Cardinal Pecci took the name Leo because he admired Leo XII (1823–29), who was pope when Pecci was a teenager. Leo XII had been a papal nuncio in a number of countries and had acquired wide and intimate knowledge of Europe and all of its changes, which led him to realize that the church must adapt itself to a newly emerging society. Leo XIII intended to follow the course of his namesake and not the ultramontane policies (those that encourage excessive loyalty to the pope) of both Gregory XVI and Pius IX. Leo realized that under both his predecessors the papacy had been extremely powerful, but only for Catholics. Leo's aim, therefore, was to restore the power and prestige of the papacy throughout the world.

The recovery of the Papal States dominated Leo's foreign policy. Nevertheless, according to J. N. D. Kelly, Anglican priest and Oxford scholar, his "main achievement was his attempt, within the framework of traditional teaching, to bring the church to terms with the modern world" (1986, 311). Agreeing with the traditional teaching, he considered most of the liberalism of his day as essentially godless, as exemplified by the principle of the separation of church and state. The real aim of his dialogue with society was to rechristianize it and to make the church what she had always been: the spiritual mentor of society (Aubert 1978, 41). In some of his encyclicals (major papal statements of theology and policy), Leo tried to show that the ideals of democracy were best served by Christian principles. He believed the lawful aspirations of freedom could only be fulfilled through Christianity.

Leo's pontificate was a period of wrenching social change. Nevertheless, the judgment of historians is that he did restore the prestige of the papacy throughout the world, mainly because he championed social reform, especially for the poor, and because he was more conciliatory toward governments than his predecessor. When he died at the age of ninety-three on July 20, 1903, flags flew at half-mast in major cities around the world. This sign of respect is in sharp contrast to the scorn heaped upon Pius IX at his funeral procession. On that occasion, a cursing, stone-throwing mob followed the funeral cortege to the body's final resting place at San Lorenzo-Outside-the-Walls and threatened to throw the pope's corpse into the Tiber River.

Pius X (1903–14)

Giuseppe Sarto was born at Riese on June 2, 1835. At the age of fifteen he enrolled in the seminary at Padua and was ordained on September 18, 1858. He spent the next seventeen years as a country priest. From 1875 to 1884, he was chancellor of the diocese of Treviso and spiritual director of the seminary. In 1884 he became bishop of Mantua and in June 1893, Leo XIII appointed him patriarch of Venice and a cardinal.

Cardinal Sarto was elected pope on August 4, 1903, at the age of sixty-eight. He chose the name Pius "out of regard for recent popes of that name who had bravely resisted persecution" (J. Kelly 1986, 313). Pius was of medium height and had a somewhat florid complexion. This simple, straighforward, and extremely pious man was capable of severity and was greatly concerned with church order.

Pius X was not distinguished for learning and had no experience with politics or the wider problems of the church and world. As one who had been a pastor during his entire priestly career, he made it clear from the start that he intended to give his pontificate a pastoral orientation rather than a political one. He adopted as his motto "to sum up all things in Christ" (Ephesians 1:10). Since his chief concerns were the internal problems of the church and the spiritual life of the people, he set three goals for his pastoral ministry: to renew religious instruction, to foster liturgical piety, and to develop devotion to the Eucharist (Falconi 1967, 20). His strategy for the church was that of defensive centralization. For example, he had a fundamental hostility toward liberalism, especially the separation of church and state. He was convinced that religion, politics, and society formed a continuous whole and their separation was a sacrilege. Any separation would divorce a nation from Christianity. He did not perceive the distinction between spheres of competence whereby the state can do certain things and the church others.

In the year 1904, four theologians were born who would make the greatest contribution to theology, the church, and Vatican II, namely, Yves Congar in France, Bernard Lonergan in Canada, John Courtney Murray in the United States, and Karl Rahner in Germany. The year 1904 could someday be known as "the year of the theologians." Congar, Murray, and Rahner attended the council. Although Lonergan did not, he was a "hidden expert," since his groundbreaking theological works influenced many bishops and conciliar theologians.

Pius X's reign of eleven years came to an end on August 20, 1914, when, it was said, he died heartbroken by the outbreak of World War I. The preliminary process of the canonization of this humble and prayerful man was initiated by Pius XII in 1943 and completed in 1953 when two miracles attributed to him were declared genuine. He was canonized on May 29, 1954, and August 21 was designated his feast day. He was the first pope to be canonized since Pius V (1566–72) was so honored in 1712.

Benedict XV (1914–22)

Giacomo Della Chiesa was born in Genoa on November 21, 1854. He earned a doctorate in civil law from the Genoa University in 1875. He then studied for the priesthood in Rome, being ordained on December 21, 1878.

After training for the papal diplomatic service (1878–82), he was assigned as secretary to the papal nuncio, Mariano Rampolla, in Spain (1883–87). When Rampolla became Leo XIII's secretary of state and a cardinal in 1887, Della Chiesa returned to Rome with him, eventually to be promoted to undersecretary of state (1901–7). Pius X appointed him archbishop of Bologna in 1907 and a cardinal in May 1914. Some three months later (on September 3) he was elected pope. He took the name Benedict in honor of his last great predecessor from Bologna, Benedict XIV (1740–58).

As mentioned, Pius X's death coincided with the outbreak of World War I. The choice of Cardinal Della Chiesa was probably due to the need for an experienced diplomat during this time of crisis. In fact, the conclave was so hurriedly called—only eleven days after Pius's death, in order to have a pope who could persuade the warring powers to stop fighting—that the cardinals from the United States did not arrive in time for the election.

Benedict was small of stature, had poor eyesight, and was matter of fact and precise, without much outward geniality and charm. On his very first day in office, he set forth his major concerns. First, was peace among nations. Benedict realized that he faced a conflict greater than any of his predecessors had confronted. As a symbol of his compassion for the suffering caused by the war, he stipulated that his installation would not take place in St. Peter's but at a simple ceremony in the Sistine Chapel. His second concern was reconciliation within the church. He personally wrote an invitation to the president of France to attend his installation Mass, despite the separation between state and church in that country during the previous ten years. Third, he inquired about Vatican finances and immediately set aside a generous sum for charitable donations to be made without delay (Falconi 1967, 114).

Benedict's pontificate of seven years and four months was overshadowed by the war and its aftermath. Because the Roman question remained unresolved, the papacy was subject to diplomatic isolation and unable to play any significant role in major world affairs. Benedict protested inhumane methods of warfare and published several peace plans, which went unheeded.

During the war he maintained strict impartiality, never condemning any of the belligerents, with the result that each side accused him of favoring the other. For example, on August 1, 1917, he sent a peace message to all the belligerents, urging them to "accept a just and lasting peace," not to strive for "victory," and to end their "useless struggle." His message antagonized just about everybody: his talk of a "useless struggle" undermined Italian morale, the Allies thought he was pro-German, and the Germans thought he was pro-French.

After the armistice, Benedict was not allowed any part in the peace settlement of 1919. In fact, "the Allies [had] secretly (treaty of London: April 1915) agreed with Italy that the Vatican should be excluded" (J. Kelly 1986, 315). Woodrow Wilson, the first United States president to be received by a pope, visited Benedict in December 1918. The two leaders had previously exchanged correspondence on Wilson's "Fourteen Points," the president's proposals for the peace that would follow the war (Hanson 1987, 42).

Benedict died unexpectedly at the age of sixty-seven on January 22, 1922, from influenza that had developed into pneumonia. Some of his initiatives were to be carried forward by two of the men he selected for diplomatic posts: in 1917 he sent Pacelli (the future Pius XII) as nuncio to Munich; in 1918 he sent Ratti (the future Pius XI) as nuncio to Poland.

Pius XI (1922–39) INAUGURATED FEAST OF CHRIST THE KING

Achille Ratti was born on May 12, 1857, at Desio, near Milan and within sight of the Alps. Vigorous in body and mind, he excelled in his youth as a mountain climber. He was educated at several seminaries, including Milan, the Lombard College, the Academy of St. Thomas in Rome, and the Gregorian University. His ordination to the priesthood took place in December

1879 at the Lateran. After a stint as professor at the seminary at Padua (1882–88), he worked at both the Ambrosian Library in Milan (1888–1911) and the Vatican Library (1911–18), becoming the prefect in 1914.

Benedict XV, recognizing Ratti's flair for languages, sent him as his emissary to Poland in April 1918. In 1919 Ratti was promoted to nuncio and made an archbishop. In 1921 he came back to Italy as the cardinal archbishop of Milan. On February 6, 1922, at almost sixty-five, he was elected pope on the fourteenth ballot taken on the seventh day of the conclave. Pius was stocky in build, had a broad high forehead, and maintained an expression at once benevolent and extremely firm.

Early in his pontificate, Pius set forth his three goals for the church: there would be a holy year (1925); he would inaugurate a new feast of universal importance (Christ the King in 1925); and he would reassemble Vatican I. This council had quickly adjourned with the outbreak of the Franco-Prussian war on July 19, 1870, having completed only two of its fifty-one proposed documents. After protracted consultations with bishops around the world, Pius decided that the reconvening of the council would be impracticable until the Roman question had been settled. Then it might not even be necessary.

Pius's motto was "Christ's peace in Christ's kingdom," expressing his belief that the church should not isolate itself from society but actively participate in it. For example, he installed a radio station in the Vatican in 1931, becoming the first pope to use the radio to teach the gospel.

During his seventeen years in office, Pius had to handle many volatile issues: communism in Russia, nazism in Germany, persecution in Mexico, civil war in Spain, and fascism in Italy. His "most significant diplomatic achievement was the Lateran Treaty (February 11, 1929), which he negotiated with Benito Mussolini [1883–1945], Italian prime minister since 1922, and which established the Vatican City as an independent, neutral state" (J. Kelly 1986, 317).

The Lateran Treaty meant that for the first time since 1870 the Vatican recognized Italy as a sovereign country with Rome as its capital. Mussolini granted the Vatican many privileges, hoping in return to obtain its support for his fascist regime. By agreement, Catholicism was accepted as the official religion of Italy and the Vatican received ninety million dollars in compensation. The Roman question had been resolved.

The treaty was revised on February 18, 1984, after fifteen years of negotiations. One major change was that Catholicism would cease to be the state religion of Italy and Vatican City would no longer be called a "sacred city," a designation that permitted the church to take such steps as banning books, plays, and films (Lavin 1984; Hebblethwaite 1984a).

Pius XI's last years were especially troubled. In the 1930s there were worldwide economic disorders brought on by the great depression; the Sino-Japanese war was fought in 1931; Mussolini conquered Ethiopia in

1936; and the French and British appeased Adolf Hitler (1889–1945) by signing the Munich Pact in 1938, which surrendered part of Czechoslovakia to Germany. When Pius died on February 10, 1939, World War II was a mere seven months away.

Pius XII (1939–58)

Eugenio Pacelli was born in Rome on March 2, 1876. After his seminary studies at the Gregorian and Lateran universities in Rome, he was ordained in 1899. He entered the papal service in 1901. In 1902 he earned a doctorate in church law (canon law) and from 1904 to 1916 he assisted Cardinal Pietro Gasparri in codifying the canon law, a project begun in 1905 by Pius X and completed under Benedict XV in 1918.

In April 1917, Pacelli was appointed nuncio to Munich and made an archbishop. As nuncio he was deeply involved in the negotiations sponsored by Benedict XV on behalf of peace. Pacelli remained in Germany, briefly in Munich but mainly in Berlin, until 1929. In December of that year he became a cardinal. On February 7, 1930, he succeeded Cardinal Gasparri, his friend and mentor, as secretary of state. This office enabled him to travel extensively, even permitting him to make an unprecedented visit to many parts of the United States in 1936.

Pacelli, a talented linguist, statesman, diplomat, and scholar, was elected the 260th pope on March 2, 1939, his sixty-third birthday. He set three goals for his pontificate: to excavate the crypt of St. Peter's Basilica for the tomb of the apostle Peter; to revise the Latin Psalter (the official prayers of the church to be recited each day by all priests); and to define the doctrine of the assumption of Mary (Hebblethwaite 1993a, 181).

Pius XII, a tall, slender man with an aristocratic yet pale and ascetic appearance, kept a tight grip on the global church, ruling with authority. Animated in conversation, often with a most winning and boyish smile, Pius made a profound impression on the thousands who attended his numerous public audiences in Rome. He gave a speech virtually every day. He ranged widely over ecclesial and world problems, giving frequent attention to medical ethics and social teachings. However, just as World War I and its aftermath dominated Benedict XV's contact with the nations of the world, so World War II and the troubles wrought by communism, fascism, and nazism preoccupied the pontificate of Pius XII. He envisioned himself as the pope of peace. He had taken as his motto: "Peace is the work of justice."

One event—one of the most shameful in world history—haunts the history of Pius's tenure: the Holocaust. The Nazis, who came to power under Hitler from 1933 to 1945, began to ruthlessly murder large numbers of Jews. In 1942 Hitler began to implement his "final solution of the Jewish question," namely, the extermination of Jews in all the countries conquered by his armies. Six million Jews were executed in concentration camps such as Dachau and Buchenwald in Germany and Treblinka and Auschwitz in Poland from 1942 to 1945. This systematic genocide shocked the world and its horrors continue to reverberate through world politics and theology. For example, when Germany's united Parliament held its first meeting in Berlin on October 4, 1990, the session opened with a minute of silence in tribute to the victims of nazism and the Holocaust.

Within the church there have been several references to the significance of the Holocaust for society and the church itself. It is not possible here to provide a history of those who examined and dialogued about the significance of the Holocaust for Christian theology. There is an extensive bibliography in the writings of John T. Pawlikowski, Servite priest and professor of social ethics (1982a, 1982b, 1988). Pawlikowski concludes that "the Holocaust has profoundly altered the very basis for morality in our time" (1988, 649). He adds a personal note: "For me the fundamental challenge of the Holocaust lies in our altered perception of the relationship between God and humanity and its implications for the basis of moral behavior" (ibid., 651).

John Paul II declared in his address to the United Nations on October 2, 1979, that the contemporary world's recognition of human rights was generated as a response to the Holocaust. Johann Baptist Metz, a priest-theologian who served in the German army as a teenager, wrote in 1989 that the Holocaust takes on "paradigmatic character through its very incomparability." The Holocaust, Metz said, points us away from any idealistic system of thought that does not take into account people. Auschwitz, more than any other event, turns theology to the people who are victims of oppression, exploitation, and other forms of human degradation. Metz's view was seconded by Nicholas Lash, professor of divinity at the University of Cambridge, just before the first Congress of the European Society for Catholic Theology held in Stuttgart, Germany, in April 1992. Commenting on the theme of the congress, "The Christian Faith and the Future of Europe," Lash wrote: "All talk of 'Christian' Europe finds its final silencing in those bleak fields that now lie in Europe's heart and center: Treblinka, Dachau, Auschwitz. In the demands that these memories lay upon our actions and imagination is to be found, I think, the key to much else that should shape European theology now and in the future" (Lash 1992).

The theses of Pawlikowski, Metz, Lash, and Pope John Paul are debatable since there were other horrible genocides in the twentieth century, for example, the seven million killed in the Ukrainian genocide of the Russian-made famine of 1932–33. The point, nonetheless, is that the Holocaust continues to resonate throughout world history, politics, and religion, and especially religion because the Nazis attempted to abolish God's covenant with the Jews, a covenant that is foundational to the

Christian and Muslim faiths. The question Catholics have to address is, What did Pius XII do about the Holocaust? And the answer is that he never publicly spoke out against the Nazi atrocities. Some angrily maintain that the pope was shamelessly silent; others argue that he did everything humanly possible to save lives. What is the truth?

One of those who said the pope was shamelessly silent was Rolf Hochhuth. In 1963 this thirty-two-year-old German Protestant wrote a play about Pius XII titled *The Deputy*. In this play, which was translated into more than twenty languages, Pius was depicted as one who knew in fine detail about the systematic annihilation of the Jews but was silent because of his own Germanophile tendencies, his concern for church property, and his obsessive fear of communism. Hochhuth's point was not that the pope did not do anything to check or halt the Holocaust but that he did not say anything about it.

Those who defend the pope point to some recent scholarship that indicates that Pius did everything humanly possible to save lives—including keeping silent. In keeping silent, he knowingly risked his own personal reputation rather than jeopardizing the day-to-day practical work of the rescue of Jews sponsored by the Vatican and others. It is estimated that the Catholic church was successful in helping save from 700,000 to 860,000 Jews from certain death, some 30,000 in Rome itself. Not only were Jews sheltered in monasteries, convents, schools, and churches, but Pius also took the advice of Roman rabbis in softening condemnation of the Holocaust atrocities. In fact, the Chief Rabbi of Rome, after seeing what Pius did to save the Jews in Rome, converted to Catholicism. When Pius died in 1958, Golda Meir, foreign minister (1956–66) and prime minister (1969–74) of Israel, declared: "When fearful martyrdom came to our people in the decade of Nazi terror, the voice of the pope was raised for the victims" (Lapomarda 1986).

J. Derek Holmes, church historian at Ushaw College, England, published a book in 1981 defending Pius XII. His arguments are based on new materials released from the Vatican archives and other sources over the previous fifteen years. For example, after the war the World Jewish Congress sent twenty million lire to Vatican charities in gratitude for the involvement of Pius XII in their cause.

Owen Chadwick, professor of history at Cambridge, wrote in 1987 about Pius and the Holocaust, based in large measure on the wartime diaries and diplomatic reports of d'Arcy Godolphin Osborne, the British Minister to the Vatican from 1936 to 1947. Chadwick quotes a letter in which Osborne criticized Hochhuth's appraisal of the pope: "So far from being a cool (which, I suppose, implies cold-blooded and inhumane) diplomatist, Pius XII was the most warmly humane, kind, generous, sympathetic and (incidentally saintly) character that it has been my privilege to know in the course of a long life." Osborne was not a Catholic.

Sister Pascalina Lehnert (1894–1984), a German nun who was officially Pius's housekeeper from 1918 to 1958 (but, in fact, was his secretary, confidant, and adviser) said in 1983 in the first interview she had granted since the pope's death that Pius condemned the Nazi massacres in the Netherlands in a scathing letter but decided at the last minute against its publication. She reported that Pius was "profoundly shaken" when the Nazis reacted to a critical pastoral letter written by the Dutch bishops by deporting another forty thousand people to concentration camps. Pius said: "I wanted this protest to be published this very afternoon. But then I thought that if 40,000 people ended up in the death camps because of the Dutch bishops' words, Hitler would intern at least 200,000 for those of the pope."[2]

Finally, there are many signs that the history of the Holocaust will continue to occupy the attention of religious and social groups for many years to come. For instance, one important question that has still to be answered satisfactorily is the following: who in the West knew in the late 1930s and early 1940s that a genocide was beginning? The thesis of theologian Ronald Modras is that neither the Catholic church nor world Jewry was institutionally and psychologically prepared to deal with the Holocaust. Once the machinery for the deliberate and systematic destruction of Europe's Jews was put into operation in 1942, "events moved so rapidly that both Christian and Jewish leadership was caught off guard" (1995, 232). Modras's thesis received some support in November 1996, when many British wartime documents were declassified. These documents revealed for the first time that the British first became aware of the mass murder of Jews in September 1941. At that time their intelligence agents were decoding messages used by the German commanders of the SS and police units that followed the German army as it occupied sections of the Soviet Union. The British analysts were under orders to glean as much as they could about the German military situation and not about the killing of Jews. In 1996, some asked why the British did not alert everyone to the merciless murder of the Jews. The response: in 1941 the British agents could hardly be aware that the Germans were beginning the systematic extermination of the Jews—a decision that was not reached until 1942. In other words, the British "could hardly be expected to reach conclusions in 1941 about events that still defy a comprehensive explanation half a century later" (Cowell 1996).

John XXIII (1958–63)

Angelo Roncalli, the third of thirteen children, was born on November 25, 1881, in Sotto il Monte, a town near Bergamo. After his seminary training in Bergamo, he studied at the Saint Apollinare Institute and graduated with a doctorate in theology in 1904, the year of his ordination.

From 1905 to 1914 he was secretary to Bishop Giacomo Radini-Tedeschi of Bergamo and also a lecturer on church history at the seminary.

During World War I he served four years in the medical corps and then as chaplain. In 1921 Benedict XV took him out of Bergamo and placed him in charge of fund-raising for the missions throughout Italy as the national secretary of the Propagation of the Faith. In his spare time he engaged in research in church history. His studies in the Ambrosian Library in Milan brought him in contact with Achille Ratti, the future Pius XI. It was Pius XI who appointed him an archbishop in 1925 and launched him on his diplomatic career, first in Bulgaria (1925–34) and then in Turkey and Greece (1934–44).

Pius XII appointed him nuncio to France in 1944, a very sensitive assignment because, among other things, Roncalli would have to deal tactfully yet firmly with the problem of the many bishops accused of collaborating with the Vichy regime. In 1953 he was made a cardinal and three days later, patriarch of Venice, at the age of seventy-one. After twenty-eight years of service outside of Italy, he was back in his native land. It looked as if Cardinal Roncalli would end his earthly days in the pastoral work for which he had always kept a strong love. However, at the conclave on October 28, 1958, he was elected pope, a month before his seventy-seventh birthday. An editorial in a New York newspaper stated: "In the secular affairs of men he would be old and ready to retire. Yet in the affairs of God, he is beginning a new and tremendously arduous task."[3]

Roncalli was elected on the twelfth ballot by the fifty cardinals present. Apparently, the cardinals were uncertain about who should succeed the powerful Pius XII. Roncalli seems to have been a neutral and compromise candidate who would provide time for the cardinals to determine the next pope. At his age, Roncalli could be nothing but a transitional pope in the temporal sense of having a brief pontificate. What no one expected was that he would be a transitional pope in the metaphysical sense: confronting the church with a totally new approach to its own identity and mission. By calling the Second Vatican Council, he forced the church to redefine its meaning for the world (Murphy 1981, 20).

Cardinal Roncalli took the name John because it was his father's name; it was the name of the church where he was baptized; and because John the Baptist, the one who prepared the way of the Lord, was one of his models. In choosing the name John, he also made a historical statement. From 1410 to 1415 there was a John XXIII (Baldassare Cossa), whose very complicated story as antipope includes his election by the Council of Pisa and his subsequent resignation and deposition at the ecumenical Council of Constance (1414–18), where he was accused of such crimes as simony and perjury. However, until 1958, historians debated his authenticity. Roncalli, a church historian, settled the matter without blinking an eye: "There have been twenty-two authentic popes called John. I will be the twenty-third" (ibid., 77).

John was a short, stout, smiling old man who radiated goodness, warmth, and gentle wit. The Vatican always prepares three sets of robes for the new pope: a small, a medium, and a large. It was a struggle to fit John into the large white robes waiting for him. He quipped: "Everyone wants me to be pope except the tailors."

When John died on June 3, 1963, after a brief pontificate of less than five years, the philosopher-journalist Walter Lippmann (1889–1974) said the pope "had reached across all the barriers of class, caste, color and creed to touch the hearts of all kinds of people" (Donohue 1981). What was it about this man that evoked such admiration and praise? At his installation Mass on November 4, 1958, John described himself in his homily. The new pope, he said, "through the events of life, is like the son of Jacob, who meeting with his brothers showed them the tenderness of his heart and, bursting into tears said, 'I am Joseph, your brother.'"

Peter Hebblethwaite believes these words tell us about the greatness of John: "This text of Genesis 45 is the key to understanding Roncalli. It is the passage in which Joseph, now powerful in the land of Egypt, reveals himself to his discomfited brothers. Roncalli used it on countless occasions: when addressing socialists in Venice, the prisoners in the Regina Coeli prison in Rome, the Jews who came to visit him in the Vatican. The message was the same each time. To paraphrase Blaise Pascal, people expected to meet a pontiff, and they met a brother human being" (1981b).

Paul VI (1963–78)

Giovanni Battista Montini was born on September 26, 1897, at Concesio, near Brescia. After his ordination in 1920, he pursued graduate studies in Rome. In May 1923 he went to Poland as an attaché in the apostolic nunciature (home of the papal representative) until ill health forced his return to Rome. In October 1924 he entered the service of the secretary of state of Pius XI, and was appointed an undersecretary of state (one who can represent the secretary of state) in December 1937. In 1952, Pius XII promoted him to pro-secretary (the assistant to the secretary of state) and then in 1954, appointed him archbishop of Milan. Why Milan after twenty-five years of close collaboration? Peter Hebblethwaite (1993a, 14, 242) offered an explanation, based on a report by Mario V. Rossi, a close friend of Montini. Rossi had been appointed by Pius XII to head the Catholic Students of Italy. Rossi related that after some time in office, he had so much trouble with the right-wing antics of Catholic Action that he decided to resign in protest. He sent his letter of resignation to Montini. But Montini decided to hold the letter since people did not normally resign from papal appointments. When the existence of the letter became public knowledge, Montini was accused of "withholding information" from the pope. This incident was the pretext for exiling Montini.

Pius XII had offered Montini the cardinal's hat in 1952. This honor Montini declined, but later accepted when offered by John XXIII in

December 1958. He actively participated in the first session of Vatican II in October 1962.

The June 1963 conclave was attended by eighty cardinals, the largest in the church's history. Montini was elected on the fifth ballot. The new pope had a high forehead, chiseled features, a strong mouth with compressed lips, and sensitive and keen grey-green eyes beneath somewhat bushy brows. He carried himself with grace and dignity. His choice of the name Paul was due in part to his keen interest in the Pauline epistles and spirituality. The name also suggested an outward-looking approach like the missionary Paul. And one of his first acts was to announce that the council would continue, thereby making John XXIII's reform irreversible.

Wilton Wynn, Vatican correspondent for *Time* magazine from 1962 to 1987, surmised that if Montini had been a cardinal in 1958, Roncalli would not even have been considered for the papacy. Montini had more extensive diplomatic experience in Rome and, at that time he was sixty-one, the right age. In 1958 the average age of the fifty-one cardinals at the conclave was seventy-four. Some irreverant observer remarked, "There is one requirement for the pope to be elected by this conclave—he must be able to walk" (Wynn 1988, 20).

John XXIII called for an ecumenical council in 1959. If Montini had been elected in 1958, would he have called a council? No one can answer this question, but it seems clear today that Paul VI was the ideal choice to steer John's council to its conclusion by putting John's spirit into church life and law.

No pope has an easy road to travel. For example, Paul had defended and reaffirmed priestly celibacy in his 1967 encyclical, *Sacerdotalis celibatus,* by describing it as a "heavy and sweet burden" and a "total gift" of the priest to God and the church. Nevertheless, toward the end of his life he admitted that his "heaviest cross" was signing the laicization papers of thousands of priests leaving the priesthood. During his fifteen years, 32,357 priests asked for laicization and he granted all but 1,033 (ibid., 248).

Paul was called "the pilgrim pope" because between 1964 and 1970, he made nine unprecedented trips overseas. Perhaps his finest hour occurred on October 4, 1965, when he addressed the United Nations in New York City. His presence was historic: it was the first time a pope had set foot in the western hemisphere. Paul's emotional speech drew a standing ovation from the general assembly. The most evocative passage was the following:

> And now, we come to the most important point of our message, which is, at first, a negative point. You are expecting us to utter this sentence, and we are well aware of its gravity and solemnity: *not some peoples against others,* never again, nevermore!

It was principally for this purpose that the organization of the United Nations arose: against war, in favor of peace! Listen to the lucid words of a great man, the late John Kennedy, who proclaimed four years ago: "Mankind must put an end to war, or war will put an end to mankind." Many words are not needed to proclaim this loftiest aim of your institution. It suffices to remember the blood of millions of men, that numberless and unheard-of sufferings, useless slaughter and frightful ruin, are the sanction of the past which unites you with an oath which must change the future history of the world: No more war, war never again! Peace, it is peace which must guide the destinies of peoples and of all mankind.

Paul died peacefully at Castelgandolfo outside of Rome, on August 6, 1978, having served the church as pope for fifteen years. "History will be generous to Paul because it possibly will say he was the first to bear the full burden of the modern papacy. John XXIII opened Catholicism's Pandora's box and left Paul with the consequences."[4]

John Paul I (August 26 to September 28, 1978)

Albino Luciani was born of poor, working-class parents on October 17, 1912, in northern Italy in the village of Canale d'Agordo in the Belluno diocese. He was the first twentieth-century pope to be born in the twentieth century. Ordained a priest in 1935, he later earned a doctorate in theology from the Gregorian University. A man of wide literary culture and of deep but simple piety, he was appointed professor of dogmatic theology for his diocese. He was consecrated bishop of Vittorio Veneto in 1958 by John XXIII. Paul VI appointed him patriarch of Venice in 1969 and a cardinal in 1973. He participated in the international synods of 1971, 1974, and 1977.

Cardinal Luciani, a man with an infectious smile and kindly manner, was elected the 263rd pope on August 26, 1978, a few months short of his sixty-sixth birthday. The vote was decisive: on the third ballot he received more than two-thirds of the 111 ballots. The decisive election took the church by complete surprise because Luciani had seldom left northern Italy and had neither curial nor international experience. At any rate, the world was captivated by this pastoral man of practical common sense and welcomed his warm and beaming smile. The first pope ever to choose a double name, John Paul did so to symbolize his esteem for his two predecessors, his desire to combine their best qualities, and his plan to continue their reform policies.

Both John XXIII and Paul VI had a great impact on Luciani's ecclesial career and vision. Both, he said, "had provided me with an example and a program" (Hebblethwaite 1978b). Unfortunately, neither the church nor the world had a chance to learn what policies he would have pursued because he died most unexpectedly on September 28, 1978, having served a mere thirty-three days as the vicar of Peter. His term was the shortest since 1605, when Leo XI served for just twenty-seven days.

Almost immediately after John Paul I's death, rumors of foul play began to circulate in Rome because of odd discrepancies concerning his sudden death. Precise answers to obvious questions were in short supply: Who found the body and when? What caused the death and when? Was there a secret autopsy or none at all? The Vatican officials had not performed an autopsy—the papal constitution forbids them—but did announce that John Paul died of a heart attack.

In 1984, David Yallop, a British journalist and author, published a controversial book that purported to be an exhaustive and thoroughly objective investigation into the death of the pope. His conclusion: the pope was the victim of an assassination plot devised by six high-ranking prelates. Allegedly, the pope was poisoned by members of a secret Masonic lodge. Yallop, invoking journalistic privilege, provided no verifiable evidence for his sensational allegations and refused to identify his alleged sources.

Yallop's irresponsible thesis that the pope was murdered provoked some Vatican officials—including John Paul II and Paul Marcinkus, a United States archbishop who had been labelled a prime suspect[5]—to invite John Cornwell, a former Catholic, former editor of the *Observer* in London, and an award-winning crime writer and novelist, to make an official investigation into the mysterious death of the pope. Cornwell used his many talents to produce in 1989 a fascinating account of the people and events surrounding the sudden death of the pope.

Having ready access to reliable Vatican officials, secretaries, funeral attendants, reporters, and relatives, Cornwell convincingly demonstrated that Yallop's fanciful murder plot was full of gaping holes. His own conclusion was that the pope died of a blood clot in the lung, possibly from not taking his anticoagulant drugs. However, although Cornwell never accused anyone of murder, he did find the papal staff culpable for the pope's death. Cornwell claimed to have uncovered evidence leading to a conclusion that he found "more shameful and more tragic than any of the conspiracy theories." John Paul died, said Cornwell, "scorned and neglected by the institution that existed to sustain him." In other words, those charged to watch over the pope never summoned medical assistance when the pope complained of feeling slightly ill on the night that he died. But this seems more like culpable incompetence than scornful neglect (Hebblethwaite 1991a).

Most people conclude that Cornwell's theory, while believable, is unsupported by concrete evidence, and thus ultimately settles nothing. Unless someone comes forward to support Cornwell's thesis, the circumstances surrounding John Paul's sudden death will remain a mystery.

The answer could simply be that the pope, who did not have robust health, was unprepared for the pressures of the office. After all, the papacy is demanding, being probably the most sensitive and public position in the world. The day before his death, John Paul jokingly asked an aide "to buy a machine that could do his reading for him" (Watson 1978). Cornwell devoted two lengthy chapters to his interviews with Archbishop Marcinkus. At one point the archbishop said: "They called him the 'smiling pope.' But let me tell you something that was a very nervous smile." Another curial official said John Paul's death "could have had something to do with passing from responsibility for a relatively small diocese of 600,000 Catholics in Venice to responsibility for the entire Catholic world."[6]

John Paul II (1978–)

Karol Wojtyla was born on May 18, 1920, in the town of Wadowice in southern Poland. When he was nine years old, his mother died while giving birth to a stillborn daughter; his father, a junior officer in the Polish army, died in 1942. In his youth Wojtyla was an outstanding student who became extremely keen about poetry, acting, and sports, especially swimming, canoeing, hiking, and skiing.

His university studies at the Jagiellonian in Krakow were interrupted by the German occupation of Poland in September 1939, but resumed after the Russians conquered the country in January 1945. He graduated with distinction in theology in August 1946, and received ordination on November 1. Sent to Rome, he obtained a doctorate in theology at the Angelicum in 1948, writing his dissertation on the concept of faith in the writings of the saintly John of the Cross (1542–91). From 1948 to 1951 Wojtyla served as a parish priest back in his native land. In 1952 he returned to the Jagiellonian to study philosophy, defending his doctoral dissertation on Max Scheler (1874–1928) in 1959. Scheler and other German phenomenologists reacted against nineteenth-century subjectivism and historicism (the identification of recorded history with history as actually lived by people), seeking a return to objectivity and the principle of human solidarity (Baum 1970a, 10–11). From 1952 to 1958, Wojtyla lectured on social ethics at the Krakow seminary and became professor of ethics at the Catholic University of Lublin.

Pius XII made him an auxiliary bishop to the diocese of Krakow in 1958; Paul VI named him archbishop of Krakow on December 30, 1963, and a cardinal on June 26, 1967.

Wojtyla was an active participant at all four sessions of Vatican II and at the five international synods called by Paul VI. During the 1960s and 1970s he had a chance to travel extensively, sometimes on curial business, to the Middle East, Africa, Australia, South and East Asia, and the United States, where he attended the eucharistic congress in Philadelphia in

1976. Cardinal Wojtyla was thus well-known and widely respected when the 109 cardinals assembled to elect a successor to John Paul I.

With twenty-seven members, the Italians were still the largest single group of cardinals. Yet they could not reach a consensus in appointing an Italian candidate. Also, the frailty and sudden death of John Paul I "may have been a symbol of the weakness of the remaining group of Italian cardinals, a signal that the time had come to break the pattern of electing Italian popes" (Wynn 1988, 262). On October 16, 1978, Wojtyla was elected the 264th pope by an overwhelming majority (103 of 109 votes) at the age of fifty-eight. He was the youngest pope since Pius IX, who was elected at the age of fifty-four. It is said that he first thought of taking the name Stanislaus, after a Polish church leader murdered by the king in 1078. Stanislaus, the Polish equivalent of the English archbishop Thomas Becket (1118–70), is, for John Paul, "the patron of church-state relations." Dissuaded by the cardinals, Wojtyla chose the name John Paul "as less nationalistic and to make the point that he would continue the work of his predecessors" (Hebblethwaite 1992b). He chose as his motto "Be not afraid."

John Paul II is an extraordinary man: intelligent, serious yet witty, charismatic, energetic. He is a talented manipulator of the media, an inspiring liturgist, an eloquent homilist, and a linguist. On his inauguration day he "addressed the world's Catholics in 11 languages, including Ukrainian and Lithuanian, which significantly are languages of restless minorities in the [then] Soviet Union."[7]

John Paul's election was marked by a series of firsts: the first Slav pope, the first non-Italian in 455 years, and the first pope to live his life as student, priest, professor, bishop, and cardinal in a communist society.

John Paul has been extremely active. His active pontificate was almost cut short when he was shot and nearly killed in St. Peter's Square on May 13, 1981, by an alleged Turkish terrorist.[8] The gunman, Mehmet Ali Agca, was caught and given a life sentence for the attack, but the investigation into who had masterminded the shooting was inconclusive. Agca claimed in 1991 that the Bulgarian secret service hired him and other Turks to kill the pope, and that there was even a Soviet connection (Simons 1991). In 1994 Agca offered a new story. He said he was convinced he acted in accordance with a divine plan. He dropped all references to alleged plots, declaring that "It's pointless to keep speculating and looking for secret plans and plots. The truth is that on that day not even I knew why I shot. I might have done it to make history."[9]

Beginning in July 1992 the pope began to have some health problems, problems serious enough to force him to cancel a trip to Belgium in May 1993 and to the United Nations in October 1993. He had surgery to remove a large intestinal tumor (July 1992), to mend a broken shoulder suffered in a fall while descending steps at the Vatican (November 1993), and to repair a thigh-bone broken during a fall in his bathroom (April 1994).

While remaining at the Vatican, John Paul was able to meet with 114 cardinals from fifty-four countries on June 13–14, 1994, to discuss specific papal proposals leading up to the year 2000. The millennium has been on John Paul's mind from the very beginning of his pontificate. He had already turned attention to it on March 4, 1979, in his first encyclical, *Redemptor hominis* (n. 1).

Each of the cardinals received a document written by John Paul titled, "Reflections on the Great Jubilee of the Year 2000." This essay of ten thousand words suggested themes and ideas for what John Paul explicitly declared the most important celebration of the twentieth century. One of the major themes is that the pontificates of the twentieth-century popes "in one way or another," as well as Vatican II have been leading to the Christian celebration of the year 2000. John Paul even stated that all the activities of his pontificate have also been leading to that celebration (T. Fox 1994a).

John Paul continued his reflections on the year 2000 in an apostolic letter signed on November 19, 1994, *Tertio mellennio adveniente* ("As the Third Millennium Draws Near"). He placed the coming jubilee year within the framework of a theology of history. He declared that the history of the world—its beginning, middle, and end—is at all points related to the eternity of God. The coming of Jesus Christ marks the fullness of time inasmuch as God became an actor on the stage of human history (n. 9). Because the risen Christ remains present through his Spirit, especially in the church, all humans since the first Christian Pentecost live in the last days, the final hour (Acts 2:17; Hebrews 1:2). This perspective does not mean the end of history is imminent. Avery Dulles (1995) explained: "Aware that we live today in a highly charged atmosphere in which the flames of mass hysteria can easily be ignited by fanciful speculations, the pope provides no basis for either utopian prognostications or dire apocalyptic premonitions." Instead, the pope calls upon the church to prepare soberly for "that new springtime of Christian life which will be revealed if Christians are docile to the action of the Spirit" (n. 18). It is the Spirit who impels Christians to preach the gospel with new power, especially to those marginalized and oppressed. Inasmuch as Vatican II was a providential event whereby the church began its more immediate preparation for the year 2000, the best preparation for the new millennium is "a renewed commitment to apply as faithfully as possible, the teachings of Vatican II to the life of every individual and of the whole church" (n. 20).

In November 1994 John Paul published *Crossing the Threshold of Hope,* a book of thirty-five brief chapters that report on such topics as the existence of God, the divinity of Jesus, the problem of evil, the nature of some of the world religions, immortality, human rights, and the dignity of women. The book became an international best-seller.

In December 1994 *Time* magazine named John Paul its "Man of the Year." It praised the pope for being "In a time of moral confusion . . .

resolute about his ideals and eager to impose them on a world that often differs from him" (Gray 1994, 53).

In December 1996 John Paul published *Gift and Mystery*, a memoir marking the fiftieth anniversary of his priestly ordination. He said he offered the book "to the people of God as a testimony of love." He recalls the strength and faith of his family, the bitter era of the Nazi occupation of his homeland, the dramatic events that surrounded his decision to become a priest, the unhappy decades under communist rule, and his exciting years of study and ministry in Rome.

Conclusion

This chapter began with Von Hügel's thesis that a religion (read: Catholic Christianity) is as strong as the individual strengths and interrelationships of its institutional, intellectual, and devotional elements. Since the papacy is distinctive of the Catholic church, vignettes of those who became popes were presented to show how their lives were inextricably intertwined with the institutional, intellectual, and devotional life of the church. Most had advanced degrees from prestigious academic institutions in Rome and were teachers. Each was an expert in some area of church life: church law, church music, philosophy, church history or theology. All were known for their solid piety and sincere commitment to Christ and his church.

Once elected to the church's highest office, each pope manifested in his own special way his devotion to the integrity of the institutional church, especially through his writings, addresses, and decrees about theological, liturgical, ethical, devotional, and social matters. As this thematic history of the Catholic tradition during the twentieth century unfolds, it will become clear that these men did not "mouth interchangeable platitudes." Each made his own distinctive contribution to the tradition, at times positive and helpful, and at other times negative and counterproductive. For example, the preconciliar popes wrote 184 encyclicals: Leo XIII wrote eighty-six and Pius XII wrote forty. Most of these documents had a tangible effect on the church. Avery Dulles, a Jesuit and prolific ecclesiologist, pointed out that in the twentieth-century preconciliar church, Catholic theology depended heavily on the papal encyclicals (1992a, 107). However, to understand more clearly the distinctive contributions of these men to the church's institutional, intellectual, and devotional life, it is necessary to turn to the historical and cultural context of the twentieth-century church, namely, the rise of modernity.

The Church and Modernity

In a 1984 book on church history, Stephen Happel and David Tracy wrote that "the most significant cultural force in our world is the spirit of modernity: the rational science born in the early modern period and the Enlightenment critique of reason, history, politics and religion" (p. 163). In 1987, a mere three years later, David Tracy declared that "we have left modernity behind" (1987b, 73). Whether modernity is still with us or behind us, the twentieth-century Catholic church and Vatican II cannot be understood unless they are placed within the context of the challenge of modernity.

Modernity is not a fully precise term or notion. In each period of history thoughtful persons attempt to be in touch with their times, that is, their modernity. For example, the attempt in the thirteenth century of Thomas Aquinas to correlate the Christian gospel with the philosophy of Aristotle was paradigmatic of the modernity of that period. The efforts of Friedrich Schleiermacher (1786–1834), "the most influential and revered Protestant theologian since the Reformation" (Pelikan 1989, 5:174), to combat the skepticism of the "cultured despisers of religion" of his century was exemplary of the modernity of that period. Schleiermacher called upon his contemporaries to look beyond the superficialities of conventional piety and official dogma to fix their regard on their "inward emotions and dispositions." Deep within themselves, especially in their aesthetic aspirations, they would find the wellsprings of an authentic religion (ibid.).

In this book *modernity* denotes the mentality or mindset that developed in the seventeenth century as a result of the scientific revolution. This mindset is associated with the eighteenth-century Enlightenment and it has continued into the nineteenth and twentieth centuries. Modernity unleashed major critiques of the past understanding of the physical sciences, politics, philosophy, economics, and religion; it was concerned with the progressive enhancement of human life by controlling the natural world; by creating a perfect society; by focusing on human reason, dignity, and autonomy; and by rejecting religion, faith, and revelation.

23

In addition to modernity, two other terms pervade this chapter: *modernists* and *Modernism*. Those Christians who tried to reconcile modernity with historical Christianity were called modernists. A modernist movement within the Roman Catholic church that was condemned in 1907 as heretical was called Modernism.

The way to modernity was opened in the fifteenth century by the Renaissance and in the sixteenth century by the Protestant Reformation—two massive cultural events opposed to the medieval world. The Renaissance rejected medievalism and called for a return to the classical humanism of Greco-Roman culture. The ideal of the Renaissance was for humans to control the natural world and create a perfect society—two goals carried forward by the Enlightenment. The Protestant reformers wanted to escape the medieval church by returning to the early church, especially its emphasis on the Bible. They protested the church's authoritarianism, doctrinal confusion, fiscal abuses, widespread ignorance, and corrupt clergy. The Reformation's insistence on the primacy of the individual conscience opened the gates for the Enlightenment's stress on human autonomy; its stress on "faith alone" helped the Enlightenment divorce faith from reason and reject faith in revelation altogether.

Can the rise of modernity be assigned a specific date? Several European and North American scholars fix on the year 1680 because this date marks the rise of modern science in which modernity has its roots (Butterfield 1966; Congar 1968; Lonergan 1974, 55). The scientific revolution of the seventeenth century—probably the greatest intellectual accomplishment in the history of the human race—was so significant that Sir Herbert Butterfield (1901–79), professor of modern history at Cambridge, did not hesitate to declare categorically that the scientific revolution "outshines everything since the rise of Christianity and reduces the Renaissance and the Reformation to the rank of mere episodes, mere internal displacements, within the system of medieval Christendom" (1966, 7).

The Scientific Revolution

Modernity began when modern science asked this radical question: Could nature "be understood as in itself a perfect system, governed by laws discoverable through repeated observation and controlled experimentation" (Clebsch 1979, 188)? Scientists believed that once the laws of nature were understood, nature could be brought into the service of humankind. Furthermore, nature would no longer need grace to perfect it.

To understand how the above scientific question was answered, we turn first to Nicolaus Copernicus (1473–1543), a Polish priest and astronomer, who published in 1543 his immortal work *On the Revolutions of the Heavenly Bodies*. In what has become the foundation for modern astronomy, Copernicus advanced the heliocentric theory of planetary motion and in the process challenged the existing Ptolemaic geocentric system. According to Copernicus, the sun is motionless at the center of the universe with the planets, including the earth, revolving around it. Copernicus's findings caused considerable consternation in part because they contradict how human senses perceive earth's place in space. More important they contradicted the world view expressed in the Bible. For example, Joshua 10:12–14 depicts Joshua in his battle with the Amorites, asking God to halt the sun in the middle of the sky for a whole day.

Galileo Galilei (1564–1642), Italian astronomer and physicist, ushered in the age of science. He examined the acceleration and deceleration of moving bodies and wrote in defense of Copernicus's hypothesis in his 1632 masterwork *Dialogue on the Two Great World Systems*. Galileo's teachings got him in trouble with the church because sixteen years earlier the Vatican had proclaimed the Copernican heliocentric view "formally heretical, inasmuch as it expressly contradicts the doctrines of holy scripture in many places, both according to their literal meaning" and the common interpretation of the early Church Fathers. Galileo, seventy years old, blind and feeble, was formally brought to trial in Rome on April 30, 1633, condemned as "vehemently suspected of heresy," made to adjure the Copernican theory, silenced, and forced to live under house arrest.

The facts surrounding the condemnation of Galileo in 1633 are controversial. Whatever the real motives for the silencing, what is most significant is that modern science, with its rigorous method of verifying experiments, undermined the medieval view that there were only two sources of the truth, namely, authority and philosophy. The church's authoritative teaching was rooted in God's word in scripture and tradition. The scriptures present a geocentric view of the universe with humans on earth the central point of the universe. The heliocentric thesis called this scriptural view into question.

The other source of truth was philosophy, especially the deductive, metaphysical methods of Aristotle and medieval scholasticism. Galileo's scientific method relativized philosophy. Science became a third route to the truth and a threat to the established order.

The findings of other major scientists also conflicted with church teachings. For example, Sir Isaac Newton (1642–1727), the English mathematician and physicist from Cambridge, was convinced the world was rational because it came from an intelligent Creator. But when he discovered the laws of gravity, his findings evoked a serious religious question: if the laws of gravity control all things and if scientists can manipulate these laws, what is God's function? Sir Charles Lyell (1797–1875), an English geologist, published a three-volume work, *Principles of Geology* (1830–33), in which he demonstrated that the earth had evolved over millions of years and not six days.

Charles Darwin (1809–82), an English naturalist, published two books, *Origin of Species* (1859) and *Descent of Man* (1871), in which he claimed that the development of both plants and animals was the result of "natural selection," a process in which random mutations in the off-spring of a species enabled some to adapt themselves to their environments more readily than others, thereby surviving in greater numbers and passing on to their offspring these invaluable assets. Such a doctrine dealt a lethal blow to the view of biological theists who regarded the plant and animal worlds as one large happy family crafted by God during the six days of creation. In contrast to this vision of nature as a peaceable kingdom of flawless specimens, Darwin's evolutionary view pitted the species against each other, each competing furiously for the limited resources available, either becoming extinct when they failed to adapt or overpopulating when they adapted too well.

When this theory was extended to humankind, it not only challenged the Genesis story that humans were created a perfect species who later fell from grace, but it also asserted that humans had a close kinship with other primates and had perhaps evolved from some other forms of life.

The condemnation of Galileo in 1633 illustrates that right from its very beginnings modern science was on a collision course with the church, and that the church retreated from science. Today most agree that religion and science need not be in conflict. Galileo himself knew this when he wrote "All that has been discovered and observed recently was due to the telescope that I invented, after being inspired by divine grace." Albert Einstein (1879–1955) also addressed this tension: "Science without religion is lame; religion without science is blind." During an address commemorating Einstein's centenniel on November 10, 1979, John Paul II said that Galileo had suffered at the hands of the church and that more study is needed "to dispel the mistrust that still opposes, in many minds, a fruitful concord between science and faith" (Hebblethwaite 1979d). That study, at least as it concerned Galileo, came to closure on October 31, 1992, when John Paul II read a formal statement before the Pontifical Academy of Sciences. In his address he asked this question: "Has not this case long been shelved and have not the errors committed been recognized?" In his answer, John Paul explained that, since the seventeenth century theologians did not recognize the formal distinction between the Bible as theology and as cultural and historical interpretations of the faith, "this led them unduly to transpose into the realm of the doctrine of the faith, a question which in fact pertained to scientific investigation" (Cowell 1992). What the pope did not acknowledge was the misuse of authority by two popes, Paul V (1605–21) and Urban III (1623–44). The former censured Galileo in 1616 for teaching the Copernican theory of the solar system and suspended Copernicus's writings "until corrected"; the latter forced Galileo in 1633 under threat of torture to adjure the Copernican system. Neither did John Paul affirm that such misuses of authority would not take place again (Spaeth 1993).

Charles Darwin's works were addressed by John Paul on October 22, 1996, when he sent a formal statement to the Pontifical Academy of Science meeting in Rome. The pope focused on the fact of evolution and the existence of a range of theories of evolution (Tagliabue 1996). He recalled that Pius XII in his encyclical *Humanae generis* in 1950 had taught that the "serious hypothesis" of the evolutionary origin of the human body does not conflict with the Catholic faith so long as it does not deny "that the spiritual soul is immediately created by God." Pius never condemned the hypothesis of evolution but cautioned that it played into the hands of materialists and atheists who sought to remove the hand of God from the act of creation. John Paul noted that "Today, nearly half a century after [Pius's encyclical], new knowledge leads to the recognition of the theory of evolution as more than a hypothesis." He added, however, that it is appropriate to speak of "theories of evolution" rather than of the theory.

This intervention of the pope is unlikely to change significantly the teaching of evolution in Catholic schools because in most schools it is a standard part of the curriculum. "But in public schools, where the teaching of evolution and creationism is a contentious issue, the statement is viewed as supporting the idea that religious faith and the teaching of evolution can easily coexist" (ibid.).

The Effects of the Scientific Revolution

Galileo and Newton introduced a radical shift in the methodology of science by rejecting the Aristotelian method, which, in its attempt to determine the universal, the necessary, and the essential, simply examined nature, recorded its doings, and profited from this information. Aristotelian science viewed nature as a finished clay vessel. It could be studied, but both its fixed nature and the intent of the potter had to be respected (Milhaven 1970, 119).

Modern science, by contrast, since it searches for the complete explanation of all the data in terms of their intelligible relationships, deals with the changing, the probable, and a pluralism of perspectives from the best scientific opinions. Consequentially, nature is not a completed clay vessel, but clay to be broken and remolded responsibly and creatively for human and social needs.

Modern science has had three major effects on human interaction with the world and nature (Johann 1968, 70–78, 154–170). First, it has allowed people to discover and explore their control over the world. Through scientific means it is people themselves who can plant crops, plan economies, dredge rivers, make rain, fly above the clouds, and eliminate illnesses. Is there any wonder, considering these accomplishments, that some would ignore or deny the presence of God? The papal nuncio to Munich reported to the Vatican in 1871 a public speech by a defrocked priest who had declared: "If twelve ignorant heads could regenerate the world, what shall we not be able to do—we who have the power of science on our side?" (Rhodes 1983, 13).

Second, it has given people a different appreciation for the scope of time that encompasses human life. Formerly, human history was viewed as short and static, with the past holding a place of honor. Modern science has helped people understand that human history is quite long and dynamic, and gives the future and its potential for greater achievements the place of honor.

The long and dynamic ages of human history have shaped the present order of the world. Consequently, moderns do not view things as having been the way they are from the beginning of time or as having been divinely established. Rather, they hold that this present world has evolved out of many cultures and traditions, and is the result of an endless series of both accidental and controlled forces. People became aware that the patterns of nature and society are open to their continued influence. Moderns see the world as a system shaped by their own technological achievements. Furthermore, since people themselves shaped their institutions, art, laws, and so on, these things are conditioned by their time and place. And so flowing from the historicity of things, moderns believe that instead of evolving from a supposed golden past, they are, possibly, progressing toward a golden future.

Third, humans have developed a different understanding of space. Science expands and intensifies the scope of communications and people's approach to truth. Formerly, people knew few traditions and conceived them as permanent and universally accepted. Communication was slow and limited. Since people lived within a limited horizon of ideas and culture, what they knew became the tradition. Traditions developed and solidified. People grew up within a tradition. They made it their own and passed it on to their children.

Modernity challenged tradition, not out of disregard or disrespect, but in order to free people "from the mystifications and ideologies inevitably present in all traditions" (Tracy 1989a, 38). Modern science invented a whole series of instruments that made it possible to discover among nations a rich pluralism of thought and cultures, all of which are relative to changing history. In our day the communications explosion offers people varied world views so that no single tradition can hold undisputed primacy over communities and individuals. As people try making important choices and decisions, especially those that orient the whole direction of their lives, they do so knowing there are other points of view and that the evidence that justifies their decisions may not be conclusive.

Classical and Historical Consciousness

The result of the rise of modern science in the seventeenth century was a new view of the world, space, and time. Beginning around 1680, people began to develop a wholly new psychological outlook or ideal, such as had happened only once before in human history (Voegelin 1956–87).

Until the time of such Greek pre-Socratics as Heraclitus (535–475) and Anaxagorus (500–428), people interpreted the interrelationships among the four constants (the created world, self, others, and the deity) in terms of myth—symbolic stories that explained the origins and inner meaning of the universe and of life, especially human life. People sought harmony among the constants. Without harmony there would be physical and psychic disasters and chaos. The four constants were considered to form a single organic whole inasmuch as a single life force was in all of them. People focused on nature as the sacred manifestation of the divine. The Greeks, especially Plato and Aristotle, differentiated the four constants in philosophical terms. Individuals were now conscious of themselves as a self distinct from the tribe, nature, time, and place. They sought harmony among science, politics, anthropology, and theology by focusing on the divine being who grounds all reality and lures humans to himself. The rise of philosophy slowly subsumed people's mythic consciousness into what is called a classical consciousness.

Classical consciousness comprised a universal and abstract way of knowing that was fundamentally applicable in all times and circumstances. It highlighted traditional ways, unchanging institutions, hierarchical rule, and authority figures. The real was a fixed order that was objective, unchanging, universal, and abstract. The ideal person was the wise person or sage.

Modern science gave rise to historical consciousness. Tradition and authority were subsumed under freedom, equality, dialogue, community, and democracy. Instead of underscoring the objective, unchanging, universal, and abstract, people concentrated on the subjective, changeable, particular, and practical. The ideal person was the free, autonomous, and rational individual.

Classical consciousness stressed philosophy; historical consciousness stresses history. To live authentically and freely, our radical historicity has to be given full play. History encompasses the past, present, and future. To appreciate some past person or event, it is essential that the cultural and temporal context be studied. History made things the way they are. To understand ourselves today, a study must be made of our social, economic, educational, and religious context. History makes us. To understand the future, we have to recognize that, to some extent, we can determine it. We make history.

The Economic Revolution

The attempt of modern science to enhance human life by controlling the natural world resulted in the Industrial Revolution. This revolution started in England around 1750 and took root in France in 1830, in Germany in 1850, and in the United States in 1860. In these countries there was an impressive improvement in living standards: better food, clothing, homes, transportation, communications, and medicine. The Industrial Revolution transformed the economy and the social structures of society. Due to the impact of science, a factory system of large-scale machine production was introduced. Although there were improvements in agriculture and breeding livestock, many people moved from the farms to the factories in urban centers. Landowners lost much of their economic importance to bankers, merchants, and industrialists.

Adam Smith (1723–70), Scottish philosopher at the University of Glasgow, is considered the primary source of theories of how societies become prosperous. He is associated with the theories of capitalism and a free market economy, ideas advanced in his two major works, *The Theory of Moral Sentiment* (1759) and *An Inquiry into the Nature and Causes of the Wealth of Nations* (1776). Smith's fundamental insight was that the virtue of charity alone, while essential, would not suffice to create prosperity. On the contrary, self-love and self-interest drive the economy. His famous words are: "It is not from the benevolence of the butcher, the brewer, or the baker that we can expect our dinner, but from their regard to their own interest."

Smith surmised that a free-market economy was so structured that it would impel people pursuing their self-interests to eventually serve the common good. Although cynical about government attempts to restrain trade and heartedly devoted to individual liberty, Smith was not an advocate of extreme laissez-faire. He accepted some restrictions on trade. His influence has lasted for almost three centuries.

The Industrial Revolution may have brought prosperity to the capitalists but not to the workers. In order to meet the problems created by the new social structures of capitalism, various theories were proposed. The most famous came from Karl Marx (1818–83), a German lawyer, philosopher, and revolutionary who founded communism, a radical form of socialism. In collaboration with Friedrich Engels (1820–95), he published the *Communist Manifesto* in 1848, and beginning in 1864 published *Das Kapital* in three volumes. Here are three of his main teachings: Progress in history does not come from Christian charity but economic greed. Economic events shape history and are the result of the class struggle between the proletariat and capitalists. The proletarian revolution will bring about communism and the end of the class struggle.

The Intellectual Revolution

The Enlightenment was first and foremost an assertion of emancipation from past views of philosophy, authority, and tradition. The very word *enlightenment* implied that if we could only throw enough light on a question, we would see things as they truly are and be free from darkness and error. Human reason became the primary focus and was viewed as the essential instrument for spiritual liberation from ignorance, superstition, and passivity. The Enlightenment also encouraged a search for a universal morality (including social justice for all) and an emphasis on respect for individuals.

The intellectual revolution was given form and substance by such famous philosophers as Locke, Hume, Kant, Hegel, Comte, and Feuerbach. In order to appreciate their thought, especially in relation to religion and the Catholic church, it is necessary to return to the seventeenth century and the father of modern philosophy, René Descartes (1596–1650).

The seventeenth century was an age of philosophical skepticism. The skeptics said certain and valid knowledge of universal truth is unattainable. According to them, people only know appearances (phenomena) and not the real thing. For example, people see colors and even patterns of color but not the being that supports or has the color. Furthermore, the skeptics maintained that the evil in the world is incompatible not only with a solid, ordered universe but also with the existence of God.

Descartes, a master mathematician and a devout Catholic, tried to answer the "mental suicide" of the skeptics. In his search for an undeniable truth, Descartes refused to appeal to religion, the philosophy of Aristotle, science, or even the senses. The latter are fallible because perceptions can mislead understanding, as is clear, for example, from our original geocentric view of the universe. Furthermore, he realized, the skeptics would simply dredge up other authorities and probable arguments. So, Descartes began with universal and systematic doubt: to doubt is to think, to think is to be. He is known for his famous assertion, "I think, therefore I am."

Concerning God, Descartes maintained that the idea of a substance that is infinite, eternal, immutable, independent, and all-powerful—in other words, perfect—is innate and not derived from sense experience. Since the notion of perfection present in this idea could not come from the ideas of other beings or have been manufactured from the subject's ideas it must have been placed there by God himself. And since we humans are finite, God is the ultimate guarantor of our search for truth.

Descartes's principle of universal doubt threatened the authority of both revelation and the church, and his demand for clear and irrefutable evidence opposed the notion of revelation and religious mysteries. In other words, Descartes argued that truth is to be found not in divine authority but in the systematic pursuit of truth through careful use of logical methods. His "turn to the subject" (i.e., a person should never accept anything as true until it is presented to the mind "so clearly and distinctively" that he has no occasion to doubt it) became an important Enlightenment theme. All philosophers after Descartes had to deal with his theories about God, innate ideas, and the relationship between spirit and matter.

John Locke (1632–1704) founded British empiricism. The term *empiricism* is derived from a Greek word meaning experience. Opposing the theory of innate ideas favored by Descartes, Locke argued instead that all knowledge is derived from experience, whether of the mind or the senses.

David Hume (1711–76), a Scottish philosopher and historian, picking up on Locke's empiricism, carried it to the extreme of skepticism. Since the only knowledge that is valid is that acquired through experience, then there is no valid knowledge of such matters as cause and effect or the idea of substance. All we can do is speak of the attributes of a thing and not of the substance behind them. For example, we see the attributes of an apple and assume there is the substance apple. But we have not experienced the substance itself. Pure reason does not allow us to affirm that there are such things as substance in which the various attributes that we perceive reside (J. Gonzalez 1984, 192).

Hume's ideas left little room for religion. He rejected natural theology—the attempt to acknowledge the existence of God through reason rather than revelation. Claims about the order of the world and a divine cause were considered improbable at best. The order of the world, he said, does not necessarily speak of a God beyond the world since there is evil as well as order, suffering as well as joy. He also denied the validity of miracles. Since matter-of-fact experience is our sole source of knowledge, what we know is that nature is uniform and regular. Since miracles violate the laws of nature, it can never be reasonable to accept them. It would be more sensible to seek other explanations that have their psychological origin in experience. For Hume, then, "Any philosophical, scientific, or religious language that required metaphysical statements, positions that once met the world of experience but transcended it, was suspect" (Happel and Tracy 1984, 115–16).

Immanuel Kant (1724–1804), a German philosopher of logic and metaphysics considered the foremost Enlightenment thinker, has influenced modern thought right up to the present. He had been a rationalist (one who holds that reason is to be granted the primary role in explanation) until, as he later acknowledged, Hume awakened him from his "dogmatic slumber." By this he meant he now also acknowledged the inability of speculative reason to establish in purely rational and objective terms the truth of theology, especially its explanation of God, freedom, and immortality. All these truths belong not to "pure reason" but to "practical reason."

Kant granted primacy to our practical reason, which knows the existence of God as the judge of our actions; of our soul and its freedom by which we choose moral actions; and of life after death when good will be rewarded and evil punished. His distinction between pure and practical reason opened the way out of skepticism and renewed the possibility of religion and morality. However, religion for Kant was primarily an ethical matter. Religion, he taught, is "the recognition of all our duties as divine commands." He reasoned that morality requires a belief in God, freedom, and immortality, for without these our sense of duty and our ability to act would vanish. Furthermore, this moral life should flow from a life of trust in oneself rather than authoritarian decrees. Kant espoused the autonomy of reason vis-à-vis any opposition from the outside. He argued that the freedom and dignity of the human person requires that the individual obey only those laws given by himself or herself. To have laws imposed from the outside, even when the outside lawgiver is God, is to lose one's autonomy.

Georg W. F. Hegel (1770–1831) was the most influential thinker of the nineteenth century. In reaction to Kant's teachings that pure reason was seriously limited, he identified the findings of the human mind with the divine Spirit. In effect, Hegel divinized human consciousness. He argued that universal reason (Spirit) is not only what distinguishes humans from the animals, but also represents the full content of our humanity. But universal reason can only be understood concretely as it objectifies itself in human institutions, laws, customs, art, science, and philosophy. Hegel thus placed humankind within history with a completeness beyond any previous thinker. Twentieth-century existentialists would eventually capitalize on his thought, declaring, "We have no nature, only a history."

Auguste Comte (1789–1857), French philosopher considered the founder of positivism, was also a sociologist who actually originated the term sociology. In his major work, *The Course of Positive Philosophy* (1842), he called for the reform of society so that both individuals and nations could live in harmony and comfort. According to Comte, science gives us our truest picture of reality because nothing real can transcend the universe of sense events and their laws. This finite world is the only absolute and everyone should contribute to the well-being of humanity. Consequently, his thesis was that history had passed from a long childhood to a recent era of change and now to a third stage of development. First there was the religious stage, with its belief in the supernatural; second was the philosophical stage, with its belief in ideas as reality; now we had reached the positive (or science of humanity) stage, in which phenomena are explained by observation, hypotheses, and experimentation. Sociology would provide a scientific basis for leading human history into a golden age. In this stage the structures of society could be changed to make life better. History, which is neither planned nor directed by a God, has its own inherent principles that can be directed toward inevitable progress.

Ludwig Feuerbach (1804–72), a German philosopher, also denied the existence of God. In his famous work *The Essence of Christianity* (1841), he declared that God is simply a projection of our best qualities. The notion of a real, personal being called God was helpful at one stage of human development because it enabled us to realize ourselves in self-transcendence. However, to remain at that stage only alienates people from themselves and one another. Feuerbach posited, then, that we are God. Feuerbach was not opposed to religion. In fact, he wanted to keep it as long as it was understood as he defined it, namely, as the glorification of the human. In other words, religion is humankind. Feuerbach's theory that alienation results when we view God as other was to influence both Freud and Marx.

The Political Revolution

The freedoms brought on by the scientific, economic, and intellectual revolutions naturally led people to seek the perfect society and liberation from various forms of oppressive inequalities. The ideas for such a political revolution were sparked by the writings of philosophers like Locke and Rousseau.

One of Locke's most important works, *Two Treatises on Civil Government* (1690), quickly established him as a leading philosopher of freedom. His predecessor, Thomas Hobbes (1588–1679), taught that it was impossible to have a stable society where men and women could be free because the world is subject to a significant scarcity of resources and people have to compete for these in order to survive. Hobbes said that because of the drive for survival, the original state of nature was nasty, brutish, and short. Locke, on the contrary, believed that the original state of nature was happy and characterized by reason and tolerance. Reason was the sovereign guide to right conduct, both private and political. Locke underscored the importance of the individual by insisting that all human beings were equal in dignity and free to pursue "life, health, liberty, and possessions." He advocated the idea that governments were formed when the people made a social contract to establish them and that they should guarantee people's inalienable rights. Locke epitomized the Enlightenment's faith in the middle class and human goodness.

Jean-Jacques Rousseau (1712–78), a Swiss-French philosopher and political theorist, was one of the great figures of the French Enlightenment. He popularized the liberal ideas for the common people. He taught that religious sentiment and intuition were more important than the rationalism of the philosophers. By this he meant that our knowledge of God rests upon a religious impulse or feeling. The inner consciousness of God and morality is first a feeling which is later aided by reason; it is not a product of cognition. It is feeling that is primary and instinctive. All thought and intellectual arguments follow from feeling. It was actually Rousseau who had set Kant in the direction of practical reason.

Rousseau also taught that the poor were the victims of the rich. His most celebrated theory was that of the natural man ("the noble savage"). His epochal work of political theory, *The Social Contract* (1762), begins with the thunderous assertion, "Man is born free, and everywhere he is in chains." Rousseau argued that humans in their natural state of innocence were naturally good and had equal rights and freedom, but were corrupted by the introduction of such things as religious dogmas and institutions, ownership of property, science, and commerce. People entered into a social contract among themselves, thereby establishing social, economic, and political structures, in order to correct the inequalities brought about by the rise of civilization. He advocated a return to our natural state with its natural religion, consisting of belief in God, the immortality of the soul, and freedom.

The political revolutions of the eighteenth century were historical consciousness in action. The American Revolution (celebrated on the anniversary of the Declaration of Independence written on July 4, 1776) called for government of, by, and for the people, and enumerated many inalienable rights. The revolution took place because, in our terms, the people wanted to control their own social and economic history. They wanted freedom of the press, speech, and religion, and freedom to vote, work, and travel. The tradition of monarchical rule had ended as far as the citizens were concerned and the people took on the responsibility of personally determining their own history.

The French Revolution (celebrated on the anniversary of the storming of the Bastille on July 14, 1789) proclaimed an end to the authority of God, the church, and the monarchy. It was Western civilization's declaration of independence from the Catholic church. It exalted the rights of the individual. Its slogans were, "No one stands above man" and "Liberty, fraternity, and equality."

Pius VI (1775–99) opposed the civil liberties of the French Revolution and condemned its August 26, 1789 Declaration of the Rights of Man and of the Citizen because it challenged the old order, encouraged indifferentism (the belief that one religion and/or church is as good as any other), and impugned Christianity.

An Evaluation of Modernity

Modernity began with the promise of science and technology to assure the progressive enhancement of human life by controlling the natural world. Science has been eminently successful. We now have better homes, food, medicine, means of communication, and travel than before 1680. On the other hand, we witness the negative results of the modern scientific promise of freedom and progress: ecological damage, more destructive warfare, genocides, and the threat of nuclear annihilation. As a result of the many ideas and ills brought on by modernity, many people have rejected a relationship with God, religion, and the traditional Christian view of life. For many there is no ultimate meaning to daily life and work, which may be why the suicide rate is higher than in the past.

Modernity began with the promise of unlimited growth through the creation of a perfect economic and political society. As a result, humankind has benefitted greatly. Never before in the history of the world have so many people enjoyed a standard of living that even medieval kings and lords would have envied. Workers have received many rights and privileges. On the other hand, we witness materialism, consumerism, the erosion of the human community, neocolonialism, labor-management conflicts, monopolies, the marginalization of the poor, and the physical impossibility of extending modern Western standards of living throughout the globe.

Modernity began with the promise of political freedoms within independent sovereign states. It insisted that people should be judged by their abilities and achievements and not by social origin or some other arbitrary measure of status. It produced major advancements in human rights, dignity, freedom, and pluralism. The principles of democracy as realized in the United States have caught the imaginations of many people around the globe—as witnessed, for example, by the collapse of the Berlin Wall on November 9, 1989. On the other hand, there has been no end to colonialism, totalitarianism, and religious oppression. Pluralism often becomes relativism, historical consciousness becomes historicism,[1] and autonomy reduces itself to self-centered individualism. Robert Bellah and his coauthors showed in *Habits of the Heart,* a 1985 study of American individualism, that, for many complex and interrelated reasons, most middle-class Americans do not even have "a moral language that transcends radical individualism." The result is that there is little sense of mutual obligation, personal or political, which leads to a crisis of community. In 1996, Bellah and his associates issued a ten-year anniversary edition of *Habits of the Heart.* The new introduction begins with this sentence: "The consequences of radical individualism are more strikingly evident today than they were even a decade ago."

Postmodern Movement

The deaths of fifty million people during World War II have given moderns a sobering view of our prospects for making this a world of peace, autonomy, and freedom. We have gone beyond such Enlightenment assumptions as "Progress is inevitable" and "Reason by itself can provide a basis for morality and society." Denise Lardner Carmody and John Carmody assert that "It is precisely the spread of this sobriety that justifies calling World War II the death-knell of modernity" (1983, 157). David Tracy added that modernity's optimistic claims of confidence and continuity were seriously called in question by the presence of all those people in the South and East who have been "set aside, forgotten, and colonized" by those in the North and West (1994, 43).

We are moving into what is being called a postmodern culture. The internationally-acclaimed Jesuit theologian Bernard Lonergan (1904–84), writing in the early 1980s, declared that the Enlightenment "still enjoys a dominant position. But, as it were, from within it there has developed an antithesis, no less massive though, as yet, it has not crystalized. To it I refer when I speak of a second enlightenment" (1985, 65). A few years later, David Tracy, a student of Lonergan, described *postmodern* as "an ever-elusive word in search of a definition." Actually, the word is "more an acknowledgment that we now live in an age that cannot name itself than that we should simply reject modernity" (1990).

This postmodern movement—this second enlightenment—did not begin in the 1980s. It was anticipated by perceptive thinkers like Kierkegaard, Nietzsche, Marx, and Freud who called into question some of the rationalist claims of the Enlightenment. "These 'masters of suspicion' forever cast doubt on the belief that the solitary autonomous rational thinker could achieve, much less had achieved, 'enlightenment'" (Tracy 1975, 8). In other words, the postmoderns posit that the modernists were self-deceived when they attempted "to ground what cannot be grounded: a secure foundation for all knowledge and life" (Tracy 1994, 3).

What binds these four masters of suspicion together is their conviction that one's primary task as a human is not to become a finely tuned rational person but to attempt something more difficult: to become a true self, that is, one who struggles to be an authentic person despite one's own radical limitations. To become an authentic, decentered self entails a willingness to enter real dialogue with others; to take sides; to start a constructive argument; to expose ideologies, frauds, and illusions; and to shape the world. Since World War II, authenticity also entails acknowledging and dealing honestly with "the radical plurality of our different languages and the ambiguity of all our histories" (Tracy 1987b, 82).

Søren Kierkegaard (1813–55), a Danish existentialist philosopher and religious writer, believed that over the course of life people normally become increasingly aware of God. But this awareness, he said, often leads to despair once they realize the antithesis between their temporal existence and eternal truth. According to Kierkegaard, the ethical person who subordinates himself to Kant's view of morality cannot bridge the "infinitely qualitative difference" that separates humans from God. Also, reason is no help in realizing the final religious state of union with God. Therefore, Kierkegaard proposed the idea that a leap of faith is required. As his model, Kierkegaard cited Abraham, the father of the Jews who obeyed the call of faith without seeking to be justified before anything less than the presence of God. Kierkegaard taught that each person must always be ready to stand alone before God without benefit of some social, even ecclesiastical, shield.

Friedrich Nietzsche (1844–1900), a German philosopher, anticipated the end of modernity by questioning the major role given to reason by the Enlightenment. What really drove "the genteel and urbane value-system of the Enlightenment thinker," said Nietzsche, was the powerful will to power. Another sign that the Enlightenment was not working was the disintegration of Western culture. Things were so bad that Nietzsche felt called to announce the death of God, arguing that the divine no longer had any effective power because it was submerged in the evils of the times. To counteract these massive evils that pervade society, he said people must reject externally imposed values and, in freedom, create their own. Nietzsche concluded that since people are on their own to survive, each person had better become a "superman," a person with aggressive self-reliance beyond good and evil.

Karl Marx maintained that the task of philosophy is not simply to interpret the world (as in the writings of both Kant and Hegel) but to change it. In order to change it, the ideologies operative in the political and economic structures of each society must be uncovered. "In the Marxian terminology, ideology is always something false, a distortion of the truth for the sake of social interest, a symbolic framework of the mind that legitimates the power and privileges of the dominant group and sanctions the social evils inflicted on the people without access to power" (Baum 1975, 34). In his day, Marx attacked the bourgeois intellectuals who refused to note or to struggle against the ideologies within the economic systems that allowed them to maintain their privileges. These privileges existed mainly because the working conditions of the proletariat were inhumane. In other words, Marx showed that there were economic conditions intertwined with hidden motives that allowed, even enforced, the illusion of the autonomy of the rational bourgeois thinkers.

Sigmund Freud (1856–1939), an Austrian psychiatrist and founder of psychoanalysis, explained that people do not live by a pure and autonomous conscious rationality. Rather, he said people are not as rational and integrated as is claimed. People are also driven and motivated by subterranean forces of the unconscious that run contrary to reason and civilization. Under our seeming civility and sense of order lurks a raging thirst for power hunkered down around a cauldron of lust. Freud argued that the natural urge for sexual gratification underlies people's entire mental life and drives them to seek as much pleasure as possible. This impulse for pleasure remains a permanent aspect of the human psychic makeup and is even the foundation of the drive toward religion. Religion, he concluded, is not a rational commitment but the result of wishful thinking for comfort and security. While religious people disagreed with Freud's conclusions, they did agree that religion is rooted in the preconscious imagination.

Modernity and Christianity

The Enlightenment was an all-out attack on Christianity (Lonergan 1974, 57). It was an attempt on the part of the principal enemies of the Catholic church—"the various atheistic groups in a number of guises: anarchists, nihilists, positivists, freethinkers, socialists" (Rhodes 1983, 193)—to demolish the church with its tradition, rituals, and doctrines, and replace them with the findings of critical reason and science.

On the one hand, specific facts justified the attacks: over many years European Christians had engaged in religious persecutions and wars; the condemnation of Galileo in 1633 alienated many scientists; and as an institution the church often came across as bureaucratic, rigidly authoritarian, and uncompromising. On the other hand, this attack was not fully justified. History makes clear that the church had made many major educational, cultural, and political contributions to the development of Europe.

The belief popular during the Enlightenment period that religion was giving way to critical reason undermined the church's roles as guardian of revelation, source of truth, and moral guide.

As guardian of revelation the church teaches about God and his son, Jesus. During the eighteenth and nineteenth centuries, reason and science were set over against Christian revelation. The Christian God was replaced by the God of the philosophers, and, eventually, with deism, agnosticism, or atheism. The teachings of the scientists, philosophers, and other scholars during these centuries rendered some Christian teachings (e.g., those concerning the creation of the world and the human race) "at worst false and at best quaint" (Clebsch 1979, 243).

It should be pointed out that not all scientists, philosophers, and historians set out to attack Christianity. For example, while it is true that Darwin's works "made fables of the notion of human uniqueness and the story of the animals in Noah's ark" (ibid., 245), Darwin himself was a devout Christian who was deemed worthy of burial with Chaucer, Newton, and other noted English heroes in Westminster Abbey, a national shrine and the place of regal coronations.

The church, since it is founded on Christ, the light of the world, professes to be a source of truth. However, with the Enlightenment, the secular state and the secular university replaced the church as the source of truth and the church's role as moral guide was undermined by the Enlightenment's assertion of freedom and autonomy, which declared the individual's moral conscience free of clerical direction and control.

Because the institutional church failed to see the positive values set forth by the modernists and because it refused to face the justifiable criticism of its own absolutism, fundamentalism, and failure to respect fundamental human rights, the church found itself on the fringes of the political, cultural, and intellectual life of society. By choice the church became an isolated fortress surrounded by an alien world made up not only of other Christian churches and other religions but also of atheists, secular scientists, and governments that had overthrown such traditional values as monarchical rule and the union of church and state in the name of liberalism and democracy. The church developed what has been aptly called "a state of siege mentality."

The Popes and Modernity

This section opens with Gregory XVI (1831–46) and Pius IX (1846–78), the two popes who governed the church for most of the nineteenth century and who set the stage for the twentieth century. Both were hardworking, morally upright, and of strong character. They rejected many of the social, economic, and political movements of the time and were unfriendly to those Catholic intellectuals and clergy who were open to new scientific and historical developments.

There were three reasons why the popes rejected liberalism and denied civil rights (Baum 1979b). First, traditional Catholic teaching highlighted the integration of the individual and society. The private good of the individual, the church taught, should be subordinated to the common good. The task of government was to enhance the common good. Liberal political philosophy, on the other hand, elevated the individual to such great heights, the popes complained, that the common good was being undermined and the traditional order of society destroyed. Furthermore, classical liberalism maintained that government should govern as little as possible and should allow maximum liberty in all spheres of activity: freedom of production and trade, religion, thought, speech, press, assembly, and so on. Second, the Catholic church regarded itself as the divinely appointed embodiment of true religion. It called for the acknowledgment of Catholicism as the religion of the state wherever possible. The popes maintained that implicit in the demand for freedom of religion was indifferentism—the belief that one religion is as good as any other. Third, the Catholic church had always expressed concern for the poor. The popes related political liberalism to economic liberalism, and so argued that in an unbridled free market system the rich could suppress the poor.

Gregory XVI

Bartolomeo Cappellari became a Camaldolese monk at the age of eighteen in 1783, and, although he eventually left his monastery in 1826 to become involved in the Vatican's international missionary ventures as prefect of the Propagation of the Faith, he had "little comprehension of the contemporary world" (J. Kelly 1986, 308). As Pope Gregory XVI, he ruled the Papal States with a heavy hand, fighting off attempts to introduce liberal reforms for the three reasons outlined above.

Many nineteenth-century Catholics, on the other hand, had come to grips with modernity's concern for freedom and strove to Christianize the culture, some by reforming it and others by transforming it (Clebsch

1979, 281). Since modernity recognized the intimate link between freedom and moral and intellectual creativity, the theme of many Catholic liberals was "There is nothing more liberal than religion and nothing more religious than liberalism" (ibid., 256). Their goal was to take the boundless opportunities offered by modernity to deliver the Christian message afresh.

Three French champions of Catholic liberalism were Father Félicité de Lamennais (1782–1854), Count Charles Montalembert (1810–70), and Henri-Dominique Lacordaire (1802–61), who became a Dominican in 1839 and was personally responsible for restoring the Dominican order in France. This group published the newspaper *L'Avenir* (The Future), from August 1820 to November 1831. In their paper they explicitly championed the role of the pope in the church but, at the same time, they also advocated social and civil liberties: separation of church and state, and freedom of the press and conscience. Gregory declared liberty of conscience "a madness." Furthermore, since he shared the view of the restored monarchs of Europe that the state existed to protect the church and since he faced rebellious conditions in the Papal States, he had little tolerance for the call for people's self-determination. Consequently, the pope condemned all these liberal attempts to reconcile the church with modern democracy in his encyclical *Mirari vos* on August 15, 1832.

Pius IX

After serving the church with a papal mission in Chile and as bishop of Spoleto and later of Imola, Giovanni Maria Masti-Ferretti (1792–1878) was named cardinal in 1840 and was elected pope in 1846. During his pontificate, Catholics made more attempts to reform the church by introducing some of the principles of liberalism. In August 1863, Charles Montalembert, the leader of the French liberal Catholics, gathered an impressive assembly of Catholics—cardinals, bishop, priests, and laity—at Malines, Belgium, to urge the church to embrace modernity and get in step with the rest of the world. He proposed that Belgium, a country both Catholic and liberal, proved that the church could flourish in a climate of religious and civil liberties.

One month later, in September 1863, Ignaz von Döllinger (1799–1890), a priest, professor of church history at Munich, and leader of the German liberal Catholics, organized a congress in Munich of eighty scholars to discuss whether or not modern culture was hopelessly secular, rationalist, and inimical to the church. He wanted Catholic theologians in Germany to unite "in scholarship, in defense of responsible academic freedom, and in opposition to the spirit of intolerance, which permeated certain segments of the European church community" (Madges 1986, 63). In his presidential address he made a personal plea as a scholar for his right to work untrammeled by authority. He argued that intervention into the work of scholars was needed only in those rare cases where their conclusions were in obvious contradiction with the dogmas of the church. The only effective weapons against error, he further declared, "were the weapons of science, not ecclesiastical censure" (G. Daly 1985). Finally, he proclaimed that post-Reformation scholasticism with its misplaced emphasis on philosophy was dead and should now be replaced by greater attention to biblical criticism and scientific history. By post-Reformation scholasticism he meant those schools of theologians and philosophers that emerged in the fourteenth century and developed after Trent and that emphasized the interpretation of texts, especially those of other theologians and philosophers, rather than the scriptures and texts of the Church Fathers (major writers of the first seven hundred years of Christianity). This theology, written particularly for seminarians, neither stimulated original inquiry nor engaged new philosophical or historical developments. The result is that Thomism stagnated.

Criticism from various quarters of society that the papacy was out of step with the enlightened views of the times as well as the meetings at Malines and Munich seem to have convinced Pius IX that he should compile a summary of the condemnations of modernity he had issued over the previous seventeen years. On December 8, 1864, he published the famous *Syllabus of Errors,* accompanied by the encyclical *Quanta cura.* The *Syllabus* listed eighty errors, including absolute rationalism, naturalism, pantheism, socialism (one that would subject the family and the school system totally to the state), liberal capitalism (one that had no other end than material gain), and freedom of religion. Error number eighty summarized the document: it is an error to think that "the Roman pontiff can and ought to reconcile and harmonize himself with progress, with liberalism, and with modern civilization." This document shocked many Catholics and angered many who were not Catholic. Were such liberties as freedom of the press, freedom of conscience, and civil rights, now considered evil?

Five years later, Vatican Council I was assembled. In 1870 the bishops declared the doctrine of papal infallibility. This teaching was controversial then and remains so to this day. For example, Döllinger spurned the dogma and was excommunicated in 1871. According to Gabriel Daly, Vatican Council I "was summoned to copper-fasten the Catholic church's radical opposition to modern thought" (ibid., 775). The doctrine of papal infallibility dramatically reminded the world of the church's claim to have a divine guarantee for its role as teacher of the truth.

Leo XIII

Leo also feared liberalism. In his inaugural encyclical, *Inscrutabili Dei consilio* (1878), he expressed this fear when he compared liberalism in the church to a "deadly plague which infects [it] in its inmost recesses." Nevertheless, he realized that the negative response of his immediate predecessors to the intellectual, economic, and political life of their times effectively pushed the church to the margins of public life. Consequently, "Leo's main achievement was his attempt, within the framework of traditional teaching, to bring the church to terms with the modern world" (J. Kelly 1986, 311). A review of Leo's sponsorship of neo-Thomism and his censure of Americanism should confirm this judgment.

Döllinger had declared post-Reformation scholasticism dead in 1863. A neoscholastic or neo-Thomist revival was launched by Leo on August 4, 1879, a year and a half after his election, when he issued his encyclical *Aeterni Patris*. This document, drafted with the assistance of the influential Jesuit Thomist Joseph Kleutgen (1811–83), officially "imposed the philosophico-theological system of St. Thomas Aquinas on the whole church. This was an unprecedented act, and its significance is often underrated" (G. Daly 1985, 775). In his encyclical, Leo called Aquinas "the chief and master" of all the scholastics and "a singular safeguard and glory of the Catholic Church" because "with his own hand he vanquished all errors of ancient times; and still he supplies an armory of weapons which brings us certain victory in the conflict with falsehoods ever springing up in the course of years."

The goal of neo-Thomism was to offer a coherent, unified, systematic philosophy and theology as an alternative to the philosophy of Kant and other modern philosophers. While some theologians were attempting to use some of the insights of Kant, the neo-Thomists judged modern philosophy intrinsically unsatisfactory for the development of Catholic theology for two reasons: because it set faith and reason in opposition to one another and it made human beings the measure of all things. Neo-Thomism became the theology of all the popes from Leo XIII to Pius XII (Gallagher 1990, 49).

Leo's decree slowed the development of historical consciousness within the church in two ways: it continued the trend begun with Vatican Council I whereby history (ancient tradition) was replaced by an appeal to the "living tradition" of papal pronouncements and authority; and it advocated the "timeless" philosophy and theology of the neoscholastics that left no room for history (Hennesey 1989, 675).

From the moment of this country's birth, United States Catholics have had to struggle to reconcile Catholicism and democratic institutions. Many Protestants "feared and mistrusted the Catholic church as an un-Christian invader of the republic" (Skerrett 1993, 128). Due to immigration, the Catholic community was the largest religious group in the United States by 1850. By 1890 the Catholic bishops had polarized into two parties over the question of how to best specify the identity and mission of the church in this country. Some bishops, led by Archbishop Michael Corrigan (1839–1902) of New York City, were satisfied with upholding the compatibility of Catholicism and democracy and opted for traditional Roman Catholic ways. Others, led by Cardinal James Gibbons (1834–1921) of Baltimore and Archbishop John Ireland (1838–1918) of St. Paul, wanted more than the compatibility approach. They believed "Catholicism should Americanize" because the church could learn from the American experience (Portier 1983, 323–28).

The Americanists claimed that, since there were obvious differences between American and European Catholics, the church in the United States should incorporate the American ideals into itself. This meant that there should be separation of church and state, that religious pluralism should be tolerated, and that the church should be remodeled along democratic lines. The latter meant that in the church there should be freedoms analogous to those enjoyed in America's liberal democracy (e.g., active participation, personal initiative, consultation, collaboration, accountability and due process); and that the church should protect individual consciences in preference to ideas such as loyalty, obedience, and uniformity. Gibbons and Ireland advocated these positions because they desired to enhance the identity and mission of the church in a pluralistic society. Americans would never respect—much less join—a church that did not value and foster the American ideals of liberty and justice.

Leo did not denounce the liberal movements with the same vigor as did Pius IX. In fact, he called on Catholics to search for practical, positive solutions to their country's social, economic, and political problems. Nevertheless, Leo XIII had little regard for the United States's principle of separation of church and state. He interpreted the American willingness to work within the framework of religious pluralism as a weakness toward indifferentism. In his encyclical *Longinqua oceani* (1895), he stated he was pleased that religious freedom had brought the church in the United States prosperity and other blessings. Nevertheless, he claimed the church would develop even more if, in addition to liberty, "she enjoyed the favor of the laws and the patronage of the public authority."

On January 22, 1899, Leo sent a personal letter, *Testem benevolentiae*, to Cardinal Gibbons about the church in the United States. In it he set forth two principles. In doctrinal matters, there can be no modification of Roman Catholic beliefs. It is wrong to foster an apologetics that would whittle down church teaching to suit modernity in order to attract those not of the faith. According to Leo, Catholicism did not "admit modifications, according to the diversity of time and place." In disciplinary matters, the church, he said, must adapt its laws to the conditions of local areas as long as they are drawn up by the responsible hierarchy.

Leo censured the church in the United States for holding views he called "Americanism," a term created by French theologians. The French distrusted the term *democracy* because in their country it was associated with the anticlericalism, skepticism, and irreligion of the French Revolution. They could not understand how a government could be neutral toward religion. In their view, governments were either supporters of religion or inimical to it. They could not comprehend the easy rapprochement between the church and the United States government. They were also baffled by the prolabor tendencies of many of the bishops, and the willingness of many of them to make decisions without necessarily looking to Rome (A. Jones 1992). Leo condemned the following views: the desire of the church in the United States to be different from the rest of the Roman Catholic world; the conviction that the church should show more indulgence to modern theories and methods; and the belief that individuals can act confidently and independently based on their natural capacities in such a way that the Catholic church's power to demand obedience to those in authority would be limited.

With this letter Leo simply cut short any conversation about the religious significance of the American system of government.

Pius X

The reform of the inner life of the institutional church was the major concern of Pius X. He promoted frequent communion, reformed the code of canon law, restored Gregorian chant, and improved the formation of priests. He also checked the smallest moves toward disobedience or doctrinal error.

During his pontificate some scholars sought to adopt the modern methodologies and findings of historians, scientists, and other thinkers to the church's interpretation of its doctrines, disciplines, and scriptures. In doing so, they rejected the unconditonal obedience that Roman authorities had come to expect. Consequently, some of their adaptations of the implications of biblical or historical criticism were deemed heretical. The scholars who believed that the church should adapt to the new situation were called modernists and their teachings were labeled Modernism (G. Daly 1980). Modernism was not a single movement or a complete system of thought. As George Tyrrell wrote: "By a modernist, I mean a churchman of any sort, who believes in the possibility of a synthesis between the essential truth of his religion and the essential truth of modernity" (1910, 5).

The underlying problem in this controversy was that traditional theology overemphazised the objective, the intellectual, and the unchangeable, whereas modernists, such as Alfred Loisy, Tyrrell, and Von Hügel, were attempting to introduce the subjective, psychological, and the changeable into the church's interpretation of Christianity.

Alfred Loisy (1857–1940), a French priest and scripture scholar, published his famous book *The Gospel and the Church* in 1902. This book touched off the conflict between Rome and the scholars. In his day the church did not conceive of itself as the product of historical development.

Loisy proposed a radically historical view of the church, explaining that the church was an historical organism that grew out of the gospel of Jesus, adapting its doctrines and itself as an institution to different circumstances in history.

Loisy published his research to refute *What Is Christianity?*, the bestseller by the German scholar, Adolf von Harnack (1851–1930). Harnack's thesis was that Jesus' basic teachings—"God as the Father, and the human soul so ennobled that it can and does unite with him"—were covered over by the church's dogmas and structures. In other words, Harnack viewed the church's dogmas and structures as distortions of Christianity. He believed the essence of Christianity was the interior and individual realization of the kingdom of God in the heart of each individual. Loisy agreed that there were historical developments of the church's structures and teachings, but these were not distortions. "To reproach Catholicism for all its developments," wrote Loisy, "is to reproach it for remaining alive."

George Tyrrell (1861–1909), an English Jesuit and philosopher of religion, wrote essays and reviews in the area of popular spirituality. He wrote for those he sensed were under a strain trying to live a spirituality that came out of the prevailing neo-Thomist theology. He identified neoscholasticism with its roots in Aristotle with intellectualism "and saw both as destructive of authentic Christianity" (D. Donovan 1985, 148). Furthermore, Tyrrell "was an eclectic rather than a systematic thinker. The recurring theme in his work is experience and how both historical and inward experience must be integrated into theology" (Haight 1990). He believed that the distinguishing note of the Catholic church was that it was the "divinely conceived fulfillment of all man's natural religious instincts." The church had amazing adaptive power whereby it could relate to any culture in which it found itself.

Baron von Hügel is often listed among the modernists because in his frequent travels he became a go-between, putting various modernist writers in touch with one another. Neither he nor his writings were ever condemned by the church whereas both Loisy and Tyrrell were excommunicated.

Modernism was condemned by Pius X in three separate documents. The decree *Lamentabili* (July 3, 1907) branded Modernism a "synthesis of all heresies." The decree was a syllabus of errors, consisting of sixty-five proscribed theses taken from publications in philosophy, theology, social theory, and, above all, biblical criticism. The encyclical *Pascendi* (September 8, 1907) condemned Modernism as a full-fledged philosophical and theological system. Pius X ordered the bishops throughout the world to see to the orthodoxy of biblical studies and scholastic philosophy in the seminaries and to extinguish the modernist movement by ridding seminaries and parishes of those sympathetic to it. The oath against Modernism was promulgated in a decree *(Sacrorum antistitum)* on September 1, 1910.

It was imposed on all clergy and was to be renewed on an annual basis. The oath opened with this sentence: "I firmly embrace and accept anything and everything defined, asserted, and declared by the inerrant magisterium of the church, especially those articles of doctrine that are directly opposed to the errors of the present time."

Some of the most adamant opponents of the new learning—called traditionalists by most writers—were Cardinal Francis Richard of Paris; Cardinal Rafael Merry del Val, Pius's secretary of state; and Monsignor Umberto Benigni, a Vatican functionary. The latter organized a spy system that made its way into many dioceses around the world. "This secret organization urged the reporting to the Holy See of the writings, sermons, speeches, and even the conversations of churchmen, from cardinals to seminarians, in which the slightest hint of divergence from true doctrines, or of non-conformity to papal policies, might be found" (Murphy 1981, 34). There occurred a veritable reign of terror.[2]

The foundations of Modernism as depicted by Pius X in *Pascendi* were the broad philosophical and theological tendencies towards agnosticism, immanentism, evolutionism, and democratism (Kerlin 1973; see also McBrien 1981, 218–19, 644–46).

The first of these, agnosticism, is the belief that it is not rationally possible to determine whether God exists and what our relationship to this deity might be. Our only means of knowing about God is by an internal personal religious experience. This experience is the real core of faith. All conceptual explications are radically changeable, like clothes covering a body. The real mystery of God is grasped nonconceptually. This is the central experience of faith.

Agnosticism is compatible with the Catholic belief in that Catholicism affirms that inner religious experience is an essential element in the act of faith. In fact, "religion in both its origins and its initial expressions is an activity of the preconceptual intellect (preconscious, creative imagination, poetic imagination, agent intellect)" (Greeley 1980). Yet inner religious experience is not the only way we come to a knowledge of God. God's revelation never occurs in a purely internal experience. It is always mediated through symbols—a person, an historical event, nature, words, or liturgical signs (Dulles 1980).

Immanentism asserts that religious beliefs are the culturally relative response to felt human needs and to the unknowable domains beyond phenomena. All people have within them a religious consciousness according to this view. They have an ever evolving personal knowledge of God that spurs them toward the divine and his salvation. Thus, the modernists downplayed the supernatural origin and process of revelation. For some of them, Jesus was a human person and God did not save us through him.

It is true that we always live in the presence of God and that God reveals himself first and foremost in order to share his creative and salvific love, rather than for the satisfaction of our intellectual curiosity. Yet Catholicism teaches that our understanding of God's revelation is not a completely natural process. It is a gift from a trancendent God whose continued guidance we need lest we distort the meaning of the gospel and the way of salvation.

Some modernists taught the theory of doctrinal evolution—that people's religious consciousness was given imperfect expression in statements called dogmas. These statements were effective if they harmonized with the general cultural situation of religious people. They can and should be changed according to the needs and culture of the people and the church because they are only statements about human perception of reality. There is no objective reality behind such dogmas as the trinity, the incarnation, and the resurrection. These terms merely point to the mysterious intuitions of God had by those persons who first coined the terms.

It is this point that aroused the greatest opposition from the traditionalists. On the one hand, it is true that the mystery of God cannot be completely captured in dogmatic statements. Also, "many dogmas are to be understood less as positive declarations of the content of revelation than as rejections of errors prevelant at a certain time" (Dulles 1986a). Consequently, all the sources of Christian tradition, especially the scriptures, must be studied according to the most scientifically critical methods at hand. Nevertheless, dogmatic statements and the scriptures, despite their cultural conditioning, do point to the definitive and unconditional character of God's revelation in Christ that Catholicism holds.

Institutional democratism was the fourth of Pius's concerns. Some modernists taught that the church came into existence when religious people tried to communicate their faith to others and to maintain it. The church did not have its source in Jesus Christ; the church's authority derived from the experience and sensitivity of its members. Faith is shaped and maintained by the conscience of the whole church community.

Catholics agree that God's revelation was only gradually unfolded in the life of the church. Yet the scriptures and dogmatic statements are more than historical documents. They are also expressions and products of the church's response to the Spirit, and need to be read and interpreted as such.

After the publication of *Pascendi,* Loisy, Tyrrell, and Von Hügel declared that the papal description of Modernism had nothing to do with their writings or beliefs (D. Donovan 1985, 146).

Benedict XV and Pius XI

Benedict XV became pope in September 1914. On November 1, 1914, he issued his first encyclical, *Ad beatissimi,* calling a halt to the bitter animosity between die-hard traditionalists and modernists. However, clergy were still required to take the 1910 oath against Modernism until Paul VI cancelled it in 1967.

When Pius X decreed in 1911 that bishops had complete authority over all Catholic organizations, he became the forerunner of Catholic Action. This term denotes the collaboration of the laity in the apostolic work of the church's hierarchy. The task of the laity was to animate society with a Christian spirit, especially the Catholic understanding of faith and morals. But it was Pius XI who inaugurated Catholic Action in his first encyclical, *Ubi arcano,* on December 23, 1922. He was eager to carry forward the theme of Pius X for two reasons. First, a major goal of his pontificate was to end the church's isolation from society. We have seen that he chose as his motto, "Christ's peace in Christ's kingdom." Second, he was concerned about the severe shortage of priests in Italy and around the world. Pius wrote "In our own time especially, when the integrity of the faith and morals is more seriously threatened each day, and the lack of priests, to our great sorrow, renders the clergy absolutely unable to meet the needs of souls, [Catholic Action] will help the priests and make up for their small numbers by multiplying their helpers among the laity."

Pius XI named Mary Ward (1585–1645), foundress of the Institute of the Blessed Virgin Mary, patroness of Catholic Action. This saintly Belgian woman maintained that women had an apostolic responsibility in society. She predicted that "it will be seen in time to come that women will do much" for the church and society. Thousands of her sisters are presently at work on six continents in thirty-four countries.

As a scholar-pope, Pius XI quietly eased the tensions arising from the modernist debate. He also enlarged the Vatican Library and founded both the Pontifical Institute of Christian Archeology (1925) and the Pontifical Academy of Sciences (1936).

Pius XII

We can get a sense of this pope's reaction to modernity from the way he dealt with scripture scholarship, the "new theology," and papal authority.

His approach to the first concern contrasted with Leo XIII's encyclical *Providentissimus Deus* (November 18, 1893), which turned a cautious eye on the historical-critical method of scripture interpretation, especially with regard to apparent contradictions between the physical sciences and the scriptures. The historical-critical method uses all the tools of criticism—archeology, history, the ancient languages themselves—to uncover fully the meaning intended by the inspired author. This method frees the reader from biblical fundamentalism, a reading that fails to consider the context of a scriptural passage, that is, its literary mode, purpose, relationship to other passages, or to the whole work in which it appears. Nevertheless, quoting Thomas Aquinas, Leo said that, concerning scientific matters, the inspired writers "went by what sensibly appeared." This understanding enabled Leo to exclude scientific matters from biblical inerrancy. The belief that scientific statements "were made according to surface appearances and so are not necessarily from a scientific viewpoint is a backdoor way of admitting human conditioning on the part of biblical authors" (R. E. Brown 1981, 14).

The Pontifical Biblical Commission Leo inaugurated in 1902 continued to be wary of the historical-critical method (Fitzmyer 1994, 14–15). Although the commission never condemned the method, its insistence on the Mosaic authorship of the Pentateuch in 1906 and its rejection of the two-source theory of the synoptic gospels in 1912 hardly inspired biblical scholars.

In 1920 Benedict XV issued *Spiritus Paraclitus* to commemorate the death in 420 of the greatest Latin biblical scholar, Jerome. Benedict took a negative view of the advances in biblical studies in his encyclical, strongly insisting on the complete historicity of the Bible.

On the fiftieth anniversary of *Providentissimus Deus,* Pius XII issued *Divino afflante Spiritu* (September 30, 1943), often considered the Magna Carta for biblical scholarship. The historical context of the encyclical was "a series of anonymous and pseudonymous pamphlets to Italian bishops attacking biblical studies" (Donahue 1993). Pius was influenced by the German Jesuit scholar Augustin Bea (1881–1968), rector of the Pontifical Biblical Institute from 1930 to 1959, and the French Dominican Jacques Marie Voste (1882–1949), secretary of the PBC. Unlike Leo and Benedict, Pius encouraged and freed scholars to pursue their research and to use the historical-critical method without threat of condemnation by the Vatican. The encyclical acknowledged an essential finding of the biblical scholars, namely, that the Bible contains many different forms of literature (myths, parables, letters, miracle stories, infancy narratives, and so forth), which must be sorted out as one reads the text (n. 12). This means the Bible should not be read as if it were modern history.

Pius also addressed the challenge of the "new theology." Even before the 1943 encyclical, some theologians were turning from the prevailing neo-Thomist or neoscholastic theology to the patristic, liturgical, and sacramental sources of the Catholic tradition. They did so in order to hear again what was said then, to reasssess the present in light of the past, and to help the church enter a dynamic conversation with the world of modernity. They found that neoscholasticism was oriented toward subtle and abstract discussions that were rather remote from the day-to-day life of people. These theologians tried to show that the ahistorical methodology of the neo-Thomists was not in accord either with Thomas Aquinas and other medieval scholastics such as Bonaventure and Vincent of Lérins or with the Church Fathers. Unlike the neo-Thomists, Thomas never dismissed the challenges of his contemporaries on the grounds that he already possessed the truth. The new theologians also opposed the dualisms that characterized the neoscholastic theology and spirituality: body and soul, profane and sacred, church and world, temporal and eternal, nature and grace. For example, in their theology of grace the neo-Thomists underscored grace as a created gift of God rather than God's personal presence; as a divine healing of the effects of sin rather than as the perfection of a human nature, which is itself God's good creation; and as a gift offered only intermittently and in certain privileged times and circumstances rather than a gift offered constantly and being universally present in the world.

The theology of these scholars was sarcastically dubbed *la nouvelle théologie* (the new theology) by Reginald Garrigou-Lagrange (1877–1964), a Dominican theologian who taught at the Pontifical University of St. Thomas in Rome from 1909 to 1960. There never was an identifiable position which could be described by the term "new theology." It was simply a convenient term of derogatory rejection applied to the "new" positions thought to be a threat to the established neo-Thomist theology. The "new theologians" were also unhappy with the word "new" because so much of their writings explored classic Christian writings.

The "new" theologians included such famous scholars as Yves Congar (1904–95); Henri de Lubac (1896–1991) and his Swiss pupil, Hans Urs von Balthasar (1905–88); Jean Danielou (1905–74); Marie-Dominique Chenu (1895–1990); and Pierre Teilhard de Chardin (1881–1955).

Most of these theologians were censured by Rome. Teilhard, a Jesuit priest and noted paleontologist, had his first brush with the Vatican in 1924 when he sent to Rome an essay on original sin that was not intended for publication. From then onward he was not allowed to publish articles in philosophy or theology without prior Roman approval. When he sought approval for the publication of *The Divine Milieu* in 1927, permission was never granted. After Teilhard's death in 1955, his scientific and spiritual writings, especially his classic on the spiritual life, *The Divine Milieu*, were translated into sixteen languages and read with great enthusiasm in the 1960s. He became something of a folk hero.

Teilhard emphasized that we encounter God primarily through the created world and not mystical union, the emphasis of the neo-Thomists. He took this position partly as a result of his attempt to integrate Christian theology with the scientific views of evolution and the origin of the universe. God, wrote Teilhard, shines through the universe and through Christ, the Alpha and Omega of evolution and the activating energy of the entire cosmos.

In place of a spirituality that divided spirit and matter, science and religion, and God and humankind, Teilhard's evolutionary humanism envisaged the whole universe as coextensive with the body of the risen Christ. In view of this relationship, he downplayed the effects of original sin and evil. He urged theologians to give serious consideration to the physical relation between Christ and the material world. He wrote "The whole of the Church's dogmatic and sacramental economy teaches us to respect matter and to value it. Christ had to assume and wanted to assume real flesh. He sanctifies human flesh by special contact and he prepares its physical resurrection. . . . Because it has been assimilated into the Body of Christ, something from matter is destined to pass into the foundations and walls of the heavenly Jerusalem."[3]

Chenu, a Dominican historian of medieval theology, was silenced in 1942 for his 1937 publication, *A School of Theology: Le Saulchoir.* In this important book, Chenu argued against a "timeless Thomism," insisting that a text could be understood only in its historical, cultural, social, and political context. He also taught that the source of theology was the involvement of the church with the changing world. This book was placed on the Index of Forbidden Books in 1942 probably because of its "apparently modernistic recognition of historicity and human experience with theology" (Schoof 1970, 104). Rome condemned Chenu's work also out of fear that any emphasis on the historical context of theology would divorce it from its foundation in revelation and would turn theology into cultural anthropology. Chenu was deprived of his title as Master of Theology, was removed from his post at Le Saulchoir (a Dominican house of study in Belgium) and was ordered to live in Paris (Komonchak 1990a).

Yves Congar was ordained a Dominican priest in 1930 and immediately began to teach and write. His writings did not go unnoticed in Rome. His first book, *Divided Christendom* (1937), a groundbreaking work on ecumenism that helped Catholics rediscover the merits of Protestantism, was scrutinized by Vatican censors. Later, several chapters of *The Mystery of the Church* (1941) were censored. During World War II Congar served as a medical orderly in the French army, was captured, and spent five years as a prisoner of war. After the war he returned to Paris to teach. He was soon the object of surveillance again (Nichols 1989). He later reported that "from the beginning of 1947 until the end of 1956, I have known only an unbroken series of denunciations, warnings, restrictions, discriminatory measures and scornful delations [secret, accusatory reports]" (cited in McBrien 1995b). In 1950 he published *True and False Reform in the Church.* This text was "submitted to 16 censors, only to finally be censured after being published" (Beauchesne 1995). In 1953 he was ordered out of his teaching position and silenced. He underwent an exile in Jerusalem, then Rome, and then Cambridge, where he was not assigned any ministerial work. In 1956 he was given a teaching position at Strasbourg. By 1958 Vatican pressure eased because the atmosphere in the church changed dramatically with the election of Pope John XXIII (Komonchak 1995).

One of the great ironies of church history is that, although almost all the new theologians were silenced by Pius XII, they were all eventually rehabilitated. For example, in July 1960, De Lubac[4] and Congar were appointed by John XXIII to the Theological Commission established to prepare texts for consideration by the council. John Paul II offered the cardinal's hat to De Lubac in 1983 and Congar in 1994. During the council, many of the new theologians served as experts to the bishops in the composition of the conciliar texts. Yves Congar, for example, worked on three of the constitutions and on the decrees on missionary activity, ecumenism, and the priesthood (Nichols 1990, 252–53). Joseph Komonchak, priest-theologian at Catholic University, suggests that "there is no theologian who did more to prepare for Vatican II and who had a larger role in the orientation and even in the composition of its documents" than Congar (1983). Although Teilhard de Chardin was dead, his spirit and writings influenced Vatican II (King 1985). Several bishops cited him during the public discussions. The document on the church in the modern world uses some of his phrases when it speaks of the impact of science and technology on human development (GS 5), of Christ as "the goal of human history" (GS 10), and when it notes that "the human race has passed from a rather static concept of reality to a more dynamic, evolutionary one" (GS 5).

Finally, Pius XII reacted to the challenge of modernity by reasserting papal authority. On August 12, 1950, he published his encyclical *Humani generis*, with its subtitle, "Some False Opinions Which Threaten To Undermine the Foundations of Catholic Doctrine." Although the encyclical did not name the new theologians, it seemed to cast suspicion on them. As we have just seen, some of those associated with the new theology were stripped of their teaching positions; some were forbidden to write or ordered to submit their manuscripts to church censors. This explains in part why Peter Hebblethwaite (1993a, 235) judged this encyclical "the most drastic and embarrassing action" of Pius's pontificate.

Pius, influenced in great part by Reginald Garrigou-Lagrange, rejected some new-theology themes. He linked them to Modernism. He believed, for example, that their emphasis on the universality of grace in history undercut both the gratuity of grace and the teaching authority of the hierarchical church. This far-ranging encyclical also pronounced that the Body of Christ and the Roman Catholic Church are "one and the same"; that Catholics owe "religious allegiance of the will and intellect" even to teachings of the pope not declared infallible; that Christian scholars should return to Thomistic orthodoxy in both philosophy and theology; and that the task of theologians is to justify the declarations of the official magisterium by showing how this teaching is found in scripture and tradition, whether explicitly or implicitly. Pius went so far as to say that once the pope expresses his judgment on a point previously controversial, "there can no longer be any question of free discussion among theologians." Finally, Pius XII asserted that the church's dogmatic formulas were unchangeable, were perfect expressions of the truths contained in the Bible, and were definitive and hence valid always. Pius declared that anyone who dared to suggest otherwise was on dangerous ground.

Modernism in Perspective

During the first half of the twentieth century two popes, Pius X and Pius XII, condemned any theology that carried the ideals of Modernism, and two popes, Benedict XV and Pius XI, tried to ease the tension arising from the debate over Modernism. Nonetheless, the condemnation of Modernism cast a pall over the intellectual and devotional life of the institutional church during these four pontificates.

In the light of Vatican II, several theologians have evaluated why Modernism took hold and what it means for the church today. Daniel Donovan, for example, stated that the Vatican "neglected to offer any positive suggestions for dealing with the new issues that developments in philosophy, history and biblical criticism were raising. This meant in practice that the problems to a large degree were simply repressed. Their return in the postconciliar context is surely a major factor in recent confusion and polarization in the Catholic church" (1985, 156). David Tracy wrote that because of the way honest scholars were dishonored, academic institutions investigated, and intellectual inquiry was silenced, "The modernist and Americanist crises should be acknowledged as Catholicism's Vietnam experience" (1987b, 271). Roger Haight, a Jesuit theologian, judged that from our vantage point today, the encyclical *Pascendi* was "a document that was politically brilliant, deadly effective, intellectually dishonest, and totally comprehensible in the historical situation" (1990). The historical situation was one of fear. Both Pius X and Pius XII feared the modernists would bring the hostile elements of modernity inside the church. "What was feared, then, were internal forces that would change the very structure of the church" (ibid.).

Conclusion: John XXIII and Vatican II

During the preconciliar period—1878 to 1962—the church solidified its identity and mission, often by challenging the intellectual, economic, and political views of society. The church was positioned over against the world, its values, and goals. The church maintained that the world needed to be rechristianized. During this period, the church also strengthened its institutional, intellectual, and devotional life by officially stabilizing these dimensions in such a way that the church as institution, especially as manifested by the papal office, was the dominant image of the church as a whole. The intellectual and devotional dimensions of the Catholic tradition were locked into the timeless philosophy and theology of neo-Thomism. Modernists within the church were marginalized, even excommunicated. However, the intellectual and devotional dimensions of the church have never been monolithic. During this period, for example, Pius XI opened the church to the physical sciences and Pius XII encouraged scripture scholars to employ the modern methods of textual analysis. The new theologians argued against a timeless Thomism, highlighted the church as Christ's community and underscored grace as God's personal and universal presence. The new theologians, those Catholic masters of suspicion, would have their say (and way) at Vatican II.

Even the future John XXIII had an encounter with the Vatican over modernity. It seems that when he was a young priest and serving as secretary to Bishop Radini-Tedeschi, he was accused of favoring some modernist positions. In his biography of the bishop, John XXIII admitted that his accusers were more anxious to get at the bishop than at him. Nevertheless, when John became pope and examined his file in the Vatican, the letter he had sent in 1914 protesting his loyalty to the gospel and the church was missing. But he had his notes among his own papers and was able to reconstruct the original letter. This unfortunate incident explains in part John's insistence that Vatican II would issue no condemnations.

With Vatican II, the institutional church's negative response to modernity came to an end. At that historic meeting, the church officially and decisively entered the age of historical consciousness. The bishops not only declared that "Ours is a new age of history with profound and rapid changes spreading gradually to all corners of the earth" (GS 4), but they also noted that "We are witnessing the birth of a new humanism, where people are defined before all else by their responsibility to their sisters and brothers and at the court of history" (GS 55). Echoing the Enlightenment, the bishops proposed that "the social order requires constant improvement: it must be founded in truth, built on justice, and enlivened by love: it should grow in freedom towards a more humane equilibrium" (GS 26). The council fathers frankly admitted that "the church is not unaware how much it has profited from the history and development of humankind" (GS 44). The bishops placed the church firmly within the modern world. They began their landmark document on the church in the modern world with these eloquent words, "The joys and hopes, the grief and anguish of the people of our time, especially of those who are poor or afflicted, are the joys and hopes, the grief and anguish of the followers of Christ as well. Nothing that is genuinely human fails to find an echo in their hearts. . . . That is why they cherish a feeling of deep solidarity with the human race and its history" (GS 1).

CHAPTER 3

Vatican Council II

The Catholic church regards twenty councils held before Vatican II to be ecumenical, the first at Nicea in 325 and the twentieth, Vatican I, from 1869 to 1870.

John XXIII had the inspiration—what he called "a flash of heavenly light"—to call a council on January 20, 1959. According to his own journal, John was in his private apartment, talking with his secretary of state, Cardinal Domenico Tardini (1888–1961), when, suddenly and unexpectedly, he exclaimed that there would be a council. Tardini was enthusiastic.

It has become a tradition that each January 18 to 25, the Christian churches pray for Christian unity. On January 25, 1959, at the Basilica of St. Paul-Outside-the-Walls, Pope John, accompanied by seventeen cardinals, presided over the prayers for unity. After the ceremony, "in a short speech he made an announcement that came as a thunderbolt: his decision to summon an ecumenical council to promote the unity of all the Christian communities" (Falconi 1967, 324). The cardinals were so struck by the announcement that they sat like statues. There were no comments and, surprisingly, not even polite applause.

John returned to the Vatican and soon realized he had to deal with Vatican officials who were on the defensive. Apparently, some feared a universal council would detract from their privileges. Others wondered if a council was even necessary since the institutional church seemed vigorous and powerful. After all, the theologians were firmly under the control of the hierarchy, there was a uniform liturgical life in the worldwide church, and there was no obvious crisis demanding the attention of all the bishops. Nevertheless, some Vatican officials gave the pope the cold shoulder or what Cardinal Giacomo Lercaro (1891–1976) called a "great institutional solitude" (ibid., 330). Even Tardini before his sudden death in 1961 expressed serious doubts—even scorn—for the proposed council, pointing to the fact that previous councils had usually been followed by times of upheaval and confusion (Murphy 1992).

Its Purpose

The Constitution on the Liturgy, the first document approved by the council in December 1963, listed four goals of the council: to revitalize Catholics in their spirituality; to adapt church observances to the requirements of the times; to unite all Christians; and to strengthen the church's mission to all peoples (SC 1).

The day Pope John announced the council, January 25, 1959, he was somewhat vague about his reasons for calling it. He told the cardinals that the purpose of the council would be "to proclaim the truth, bring Christians closer to the faith, and contribute at the same time to peace and prosperity on earth" (cited in MacEoin 1966, 9). Over the next few months and with the advice of his associates, however, John made the goals of the council much clearer. The immediate goal was to modernize the church and to involve it in the concerns of the world, especially those efforts at strengthening unity and peace. The ultimate goal was the unification of all Christians.

John also wanted Vatican II to be a "new Pentecost" for the church. He himself composed a prayer to the Spirit, asking blessings on the council. He prayed that the Spirit would renew its wonders "in this our day, as by a new Pentecost" (Abbott 1966, 793). John was convinced that the church had to respond to God's presence in the world as manifested through the "signs of the times." When John formally convoked the council with the apostolic constitution *Humanae salutis* on December 25, 1961, he used the biblical phrase "signs of the times" in an optimistic sense; that is, there were special signs of the presence of God in history that required the attention of Christians. This meaning is quite different from the scriptural usage, which highlighted the apocalyptic events said to precede the end of history (as in Matthew 16:1–4).

John used the term again in his encyclical *Pacem in terris* (1963) when he indicated that there were developments taking place in history that Christians ought not to fear or resist because some of them "augur well for the fate of the church and humanity." John, whose "great gift to the church was his ability to read the signs of the times" (Lernoux 1989, 21), singled out three signs: the struggle of colonial people to determine their own future, the effort of workers to obtain their socioeconomic rights, and the quest of women for equality in domestic and public life. At Vatican II the bishops picked up on John's usage, in great part because "Paul VI missed no opportunity to speak of the significance of the signs of the times" (Häring 1992, 49). The bishops declared that "In every age, the church carries the responsibility of reading the signs of the times and of interpreting them in the light of the gospel. . . . We must be aware of and understand the aspirations, the yearnings and the often dramatic features of the world in which we live" (GS 4).

John's word for modernizing the church in light of the signs of the times was the Italian word *aggiornamento,* meaning an updating. Aggiornamento became the guiding principle of Vatican II. For the longest time the church had followed the principle set forth by Giles of Viterbo (1469–1532) at the Fourth Lateran Council (1512–17) that "men must be changed by religion, not religion by men." What John's aggiornamento called for was precisely the opposite. Aggiornamento meant the church had to change to meet the needs of the times, that is, the changes taking place outside itself. Aggiornamento looked to the needs and legitimate demands of people. It was not a simple-minded rejection of all that was old and a breezy acceptance of everything new, but rather a disengagement from the limitations of the past and from a culture no longer viable. Aggiornamento denoted critical involvement in the new culture without denying its evils and its need for transformation (Lonergan 1974, 113).

The ultimate goal—church unity—was a Promethean and revolutionary project. While it is true that on the eve of Vatican I in 1869, Pius IX wrote a letter inviting all who were not Catholic to enter the church and to let the council be the occasion to respond to the needs of their hearts and "to extricate themselves from that state in which they cannot be certain of their salvation," nevertheless, once the council got underway, it "operated at an almost total removal from the concerns, or even the very existence, of other Christians" (Hennesey 1971). In June 1960, John XXIII created the Secretariat for Christian Unity and gave it the task of inviting leaders of the other Christian churches to attend the council as observers. By calling Vatican II, John thrust the Catholic church into the midst of those Christians who were in the vanguard of the ecumenical movement.

Its Preparation

Between the announcement of the council on January 25, 1959, and its opening on October 11, 1962, there were three years and eight months. A great deal of preparation was needed.

The Roman curia, under the leadership of Cardinal Alfredo Ottaviani (1890–1979), Prefect of the Holy Office, was given the task of organizing the council. Twelve preparatory commissions were set up to deal with different aspects of the church such as the sacraments, the clergy, the bishops, and the religious orders. These commissions eventually produced seventy decrees and dogmatic constitutions. The opinion of many is that "The preparatory documents were consistent in their analysis and in their response: against the threats of subjectivism and historicism, the council was to provide a massive reaffirmation of authority, the authority of God in revelation, of Christ as his chief legate, of the church as Christ's juridically empowered agent in the world, of the tradition of objective verbal statements which articulate the Christian mysteries" (Komonchak 1985b).

Pope John was aware that the preparatory drafts were of a neoscholastic, juridical (an emphasis on the legal and organizational), and moralistic bent—not his emphasis—but he was not discouraged. After all, the work was getting done at the rate envisaged and the council would begin on time. Furthermore, the curia's "great institutional solitude" was broken by the interest and support for the council that came from individual bishops in Europe, the United States, and from the African and Asian countries.

"The most impressive and decisive help" came, however, from some of the other Christian churches—the Orthodox and Protestant churches (Falconi 1967, 333). For example, there was exuberant praise for Vatican II from Athenagoras, the Orthodox Patriarch of Constantinople. Similarly, many church leaders visited John at the Vatican, including Dr. Geoffrey Fisher, Archbishop of Canterbury, on December 2, 1960. This was a historic meeting: the first by the leader of the Anglican churches to Rome.

Its Opening

Vatican Council II—the decisive ecclesial event of this century—opened with a solemn liturgy on October 11, 1962. Present were twenty-seven hundred bishops, "the greatest gathering of bishops in the history of the Roman Catholic church" (Cortesi 1962). In 1869 at Vatican I there were forty-eight United States bishops; in 1962 there were two hundred seventeen. Also present were ninety superiors of religious communities of men. Present, too, were some four hundred *periti* (experts or advisors), thirty-nine representatives from other Christian communities, and some eighty-five ambassadors from different countries (Hebblethwaite 1982).

In his official opening address of October 11, 1962, John gave "the most important speech of [his] life and the most important speech in church history in the twentieth century" (ibid.). John made three points: First, the council was to be a celebration of Christian faith, of its unity in diversity, and catholicity.

Second, John expressed his optimism about the presence of the Spirit in the world. He complained that there were present in the church certain "prophets of doom who continually announce baleful events as if the end of the world were impending." He added that these prophets see an evil world where there is "only prevarication and decay" and that they fail to see that the church, herself a daughter of time, needs to be changed or modernized. John's hopeful message affirmed that "at the present moment in history, Providence is leading us towards a new order in human relations." John admitted that there were many errors in the contemporary world, but he believed these "often vanish as swiftly as they arise, like mist before the sun." To meet the needs of the modern age, John knew the church should show "the validity of her teachings rather than by [issuing] condemnations."

Third, the council must be pastoral. Instead of simply repeating the church's doctrine, stated John, the council must reclothe it to meet the needs "which our era demands." He said, "It is one thing to have the substance of the ancient doctrine of the *depositum fidei* [The Christian gospel originating in Christ and handed on over the ages] but quite another to formulate and reclothe it: and it is this that must—if need be with patience—be held of great importance, measuring everything according to the forms and proportions of a teaching of pre-eminently pastoral character." With this latter distinction, John effectively paved the way for accepting legitimate, though differing cultural expressions of the Christian gospel. It is just possible that the spirits of those modernists excommunicated by Pius X encircled the throne of John XXIII with smiles on their faces.

Most ecumenical councils have been polemical and juridical. The Council of Trent met for two reasons: to root out heresies and to reform the church's organization, discipline, and doctrines; Vatican I set out to condemn rationalism and define papal infallibility. Vatican II, however, was pastoral, that is, it intended to bring out the enduring relevance of the gospel by proclaiming Jesus' word and Jesus himself in order to meet the needs, hopes, joys, and fears of all people.

Its History

No one knew how long the council would last. Pope John seems to have anticipated a short, harmonious event. On October 10, 1962, he said he hoped it "will finish before Christmas," but that there might be another session "if we are not able to say all that we would like to in this period" (Cortesi 1962). By November 12, there was talk of a recess on December 8, with a resumption on May 12, 1963 (Dugan 1962b). When it was clear that more time was needed to permit the various working commissions to complete the greater part of their tasks, John ordered a switch in dates. The second session would begin on September 8, 1963 (Dugan 1962c). Eventually, four sessions were held: the first from October 11 to December 8, 1962; the second from September 29 to December 4, 1963; the third from September 14 to November 21, 1964; and the fourth from September 14 to December 8, 1965.

Most of the opening and closing dates were chosen for symbolic reasons. Several of the dates are Marian feast days. For example, in the Orthodox churches, October 11 is the feast of the Motherhood of Mary, an infallible declaration made at the ecumenical Council of Ephesus in 431. Since Mary receives special honor in all the Eastern churches, Catholic and Orthodox, the date served as a point of unity between the West and the East.

Its Mind

There were three events during the first session (October 11 to December 8, 1962) that indicated that there were serious divisions among the bishops. First, within twenty minutes of the first working session on October 13, 1962, when the curia presented its nominations for the working commissions, "frail looking Cardinal Achille Lienart [1884–1973] of Lille arose to propose that, on so crucial a point, the council should be given enough time to nominate and elect the members of these commissions on its own" (Outler 1982). He was promptly seconded by Cardinal Joseph Frings of Cologne—to the applause of the junior bishops at the far end of the assembly. In just twenty minutes the council passed from the tight grip of the Roman curia to the hands of the bishops, becoming an autonomous parliament with a mind of its own. It has been reported that John XXIII was pleased and even excited by this turn of affairs (Häring 1992, 49).

Second, the debate on the first document, the Constitution on the Liturgy, revealed two main trends among the bishops. To state it generally, the conservative, traditional point of view—one based on a classical consciousness—believed the troubles in the church stemmed primarily from a growing secularization in the world, a decrease in faith, and a lessening of respect for authority. The council's task, they maintained, was to repeat and clarify the traditional teaching. Its first priority was the internal organization of the church and its rights. The progressive point of view—based on an historical consciousness—maintained that the institutional church needed restructuring and reform because it was too hierarchical, too impersonal, and too detached from modernity. Service to all humankind in the name of the gospel should be the church's first priority. Therefore, the council had several tasks: to reclothe the church's teachings and disciplines to meet the modern world and its needs; to reform the liturgy; and, as a result of the example and urgings of John XXIII, to reunite the Christian churches (Komonchak 1990b).

Third, during the final week of the session the bishops discussed the initial draft of a document on the church. Although there was some praise for the document, several bishops found the neoscholastic document too juridical, triumphalist, and clerical. It left little room for the pastoral questions facing the church. On December 4, 1962, Cardinal Leo Joseph Suenens (1904–96) of Belgium proposed that the bishops first consider internal reform of the church and then the church's relations with the rest of the world. His proposal was a turning point in the bishops' deliberations. John XXIII gladly accepted Suenens's program and appointed him to a new coordinating committee that reviewed all the preparatory material before the second session in September 1963. This committee essentially set the agenda for the entire council.

Although Vatican II took a pastoral direction, bishops with a traditional perspective clashed with those with a progressive mindset over issues that are discussed here in later chapters—problems such as collegiality, religious freedom, marriage and family, priesthood, ecumenism, mariology, and so forth. Because of the presence of these two mindsets, it is not surprising that the bishops produced documents marked by different emphases, some inconsistencies, and some compromises. For example, the bishops maintained some of the dualisms that characterized the neoscholastic spirituality of the times: body and soul, profane and sacred, church and world, and temporal and eternal. Similarly, the bishops declared that the church has a mission in the world and the faithful were urged to engage in social action (GS 9), and yet the bishops said that "Christ did not bequeath to the church a proper mission in the political, economic, or social order: the purpose he assigned to it was religious" (GS 42). In the postconciliar church both conservatives and progressives have been able to cite the documents selectively, pressing either for change or the status quo.

Its Results

The conciliar bishops produced sixteen documents (approximately 103,000 words) on internal church reform and the church's relations with the rest of the world. The order and the dates are listed here:

> **December 4, 1963**
> Constitution on the Liturgy
> Decree on Communications
>
> **November 21, 1964**
> Constitution on the Church
> Decree on Ecumenism
> Decree on the Eastern Catholic Churches
>
> **October 28, 1965**
> Decree on the Bishops
> Decree on Priestly Formation
> Decree on Religious Life
> Declaration on Christian Education
>
> **November 18, 1965**
> Constitution on Revelation
> Decree on the Laity
>
> **November 28, 1965**
> Declaration on Non-Christian Religions
> Constitution on the Church in the Modern World

December 7, 1965
Decree on Priests
Decree on the Church's Missionary Activity
Declaration on Religious Freedom

There was another significant result of the council, but it took a few years for it to be recognized. The church, which had always been global, was perceived as being what was called a "world church."

The church is essentially global: its mission has always been to all people and nations. While it is true that Jesus instructed his disciples not to enter "pagan territory" or Samaritan towns but to go "only to the lost sheep of the house of Israel" (Matthew 10:5–6), nevertheless, the inner dynamism of his message of the universal reign of God made it inevitable that Christianity would be a faith with world-encompassing claims. The thrust to all corners of the globe is clear in other New Testament passages, especially in Matthew 28:18–29, Luke 9:1–6, and Acts 1–2.

In Germany in 1974, Walbert Bühlmann, a Capuchin missionary and theologian, published *The Coming of the Third Church*, a phenomenological study of the notion that Vatican II marked the emergence of the global church as a world church. The book created a stir in Europe because Bühlmann provided statistics that indicated that there were now more Catholics in Latin America, Africa, and Asia than in Europe and North America. He concluded that the West, while remaining influential within the church, was no longer the center of religious and cultural unity for the universal or global church. Karl Rahner (1904–84), a prolific and eminent Jesuit theologian, gave the book a stunning tribute, calling it "the best Catholic book of the year." However, it was Rahner himself who produced a brief essay in 1979 that has become the locus classicus for the discussion of this question and its far-reaching consequences.

Rahner divided church history into three periods. The first was that short period of Jewish Christianity (A.D. 30–49) when Christianity was proclaimed within one culture only: Israel. The second was that very long period (49–1962), when the gospel was proclaimed not in Jewish culture but in the Roman-Hellenistic culture in European and, eventually, North American culture and civilization. Christianity and western culture were goods exported to the cultures of Africa, Latin America, India, and the Orient. The third period began with Vatican II, when, due to the Spirit and the rise of historical consciousness, the church appeared for the first time as a world church in a fully official way. The church had found ways to formulate and incarnate the gospel within the traditions and customs of each culture. Rahner pointed out a number of signs of this change: the council brought together indigenous representatives of all the world's countries and cultures; it advocated the vernacular in the liturgy; it highlighted the authority of bishops in their dioceses; it recognized the autonomy and independence of regional or national churches; it expressed an opening to the world and historical consciousness; it made the first truly positive statements about other religions; and it produced the document on religious liberty.

The acceptance of other cultures relies on a transformational model and not simply a synthesis model, whereby the church merely adapts itself to other cultures, their beliefs and practices. Rather, the church must discover the Christian values already present in the nonwestern cultures. Rahner ended his essay by warning that if the church did not become de-Europeanized and de-Romanized, it would remain a western church and, in the final analysis, betray the meaning of Vatican II and aggiornamento. The recognition of the church as a world church is perhaps the most far-reaching effect of aggiornamento.

Its Decisions

"From the viewpoint of church history, it can be asserted that never before in the history of Catholicism have so many and such sudden changes been legislated and implemented which immediately touched the lives of the faithful, and never before had such a radical adjustment of viewpoint been required of them," commented Jesuit historian John O'Malley (1989, 17).

A list of the principles endorsed by Vatican II is too lengthy to produce here. These ten are some of the most important ones. The first five concern the church's relations with the rest of the religious and secular world; the second five deal with the church's internal reform.

1. Aggiornamento. Instead of being hostile and suspicious of the modern world, the church should update itself, that is, live in close union with its contemporaries, since the risen Christ is with us, calling his church to witness his gospel in today's world.

2. Religious freedom. The church, instead of seeking a privileged status and insisting that all belong to it, should foster religious freedom: it should respect the right and duty of each person to choose his or her religion.

3. Ecumenism. Instead of viewing the other Christian churches with hostility, Catholics should respect the heritage of other churches, note their salvific importance, and admit they possess true elements of the one and only church of Christ.

4. Interreligious dialogue. Instead of viewing other religions as false and harmful, Catholics should acknowledge the truths and goodness they manifest, even as Catholics continue to

proclaim that Jesus Christ is universal Lord and savior of all humankind.

5. Social mission. Instead of overemphasizing that individual salvation is to be achieved in the next world, the church must carry out on earth the mission of Christ, especially among the poor. Earthly affairs should not be divorced from religious life. The bishops said: "One of the gravest errors of our time is the dichotomy between the faith which many profess and their day-to-day conduct" (GS 43).

6. Reform. Instead of regarding itself as spotless and all holy, the church must acknowledge its errors, failings, and sins and continually reform itself.

7. The scriptures. Catholics should not limit their spirituality to sacraments, ritual, and law. Rather, the faithful must also immerse themselves in the scriptures because here the Spirit speaks in a special way.

8. Laity. Instead of reinforcing the principle behind Pius XI's Catholic Action (namely, that the faithful are called to the apostolate by a mandate from the hierarchy), the bishops said the faithful should exercise their ministry both in the church and in society based on their baptismal faith and commitment to Christ (LG 33). This put an end—in theory at least—to episcopal control over all forms of apostolic activities.

9. Collegiality. Instead of viewing the church primarily as a pyramid (bishops subordinate to the pope, priests subordinate to bishops, and people subordinate to priests), all Catholics should work together according to their proper roles for the common good of the church and its mission.

10. Regional and local diversity. Instead of emphasizing itself as a monolithic society, the church should stress the local churches in communion with the universal church.

Its Nature

What did Vatican II do for the universal and local church? How was the church different after the council from what it had been before 1962? What process did the council set in motion—was it a renewal, a reform, a reformation, or a retrieval and reinterpretation of the Catholic tradition?

We have seen that John XXIII had several specifics in mind: a new Pentecost; aggiornamento and Christian unity; the presence of leaders of other Christian communities as observers; a statement on Catholic-Jewish relations; and a policy prohibiting condemnations. Otherwise, declared O'Malley, "there is not the slightest shred of evidence that he foresaw or intended the direction it took" (1989, 116). There are several indications that John XXIII leaned toward the progressive outlook while holding onto some traditional views. For example, he issued an apostolic constitution on the importance of the use of Latin in the education of seminarians; on June 30, 1962, he issued a general warning against "numerous ambiguities and serious errors" in the writings of Teilhard de Chardin; and in 1962, he approved the dismissal of some professors from the Pontifical Biblical Institute in Rome who advocated the historical-critical method of scriptural interpretation.

Was the council a renewal? To renew is to restore something to its original state. Renewal takes place when "the church looks to its origins and revitalizes itself by contact with its spiritual sources" (Hebblethwaite 1975, 19). The council did that, particularly in its decisions about the church's identity and mission and about the laity, ecumenism, and religious liberty.

Was the council a reform? Reform entails a process to correct what is wrong, to remove defects, correct errors, and improve by alteration. The conciliar documents hardly use the word *reform*. The church never admitted that its teachings on religious liberty were a reversal or that it was guilty of persecuting Jews over many centuries. Yet, the bishops were aware of changes in society and, therefore, progress and development became major conciliar themes. The Decree on Ecumenism acknowledged that "Christ summons the church, as she goes her pilgrim way to that continual reformation of which she always has need, insofar as she is a human institution here on earth" (UR 6). Similarly, the council called for a number of reforms—for example, instead of having one liturgy for the whole church, the liturgy must be adapted to the genius and traditions of people (SC 37–40); and members of religious orders were instructed that instead of holding on to antiquated rules and constitutions, they should adapt "to the needs of our time" (PC 18).

On the other hand, while a reform involves changes and corrections, the changes take place within a given frame of reference and do not change the church's self-understanding. Reform steadies the church on its course. Did the self-understanding of the church actually change at Vatican II? Not drastically. The council failed to do away with its "absolutistic claims and its antiquated class structure" (Dulles 1988a, 19). In other words, the church never made a decisive break with juridicism, clericalism, and triumphalism. The latter term indicates that the church highlighted its successes in such a way that it assumed privileged status and superiority over the rest of the world's institutions and religious bodies. We have seen that the sixteen documents reflect the huge committees in which they were hammered out. They are marked by qualifications and ambiguities. The result, said O'Malley, was that many of the bishops "went home to resume life pretty much as usual once the work was done" (1989, 116). The reform, then, is ambivalent. There were some important changes, but others were not made—for example, the council did not restructure the Roman curia so that all authority would not be centralized in Rome.

Was Vatican II a reformation? This is O'Malley's thesis. By reformation he means "reform by transformation or by revolution." Such a reformation entails "a partial rejection of the past in the hope of creating something new" (ibid., 73). Reformation is "a self-consciously induced change in ecclesial life or consciousness that is based on principles that tend to dislodge old ones" (ibid., 88). In other words, a reformation is an event or period in which the church's self-understanding has changed radically.

To defend his thesis, O'Malley refers to two previous ecclesial reformations. First, the reformation of Gregory VII (1073–85) over the issue of investiture, that is, whether bishops and other ecclesiastical leaders would be appointed by the church or by the state. At that time many church buildings and property were controlled by kings and other feudal lords for economic reasons. Gregory insisted that bishops were to be appointed by Rome. This decision freed the church from the state and resulted in the emergence of a strong and centralized papacy that protected local churches from the state. Second, from the reformation of Martin Luther (1517) there emerged a new church that separated the scriptures from the papacy, grace from merits, and faith from works. O'Malley admits that these two reformations "are in no way prescriptive or normative" for other reformations (ibid., 121). Vatican II, he maintains, is a special reformation. The council fathers knew that they were experiencing a new Pentecost and that the council had radical implications. Also, Vatican II stands in marked discontinuity with the councils that preceded it because of the principle of aggiornamento: the church is in a new era, and religion is to be changed by and for people "in order to accommodate these new historical and cultural differences" (ibid.). The main example O'Malley gives to defend his thesis is that "the laity is doing things once reserved exclusively to priests" (ibid., 119).

Is this shift from priests to people a reformation? Evidence indicates otherwise. For example, in his monumental book on the various forms of ministry in the history of the church, Bernard Cooke demonstrated that the charisms of ministry have always been plural (1977). In the first centuries these charisms did not exist uniquely in any one ministry, whether bishop or priest. What eventually happened in the history of the church, added John Coleman, is that there developed "what has been called a 'ministerial moloch,' whereby the priesthood gobbled up all ministries in itself" (1981). In the postconciliar church many wonder if the shift has actually taken place. Although many bishops encourage the laity to participate in the life of the church because they agree with the scriptural teaching that all the faithful participate in the one priesthood of Christ (LG 10), many bishops continue to keep "all real power in the hands of the clergy" (Dulles 1988a, 11). Consequently, what is happening in the church is that many people are looking past the post-Tridentine, hierarchical, and sacerdotal patterns based on ordination and a celibate lifestyle to the tradition of ministry based on the priority of baptism and ministerial competence rooted in charisms (Cooke 1985). In other words, all ministries in the church—liturgical, educational, social, ecumenical, and special ministries to the sick and dying—are ultimately the reponsibility of the entire Christian community. The ecclesiastical categories of clergy and laity inherited from the classical tradition of Christianity are increasingly irrelevant in the church as she renews herself by retrieving a modified hierarchical view from the past.

To call the council a reformation seems an exaggeration. What seems more accurate is Robert Imbelli's thesis that the "major theological achievement of Vatican II" was "the recovery of tradition" (1982). A thorough review of the sixteen documents makes clear that the church did recover its ancient tradition, reclothing it for our era as requested by John XXIII. "To reclothe" does not mean to reformulate or merely to translate "traditional dogmas into a new idiom" (Baum 1970b). To reclothe is to recover the tradition by reinterpretation for the present age. At Vatican II the church was doing theology: it was seeking an understanding of its faith in the Christ-event for modernity. Good theology has two constants: it is always an interpretation of the Christ-event and an interpretation of the contemporary situation (Tracy 1981, 79, 340). At Vatican II the church turned from neoscholastic theology to its venerable patrimony, attempting to articulate a clearer sense of its own identity and mission in view of such factors as the new humanism, historical consciousness, social justice, ecumenism, and religious and cultural pluralism. As explained in chapter 2, the dominant theologians at Vatican II were the so-called new theologians (Yves Congar, for example), who returned to the sources of Christianity not only to rehear what was said then but also to reinterpret the present in light of the past.

In addition to the recovery of the importance of scripture, collegiality, religious freedom, and the role of the laity, there are several other instances of this recovery of the tradition. Consider the following three. First, the church recovered the view that the whole church is both a teaching and a learning church. This perspective had been lost, especially under Pius XII. In *Humani generis* (1950), he wrote that Catholics owe "religious allegiance of the will and intellect" even to non-infallible teachings of the pope. The conciliar bishops wrote: "With the help of the holy Spirit, it is the task of the whole people of God, particularly of its pastors and theologians, to listen to and distinguish the many voices of our times, and to interpret them in the light of God's word, in order that the revealed truth may be more deeply penetrated, better understood, and more suitably presented" (GS 44). Second, the Declaration on Religious Freedom reversed the teachings of the *Syllabus of Errors* (1864) by returning to biblical insights about human dignity. In this document, the bishops declared "that the right to religious freedom is based on the very dignity of the human person as known through the revealed word of God and by reason itself" (DH 2). Third, the members of religious orders were told that "the up-to-date renewal of the religious life comprises both a constant return to the sources of [C]hristian life in general and to the primitive inspiration behind the institutes and their adaptation to the changed conditions of our times" (PC 2).

In my judgment, Imbelli is correct: at Vatican II the true Catholic tradition was recovered or retrieved. I would add that once the true tradition was recovered, the bishops built on it their renewal and reform of the church.

Its Successes

Vatican II was a stunning success. In Von Hügel's terms, the theologians (the intellectual) discussed with the pope and bishops (institutional) ways to update the devotional life of the church (mystical). "Historians may indeed decide that open discussion within the church was the decisive gain registered by Vatican II. Without it nothing would have changed" (MacEoin 1966, 72). This pastoral council made many dogmatic and disciplinary decisions: it renewed and reformed the church; it emphasized the community and power-sharing aspects of the church (collegiality); it formalized cooperation with the other Christian churches; it legitimated the transformation of the rites of the various sacraments, especially the Eucharist; it repudiated anti-Semitism; it acknowledged the rights of people to choose their own religion; and it directed Catholics to dialogue with the modern world. If it were not for Vatican II, said one bishop, "the church would have been like the Loch Ness monster: rumored to exist, of venerable antiquity, actually seen by some, but not of much relevance in the contemporary world" (Hebblethwaite 1975, 13).

A few cautions are necessary. During the council, considerable tension and even fierce resistance permeated the formal and informal discussions as the progressive and traditional mindsets attempted to hammer out the sixteen documents. The documents, as we have seen, are compromise statements. Also, the full success of the council will take time, as history teaches. Walter Kasper, a German bishop-theologian, was probably correct when he wrote several years ago: "I myself have no doubt that the council's hour is still to come, and that its seed will spring up and bear rich fruit in the field of history" (1989, 176).

Its Failures

Some of the conciliar failures—scores of articles and books have explained many of them—relate to the pastoral purposes of the council and its affirmation of the modern world.

Andrew Greeley, a priest, sociologist, and novelist, has written extensively on the failure of the council to be pastoral, that is, "a council concerned about the reformulation [sic] of the gospel message" (1970). Greeley maintains that no attempt was made at Vatican II to develop catechetical styles for presenting the Christian gospel for people today. To present the gospel today the religious needs of people must be monitored. The bishops turned instead to administrators and scholars for their agenda. As a result, wrote Greeley, "The council was concerned with institutional structures and doctrinal propositions (the role of bishops, the nature of revelation, collegiality, etc.), and not with religion. . . . Despite its claim to be pastoral, Vatican II was perceived to be (and in fact was) concerned mostly with the distribution of power in the church and (though by silence) with sexual morality. The postconciliar controversies have been almost totally preoccuppied with these issues" (1982a).

Greeley was most annoyed that the council "did not produce a positive statement on sexuality and did not debate the question of human reproduction" (1982b). Greeley's accusations are disturbing because they make such an ugly contrast with the council's enunciations about ministry as service and the church as a participatory community. On the other hand, it could be that Greeley expected the council to undertake a theological and hermeneutical task beyond its competence. How can two thousand bishops from a world church have organized one language that would meet the deep religious needs of the faithful? Even the 204 bishops and delegates assembled for the Synod of 1977 on catechetics did not tackle this project.[1] Similarly, when the two thousand bishops addressed the pastoral issues of liturgy and moral theology, the most they could do was to set forth principles for a liturgical reform and to declare that "Special care is to be taken for the improvement of moral theology" (OT 16).

It must be noted to Greeley's credit that he has successfully attempted—and not without arousing considerable controversy—to reclothe the gospel message in the articles cited here, in several books on religion, and in dozens of novels.[2]

As to the council's failure to affirm the modern world, Gregory Baum, a theologian and sociologist, argued that the bishops, by buying into the liberal confidence that the economic, social, and political problems of the world could be gradually solved by human ingenuity, "paid insufficient attention to the limits and ambiguities of the liberal tradition. While the new emphases on personal conscience and personal development represented an undeniable progress, Catholics had not sufficiently thought through the problematic link of these ideas to individualism, the breakdown of social solidarity, the replacement of human values by the exchange value, the utilitarianism of public policies, and the cultural impact of capitalism" (1985).

Baum delineated four weaknesses in Vatican II's optimistic acceptance of liberalism (1984a, 75–104). They are as follows: First, Vatican II affirmed modern industrial, technical, and developmental society as the instrument of justice and said all peoples should share in the positive benefits of modernity. However, it was the bishops and theologians from western Europe, the United States, and Canada who most influenced this vision. They were naturally influenced by the extraordinary economic progress made in the West after World War II. In other words, the bishops of the West viewed the world through the eyes of capitalists and not through those of the poor, the underdeveloped, and the oppressed in the South and the East.

Second, Vatican II encouraged Christians to engage in social action and criticized a purely individual ethic. However, the council did not go far enough. It said people must change so society would change. While this is true, what is often the case is that societal structures must be changed before people can even have a chance to change and to live more authentically.

Third, Baum pointed out, Vatican II acknowledged the presence of personal sin in society, especially the neglect of the poor. However, Vatican II said not a word about social sin, that is, about our past, personal sinful choices that give rise to systematic institutions of socioeconomic and political oppression and deprivation. In other words, it is people who create ghettos, homelessness, hunger, disease, racism, and sexism.

Finally, Vatican II declared the church to be in solidarity with the whole human family. However, Baum argued that the church was too identified with the wealthy and the middle-class and hardly at all with those people involved in emancipatory struggles for basic human dignity and rights.

Vatican II: Twenty-five Years Later

In 1990 the church celebrated the twenty-fifth anniversary of the closing of Vatican II. The celebration was muted, even somewhat neglected. There was praise and gratitude for all the successes mentioned above. After all, had not these movements, ideas, and actions been inspired by the Spirit?

On the other hand, several concerns were raised. The editors of *Commonweal* complained that the fierce resistance by the Roman curia to the thrust of the council still survives and "has been given new life by Pope John Paul II and Cardinal Joseph Ratzinger."[3] (Ratzinger has been the prefect since 1981 of the Congregation of the Doctrine of the Faith, the Vatican office that oversees the integrity of the church's teachings on faith and morals.) Restorationists and reformers are painfully divided over the best way to deal with papal and episcopal authority, participation in the liturgy, collegiality, ecumenism, religious education, and how faith should permeate daily life.

Rembert Weakland, archbishop of Milwaukee, worried that the enthusiasm generated twenty-five years ago by the council "has spun itself out." He hoped that the church would recapture the attitude that it is "but a humble partner, an imperfect society, engaging this world in dialogue." He regretted that "tensions have arisen between the role of the clergy and the laity. One simply has to admit that these tensions do exist and that the aspirations created by the Vatican II documents are not going to go away simply by edicts that reinforce the power of the hierarchy" (Vidulich 1990).

The view that Vatican II's momentum had diminished was shared by 431 American and Canadian theologians who, on December 8, 1990, endorsed a statement by a committee of the CTSA that accused the Vatican of obstructing changes in the church.[4] The twenty-four hundred-word statement, titled "Do Not Extinguish the Spirit," claimed that the church's leadership had failed to carry out the changes called for by the council in four areas that are of specific concern in North America: collegiality of the bishops, cooperation between the magisterium and theologians, ecumenism, and the development of legitimate public roles for women in the church. Concerning the latter, the CTSA readily acknowledged "the insights on women shown in some teaching documents of this pontificate," but declared that there was still a glaring disparity between the roles of women and men in society and in the church. Feminism, then, was not being recognized as a sign of the times (see GS 9) but was "consistently viewed with suspicion." Furthermore, "Candidates for the episcopacy are screened to insure their unqualified opposition to the ordination of women to the priesthood."

Conclusion

The preconciliar church offered Catholics a religion of beauty, order, and goodness, however imperfectly realized. At Vatican II—the decisive ecclesial event of the twentieth century—the Catholic church emerged as a world church in a polycentric global culture. These developments brought necessary changes in the institution, in theology, and in spirituality. For example, the preconciliar spirituality was otherworldly, ahistorical, anti-secular, and individualistic, whereas the council moved Catholics toward a spirituality that is of this world, personal without being private, prophetic and countercultural without being partisan, and communal. The rest of this book examines how the church, in view of the signs and needs of the times, reshaped its intellectual, devotional, and institutional life at and since Vatican II and evaluates whether the changes have helped or hindered the church in clarifying its identity and fulfilling its mission.

CHAPTER 4

The Identity and Mission of the Church

Vatican II had several important goals, but it was primarily concerned with the identity and mission of the church in the modern world.

The Christian religion has a distinctive identity. When the identity became a problem in the fifth century, the noted theologian Vincent of Lérins maintained that the essence of Christianity is what has been proclaimed "everywhere, always, and by all" (Pelikan 1971, 1:333). Today, because the Christian religion is divided (tragically) into thousands of denominations, it is very difficult to pinpoint what meets Lérins's three criteria of universality, antiquity, and consensus. Each church has its own list of essentials. Nonetheless, it is safe to state that Catholic Christians have believed, taught, and confessed that they are a community of people who personally accept in faith, hope, and love the good news that the eternal reign of God the Father has been manifested in an unsurpassable way in the life, death, and resurrection of his son Jesus, and in the power, presence, and gifts of the Spirit and with the church community.

Community is an analogous term; it has many univocal definitions, depending on concrete situations. Today it is used so widely that it can refer to a family, a city, a political organization, a voluntary association, a religious order, and other groups (e.g., a college, African Americans, Latinos, gays, lesbians). All these groups are somewhat the same and yet entirely different from one another. The church, too, is a voluntary association, a society, a family, and an interest group. Nonetheless, it is *sui generis*, because its source is Christ, its ground the Spirit, and its goal the reign of God.

The New Testament narrates the complex stories of the churches the apostles organized and left behind (R. E. Brown 1984). There was a great deal of variety, partly because the churches had different needs and goals. Nevertheless, there are four basic interrelated structures to all the church communities that form the one church of Christ.

First, the church is a visible society or institution or organization that mediates the risen Jesus and his Spirit. The institution has its own leaders, officeholders, laws, customs, rituals (especially baptism and

Eucharist), and special doctrines or teachings, many found in the scriptures. The institutional church is regarded as a means of grace; it is a conditional reality subordinated to the reign of God.

Second, the church is an interpersonal community or communion, bound together around the risen Christ and his Spirit. The community enjoys fellowship, prayer, goods in common, mutual concern, and love. The New Testament word for communion, *koinonia,* encompasses a wide variety of meanings and does not translate easily into any language. It has nuances not captured by our word *communion.* It connotes sharing, fellowship, or a deep spiritual union, thus projecting "an organic, participating image of unity" (Heim 1993).

Third, the church is a missionary community. Led by the risen Jesus and his Spirit, it shares the good news and its life with the whole world.

Fourth, the church is made up of individual disciples. Each makes his or her personal commitment in faith, hope, and love. Each has charisms (gifts) to be used to foster the church's identity and mission.

The Relationship of Identity and Mission

A fundamental theological question is the relation of identity to mission. Some claim that mission is a consequence of community; others that mission and community exist side by side as coequals. A third answer—one that reflects the facts both historically and existentially—is that not only is it impossible for identity and mission to be separated, but also that mission is constitutive of the community. The community was formed for its mission. The resurrected Jesus said: "As the Father has sent me, so I send you" (John 21:22). Eugene Hillman, a theologian, author, and missionary, suggests, "Instead of thinking of the church as having a mission to the nations, it is more helpful to think of the mission of Jesus Christ having a church as its instrument" (1989, 73). The identity and mission roles should not be viewed as two successive movements, but, rather, as "simultaneous and dialectically related dimensions of a single hermeneutical process" (Komonchak 1985a, 30).

The Church's Proper Mission

At Vatican II the bishops declared, "The church on earth is by its very nature missionary" (AG 2). But this statement raises another theological issue: the extent of the church's mission. What is the church called to do? What is the church's proper mission?

Before Vatican II it was customary to teach that the church had two missions: one supernatural and the other natural, the latter subordinate to the former (Baum 1986a). The supernatural mission consisted in preaching the gospel (evangelization) so that nonbelievers would believe and enter the community and thus share its worldview, participate in its worship, and spread its teachings. The natural or temporal mission was to contribute to the building of a just society through the spiritual and corporal works of mercy. An example of this point of view is found in a letter Pius XI wrote to a French priest: "It is necessary never to lose sight of the fact that the objective of the church is to evangelize, not to civilize. If it civilizes, it is for the sake of evangelization."[1] The teaching that the church had two missions, one supernatural and the other natural, flowed from the many dualisms between natural and supernatural, body and soul, profane and sacred, and church and world that characterized the preconciliar church and its neo-Thomistic theology and spirituality.

At Vatican II the church declared an end to its siege mentality and placed itself in solidarity with the whole human family. The bishops stated that a free social order "must be founded in truth, built on justice, and enlivened by love; it should grow in freedom toward a more humane equilibrium" (GS 26). The bishops defined the mission of the church largely in terms of service. Just as Jesus was servant, so the church was sent to be servant of the world. The bishops urged the faithful "to play their due role in organizing economic, social, political and cultural life" (GS 9). They said there should be no dualism for Christians between their faith and their daily lives (GS 43). Nevertheless, Vatican II reiterated the preconciliar teaching of two missions. The bishops wrote that, "Christ did not bequeath to the church a mission in the political, economic, or social order: the purpose he assigned to it was religious" (GS 42).

Commenting on this last statement as translated by Abbott (1966, 241), Richard McCormick, a Jesuit moral theologian, declared with justifiable frustration, "Terms such as 'proper mission' and 'strictly religious' cry out for clarification: for they are capable of yielding a very dualistic meaning which ends up restricting the mission of the church to instruction in the faith, liturgy, preaching and sacraments—in brief, a kind of 'sanctuary Christianity.' In this view those directly concerned in one way or another with righting unjust social structures would not be involved in the church's 'proper mission' or with something 'religious'" (1976b, 108).

In addition to saying that the church had no proper mission in the political, economic, and social order, however, the bishops also insisted that the church should not be relegated to the margins of society. This would be inconsistent with its unique religious mission, which "can be the source of commitment, direction, and vigor to establish and consolidate the human community according to the law of God. In fact, the church is able, indeed it is obliged if times and circumstances require it, to initiate action for the benefit of everyone, especially of those in need, such as works of mercy and the like" (GS 42).

The conciliar statements just quoted reflect a compromise between the two mindsets at the council. The traditionalists, relying on such neoscholastic dualisms as natural and supernatural, church and world, insist that the church has no proper mission in the political and social order, while the progressives, building on the new theology's rejection of the dualism of church and world, insist that the church's mission is to serve the world.

The decisive turning point in mission theology came during the international Synod of 1971, which addressed both priesthood and social justice in the synod's famous document *Justice in the World.* The bishops reiterated the conciliar teachings on social justice but also made them more explicit. They declared that "action on behalf of justice and participation in the transformation of the world fully appear to us as a constitutive dimension of the church's proclamation of the preaching of the gospel, or in other words, of the Church's mission of the redemption of the human race and its liberation from every oppressive situation" (n. 6). The bishops went on to emphasize that "the mission of proclaiming the gospel in our times requires that we commit ourselves to man's integral liberation, here and now, in our earthly existence" (n. 35). At this historic meeting, the church acknowledged that it does indeed have a proper mission in the social, political, and economic areas.

Paul VI continued this theme in *Evangelii nuntiandi* (December 8, 1975)—an apostolic exhortation that reported on the Synod of 1974 on evangelization. He wrote that "the Church is certainly not willing to restrict her mission only to the religious field and dissociate herself from man's temporal problems" (n. 34). He also discussed the church's one mission that embraced in an inseparable manner both evangelization and public witness to social justice. He took the two missions of the preconciliar theology and combined them as dimensions of one mission. John Paul II endorsed this teaching in his first encyclical, *Redemptor hominis* (1979). Both pontiffs reject the neoscholastic dualism of church and world and both "emphasize human dignity and love for humans as the link between evangelization and liberation. They refer to the transcendence of eschatology to show that evangelization should not be identified totally and exclusively with human progress" (Fiorenza 1982, 209).

However, is one mission with a twofold dimension a complete picture of the church's mission? At the Synod of 1971 the bishops stated in *Justice in the World* that "while the church is bound to give witness to justice, she recognizes that anyone who ventures to speak to people about justice must first be just in their eyes. Hence we must undertake an examination of the modes of acting, of the possessions and lifestyle found within the church herself" (n. 40). Consequently, many theologians prefer to speak of one mission with a threefold dimension: not only evangelization and service for social justice, but also witness (McBrien 1973, 140; 1981, 716). These three—evangelization, witness, and service—are continuations of Jesus' threefold mission as prophet, priest, and servant-king. The church's mission is to proclaim the kingdom of God the Father of

Jesus Christ, to witness to the presence of this kingdom, and to serve the kingdom by serving the needy and oppressed.

At Vatican II the church highlighted its sacramental role. "The words 'testimony' and 'witness' (both as noun and verb) are found over one hundred times in conciliar documents" (Latourelle 1988b, 408). Not only must the church teach the gospel and promote justice in the world, but it must exemplify this gospel and this justice within the community and for all to see. In other words, the church must practice what it preaches. Jesus did pray "that they may all be one, as you, Father, are in me and I in you . . . that the world may believe that you sent me" (John 17:21). The lifestyle of the first Christians had a major impact on the spread of the church: "See these Christians. How they love one another."

Finally, there has been another significant development in the understanding of mission, this one involving the term *evangelization*. Before Vatican II, Catholics spoke rarely of evangelization. When they did, it usually meant the special vocation of a few priests and religious sisters and brothers to gain new adherents for the church in a foreign land. At Vatican II the bishops referred to evangelization thirty-one times. When they did so, they seem generally to have meant the preconciliar understanding: the proclamation of the basic Christian message to those who did not yet believe in Christ (Dulles 1992b).

After Vatican II, Paul VI began to focus on evangelization. However, he broadened the concept, identifying it with the total mission of the church. In 1967 he changed the name of the Congregation for the Propagation of the Faith to the Congregation for the Evangelization of Peoples. He made nine unprecedented, evangelical visits to other countries. He chose evangelization as the theme for the Synod of 1974. He explained in *Evangelii nuntiandi* (1975) that "Evangelization is in fact the grace and vocation proper to the church, her deepest identity. She exists in order to evangelize, that is to say in order to preach and teach, to be the channel of the gift of grace, to reconcile sinners with God and to perpetuate Christ's sacrifice of the Mass, which is the memorial of his death and glorious resurrection" (n. 14). Evangelization, he taught, includes human development and liberation for the millions of people condemned to remain on the margin of life because of such factors as famine, chronic disease, illiteracy, and "situations of economic and cultural neocolonialism sometimes as cruel as the old political colonialism" (n. 30). In addition, he said evangelization should not be directed simply at individuals but also at both culture and cultures because they need to be regenerated by contact with the gospel (n. 20). Finally, he proposed as the theme for the episcopal conference of Latin America scheduled for 1979, "Evangelization in the Present and Future of Latin America."

John Paul II has also emphasized evangelization, but he speaks in terms of a "new evangelization" and "re-evangelization." He first mentioned the term "new evangelization" on March 9, 1983, while in Haiti addressing Latin American bishops. Later, he and the Latin American bishops chose as the theme for their conference to be held in Santo Domingo in 1992, "New Evangelization, Human Advancement and Christian Culture."

New evangelization has several dimensions. First, it includes teaching the gospel. In his encyclical *Redemptoris missio* (December 7, 1990), John Paul said the name of Jesus Christ must be explicitly proclaimed. If the name of Jesus is not taught, there can be no evangelization in the true sense (n. 44). Second, evangelization can never be a matter of words alone. "The witness of a Christian life is the first and irreplaceable form of mission" (n. 42). Third, evangelization involves the humanization of political and economic systems so that people can truly live in the image of God. Those who evangelize by insisting on the dignity and integral development of humankind help to build a new civilization of love (n. 51). In his encyclical *Sollicitudo rei socialis* (December 30, 1987), John Paul had already stated that "Teaching and spreading her social doctrine are part of the church's evangelizing mission" (n. 41).

This emphasis on evangelization prompted Avery Dulles to state (1992b) that "In my judgment, the evangelical turn in the ecclesial vision of Popes Paul VI and John Paul II is one of the most surprising and important developments in the Catholic Church since Vatican II." However, Dulles does not explain what is so new or special about these important developments. It seems that what is new about the "evangelical turn" of both popes is that this is their way of endorsing and highlighting the church as a missionary community with a threefold mission. The new evangelization involves participation in the threefold mission of Jesus who taught, witnessed, and served. In his encyclical *Evangelium vitae* (1995), John Paul wrote that "evangelization is an all-embracing, progressive activity through which the church participates in the prophetic, priestly and royal mission of the Lord Jesus. It is therefore inextricably linked to preaching, celebration and the service of charity" (n. 78). In other words, John Paul means by "new evangelization" that the signs and needs of the times demand that the church herald the gospel not only by proclamation but also by witnessing the gospel and serving those in need, especially the poor and marginalized.

From Mission to Ministry

Since Vatican II, the meaning of the word *mission* has been broadened. Before the council, mission was often understood in a narrow sense: it applied to those men and women who made a distant journey to teach the gospel to a foreign people. This understanding of mission is essentially heroic, denoting an extra thrust beyond normal Christian concern for the gospel. In the postconciliar church, mission is not regarded as something heroic or extra. Rather, every Christian shares in the threefold mission of Jesus and his church. The question is not *who* is called but *how* each is called.

Ministry is the word used to specify the outward reach of Christians. People are engaged in many ministries: liturgical, eucharistic, and ecumenical. In addition, there are special ministries to the divorced, the imprisoned, the sick, and dying. There are also "parochial ministers," that is, nonordained who direct parishes where there are no priests. It is interesting to notice a significant vocabulary change regarding the mission of priests. Vatican II spoke of "the ministerial priest" (LG 10), whereas the Synod of 1971 on priesthood had as one of its themes "the priestly ministry." On September 14, 1972, Paul VI reformed the so-called "minor orders" of priesthood in *Ministeria quaedam*. He abolished five of them, and the two that remained, lector and acolyte, were given back to the laity from whom they had been removed. Paul VI called them "lay ministries." It is against this background that Eugene Kennedy wrote in 1976: "The most exciting religious awareness of this era centers on ministry as the vocation shared by all believers in virtue of their baptism. It is the theme that has been repeated by Pope Paul VI all through his years as head of the church, the notion he has underscored verbally and symbolically in a thousand different ways" (1976b).

Distinctively Catholic

All the Christian churches would agree, *mutatis mutandis*, that the four interrelated structures described above are what make a community distinctively Christian. The next question is: what makes the Catholic church distinctively Catholic?

The word *catholic* can be spelt with a small *c* or with a capital *C*. Catholic with a small *c* designates a property of the one true church of Christ, namely, its universality (see LG 13, AG 4, 8, 10). Catholic with a capital *C* refers both to the Roman Catholic church as a distinct Christian community and to a particular *type* or *style* of Christianity. The latter is what is being explained here.

Before beginning, however, it is necessary to state that the style that is distinctively Catholic is not found exclusively in the Roman Catholic church. Some of the characteristics that describe Catholicism are found not only in some other Christian communities but also in some other religions, though not to the same extent.

We express our consciousness or sensitivity in language. The word *God*, for example, refers to that supreme being who is all holy, who is the originator and creator of all, and who is different from all persons and things (animal, vegetable, or mineral). Since human language denotes only persons or things, when we describe God, who is not a thing (but real) nor a person (but personal), we naturally have to use our imagination. On the one hand, we can say God is unlike any thing or person. In this instance we focus on what is distinctive of God, and, therefore, the radical dissimilarities between the divine and his creatures, human and non-human. For example, since God cannot be limited by time and space the way we are, we say he is eternal and omnipresent. This is a dialectical imagination. On the other hand, we can say God is like things (my wisdom, rock, star, lion) or persons (my father, king, shepherd, mother). This is an analogical imagination.

All Christians use both imaginations. However, Protestants tend to emphasize the ways the transcendent God is unlike us (dialectical imagination) and Catholics tend to emphasize the ways the providential God is like us (analogical imagination). It is that simple—but the implications are profound (Tracy 1977, 1981; McBrien 1978a; Kennedy 1988a).

This is not to say that there are no doctrinal differences that separate Protestants and Catholics. It does denote that the problems that separate the two groups are not primarily doctrinal but differences in the religious imagination.

To say God is like things and persons is to have a sacramental consciousness. Sacraments are signs and instruments of God. Catholics have a sacramental consciousness: every thing and person can be a sign and instrument of God's presence or love or judgment.

Hilaire Belloc (1870–1953), a Catholic apologist and author, wrote this little ditty: "Wherever the Catholic sun does shine/ There is music, laughter and good red wine. At least I've always found it so. *Benedicamus Domino*" (Greeley and Greeley Durkin 1984, 62).

Catholics enjoy good red wine and other alcoholic drinks. For this reason, Catholic Europe was bewildered when the United States prohibited alcoholic beverages in the 1920s. Several Protestant communities (including Baptists, Methodists, and Mormons) discourage the use of alcohol. Catholics enjoy and encourage music and dancing. Some Protestants do not. For example, Baylor University, founded as a Baptist college in 1845, prohibited dancing for 151 years. It lifted its prohibition in January 1996. The ruling by the president came after years of surveys and votes, and months of preparation by a thirty-member committee of students, professors, and alumni. The change had the blessing of many Baptists, on and off campus, but not all. One Baptist pastor declared that the university "has been on the slippery slope for some time, and this is just one more slip. Wherever modern dancing is, there is alcohol and promiscuousness" (Meyerson 1996).

Another example of the difference between Protestant and Catholic imaginations is found in "Amazing Grace," an eighteenth-century Protestant hymn. "Amazing grace, how sweet the sound, that saved a wretch like me." Protestants highlight that, as sinners, people are quite unlike the all-holy God. A fundamental starting point of the Protestant reformation was the contrast between sin and grace. This hymn offends a Catholic sacramental consciousness, which proceeds from the assumption of harmony between nature and grace. In many Catholic hymnals the words are often adjusted: "Amazing grace, how sweet the sound, that saved and strengthened me." *Wretch* is seldom used in the Catholic vocabulary! But this does not mean Catholics deny their sinfulness and need for conversion and reform.

It must be admitted that contrasting the Protestant and Catholic imaginations and language in this way can lead to caricature. If so, this would be unfortunate. One reason for the contrasts follows from the present ecumenical atmosphere. The churches need to understand one another clearly so they can dialogue honestly. Many Lutherans enjoy drinking, smoking, and dancing. But most Protestant theologians agree that the basis of their tradition is what Paul Tillich (1886–1965), an influential Lutheran theologian, called the "Protestant principle" i.e., "the divine and human protest against any absolute claim made for a relative reality." He meant that no representations of the divine—either visual or verbal—are finally adequate to the splendor of God, and that failure to accept this judgment leads to idolatry. He meant that no ritual system, doctrines, or moral code can be equated with the saving intervention of God in the cross and resurrection of Jesus Christ (Braaten 1992, 6). Tillich's very valid principle is rooted in a dialectical imagination. We have already explained that an analogical and dialectical imagination are two sides of the same coin. Both the Protestant principle and the Catholic sacramental principle are essential aspects of the Christian tradition.

In most dictionaries *catholic* is defined as universal. This definition is not quite exact. The Latin word for universal is *universalis,* yet when the church wanted to talk about being "all-encompassing" it preferred instead the Greek word *katholikos.* The etymological history of these two words is not clear in every detail. Nevertheless, universal is an inclusive concept. It suggests a circle that includes everything within it. However, it always carries the negative implication that everything outside the circle is excluded. *Katholikos,* on the other hand, is more positive. It means "throughout the whole" or "through the whole." Thus *Catholic* means through or throughout everything, with nothing excluded. It opposes sectarianism, that is, when a church group separates itself from the larger or universal community, and to some extent, from society itself.

Since *Catholic* means "throughout everything, with nothing excluded" then a sacramental consciousness will, indeed, include everything and everyone without exception. For Catholics, all of life is sacramental. Scholars like Dulles (1985a, 1988a, 51–74) have listed and explained the characteristics of Catholicism. According to Robert Imbelli, a sacramental consciousness has five dimensions and anything less fails of Catholicity (1982). The five characteristics are corporeal, communal, cosmic, global, and transformational, or what I call tradition-centered. These five terms, it seems to me, can be incorporated into one simple sentence: I am a body-person (corporeal) with others (communal) in this world (cosmic) of space (global) and time (tradition-centered).

A sacramental consciousness respects and appreciates everyone's corporeal reality. The body—the whole body—is good. Music, dancing, gambling, sexuality, drinking good red wine are all good. Catholics enjoy them, saying *"Benedicamus Domino."* As body-persons we have minds. Our body is animated and our soul embodied. A Catholic sacramental consciousness has always fostered "the drive toward rationality" (Gilkey 1975, 17). Faith is not blind, but is to be informed by reason. The Christian foundation for respecting each and every body-person is the fact that the Word of God assumed a full body and a full human mind in the person of Jesus of Nazareth, and the risen Christ pours out his Spirit on everyone. A corporeal, sacramental consciousness opposes whatever dehumanizes: abortion, euthanasia, the death penalty, and every oppression: racial, sexual, political, economic, religious.

A sacramental consciousness is communal—each of us is a body-person with others. Community is a sign and instrument of God. Catholics maintain that Christ is encountered in the living community and the community can respond to him together. Catholics believe in Jesus Christ, but *with* the Twelve and all those who joined them in passing on the faith. As we have seen, it is, perhaps, the vicars of Peter who have been the single most powerful force holding the community together. Catholics also revere the scriptures, the word of God in the words of men and women of the community. The Bible is the book of the community, interpreted in and through the community. Furthermore, when Catholics assemble it is often for music, dancing, and good red wine; but most frequently it is to celebrate some aspect of life or rite of passage by means of one or more of the seven ecclesial sacraments, especially the Eucharist. The Christian foundation for the sacramentality of the community is the trinitarian life of God and the risen Christ's promise to be with the community until the end of time, especially when Christians discern the Spirit, serve the poor and needy, and eat the bread and drink from the cup. A communal, sacramental consciousness opposes individualism, moral relativism, elitism, divisions, and a privatized spirituality.

The cosmic aspect of a sacramental consciousness is well expressed by a quote from Gerard Manley Hopkins (1844–89), the English Jesuit poet. The created world, he said, is "charged with the grandeur of God." Francis of Assisi (1182–1226) wrote poetically of brother sun and sister moon. Again, everything can be a sign and instrument of God. Catholics are steeped in the earth's elements, using many of them in their liturgies: water, fire, oil, bread, wine, stone, light, darkness—and even ashes. In principle, the Catholic tradition has always had a creation spirituality.

The Christian foundation for this cosmic dimension of a sacramental consciousness is the uniqueness of Christ and his relationship to the cosmos. The scriptures proclaim that the Father chose us in his Son before the creation of the world and God's plan is to unite all persons and things in the risen Christ (see Ephesians 1:3–10).

Any abuse of the ecology is contrary to a sacramental consciousness. For example, just because some people drink a lot of beer and good red wine does not mean they have a sacramental consciousness. Actually, overindulgence indicates a lack of reverence for the body-person as well as the beer and good red wine.

Belloc described the global aspect of sacramental consciousness: "Wherever the Catholic sun does shine." The Catholic sun shines everywhere. The church has always been global—at least in intent. The church goes out to every person and every culture (it is a world church). If a person has a sacramental consciousness, she or he spreads the gospel by teaching, witnessing, and serving others, in the tradition beginning with Peter and Paul and reaching to our day. Thomas Merton (1915–68), a Trappist monk, religious writer, and poet, said that even monks and nuns hidden away in monasteries are called to be everywhere by compassion.

The Christian foundation for this global dimension of the sacramental consciousness is the risen Christ's injunction to teach all nations in the power of the Spirit.

Unfortunately, the church has not always been that Catholic. There have been solar eclipses, even arctic nights. The church has not always taken into account all dimensions of its sacramental consciousness. For example, there have been puritanical and elitist groups that disrupted church devotion and life: Manichaeans, Albigensians, and Jansenists. Today, it is obvious that the church is still too western, too masculine, too clerical. Those with a sacramental consciousness oppose these misplaced emphases.

Finally, a sacramental consciousness is tradition-centered. The Catholic sun has been shining for two thousand years and over these years the church has been handing on the gospel from one generation to another, meeting new situations, new experiences, new questions. Catholics have an ecclesiastical order and process that helps the community understand the meaning of the gospel. This handing on of the tradition has been accomplished by millions of faithful parents, hundreds of councils (twenty-one being ecumenical), hundreds of synods (eleven international synods between 1967 and 1994), hundreds of popes, thousands of bishops, outstanding theologians in each century, and a countless succession of catechisms, books on spirituality, retreats, sermons, and so forth. The richness of the living tradition is staggering.

The Christian foundation for this tradition-centered, sacramental consciousness is the risen Christ's gift of the Spirit, who as Paraclete, leads and defends the church. However, the church has not always been without fault in its interpretation of the gospel. For example, we have seen that the major theological achievement of Vatican II was the recovery of some of the tradition that was lost or blurred in post-Reformation and neoscholastic theologies.

At Vatican II the bishops expressed concern about the strength and depth of this sacramental consciousness among Catholics when they noted that "One of the gravest errors of our time is the dichotomy between the faith which many profess and their day-to-day conduct" (GS 43). Just as the papacy has been the single most powerful and visible force holding Catholics together at the institutional level, a sacramental consciousness has been at the core of the Catholic tradition at the devotional level. Even such aberrations as the Manichaean and Jansenist heresies are exceptions which prove the rule. The future identity and mission of the church depend upon a revitalized sacramental consciousness among all the disciples of Christ.

The Preconciliar Catholic Church

Christians believe in God's saving love manifested in the death and resurrection of Jesus and incarnated in his church through the Spirit. This multilayered and complex relationship is polycentric: Christians believe God's eternal, saving love and kingdom (theocentric) is manifested in a special way in Jesus and his Spirit (christocentric) with and through the first disciples and apostles (ecclesiocentric). At various times the polycentric church has had different emphases. All three centers are always operative but, at different times, one center is underscored, often because of societal and/or ecclesial conditions and needs.

The institutional character of the Catholic church makes it unique among the other Christian churches and the world's great religions. Most religions and churches have only minimal national or international organizations. In some Protestant denominations the word *church* refers only to the local place of worship. The Catholic church is a worldwide institution with an administrative apparatus that dwarfs those of most modern governments. The vast hierarchical machinery, besides supporting a vast network of public services like hospitals and schools, oversees the theological and devotional practices in thousands of dioceses and parishes.

In the preconciliar period, the institutional church was in a "state of siege mentality." As a result, the church was ecclesiocentric and the emphasis was on the church as an institution. The institution was conceived as an autonomous and sovereign society, one opposed to the rest of society. For example, when Pius XI issued his encyclical *Quas primas* (1925), in which he instituted the feast of Christ the King, he stated that as the church was divine in origin, its rights were inviolable, above and beyond the judgment of secular society.

The church's government was centralized and bureaucratic. Prized were clarity, unity, and order. The order was hierarchical—the Greek root of this word means literally "priest-rule." Being hierarchical, the church is "an 'unequal society,' in which the members, located on different levels, know their place and through the interplay of authority and obedience serve the well-being of the whole" (Baum 1989c, 725–26). The Catholic church regards the papal-collegial structure of ecclesiastical government as of divine origin.

Pius XII, with the aid of the Jesuit theologian Sebastian Tromp, wrote *Mystici corporis* (June 29, 1943), "the most comprehensive official Catholic pronouncement on the church prior to Vatican II" (Dulles 1989, 422). At first it seemed he was breaking with the overly juridical understanding of the church as a "perfect society" (n. 63), a notion dating to the saintly Jesuit theologian, Robert Bellarmine (1542–1621). According to Bellarmine, the church was perfect because it had everything it needed in order to achieve its ends; it stood over against a "corrupt world"; and it could (and even should) impose its "rights" over civil society. But *Mystici corporis* really protected the institutional nature of the church in all its dimensions.

Pius had two main points. First, he addressed those theologians, who, in their efforts to highlight the church's supernatural or mystical qualities, were neglecting the visible, organized, and juridical institution. To counteract this overemphasis, Pius tried to synthesize both dimensions by writing at length about "the doctrine of the Mystical Body of Christ, which is the Church" (n. 1). This identity of the Catholic church with the Mystical Body meant that one had to be a member of the Catholic church to belong to the Mystical Body. Christians not united to the visible institution were cut off from communion with Christ. Nevertheless, these Christians, if they were living by the grace of Christ and were in good faith (even in their "errors"), could be in communion with Christ by desire. Second, while underscoring the church as institution, Pius did not want the individual Catholic to be lost within the totality. He warned that the biological analogy for the church should not be carried so far that the totality was more important than the individual.

The encyclical evoked intense discussion in theological circles among liturgists, biblical scholars, canon lawyers, and ecumenists. Important questions were raised. Did the identification of the Catholic church with the Mystical Body of Christ contradict ecumenical experience? Did the encyclical actually put other Christian communities in the same spiritual category as those who belonged to other religions? And did the too solid identification of Christ and the Catholic church make it difficult to accept the church as it is: a community of both saints and sinners?

The hierarchically ordered society has a purpose: it should stand in the service of the community and each individual in the community. Few have expressed this more clearly than Karl Rahner:

In a chess club the main thing is that chess should be played well, and that masters of the game should be trained there. Everything else, the functionaries, the cashiers, the president, the club meetings and statutes are, indeed, necessary and cannot be abolished; but their true meaning is to serve playing chess. The true stars of a chess club are the best players, not the cashier or the president who may, indeed, be players who have failed. Exactly the same is the case in the Catholic church. . . . All presiding ministers of the church, from the pope and the bishops down to the parish priests and chaplains, exist only so that there may be Christians, that is, men and women who believe, hope and love, who bear their cross, who see light even in darkness, who firmly hope even against hope, men who have the folly and the courage to love in a loveless world. All sermons, all papal decrees, all canon law, all sacred congregations in Rome, all bishops—in short, the whole organization of the church exists only to assist the true Christian life in the hearts of men. Where this meaning is lost it becomes only man's ridiculous presumption before God (1969, 18–19).

Few Catholics are opposed in any absolute sense to the church as institution. Institutions are indispensable to human development and order. Moreover, the church has changed its governmental structures over the centuries from Jewish presbyterial government, feudal fealties, and monarchical nation-state. In all these forms the hierarchy has the responsibility to govern, legislate, and judge. What the faithful disapprove of is "a disproportionate sacrifice of individual freedom to collective discipline. . . . They disapprove despotism and absolutism" (Gaffney 1986).

The Conciliar Church

During the two decades preceeding Vatican II, extensive ecclesiological scholarship was taking place, especially in France and Germany. The so-called "new theologians" returned to the biblical and patristic sources where they found many images of the church that highlighted the life of grace and charity at the heart of the church rather than a juridical view of the church. Some argue that this shift from institution to communion by the progressive preconciliar ecclesiologists was "the single most important concept leading to Vatican II's reforms" (Doyle 1992). The scholars produced studies on the church as Mystical Body (by Emile Mersch and Sebastian Tromp), as people of God (by Lucien Cerfaux and Joseph Ratzinger), as temple of the Spirit (by Yves Congar), as the sacrament of Christ (by Henri de Lubac, Otto Semmelroth, and Karl Rahner) and as a pilgrim people (by Rudolf Schnackenburg) (Dulles 1989, 425–29).

Vatican II did not make a sharp break with the official teaching of the recent past regarding the identity and mission of the church. It did make a substantial shift in emphasis. The preconciliar stress on the church as institution, while understandable at the time, did lead to institutionalism, one deadening effect of which was the creation of a wide gap between the faithful and the hierarchy. The latter were so identified with the whole church that it was not uncommon for the faithful to refer to the church as "they."

As a result of the "new theology" as well as the explosion of historical consciousness and the general trend in Western society toward freedom, equality, dialogue, community, and democracy, there was a desire to view the church more personally. At Vatican II the church shifted from an ecclesiocentric view of its identity and mission to a christocentric view. Recovered from the tradition was the presence of the risen Christ as the personal center of the church, and the church as the sacrament of his redemptive presence. The bishops wrote that "it is the function of the church to render God the Father and his incarnate Son present and as it were visible, while ceaselessly renewing and purifying itself under the guidance of the holy Spirit" (GS 21).

Vatican II was a council by the church about the church. There were two major documents on the church: a constitution on the church's identity, structures, and disciplines *(Lumen gentium)* and a constitution on the church and modern society *(Gaudium et spes)*. The former dealt with the identity of the church; the latter with its mission.

Volumes have been written about the shifts in emphasis concerning the identity and mission at Vatican II. Summarized here are six of the council's major ecclesiological themes.

First, the council emphasized the church as sacrament or mystery. In the preconciliar days, the church was regarded as a plank of salvation for a shipwrecked humanity. At Vatican II the church was described as the visible sign and instrument (sacrament) of Christ's salvation of the whole world, that is, for all those who did not belong to the community (LG 1). This change from plank to sacrament more clearly explains the identity and necessity of the church. It shows that the triune God's salvific will is universal and can be thwarted only when people make personal decisions contrary to it.

The theme of mystery was a favorite of Paul VI. In his opening address at the second session (September 29, 1963), he said, "The church is a mystery. It is a reality imbued with the hidden presence of God."

Second, the council moved to describe the church as the people of God. The church is both an institution and a communion. The preconciliar church stressed the institution and its hierarchical officers and specialists. Vatican II turned to the image of the church as the people of God. In 1870 at Vatican I the majority of bishops favored the hierarchical model but there was a minority who advocated the communion model. "What is certain is that the ecclesiology of the minority at Vatican I was transformed into the majority at Vatican II" (Anton 1988, 422).

Of all the images used at Vatican II, the bishops gave pride of place to people of God. The second chapter of the Constitution on the Church is devoted to exploring the ramifications of this image. Chapter 1 explores the mystery of the church and chapter 3 discusses the hierarchical structures of the church. Yves Congar called this sequence and placement a Copernican revolution because it radically moved from identifying the church as an institution to identifying it primarily as a communion (ibid., 413). Communion became "the key concept for interpreting the ecclesiology of Vatican II and the one that best summarizes its results in ecclesiological doctrine and in the renewal of the church" (ibid., 416).

There are many reasons why the conciliar bishops chose the communion model. It focuses attention on the church as Christ's community; it avoids the controversy over whether the church is a mystical community or an institution of discipline and government; it highlights the historical and dynamic nature of the church as a pilgrim community gathered and led by Christ; and it is ecumenical, evoking an association with Israel, God's chosen people.

Third, the council described the church as servant. The preconciliar church spoke of two realms: the church and the world. The church was a fortress of truth in an alien world. Vatican II, on the other hand, unambiguously established solidarity between the church and the whole human race, especially in the Constitution on the Church in the Modern World, the longest of the sixteen documents at 23,335 words.

The bishops declared that the church, while not bound to any particular form of human culture, nor to any political, economic, or social system, "is obliged, if times and circumstances require it, to initiate action for the benefit of everyone, especially of those in need, such as works of mercy and the like" (GS 42). All this activity the church does in imitation of the work of Christ himself "who came into the world to bear witness to the truth, to save and not to judge, to serve and not to be served" (GS 3).

Fourth, the council portrayed the church as collegial. The preconciliar church stressed the universal church governed and directed by the papacy and the Roman curia. Vatican II said the church is realized and expressed not only at the universal level, but also the local level (LG 26; CD 11). There is a dialectical balancing between the church as a worldwide international community and the local congregation. Each exists only in the other.

The term *local church* encompasses parishes, dioceses, regions, and nations. In the Catholic tradition each of these levels works together with their bishop(s) according to their proper roles for the common good of the church in its identity and mission. The local churches are church in the full sense and not as part of the universal church. The universal church is a communion of local churches and can act only in and through them. Collegiality, then, is the shared responsibility of pope and bishops for leading and governing the church.

Yves Congar commented on the church's rediscovery of the local church at Vatican II: "Universal is the opposite of particular or local, but Catholic is not the opposite of anything. A local church is Catholic, and even an individual is Catholic; a small community is Catholic, but it is obviously not universal. I believe that this rediscovery of the local church . . . is extremely important. Karl Rahner even thought it to be the most important part of all the council's work on ecclesiology" (Lauret 1988, 11).

Fifth, the council also affirmed the church as ecumenical. The preconciliar Catholic church declared itself the one true church of Jesus Christ. It alone possessed the marks of the true church—one, holy, catholic, and apostolic—and it alone had preserved the vicars of Peter. The other Christian communities had broken from the true church through schism or heresy.

Vatican II stressed what unites all Christian communities: the presence of the Spirit and the common belief that Jesus is Lord and Christ. The council's perspective was christocentric. The other churches were addressed as separated brethren or sister churches, and not strangers or enemies. The elements that constitute the one true church of Christ are distributed in varying degrees throughout the other Christian communities. Due to the presence of the Spirit and his gifts of faith, hope, and love, there is already an ecclesial communion among the Christian churches that is real, even if incomplete (LG 15; UR 3–4). The council committed itself to ecumenism "so that the sign of Christ may shine more brightly over the face of the church" (LG 15).

Sixth, the council perceived the church as eschatological, that is, it is oriented toward the future and development. The preconciliar church referred to itself as a perfect society and the earthly embodiment of the kingdom of God. Vatican II declared that the kingdom was already present in Christ but, as for the church, it was but the sacrament of Christ and the kingdom. Some theologians consider this shift from embodiment of the kingdom to sacrament of the kingdom the "single most significant reversal of ecclesiological perspective brought about by Vatican II" (Van Beeckx 1985, 34).

The earthly church is a sacrament of the one true church of Christ but in a pilgrim state and in constant need of development and reform. *The one true church of Christ will not be wholly one and holy until human history as we know it ends.* "It is unreasonable to ask for perfect faith, hope undimmed, inexhaustible charity in the church. . . . The church is the flawed embodiment of faith, hope and charity" (Hebblethwaite 1975, 238).

The Conciliar Images in the Postconciliar Church

The council's images of the church as sacrament, people of God, and servant at first evoked considerable enthusiasm. Unfortunately, they could not capture the imaginations of people in a lasting way because of three factors: the ambivalence of the images, the situation in the world, and the changes the church underwent after the council.

Sacrament suggested either "an impersonal reality, such as baptismal water; or a ritual action, such as anointing" (Dulles 1981). Also, the image suggested a conspicuousness the church just did not have. Even in the United States where the Catholic church was some 20 percent of the population, the church had only a minor impact on the political and economic life of the country. Finally, there was some uncertainty about what the church as sacrament represented since the church was not a convincing sign of the unity, peace, justice, and love that the council announced.

People of God, the favorite image of the council fathers, proved to be embarrassing for two reasons. First, it suggested that the rest of humanity was not included in God's love. Second, it proved difficult for Catholics to regard themselves as a people. The Jewish people had a religious, ethnic, and political heritage that made it easy for them to cherish the image people of God. Not so for the global and world church.

The servant model, when it specified the gospel injunction to make this a better world by healing, feeding, and reconciling in imitation of Jesus, met with less opposition than the other two images. However, in democratic societies like that of the United States, the term *servant* had taken on pejorative connotations. Today those who do the kind of menial tasks once done by servants are called "staff" or some other neutral term. In church parlance, the term servant was soon replaced by *stewardship* or *ministry*, words that evoke the notions of inventiveness and originality.

The Community of Disciples

After Vatican II considerable reflection and discussion was given to the models of the church, especially the five enumerated by Avery Dulles in 1974, namely, mystical communion, herald, sacrament, servant, and institution.[2]

As is his style, Dulles explained the models most carefully and with balance. He did this by emphasizing these principles: the church is irreducible to any single image or model; no model should be absolutized; and the five models are sufficiently flexible to be mutually open and complementary. He went on to show that the five models can conflict with one another and so ecclesiologists should incorporate the major affirmations of each model without carrying over their distinctive liabilities. An ecclesiology would be truly adequate to the extent that it took into account the insights contained in each of the five models.

Something Dulles did not develop is the relationship of the five models to the four interrelated structures of the church. When the models are so related, they denote that the visible society (institution) is an interpersonal community (mystical communion) with a threefold mission: to teach the gospel (herald), to witness the gospel (sacrament), and to serve the needy and oppressed (servant).

Something else is lacking in Dulles's models: the personal dimension. At the beginning of this chapter, I indicated that one of the four essential dimensions of the church is the presence of individual disciples who personally respond to the God of Jesus in faith, hope, and love. This personal dimension is essential because at this level, although all men and women receive different gifts of the Spirit, all are equal in dignity and freedom. At this level, all women and men are followers and learners, all must embrace the cross of Christ, and all must appropriate their mission. *Gaudium et spes* stated that "When [people] are drawn to think about their real selves they turn to those deep recesses of their being where God who probes the heart awaits them, and where they themselves decide their own destiny in the sight of God" (GS 14). The document also taught that "conscience is people's most secret core, and their sanctuary. There they are alone with God whose voice echoes in their depths" (GS 16).

Karl Rahner wrote perceptively of the personal dimension of ecclesial life. He insisted that the nature of both the church and the person demanded that a legitimate private sphere be left for individual inspiration, initiative, and responsibility on the part of each member of the church. For example, the church cannot force prayer, faith, or vocation upon the unique individual member, nor can it decide upon the individual's moral standing in the sight of God. Finally, there is Rahner's oft-quoted prophecy: "The Christian of the future will be a mystic or he or she will not exist at all" (1964b, 217–34).

In his first encyclical *Redemptor hominis* (March 4, 1979), John Paul addressed the personal, mystical dimension of ecclesial life. He reminded his readers that membership in the church has its source in "a particular call" from Christ. The church "is the community of the disciples, each of whom in a different way—at times very consciously and consistently, at other times not very consciously and very consistently—is following Christ. This shows also the deeply 'personal' aspect and dimension of this society."

Dulles wrote an essay two years later about the church as a community of disciples. He outlined its biblical basis (e.g., Acts 6:2) and explained at length why this model is needed more today than in previous generations. He said that since we live in a world where atheism is pervasive, the world religions are attractive, and the lure of wealth, military power, and status are corrupting, then anyone coming to the church (or persevering in it) will be "obliged to hear a personal call and respond in a free, self-conscious manner, somewhat as the first disciples responded to the summons of Christ. The call, if it is to be efficacious, must be heard as coming not simply from the church but from the Lord of the church, so that Jesus himself is seen as the focal point of the Christian's life" (Dulles 1981, 129).

Dulles appreciated the significance of the community-of-disciples model for our times. However, he never allowed this model to stand separately from the others. That is, Dulles believed this model was able to test and perfect the five he advocated. He said the discipleship model could only be adequately understood in light of the other five, "all of which were useful for illuminating different aspects of community and discipleship themselves" (1992a, 50). While it is true that all the models are interrelated and shed light on one another, I contend that this sixth model is needed to complete the picture of the four basic structures of the church.

The Postconciliar Identity and Mission of the Church

We have seen that the conciliar theology was christocentric. This was manifested in the images of sacrament, people of God, and servant. We have seen that these images did not resonate fully with people's experiences. Are there any dominant images or models in the postconciliar church? Unfortunately, Vatican II largely ignored the symbol of the kingdom of God. "Any attempt to discuss the church in the world without spelling out the church's role in discerning, promoting and realizing the kingdom in the world is bound to be limited and frustrated" (E. McDonagh 1991, 111). It seems that many in the postconciliar church experienced this frustration and found the church's identity and mission in terms of the kingdom of God—the most important New Testament image. There has been a shift from christocentrism to theocentrism. Jesus said, "He who believes in me, believes not in me but in him who sent me" (John 12:44). As Eugene Hillman explained (1989, 56), "A shift from christocentrism to theocentrism would conform more with the teaching of Jesus. . . . Christocentricism is not an end or a goal; it is a means or 'way' to theocentrism (John 14:6)."

Although neither Pope John Paul II nor Avery Dulles have highlighted the community-of-disciples image since the early 1980s, I would suggest that this model of the church's identity and mission captures the direction and spirituality of many in the postconciliar church (Osborne 1993). The church, the sacrament of the kingdom of God, is a world church of communities of disciples with a threefold mission, especially service to and with the poor. The implications of this view for liturgy, authority in the church, social justice, and morality will be examined in later chapters.

The Synod of 1985

In order to promote collegiality between the pope and bishops, Vatican II recommended that international synods be held periodically (CD 5). Synods serve three purposes: they encourage closer union between bishops and the pope; they provide information about matters affecting the life and mission of the church; and they facilitate agreement about essential points of Christian faith. Paul VI began them on a three-year cycle with the Synod of 1967 on the doctrinal and historical coherence of the faith. On the agenda were canon law, seminary reform, doctrinal dangers, liturgy, and mixed marriages—too many topics for a six-weeks meeting. The seventh synod was held in 1983. On January 25, 1985, John Paul II was in St. Paul-Outside-the-Walls, presiding at prayers for Christian unity, just as John XXIII had done on January 25, 1959. John shocked the church by announcing the twenty-first ecumenical council; John Paul surprised the church by announcing the eighth synod—an extraordinary one—to be held later that year, November 25 to December 8, to mark the twentieth anniversary of the conclusion of Vatican II. A synod is labeled "extraordinary" when the delegates are presidents and leaders of episcopal conferences rather than elected members.

John Paul said that Vatican II "remains the fundamental event in the life of the modern church" and that for himself it has been "the constant reference point of my every pastoral action." He hoped the synod would revive the "extraordinary atmosphere of ecclesial communion" and "mutual sharing" expressed at the council, review the experience of the council's application, and continue to apply its insights "in the light of the new exigencies as well."

Commentators agreed that there were reasons this synod was needed. The sixteen conciliar documents were either poorly known or simply ignored. Also, the synod might be able to address two groups in the church: those who disapproved of Vatican II and those who believed the church had changed even more than the council had mandated.

The synod assembled 165 bishops, 40 percent of whom had been at Vatican II and 60 percent of whom were from the third world—a sign of the world church. There were ten male observers from other Christian churches.

The synod produced two documents on December 9, 1985—a *Final Report* and a *Message to the People of God*—and offered four main recommendations: the completion of a code of canon law for the Eastern Catholic churches, a clarification of the status of episcopal conferences, a study of the principle of subsidiarity, and the preparation of a universal catechism.

Most synods command three years of preparation and continue for more than a month in duration. This one opened ten months after its announcement and lasted two weeks. It had its shortcomings, for example, no women were invited (Schüssler Fiorenza 1986), and it abandoned the image of the church as the people of God. Probably its real achievement was its very strong affirmation of Vatican II. It correctly understood aggiornamento which it described as "a missionary openness to the integral salvation of the world."

The history of the synod was written up in journals and books.[3] There was general agreement that three main tendencies emerged at the synod. Dulles called the first group "neo-Augustinian" (1988a, 191).

The saintly Augustine of Hippo (354–430), one of the church's most influential theologians, wrote the *City of God*, a book written against the background of the invasion of the Roman Empire by the Visigoths and Vandals. Augustine wrote in response to the charge that the growth of Christianity was the cause of the decline and eventual fall of Rome to Alaric, king of the Visigoths, in 410. Augustine argued that Rome fell because it lost a comprehension of virtue and the common good. In his book, Augustine pictures Jesus as the one who redirects, reinvigorates, and regenerates human life which has been corrupted by sin. He also identified the church with the kingdom of God, the heavenly city, because the world, the earthly city, will one day pass away.

According to David Hollenbach (1989, 79), the *City of God* is "marked by a deep sensitivity to the fragility and incompleteness of the political order and the dangers which beset it as a result of human arrogance. . . . Both historical circumstances and deep theological insight into human psychology gave Augustine a right to be . . . pessimistic about politics." As Augustine lay dying in 430, the Vandals were at the very gates of Hippo.

The neo-Augustinians—mainly curial bishops—underscored the church as "mystery." By "mystery" they meant what it meant at Vatican II, especially in the constitutions on the church and revelation. That is, Jesus (and not the church) is the light of the world who not only mediates the very life of the triune God to the church but also "fully reveals humanity to itself and brings to light its very high calling" (GS 22). All Christians are invited to participate in this mystery of communion with God.

Robert Imbelli (1986), employing Von Hügel's triad, applauded the synod's stress on the mystical and its focus on the trinitarian and christocentric character of the church. He found that many pre-synodal articles made no reference "to Christ in the many expectations advanced and programs proposed. Management, not mystery, seemed the order of the day." He believed that, although Vatican II stressed the mystical element of the church, "much of the subsequent interpretation and implementation of the council was neglectful of it and concentrated upon the critical [intellectual] and institutional."

There are several conclusions that can be drawn from the theology of the church as mystery. The neo-Augustinians drew a pessimistic conclusion. For them the church was "an island of grace in a world given over to sin" (Dulles 1988a, 191). It was obvious, said these bishops, that the world of 1985 was not converging toward greater freedom, prosperity, or universal harmony as the council had said it was in 1965. Furthermore, those Catholics who seek friendship with the world easily fall into materialism, consumerism, and religious indifference. The bishops, influenced by Augustine's pessimism, insisted that the church must shun the secular world and must seek to arouse the sense of God's holy mystery. The world is so darkened by sin that it is only with the guidance of the church that it can attain truth.

The neo-Augustinians refused to let the church be reduced to an instrument for the rebuilding of secular society. They viewed the church as a divinely animated organism that directs people to eternal life. They were deeply convinced that special graces are attached to the church's officeholders, especially the pope. While approving of the accomplishments of the council, they regarded the postconciliar period as one of turmoil. They strongly resisted all proposals to reform the structures of the church according to contemporary management theory. The church, in their view, was being excessively politicized. They observed that the very people who protest against the power of the papacy were seeking to gain power for themselves and their constituencies. True reform, these bishops maintained, is interior and spiritual, requiring humility, obedience, and respect for authority and tradition.

The second group, the bishops from Canada, Britain, and the United States, Dulles called communitarians. They viewed Jesus as servant of the world, declared that the church and the world have the same frontiers, and underscored the church as sacrament or communion of Christ. The synod's final document said the "ecclesiology of communion is the central and fundamental theme of the council's documents."

In the opinion of these bishops Vatican II effected great progress, but the failure to achieve communion stemmed from those conservative prelates who failed to carry through the reforms. Some bishops had either resisted the reforms or had partly blocked them. The communitarians said, for example, that the laity still did not have an adequate sense of participation in and shared responsibility for the mission of the church. They said the church needed more development in its collegial and synodal structures. The communitarians wanted a church more internally diversified and, at the same time, one more involved in the promotion of peace, justice, and reconciliation.

The third group, bishops from Asia, Africa and Latin America, Dulles labeled liberationist. Since these bishops viewed Christ as primarily a liberator, they envisioned a politically involved church that was confrontational and militant. The church must not retreat into itself, they held, but must fearlessly defend and promote authentic human values, such as personal dignity and freedom from oppression, including the right to life. This group favored a preferential option for the poor.

Dulles explained (1988a, 195) that the image of the church as sacrament was used to unify the diverse views of the three groups: "Sacrament may be seen as a manifestation of mystery, as a source of communion, and as an instrument of transformation." He also believed that the *Final Report* captured all three groups in this "pregnant sentence": "The church as communion is the sacrament for the salvation of the world."

All the commentators on the synod agree that the *Final Report* is a compromise document, written so that no one of the three positions advanced at the synod would either be rejected or allowed to prevail. As Dulles put it, the synod "made it clear that the favorite themes of particular schools can and must be harmonized in the interests of depth, completeness, and unity." But is this true? Does not the sentence Dulles called pregnant reflect the communitarian view? The neo-Augustinians might have preferred the statement to read: "The church as sacrament of the world's salvation should be a strong communion that confronts the evil world." The liberationists might have preferred: "The church as liberator is a communion that itself must be a sacrament of the transformation it preaches." Dulles believed the synod's pregnant sentence leads to "depth, completeness, and unity." But is this true?

A compromise document is quite different from the actual life of the church. These mindsets are in tension and offer different views of the intellectual and devotional life of the church. The neo-Augustinians offer a pessimistic view of the signs and needs of the times. They believe the church is still in a state of siege against a sinful world; that Christ is the light of a world that is pervaded with darkness; and that Catholics should be known for their life of prayer, humility, and obedience to the church's authority and tradition. The communitarians see the church as a communion or sacrament of Christ, who is the servant of the world, and believe that Catholics should take responsibility for the life and mission of the church and be involved in the transformation of society. To the liberationists, the church is a prophet of Christ's message of liberation and the church must confront society the way Jesus confronted the evils of his society, especially patriarchalism, violence, and greed.

Conclusion

The Acts of the Apostles narrates the struggles the early church experienced with its identity and mission, especially once the Jewish disciples began to accept gentiles. Since those days, identity and mission have been basic theological and practical issues, often causing confusion and even crisis.

Some believe that the present crisis of identity within the church is "probably the major theological issue of this century" (Mahoney 1990,

300). The postconciliar church is in turmoil because there does not seem to be a dominant image of the church in the imagination of the people and the clergy, and because it is struggling to assimilate Vatican II and its consequences, especially its acceptance of modernity. There is a measure of truth in the judgment that the council documents, given their ambiguity and compromise, "helped to provoke postconciliar confusion. Therefore, the council itself cannot provide a sufficient criterion for the problems of the church [these many] years after the council closed" (Komonchak 1985b). Meanwhile, the three theologies of the identity and the mission of the church outlined in this chapter—preconciliar, conciliar, and postconciliar—exist in local churches throughout the universal church. As is clear from this survey of the Synod of 1985, these three theologies and spiritualities exist at the highest levels of the church. The three synodal tendencies are basically the three conciliar theologies. Instead of calling them preconciliar, conciliar, and postconciliar, Dulles labeled them neo-Augustinian, communitarian, and liberationist.

The bishops at the Synod of 1985 were divided. Yet they were able to work together reasonably well. Why? The answer to that question is probably what will help our divided local churches to live and work in harmony as true disciples of Christ. Perhaps the answer is found in the striking insight in the final paragraph of the synod's *Message to the People of God*. The bishops prayed: "Finally, may there come in our day that 'new Pentecost' of which Pope John XXIII had already spoken and which we, with all the faithful, await from the Holy Spirit."

C H A P T E R   5

The Church and Authority

Authority is a sound and indispensable element in human growth. The word means at its root "to make able to grow" or "to enable another to grow."

Today most Christian churches are experiencing an unprecedented crisis of authority. As Martin Marty explains, "The Christian church seems to have one great thing on its mind in each epoch. In one period it was the Trinity; in another, christology, and the two natures of Christ; in still another it may have been sacraments or the realization of grace. In our time it is authority. The fact that papal 'infallibility' and Protestant biblical 'inerrancy' came to be defended in the nineteenth century and used as weapons between the parties in the twentieth century is an indicator of their issue of authority" (1988).

The word *authority* is usually linked with two others: *power* and *leadership*. Power is "the ability to produce effects" (Provost 1985, 195). A person or group can accomplish something. Power also "describes the ability to compel others to do something, whether legitimately or not" (Rausch 1989a, 38). Authority is the legitimate exercise of power. A person or social unit can direct something to be accomplished. One possessing authority "can bring about some effect, whether of persuasion, definition, or compliance" (ibid.). A person in authority has the right to speak and to decide for a particular group. Leadership is the actual guiding or escorting of others in some direction or goal, relying on one's credibility. "Leadership can assume any number of forms: administrative, executive, charismatic. But beneath all of them and common to all of them (insofar as they are leadership and not merely control) is a singular element: the release, stimulation, evocation, maximization of the potential of the individual. True leadership, in whatever form it is found, calls forth the best in those led. It liberates them into the fullness of their potential as individuals and as a group" (McCormick 1996).

The Source of Church Power

The nature of power, authority, and leadership is less important than their source, exercise, and purpose. In Christianity, the source of power and leadership is the authority of the risen Christ. Only Jesus is Lord (Romans 10:9) and no one else is to be called teacher, father (a rabbinic title), or master (Matthew 23:8–10).

The risen Christ is alive and powerfully present in human history with and through his Spirit. The Spirit, the personal center of the church, is the basis of the church's authority. Vatican II states that the Spirit "guides the church in the way of all truth (see John 16:13) and, uniting it in fellowship and ministry, bestows upon it different hierarchic and charismatic gifts, and in this way directs it and adorns it with his fruits (see Ephesians 4:11–12; 1 Corinthians 12:4; Galatians 5:22)" (LG 4).

The Christian scriptures do not provide a systematic theology of the Spirit. However, biblical scholars discern five major activities of the Spirit as follows: it distributes charisms; directs the church's mission; as the Paraclete-Spirit in John's gospel it both defends the cause of Jesus against the world and guides each believing Christian; and it assists the church's officeholders (R. E. Brown 1985, 101–13).

The subject of John Paul II's fifth encyclical, *Dominum et vivifican-tem*, is the Spirit. This long encyclical, dated May 18, 1986, is not concerned with exegesis but with a philosophical reflection on the scriptural texts. While the letter does provide a sterling defense of human conscience laboring to carry out the work of the Spirit in the world, some commentators judged it an example of a pessimistic view of life because it one-sidedly portrays the main work of the Spirit as "convincing the world of sin" in a dramatic struggle with Satan (Hebblethwaite 1986c). It reflects a neo-Augustinian outlook on the relationship of church and world.

The thesis of this chapter is that the Spirit operates in the world (or society) through the signs of the times and in the church through seven interrelated bearers or voices of authority: papacy, bishops, tradition, scripture, theologians, the community of the faithful, and each individual's conscience. What this means is that in the church there are not one or two agencies of authority but rather "a plurality of complementary authorities" (Mahoney 1990, 172).

Each voice is distinct and not fully reducible to any other. Yet not one of them is autonomous and self-sufficient. Each has its limits (Granfield 1987). To function properly, all depend on one another. For example, the faithful and hierarchy are interdependent. They are not antithetical, nor can one be understood without the other. Similarly, the faithful and theologians are interrelated. "Theological research examines, draws upon, challenges, deepens the faith of people—and therefore must interplay with, be available to, be tested by, make sense to those whose faith is involved" (McCormick 1986b).

The Exercise and Purpose of Authority

The improper exercise of authority is called authoritarianism. Authoritarianism demands uncritical, servile, or absolute obedience but offers no solid reasons for its directive or law (Kennedy 1988b). The bottom line, therefore, is that those exercising proper authority must do so within the community and not above it.

The church is a hierarchical community with many levels of power, leadership, and authority. Without authoritative structures, the church would lapse into either narrow sectarianism (adhering to a factional viewpoint) or a vapid latitudinarianism (allowing complete freedom of thought or behavior). Presently the United States is afflicted with a deadly individualism, which in its extremes, even within the church, denies the very notion of communal authority.

John Courtney Murray (1904–67), American Jesuit expert at Vatican II, wrote a seminal article in 1966 on authority in the church (1966b). He demonstrated that those in authority in the church have one purpose or function: to unify the church as an interpersonal and missionary community. The officeholders do this by dialogue and consultation. He added that the unitive function has two modalities. First, it is directive. The church is a faith community with its own tradition and so the officeholders should ensure that the discipline and work of the community truly coincide with the true identity and mission of the church. Unity requires direction. Second, the unitive is also corrective. Since the church is a community of weak and sinful disciples, the officeholders should ensure that nothing hinders the unity and mission of the church. Unity will require corrections.

Presently, authority is under attack in the Catholic church. Disaffection with officeholders is widespread. Many of the faithful feel alienated, others apathetic, and many have withdrawn from the church. Eugene Kennedy suggested that the issuance in 1968 of the controversial encyclical on birth control, *Humanae vitae*, "will be noted one day as the event that killed authoritarianism in the church" (1976a). Unfortunately, authoritarianism—the control of people's conduct—still exists, especially about sexual, marital, and feminist matters, both within and outside the church community.

There are seven interrelated agencies or voices of authority: the episcopacy, the papacy, tradition, scripture, theology, the sense of the faithful, and individual conscience. They are distinct, yet not one of them is an autonomous source of authority.

Bishops

Kenneth Untener, Bishop of Saginaw, Michigan, wrote in 1984, "Our Western theology tends to start with the universal church and then see local churches as concrete realizations of this. Eastern theology, on the other hand, starts with the local church as the fundamental reality and then sees the universal church as a reality realized by the communion of local churches. The difference may seem subtle, but it can have a major effect on our theology." Vatican II declared that neither the universal church nor the local church has priority over the other because each arises out of the other. The bishops declared that "Individual bishops are the visible source and foundation of unity in their own particular churches, which are modelled on the universal church; it is in and from these that the one and unique [C]atholic church exists. And for that reason each bishop represents his own church, whereas all of them together with the pope represent the whole church in a bond of peace, love and unity" (LG 23).

Despite these clarifications, there is widespread confusion among many people inside and outside the church about the authority and power of bishops in relation to the pope. Some imagine the church as a religious empire directed by an absolute sovereign or as a multinational corporation with the pope as the chief executive officer. The corporation's headquarters are in Rome, with bishops as branch managers around the globe.

According to Yves Congar, this centralized view of the church is not the ancient and, therefore, traditional view of ecclesial authority (see Lauret 1988, 40–42). The existence of the Papal States aggrandized papal prerogatives to the detriment of collegiality. The centralized model received further impetus in the eleventh century under Gregory VII (1073–85) when the church appropriated great legal and political power during the investiture controversy. This model picked up theological support through Bonaventure (1221–74) and continued right up to Vatican II, when, with the idea of reversing the trend, "the relationship between pope and bishops was the primary item on the agenda" (Cooke 1989, 3).[1]

Bonaventure is an important figure in church history. This saintly Italian Franciscan was a theologian at the University of Paris, a cardinal, the general of the Franciscans (1257–74), and declared a doctor of the church by Sixtus V (1565–90). He taught that the pope possessed the fullness of power, while bishops and priests only had power derived from the pope. He defended this teaching by distinguishing between the power of orders and the power of jurisdiction. Bishops had the power of orders but this was of no avail to them until the pope granted them the power of jurisdiction, of which he possessed a monopoly. Bishops were, in Bonaventure's words, "vicars of the pope," that is, deputies empowered to implement his teachings. One of the reasons Bonaventure took this position was to safeguard the newly founded Franciscans and Dominicans from episcopal control.

Vatican II generally retrieved the traditional view. According to the Catholic tradition, each local church is distinct and equal as church; each local church is *an* entire church but it is not *the* church (LG 26). Bishops are "vicars and legates of Christ" (LG 27). Bishops have full responsibility for their dioceses by exercising their offices of sanctifying, teaching, and governing. Bishops possess authority and power in virtue of the sacrament of orders, are not the pope's instruments and functionaries, and exercise pastoral authority within their dioceses based on the principle of subsidiarity. It was Pius XI who gave subsidiarity a classic definition in *Quadragesimo anno*, his influential encyclical of 1931: "Nothing should be done by a larger and higher institution that can be done equally well by a smaller and lower institution" (n. 79). For example, today some would insist that if a bishop gives an imprimatur to a book and it is ordered withdrawn by the Roman curia, the bishop has both the right and responsibility to demand specific reasons. If the reasons given are not persuasive, the bishop should not withdraw the imprimatur.

Vatican II countered the notion that bishops are vicars of the pope, for "they exercise a power which they possess in their own right and are most truly said to be at the head of the people they govern. Consequently, their authority, far from being damaged by the supreme and universal power, is in fact defended, upheld and strengthened by it, since the holy Spirit preserves unfailingly that form of government which was set up by Christ the Lord of his church" (LG 27). The bishops, as successors of the apostles, together with the pope, "govern the house of the living God" (LG 18). The universal church (the house of the living God) is a reality realized by the communion of local churches. The bishops, then, are neither independent of nor separated from the other bishops and the pope. Apostolic authority rests in the entire college of bishops in union with the pope. If a pope ever separated himself from the entire college of bishops, he could not claim to possess the fullness of apostolic authority. The same applies to an individual bishop or a group of bishops.

In conclusion, a bishop has three essential interrelated relationships: to the pope, the bishop of Rome and head of the episcopal college; to the entire college of bishops; and to the people of his diocese.

Collegiality

Collegiality denotes the corporate responsibility of the whole body of bishops for the unity and mission of the whole church. The word indicates that the church is a community or college of local churches that together make up the universal church. Collegiality is exercised in many ways, two of which are special: ecumenical councils and international synods.

Since the pope is "pastor of the entire church" and "has full, supreme, and universal power over the whole church" (LG 22), there naturally arises tension between the primacy of the pope and the power of the bishops. For example, Paul VI believed firmly in both papal primacy and collegiality. During the council his speeches showed him "plainly struggling to hold these concepts in balance, unwilling to abandon either primacy or collegiality" (Hebblethwaite 1988a).

In September 1965, Paul VI set up the international synods—but did not use the word *collegiality* (Dulles 1985b). These assemblies are advisory to the pope. The bishops enjoy no deliberative powers. It is the pope who calls them and determines the agenda. Paul VI held five synods between 1978 and 1994; John Paul has assembled six.

Paul VI never let collegiality restrict his primatial powers. He went his own way on certain issues: he reinforced the teachings about priestly celibacy in 1967 and contraceptive birth control in 1968. The theme of the Synod of 1969 was collegiality. This topic called for serious discussion in light of the aftermath of *Humanae vitae* in 1968. However, no practical directives came from the synod to make collegiality a more significant part of church governance.

John Paul II, too, continues to exercise the primacy in a highly personal style. For him the synods are "instruments of collegiality." On a visit to Ireland in 1979, he called the postconciliar church "the synodal church," meaning synods have become part of the mainstream of the church's life. Nevertheless, for both these postconciliar popes, ecclesiastical authority resides in the pope and bishops, but especially in the pope, who makes use of the bishops at his own discretion.

Until the popes learn to deal collegially with the bishops, the authority tension will erode the identity and mission of the church (Granfield 1985). Church historian Brian Tierney wrote that the sixteenth ecumenical council, Constance (1414–18), tried to give the church a constitutional structure in accord with the church's own intrinsic collegial nature. But it failed. And the failure was disastrous for the church. "Now we live in the shadow of another great council. The doctrine of collegiality has been defined afresh. But the problem of constitutional structure remains quite open and unresolved. We have a second chance to solve it. And we have less excuse for failing than the men of the fifteenth century. We have not forgotten our history, and we are not condemned to repeat it," Tierney advised (1988).

Episcopal Conferences

Bishops exercise collegiality through national or regional conferences. Such meetings have a long history in the church. Vatican II underscored and reinvigorated them on October 28, 1965 with this statement: "[T]his sacred synod judges that it would be in the highest degree helpful if in all parts of the world the bishops of each country or region would meet regularly, so that by sharing their wisdom and experience and exchanging views they may jointly formulate a program for the common good of the church" (CD 37).

The conferences serve several functions. First, they link the local churches to one another in mutual charity and care. Second, they become the occasion for the bishops to authoritatively teach the nation and set policy on moral and disciplinary issues. The United States bishops, for example, issued two masterful pastoral letters, "The Challenge of Peace" in 1983 and "Economic Justice for All" in 1986. In these letters the bishops distinguished between the church's social teaching and the application of its principles to the concrete circumstances of the times. The applications, as prudential judgments, are not binding in conscience on the faithful. The bishops did ask Catholics seriously to consider the bishops' perspectives when forming their own opinions in the light of the gospel. Third, the conferences can also include doctrinal teachings. It seems clear that "within the church of Christ all pastoral activity has, or should have, a doctrinal basis" (Dulles 1983; see also Dulles 1990). Furthermore, the church's doctrines, customs, and disciplines can be incarnated within national and regional cultures. Technically, this is called inculturation. Inculturation is more than adaptation. It takes place "when an indigenous culture profoundly influences a culture of foreign origin" (Donders 1990, 32). Those from a foreign culture discover Christian values already present in the indigenous culture.

The term inculturation became widespread in the 1970s through its frequent usage by the Jesuits, especially in the letters of Pedro Arrupe (1907–91), their renowned and saintly Superior General. Cardinal Jaime Sin of the Philippines built on the Jesuit use of the term by making specific references to inculturation at the Synod of 1977 on catechetics (Azevedo 1984, 122–27). John Paul II gave papal approbation to this neologism in *Catechesi tradendae*, his authoritative response to that synod (see n. 53).

Paul VI decreed in 1966 that all nations (or regions) should have episcopal conferences. He even convened the extraordinary Synod of 1969 to discuss collegiality—but no solution was reached. But by then, Paul had become wary of episcopal conferences because Vatican II had left their theological basis and power rather vague (Dulles 1988a, 209–10). Some argued that the conferences tended to undermine the teaching authority of the pope; others feared that the conferences introduced an unnecessary nationalism into the church; and still others cautioned that they could conflict with the teaching authority of individual diocesan bishops.

Concerning inculturation—the making of the church into a genuine world church by incarnating the gospel in different cultures—Paul was at first open to it. In 1971 he made clear in his apostolic letter, *Octogesima adveniens* ("Call to Action"), that it is virtually impossible for himself as pope to specify in detail the relevance of the gospel for all the different cultural contexts in which the various local churches find themselves. "Such is not our ambition, nor is it our mission," he said. "It is up to the Christian communities objectively to analyze the situation which is proper to their own country, to shed on it the light of the gospel's unalterable words, and to draw principles of reflection, norms of judgment, and directives for action for the social teaching of the church" (n. 4). By the time of the Synod of 1974 on evangelization, he became cautious about inculturation, saying it would be "dangerous to speak of diversified theologies according to continents and cultures."

Although he has encouraged regional meetings, John Paul II maintains a highly centralized control over the church. He, too, is wary of inculturation. He prefers the phrase "the evangelization of cultures" and is reluctant to authorize regional liturgical innovations. The pope's theologian, Cardinal Joseph Ratzinger, has written that "episcopal conferences have no theological basis" (Ratzinger with Messari 1985, 23; see also Lindbeck, Hellwig, and Higgins 1985).

The Synod of 1985 on Vatican II discussed episcopal conferences. The assembled bishops were unable to solve the theological debate and so mandated in their *Final Report* that "since bishops' conferences are so useful, indeed necessary in the present pastoral work of the church, a study of their theological standing is desired, and especially a clearer and more profound explanation of their doctrinal authority."

Such a study was undertaken and a draft statement titled "Theological and Juridical Status of Episcopal Conferences" was circulated in the spring of 1988.[2] This CDF text offered essentially the same debate that took place during the council. It declared that episcopal conferences have no theological basis, "have no competence to establish doctrinal and moral contents," and do not have the teaching authority that individual bishops have in their dioceses. The United States bishops reviewed the Vatican draft statement and criticized it for being "defensive, negative . . . and polemical." The editors of *Commonweal* wrote that the bishops also "found it deficient on historical, juridical, experiential, and thematic grounds. Taking a leading role within the universal college of bishops, they called for the complete revision of the document."[3] As of now, this issue remains unresolved.

Appointment of Bishops

In addition to the tension between the pope and bishops over synods and episcopal conferences, a third issue has become increasingly problematic: the appointment of bishops.

The election of bishops by the clergy and people of their dioceses is a venerable and authentic Catholic tradition. However, the church's mechanisms for choosing bishops have changed numerous times, usually in response to changes in the secular world. At one time, kings and other national leaders had a decisive part in the appointment of bishops.

The present practice is that bishops are appointed by the pope (Reese 1984). This practice is relatively recent, a product of the centralization that followed Vatican I.

There is a positive side to the system of Rome making the appointments: it makes bishops more independent of governments. In the past, many governments demanded a say in the appointment of bishops. However, today there is a measure of dissatisfaction with the present process in certain parts of the world. For instance, in Germany on January 27, 1989, 163 German-speaking theologians from Germany, Austria, the Netherlands, and Switzerland signed the "Cologne Declaration."[4] These theologians complained that vacant episcopal offices around the world were unilaterally filled "without regard for the recommendations of the local church and without respect for their established rights." The theologians were disturbed by "the following changes in the postconciliar church: a creeping extension of exaggerated hierarchical control; progressive undermining of the local churches, suppression of theological debate, and reduction in the role of the laity in the church; antagonism from above which heightens conflict in the church through means of disciplinary measures." These concerns were later ratified by a large number of Spanish, French, Italian, Belgian, and Brazilian theologians.

The catalyst in this case was the appointment of Cardinal Joachim Meisner as archbishop of Cologne, in opposition to the recommendation of the Cologne Cathedral Chapter. According to Bernard Häring, the theologians took this very bold step of publicly voicing their grievances because the bishops "seemed not to dare to play their role of collegiality and subsidiarity" (Windsor 1989).

The Papacy

The Catholic tradition has always recognized the centrality of the Petrine office. Nonetheless, biblical scholars, historians, and theologians agree that the papacy is an evolving institution in a living church (R. E. Brown 1970, 1984; Brown, Donfried, and Reumann 1973; Tillard 1983; Miller 1983; Fiorenza 1984). Some of its authority and power is of divine design, hence permanent; and some of human design, hence changeable.

At Vatican I it was declared infallibly in *Pastor aeternus* of July 18, 1870, that Christ made Peter the "visible head of the church," and gave him "a primacy of true and proper jurisdiction," and "perpetual successors." Peter's successors have "full and supreme power of jurisdiction."

Such infallible statements are studied, explained, and interpreted by theologians. What did they mean in 1870 and what do they mean today? As a living community, the church holds on to its tradition by interpreting it for the contemporary situation. To simply repeat doctrinal statements without reinterpretation would freeze them into the language of one historical era, cripple the church's teaching function because she would be teaching in a language the people do not understand, and disallow any doctrinal development.

The magisterium has officially taught that the gospels are not biographies or lives of Jesus. The PBC issued an *Instruction on the Historical Truth of the Gospels* in 1964, declaring that the gospels contain the words and deeds of Jesus as theologically interpreted by Jesus' disciples, especially the four evangelists who edited, synthesized, and explicated the apostolic traditon that came down to them. For example, what specifically do the gospels say about Peter during and after the ministry of Jesus? According to tradition, Peter founded the church in Rome and was its first bishop. But these "facts" are not found in the gospels. How did they get into the tradition?

In 1973 the CDF published another landmark document, *Mysterium ecclesiae.* Here the church explained that there is a fourfold historical conditioning of all faith documents. These infallible statements are affected by the presuppositions of the authors, the concerns ("the intention of solving certain questions"), the thought categories ("the changeable conceptions of a given epoch"), and the available vocabulary of the times. In light of these principles, theologians examined the statements of Vatican I about the papacy, asking if they have biblical and historical limitations in view of the Vatican standards.

The consensus of Protestant and Catholic scholars is that in the New Testament "the image of Peter was adapted to meet the needs of the church after his death" (R. E. Brown 1975a, 77–78). Peter became a symbol for those leaders who had to interpret the Christian and apostolic message for their times and their church community. Furthermore, the "emergence of a single bishop, distinct from the college of presbyter-bishops, came relatively late in the Roman church, perhaps not until the second century. Leaders such as Linus, Cletus, Clement, known to us from the early Roman church, were probably prominent presbyter-bishops but not necessarily 'monarchical' bishops" (R. E. Brown 1970, 53).

This brief historical account seems to suppose the possibility of continued adaptability of the papacy to meet church needs. Vatican I underscored the pope's jurisdiction over all Christians. Why? "Jurisdiction may have been a very appropriate expresssion for Petrine authority in the nineteenth-century–European context where the legitimate rights and claims of religion were trampled upon by the emerging national states," (R. E. Brown 1975a, 78).

Vatican II did not substantially change Vatican I's teaching on the papacy: "For the Roman Pontiff, by reason of his office as Vicar of Christ and as pastor of the entire church, has full, supreme and universal power over the whole church, a power which he can exercise freely" (LG 22). Nevertheless, something new happened at Vatican II (Rausch 1986, 168). The council shifted emphases, setting Vatican I in a new context and, therefore, making clear that there are limits to papal authority. First, the monarchical authority of the pope was tempered by collegiality, whereby all the bishops share responsibility for the identity and mission of the church. Second, the teaching that episcopal power was delegated by the pope shifted to sacramental theology, whereby episcopal power flowed from the episcopacy as a sacrament, in fact, "the fullness of the sacrament of Orders" (LG 26). In other words, bishops are not the pope's instruments and functionaries, but they exercise pastoral authority within their dioceses based on the principle of subsidiarity.

With these shifts, the pope was more securely located within the church rather than over against it as its juridical head. In other words, the stress of Vatican I was on the church as a juridical institution with the rights of authority united in the pope at the very top of the church. At Vatican II the church's structure was viewed not from the top down to the bottom but from the people of God to the pope, with the pope called to use his supreme authority, extensive power, and charismatic leadership to unify and serve the "house of the living God."

Papal Authority

The pope has authority in three interrelated spheres. First, as the bishop of Rome, he, like other bishops, is responsible for his diocese. John XXIII, for example, convened a synod for his diocese in January 1960—the first in Rome's history—which made its own rules affecting only the diocese of Rome.

Second, as the vicar of Peter, the pope is leader of the college of bishops and the universal church. He can convene the bishops to implement what he believes is essential to the unity of the "house of the living God." The pope is the rock of unity and the strengthener of his brothers. In addition, the pope is the universal teacher and guide of the church. He can teach through apostolic letters, encyclicals, and other educational tools, such as catechisms. The Greek word for catechism means "to make hear," hence "to instruct."

John Paul II approved the *Catechism of the Catholic Church* in 1992. This landmark document had its origin at the extraordinary Synod of 1985 on Vatican II. At that time, Cardinal Bernard Law of Boston recommended the development of an authoritative catechism or compendium of doctrine for the whole church. Law said that it was time for a catechism that would set out and clearly explain the entire body of authentic Catholic teaching. Many bishops, priests, and faithful agreed that, given the somewhat tumultuous period following Vatican II, there was a need for some standard of the faith. The synod adopted Law's recommendation and proposed it to John Paul II, who immediately agreed.

On June 10, 1986, the pope appointed a commission of cardinals and bishops under the direction of Cardinal Ratzinger of the CDF to oversee the production of the catechism (L. Cunningham 1993; Boys 1994). The principal author of the text was Christopher Schonborn, auxiliary bishop of Vienna. The catechism, which went through several drafts and revisions, was written in French, the working language of the drafting commission. The French text was approved by the pope in June 1992 and published on November 16 in France (Riding 1992). Some translations went through a tortured course. For example, the English translation was delayed by two years when its gender-inclusive language was returned to all-male pronouns and other language closer to the original French version (Gibeau 1994; Hebblethwaite 1994d). The *CCC* was finally published in the United States on May 27, 1994, almost nine years after the synod. The gender-exclusive language affected the reception of the text in several places because many found it unnecessary, very painful, and quite offensive. How this universal document will affect the intellectual and devotional life of the church remains to be seen.

The *CCC* contains four parts organized around creed, sacraments, commandments, and prayer. It is designated primarily for bishops as teachers of the faith and, from them, to those charged with a catechetical ministry under their guidance. The book became an instant best seller, despite the fact that it was not intended as a handbook for popular use. Shortly after its publication there were more than two million copies in print.

The *CCC* received both positive and negative reviews. For instance, some claimed the text draws its inspiration from Vatican II, but others said this is only superficially true. It is beyond the scope of this chapter to evaluate the theological, scriptural, and doctrinal content of the *CCC*. It is enough to state that the text is an authoritative work that serves three purposes. It is intended to counter the challenges posed by the socioeconomic, political, and scientific changes that have taken place since the council; to check the growing religious illiteracy in the church; and to correct a widespread uncertainty about Catholic beliefs stemming from the theological debates and changes in church teaching, discipline, and practices since Vatican II. In Cardinal Ratzinger's words, the *Catechism* "was suggested by a world synod of bishops, desired by the Holy Father, written by bishops and the fruit of consultation with the episcopate, and approved by the pope in his ordinary magisterium" (Hebblethwaite 1992c).

Third, the pope exercises authority—primacy of jurisdiction—as the successor of Peter. Jesus placed Peter "over the other apostles, and in him set up a lasting and visible source and foundation of the unity both of faith and of communion" (LG 18). The pope is not the bishop of the world as though the world were all one diocese. Supreme authority and power in the church reside, therefore, in the college of bishops—with the pope as its center and leader. Nonetheless, in his role as the visible foundation of unity, the pope has the discretionary power to intervene directly into a particular diocese or in differences between bishops. Such interventions are considered proper if they are necessary for the church's unity and mission.

On January 12, 1995, the Vatican made an intervention in a diocese in France that resulted in the abrupt removal of its bishop. Since the removal seemed inappropriate to many in the global church, it received international attention. Jacques Gaillot, bishop of Evreux since 1982, was removed from his diocese without any canonical process or any formal review of his case by the national episcopal conference of France. When he was called to Rome on January 12 to meet with Cardinal Bernardin Gantin, head of the Congregation of Bishops, he was told to retire (Farrell 1995a). The Vatican declared that the fifty-nine-year-old bishop "has not shown himself able to exercise the ministry of unity that is the bishop's first duty." The dismissal provoked demonstrations in France. The Vatican may have miscalculated the far-reaching consequences the removal would have on the church. No one expected some twenty thousand people from France, Belgium, and Germany to rally at the cathedral in Evreux on January 22, the day Gaillot presided at his last Eucharist in his diocese, or that simultaneous demonstrations would be held in other French cities, including Lyons, Bordeaux, and Strasbourg (Whitney 1995). In Italy the nation's second largest newspaper published a front-page editorial sharply criticizing the Vatican.

According to reports, Gaillot had made many public statements on a variety of controversial matters. Undoubtedly, the gravest charge against the bishop is that he spoke against some Vatican policies. For example, he endorsed the use of condoms to prevent AIDS and also the controversial French-made abortion pill, called RU-486. He supported the ordination of married men as priests because, he explained, there was a severe shortage of priests in France. In 1965 there were thirty-five thousand priests; in 1995 there were about nine thousand. In 1991 he publicly demanded that Rome and the French bishops change sides in Haiti and support its president, Jean-Bertrand Aristide. He even argued with the French government. He opposed the country's immigration laws and demonstrated for financial support for homeless people. He tirelessly championed the causes of the poor, the marginalized, and people with AIDS. He lived the option for the poor.

The Gaillot affair provoked more than a few reactions in the United States. For example, according to Richard McBrien (1995a), there was no "single compelling reason why Gaillot was dismissed from office. What seems to have done him in is his overall public profile, which proved a source of serious irritation to conservative forces with the French government and church."

Others maintained that the dismissal was justified. Steven Englund, an American who specializes in French history and culture, spent six weeks in France trying to sort out the issues. In a long, well-balanced report in 1995, he explained that "the most common complaint voiced against Gaillot was his abuse of the media. He is said to speak out too often too unthinkingly." While Englund found many who defended Gaillot, many others raised legitimate questions about his suitability for being a bishop. Englund notes that, although nearly all the French bishops were shocked by his dismissal, none publicly sided with Gaillot against Rome. It seems that Cardinal Gantin "had warned Gaillot on three occasions about dividing his flock and isolating himself from his brother bishops." Gaillot "never joined episcopal committees or networked or even bothered to be in touch with his colleagues."

When Gaillot met with John Paul II and top Vatican officials on December 21, 1995, he was told a place would be found for him in the church with close ties to the French episcopal conference. It is said that the pope gave the bishop "a fraternal reminder that a bishop must be a faithful witness of the church, a witness of its doctrine."[5]

As bishop of Rome, the pope witnesses to the church in his diocese, with the college of bishops, and as primate. Exercising his primacy of jurisdiction has become problematic in the postconciliar church. John Paul himself acknowledged this in 1995 in an encyclical, *Ut unum sint*. He challenged bishops and theologians to help him "find a way of exercising the primacy, which while in no way renouncing what is essential to its mission, is open to a new situation" (n. 95). Since the encyclical is about ecumenism, the discussion of the pope's primacy of jurisdiction will be continued in chapter 7.

Papal Teaching

Church teachings are classified either as infallible or noninfallible. The former, always made with the consent of all the bishops (the extraordinary magisterium), comprise doctrines of the church to which the church irrevocably commits itself under certain circumstances (LG 25). These are divinely revealed truths and demand the assent of faith. In modern times infallible statements are very rare. The last three were Mary's immaculate conception (1854), the infallibility of the pope (1870), and Mary's assumption (1950).

Noninfallible teachings (ordinary magisterium) are the day-to-day interpretations by the pope and bishops of the church's faith and morals. These teachings are provisional and reformable. They are not necessarily inerrant. However, they are not to be treated lightly since the pope and bishops are Spirit-guided officeholders commissioned to teach in Jesus' name. In fact, at Vatican II, the bishops said the faithful should adhere to the teachings of the bishops in matters of faith and morals "with a religious docility of spirit" (LG 25). Furthermore, "this religious docility of the will and intellect must be extended, in a special way, to the authentic teaching authority of the Roman Pontiff, even when he does not speak *ex cathedra*" (LG 25).

The concept of religious docility denotes that the noninfallible teachings are to be accepted even if there are doubts about the reasons proposed by the magisterium. In other words, the reasons offered by the magisterium do not have to be conclusive before a person is required to give religious assent. If, in fact, the arguments or reasons were conclusive, no rational person could doubt the teaching anyway. Nonetheless, assent to and dissent from the ordinary magisterium have been hotly debated in the postconciliar church for two reasons. First, it is not clear in an age of historical consciousness that the truth can be fully expressed once-for-all in ecclesial statements. Second, important ordinary teachings of the magisterium—such as the May 1994 statement that the ordination of women priests is impossible—affect both the very nature of the church and the spirituality of people as they respond to the Spirit in light of the signs and needs of the times. Such existential questions cannot be shelved.

Interpreting Papal Teaching

Today the global church is struggling over two diametrically opposed interpretations of Petrine authority. One group regards some of the papal and curial pronouncements as historically and culturally conditioned documents open to investigation and, if warranted, even to dissent. The second group disagrees vehemently with this approach. They appeal "to a literal, ahistorical, and nonhermeneutical reading of papal and curial pronouncements as a sure bulwark against the tides of relativism, the claims of science, and other inroads of modernity" (J. Coleman 1989). This second group is labeled Catholic fundamentalists or "integralists." Integralists assert "that Catholic orthodoxy is expressed in, and bound up with, a logically organized system of interconnected doctrines each of which goes to make up a divinely guaranteed whole" (G. Daly 1985, 776).

The term *integralists* has its origins around 1907, when Pius X condemned Modernism. At that time, as we have seen, the modernists were considered unfaithful to the church and especially the Petrine ministry. Those attached to the papacy and papal teachings in the manner described above called themselves "integral Catholics."

In the United States there are two well-known organizations with an integralist perspective. Catholics United for the Faith (CUF) was founded in 1968 by H. Lyman Stebbins. Their magazine is *Lay Witness* (McClory 1996a). The *Wanderer* is a magazine based in Minnesota that is edited by A. J. Matt, Jr. Integralist associations in Europe include Confrontatis in the Netherlands, Schönstadt in Germany, Communione e Liberazione in Italy, the Fraternity of St. Pius X in France and Switzerland, and Opus Dei. The latter was founded by Josemaría Escrivá de Balaguer (1902–75) in Spain in 1928 (Lernoux 1989, 302–24; Martin 1995). Several of the European organizations have chapters in the United States.

The integralists attribute inerrancy to all papal teachings. They emphasize that all teaching authority is in the final analysis papal teaching authority. Their litmus test for orthodoxy is uncritical adherence to papal and curial documents. They are quick to report any deviations from these norms on the part of priests, theologians, and bishops, or in religion texts, catechism classes, and liturgical practices. The conflict between the integralists and those who seek an integrated balance among the seven fonts or sources of the Christian faith has prompted essays about a "chill factor" in the church (see McCormick 1984) and about a "psychological exodus" from the church (see Windsor 1989).

John Paul II tends towards the integralist view. For example, the Cologne Declaration objected to the manner in which the pope sometimes teaches. There is a long tradition in the church to group teachings according to their importance for salvation. The technical expression is a "hierarchy of truths." Vatican II reminded Catholics "that in Catholic doctrine there exists an order or 'hierarchy' of truths, since they vary in their relation to the foundation of the Christian faith" (UR 11). The signers of the Cologne Declaration accused John Paul of violating this order of precedence, specifically when, in addresses to theologians and bishops, he "has connected the teaching on birth control with fundamental truths of the faith, such as the holiness of God and salvation through Jesus Christ." To give the ordinary magisterium the same prerogatives given the extraordinary magisterium is referred to by some theologians as "magisterial maximalism" or "creeping infallibility." These terms indicate that some believers will stretch the infallibility of the pope to such an extent that no dissent, even in the realm of noninfallible teachings, would be permitted. Integralists accuse dissenters of attacking fundamental cornerstones of Catholic doctrine.

Some wonder why John Paul teaches as he does. The answer may rest in his interpretation of Vatican II. We have seen that the council insisted that a "religious docility of will and intellect must be extended in a special way to the authentic teaching authority" of the pope, even when he is not speaking infallibly (LG 25). Since Vatican II upheld this principle, John Paul adheres to it. Peter Hebblethwaite firmly believes that for John Paul the council "was an end and not a starting point; it settled questions rather than opened them up; it changed the vocabulary, but it did not result in any substantial change; it poured old wine into new bottles" (1979b).

Tradition

Christians believe the church's long and rich tradition originated when the first apostles began to proclaim and celebrate that God's saving love had been definitively revealed or manifested in the life, death, and resurrection of Jesus Christ and through his Spirit.

The origin and development of this tradition creates a tension between the past and the present, that is, between what the Father has done for our salvation in Jesus Christ and what the Spirit is still doing today. Since the two poles of the tradition "evoke each other and complement each other," (Schoof 1970, 197), both must be retained lest the church fall into primitivism (which accepts only the tradition of the apostolic church) or modernism (which rejects continuity over the ages). Both of these extremes lead to traditionalism: the attempt to freeze the living tradition at a specific stage of the church's history (Pottmeyer 1992). "Tradition is the living faith of the dead; traditionalism is the dead faith of the living" (Pelikan 1971, 1:9).

The nature of tradition and its relationship to both scripture and the magisterium has been the subject of considerable study and development. In the preconciliar period the Tridentine explanation prevailed. In order to counteract the Lutheran emphasis on "scripture alone," Trent taught that scripture and tradition were "two sources of revelation," the one written and the other unwritten. It also said that the living magisterium was the divinely authorized custodian and interpreter of both scripture and tradition.

Unfortunately, during the preconciliar period many Catholic theologians interpreted Trent to mean that scripture and tradition were two separate sources of revelation so that revelation was partly in scripture and partly in tradition. Consequently, tradition was the final judge of the scriptures (McBrien 1981, 64–65).

At the first session of Vatican II, a document with this inadequate theology was presented to the bishops by Cardinal Ottaviani. In the debates of November 14–20, 1962, this document met with severe criticism. The document emphasized the Tridentine view that tradition consisted in an objective set of doctrines or precepts that came down from the first apostles and were passed on verbally, especially by the magisterium. Many bishops—almost two-thirds—judged this theology to be inadequate because its view of tradition was too static and unecumenical. These bishops wanted more emphasis on the subjective, dynamic, and nonverbal aspects of tradition, so that it could be identified with the total life and mission of the church. In other words, these bishops believed that all the disciples of Christ must be conscious bearers of the Christian tradition.

The debate became so heated that John XXIII intervened on November 21 and appointed a new commission to prepare a different text for discussion. Yves Congar, whose masterly study, *Tradition and Traditions: An Historical and a Theological Essay*, was published shortly before the council, exerted a major influence on the document on revelation—a document that was finally promulgated in the last session of the council on November 18, 1965 (Dulles 1992a, 87–104).

For the purposes of this chapter, it is sufficient to point out two distinctions made in the conciliar document. First, it declared that tradition involves more than objective doctrines or precepts. It also involves a process whereby the sacred history of Jesus is revealed in the scriptures and celebrated in the liturgy. From generation to generation the church hands on and perpetuates "all that it itself is, all that it believes" (DV 8) through liturgy, religious education, devotions, doctrines, saints, art works, and the scriptures. Scripture and tradition "make up a single sacred deposit of the word of God, which is entrusted to the church" (DV 10). Since Christianity is a distinct religion with its own beliefs about God, the world, community, and the individual, tradition consists of content about Jesus Christ and his church which is handed down consciously and purposefully from one generation to another. Each generation is its heir and continues the process by holding fast to the faith and bearing witness to it. At Vatican II, for example, all the documents quoted not only the scriptures but also previous councils, doctors of the church, and popes.

Both process and message are intrinsically interrelated. Edward Schillebeeckx, internationally-known Belgian Dominican priest and theologian explained: "Christianity is not a message which has to be believed, but an experience of faith which becomes a message, and, as an explicit message, seeks to offer a new possibility of life experience to others who hear it from their own experience of life" (1981a, 50). Rahner wrote that "revelation is an historical dialogue between God and man in which something happens, and in which communication is related to the happening, the divine action. . . . Revelation is a saving happening, and only then and in relation to this a communication of truths" (cited in Nichols 1990, 221–22).

The writings on revelation by Schillebeeckx, Rahner, Congar and others were creatively synthesized right after Vatican II by Gabriel Moran, a professor of religious education. The thesis of his books on revelation and religious education—that revelation is a present, personal, social, and historical happening—revolutionized the intellectual and devotional lives of many English-speaking Catholics, especially in the United States (1966a, 1966b, 1972).

Second, there is a difference between tradition and traditions—a distinction not made at Trent. Tradition is the living faith of the church that establishes the community's identity and mission; traditions are customary ways of doing or expressing matters related to the faith. The church is protected by the Spirit who prevents it from deviating fundamentally from its life of faith and from the truth of the gospel. Traditions develop as each generation lives the faith within its cultural experiences in the Spirit. A rich variety of traditions has developed, for example, priestly celibacy, Mass in Latin, election of the pope by cardinals, and Marian devotions. Believers learn to select from these nonessential traditions and when to modify them. This process will continue until the end of time: "Thus, as the centuries go by, the church is always advancing toward the plenitude of divine truth, until eventually the words of God are fulfilled in it" (DV 8). A perennial temptation in Christianity is to confuse nonessential traditions with tradition—and vice versa. It is tradition that is authoritative.

Scripture

Tradition is logically and chronologically prior to scripture, but is never independent of scripture as a source of revelation. Both "must be accepted and honored with equal devotion and reverence" (DV 9). Both work together so that we find normative tradition within scripture. The New Testament books are the living tradition of the first generation Christians written under the inspiration of the Spirit. These twenty-seven books bind the church so that it is in them that it finds the meaning of its life and mission. Since these first-century texts were written for their respective churches, we cannot expect to find in them answers to such contemporary problems as nuclear war, homosexual orientation, and the legalization of drugs. Nevertheless, they do provide Christian principles with which to evaluate our personal and communal problems. The church listens to the scripture "devoutly, guards it reverently and expounds it faithfully. All that it proposes for belief as being divinely revealed it draws from this sole deposit of faith" (DV 10). It is the scriptures that should be the "very soul of sacred theology" (DV 24).

The Bible, the book of the church, is interpreted in and through the church. The magisterium has been entrusted exclusively with the task of authoritatively interpreting the scriptures, even as it "is not superior to the word of God, but is rather its servant" (DV 10).

Because the inspired books are historically and culturally conditioned, the magisterium should interpret them in association with the scholars trained to do so—the theologians, exegetes, and historians. The collaboration of the magisterium and theologians in interpreting the scriptures has not been a smooth relationship during the twentieth century. For instance, at the heart of the Modernism crisis was the question of authority—the authority of the hierarchy to interpret scripture versus the authority of scientific and historical scholarship.

In fact, the magisterium, tradition, and scripture are interrelated voices of authority. The council addressed this point: "It is clear, therefore, that, in the supremely wise arrangement of God, sacred tradition, sacred scripture and the magisterium of the church are so connected and associated that one of them cannot stand without the others. Working together each in its own way under the action of the one holy Spirit, they all contribute effectively to the salvation of souls" (DV 10).

Theology

The Christian faith does not exist in some "pure" state. As soon as the Christian experience of God and his intentions is brought to expression by explanation, interpretation, and questions, theology begins. Theology, in the classic expression of Anselm of Canterbury (1033–1109), is "faith seeking understanding."

"During the years 100 to 600, most theologians were bishops; from 600 to 1500 in the West, they were monks; since 1500, they have been university professors. Gregory I, who died in 604, was a bishop who had been a monk; Martin Luther, who died in 1546, was a monk who became a university professor" (Pelikan 1971, 1:5).

In the medieval universities, theology was honored as the "queen of the sciences." Its intellectual methods and criteria compared well with the methods of other sciences. With remarkable intellectual courage, theologians engaged the theories and challenges of their contemporaries. In doing so, they did not simply repeat magisterial teaching. Rather, they also used the new philosophical and historical resources recovered from the ancient world to reinterpret the tradition. They knew that without dialogue about contemporary philosophical and historical problems, their theology would be conducted "from deep within the hinterland of faith, safely but irrelevantly" (Hebblethwaite 1975, 114). Theologians worked within and for the church and without need of an ecclesiastical mandate.

John XXIII reminded the church community in his encyclical *Ad petri cathedram* in 1959 that the official church leaves many questions open to the discussion of theologians because its answers "are not absolutely certain." Such discussion paves the way for the unity of the church and "can lead to fuller and a deeper understanding of religious truths." John then quoted an ancient saying: "In essentials, unity; in doubtful matters, liberty; in all things, charity" (n. 71).

In the postconciliar church there is a Vatican view of theology that is clearly at odds with the traditional understanding. The Vatican, continuing the policy of Pius XII in *Humani generis* (August 12, 1950), urges theologians to show how a truth of faith or a theological statement is grounded in scripture and the tradition of the church. For example, John Paul II in his first encyclical, *Redemptor hominis,* stated that theologians are called to "serve the magisterium, which in the church is entrusted to the bishops." While "a certain pluralism of methodology" is legitimate, theologians may not depart from "fundamental unity in the teaching of faith and morals." "Close collaboration by [theologians] with the magisterium is indispensable." Nobody "can make theology, as it were, a simple collection of his own personal ideas." From this, one might conclude that John Paul II would describe a theologian as "a person who is formally authorized to teach what the church teaches and to do so in the name of the church" (Komonchak 1987).

Why this radical shift from the traditional view to the present Vatican understanding of the work of theologians? There are two causes (ibid.). First, the advent of modernity. With the rise of modern science in the seventeenth century, the church lost much of its power, leadership, and authority in society. Science promised to enhance human life by providing social, economic, and political advantages. As described earlier, the official church reacted negatively and adopted a siege mentality whereby it became a countersociety, centralized and bureaucratic. Within this defensive context, theology's main function became the defense and explanation of the official teachings of this countersociety.

Second, once Vatican II accepted the positive values of modernity, theology was free to take many creative directions. In bringing the church out of its countercultural and anti-modernity mindset, Vatican II inaugurated many changes in the life of the church and in its relations to both society and the other religious communities. Uniformity and centralization were undercut when local and regional churches were encouraged to adapt the gospel in their various cultural circumstances. These changes in doctrine and discipline involved changes in theological methodology. Following the lead of Vatican II, many theologians abandoned the language and methods of neoscholasticism. New theologies developed: political, liberation, feminist, black, and process. Encouraged by the council's concern for such issues as the needs of the modern world, atheism, and ecumenism, theologians addressed these and other public issues.

The effects of Vatican II on theology, as just described, are ambiguous. Some rejoiced with the changes brought by new theologies; others did not. Jacques Maritain (1882–1973), a renowned Catholic philosopher, believed that the theological developments and controversies that arose after the council were so terrible that, by comparison, the crisis of Modernism was only a mild case of hay fever. Similarly, George A. Kelly, priest-sociologist at St. John's University in Jamaica, Long Island, vehemently argued (1976, 1979, 1982) that the chief responsibility for the ongoing difficulties of the postconciliar Catholic church in the United States rested not with this or that bishop, but with the body of the United States bishops. Kelly charged all the bishops with a "religious crime": disloyalty to the pope and "appeasement" of the theologians. Kelly complained that the hierarchy "frequently loses from too much dialogue accompanied by too little decision making, by decisions made too late, or too little enforced." He was convinced that the majority of United States theologians and biblical scholars fully intend to "dismantle the Catholic church."

Cardinal Ratzinger, prefect of the CDF, also interpreted the postconciliar years as disastrous for the church. The church, he said, had passed from "self-criticism to self-destruction."[6] The unity the council expected had not materialized because many went beyond what Vatican II actually recommended. Theologians and others invoked a false "spirit of the council" to justify their teachings and practices. Ratzinger called for a return to the council's letter and true spirit. He called for a "restoration," by which he meant that the church must now "search for a new balance after all the exaggerations of an indiscriminate opening to the world, and after the overly positive interpretation of an agnostic and atheistic world" have been considered (Ratzinger 1985, 37). This search involves a turning back "beyond the preconciliar attitudes to an earlier, pre-modern vision of the faith." His vision comes from Bonaventure, the noted thirteenth-century Franciscan, whose theology was outlined earlier in this chapter.

To achieve this restoration, Ratzinger has fostered a series of actions: greater recourse to the 1983 Code of Canon Law; a reassertion of Vatican authority; the appointment of bishops favorable to a centralized view of church authority; and the censuring of theologians considered harmful to the church. It should not come as a surprise that some fear that "restoration" is simply a code word for undoing the deeper thrust of the postconciliar renewal and reform (Hebblethwaite 1979b). This explains in part why the tension between the Vatican and so many theologians in almost every country in the world has risen to an unusually acrimonious peak.

Doctrinal Control and Dissent

At Vatican II the bishops declared that "the task of giving an authentic interpretation of the word of God, whether in its written form or in the form of tradition, has been entrusted to the living teaching office of the church alone. Its authority in this matter is exercised in the name of Jesus Christ" (DV 10). Since the church is a community of disciples, theologians should assist the hierarchical magisterium with its teaching. However, it is obvious that there is going to be a measure of tension between them. At Vatican II when the hierarchy was unduly exalted (as the quote above indicates), the result was "a certain downgrading of other teachers in the church. Unlike the scholastic theology manuals, Vatican II made no allusion to the scholarly magisterium of theologians" (Dulles 1985b). Nevertheless, theologians believe there is room for dissent—theological views by an individual or a group that question or challenge the church's authoritative, noninfallible teachings.

There is tension between the magisterium and theologians because the Christian tradition, even though Spirit-guided, is ambiguous; fundamentally it is to be trusted, but yet it is ever in need of self-reform, self-correction, and self-clarification because all human knowledge that is concerned with specific human actions is imperfect and contingent. Despite the continuity it often claims for its teachings, the hierarchical magisterium has struggled with this ambiguity and frequently changed its explanation and/or attitude in many of its theological pronouncements and disciplinary practices. Here are three modern examples: (1) Pius XII identified the Mystical Body of Christ, the church, with the Roman

Catholic church, but Vatican II did not; (2) John Courtney Murray was silenced for his teachings on religious freedom in the 1950s, but Vatican II endorsed and promulgated his foundational ideas; (3) In the early church, priests administered confirmation, but in the preconciliar church, the authoritative teaching and common theological opinion was that only bishops could administer this sacrament. Vatican II restored the practice to priests (OE 13).

Paul VI and Theology

Paul VI, in keeping with his two most constant concerns—prudent change of church life and discipline, and a faithful safeguarding of the papal office—made great efforts to smooth the relationship between the magisterium and theologians. On December 6, 1965, two days before the closing of Vatican II, he changed the name of the Holy Office (1542) to the CDF. His motive was to encourage sound doctrine. At the first of the international synods, the Synod of 1967, he set as the topic of discussion the doctrinal and historical coherence of the Catholic faith. The assembled bishops recommended that there be set up an International Theological Commission to assist the CDF. Paul VI inaugurated this commission on October 6, 1969, appointing such prominent theologians as Karl Rahner and Bernard Lonergan. In 1971 the CDF instituted new procedures for the examination of doctrinal cases of alleged errors. It also issued a number of instructions on controversial issues: incarnation and Trinity (1972), infallibility (1973), sexual ethics (1975), and the ordination of women (1976). Most of these instructions were theologically incisive; some, like the one on the ordination of women, evoked controversy and dissent (see chapter 12). As we will see in chapter 10, despite Paul VI's efforts to work with theologians, his 1968 encyclical on birth control evoked worldwide dissent. He was profoundly shaken by the critical international reaction to it during his last ten years in office.

John Paul II and Theology

John Paul II is a man of moral passion and religious conviction. He regards himself as the one elected to hand on and protect the Catholic tradition. He has kept a very close eye on theologians. When any of them are judged to be beyond the limits of orthodoxy, they have been confronted by Rome.

The confrontations began in earnest once Cardinal Ratzinger was appointed prefect of the CDF in November 1981. Since then the CDF has silenced many famous theologians, condemned their books, removed them from their teaching or editorial posts, and, in some instances, deprived them of their right to preside publicly at the Eucharist. Censured were Jacques Pohier of France (Jossua 1987, 205–11); Edward Schillebeeckx of Holland; Hans Küng of Germany; Leonardo Boff and Ivone Gebara of Brazil (Molineaux 1995); Jose María Castillo, Juan Antonio Estrada, and Benjamin Forcano of Spain (Goslin 1988); Tissa Balasuriya of Sri Lanka (Schaeffer 1996f, 1997a); and Charles Curran and Matthew Fox of the United States.

The case histories of these men and women make interesting but disturbing reading, especially of the two that received international media attention: Charles Curran and Hans Küng. Curran's case is discussed in chapter 10; a review of Küng's case follows.

Hans Küng, a priest born in Switzerland in 1928 and a teacher at the University of Tübingen in Germany since 1960, has been in controversy with the Vatican ever since his doctoral dissertation from the Sorbonne was published in 1957. In his dissertation, an ecumenical work, he argued that Luther's doctrine of justification as explained by the prominent Swiss Reformed theologian, Karl Barth (1886–1968), was fundamentally the same as the Council of Trent's. Küng subsequently produced books, some of them best sellers in Europe, in which he questioned such teachings as papal infallibility, the virginal conception of Jesus, and Mary's title as Mother of God. On December 18, 1979, the Vatican informed him that he "can no longer be considered a Catholic theologian or function as such in a teaching role." The immediate occasion of the Vatican's action was Küng's attack on the doctrine of papal infallibility that began in 1970 with his book, *Infallible? An Inquiry* (J. Hughes 1971, 1980a; Swidler 1987, 193–204).

In the past when theologians fell into severe disfavor with Rome they "were either censured, silenced, made to recant, suspended from priestly office, excommunicated, burned at the stake—or all of the above" (Swidler 1987, 198). Küng suffered none of these punishments. The quasi-silencing of Küng was something new. It did result in the loss of his membership on the Catholic theology faculty at the University of Tübingen. Nevertheless, since he enjoyed tenure in the German (state) university system, he remained at Tübingen as professor of ecumenical theology and the director of its ecumenical institute. As such, his position was not connected with the Catholic theological faculty. Küng taught at Tübingen until his retirement in January 1996.

In order to clarify the role of theologians in the church, the CDF put out two documents, one in 1989 and the second in 1990. On March 1, 1989, the CDF issued a "Profession of Faith and Oath of Fidelity." It declared that the profession of faith and oath were to be taken by all new pastors, teachers and rectors of seminaries, heads of religious communities, and teachers of philosophy and theology in seminaries and on ecclesiastical faculties. The latter included, as in the case of Küng at Tübingen, Catholic faculties of theology that have been established in state universities in Switzerland, Austria, Germany and other countries where theologians "have a mandate [to teach] from the competent ecclesiastical authority" (see canon 812).

Although canon 833 states that the profession of faith must be made by rectors of ecclesiastical universities and by "teachers in any universities whatsoever who teach disciplines which deal with faith and morals," the profession of faith has not been forced on theologians and the presidents of Catholic universities in the United States because they have not received a canonical mission from an ecclesiastical superior to teach in the name of the church (Orsy 1989).

The second document, *Donum veritatis* (translated in English as "Instruction on the Ecclesial Vocation of the Theologian"), was issued by the CDF on May 24, 1990. This twenty-eight-page document was addressed primarily to bishops and through them to theologians. It encouraged bishops to "maintain and develop trust with theologians in the fellowship of charity." Avery Dulles called the document "quite good," saying, "I've never seen a Vatican document give so much attention to the difficulty theologians have in accepting certain authoritative teachings."[7]

The instruction said some positive things about theology. It said, for example, that theology is a valid "scientific" pursuit, and should use history and other human sciences as well as the surrounding culture as instruments for understanding the mysteries of faith. On the other hand, its points about the mission of the magisterium and the ban it placed on public dissent promoted alarm and even furor in some places. In Europe, Küng, Schillebeeckx, and others responded in the so-called Tübingen Declaration of July 12, 1990, which accused the Vatican of attacking the legitimate freedom and autonomy of theologians in a repressive and dictatorial fashion. A *Commonweal* editorial said the instruction "may be the prelude to further steps that could provoke—we choose our words carefully—forced schism, forced apostasy, or widespread hypocrisy."[8] Charles Curran promptly declared that the instruction was "akin to Rome's denunciations of Americanism and Modernism" (cited in Feuerherd 1990). Then more than a year later, Richard McCormick and Richard McBrien argued at length that the document attempted to impose "the privatization of theological reflection." By privatization they meant that the document restricted theology's critical and creative function to the hierarchical magisterium and theologians, and thereby removed theology from the scrutiny of the public and the rest of the believers in the church community (McCormick and McBrien 1991). What did the document say to provoke such strong critical reactions?

The document explained the important mission the magisterium has in the church. The church, the people of God, has been gifted with God's own infallibility. However, the people can participate in this infallibility only under the guidance of the magisterium, "the sole authentic interpreter of the word of God." The "magisterial teaching, by virtue of divine assistance, has a validity beyond its argumentation." The magisterium's mission is threefold: "to affirm the definitive character of the covenant";

to "protect God's people from the danger of deviation and confusion"; and to guarantee them "the objective possibility of professing the authentic faith free from error."

Theologians, the document said, should "submit loyally" to all the teachings of the magisterium. If a theologian has difficulties with a teaching, he or she "has the duty to make known to the magisterial authorities the problems raised by the teaching in itself." In any case, the theologian should avoid turning to the mass media. Dissent is forbidden. "One cannot speak of a 'right to dissent' in the church." Dissent in opposition to and in competition with the church's magisterium only creates "a kind of 'parallel magisterium' of theologians." If dissent occurs, the magisterium has the right and duty to intervene by taking serious measures to guard the integrity of the faith. In doing so, the church condemns intellectual positions publicly taken, not the individual theologians. "The fact that these procedures can be improved does not mean that they are contrary to justice and right."

There was widespread disagreement with this integralist document, which equated dissent with disrespect for, and even rejection of, the hierarchical magisterium. Many questions were raised. Why was nothing said about the episcopal magisterium? The document's exclusive concern was with the papal magisterium (Hebblethwaite 1990c). Ladislas Orsy asked, "How far can the magisterium bind the faithful (including theologians) in matters that are not of faith?" (1990). Why were the theologians not treated with trust? Why were they presented as troublemakers who challenged the magisterium, did not love the church, and had sold out to worldliness? And why were the theologians cast as, at best, supercatechists and at worst, as mouthpieces for approved Vatican theology?

The Function of the CDF

How effective is this attempt by the Vatican to mediate theological disputes through the CDF? On the one hand, some see its positive side. Edward Cuddy, historian and political scientist, wrote in 1979 that "the church needs her rebels. But rebels also need the church. Her living tradition, nourished by many intellectual currents, often provides the vision underlying their commitment. Church authorities are the friction points which force dissenters toward greater intellectual clarity and intensity. Catholicism provides a structure to harness creative energies and a living community to test and assimilate (however painfully) new ideas." Jeffrey Gros, a Christian Brother and ecumenist, wrote in 1990 that the oversight of the CDF can be healthy. He believes that having a centralized body oversee its teachings attests to "the church's intellectual vitality, its commitment to seriousness in discerning God's truth in Jesus Christ, and its healthy dialectic between continuity and change."

On the other hand, some have been deeply disturbed by the silencing of theologians. The Cologne Declaration was written to express "solidarity with all Christian women and men who are scandalized by the latest developments in our church." Gregory Baum pointed out that the key concept in several of John Paul's encyclicals is the individual as a "subject," that is, the individual person as a responsible agent in society and in all relevant institutions. For example, in *Sollicitudo rei socialis* (1987), the pope wrote: "No social group—for example, a political party—has the right to usurp the role of sole leader, since this brings about the destruction of the true subjectivity of society and of the individual citizens, as happens in every form of totalitarianism. In this situation, the individual and the people become 'objects,' despite all the declarations to the contrary."

Baum commented on this passage that "we have then the curious contradiction that at the very time the Vatican tries to return to centralization, control and authoritarian rule, the church's magisterium affirms the divinely grounded human destiny to be 'the subject of society and its institutions.'" [9]

The critique of Sidney Callahan, professor of psychology, was even more trenchant: "We also appear absurdly hypocritical in preaching freedom of conscience to the world when we do not live by those same standards within our own community. Who will stay in a church that seems to demand that the free assent of conscience needed to enter the church will be the last free decision one will ever make?" (1986)

Dissent: Public and Private, Individual and National

Dissent from noninfallible teachings has always had a place in the church (Orsy 1987; Fauss 1989). But it remained in the realm of theory inasmuch as it had to be carried out privately. Since Vatican II, and especially since *Humanae vitae* in 1968, dissent has become a public reality, often receiving considerable notoriety because of the media. Charles Curran was sensitive to this fact and admitted that, on the eve of the impending 1968 encyclical, he himself was alarmed at the crises of conscience he anticipated for both priests and laity. He said: "I was convinced that most Catholics and priests did not even know about the right to dissent from authoritative noninfallible, hierarchical teachings" (Cuddy 1979).

Shortly after the encyclical was issued and dissent became quite public, the United States bishops were forced to propose norms for theological dissent. They did so on November 15, 1968, in their pastoral letter "Human Life in Our Day." They set down three conditions: "The expression of theological dissent from the magisterium is in order only if the reasons are serious and well-founded, if the manner of dissent does not question or impugn the teaching authority of the church, and is such as not to give scandal."

Theologians have delineated principles that permit dissent. First, since critical theology involves the interpretation of the faith for its own times, dissent about what the faith means today is inevitable. However, dissent as such is not the problem. The problem is how to use it for the unity and growth of the church's identity and mission. Dissent is the church's self-correcting source of reform and renewal.

Second, "Since [theology] is of the public, with the public and for the public, it must be done in public," argues Richard McCormick (1986b). The media can actually assist in this process. Moreover, theologians should be able to engage in their task with freedom so that there is room for trial and error and mutual criticism. "In a pluralistic society, a non-pluralistic church would be an anachronism" (Modras 1979). Where the self-correcting processes of theological debate do not suffice, the hierarchy should intervene. This should begin at the local or regional level and only later at the Vatican level.

Third, since theology is an academic discipline, the signers of the Cologne Declaration asserted that judgments against theologians must rest on legitimate reasons and be substantiated in accordance with recognized academic norms.

And finally, since there is a major difference between infallible and noninfallible teaching, it is wrong to expect the same kind of uncritical and unqualified obedience for noninfallible teachings as is expected for infallible teachings. Canon 752 says official magisterial texts do not require an assent of faith in the area of noninfallible teaching, but, rather, a *religiosum obsequium* of intellect and will. The English translation reads "a religious respect of intellect and will." Bernard Häring believes the respect expected has two dimensions. First, out of religious loyalty a believer will honestly and sincerely endeavor to understand and appropriate the teachings. Second, again out of religious loyalty, a believer will "examine the teachings critically and, should the situation arise, assert those reservations which seem necessary without rebellion against authority" (Häring 1987, 238).

Based on the four principles just outlined, public dissent erupted across Europe within national churches in 1995 and spread to the United States in 1996. In June 1995, the Austrian church called for sweeping reforms in the church in a petition signed by more than five hundred thousand Catholics. The petition called for such changes as the building of a church of sisterly and brotherly love based on the coresponsibility of laity and clergy and on the people's right to have a voice in choosing their bishops; full, equal rights for women, including ordination; and free choice of a celibate or married lifestyle for priests (Shafer 1995a). One reason for the drive: statistics showed that a large number had recently withdrawn from church participation (Shafer 1995b). John Paul II lashed out at dissident Austrian Catholics on September 14 in a three-page letter. He called the petition an "effort at destruction" of the church and urged the bishops to unite to stop the spread of criticism and discord among Catholics (Bono 1995).

In Germany the laity, led by a group called We Are Church, conducted a nationwide drive from September 16 to November 12, 1995, to express their discontent with some of the church's teachings and disciplines (Shafer 1995b). They appealed for a more democratic church. They asked for the ordination of women, greater laity participation in church decisions, and local consultation in the appointment of bishops. Approximately 1.5 million German Catholics signed the petition (Bohlen 1995b). Similar petition drives occurred in France, Spain, Canada, and Belgium. The Italians conducted a drive from January 16 to May 26, 1996. They observed that the hopes raised by Vatican II were unfulfilled since the hierarchy imprisoned "the spirit of renewal." The Italian statement called for full participation of women in ministries but was less explicit about the ordination of women than the Austrian and German petitions. It was very clear in its demand for structures to facilitate communication at diocesan, national, and international levels; diocesan involvement in selecting bishops; an end to divisions between clergy and laity; optional celibacy for priests; a review of norms that exclude the divorced-remarried from the Eucharist; an end to discrimination against homosexuals; and a commitment to work ecumenically for justice, peace, and improvement of ecology (G. O'Connell 1996).

In April 1996 Dutch Catholics mounted a nationwide petition drive calling for reform of the church, including opening the ministry to women and making priestly celibacy optional. Organizers of the drive said that public discussion of church reform has been suppressed for such a long time by the leaders of the church. The Dutch bishops warned that the campaign could polarize the church community.[10]

In the United States a coalition of ten reform groups, coordinated by the Women's Ordination Conference and Catholics Speak Out, launched a national campaign on May 22, 1996 (Filteau 1996). They hope to gather a million signatures between Pentecost, May 26, 1996 and October 11, 1997, the thirty-fifth anniversary of the opening of Vatican II. Their statement, titled "We Are Church: A Catholic Referendum," is said to be "in union with our Austrian and German sisters and brothers, and those in other lands." Like the other referenda, the purpose of the drive is to bring about "long overdue reforms." They call for equality of all the faithful, closing the gap between clergy and laity, participation in the process of selecting bishops and pastors, equal rights for women, full participation of women in all official decision making as well as in all ministries, including the diaconate and the ministerial priesthood. They declared that "these changes are necessary for the gospel message to be heard by the whole people of God as we enter the new millennium."

On November 25, 1996, organizers of petition drives from ten countries met in Rome to plan future moves. The coalition named itself the International Movement of We Are Church. They announced that there would be a massive pilgrimage to Rome to demonstrate for reforms on October 11, 1997.

The Sense of the Faithful

The sense of the faithful *(sensus fidelium)* means that the people have a certain "collective consciousness" or an existential affinity or "connaturality" or "a deep sure-guiding feeling" with the realities of the faith so that they can spot what is true (orthodoxy) and what is error or heresy (heterodoxy). This teaching has a long and varied history in the Christian tradition. At Vatican II the bishops reaffirmed this ancient doctrine:

> The whole body of the faithful who have received an anointing which comes from the holy one (see 1 John 2:20 and 27) cannot be mistaken in belief. It shows this characteristic through the entire people's supernatural sense of the faith, when, 'from the bishops to the last of the faithful,' it manifests a universal consensus in matters of faith and morals. By this sense of the faith, aroused and sustained by the Spirit of truth, the people of God, guided by the sacred magisterium which it faithfully obeys, receives not the word of human beings, but truly the word of God (see 1 Thessalonians 2:13), 'the faith once for all delivered to the saints' (Jude 3). The people unfailingly adheres to this faith, penetrates it more deeply through right judgment, and applies it more fully in daily life. (LG 12).

Many were disappointed with the council's explanation of the sense of the faithful. For example, the last two sentences in the above quotation actually downgraded the *sensus fidelium* because nothing is said about how, in its own way and as directed by the Spirit, it is a separate source of Christian faith.

Today because we are perhaps more conscious than previous generations of the social, historical, and psychological conditioning of human ideas, we have several questions about the way the sense of the faithful has and does function. For instance, can we name a significant doctrine (e.g., Mary's immaculate conception or assumption) that has truly had a universal consensus? Can we credit the faithful over the past two thousand years with the kind of scriptural and theological expertise that go into explaining even the two Marian doctrines just mentioned? Can we gauge the motivation of the faithful in their assent to certain doctrines? Were they impelled by prayerful familiarity with the gospel or were their opinions shaped by prejudice or passion or ideology?

Despite these theological questions, Dulles points out that we must ultimately rely on a prayerful discernment of the Spirit: "If we have identified the word of God, it serves as a criterion for recognizing God's people, and if we know who God's people are, we have a clue for ascertaining the word of God" (1986b).

It seems impossible to overestimate the importance of the community of disciples in fostering the faith century after century. Their authority rests in the quality of their witness. John Henry Newman (1801–90), a priest, cardinal, and the leading Catholic apologist of the nineteenth century, was asked how truth is maintained in society. His answer applies to Christ's communities of disciples. The truth, Newman wrote, "has been upheld in the world not as a system, not by books, not by argument, not by temporal power, but by the personal influence of such men [and women] as are at once the teachers and patterns of it." [11] At Vatican II the bishops declared: "One is right in thinking that the future of humanity rests with people who are capable of providing the generations to come with reasons for living and for hope" (GS 31).

The ninth international synod, the Synod of 1987 on the laity, addressed this perennial problem of active witness. The bishops appealed to Catholics to become more active participants in church and social matters. They urged the faithful to carry the gospel into the world without assuming semiclerical roles. However, despite all the talk of shared responsibility and equality based on baptism, the 230 bishops never really offered an adequate theology for understanding the role of the laity in either the church or world. For example, the United States delegation had hoped the synod would call specifically for the acceptance of women in all liturgical roles short of ordination. Instead the synod offered a vague statement urging an end to discrimination against women. The same criticism can be made of *Christifideles laici*, the document issued in late January 1989 to follow up the synod. John Paul himself admitted that his apostolic exhortation adds little to the teaching on the laity found in Vatican II.

Individual Conscience

According to Christian tradition, the grace of Christ is *not* made available to individuals primarily in prayer, rituals, readings, and laws. It is true that these are important for helping a person focus upon the reality and meaning of the Christian life. Nevertheless, they remain secondary occasions of grace. It is in the common and ordinary events of daily life when people obey or disobey the dictates of conscience that the grace of Christ is primarily available. Conscience is a permanent natural disposition that summons us to seek the good and to avoid evil. It is not an impersonal oracle that confirms or negates our decisions. Rather, it is the result of hard, honest, and practical thinking about a particular decision. Conscience (the root meaning of the word means "with knowledge") is human reasoning applying to individual situations both moral principles and the teachings coming from the other six complementary authorities discussed above. The conciliar bishops reminded Catholics that "their conscience is [their] most secret core, and their sanctuary. There they are alone with God whose voice echoes in their depths" (GS 16).

The Christian tradition has always respected the autonomy of conscience, declaring that it is the ultimate judge in decision making. This teaching was reiterated at Vatican II: "All are bound to follow their conscience faithfully in every sphere of activity so that they may come to God, who is their last end. Therefore, the individual must not be forced to act against conscience nor be prevented from acting according to conscience, especially in religious matters" (DH 3). The present crisis in the church over conscience and dissent "comes down to disagreement over how an integrated human personality functions and how the holy Spirit works within individuals and within the church" (S. Callahan 1986).

In the preconciliar church the hierarchy's moral authority was quite direct. Individuals were told what they should and should not do. The truth content of a teaching was assumed. Teaching "was a disciplinary issue, calling for a response of will rather than intellect" (Vacek 1983). Those who disagreed were simply being disobedient.

With Vatican II the magisterium did not stop trying to educate the consciences of the faithful, but it stopped directing them with the same force. The conciliar bishops acknowledged that "People nowadays are becoming increasingly conscious of the dignity of the human person; a growing number demand that people should exercise fully their own judgment and a responsible freedom in their actions and should not be subject to external pressure or coercion but inspired by a sense of duty" (DH 1). The bishops also said that the laity should "realize that their pastors will not always be so expert as to have a ready answer to every problem, even every grave problem, that arises; this is not the role of the clergy: it is rather the task of lay people to shoulder their responsibilities under the guidance of Christian wisdom and with careful attention to the teaching authority of the church" (GS 43).

The bishops also agreed that "the truth can impose itself on the human mind by the force of its own truth, which wins over the mind with both gentleness and power" (DH 1). This means that religious leaders have to present their moral teaching so that their basic authority lies in the truth of the claims they make. The truth has its own authority and can command assent to itself. The teachings of the hierarchy will have authority to the extent that they illumine the doctrinal and moral issues they address.

Recapitulation

This chapter has surveyed Von Hügel's triad from the perspectives of authority, power, and leadership. The institutional church was given new directions in its authoritative structures by Vatican II when it called upon the pope to work more closely with the bishops within the principles of collegiality and subsidiarity. However, neither Paul VI nor John Paul II have decentralized the papacy within the episcopate. Both popes kept a tight grip on the universal church by issuing encyclicals, approving CDF documents, controlling the international synods, overseeing episcopal conferences, appointing bishops receptive to the Vatican policies, and silencing theologians. Even while John Paul's numerous overseas pilgrimages help to symbolize the church as a world church, they also keep the focus on papal power and jurisdiction.

It is no secret that there is widespread dissent from official teachings among many laity, clergy, and theologians. Many of the faithful are hard-pressed to know where to turn. A certain relativism has crept into the church; many simply go their own way, making decisions in their conscience that are pragmatic, utilitarian, and individualistic. In the Catholic tradition, conscience is the ultimate judge in decision making, but it is not autonomous and each Christian must always decide in the context of faith and the faith community. According to the Catholic tradition, the authoritative voices in the faith community include the pope, the bishops, scripture, tradition, theologians, and the whole body of the faithful. Consequently, all Christian disciples are teachers and learners. Until these perspectives are taken, the institutional, intellectual, and devotional life of the church will be in disarray.

Finally, it has been explained that all members of the church should also learn from society by scrutinizing the signs of the times because, as is now clear, the world's "joys and hopes, [its] grief and anguish" are the joys, hopes, grief, and anguish of the church (GS 1). Vatican II reminded the faithful about dialogue with society: "Through loyalty to conscience, Christians are joined to others in the search for truth and for the right solution to so many moral problems which arise both in the life of individuals and from social relationships" (GS 16). In short, the council directed Catholics to find God working directly in society, and not simply through the action of the church upon society.

Conclusion: Catholics Seeking Common Ground

Cardinal Joseph Bernardin (1928–96) of Chicago wrote in 1996 that "It is widely admitted that the Catholic church in the United States has entered a time of peril" (1996a). Catholics are polarized over issues like changes in liturgical worship and texts, a celibate clergy, women deacons and priests, contraceptive birth control, the legalization of abortion, and the extent of Vatican authority over bishops and theologians. Consequently, said Bernardin, a "discordant and disheartened atmosphere" pervades the church. The present polarizations hobble leadership, hinder mission, and inhibit dialogue.

This situation has its roots in Vatican II. We have seen that shortly after the council began, it became clear that the bishops had opposite mindsets. Some made decisions based on a classical consciousness while others operated out of an historical consciousness. Consequently, the bishops clashed over many of the topics already addressed in this book, namely, the identity and mission of the church, the exercise of papal jurisdiction in relation to collegiality and subsidiarity, the role of theologians, the nature of revelation, the dynamics of tradition, and the place of dissent from noninfallible teachings.

In itself there is nothing wrong with the presence of different views contending within the church. Reasonable debate, multiple rites, various ethnic practices, and cultural adapations have been present in the church ever since Peter, Paul, Barnabas, and other disciples met in council in Jerusalem in 49 to seek the terms (common ground) under which Gentiles could be admitted into the church (Acts 15:1–22). Indeed differences of opinion are essential to the process of attaining the truth. However, since the bishops at Vatican II were unable to determine a specific answer or precise direction to all the challenges they faced, compromises were written into the sixteen documents. Inevitably, the church has been divided by different responses to Vatican II. Opposing interpretations have spread throughout all regions of the global church. The result is that "a mood of suspicion and acrimony hangs over many of those most active in the church's life" (ibid.). Many find that it is almost impossible to hold peaceful and productive meetings—whether communal, parochial, diocesan, or regional—about the church's mission, needs, and concerns. There is too much "distrust" and "mean-spiritedness."

To counteract the distrust and acrimony, Bernardin introduced on August 12, 1996, a document and a related project aimed at restoring unity (Niebuhr 1996g). Bernardin announced to the press: "I have been troubled that an increasing polarization within the church and, at times, a mean-spiritedness, have hindered the kind of dialogue that helps us address our missions and concerns. As a result, the unity of the church is threatened, the great gift of the Second Vatican Council is in danger of being seriously undermined, the faithful members of the church are weary, and our witness to government, society and culture is compromised."

Bernardin inaugurated a project called Catholic Common Ground Initiative and presented a three thousand-word document titled "Called to Be Catholic: Church in a Time of Peril." This text, signed by twenty-four prominent Catholics, laments the hardening of "party lines" within the church. It calls on Catholics to show each other "civility, charity and a good-faith effort" at understanding differences.

The Common Ground Initiative had its genesis around 1992 when varying groups of Catholics met to exchange articles and ideas and to support one another in their work (A. Jones 1996). They realized that the church had to be revitalized and renewed to meet its own needs and those of society in the next millennium. Eventually, they agreed to produce a statement. A text was prepared by Philip Murnion, a priest-theologian from New York City, in consultation with a number of Catholic men and women serving the church and society in a variety of callings. The opening paragraph of the initiative's statement does not place its priorities in politics or ideologies or cultural attitudes. Rather, it declares that a Catholic common ground must be "centered on faith in Jesus, marked by accountability to the living Catholic tradition, and ruled by a renewed spirit of civility, dialogue, generosity and broad and serious consultation" (Bernardin 1996a). Later, reinforcing the centrality of Christ, it says, "Jesus Christ, present in scripture and sacrament, is central to what we do; he must always be the measure and not what is measured. Around this central conviction, the church's leadership, both clerical and lay, must reaffirm and promote the full range and demands of authentic unity, acceptable diversity and respectful dialogue, not just to dampen conflict but as a way to make our conflicts constructive."

This initiative has limited but vital objectives. It does not propose to provide answers but to promote dialogue by sponsoring conferences at which people of differing views can discuss issues affecting church and society. Its focus is pastoral not doctrinal, said Bernardin, because it is "primarily concerned with building up the church's unity by addressing many serious questions where Catholics may understandably disagree among themselves" (Bernardin 1996b). The object of the initiative, said Bernardin, is not "to challenge or supplant the authority of diocesan bishops" by bringing "contending sides, like labor-management negotiators, to a bargaining table and somehow hammer out a new consensus on contentious issues within the church." Rather, the object is to create a "space of trust within boundaries" wherein we can "learn how to make our differences fruitful" (McClory 1996b). The committee recommends "some conditions for addressing our differences constructively." It urges that when people come together they should recognize that no single group or viewpoint in the church has a complete monopoly on the truth; they should presume that those with whom they differ are acting in good faith; they should put the best possible construction on differing positions; and they should be cautious in ascribing motives.

Reactions to both the initiative and the document came quickly. Many welcomed them, including Bishop Anthony Pilla, president of the National Conference of Catholic Bishops. Many were critical, such as Catholics Concerned, a conservative organization in Baltimore, which called the initiative "a plot against the church and the teachings of Christ" and "a last ditch effort by 'reformers' to push support for their misinterpretation of the Second Vatican Council" (Schaeffer 1996e). Avery Dulles said that even if Bernardin did not wish to legitimize dissent, his statement "could easily be interpreted as favoring the view that the teaching of the church is not binding in conscience. . . . The support given to these statements by individuals and groups who are known to diverge from current teaching confirmed this decision." He added that polarization did not usually arise "from clear and confident teaching of the church's faith," but from "indulgence of contrary opinions."[12]

Some found the composition of the advisory committee faulty. Among the twenty-four who joined Bernardin are seven bishops (including the cardinal archbishop of Los Angeles), seven laymen, five priests, and five women (three of them nuns). Some proposed that the committee include more women. Others complained that the committee did not represent the full spectrum of Catholic opinion. Frances Kissling, president of CFFC, said dissenters were excluded (Niebuhr 1996g), and Maureen Fiedler, a Loretto Sister and spokeswoman for the We Are Church Coalition, complained that representatives of "church reform organizations" were not included (Schaeffer 1996e). Richard McBrien (1996) stated that, since all the committee members "are conservative or moderately conservative," there are "too few members who can accurately and forcefully give voice to views of the church's more liberal and moderately progressive constituencies."

The text of the initiative received criticism from groups and individuals. Four cardinals said the document failed to give sufficient weight to authoritative church teaching and gave too much weight to dialogue and debate. Seeking common ground, they warned, cannot be a back door to compromise on doctrinal matters (Niebuhr 1996h). It seems that for the cardinals, "the only legitimate purpose of dialogue is to give the magisterium a chance to explain better to dissenters established church teaching, since the magisterium is in possession of the truth" (Reese 1996). Bishop Kenneth Untener (1996) wrote a strong defense of the initiative by explaining how the four cardinals misread the initiative's statement. Some liberal groups said the statement adheres too closely to official church teaching. It speaks only in general terms of "the changing role of women." There is no mention of the abortion controversy or the ordination of women. The editors of *America* suggested that the initiative does not go far enough. Eventually, those principled adversaries on the far right and far left will have to be brought into the conversation. And when this is done, the model of academic or ecumenical dialogue will not suffice. "What we will need then is the model of conflict resolution or (why not?) of family therapy—which focuses on changing relationships rather than solving problems, which pay attention to the sticking points in the process rather than the outcome, which is acutely sensitive to context and the subtleties of language."[13]

Two individuals who questioned some aspects of the statement are Richard McBrien (1996) and Thomas Reese, a Jesuit political scientist (1996). McBrien argued that the statement did not adequately explain how, "given the high promise of Vatican II and the new spirit of energy and hope it released," we got to our present situation of mean-spiritedness and polarization. He believes the answer lies in Rome with John Paul II and "the manner in which authority is exercised in this pontificate." McBrien noted that the pope is not even mentioned in the statement. According to McBrien, there are "factors that have generated the polarization, especially the use of ecclesiastical power to prevent such conversation [as the initiative calls for] and even to punish such conversation and even to punish those who would presume to initiate or engage in it." McBrien then names three theologians censured by the pope: Leonardo Boff, Charles Curran, and Hans Küng. Reese pointed out that Bernardin "needs to explain more clearly his distinction between pastoral and doctrinal questions; most of the important issues are both." He also wondered about the exclusion of the abortion issue and women's ordination. He asked, "Were these left out for political reasons or for reasons of principle?"

On August 29, Cardinal Bernardin released a 2,500-word formal reply to criticisms of the Common Ground Initiative from among his fellow church leaders (Niebuhr 1996i). He said, for example, that the committee recognized the primacy of church teaching and did not legitimize dissent. He also pointed out that the committee wants to address "serious questions where Catholics may understandably disagree among themselves. These questions are not directly doctrinal, but they do require consideration of any doctrinal implications" (Bernardin 1996b).

On October 24th, the entire advisory committee met and changed its focus by taking the most controversial issues off the table. It no longer aims at patching up differences among moderates, liberals, radicals, conservatives, or neoconservatives, but it seeks to revitalize the vast middle among American Catholics. The "middle," the overwhelming majority of active parishioners throughout the country, has been dismissed by the militant partisans. To meet the pastoral expectations of "middle" Catholics is an important and necessary project. However, the shift in focus makes the initiative less ambitious than first announced in August. It "also leaves the really divisive issues without a legitimate forum within the church" (Reese 1996).

Unfortunately, Bernardin, who had been suffering from inoperable pancreatic cancer, died on November 14, 1996. He said before his death that the initiative "does not depend upon me personally" and he requested that Archbishop Oscar Lipscomb of Mobile, Alabama, a member of the committee, succeed him as chair.

For the church to exist as a distinct community, there must be boundaries, limits, and a common authority. Sidney Callahan correctly noted that at this time of distrust and mean-spiritedness, what is at stake "is not individual morality and good will, but what institutional structures and operational procedures are appropriate in our post-Vatican II church. Consequently, we cannot avoid engaging in fundamental dialogues about the nature of the church and the exercise of Christian authority" (1996). In February 1997, when Andrew Greeley analyzed the Common Ground Initiative, he also pointed to the authority issue as the more basic problem in the church today. Based on studies by himself and other sociologists on the existence of polarization during the past two decades in both society and among Catholics, Greeley's thesis is that the existence of polarization is an "inaccurate and misleading" assumption. Catholics, argues Greeley, are even less divided than the rest of society "on issues of morality, the role of women, divorce and especially abortion." Actually, Catholics are drifting to the left and "have done so in such a way as to diminish polarization instead of increasing it." Consequently, "the 'right wing' segment of the Catholic population is declining."

Greeley offers several reasons why everyone thinks polarization is increasing when it is actually declining. He says, for example, that, since bishops, priests, and magazine editors hear most from the hard line right and the hard line left, they assume that all Catholics are polarized. Similarly, "as they compete for public attention, leaders of various factions have become increasingly shrill and hence create the illusion of polarization." Another reason: "There is political capital to be gained in posing as 'moderates' and 'mediators' between the left and the right." Greeley argues that what has increased in the past twenty years is "the alienation of the body of the Catholic population from the leadership." He considers it a tragedy that "the laity as a body are less likely to take seriously what the pope or the bishops say." The assumption of the Common Ground Initiative that "the Catholic population is splitting into two polarized groups obscures this deeper and more serious problem. There is no evidence that a polarizing split is happening. To the extent that this assumption continues to dominate the discussion, the basic goal of the project will be perverted and the project itself will become mischievous." The dialogue needed today is between the hierarchical magisterium and the people.

Those who support the Common Ground Initiative hope it can assist those in authority to exercise their unitive, corrective, and directive roles in imitation of Christ.

CHAPTER 6

The Church and
the Other Religions

At the heart of the Christian tradition is the risen Christ's command to teach all nations. Right from the first generation of disciples when Peter, Paul, Barnabas, and other Jewish Christian men and women discussed the evangelization of the Gentiles (Acts 15:1–29), this mission has been a daunting and controversial enterprise. Today, since we live in a polycentric global culture, many agree with David Tracy's judgment that "there is no more difficult or more pressing question on the present theological horizon than that of interreligious dialogue" (1991, 27). In light of Von Hügel's triad, it is clear that the existence of many vital religions challenges the Catholic church in a way that no other issue can to clarify its identity and to explain its understanding of the person and mediatorship of Christ and its devotion to him.

In the history of humankind, there have been thousands of religions. These can be classified either as indigenous or as "world religions." An indigenous religion originates within a culture and, for the most part, is identified with that culture. When the culture dies out, so does the religion. A religion becomes a world religion when it has a universal message which it both adapts to and incarnates within other cultures. The major religions—Christianity, Buddhism, Hinduism, Judaism, and Islam—have been especially good at this.

Some claim that our world is "post-Christian." But this is far from true. Actually our world is "pre-Christian" (Ong 1996), inasmuch as Christianity is professed by about 34 percent of the world's people.

Since 66 percent of the world has not yet accepted Christ as savior, the Christian mission to the rest of humankind is a major challenge. Two factors complicate this mission. First, "for an increasing number of people today, the chief obstacle to being fully convinced of the truth of Christianity is not a scientific view of the world that has no room at all for religion, but the existence of rival religions" (Allen 1990, 22). Second, it has become clearer today that the mission to spread Christianity through interreligious dialogue is inextricably related to two other issues: cultural pluralism and global social justice. In other words, concerned people ask how the church can witness to Christ, who said, "I came so that they might have life and have it more abundantly" (John 10:10), if it does not address the legion of problems—such as hunger, genocide, militarism, sexism, and war—that prevent people from living a decent life. In view of the oppressive poverty and suffering present in so many developing lands, it seems that missionaries "have to place work for justice and material sufficiency at the heart of [their] agenda, even, perhaps, before the name of Christ is mentioned" (M. C. Riley 1978; also 1979).

Cultural Pluralism and Ethnocentrism

Culture denotes the set of customs, rules, institutions, and values inherent in the way of life of a community that express the aspirations of the society and the norms for the interactions of peoples and groups in that society. The church always expresses its faith in cultural forms. The modern church acknowledges, especially now that it is a world church, that it should never be identified with one particular culture. Joseph Fitzpatrick (1913–95), a renowned Jesuit sociologist, wrote that "*the* fundamental problem of the church from its very beginning to the present has been its reaction to culture" (1978).

Most missionaries in the preconciliar church believed they were conferring in God's name both the true religion and a better culture when they imposed their own culture as a precondition for admission to baptism. Believing one's own culture and people to be superior to others is called ethnocentricism (AG 23). Fortunately, not all missionaries were so psychologically insensitive and sociologically exploitative. There were some significant and heroic attempts to respect the autonomy of foreign cultures. For example, in the seventeenth century, the Jesuit missionaries, Matteo Ricci (1552–1610) in China and Roberto de Nobili (1577–1656) in India, believed that Christ's grace was available outside the church and respected the non-European cultures they entered. Ricci adopted the lifestyle and clothing of a Chinese scholar and accepted into the liturgy not only the traditional Chinese names for God but also the honors paid to Confucius and ancestors. His liturgical efforts were squelched by Rome. De Nobili lived like an Indian holy man (sannyasi) for thirty-seven years. He dressed in ochre robes, ate no meat, learned classical Sanskrit, and mastered the Hindu scriptures in order to convert Brahmins, the priestly caste.

A modern illustration of the problems created by cultural pluralism and ethnocentrism is the controversy in 1987–88 that centered around the beatification of Junipero Serra (1713–84). This Franciscan missionary built nine of the twelve California missions and baptized thousands of Native Americans (De Nevi and Moholy 1985). When John Paul II's scheduled visit to Monterey, California, on September 17, 1987, had been planned, he was supposed to celebrate a Mass of beatification for Serra. However, this ceremony never took place. It was reported that the process of verifying the two miracles required for beatification had been slowed down. Others said the change was due to the protests of Native American activists. Many Native Americans consider Serra a brutal conqueror who physically mistreated their ancestors and was part of the colonial system that eradicated their culture.

The overall effect of mission rule on the indigenous people is debated. Some church historians portray the results in idyllic and romantic terms; some anthropologists compare the mission compounds to concentration camps; some theologians decry Serra's beatification as a legitimization of a racist and paternalistic system. It is estimated that European diseases such as measles and syphilis reduced the Native American population during the mission period from approximately 130,000 to 83,000. The nomadic Native Americans were forced into menial labor at the missions, and those who escaped or were caught stealing were flogged, often by order of the priests, including Serra.

When it was announced in May 1988 that Serra's beatification would take place in September, a spokeswoman for the American Indian Historical Society said, "It's not surprising. The pope doesn't care what's been done to us. We thought we could expect something better—that he would hold up beatification until we could make our case" (Bishop 1988). Serra's beatification took place in Rome on September 25, 1988. At the celebration, John Paul said that in his dealings with the Indians, Father Serra "was well aware of their heroic virtues" and that he "sought to further their authentic human development on the basis of their new found faith as persons created and redeemed by God" (Suro 1988).

The Popes and Missiology

During the pontificate of Leo XIII, the global church developed significantly: 248 new dioceses were established outside Europe, including twenty-eight in the United States. Pius X promoted missionary activity. He recognized that countries like the United States, Canada, and Ireland were no longer mission lands and removed them from the jurisdiction of the Congregation for the Propagation of the Faith.

BENEDICT XV

Benedict is often called "the pope of the missions" because his landmark encyclical, *Maximum illud* (1919), set forth three principles for missiology, the theology of missionary activity. He called for the promotion of the formation of native clergy. He told missionaries to renounce nationalism, that is, they must seek the good of the people among whom they worked and not the imperialist interests of their own country of origin. He urged missionaries to show appreciation for the cultures among which they worked. Benedict's vision had an important effect on Vatican II—many of the bishops from Asia and Africa were natives of their own countries. The seeds of the world church germinated during Benedict's pontificate.

Even before Benedict's encyclical, missionary endeavors had been underway in the United States. For example, in 1911 two priests, James A. Walsh (1867–1936), a Harvard-educated priest from Boston, and Thomas Price (1860–1919) of North Carolina, founded the Catholic Foreign Missionary Society, popularly designated Maryknoll. They built a seminary thirty-five miles north of New York City on a hill which came to be called "Mary's knoll." Over time, Maryknoll became the popular title of their community, a community that was the first American group designed uniquely for mission work in foreign lands. The first Maryknollers went to China in 1918. In 1912 the Maryknoll Sisters were founded by Mary Joseph Rogers (1882–1955). Their first mission took place in 1921, when six sisters went to China. Today, Maryknoll sisters, brothers, and priests are working in thirty countries around the world.

Pius XI

Pius XI was ardently involved in overseas missions, even requiring religious communities to get more involved. He continued Benedict's call for native priests and cultural adapation in his encyclical *Rerum ecclesiae* (1926). That year he personally consecrated the first six Chinese bishops and in 1927 a Japanese bishop. He also ordained numerous native priests from India, southeast Asia, and China. He founded a faculty of missiology at the Gregorian University and a missionary museum in the Lateran. Thérèse of Lisieux (1873–97), a French Carmelite nun whose autobiography captured the attention of so much of the world, was canonized in 1925 and declared patroness of the missions.

In 1938 the pope had a premonition of the war about to ravage Europe. Commenting on the canon of the Mass to a group of Belgian pilgrims, he said: "Anti-Semitism is not compatible with the thought and the sublime reality expressed in the Mass. . . . Through Christ and in Christ, we are the spiritual descendants of Abraham. Spiritually, we are Semites" (cited in Castel 1994, 13).

Unfortunately there is a negative side to the efforts of Pius XI. He was intolerant of other Christian communities and other religions. His belief was that the other Christians should be absorbed within Catholicism and the other religions should be conquered.

Pius XII

His first encyclical, *Summi pontificatus* (1939), had as its theme the evil of aggressive nationalism. Pius included in his discussion of this theme long passages about the need for missionaries to respect all that is good in the cultures and traditions of other tribes and nations. In *Evangelii praecones* (1951), an encyclical on the overseas missions, he reiterated the themes of Benedict XV and Pius XI about respecting the culture and traditions of the indigenous peoples. Pius XII was progressive about this issue. For example, he published a decree in December 1939, tolerating the honors paid to Confucius and ancestors that were promoted by Ricci in the seventeenth century. His decision was certainly historic—but one tragically and disastrously too late for China and the rest of the East. More than 50 percent of the world's population lives in Asia but only about 3 percent is Christian.

Pius's encyclical *Mystici corporis* (1943) contained an important sentence about the relation of those not Christian to the Catholic church. These persons, although not explicitly united to the church, can be related to the Mystical Body of the Redeemer "by an unconscious yearning and desire" (n. 103).

Despite this concession in the encyclical, an unfortunate controversy broke out in the United States over the necessity of the church for salvation. Leonard Feeney (1897–1978), a Jesuit from Boston and a respected essayist and poet, took the church's infallible statement, "outside the church there is no salvation" and taught it literally. He insisted that all are lost who do not belong explicitly to the Catholic church.

In a letter to Boston's Archbishop Richard Cushing, dated August 8, 1949, the Vatican explained that, although the church is a necessary means of salvation, actual membership in the church is not required in all circumstances. What is required is that a person belong "at least in desire and longing. . . . When a man is invincibly ignorant, God also accepts an implicit desire, so called because it is contained in the good disposition of soul by which a man wants his will to be conformed to God's will." The letter maintained that these points had been clearly taught in the 1943 encyclical. When Father Feeney persisted in his position, he was dismissed from the Jesuits in 1949 and excommunicated in 1954. He returned to the church before his death.

The Feeney case challenged theologians to retrieve the infallible statement "outside the church there is no salvation." This principle had its origin in Cyprian, the fourth-century bishop of Carthage. Cyprian had in mind those Christians who had abandoned the church in bad faith during persecution. He believed a person "cannot have God for his Father who has not the church for his mother." Cyprian formulated this statement for a particular situation. Hence, it seems unreasonable to extrapolate his historically-conditioned statement to a blanket condemnation of all who are not Christian. But in later centuries this extension is exactly what happened at the councils of Lateran IV (1215) and Florence (1442). Consequently, today this doctrine is reinterpreted as follows: The redemptive action of God among the thousands of religions prefigures and prepares for the church. The triune God cannot be separated from the church. Wherever grace is given, therefore, it is given in view of the church—and in this sense there is no salvation apart from the church (see LG 16). In other terms, instead of insisting that "where the church is, there is Christ," Christians say, "Where Christ is, there is the church." Whoever is graced by Christ belongs to the church.

John XXIII

His encyclical on overseas missions, *Princeps pastorum* (1959), commemorated the fortieth anniversary of Benedict XV's letter and covered the same concerns. But John also did the groundwork for a multicultural church by acknowledging that the church was not bound to any one culture to the exclusion of the rest, even the European and Western culture to which it was so closely linked over history.

While John was an apostolic delegate in Turkey, he was instrumental, following the instructions of Pius XII, in saving some twenty-seven thousand Jews from the Nazis. He liked to repeat Pius XI's teaching that "spiritually, we are Semites." It is not too surprising, then, that on Good Friday in March 1959, John dramatically interrupted the liturgy, ordering then and there that the phrase "the perfidious Jews" be deleted. The adjective perfidious implied that Jews were a people without faith or were guilty of a deliberate breach of faith.

Paul VI

On Pentecost Sunday, May 1964, he created the Vatican Secretariat for Non-Christian Religions. The purpose of this office was "to search for methods and ways of opening a suitable dialogue with non-Christians," so that both sides will come to know and esteem one another's teachings and life. This dialogue can take place without the church compromising its faith in Christ.

Three months later, Paul published his first encyclical, *Ecclesiam suam*. This letter picked up the themes associated with the Secretariat for Non-Christian Religions, especially the desire of Catholic Christians to join with the other religious communities "in promoting and defending common ideals in the spheres of religious liberty, human brotherhood, teaching and education, social welfare and civil order." However, Paul VI reiterated that Christianity is the one true religion and he hoped everyone would acknowledge this belief.

In the 1960s missionaries were describing one of their major tasks with the term *pre-evangelization*. This term was popularized by the Jesuit missionary Alfonso Nebreda both at the international catechetical meeting held in Bangkok in 1962 and through his book *Kerygma in Crisis?* The term meant people had to be prepared to hear the gospel; that is, missionaries had to meet people's physical needs first. Often, said Nebreda, the culture and lifestyle of the indigenous peoples were too pagan or primitive or poor to permit them to be receptive to Christianity. These social, religious, and economic obstacles had to be removed before the people could hear the gospel and celebrate the sacraments. In short, pre-evangelization was concerned with humanization, i.e., helping people become more aware of themselves as body-persons who are social, rational, and free.

On December 8, 1975, the tenth anniversary of the closing of Vatican II, Paul issued *Evangelii nuntiandi*. This document, his last apostolic exhortation, was the follow-up document to the Synod of 1974 on evangelization. In it Paul brilliantly eliminated pre-evangelization as a viable term. He declared that all actions that fostered human growth and dignity—education, health care, freedom, food—were already evangelization, albeit in "its initial and incomplete stage. . . . The church promotes the human by evangelizing, and the church evangelizes by promoting the human." Humanization, therefore, is itself a dimension of salvation and not simply a tactical prelude to teaching the Christian gospel. Paul also broadened the scope of evangelization by indicating that it should be directed not simply to individuals but also to cultures. He wrote that "the split between the gospel and culture is without doubt the drama of our times" and that "every effort must be made to ensure a full evangelization of culture, or more correctly, cultures" (n. 20). The term *evangelization of cultures* means that the church cannot simply accept cultures as they stand but must renew and transform them (Dulles 1984, 6).

Vatican II

The council produced two documents that dealt with the church's relationship to the other religions. The Declaration on Religious Liberty affirmed religious freedom as a human right (see chapters 7 and 9); the Declaration on the Non-Christian Religions *(Nostra aetate)* called for interreligious dialogue.

The history of the latter document began in June 1960 when John XXIII created the Secretariat for Christian Unity. When the pope saw that the secretariat was received so favorably, he decided the church should do something about Catholic attitudes towards non-Christians. The logical place to start was with the Jews. Their religion is closer to Christianity than any other. In addition, the Holocaust demonstrated the need for better understanding of the Jews on the part of the Christian world. In September 1961, the pope turned this project over to Cardinal Augustin Bea, prefect of the Secretariat for Christian Unity and a German biblical scholar. Robert Graham (1913–97), a Jesuit and Vatican historian, declared that "between that beginning and the outcome there is perhaps the most dramatic story of the council" (1966, 656). Thomas Stransky added: "To those of us who were directly involved in the preparations and the four sessions of Vatican II, no draft had a more unplanned, tortuous and threatened journey than did *Nostra aetate,* especially no. 4 on the Jews" (1986b). Journalist Gary MacEoin described (1966, 10–17) the intrigue and political problems that surrounded the deliberations over the section on the Jews (NA 4), the details of which are beyond the scope of this book.

The document that became the Declaration on the Non-Christian Religions was at first part of the Decree on Ecumenism. Later the bishops voted that a separate document on Jewish-Catholic relations be published. Finally, the scope of the proposed document was expanded to include the other world religions in order to give it a global view. On October 28, 1965, the day of the promulgation, the final vote in favor was impressive: 2,312 to 88 (see Oesterreicher 1969). John XXIII's concern for interreligious dialogue—called wider ecumenism—"may prove to be, because of its far-reaching implications, the council's most revolutionary act" (Hillman 1989, x). The implications of this wider ecumenism profoundly enriched the self-understanding of Christians and also encouraged the extensive transformation of the church's missionary outreach.

Nostra aetate is a compact and clear essay, the shortest of the sixteen documents at approximately 1,120 words. It has three major points. First, all peoples share much in common: all have a single origin and a final goal, and constitute a single community. It also pointed out that people ask the same religious questions about the nature of the human, the meaning and purpose of life, and "that ultimate and unutterable mystery which engulfs our being."

John Oesterreicher (1904–93), a convert from Judaism who became a Catholic priest and a consultant to the Secretariate for Christian Unity from 1961 to 1968, was one of the authors of *Nostra aetate.* He explained that Vatican II marked the first time in history that an ecumenical council acknowledged the search for the absolute by whole races and peoples, and honored the truth and holiness in other religions as the work of the one loving God (Osterreicher 1969, 1).

Second, in its brief reflections on Hinduism, Buddhism, and Islam, the document says the church "rejects nothing of what is true and holy in these religions," which "often reflect a ray of that truth which enlightens all men and women" (n. 2). This is an ancient teaching reaching back to the gospels (see John 1:9) and the Church Fathers. The apostle Paul challenged the Athenians to worship Jesus Christ, the one he explicitly identified as the one they worshiped unknowingly (Acts 17:23). Similarly, in the second century, the apologist Justin Martyr wrote that Christ is Logos or the wisdom of God imprinted in the mind of every person. As such, "whatever has been uttered aright by any men in any place belongs to us Christians."

In our times it is Karl Rahner who defended and developed the ancient teaching that all people have been saved in Jesus Christ. He explained that the church is faced with two teachings that are hard to reconcile. On the one hand, the church must preserve the belief that the human race is saved only in Jesus Christ (Acts 4:12; 1 Timothy 2:5; John 3:16). This is called Christian exclusiveness. On the other hand, it must teach at the historical and practical level that salvation takes place outside of Christianity. The grace of Christ flows primarily from the world to the church and not the other way around. The world is the primordial arena of experiencing grace (God's universal love). Rahner brought these two teachings together by coining the term "anonymous Christianity." While Rahner's term never appeared in the council documents, it is his theology that Vatican II espoused. Its influence is clear in one of the bishops' more famous sentences: "For since Christ died for everyone and since all are in fact called to the one and same destiny, which is divine, we must hold that the holy Spirit offers to all the possibility of being made partners, in a way known to God, in the paschal mystery" (GS 22; see also LG 16, NA 2, AG 7).

Rahner used the term *anonymous* to indicate that the "first beginnings of Christianity are already given, but have not yet grown to the real fullness of their nature, have not yet attained their historical and social specificity and tangibility" (Rahner 1966, 120; see also Rahner 1974). A person may already possess the grace of Christ even before he or she has explicitly come into contact with Christianity. The life of Jesus of Nazareth indicated that he was a man who accepted his existence as drawn and claimed by God, who loved his neighbor, who was open to the true and the good, who hoped for the future in spite of circumstances that suggested fear or even despair, and who accepted his death not as the victory of emptiness but as an openness to life. People who freely accept these attitudes or dimensions of human existence are at the beginning of faith in Christ who is the goal and crown of God's plan for human history (Maloney 1970).

Rahner's thesis met with opposition from several theologians. Hans Küng (1967, 25–66), Heinz Robert Schlette (1966, 1976), and Johann Baptist Metz (1985, 5) said his explanation was filled with the same old Christian imperialism that had long been a barrier to authentic interreligious dialogue. When Christians maintain that they know others better than they know themselves, there can be little dialogue. Rahner's response to his opponents speaks for itself: "The non-Christians may think it superfluous that the Christian attributes all that is good and whole in every man to the fruit of the grace of his Christ and regards the non-Christian as a Christian who has not yet found himself. But the Christian cannot do otherwise. And actually this seeming superiority is the way in which his greatest humility is expressed, both as regards himself and his church. For it lets God be greater than both man and the church" (1969, 86).

Third, *Nostra aetate* also discussed Judaism, declaring that Christianity has its beginnings in the faith of Abraham. Jesus, who was a Jew, "reconciled Jews and Gentiles, and made them one in himself (see Ephesians 2:14–16)" (NA 4). The document repudiated the persecution of any people and deplored all forms of anti-Semitism (NA 4). It also disavowed the thesis that the Jewish people are guilty of the death of Jesus and reiterated the Pauline teaching (Romans 11:28–29) that God's covenant with the Jews perdures even to this day. Oesterreicher observed, "It [was] the first time that the church [had] publicly made her own the Pauline view of the mystery of Israel" (1969, 1).

Nostra aetate was a major step by the Catholic church to reach out to the other religions. But it was only the start of a long and difficult journey. Cardinal Bea declared that "it is an important and promising beginning, yet no more than the beginning of a long and demanding way towards the arduous goal of a humanity whose members feel themselves truly to be sons of the same Father in heaven and act on this conviction" (cited in Oesterreicher 1969, 130).

Mission Theology Today

The Christian community emerged in the midst of Jewish, Greek, Roman, and Oriental religions. The first missionaries went forth at Christ's command and the Spirit's direction to evangelize and baptize all these people. The missionaries proclaimed to all men and women the gospel of Jesus and the belief that he is the principle of eternal life and "the key, the center and the purpose of the whole of human history" (GS 10).

One of the results of *Nostra aetate* is that mission theology is very concerned with two major weaknesses in preconciliar mission activity and theology (Richard 1981). First, missionaries brought the Christ of their own culture to the persons they were evangelizing without incarnating Christianity within the foreign culture. The church lacked an appreciation of cultural pluralism and was not a world church in a fully official way. Second, missionaries strove to convert all nations and all religions to Christianity, based on the conviction that Christianity was true and the other religions were incomplete or false. Judaism was incomplete and had been superceded and invalidated by Christianity, and the other world religions were "merely natural at best, satanic at worst" (Hillman 1989, 46). The church lacked a theology of religious pluralism. The search for some resolution to these two central problems of missiology—cultural and religious pluralism—has occupied the attention of missiologists in the postconciliar church.

Christ and Cultural Pluralism

Evangelization is the activity whereby the church proclaims the gospel in order to awaken living faith among those who do not know Christ. Paul VI declared in *Evangelii nuntiandi* in 1975 that evangelization "is in fact the grace and vocation proper to the Church, her deepest identity" (n. 14).

Today there is considerable discussion about the methodology of evangelization. In the past there was widespread disregard for the autonomy of each culture. When missionaries went from the West to the East, it was understood that they brought the Western image of Christ and the church to the foreign culture, creating their own type of society artificially rather than respecting the values and traditions of the culture they were entering. The Christ whom Western missionaries taught was a replica of the Christ they knew in their own culture (MacEoin 1973). This ethnocentric approach became, unfortunately, a positive sign that the Catholic church, far from being a world church, was essentially bound to the civilization of the West.

Today there is a greater appreciation of inculturation, the process of discovering and developing those Christian values that are already present in a culture. "In the same way that Christ by his incarnation committed himself to the particular social and cultural circumstances of the women and men among who he lived" (AG 10), so the church must incarnate or implant itself in each culture. Not only can Western Christianity be enriched by the incorporation of the customs and traditions of a nonwestern culture, but the missionaries' own relationship to Christ can be enhanced as they discover Christ and his Spirit already present to the people and their culture (Ranly 1977). If, in the past, missionaries thought they had much to give and teach, they now acknowledge that they have much to receive and learn about diverse ways of being human, religious, and holy.

It should be noted that this inculturation process is actually a manifestation of greater changes taking place throughout the world as a result of several manifestations of historical consciousness: communication technology is improving, nationalism is on the rise, and people are becoming aware of the obstacles in their society that prevent them from assuming responsibility for themselves (conscientization). For example, the countries of the third world have challenged the success of the first world for placing themselves at the center of the earth, for controlling the greater share of the earth's resources, and for understanding human history and culture along an axis that passes through their own immediate past. Langdon Gilkey remarked: "I do not think this new sense of rough equality among religions comes from any new and sharper *dogmatic* critique of Christianity, for instance, of its christological claims," but rather because "the cultures have become roughly equal." Since the cultures "are now perceived *on both sides* as equal, so the religions of the cultures are perceived differently than they were" (1989, 380–81).

Christ and Religious Pluralism

In recent times a Christian theology of other religions has moved through two paradigms to a third in its understanding of Christ's relationship to the world religions (Schineller 1976).[1] These changes pivot around Vatican II and are usually labeled preconciliar, conciliar, and postconciliar.

Roman Catholic missiology has moved to new plateaus because new consideration has been given to some of the most basic concepts of evangelization (Hillman 1980). It will be possible to understand the postconciliar missiology after examining the changes that have taken place in the understanding of four interrelated areas: salvation, the mediatorship of Christ, conversion, and true and false religion.

Salvation

All men and women have found themselves in a state of alienation from self, others, nature, and God. Salvation delivers us from the restraints that bind and alienate us from ourselves, the human community, and divine love and life. The Catholic tradition holds that Jesus of Nazareth brought universal salvation through his life, death and resurrection, and his salvific grace and life are found in his Catholic church.

The preconciliar view of salvation held that members of the Catholic church had available to them all the means of salvation. Membership in the visible church was the ordinary way to be saved. The duty of the church was to preach Jesus' message of salvation to all people so that they could be converted and saved. If followers of other religions remained in their religion, they could be saved if they practiced their religion sincerely and honestly. However, their salvation did require the extraordinary intervention of God.

At Vatican II, the church moved away from this ecclesiocentric view and acknowledged the salvific value of the other religions (LG 16). It declared that God and his Spirit have been working through these religions and not in spite of them. The other religions were legitimate and had a proper place in God's salvific plan (I Timothy 2:4–6).

In the postconciliar period theologians like Heinz Robert Schlette and Hans Küng proposed that the world religions were the normal and ordinary way of salvation and that Christians, being so overwhelmingly outnumbered during the hundreds of thousands of years humans have been on earth, had been given the extraordinary grace of knowing Christ. Christians should be a sign that all people are saved in Christ (O'Grady 1977).

The postconciliar understanding of salvation for those not Christian is much more radical than the conciliar view. It developed in part because there was a certain uneasiness and even dissatisfaction with Rahner's theology of the anonymous Christian. When Christian theologians, mystics, and missionaries started using Rahner's phrase in interreligious dialogue, Jews and Muslims found it offensive. For them Jesus is simply a prophet; to consider him divine is idolatrous. Hindus and Buddhists found the term incomprehensible because they believe all humans are destined for either nirvana or union with the divine, and not a personal relationship with a fellow human being. Foisting anonymous Christianity on the other religions would be like whites trying to express esteem for Martin Luther King, Jr. by saying that he was anonymously a white man—or for men to say that women are virtually as good as men. Furthermore, it seems that to read Christian ideas into the world religions does not do justice to the distinctiveness of these faiths. What we encounter in each religion is a different faith and different patterns of behavior; different standards and ideals of ultimacy, happiness and salvation; and different claims to the truth about God, the universe, and the nature of humanness.

Faith is the basic foundation of each religion. Each religion has its own identity and autonomy because of the specific epistemological nature of faith and because of the certitude that faith confers upon the believer concerning the content of her or his religion. When a Muslim, for example, makes an act of faith, he or she stands in a relationship to Allah which is in no way less immediate than that of the Christian to the Trinity.

We have also learned to distinguish faith from beliefs. This very important distinction provides a means for ecumenical encounter. Beliefs are intellectual explanations of one's faith. They are often held with firm conviction, but can change when knowledge changes. For example, a person's faith in God the Creator does not change significantly when the person's belief changes from creation within one week to creation involving millions of years. While each religion has different beliefs and practices that are culturally fashioned and historically circumscribed, common to all religions is faith. Faith—a commitment supported by conviction and confidence—is the most basic and dynamic feature of each religion. This explains why all the religions of the world may be understood as communities of faith.

The postconciliar theology of salvation states that the gospel of Jesus Christ is only one way of salvation. The preconciliar view of salvation was ecclesiocentric and exclusivist: salvation was to be found in the Catholic church alone. The conciliar view was christocentric but inclusivist: salvation is found in Christ alone. The postconciliar view is theocentric and pluralistic: salvation is found in God who works in the heart and history of each person and in all the religions. All religions are valid means of salvation. This theology—a theocentric religious pluralism—is so radical that John Hick (1973, 131) and Paul Knitter (1985, 145–46) did not hesitate to call it "a Copernican revolution in theology." However, most Catholic theologians reject the pluralistic view of Hick and Knitter because of its radical indifferentism. Hick, a Presbyterian, and Knitter, a Catholic (1988), place all the world religions on the same level, holding that the great faiths are different but equally valid ways of experiencing, conceiving, and responding to God or an Ultimate Reality (D'Costa 1984, 1986, 1990). In addition, Hick and Knitter want interreligious dialogue to center on God apart from Christ. For them, "Christ is a liability in the Christian dialogue with other religions. Christ divides, God unites!"

(Bratten 1992, 21). Their approach effectively eliminates the doctrine of the Trinity. But in Christian faith, God is always the God of Jesus Christ.

Although most Catholic theologians reject the radical theocentric pluralism of Hick and Knitter, many uphold a theocentric view of missiology. They have two reasons: the church is relative to the kingdom of God, and the mission of Jesus is relative to the work of the Father. In other words, a Catholic theology of salvation first shifted its focal point from the specifically Roman Catholic to the total Christian community—and, now, to the entire human family. One reason for this shift is the undeniable universalist cast of many sayings in the Christian scriptures: "through [Jesus'] one righteous act acquittal and life came to all" (Romans 5:18); "For God delivered all to disobedience, that he might have mercy upon all" (Romans 11:32); and the plan of God is "to sum up all things in Christ, in heaven and on earth" (Ephesians 1:10). Another reason is the retrieval of a basic fact about Jesus: He calls all people to be totally open to their humanity so as to receive the grace of his Father. Jesus says all people are of infinite worth to the Father and it is his kingdom which is absolute. "Neither historical Christianity, nor the church, nor Jesus himself, are absolutes. The historical vocation of churches is not the maximum extension of Christianity itself, but rather—in dialogue with other religions and spiritual families—to bear witness to the kingdom of God anticipated in the paths of history" (Geffre 1989, 394).

From the theocentric theology just outlined one can conclude that the statement quoted earlier, namely, that "Jesus is the principle of eternal life, the meaning of history, and the perfect man," is a faith conviction that can be made only through the power of the Spirit. There does not seem to be any way in which these claims to Jesus' absolute uniqueness can be objectively verified. Eugene Hillman points out that there is no objectively reliable evidence for any religion to make "sweeping generalizations concerning its answers to life, death, and salvation" (1989, 52–53).

Some question this theology of religious pluralism. It certainly seems like a form of the radical indifferentism of Hick and Knitter. It also smacks of relativism (a denial of the primacy of Christ) and reads like a capitulation to those secularists who say that the Christian belief that Jesus is the universal savior is both arrogant and imperialist (Gorday 1989). This is not so. First, Christian religious pluralists do not see evangelization as religious imperialism or a betrayal of open dialogue. "To discuss one's firmly held beliefs with non-believers is not the same thing as trying to impose such beliefs upon them" (Hillman 1989, 58). Second, Christians evangelize knowing that every religion affects the quality of a person's personal and communal life. Missionaries tell those of other religions how Christian life is distinct from their religious life. The adherents of other religions learn that Christianity creates a transformation of consciousness whereby a person acquires a new and distinct awareness of self, others, the world, and God. They learn also that Christian life consists in living with and for Christ as one lives with and for others. Third, a theology of religious pluralism directs missionaries to free the adherents of other religions for full contact with the best of their own religious traditions. The missionary helps these people solve their own problems, humbly, genuinely, openly, and with respect for their traditions and a willingness to learn about God from them.

The Mediatorship of Christ

The church teaches that Jesus is the world's unique savior. There is salvation in no one else (Mark 16:15–16; John 3:16; 15:5). He is the mediator, the representative before God in the process of atonement (1 Timothy 2:5). In the preconciliar church, the missionary taught that Jesus founded the Catholic church—the one true church—and this is where he is present, mediating the Father's kingdom and sending his Spirit. There was a radical discontinuity between Christianity and the world religions. Jesus was the exclusive savior of the world (Acts 4:12). To cooperate with the other religions was virtually a betrayal of Christ and his church.

At Vatican II the bishops refocused their view of the scriptures. They began to see Jesus as the fulfillment of the religions of the world (1 Timothy 2:5; Acts 4:12; 17:23). The authentic seeds of the gospel are contained within the other religions. Christianity is not discontinuous from the world religions, but the leaven in all of them. The relation of the church to the other religions of the world is not one of competition nor an effort at substitution. It is one of sublimation. The mission of the church is to take what is holy and true in the other religions and show its fulfilment in Christ. He is constitutive of these religions.

Postconciliar theology still teaches Christ's universal and decisive mediatorship even while respecting the other religions (Watts 1989). This is a difficult balance, since a theocentric religious pluralism accepts a diversity of mediators and avatars (earthly mainfestations of the deity) whose relationships to God are more equal to Christ's in a way that had not been thought possible before now. Postconciliar theology retains Christ's universal and decisive mediatorship (and does not embrace the nontrinitarian theocentricism of Hick and Knitter) because it maintains that the crucial decision regarding the divine is made by people in their relationship to the human community (Romans 13:8–10). The gospels say that in the human community people are open to the Spirit, are addressed by the Spirit, and can commit themselves to the Spirit. When missionaries teach people to love all people, especially one's enemies, they are evangelizing them.

Postconciliar theology's identification of Jesus as the normative mediator may seem to be no more than another version of the "exclusive mediator" of preconciliar theology. The difference is that postconciliar theology views Jesus as normative because he is the one who illumines for the missionary "other ways in which God has saved and is saving people" in other religions. In other words, Jesus, for Christians, is the touchstone or criterion by which other religious experiences are examined and related (Redington 1983).

Conversion

Conversion involves a transformation or reorientation of the person and his or her worldview, that is, a person makes a total change from one way of living to another. Christian conversion entails a commitment of faith, hope, and love to Jesus Christ, the sacrament of the Father and the source of the Spirit. This conversion has affective, intellectual, moral, religious, and ecclesial dimensions.

Preconciliar missiology sought overt conversion to Catholic Christianity as its goal (John 3:16; Acts 4:12). At Vatican II the Catholic church adopted a policy of "mergerism." Since the other religions prepared the way for Christianity and since they possessed elements that could be fulfilled in Christ, the bishops' dream was for a gradual convergence of all religions into Catholic Christianity.

This theology was hardly acceptable to non-Christians, because, like the preconciliar approach, it entailed a union by absorption. The non-Christians knew that, since the Christians regarded their religion as inferior, their efforts at conversion were often based on condescension and contempt. When non-Christians resisted conversion, Christians often turned to coercion through crusades or inquisitions or pogroms. Postconciliar missiology begins with respect for the autonomy of each religion, and, in view of the tenacious persistence and steady numerical growth of many religions, tends increasingly to accept religious pluralism as part of the divine dispensation. Consequently, the primary conversion that the missionary tries to effect is to convert each believer within the framework of the religion she or he already professes. The initial task of the missionary is to help believers live their religion more integrally and honestly.

True and False Religion

Religion pertains to the relationship of God with humans. Every religion declares that God has revealed himself through its sacred persons, signs, and symbols. Each religious group thinks that it is the true way (Cox 1988b). Many religious groups have little use for the other religions. Historically, Christianity has probably made the strongest claims that it is the one true faith.

In preconciliar theology, the Catholic church professed to be the home of the one true religion. It could point to the "marks of the church" as the sign of its veracity. It alone was one, holy, catholic, and apostolic. The other religions were considered to be natural, imperfect, and, ultimately, erroneous. Missionaries attempted to prove the superiority of Christianity over the other religions against the measurement of the "marks" of the true church.

In conciliar theology, the church moved from an ecclesiocentric to a christocentric position in which it acknowledged some truth in the other religions. This truth had its source in Christ. If these religions developed their principles to their logical conclusions, they would naturally culminate in Christianity.

Postconciliar theology shifted the concept of true or false religion from measurement (special criteria of validity) to function or value. Paul Knitter suggests "that many religions may have equally meaningful and valid messages for mankind and that it may be the case that no one religion has the final or normative word for all the others" (1990). A corollary to this position is the conviction that true religion humanizes and reconciles people, whereas false religion dehumanizes and fragments the human community. This is a theocentric approach to religion. It begins with the fact that God incarnates himself in every human person, above every religious barrier.

Jesus taught a theocentric religion. He said people do not relate themselves to God in worship (a religious practice) and then, as a second step, seek the right relationship to their brothers and sisters (Matthew 5:23–24). Rather, as people relate to the human community, they also relate to the Father. The Father is love and anyone who does not love his brother and sister does not know God (Matthew 25:31–46). The ultimate test between true and false religion, then, is the reconciliation of people in community. Anything in the church that hinders human community is false religion.

This understanding of true and false religion does not demand that the members of another religion become Christian. When missionaries help people overcome whatever fosters egotism, hatred, and injustice, they are evangelizing. Perhaps, then, a common ground for interfaith dialogue is the goal of liberating the countless people in the world who suffer poverty and injustice (Collinge et al. 1986). In fact, this is the thesis of Paul Knitter who suggests that since there has been "an evolution from ecclesiocentrism to christocentrism to theocentricism, it is now time to move on to soteriocentrism" (1986, 135).

It is possible to appreciate the dramatic shifts that have taken place in interreligious dialogue by comparing the purposes and goals of two meetings of the Parliament of the World's Religions held in Chicago, the first in 1893 and the second in 1993.

The 1893 meeting—the first time the major religions met together in a public forum—was planned and hosted by Protestant Christians. The great majority of the four hundred official delegates representing forty-one religious communities were Christian. Although there were appeals during the seventeen days of meetings and more than two hundred presentations for the end of religious fanaticism and warfare and for respect for the essential dignity of each person, the "purpose was more evangelical than ecumenical" (Briggs 1993). Christian missionaries hoped to become better acquainted with the other religions in order to more easily convert them to Christianity. "The universal gathering of the religions was nothing more than an extension of the vision of a united Christendom" (Eck 1993, 93).

The 1993 Parliament met for eight days beginning on August 29. It drew six thousand delegates and represented over 120 religions. Present were not only representatives of the major religions but also self-styled "neo-pagans" and goddess worshipers. The underlying theme was not theological unity but unity for peace and justice in a world marked by violence and war, much of which had (and has) religion at its core. The delegates agreed that unless humans were guided by an overarching global ethic, the future of the planet and the human race would be bleak (Stammer 1993). Approximately 250 religious leaders signed *Towards a Global Ethic: An Initial Declaration,* a five thousand-word document which expresses such an ethic (Küng and Kuschel 1994).

Hans Küng was the principal writer of this document. He did not use the word God, a step necessitated, he said, to respect Buddhism and other faiths that are nontheistic (i.e., they accept a spiritual dimension to reality but not the personal involvement of a divine creator in their lives). Küng said he took this position because the religions are not ready to talk about unity of religion. "I talk about peace among religions. That would be enough."

Küng also stated that "we have to answer questions that Jesus or Moses never thought about. We are at a transformation of consciousness with regard to nature." He also admitted that the declaration offered a "minimum ethic," but one to which all religions could hold themselves and others accountable (P. Steinfels 1993b).

Although the declaration professes to be, in Küng's words, "a minimal, fundamental consensus concerning binding values, universal standards and moral, fundamental attitudes," nevertheless, the text makes some very firm statements about fanaticism and violent, bloody conflicts incited by religious leaders; the misuse of religion "for purely, power-political goals, including war"; and sexual discrimination, "one of the worst forms of human degradation." In short, the document affirms the religious wisdom of the ages and declares that much of it should be applied to modern circumstances. The document is also a clear indication that interreligious dialogue can have a certain measure of success if it begins with soteriology, that is, persons turning away from whatever alienates them from one another, the created world, themselves, and God.

Recapitulation

Is Jesus indispensable for salvation? To this crucial question there are five different answers. First, a relativist approach maintains that there should be no Christian missionary activity because this is an age of religious pluralism. Jesus is one of many ways to God and not *the* universal mediator. Jesus is not indispensable for salvation.

Second, the Orthodox, evangelicals, and some other Christian communities view dialogue with other religions as an affront to the centrality of Christ. These groups insist that missionary activity directed toward conversion to Christ is absolutely necessary because Jesus is the way and none of the other religions are salvific. The scriptures declare that Jesus alone is savior (Acts 4:12; John 14:6). Nonbelievers face hellfire.

Third, the preconciliar position holds that Jesus is the exclusive way to salvation, yet God in his compassion can and does save others (Acts 4:12).

Fourth, the conciliar position maintains that Jesus is the inclusive savior. The other religions are united anonymously to Christ and his final and unsurpassable salvation (John 3:16).

Fifth, the postconciliar position holds that Jesus is the normative savior. This pluralistic view accepts that God has manifested himself to others, but Jesus' salvation remains universal and decisive (1 Timothy 2:5). One significant nuance is that, while for the Christian, Jesus is the indispensable and normative way to God and the meaning of life, this faith position cannot be the basis of ecumenical dialogue. Such a faith claim would seriously obstruct the dialogue.

Christianity can never drop its belief in the universality of the salvation brought by Jesus. Nevertheless, it so happens that many are letting go of both the exclusivist and inclusivist understandings of that universality.

The church can never cease its missionary activity. The postconciliar missiology of religious and cultural pluralism explained here states that, from one point of view, Christian evangelization has three dimensions: human, religious, and Catholic Christian. The missionary evangelizes on any or all of these levels, depending on the circumstances and the needs of the people.

The church evangelizes on the human level when it teaches moral values and urges people to accept their humanity and to treat others lovingly and justly as their brothers and sisters. To repeat what Paul VI said in *Evangelii nuntiandi* in 1975, "The church promotes the human by evangelizing, and the church evangelizes by promoting the human."

The church evangelizes on the religious level by teaching that any religion is true to the extent that it contributes to humanization, liberation, and reconciliation in community (James 1:27), and any religion is false to the extent that it contributes to fear, superstition, injustice, and exploitation.

JESUS — MOST PROFOUNDLY ANTIRELIGIOUS PERSON IN HISTORY

The church evangelizes on the Catholic Christian level when it teaches that people can know Jesus Christ through a living tradition that is guarded by a community of disciples, and people can respond to Christ through and with this community of disciples.

John Paul II and Judaism

John Paul always acknowledges that there is a spiritual relationship between Christians and Jews. Is not the God of Abraham and the prophets the God of Jesus Christ? Nevertheless, John Paul's dealings with the Jews have been uneven. For example, in 1987 critical headlines greeted not only the presence of a Carmelite convent on the site of the Auschwitz concentration camp, but also the June 25 visit to the Vatican by President Kurt Waldheim of Austria, a man accused, but never tried for nor convicted of, Nazi war crimes. Waldheim was accused of rounding up Jews for concentration camps. John Paul was the only Western leader to officially receive Waldheim as a head of state.[2] The Vatican and Waldheim were in the news again on July 6, 1994, when the Vatican conferred knighthood on the former Austrian president. This honor, which comes directly from the pope, was awarded for his service as secretary general of the United Nations from 1972 to 1980. The Vatican stated that Waldheim's service was marked by "the safeguarding of human rights, aid for refugees and solidarity with the numerous problems of humanity in the Third World." Some officials of the Jewish community said the honor reopened old wounds because the Vatican seemed insensitive to the atrocities of the Holocaust (Roberts 1994).

On the other hand, John Paul has had many positive contacts with Jewish groups, so much so that Richard McBrien (1994b) did not hesitate to declare that, when the history of John Paul's pontificate is written, his "outreach to the Jews may be among his most enduring achievements."

On April 13, 1986, the pope visited the central Roman synagogue. This was a meaningful and historic occasion for the Catholic church because it was the first recorded appearance at a synagogue by a pope since Peter. John Paul said, "With Judaism we have a relationship which we do not have with any other religion. You are our dearly beloved brothers and, in a certain way, it could be said you are our elder brothers."[3] Some Jewish leaders had hoped that the pope would take this occasion to set up diplomatic relations with Israel. But John Paul did not address politics except to express his abhorrence of anti-Semitism and to condemn the Holocaust.

On October 28, 1985, John Paul met with a group of Jewish leaders to celebrate the twentieth anniversary of *Nostra aetate*. This conciliar document declared that God's covenant with the Jews still stands, that the Jews as a people could not and should not be held responsible for the death of Jesus, and it denounced anti-Semitism. A rabbi told John Paul, "October 28, 1965 was both a historic and revolutionary date. It marked a turning away from eighteen centuries often characterized by both misunderstanding and persecution" (Dionne 1985).

In December 1990 the pope received an international delegation from Jewish organizations to endorse their "Prague Statement." This candid document, drawn up in September, acknowledged that some aspects of Catholic teaching and practice had fostered anti-Semitism and the church should repent for this (P. Steinfels 1990e).

For over four decades there was one issue that resulted in diplomatic aloofness and prevented open dialogue between Israel and the Vatican, namely, the Vatican's persistent refusal to recognize the state of Israel.

Palestine became a Jewish state on May 14, 1948. The modern attempt by the Jews to establish a homeland goes back to the time of Leo XIII. In 1894 there was a military trial in France that involved Captain Alfred Dreyfus (1859–1935), an Alsatian Jew who was accused of betraying French military secrets to the Germans. On the basis of forged evidence, Dreyfus became an easy scapegoat for the anti-Semitic French right, including many Catholics. Dreyfus was convicted and condemned to life imprisonment on Devil's Island, off French Guiana. It was later proved that Dreyfus had been framed. He was exonerated and granted amnesty in 1899.

Theodore Herzl (1860–1904), a Jew and Viennese journalist, covered the Dreyfus trial for his newspaper and came to the conclusion that, regardless of the liberal facade of European countries based on the Enlightenment ideals of freedom, the Jewish people would never be treated justly until they had their own land. He was inspired to begin a crusade to secure a homeland for the Jews. There was a second factor that contributed to his crusade: the growing anti-Semitism in Vienna. In 1897, Karl Lueger, a Christian socialist, was elected mayor of Vienna. Lueger was known for his virulent anti-Semitism. "It was Lueger who was later to become the idol of the young Adolph Hitler" (Küng 1992, 286).

In 1896, Herzl published *The Jewish State,* a pamphlet calling for the establishment of an exclusive Jewish homeland to serve as a haven for Jews. His major concern was not the Jewish religion but the Jewish people. His slogan was "We are a people—one people." In 1897, he organized the first Zionist World Congress. The delegates insisted that the homeland be "in Palestine." In 1904 Herzl visited Pius X to discuss the return of the Jews to Jerusalem and to request Vatican support. Pius X bluntly told him: "We are unable to support this movement. . . . The Jews have not recognized our Lord, therefore we cannot recognize the Jewish people" (cited in Stransky 1993).

In the postconciliar church Jewish and Catholic authorities were not so antagonistic due in part to *Nostra aetate* and because both parties were deeply concerned with ending the useless killings of both Jews and Palestinians in Israel. Consequently, after years of negotiations, the Vatican approved on July 29, 1992, the establishment of a bilateral permanent working commission aimed at achieving normalized relations with Israel (ibid.). Shortly after the Jewish state was created on May 14, 1948, the Vatican acknowledged its right to exist. Nevertheless, it withheld full recognition for several reasons. First, the Vatican insisted that Jerusalem, a city sacred to Jews, Muslims, and Christians, be under international control. This requirement became more complicated by two important events: in 1967 Israel captured East Jerusalem from Jordan and in 1980 the Israeli government declared Jerusalem its "united and eternal capital." Second, the Vatican insisted that the Palestinians have "their own homeland, in which they live in freedom, dignity and security with their neighbors" (Baum 1988). Until this situation was resolved the Vatican feared that formal diplomatic ties with Israel would not only alienate Arab Christians but would also jeopardize Christian minorities dotted across the Arab world in Egypt, Jordan, Syria, and Iraq.

By the end of 1993, these two conditions were somewhat resolved. Israel maintained that Jerusalem did not have to be internationalized because there was complete freedom of access to places of worship in the sacred city; on September 13, 1993, Israel and the Palestinian Liberation Organization signed a "Declaration of Principles" in Washington to bring about peace and Palestinian autonomy in Jericho and the Gaza Strip in early 1994. Consequently, the Vatican and Israel signed an agreement consisting of fifteen articles in Jerusalem on December 30, 1993, declaring their willingness to establish diplomatic ties, to combat anti-Semitism, and to safeguard Christian pilgrimages to the Holy Land in the hope that these pilgimages "will provide an occasion for better understanding between the pilgrims and the people and religions of Israel."

Not everyone welcomed this historic event with its ecumenical potential. Protesters stood across the street from the Foreign Ministry, some carrying signs that read: "The Holocaust" and "Blood Libel." A commentary in the largest selling newspaper in Israel said in part: "The Catholic Church is one of the most conservative, oppressive and corrupt organizations in all human history. Israel has no reason to court the Vatican. The reconciliation can be done only if the Catholic Church and the one who heads it fall on their knees and ask for forgiveness for the souls of millions of tortured who went to Heaven in black smoke, under the blessing of the Holy See" (Haberman 1993). Despite such objections, the Vatican and Israel established full diplomatic relations on June 15, 1994 (Haberman 1994).

Because of the Vatican-Israeli pact, relations between the Vatican and Israel became more amicable. April 7 has been designated by the Jews as the day for their annual remembrance of the Holocaust. On April 7, 1994, John Paul invited the Chief Rabbi of Rome, Elio Toaff, as guest of honor at a concert to honor the memory of the victims of the Holocaust. This was the first time that a pope had officially honored the memory of the millions of European Jews killed by the Nazis. The London Philharmonic Orchestra played at a service of mainly Jewish inspiration. A large menorah with six candles was lit to represent the estimated six million Jews who perished in the Holocaust. Among the five thousand invited guests were some one hundred Holocaust survivors who heard the pope declare, "The candles lit by some of the survivors seek to demonstrate symbolically that this hall has no narrow limits, but that it contains all the victims: fathers, mothers, sons, brothers, friends. In our memory they are all present. They are with you; they are with us." Rabbi Toaff said that the pope's effort to commemorate the Holocaust "was much appreciated by the Jews." He asserted that the concert "assumes a significance that goes beyond that of a simple artistic event" (Tagliabue 1994).

The Holocaust was in the news once again on January 28, 1995, the fiftieth anniversary of the liberation of Auschwitz. The camp's four gas chambers and crematorium ovens claimed twenty thousand victims a day: not only almost one million Jews but also twenty thousand Gypsies, fifteen thousand Soviet prisoners of war, and twenty-five thousand victims of other nationalities. Germany's Roman Catholic bishops stated that Catholics share responsibility for the Holocaust. The bishops deplored the failure of German Catholics to act against Nazism, and asserted that they now bear a special responsibility to speak out against anti-Semitism. They said: "The denial and guilt that was prevalent in those days also came from the church. During the period of the Third Reich, Christians did not carry out the required resistance to racist anti-Semitism" (Kinzer 1995). Pope John Paul II also denounced anti-Semitism and called on the world to work and pray to prevent "other modern-day Auschwitzes." The pope stopped short of the kind of explicit admission of guilt on the part of the church as made by the German bishops. He did say, "Let us pray and work so that this doesn't happen. Never again anti-Semitism. Never again the arrogance of nationalisms. Never again genocides" (Bohlen 1995a).

John Paul and Missiology

The relation of the Catholic church to the other religions is important to John Paul. He has written about missiology in two major encyclicals, attended an unprecedented day of prayer with representatives of other religions, and discussed the world religions in his best seller, *Crossing the Threshold of Hope.*

On March 4, 1979, he issued *Redemptor hominis,* his first encyclical and the first papal letter since *Humanae vitae* in 1968. He recommended activities that can bring Catholics closer to followers of other religions: "dialogue, contacts, prayer in common, investigation of the treasures of human spirituality in which . . . the members of these religions are indeed not lacking." The pope also insisted again and again that Christ is united to each person without any exceptions whatsoever. Commenting on the letter, Gregory Baum declared, "What is new and startling in the encyclical is the emphasis, many times repeated, on the redemptive presence of Jesus Christ to the entire human family—to people everywhere, to every single human being in his or her concrete, historical situation" (Baum 1979a).

On October 27, 1986, John Paul met at Assisi, Italy, with one hundred representatives of religions from around the world for a day of prayer, fasting, and silence for world peace. The pope called these leaders together because "the challenge of peace, as it is presently posed to every human conscience, transcends religious differences." One fear—that of papal dominance—haunted the preparations for the gathering. However, John Paul promised, "I shall be at Assisi as a brother among brothers and sisters" (Crow 1986).

John Paul addressed mission theology once more in his eighth encyclical, *Redemptoris missio,* published on December 7, 1990—the twenty-fifth anniversary of Vatican II's Declaration on the Church's Missionary Activity. This long document of 153 pages represents the first major papal statement on missionary work since 1959.

John Paul wrote this encyclical "to clear up doubts and ambiguities" regarding missionary activity both within and outside the church (P. Steinfels 1991). Within the church, said the pope, there are semantic confusions around the word mission and he deplored any move toward a God-centered rather than a Christ-centered understanding of interreligious dialogue. Christ, the Word of God made man for the salvation of all, has, he wrote, "an absolute and universal significance, whereby, while belonging to history, he remains history's center and goal" (n. 9). However, the pope regretted that some theological trends seem to dampen missionary activity, motivation, and vocations. Furthermore, some so stress interreligious dialogue and involvement in political and economic struggles that they neglect spreading the faith and seeking converts to Christianity. Indifferentism is widespread. Also, missionary activity is waning whereas it should be the concern of all Christians. Evangelization is the "primary service" of the church to the world. The duty of the church is to proclaim without fail wherever there is no local church that Jesus Christ is the source of salvation. Catholic Christians should be concerned that millions of people live in ignorance of God's love as manifested in the life and death of Jesus Christ. In fact, the number of people who do not know Christ has doubled since 1965.

The pope also complained that some Middle Eastern, African, and Asian countries refuse entry visas to missionaries and that some Islamic countries forbid converts and any cult that is not Muslim.

John Paul made his sixty-third overseas pilgrimage in January 1995, a four-nation Asian trip that included Sri Lanka, a country that is 7 percent

Catholic and 70 percent Buddhist. Before his arrival, Buddhist monks pledged to boycott the pope's visit unless he apologized for statements made about Buddhism in *Crossing the Threshold of Hope.*

John Paul wrote that Buddhism "is in large measure an atheistic system," because it does not recognize the concept of a personal God. "We do not free ourselves from the good which comes from God; we liberate ourselves only through detachment from the world, which is bad," the pope declared in describing his understanding of the Buddhist system. The Buddhists claimed the pope misunderstood their beliefs, especially their belief in nirvana. The pope called their doctrine of salvation through nirvana as "almost exclusively negative." This suggests that the transcendent state of nirvana is really a state of "indifference." Nirvana to Buddhists requires not only detachment from the material world but also compassion and self-discipline in the pursuit of enlightenment.

When John Paul arrived in Sri Lanka on January 20th, he sought to soothe the Buddhists (Cowell 1995a). He said: "I come as a pilgrim of good will with nothing in my heart but peace." He added: "In particular, I express my highest regard for the followers of Buddhism. I ardently hope that my visit will serve to strengthen the good will between us, and that it will reassure everyone of the Catholic church's desire for interreligious dialogue." Nonetheless, the Buddhist leaders boycotted a scheduled meeting with the pope, injecting a sour final note into what had otherwise been a successful trip (Cowell 1995b).

In light of the explanation of preconciliar, conciliar, and postconciliar missiology outlined here, it is clear from John Paul's two encyclicals that his perspective is conciliar. He states that the church alone possesses the fullness of the means of salvation; that the primary missionary activity is the proclamation of the gospel; that conversion and the planting of new churches throughout the world is required of the church. Needless to say, missionaries and theologians with a postconciliar missiology disagree with these views of the church's missionary activity.

Tissa Balasuriya, a Sri Lankan Oblate of Mary Immaculate, took issue with John Paul's encyclical on the question of Jesus' "absolute and universal significance" because some have used this christology to negate other religions (1991). In 1993 the bishops in Sri Lanka and later the Vatican examined the writings of Balasuriya, a priest-theologian and sociologist, on such issues as original sin, women's priesthood, and missiology. His missiology was labeled "religious relativism," according to which no religion has a unique claim to the truth, and no religious figure can claim to be the only savior (Bohlen 1997a; Cloney 1997). Balasuriya insisted that his critics have misunderstood him and complained that he was never given a face-to-face hearing in Rome. Cardinal Ratzinger considers relativism "the central problem for the faith at the present time" (Thavis 1996). He said that "Balasuriya does not recognize the supernatural, unique and irrepeatable character of the revelation of Jesus Christ, by placing its presuppositions on the same level as those of other religions. In particular, he maintains that certain 'presuppositions' connected to myths were uncritically assumed to be revealed historical facts and, interpreted ideologically by the clerical 'power holders' in the church, eventually became the teaching of the magisterium" (cited in Schaeffer 1997a).

In May 1996, the Vatican sent Balasuriya a long "profession of faith," which it insisted he sign by December 8 under penalty of automatic excommunication. The CDF statement was sent "to verify" if Balasuriya accepts the truths taught by the Catholic church. Balasuriya signed instead a profession of faith composed by Paul VI in June 1968 (Schaeffer 1996c). On December 15, eighty theologians meeting in the Philippines voiced support for Balasuriya and wrote the pope asking that he be granted a public hearing (Schaeffer 1996f). On January 2, 1997, Balasuriya was formally excommunicated under canon law 1364. Excommunication means that the person remains a member of the church but is forbidden to celebrate and receive the sacraments. Balasuriya's response to this harsh penalty: "Since 1945, I have given all my adult life to the service of the church. . . . At the age of 72, after 51 years in the Congregation of the Oblates and 44 years a priest, I wish to remain a member of the Catholic church. I will be in ecclesial and spiritual communion with the church of Jesus even if legally excommunicated by ecclesiastical authorities" (ibid.).

News of the excommunication elicited predictable responses. Those who favor the past steps taken to discipline dissenters rejoiced at the escalation in the penalties imposed on dissenters. Others pointed to weaknesses in Balasuriya's theology. For example, Balasuriya argues that the doctrine of original sin has no basis in the gospels, but evolved as the church began to define itself as the sole mediator of salvation. In an Asian context, he says, "this idea of humanity being born alienated from the Creator would seem an abominable concept of the divine . . . repugnant to the notion of a just and loving God" (see Toolan 1997). But Balasuriya's critics note that the Hindu and Buddhist doctrines of karma and reincarnation have a deep sense of inherited evil that is almost the equivalent of original sin (ibid.).

Other Catholics found the penalty excessive, the methods antiquated, the message unduly harsh and unecumenical (Orsy 1997). Charles Curran (1997), feeling "a bond" with Balasuriya, wrote him a long letter, decrying "the process and final action." He expressed sympathy with what Balasuriya is "trying to do in [his] culture and circumstances," stated that "excommunication is a last resort that is appropriate only in the most extreme cases," and hoped that Balasuriya would receive support from other Catholic theologians.

Many hope that just as reconciliation was achieved in the Leonard Feeney affair earlier in the century, so reconciliation will take place for Tissa Balasuriya.

Conclusion

In a book on the religions of the world, Huston Smith writes, "When historians look back on our century, they may remember it most, not for space travel or the release of nuclear energy, but as the time when the peoples of the world first came to take one another seriously" (1991, 7). At Vatican II the bishops acknowledged this interdependence as one of the signs of the times: "In our day, when people are drawing more closer together and the bonds of friendship between different peoples are being strengthened, the church examines more closely its relations with non-Christian religions" (NA 1). This chapter has reviewed the ways in which the conciliar and postconciliar church has taken seriously the other religious communities.

Any contact with the other religions will focus on christology and Christ's role as universal mediator (Acts 4:12; 1 Timothy 2:5). We have seen that, although interreligious dialogue is still in its early phase, it is complicated. For example, there are five approaches to the indispensibility of Jesus for salvation: relativist, fundamentalist, exclusivist, inclusivist, and pluralistic.

Catholic theologians and missionaries have developed different understandings of the other religions. In the preconciliar days most Catholics judged the other religions to be false, that is, futile attempts to reach God. However, when missionaries and mystics came into close contact with the world religions, they soon learned that this judgment was not true. For example, Bede Griffiths (1906–93), the trailblazing Camaldolese Benedictine from England, spent some thirty-eight years in India defending Eastern spirituality and trying to bridge Christianity and Hindu and Buddhist traditions (Toolan 1993; Teasdale 1995). As early as 1954 he wrote in *The Golden String* (his autobiography about his conversion to Catholicism in 1932 and his entry into the Benedictine community) that all Christians should recognize "all that is valid and true in all the different religious traditions."

In the conciliar period, there was a shift in theology: the other religions were called anonymous Christians, a term which ultimately they rejected. In the postconciliar period there was a Copernican shift in missiology: some Catholics have come to regard the world religions as autonomous bodies, as valid ways to God, and as sources of new religious awareness.

Pope John Paul does not favor the postconciliar view. In the Catholic church, then, this discussion between the magisterium and the theologians, mystics, and missionaries will continue. For now, the suggestion of Ralph Mecklenburger, a rabbi from Michigan, deserves serious consideration: perhaps the best attitude Christians can have toward the other religions is to call them "honorary Christians." "Think of a foreign visitor being declared an 'honorary citizen' of a city; the term connotes appreciation, fondness, respect" (1979). Certainly, this world would be a much more peaceful place if every Jew, Muslim, Buddhist, and Hindu were considered an honorary Christian and every Christian considered an honorary Jew, honorary Muslim, honorary Buddhist, and honorary Hindu.

CHAPTER 7

The Church and
the Other Christians

Applied to the Christian religion, Von Hügel's triad reveals a religion in disastrous disarray. Christianity is like a precious mirror that has been shattered into thousands of pieces. The Christian churches hardly honor one another. They are deeply divided over such issues as identity, mission, authority, theology, interreligious dialogue, the role of women, and Christian ethics. This chapter investigates the whole Christian church and ecumenism: the efforts to reconcile "all Christians in the unity of the one and only church of Christ" (UR 24). Ecumenism, acknowledged as one of the signs of the times (UR 4), was one of the purposes of Vatican II (SC 1).

Most Catholics living in the West know only the Catholic churches of the West united with Rome. What they often overlook is that the church originated in the Middle East and then spread from the mother church in Jerusalem to such centers as Antioch, Alexandria, and Damascus. Even today there are churches in such countries as Greece, Egypt, Syria, Russia, and the Ukraine that are united with Rome and called Eastern Catholic churches.

Eastern Catholics have their own institutions, disciplines, theologies, liturgies, and spiritualities, all rooted in their own cultures and traditions. The Catholic church has always had this diversity-in-unity. Unfortunately, the Eastern churches have lived under a twofold shadow: their separation from their Orthodox mother churches, and their administrative and cultural domination by Rome. Because of the latter, Eastern Catholics have often been overlooked or slighted by the West. For example, Pius IX placed them under the Propagation of the Faith in 1862. On May 1, 1917, Benedict XV corrected this insult by establishing an autonomous office, the Congregation for the Eastern Churches. Similarly, the Eastern churches allow married men to be ordained as priests. Once a man is ordained he may not marry and if a married priest loses his wife through death, he may not remarry. Pius XI decreed in 1929 that in the United States married men cannot be ordained to the priesthood of the Eastern churches. He believed American Catholics would find this scandalous. Needless to say, the Eastern churches find this restriction of an age-old tradition unjust. Finally, at the first session of Vatican II in 1962, the Eastern patriarchs were given seats behind the cardinals; later they sat opposite them.

Vatican II promulgated a document on the Eastern Catholic churches on November 21, 1964. It solemnly declared that "the churches of the east like those of the west have the right and duty to govern themselves according to their own special disciplines" (OE 5; cf. UR 16). It also affirmed the equality of the eastern and western traditions of Christianity (OE 3) and the importance of preserving the spiritual heritage of the East (UR 14–15).

Jesus prayed that his community of disciples would be one so "that the world may believe that you have sent me" (John 17:21). Throughout its history, however, the church has not been "the seamless robe of Christ" (UR 13). The conciliar bishops noted that "In this one and only church of God from its very beginnings there arose certain rifts" (UR 3; cf. 1 Corinthians 11:18–19; Galatians 1:6–9; 1 John 2:18–19). In 1054, however, there was a major rift between the church of the West and the East; and in 1517, a devastating division within the churches of the West. These divisions are a shameful contradiction of the nature of "the one and only church of Christ" and a stumbling block to its mission. A divided church scandalizes the world and divided Christians become unconvincing messengers of peace and fellowship. Ecumenism has a "holy objective—the reconciliation of all Christians in the unity of the one and only church of Christ" (UR 24).

Eastern Schism: Leo IX and Michael Cerularius

Pope Leo IX, a man of spirituality, gentility, and courtesy, was a reformer and disciplinarian. This able pope was more a bystander than an actor in the great schism that took place on July 16, 1054, because he died on April 19, 1054, and his successor, Victor II, was not elected until April 13, 1055. Nevertheless, since his legates were acting in his name, the East-West schism is attributed to his pontificate. A schism is a formal separation or division based on different understandings of official teachings, disciplines, and/or authority.

Leo IX wanted the churches of the East to help him control the growing power of the Normans who had been invading the Papal States from southern Italy. He appealed for help to the Patriarch of Constantinople, Michael Cerularius (1043–58), but the patriarch refused to get involved in the pope's political problems. The patriarch then added fuel to the estrangement by imposing the Eastern rite on Latin churches in Constantinople and by condemning several Western practices. To seek reconciliation, Leo sent legates to Constantinople under the leadership of Humbert of Mourmontiers (1000–61), an archbishop. By all reports, Humbert was a fiery competitor with little charity of spirit. He hated Greeks and could not communicate adequately in their language.

Michael Cerularius was an arrogant, ambitious yet popular leader who hated Latins and was concerned for the ecclesiastical supremacy of Constantinople. With their sophisticated liturgy, theology, and spirituality, the Greeks felt superior to Rome. When Cerularius and Humbert met, the two very irreconcilable personalities clashed. In addition to linguistic and cultural differences, the Latins and Greeks were divided over disciplinary practices; for example, the Greeks fasted on Saturdays instead of Fridays, used leavened bread in the Eucharist, and allowed married men to be ordained as priests. However, it was at the level of theology—especially that of the holy Spirit and the nature of the church—that their differences were more significant.

The Greeks taught that "the Spirit of Truth . . . proceeds from the Father" (John 15:26). This wording was made part of the creed adopted by the ecumenical councils of Nicea in 325 and Constantinople in 381. The Latins, relying on the saintly Augustine of Hippo (354–430) and a local council held in 589 in Toledo, Spain, said the Spirit proceeds from the Father *and the son (filioque)*. Rome adopted the *filioque* theology around the year 1000 and added it to the Nicene-Constantinopolitan creed without consulting the Greeks.

Filioque is theological theory. Who can ever know about the essence or inner life of the triune God? Are not all descriptions of God symbolic communication? The Greeks preferred "from the Father" because, since the Father alone is the principle, source, and cause of all things, the Spirit cannot proceed from the Father "after the Son" but rather "with the Son" (Pelikan 1989, 5:22). The Greeks thought *filioque* was too rational. It diluted the essential incomprehensibility of God by making God one with three aspects of being. The Latins preferred *filioque* because it expresses the communal and dynamic sense of God's three-in-oneness and mutuality. *Filioque* might be a better explanation of the eternal, ontological bond among the Father, Son, and Spirit than the one based on John 15:26, but it is still the refinement of an idea or an interpretation of dogma. As such it does not belong "in a creed intended to express the common faith of the East and West" (Kilmartin 1979, 57–58).

Beneath the cultural and theological differences lurked the ecclesial problem of authority. Who can authoritatively explain the nature and mission of the Spirit? The Spirit is central to the Christian scriptures, church doctrine, and creeds. However, the creeds say little about the Spirit. These theological and historical facts prompted Raymond Brown to say "with permissible exaggeration" that the Spirit "has been the most divisive feature in the history of Christianity" (1985, 102).

The authority issue also involved the interrelationship of conciliar and papal authority. The Greeks questioned the extent of papal jurisdiction, arguing that ecumenical councils were the one sure source of inspired doctrinal authority. Their model was the church's first council in

Jerusalem as related in Acts 15. After deliberation, the Jerusalem church announced its understanding of its mission in consultation with Peter, James, and Paul: "It is the decision of the holy Spirit and of us." This process carried over to the deliberations of the first seven of the ecumenical councils which "had been held in the East and not under any direct papal authorization" (Pelikan 1989, 5:249).

The above summary of the personal, political, theological, disciplinary, and jurisdictional differences between the Roman and Greek participants is the background to the heated exchange that took place between Humbert and Cerularius in full view of the congregation in the Santa Sophia on July 16, 1054. Humbert placed on the altar a decree, excommunicating the patriarch and his supporters. Cerularius responded with his excommunication on July 24.

Conventionally, if somewhat inaccurately, the East-West division is dated 1054. Actually, some of the successors of Leo IX attempted reconciliation with the patriarchs. Most of the patriarchs of the East were better disposed toward Rome than toward Constantinople. But two events solidified the division. In 1098, the Greek patriarch of Antioch was expelled from the city and replaced by a Latin patriarch. There still may have been reconciliation, but the ruthless sack and pillage of Constantinople by crusaders in 1203 ended all hopes of reunification.

The Eastern churches that were excommunicated are called Orthodox, a term which means "right praise" or "holding the correct faith." In 1993 it was estimated that the Orthodox population worldwide was some ninety million. However, as a result of the Christian revival in the former communist countries, the total world membership was estimated in January 1996 to be from two hundred to two hundred fifty million.[1]

Although the Orthodox churches are growing numerically, several of the Eastern Catholic communities are declining. For example, in Lebanon, as a result of emigration, a declining birth rate, and a civil war between Christians and Muslims (1975–1990), the Lebanese Christians, and especially the seven hundred thousand Maronite Catholics, have seen their numbers, influence, and political and economic power wane. By 1997, Christians were no more than 30 percent of Lebanon's four million people (Jehl 1997). They also felt marginalized by the Syrian-dominated government which was backed by thirty-five thousand Syrian troops.

John Paul visited Lebanon on May 10–11, 1997. This was his seventy-seventh overseas visit but his first to the Middle East. A previous visit planned for 1994 was canceled after the bombing of a Maronite church north of Beirut in which eleven Sunday worshipers were killed and fifty-nine wounded. The Middle East has always represented a challenge to the Vatican, especially since 1993, when Rome established formal diplomatic ties with Israel. The Vatican's relations with the Arab countries are dominated by two concerns: support for the local Christian minorities and a nuanced treatment of Muslim-Christian relations.

When the pope visited Lebanon, he had several goals: to comfort the beleaguered Christians, both Catholic and Orthodox, to highlight Lebanon's need for independence and sovereignty, and to appeal to all for forgiveness, reconciliation, and peaceful coexistence (Bohlen 1997d, 1997e). It will take time before it can be known how and if the pope's visit aided in building the political and civic institutions necessary to achieve these social, moral, and religious goals.

The Reformation: Leo X and Martin Luther

Leo X (Giovanni de'Medici), Bishop of Rome from 1513 to 1521, was a polished yet devious politician. This Renaissance pope was immersed in literature, the arts, and music, and, consequently, was generous to artists and scholars because of his interest in furthering humanist culture. Nevertheless, he damaged the papal finances by his lavishness. To recoup his treasury and in order to build St. Peter's Basilica in Rome, he permitted the sale of indulgences and sold church offices, even cardinal's hats. Indulgences are the partial or full remission of the temporal punishment still due to sins that have already been forgiven.

Leo was unconcerned about the church's spiritual welfare; unaware of the intellectual ferment brought on by the printing press in 1455; and insensitive to the widespread desire for reform of the corruption, ignorance, and doctrinal confusion in the church. When Luther was first brought to Leo's attention, he dismissed the controversy between Luther and the sellers of indulgences as "a monkish squabble." He eventually condemned Luther in 1520 and excommunicated him on January 3, 1521.

Martin Luther (1483–1546), a German Augustinian monk, was a man of violent temper, rough manners, and coarse language. At the same time, this complex man was well-educated, intelligent, honest, and a devout priest with extraordinary powers of persuasion, both written and oral.

Luther's world was marked by an emphasis on human sinfulness. God was imagined as a stern judge. The world was filled with demonic spirits who roamed everywhere seeking to ensnare sinners. Luther was caught up in this way of thinking. Nevertheless, he sought relief from these horrors within his monastic life of prayer, fasting, and discipline. Even after ten years as a monk, 1505 to 1515, he found no relief to his personal twofold search for certitude about his salvation and for a gracious God. However, in 1515, Luther found in the scriptures, especially Romans 1:16–17, the answers he needed (Woodward 1983). Luther taught that humankind is declared "justified" by God, not on the basis of their own "strength, merits or works," but by faith alone. Today Luther's theology is often summarized as follows: humankind is saved (justified) by the grace of Christ alone through scripture alone, appropriated by faith alone. This theology brought Luther into conflict with the popular theology of the day and its misplaced emphasis on works (e.g., the selling of indulgences), the authority of popes and councils, the acquisition of merit, and the excessive veneration of saints and Mary. Luther challenged this theology by posting his ninety-five theses of protest on the church door at Wittenberg on October 31, 1517. These were quickly printed and disseminated.

As in the 1054 controversy, the deeper issue was authority, especially that of the Spirit and the papacy. How does the Spirit of truth function in the church, its officeholders, and the scriptures? The Catholic church has consistently taught the infallibility of the church—that Christ delivered the truth about himself to the church, which is infallibly protected when discerning the truth collectively. This teaching was reiterated at Vatican II: "The whole body of the faithful who have received an anointing which comes from the holy one (see 1 John 2:20, 27), cannot be mistaken in belief. It shows this characteristic through the entire people's supernatural sense of the faith, when 'from the bishops to the last of the faithful,' it manifests a universal consensus in matters of faith and morals" (LG 12). Edward Norman, an Anglican priest and historian, believes that it is the Catholic understanding of the infallibility of the church itself "which is the major difference between Catholics and Protestants" (1991, 459). The Catholic tradition also maintains that the pope and bishops are the official interpreters of the Christian faith and scriptures. The Spirit does not speak through the scriptures in such a way that individual readers could indiscriminately challenge the teachings of the officeholders.

Protestant Christianity divided further over the theology of the Spirit. Although both Luther and John Calvin (1509–64) taught that "the Spirit speaks through the scriptures *in the church*," some of their followers later taught that the Spirit speaks "so *individually* in the heart of every Christian that the Bible read in a personal way, without church tradition or church setting, is an adequate guide" (R. E. Brown 1985, 103).

The conflict between Luther and Rome started as a protest in the name of the scriptures and salvation. Because of a whole series of factors— some political, some economic, some the result of ignorance, stubbornness, and poor communication—the church of the West was divided beyond the imagination of any of the participants. Luther never intended to shatter the church of the West. His revolution is probably the most devastating event in the history of the church. The devastation continues as new denominations continue to split off from one another for institutional, intellectual, or devotional reasons. Ernst Käsemann, a Lutheran biblical scholar, has indicated the very ambiguous role the scriptures play in the one and only church of Christ: "The New Testament canon does not, as such, constitute the foundation of the unity of the church. On the contrary, as such, it provides the basis for the multiplicity of confessions" (cited in Toolan 1982).

The Vatican's response to the Protestant Reformation is called the Counter-Reformation. At its center was the Council of Trent (1545–63). Its disciplinary decrees, doctrinal definitions, and condemnations of

Luther's theology shaped the church until Vatican II. After Vatican II and as a result of many amicable Lutheran-Catholic dialogues, the possibility of lifting Luther's excommunication has been discussed several times. In 1970, a group of German Lutheran bishops stated that the excommunication had already become history and that historical facts could not be abolished retroactively by formal legal acts. In 1980, when Cardinal Joseph Ratzinger was archbishop of Munich, he concurred with the Lutheran view saying that he was "in principle against such posthumous cleansings of history."[2]

Of all the productive Lutheran-Catholic dialogues, those dealing with the fundamental "doctrine of justification" have been the most important. Both churches had planned to issue a joint declaration on justification in 1997 to mark the 450th anniversary of the Council of Trent, a council that condemned the Lutheran doctrine. The basic thrust of the proposed text states that, while differences remain between Catholics and Lutherans on justification, the consensus of the two churches is so far-reaching and fundamental that "the remaining differences are not church-dividing." However, on September 30, 1996, the Lutheran World Federation (LWF), the international body of Lutheran churches, announced that the proposed joint declaration must be revised again in order to clarify formulations regarding the Lutheran understanding of sin. After the amended document is reviewed by the LWF and the CDF, it will probably be promulgated in 1998.[3]

Ecumenism

Thomas Stransky, a Paulist priest who served on the Vatican Secretariat for Promoting Christian Unity from 1960 to 1970, wrote in 1986 that "The main flaw in the present ecumenical movement . . . is a lack of vision . . . of what ecumenism is" (1986a). A faulty understanding of ecumenism can only create fear and further divisions.

Ecumenism is the quest by Christians for full visible unity for mission through personal and church renewal and reform. The Greek root of the word means "the inhabited world." Ecumenism, then, points to the whole world and wholeness. This meaning prompted Arie Brouwer (1935–93), a former General Secretary of the National Council of Churches, to state in 1986 that ecumenism "is the shaping and nurturing of the whole person committed to the whole ministry of the whole gospel through the whole church for the whole world."

The phrase, "full visible unity," assumes that since all Christians are disciples of Jesus Christ, a real but imperfect union already exists among them. However, this view of unity can point to an invisible and spiritual union, whereas the union should also be visible and juridical. Christians should have the same altar, a shared life, a common worship, and a single mission.

Two developments have taken place to deepen the understanding of unity. First, the Catholic church and the Russian Orthodox church, two communities that emphasize catholicity, have become more substantially involved in the ecumenical movement since Vatican II. Second, "many ecumenists are realizing afresh that the ground of unity is the apostolic faith" found in the scriptures and the early creeds (Deschner 1986). The result of these two developments has been a striking emphasis on apostolicity and catholicity alongside unity as primary ecumenical themes. There can be no unity unless the churches are grounded in the apostolic faith. Similarly, this apostolic faith must be articulated in such a way that it will be catholic, that is, "open to the pluralism, the mutual surprise and joy of discovery which belongs to an adequately diversified unity" (ibid.).

This unity should occur for the purposes of mission. Thomas Stransky defines ecumenism as "a commitment to the unity of the church-in-mission." The church's mission is threefold: to evangelize, to witness, and to serve. Mission is "the obligation of the whole church to proclaim, by word and act, the whole gospel to the whole world" (Stransky 1986a). Stransky fears that our ecumenical pedagogy is weakest at the point of mission: "Few Christian persons or groups enter the ecumenical movement because of a commitment to the unity of the church-in-mission" (ibid.). Most get involved in specific common ministries (e.g., social justice projects, Bible study), but in doing so they often miss the wider implications of their specific projects: "the vision of Christ's revelation for the whole church in the whole world" (ibid.).

Renewal and reform are conditions for the possibility of unity. Christians cannot bring about the one and only church of Christ by their own efforts. This is the work of the Spirit. Yet, all Christians are obliged to work with the Spirit for unity, until it is fully accomplished by the Spirit. This work, which should be a priority, requires the "continual reformation" of the church (UR 6), which begins with "interior conversion. For it is from newness of attitudes of mind, from self-denial and unstinted love, that desires of unity take their rise and develop in a mature way" (UR 7). The bishops called "this change of heart and holiness of life, along with public and private prayer" for the unity of Christians "spiritual ecumenism" and regarded it as "the soul of the whole ecumenical movement" (UR 8).

The ecumenical movement has achieved a measure of success. However, most Catholics of this generation have escaped the scars of religious bigotry. They do not realize how much fear, hatred, and ignorance of Catholics existed in many countries, including the United States. Most modern Catholics are tolerant of other Christians and other religions. Consequently, they are puzzled or shocked to read of public insults to the pope. For example, in 1988, when John Paul was in Strasbourg to address the European Parliament, he was interrupted by Ian Paisley, a Northern

Ireland Protestant minister and leader of the Democratic Unionist Party. While holding up a placard that read, "Pope John Paul II—Antichrist," Paisley kept yelling, "I renounce you and all your cults and creeds."[4]

Catholics are also shocked to read of conflicts among other Christian communities. For example, in January 1990, at a week of prayer for Christian unity held at Westminster Cathedral, a group of Welsh Presbyterians protested the services, presided over by the Anglican Archbishop Robert Runcie of Canterbury. They said: "We wish to defend our Lord and Savior, Jesus Christ, against the blasphemy and idolatry of the papist Mass and the treachery of Dr. Runcie. We believe the ecumenical movement comes directly from hell."[5] Here is another example: the primarily white Southern Baptist Convention (SBC) and a denomination within the African-American Baptist church (AAB) were at odds in the fall of 1995. The background of their tension goes back to June 25, 1995, when the SBC renounced its racist roots and apologized for its defense of slavery at the time of the Civil War. The president of the second-largest AAB denomination rejected the SBC's apology, insisting that more action is needed. His point: "The civil rights struggle is still going on and we need more than an apology."[6]

The Papacy and Ecumenism: Leo XIII

The preconciliar church had developed a "state of siege mentality." Orthodox and Protestant Christians were regarded as schismatics and heretics who had broken from the true church. Nevertheless, Leo was the first pope to speak of these other Christian communities as "separated brothers" and in his encyclical *Praeclara* (1894), he invited both communities to return to Rome (J. Kelly 1986, 312).

The Armenian and Chaldean churches did return. Leo had no success with the other Orthodox communities, especially the Russian Orthodox, mainly because of his insistence on obedience to the Bishop of Rome and because they did not want to be latinized (Murphy 1981, 28–29).

Leo's encyclical *Ad anglos* (1895) revealed special interest in the reunion of the Anglican churches with Rome. That same year he appointed a commission to investigate the validity of Anglican ordinations of bishops and priests. After receiving a negative report, he declared in September 1896 in *Apostolicae curae* that Anglican ordinations "have been and are absolutely null and utterly void." This means that the ordination of the ministers was invalid, making their sacraments valueless and amounting to nothing in the eyes of the Catholic church.

Modern theologians and historians have argued over the accuracy of the "proofs" presented to Leo by his expert commissioners. Francis Clark, a British theologian, defended the papal decision in his book, *Anglican Orders and Defect of Intention* (1956), while John Jay Hughes disagreed with both Leo XIII and Clark in his 1970 publication *Stewards of the Lord: A Reappraisal of Anglican Orders* (see Fichter 1988b). When the Vatican archives were opened in 1978, new sources of information became available. It seems that Leo's commission of eight experts was evenly split on the issue. However, Cardinal Rafael Merry del Val (1865–1930) drafted the final report. Upon investigation, many historians have criticized the way he handled history to support his arguments.

John Jay Hughes, the church historian cited above, was ordained an Anglican priest in 1954, became a Catholic in 1960 and a Catholic priest in 1968. His ordination (not reordination) in 1968 was performed *conditionally* by the then-bishop of Münster and later Cardinal of Cologne, Joseph Hoffer, who declared: "We have given you the orders of deacon and priest conditionally. . . . We leave it to God what has really happened" (Lefevere 1995b).

Hughes and Hoffer were convinced that today's Anglican orders are no longer identical with those declared invalid in 1896. Their judgment is based on their rejection of a sacramental theology of orders which is based on the names in a bishop's table of succession—the theology of apostolic succession favored by Rome. In this view, bishops form a "continuous chain" back to the twelve apostles. Nevertheless, in Hughes' case, the Episcopalian bishops who had ordained him "had in their tables of succession consecrators whose orders are recognized by Rome as valid" (J. Hughes 1980b).

Today, most Catholic and Anglican theologians prefer a sacramental theology of ordination that attaches greater importance to the faith and sacramental life of the ecclesial communities in and for whom bishops and other ministers are ordained. In this view, rather than a "continuous chain" of bishops, there is "functional succession," that is, bishops are considered validly ordained because they carry on the special apostolic mission of founding and leading churches. As of now this issue has not been resolved and it continues to block ecumenical relations.

Despite the debacle of 1896, Leo's overall perception of ecumenism was honorable. In a discourse on March 9, 1895, he said: "Our eyes will never see the union of the churches that we are working for, but let us not be so faint-hearted as to regard this unceasing effort as a fanciful dream. Such a sentiment would be unworthy of a Christian" (Tavard 1960, 113).

During Leo's pontificate, there were no major ecumenical efforts as such on the part of other Christian communities. There were stirrings, however. The most significant initiative came from Patriarch Joachim III of Constantinople, who in 1902 sent an encyclical to all the Orthodox churches, expressing concern about possible rapprochement among those who believe in God as Trinity so that the union of all Christian churches might eventually come about. The patriarch hoped for two things: a union of Orthodox churches and programs whereby the Orthodox could make contacts with other Christian churches.

Pius X

The goals Pius X set for his pontificate were religious rather than political or ecumenical. One of his actions offended Christians, especially in the United States. In 1910, former-President Theodore Roosevelt was in Rome to lecture at the Methodist church there. When he requested a papal audience, he was refused because he was a Protestant.

It is ironic that during the pontificate of this unecumenical pontiff, "spiritual ecumenism" began in the United States in 1908 and the actual ecumenical movement was organized by an American in 1910.

Spiritual ecumenism began through the efforts of Paul Francis Wattson (1863–1940) and Lurana Mary White (1870–1935). They were Episcopalians who in 1898 founded in Garrison, New York, the Society of the Atonement, a Franciscan community of friars and nuns with a special ecumenical dedication. This community of fifteen was corporately received into the Catholic church on October 30, 1909.

In 1908, they had initiated eight days of prayer—from January 18 to 25—for church unity. They called this the Church Unity Octave. For some time, this octave focused firmly on reunion with Rome. The prayers were rather sternly phrased. For example, on January 20, there were prayers for "the submission of Anglicans to the authority of the Vicar of Christ." On January 22 the prayers asked "that Christians in America may become one in union with the chair of St. Peter."

Pius X approved the octave in 1909, and Benedict XV extended its observance to the universal church in 1916. In 1934, Paul Couturier (1881–1953), a priest active with the Orthodox in Lyons, France, suggested that prayers simply be offered for "the unity Christ wills by the means he wills."

In the early 1960s, the name of the week of prayer was changed to the Chair of Unity Octave. Finally, in 1966, in keeping with a greater ecumenical awareness, the present name was given: the Week of Prayer for Christian Unity. The title changes are significant for two reasons: Catholics had learned to pray with others and not simply for them; the emphasis was no longer church reunion but Christian unity.

It is plausible to date the beginnings of the modern ecumenical movement to the World Missionary Conference at Edinburgh, January 13–23, 1910. There were twelve hundred delegates from the Protestant missions from around the world, except Latin America and Africa (Desseux 1983, 46). The main concern of the delegates was their common task: the evangelization of the world. One of the conference's eight commissions was designated to study cooperation and the promotion of unity. Several speeches alluded to the regrettable absence of Roman Catholic and Orthodox representation.

The organizer and president of the conference was the American Dr. John Raleigh Mott (1865–1955), a Methodist layman who later received the Nobel Peace Prize in 1946. In his first address he asked, "Has it not humbled us increasingly as we have discovered that the greatest hindrance to the expansion of Christianity lies in ourselves?" He meant that they now realized they could not evangelize effectively as long as they were aggressively competing with one another for converts. Nonetheless, the meeting was an optimistic and unanimous affirmation of their task to evangelize the world.

During the conference, Bishop Charles Brent (1862–1929), a Canadian who at that time was an Episcopal bishop in the Philippines, was disturbed because questions of faith and church order were considered to be outside the competence of a missionary conference. He argued that Christians could not be content with cooperative efforts. In addition to cooperation a forum was needed so the churches could study the causes of division with the purpose of removing them. He had in mind the divisions over such theological issues as the validity of each other's sacraments and ministries, the nature of authority, and the interpretation of tradition and scripture. Brent was to be the chief instrument in bringing about the Faith and Order Movement. A committee was approved, eventually set up in Geneva, and the first world conference was held in 1927 in Lausanne, Switzerland.

Benedict XV

Like his predecessors, he dreamt of reunion with the Orthodox. As a way to achieve this very goal, he moved to strengthen the ties between Rome and the Eastern Catholics, especially when "the outbreak of the Russian Revolution made him think that the moment for this [reunion] had arrived" (J. Kelly 1986, 316). He created the Congregation for the Oriental Churches in May 1917 and set up the Pontifical Oriental Institute in Rome that October.

The Orthodox themselves became involved in ecumenism. On January 10, 1919, under the leadership of Patriarch Germanos of Constantinople, they called for all Christian churches to form a "league of churches." They "became the first church to call for a permanent organ of fellowship and cooperation between the churches" (Rusch 1985, 27).

In January 1920, they sent an encyclical to all the churches of the world, calling for the formation of an ecumenical council of churches (Visser't Hooft 1982, 1–2). The encyclical recognized both the new opportunities and the dangers of the times. It underscored the need for discussions at the practical level, insisting that doctrinal differences did not doom the enterprise to failure. By taking common action, it was stated, the churches would gain mutual knowledge, eliminate prejudice, and create a spirit of trust that would militate against disagreements and distrust. Unfortunately, the document did not receive wide circulation. Yet, it was a significant contribution.

Meanwhile, Protestants were organizing an interchurch and international forum to examine doctrinal causes of disunity. In May 1919, they sent a delegation to Benedict to invite him to attend. He politely declined, but said he would pray for the success of the conference and, especially, that "those who participate in it may, by the grace of God, see the light and become reunited to the visible Head of the church, by which they will be received with open arms" (Tavard 1960, 117; see also Jay 1978, 299).

On July 4, 1919, the Holy Office forbade Catholics to participate in ecumenical congresses organized by other Christians, unless by express permission of the Vatican.

Pius XI

Pius had little sympathy for the other Christians other than as potential returnees to the Catholic church (Murphy 1981, 56). The Orthodox gave little response to his calls for reunion. On the other hand, he did approve the conversations between Catholics and Anglicans held at Malines, Belgium from 1921 to 1926 (J. Kelly 1986, 318).

In 1927, Protestant emissaries preparing for the first ecumenical conference on Faith and Order to be held at Lausanne, Switzerland, visited the pope, seeking his blessing and cooperation in the search for Christian unity. Pius declined any interest in the "distinctive witness" they sought to bring intact into "the coming great church." Rather, the pope politely reminded them that their search could be immediately finalized right there on the spot by a return to the Catholic church.

After the meeting, the Holy Office announced in July 1927, that Catholics could not take part in the Faith and Order Conference at Lausanne. Just after the Lausanne conference, Pius issued his encyclical, *Mortalium animos* (January 1928) in which he denounced ecumenical congresses, meetings, and addresses because they led to indifferentism. Catholics could not take part in these assemblies, he wrote, nor should they encourage or support them, since "there is but one way in which the unity of Christians may be fostered, and that is by furthering the return to the one true church of Christ of those who are separated from it; for from that one true church of Christ they have in the past fallen away." Furthermore, since the other Christians are themselves so divided in belief on many points, Pius wondered how, with their wide variation of opinions, they "can open up the way to unity of the church when this unity can be born of but one single authority, one sole rule of faith, and one identical belief."

Finally, during Pius's pontificate another Protestant conference was organized: Life and Work. Its actual origins go back to 1919, followed by a preparatory conference at Geneva in 1920. Nathan Söderblom (1866–1931), Lutheran Archbishop of Uppsala, Sweden, was the organizer and leader. This outstanding Christian was to receive the Nobel Peace Prize in 1930.

The purpose of Life and Work was to relate the Christian faith to the social, political, and economic problems of society. They believed the churches should first unite and then discuss doctrines. Their motto: "Service unites; doctrines divide."

Their first meeting was held at Stockholm in 1925, with 600 delegates from 37 countries. Some consider it *the* first ecumenical conference because it was composed entirely of delegates who were representatives of their churches (Visser't Hooft 1982, 10).

Pius XII

The ecumenical movement, which began among the Protestant churches in 1910, reached a major landmark in 1948 during the pontificate of Pius XII. Within both the Faith and Order and the Life and Work movements there grew an awareness that their concerns were so intertwined that they needed to be brought together in a single council. In 1937, these councils met at Edinburgh and Oxford, respectively. Both recommended unity in a World Council of Churches. A provisional WCC was set up at Utrecht, Holland, with Willem A. Visser't Hooft (1901–85) as its general secretary. He gave the council its name and is considered "the supreme architect of the ecumenical movement" (Thompson 1985a).

World War II prevented the WCC from holding its first meeting until August 22–September 4, 1948. The meeting in Amsterdam attracted 351 delegates from 147 churches from 44 countries. Visser't Hooft was elected the first general secretary, a post he would hold until 1966. Geneva was chosen for their headquarters.

Their theme was "Man's disorders and God's design." Right from their first meeting, concern for church unity and for social questions were inextricably linked; they are two sides of the same ecumenical coin. For example, the most controversial statement made in the Amsterdam assembly was its criticism of laissez-faire capitalism and Marxist communism. "The Christian churches should reject the ideologies of communism and laissez-faire capitalism and should seek to draw men away from the false assumptions that these extremes are the only alternatives. Each has made promises which it could not redeem."

At Amsterdam, the delegates committed themselves to stay together, having defined themselves as "a fellowship of churches which accept our Lord Jesus Christ as God and Savior." The last two words in the statement were never defined. Incarnation and atonement were underscored, but each church was free to interpret them in its own way.

The WCC does not pretend to be or become a "super church." It is an instrument for the union of the churches; only particular churches can choose to unite with others. The WCC provides a forum for speaking and acting together, hoping to create the conditions for the possibility of visible union. The WCC "is not a church but a confederation of independent churches, each of which remains free to disassociate itself from any WCC position or statement" (Rausch 1985).

In December 1949 in *Ecclesia sancta,* Pius XII relaxed his predecessor's negative views of the ecumenical movement by formally recognizing it and by permitting Catholic scholars to dialogue with other Christians on matters of faith and morals. He even allowed that such meetings could begin and end with shared prayer. This permission came as a very considerable shock to moral theologians and ecumenists because in the previous year Pius had reiterated the church's position that any sharing in worship with those not Catholic was "entirely forbidden."

The second WCC assembly was held in Evanston, Illinois, in August 1954. There were 502 delegates from 161 member churches. Their theme was "Jesus Christ—the hope of the world." They committed themselves not only to stay together (as had been agreed at Amsterdam) but also to grow together. They stressed service to the world and said less about evangelization and missionary activity than had been said at Amsterdam.

On June 24, 1985, the seventy-fifth anniversary of the World Missionary Conference, a meeting was held in Edinburgh with some 500 delegates present. The meeting was not a triumphalist celebration. A delegate from Nigeria reminded the assembly that "there were Christians in Africa before they were in Edinburgh." Emilio Castro, secretary general of the WCC, did not spare his predecessors. He criticized the way they had married missionary activity with colonialism, and noted the irony that by 1914 the armies of the missionary countries were killing each other. Finally, he observed that the regions whose representatives dominated Edinburgh in 1910—the United Kingdom and western Europe—had reached the point in 1985 where they now needed re-evangelization. In fact, to the dismay of many, neither the Church of England nor the Church of Scotland had sent delegates (A. H. Jones 1985).

John XXIII

One of the chief concerns of Vatican II was the restoration of unity among all Christian churches. In John's first encyclical, *Ad petri cathedram* (June 29, 1959), he greeted the other Christians as "separated brethren and sons." However, his ecumenical theology echoed that of his predecessors. He invited the other Christian churches "to take or resume that place [in the Catholic church] which is yours, which for many of you was your father's place."

In June 1960, John created the Secretariat for Christian Unity. This office was given responsibility for inviting leaders of Christian churches as official observers at Vatican II and for initiating interchurch dialogues.

The original members of the secretariat included Cardinal Augustin Bea and Monsignor (later cardinal) Jan Willebrands, and two staff members, Thomas Stransky (later Superior General of the Paulist Fathers) and

Monsignor Jean-Francois Arrighi. This team won the respect of ecu-menists worldwide. Bea was the first president (1960–68) and Willebrands succeeded him (1968–89). The present president is an Australian, Cardinal Edward Idris Cassidy (Hebblethwaite 1989h). On March 1, 1989, the Sec-retariat was renamed the Pontifical Council for Promoting Christian Unity and made an arm of the CDF.

During John's pontificate there were two important developments: the founding of another ecumenical organization and the third assembly of the WCC. On December 4, 1960, at Grace Episcopal Cathedral in San Francisco, Eugene Carson Blake (1906–85), stated clerk of the (then) United Presbyterian church, gave a landmark sermon, "A Proposal To-ward the Reunion of Christ's Church." This sermon marked the tenth an-niversary of the National Council of Churches in the United States and attracted such nationwide attention that it rated Blake a spot on the cover of *Time*. Blake's sermon called for a church "truly catholic, truly evangel-ical, and truly reformed" (Thompson 1985b), and launched the Consulta-tion on Church Union (COCU).

COCU "is not a denomination but a movement created by the nine denominations that participate in it. Its one task is to hammer out theo-logical underpinnings and practical details of a possible united and unit-ing church" (Penfield 1980). Its foundation document, "The COCU Consensus," sets out areas of theological agreement and has been ap-proved by eight of the nine member denominations.

In December 1989, the members voted unanimously to adopt a second document, "Churches in Covenant Communion." The thesis of this one hundred-page document is that churches in covenant are not at an interim step on the way towards one big church but the covenanting process is a new form of church union. In its outline of ways for churches to achieve unity without structural merger, it focuses on mutual recognition of min-isters and also shared communion, membership, and mission. By mission they mean the churches should work together on projects that enhance the social, political, and economic life of the community. The plan stops short of calling for an organic merger. That meant each church could re-tain its own governing structures and worship. Many churches were not ready to give up their identity as Methodists or Episcopalians or Presby-terians. They scaled down their plans and proposed a partial church union to be called the Church of Christ Uniting, also called COCU.

By June 1993 (ecumenism is a long, slow process), three of the churches had endorsed the document: the International Council of Com-munity Churches, the Christian Methodist Episcopal church, and the United Church of Christ. The Disciples of Christ endorsed the proposal in November 1995 and the United Methodist church in April 1996. The Presbyterian church (U.S.A.), the African Methodist Episcopal church, and the African Methodist Episcopal Zion church have delayed a final vote on the plan until 1997. The other denomination, the Episcopal church, has yet to set a time to vote.[7] The reasons for the delays are doctrinal and disciplinary. The Presbyterians, for example, are resisting the COCU requirement that member churches have an office of bishop. Some groups who oppose gay clergy are afraid that COCU churches that ordain gays and lesbians, such as the United Church of Christ, will be allowed to minister in their denominations.

The WCC held its third assembly at New Delhi in 1961 with 577 delegates from 197 member churches. Its theme was "Christ, the Light of the World." The delegates affirmed their intention not only to stay together and to grow together, but also to assume new tasks together. They revised their self-definition as presented at Amsterdam: "The WCC is a fellowship of churches which confess the Lord Jesus Christ as God and Savior according to the scriptures and, therefore, seek to fulfill their common calling to the glory of the one God, Father, Son, and Holy Spirit."

Four Orthodox churches—Russian, Romanian, Polish, and Bulgarian—became members. This gave the Orthodox more influence in ecumenism. Their presence, said Visser't Hooft, did not make the ecumenical task easier, but their presence enriched it. John XXIII approved Roman Catholic observers at the New Delhi meeting, leaving it to Cardinal Bea to choose the delegates.

Vatican II

The council produced two documents that dealt with ecumenism: the Decree on Ecumenism and the Declaration on Religious Freedom. Paul VI signed the ecumenism decree on November 21, 1964. In the final vote, it received only eleven negative votes. From what has been reported about the preconciliar popes, it should come as no surprise that this decree was not based on experience in ecumenical matters; actually, it became the source of a new tradition. It marked the beginning of Catholic openness to ecumenism. Wider horizons and urgent tasks would become clearer as the church's involvement developed.

The decree is new because it acknowledged that both sides were responsible for the divisions and because it overcame the simple identification of "the one and only church of Christ" with the Catholic church, as had been claimed by Pius XII in *Mystici corporis* (1943). Nevertheless, the bishops reaffirmed the special claim of the Catholic church to be the church of Christ: "For it is through Christ's Catholic church alone, which is the universal help toward salvation, that the fullness of the means of salvation can be obtained" (UR 3). But then the bishops went on to add significant qualifications: (1) They recognized the unity already created by baptism, faith, hope, and love, and spoke of "obstacles to perfect ecclesiastical communion"; (2) they acknowledged the ecclesial character of the other Christian communities—until the publication of this conciliar decree, other Christian churches, with the exception of the Orthodox, were officially referred to as "societies" and not churches; and (3) they stated that the church of Christ "subsists in the Catholic church, which is governed by the successor of Peter and by the bishops in communion with him" (LG 8; see UR 3–4).

The phrase "subsists in" has been controversial since the council because it smacks of ecclesial superiority. In March 1985, the CDF, in criticizing a book by Leonardo Boff, argued that the authentic meaning of "subsists in" was that "only elements of the church" exist outside the "visible structure" of the Catholic church. In May 1987, Cardinal Jan Willebrand, president of the Secretariat for Christian Unity, questioned this interpretation of the CDF.[8] Avery Dulles concurred, insisting that "subsists in" is quite different from "is" and that the phrase "subsists in" was "an expression deliberately chosen to allow for the ecclesial reality of the other Christian communities" (1989, 430). Gregory Baum had already written along these lines in 1972: "Whoever speaks of the Catholic church as the one true church must qualify this doctrine by the complementary teaching that the one true church transcends the Catholic church and cannot be simply identified with it" (1972b).

The Declaration on Religious Liberty was the most controversial conciliar document because it raised the question of doctrinal development. Pius IX's *Syllabus of Errors* (1864) had rejected religious liberty, declaring that it is erroneous to hold that "every person is free to embrace and profess that religion which, led by the light of reason, that person may have thought true." But the experience of religious pluralism in the United States—perhaps the greatest contribution the United States has given to world civilization—made its impact on the development of doctrine and policy at the council, thanks to the brilliance of John Courtney Murray. This conciliar document was the distinctive contribution of the United States to Vatican II. During the council it was this document that "had become a Protestant litmus test of the sincerity of the council's ecumenical resolve" (R. M. Brown 1987a, 178). The declaration received a final approval by a vote of 2,308 to 70.

Despite the controversy, it is generally acknowledged that Vatican II marked a fundamental shift in Catholic appreciation of the other Christian communities. Before Vatican II, Catholics emphasized what divided the churches. The other churches were strangers or enemies. The council underscored what united Christians: all are brothers and sisters baptized in Christ, joined in the Spirit, and exist for one another. All Christian communities belong to the one and only church of Christ. This new perspective reflected a shift from an ecclesiocentric to a christocentric theology—instead of unity through return to the Catholic church, there should be unity by deeper and more explicit regrafting into the "one and only church of Christ," especially as this is manifested in the Roman Catholic church.

Evaluations of the Council: 1979–90

Writing in 1979, Richard McBrien judged ecumenism "almost dead in the water, at least at the officially approved levels." He based his judgment on two points: many bishops ignored reports from bilateral consultations and there was hardly any positive action being taken about intercommunion and the mutual recognition of ordained ministries.

In 1982, Kilian McDonnell wrote that the conciliar decree was cautious, reticent, and even fearful. It gave a careful answer to the realities of 1964 when the question was about how the church could take part in ecumenical meetings, he explained. But in the meantime, the question had changed. Ecumenists asked how the unity of the church could become a reality. How can unity be manifested today? The decree had no answer to this question.

In 1986, Thomas Stransky highlighted some of the surprises in ecumenism since the council. Vatican II had recommended interchurch dialogues. The extent and pace of the dialogues, both bilateral and multilateral, had far exceeded all expectations. The council also recommended that "ecumenical dialogue could start with the moral application of the gospel" (UR 23). When this statement was made, the bishops were not unaware of the sharp and serious differences between Catholics and other Christians about moral matters. A real surprise is that twenty years after the council, the personal and social ethical issues would be more divisive than they were in the 1960s (Stransky 1986a). However, after a look at the list of issues, it is easy to see why there is so much division. Part of the long list includes abortion, birth control, the death penalty, euthanasia, divorce and remarriage, and active homosexuality. As Thomas Rausch, a Jesuit ecumenist, observed: the moral issues now constitute "the Achilles' heel of the ecumenical movement" (1989b).

In 1986, Stransky was disappointed with the reception of ecumenism: "Authentic ecumenical thinking, attitudes and practices have entered the bloodstream of only a minority of Catholics," he remarked (1986a). A few years later, Thaddeus Horgan, an Atonement friar, was more optimistic. He stated that since the council, "the church has wholeheartedly committed itself to the ecumenical quest, particularly in its leadership at the international and national levels" (1990).

In another 1990 assessment of ecumenism, Thomas Rausch wrote, "Perhaps the greatest obstacle to ecumenical progress remains the fact that far too few Christians really long for reconciliation. The churches today seem content to live in peace as they follow their separate paths. There is a new level of mutual respect. Occasionally they cooperate on practical matters. . . . But for the vast majority, Christians in different churches remain strangers to each other."

Paul VI

Paul and Patriarch Athenagoras of Constantinople met in Jerusalem on a common pilgrimage on January 5 and 6, 1964, praying that "this meeting may be the sign and prelude of things to come for the glory of God and the illumination of his faithful people." On December 7, 1965, the day before the closing of the council, the two leaders mutually lifted the excommunications of 1054. Since Vatican II had Christian unity as one of its goals, this act was a dramatic symbol of the intent of the institutional church. In 1967, the two leaders exchanged visits, July 25 in Constantinople and October 26 in Rome. These religious encounters helped smooth the way for many productive Catholic-Orthodox dialogues. A few years later, Paul wrote a letter to Patriarch Athenagoras on February 8, 1971, stating that the Orthodox churches are "in almost complete communion" with the Catholic church (Dulles 1986a, 35).

Paul visited the WCC in Geneva on June 10, 1969, a visit unthinkable in 1948. The visit proved his esteem for the work of the WCC, and yet he made it clear that the Catholic church was still reluctant to enter fully into the organization.

There are several reasons for this reluctance. First, the Catholic church is so hierarchically and solidly structured and organized that it would be very difficult to diffuse its identity and independence of action within another organization. Second, there are theological and jurisdictional problems that must be considered, especially those concerning the future role of the papacy. Third, the sheer size of the Catholic church is such that it would so overwhelm the WCC as to call into question its very identity. In short, presently the Vatican says it is "inopportune" for the Catholic church to officially join the WCC.

The WCC held two general assemblies during Paul's pontificate. Its fourth assembly was held at Uppsala, Sweden, in July 1968, with Eugene Carson Blake as general secretary (1967–72). The assembly met against the background of the many challenges of the 1960s: the ambiguity of new scientific and technological progress, the growing gap between poor and rich nations, and racism. Its theme was "Behold I make all things new" (Revelation 21:5). There were 704 delegates from 235 churches from 84 countries, one-third from the third world. The largest group of delegates came from Orthodox churches. The Catholic church sent fourteen observers and also had two firsts: nine theologians joined the Faith and Order Commission and Roberto Tucci, a Jesuit theologian and editor of *Civilta Cattolica*, gave a major address to the assembly. In his talk he referred to the possibility of the Catholic church joining the WCC.

The fifth assembly was held in Nairobi in 1975 (J. R. Nelson 1976; Gibeau 1976a). There were 676 delegates from 285 member churches. The general secretary was Philip Potter (1972–84). The delegates agreed that in addition to staying and growing together, they would struggle together. Their theme was "Jesus Christ frees and unites." The delegates declared that faith in the triune God and socio-political engagement and also conversion to Jesus Christ and active participation in changing social and economic structures belong together and condition one another. They wrote a major amendment into their constitution. They declared that the churches are called "to the goal of visible unity in one faith and in one eucharistic fellowship expressed in worship and in common life in Christ, and to advance toward that unity in order that the world may believe."

New Delhi (1961) had called for the unity of all in each place; Uppsala (1968) had underscored the depth and extent of catholicity. Nairobi (1975) complemented those two meetings by acknowledging there can be unity-in-diversity and diversity-in-unity.

John Paul II and the Orthodox Churches

On October 17, 1978, the day after his election, John Paul committed himself to the work of ecumenism without reservation. He expressed hope that with common effort "we might fully arrive at full communion."

In 1979, when John Paul visited Turkey, he and the Patriarch of Constantinople attended each other's liturgies, without, however, sharing communion. Some commentators felt this visit signaled John Paul's keen interest in the East, so much so that he seems to have relegated dialogue with the West to second place (Hebblethwaite 1980a, 1980b).

It is natural for John Paul to be drawn more to the East than the West. First, he is a Slav. His fourth encyclical, *Apostles of the Slavs* (1985), was a commemoration of the two Greek missionary brothers to the Slavs in the ninth century, Cyril and Methodius, and an appeal for spiritual unity between eastern and western Europe. Second, the Orthodox tradition confirms many of John Paul's own concerns: his insistence on high christology, sacramental piety, Marian devotion, monasticism, a "sacred" view of the priesthood, and resistance to "secularizing" trends (Hebblethwaite 1980c).

Nevertheless, those involved in Catholic-Orthodox dialogues admit that their concerns are just as demanding and complicated as those that engage Catholic-Protestant dialogues. For example, it is unthinkable to hope for a successful dialogue with the Orthodox unless claims to universal papal jurisdiction are reconstituted and the papacy functions mainly as a quasi-sacrament of unity for the whole church. Also, Orthodox-Catholic union is impossible until the churches first work out how it will be possible for Eastern Catholics and Orthodox to exist in communion. Finally, as long as Eastern Catholics are treated as second-class members of the Roman Catholic church, Orthodox churches will suspect and disregard the Catholic church's declaration to be a sister church to the Orthodox.

Some of the deep-seated problems between the Orthodox and Catholics surfaced in 1991 when John Paul II called a special synod of European bishops to discuss "a new evangelization of Europe" in light of the collapse of communism and the sudden fall of the Iron Curtain. About 137 bishops gathered in Rome from November 28 to December 14. In addition to the European bishops, the pope invited episcopal observers from different continents and also Protestant and Orthodox church leaders. The synod got off to a poor start when concerns raised by the Orthodox leaders took center stage as five Orthodox churches rejected the papal invitation to attend. Alexsie II, the Russian Orthodox Patriarch, declared that the Catholic church had created "rival missionary structures" in Soviet territory by appointing bishops in regions where there had been none before and by conducting a proselytizing campaign of "conversion."

The meeting, although tense at times, ended with attempts at reconciliation. Both sides agreed that more ecumenical dialogues were needed so that unfortunate differences such as the one that disrupted this meeting would not erupt in the future. And the concluding document stressed the valiant testimony to Christ exhibited by the Orthodox churches under decades of communist regimes (Cowell 1991; Rosato 1992; Weakland 1992).

The perennial tension between the Orthodox and the Vatican emerged again during a 1994 papal visit to the Balkans, John Paul's sixty-second international pastoral visit. The pope had planned to visit several areas in the former Yugoslavia, despite the armed conflicts that were in place among the Croatian Catholics, Serbian Orthodox, and Bosnian Muslims since April 1992. The Croatian and Bosnian wars had been marked by a religious fanaticism expressed in the widespread destruction of Muslim mosques, Orthodox monasteries, and Catholic churches. The Bosnian Serbs were ruthlessly driving Bosnian Muslims from Bosnia and Croatians from occupied territory in Croatia in what was called "ethnic cleansing."

The Serbian Orthodox church resisted the pope's visit to Belgrade and the Bosnian Serbs forced the cancellation of a visit to Sarajevo because they could not (or would not) guarantee the safety of the people assembled to pray with the pope. This left the pope with a one-sided visit to Roman Catholic Croatia on September 10–11, 1994.

The cancellation of the visit to Sarajevo was particularly distressing to John Paul, not only because he wanted to visit this city that had been terribly devastated by war but also because it was the testing ground for good relations with Islam in Europe. Before the war significant dialogues had taken place among Catholic, Orthodox, and Islamic leaders. A Catholic theologian in Sarajevo surmised that "the pope had intuited that the dialogue between religions is the most important spiritual need of the late 20th century" (Hebblethwaite 1994f).

The animosities between the Serbian Orthodox and the Croatian Catholics date back to World War II. The Serbs could not forgive the Croatian Fascists for fighting alongside German troops against those Serbs, Muslims, and Croats who tried to block the Nazi conquest of Yugoslavia. Once the Nazis subdued the country, the Croatian Fascists embarked on a policy of genocide and forced conversions. Five hundred thousand Serbs were massacred and two hundred thousand Serbs were compelled to become Catholics.

When the pope arrived in Zagreb, Croatia, he came, he said, as a "defenseless pilgrim" who urged reconciliation, peace, and unity. He called on the people to shun nationalism and pursue a "culture of peace." He declared, "It is necessary to promote a culture of peace which does not reject a healthy patriotism but keeps far away from the exasperations and exclusions of nationalism" (Cohen 1994a). Religious tolerance, he asserted, was part of the heritage of the region. He even appeared to stretch historical facts to promote reconciliation and peace. "No, the phenomenon of nationalist intolerance which has swept over this region cannot be attributed to religion" (Cohen 1994b).

On May 2, 1995, John Paul issued a fifty-four-page apostolic letter, *Orientale lumen* ("The Light of the East"). The context of the letter was the collapse of communism and the revival of religion-based ethnic tensions. The pope called all Catholics and Orthodox to speed the quest for unity and to end the "sin" of a nearly one thousand-year schism between the two branches of Christianity. The pope wrote: "The sin of our separation is very serious. I feel the need to increase our common openness to the Spirit who calls us to conversion, to accept and recognize others with fraternal respect, to make fresh, courageous gestures able to dispel any temptation to turn back." John Paul offered no concrete proposals for realizing the unity of the two branches of the one church of Christ.

A concrete expression of unity did occur some two months later during a Mass at St. Peter's Basilica on June 29, the feast of the apostles Peter and Paul. The Patriarch of Constantinople, Bartholomeos I, joined the pope at the altar. The Mass was the highlight of the patriarch's four-day visit to promote reconciliation and full communion between the two churches. John Paul reiterated that "we cannot remain separate" and recalled the "common traditions" of the churches. Bartholomeos said that "humility and repentance" are the means to overcome the longstanding division between the churches. He added: "With God's help, today we reached an apostolic maturity of conscience which impels us to seek not primacy among persons but among the church's ministries of service." After stressing that "integrity of faith" is linked to true Christianity, the patriarch said that being faithful to God requires "self-criticism" and, to restore the unity of the church, "the primacy of humility."[9]

The two leaders declared in a joint statement that unity between the churches would "increase the influence of the church for peace and justice in zones of ethnic and religious conflict." Even as they were talking, deadly fighting continued between Catholic Croats and Orthodox Serbs in the former Yugoslav federation.

The patriarch also spoke about the need for ecclesial diversity and serious reflection about the roots of religious discord. He may have had in mind that he and the pope shared the altar until after the Nicene Creed, but not during the canon of the Mass. But most of his comments appeared tailored for his own people who are divided over attempts to strengthen ties with the larger and more politically active Roman Catholic church. Greek and Russian Orthodox clerics have been particularly critical of overtures to the Vatican, which they perceive as interested in expanding its mark in the former communist countries of Eastern Europe. [10]

On November 29, 1995, the annual November meeting between the Greek Orthodox and Catholic church was held in Istanbul. Present were Bartholomeos I and Cardinal Edward Cassidy. The dialogue went well. However, at the conclusion it was clear that it will be quite some time before the two churches share the Eucharist—the main focus of spiritual life in both communities. The patriarch noted that "Intercommunion doesn't seem closer because we have first to agree on matters concerning faith. We have different ecclesiologies, and the place of the bishop of Rome in the universal church of Christ constitutes the principal obstacle." He also pointed to current difficulties between the two churches, namely, the relationship of the Orthodox to the Eastern Catholics regarding proselytism. The Orthodox object to the establishment of Catholic churches in the traditionally Orthodox countries of Eastern Europe since the fall of communism. [11]

Little did the Patriarch of Constantinople (now Istanbul) know in November 1995 that his ecumenical efforts would receive another setback—this time within the Orthodox communities themselves. On Sunday, February 25, 1996, the Russian Orthodox church severed ties with Constantinople. On this day, as Patriarch Aleksie II of Moscow celebrated liturgy with fifty other Russian Orthodox bishops, he omitted the name of Patriarch Bartholomeos I from the list of Orthodox leaders normally commemorated in the rite. It was the first time since the origins of Russian Orthodoxy in 988 that the Russian church refused to commemorate the patriarch in Constantinople (Steinfels 1996).

This breach reflects the same national conflicts that have unsettled the political life of Russia and Eastern Europe since the collapse of communism. The cause of the breach involves the Orthodox church in Estonia. At one time it was under the jurisdiction of Constantinople but, after Russian occupation in 1944, it was attached to Moscow. In 1996 the Estonian church asked that it be answerable once again to Constantinople. The Russian church denounced this move as a completely unjustified incursion into its own historic jurisdiction. It is beyond the scope of this book to trace the very complicated history of these Orthodox churches and the way this squabble was resolved through compromise in 1996 (Webster 1996). The main point is that these political and religious conflicts among the Orthodox themselves and between the Orthodox and Catholics are additional stumbling blocks on the road to ecumenism.

Finally, since the Bosnian war of forty-three months had ended in 1995, John Paul was able to visit Sarajevo, a predominantly Muslim city, on April 12–13, 1997, his 75th overseas pilgrimage. The pope urged the people to turn their backs on war and intolerance and to continue trying to rebuild their shattered community. He said, "It is not a matter of material reconstruction alone. What is needed above all is to provide for the spiritual rebuilding of mind and hearts."

This was not an easy pilgrimage for the pope because his message of reconciliation and democracy was offered to a region where tensions continue to linger. Not only do hard-line Catholic Croatian nationalists oppose the unified Bosnia that the pope's visit inevitably blesses, but the Muslims, Catholic Croats, and Orthodox Serbs have yet to find a solution to their mutual hostilities. In fact, just hours before the pope arrived in Sarajevo, police discovered a powerful batch of explosives along the route his motorcade was scheduled to take. The cache apparently was planted under a bridge overnight and would have caused enormous damage. Also, when the pope arrived in Sarajevo, two members of Bosnia's collective presidency were present but the Serbian president "was conspicuously absent, reportedly because of security reasons" (Bohlen 1997b).

At the conclusion of the pope's visit, people said they hoped that the visit will insure a peace that they still see as tenuous (Bohlen 1997c). One priest said that, since extreme nationalism is so pervasive, the pope's visit will either mark "a new beginning in the search for a true, multireligious character" for Bosnia or it will be "a liturgical act, a spiritual parade" and nothing else (Wilkinson and Boudreau 1997).

John Paul II and Protestants in the Americas

John Paul has made several visits to North, Central, and South America. His very first overseas visit was to Puebla, Mexico, in January 1979—a visit that will be described at length in chapter 9. His fourth overseas pilgrimage was to the United States, which he visited for a week in 1979 (October 1–7). During this important visit, the pope never met with Protestant leaders nor did he learn about the ecumenical progress taking place in the United States. He did give a talk to ecumenists at a prayer service in Washington on October 7. In his address, John Paul referred to such topics as intercommunion and the deep division over moral and ethical matters. He said, "The moral life and the life of faith are so deeply united that it is impossible to divide them." Some Protestant leaders were disappointed with the visit, but most agreed that while the visit did not further ecumenical relations, neither did it hinder them (Winiarski 1979b).

On September 11, 1987, during his second visit to the United States, John Paul prayed with evangelical Protestants in Columbia, South Carolina. This was a highly public approach to this group, especially the Southern Baptist Convention (SBC), who at thirteen million are the second-largest denomination in the United States. Since the SBC has not participated with the National Council of Churches, the visit was "a step toward bringing evangelical Protestants more comfortably into pan-Christian discussions" (A. Jones 1987). On the negative side, "A number of perceptive Protestants . . . see Pope John Paul II as being more concerned with reasserting the identity and integrity of the Roman Catholic church as a worldwide community" than with ecumenism (Rausch 1985). It is not that John Paul is unecumenical; he is ecumenical in his own way.

In May 1990, John Paul made his second visit to Mexico. This predominantly Catholic country has had a rapid growth of Protestant denominations, especially among such churches as the Assemblies of God, Pentecostals, and Seventh-day Adventists. The Catholic hierarchy in Mexico perjoratively refers to these churches as "sects." On the occasion of the pope's visit, the local hierarchy refused to invite their leaders to an ecumenical meeting with the pope. One Mexican bishop was quoted: "You do not have dialogue with bandits." In one of his homilies John Paul noted that some Catholics had "broken the link of saving grace, joining the sects. . . . No Catholic in Mexico can consider himself exempt" from the obligation to bring defectors back to the church. He continued: "I would like to meet with you one by one to tell you: come back to the fold of the church, your mother" (Rother 1990).

In the twenty-first century, 50 percent of the world's Catholics will be in Latin America. Cardinal Edward Cassidy, president of the Pontifical Council for Promoting Christian Unity, predicts that "The commitment of the Latin American church to ecumenism will be the key to the strength of the church overall" (Lefevere 1996).

John Paul II and the Anglican Community

Geoffrey Fisher, Archbishop of Canterbury, met with John XXIII in 1960. Since that historic meeting, contacts between Rome and the leaders of the Anglican church have occurred with relative frequency. Archbishops Michael Ramsey (1961–74) and Donald Coggan (1974–80) met, respectively, with Paul VI in 1966 and 1977. Archbishop Robert Runcie (1980–91) met John Paul five times between 1980 and 1989. Their first meeting took place on May 9, 1980 in Accra, Ghana. They issued a common statement: "The time is too short and the need too pressing to waste Christian energy pursuing old rivalries. The talents and resources of all the churches must be shared if Christ is to be seen and heard effectively."[12] At their last meeting, this one held in Rome in 1989, Runcie announced that the papacy had to be more than a symbol of unity: "Today the divisions among Christians require that the primacy of the Bishop of Rome should also be a primacy of action and initiative in favor of that unity for which Christ so earnestly prayed" (Hebblethwaite 1989e).

In response, John Paul acknowledged his ecumenical mission but also frankly and honestly pointed to differences between Rome and Canterbury. He said: "Events in recent years have seriously aggravated the differences between us, making the work of unity more difficult" (Hebblethwaite 1989g). John Paul was referring to the ordination of women as priests, and even bishops, a practice rejected out of hand by the institutional Catholic church.

This issue surfaced again when, on November 11, 1992, the mother church of the Anglican community voted by a narrow margin to ordain women to the priesthood. The Vatican's reaction came quickly and was uncompromising: "This decision by the Anglican Communion constitutes a new and grave obstacle to the entire process of reconciliation."

Anglican and Catholic relations are ambivalent. The ordination of women priests creates very negative feelings; other relations are somewhat more positive. For example, shortly after Vatican II on March 26, 1966, Paul VI and Michael Ramsey, Archbishop of Canterbury, announced their intention "to inagurate between the Roman Catholic church and the Anglican Communion a series of dialogues that, founded on the gospels and the ancient common tradition, may lead to that unity in truth for which Christ prayed."

In 1967, a preparatory commision on Anglican-Catholic unity was established. By 1968, the commission was able to issue its "Malta Report," which said there were large areas of agreement between the two communities and three areas of disagreement: the Eucharist, ministry and ordination, and authority in the church. Those who disagreed on the issue of authority were particularly concerned with the role of the papacy.

The first Anglican-Roman Catholic International Committee (ARCIC I) met in 1970, studied these areas of disagreement and twelve years later (March 12, 1982) published its *Final Report*. This document has been called "The most dramatic achievement toward Christian unity in the realm of international ecumenical consultations" (A. Cunningham 1986, 69). In the report the theologians of ARCIC I declared that they had reached "substantial agreement" on major doctrinal issues concerning authority, Eucharist, and ministry and ordination. They believed the report was "consonant with the faith" of both communities.

The CDF praised the report in its initial response in 1982 for "the quality of doctrinal rapprochement achieved," but sharply criticized it as being ambiguous or inadequate on several key points. The CDF said it had reservations because the Anglicans explicitly acknowledge that they cannot accept such Catholic teachings as infallibility, the Marian dogmas, eucharistic adoration, and the primacy of the bishop of Rome (McDonnell 1982). The CDF sent its initial eleven-page response to the international episcopal conferences for their responses. The Vatican's response evoked surprise since the Catholics on the committee had helped produce and consented to the *Final Report.*

In 1988, the Anglicans accepted the committee's document. The Vatican's long overdue response came on December 5, 1991. The response began enthusiastically, saying that the report achieved "points of convergence and even of agreement which many would not have thought possible." It commented on the "notable progress toward a consensus" on the Eucharist and on the ordained ministry. It saw "convergence" but "no substantial agreement" on authority in the church, the Marian dogmas, or Roman primacy. It also noted that "convergence has eluded ARCIC I on such issues as papal infallibility." And it concluded with these words: "The objection may be made that this reply does not sufficiently follow the ecumenical method. . . . It must, however, be remembered that the Roman Catholic Church was asked to give a clear answer to the question: Are the agreements contained in this report consonant with the faith of the Catholic Church? What was asked for was not a simple evaluation of an ecumenical study, but an official response as to the identity of the various statements with the faith of the church."

The Catholic church appears to be asking that the ARCIC I report express a theology that is identical (rather than consonant) with its own teachings. But if either church community requires that the other conform to its own theological formulations, further progress will be hard to achieve. Both churches need to concentrate on "the substance of the ancient deposit of faith"—the message of John XXIII at the opening of Vatican II.

ARCIC II was convened in 1982 by Archbishop Robert Runcie and John Paul II. It has to deal with these documents and the differences that surfaced so that the debilitating division of these two international communions will be healed.

George Carey, Archbishop of Canterbury since 1991, made his first formal visit to the Vatican and John Paul II in December 1996. Their meeting, while amicable, was not satisfying for either leader because they could not agree about the difficult and, so far, irreconcilable issue of the priestly ordination of women (Bohlen 1996).

John Paul II and the WCC

On June 12, 1984, almost six years after his election as pope, John Paul visited the WCC headquarters in Geneva to show that the search for unity was still among Rome's pastoral priorities. Meanwhile, the WCC was earnestly working towards Christian unity. There were several significant results of its efforts. For example, in January 1982, the Faith and Order Commission met in Lima, Peru, and by a unanimous vote of more than one hundred theologians, accepted its document "Baptism, Eucharist and Ministry" (called BEM, or the Lima document). BEM is unique in the history of the ecumenical movement. It is probably the most significant ecumenical document to appear since the Decree on Ecumenism of Vatican II. It represents almost fifty years of development in the Faith and Order Commission. The assembled theologians believed BEM expresses "the faith of the Church through the ages" and provides a basis for each church's "relations and dialogues with other churches." However, since BEM is the work of theologians and does not represent official church positions, then "the next chapter of the history of the ecumenical movement may well be written on how the churches respond to this statement" (Rusch 1985, 31).

It is not possible to give a lengthy summary of this thick text (World Council of Churches 1992; see Dulles 1982; Fahey 1986; Heim 1986; McCarthy 1996, 96–8, 169–71, 201–3). Some significant points of agreement are the following. The statement on baptism maintains that the difference between infant and adult baptism becomes less sharp when Christians recognize "that both forms of baptism embody God's own initiative in Christ and express a response of faith made within the believing community." The section on Eucharist states that Christ's presence in the Eucharist is real, living, active, and unique, and should be celebrated "at least every Sunday." It also stated that "The very celebration of the Eucharist is an instance of the church's participation in God's mission to the world." The statement on ministry singles out the threefold ministry of bishop, presbyter, and deacon. Those churches with this ministry "will need to ask how its potential can be fully developed for the most effective witness of the church." Those churches without this threefold ministry "need to ask themselves whether the threefold pattern as developed does not have a powerful claim to be accepted by them."

BEM has become a part of church life at the local and denominational levels. By 1990, some four hundred and fifty thousand copies of the document were in print around the world in thirty-one languages. It has evoked a new level of interest and involvement in ecumenism at the grass roots. There are, however, some concerns and reservations. Many in the United States argued that the ordination of women should have been dealt with in a more positive and forthright way. Also, some churches without the threefold ministry expressed some reluctance to endorse such a ministry, mainly because of uncertainty about how these categories—especially that of the episcopate—are to be understood.

The Catholic church responded to BEM in the summer of 1987 through the Secretariat for Promoting Christian Unity in consultation with the CDF and after advisement with episcopal conferences and theological faculties.[13] The Vatican declared that "BEM is a significant result of and contribution to the ecumenical movement. It demonstrates clearly that serious progress is being made in the quest for visible Christian unity." It added that "Catholics can find in BEM much that they can agree with." On the other hand, the Vatican explained why "we think the text falls short at certain points." The major problem seems to be that the "focus of BEM is not ecclesiology as such." The "study of ecclesiology must come more and more into the center of the ecumenical dialogue." The Vatican observed that "full agreement on the sacraments is related to agreement on the nature of the church. The sacraments, including baptism, receive their full significance and efficacy from the comprehensive ecclesial reality on which they depend and which they manifest." Furthermore, the BEM document does not offer "a clear concept of sacrament (and sacramentality)."

In light of what it considered faulty ecclesiology and sacramentality, the Vatican outlined many of its concerns regarding the three parts of the BEM text. Some significant concerns are the following. With respect to baptism, the Vatican said BEM does not "give reasons to show why baptism is an unrepeatable act." As for the Eucharist and the real presence of the risen Christ, the Vatican stated that "the description of the change that takes place is ambiguous and open to several interpretations." Regarding ministry, the Vatican claimed that the description of ordination does not reflect the faith of those Christians "for whom ordination is clearly a sacrament." It added a question: Does "the threefold ministry belong to the constitutive being of the church or only to the ecumenical well-being of the church?" These points indicate that the dialogue between the Vatican and the Faith and Order Commission will involve many lengthy and difficult sessions.

The WCC held its sixth assembly at Vancouver, July 24–August 10, 1983 (see Geyer 1983; Moore 1983; Lyles 1983; Misner 1983; and Rausch 1984). There were 847 delegates from 301 member churches from one hundred countries. Twenty Roman Catholic observers, including six bishops, were approved by the Vatican. The theme of the assembly was "Jesus Christ—the life of the world."

The WCC has been a controversial body because it deals with controversial issues in which theology and ethics impinge on political, economic, and social policies. Its Vancouver meeting was as faithful as previous assemblies had been to the ecumenical pioneers who emphasized the importance of the work of Christian unity not in a political or social vacuum, but in relation to the continuing worldwide struggle for a greater measure of justice, peace, and human dignity. The delegates were reminded that peace and justice belong together with baptism, Eucharist, and ministry. These two strains must mutually reinforce one another rather than become parallel tracks which might split apart. Keeping them together is no easy task.

In 1984, Emilio Castro of the Evangelical Methodist Church of Uruguay was elected the fourth general secretary of the WCC (Howell 1984). He presided over the seventh assembly which met in Canberra, Australia, February 7–20, 1991. The 842 voting delegates from one hundred countries represented 311 churches—a major increase over the 147 churches present in 1948. In 1983, 31 percent of the delegates were women; in 1991, women comprised 35 percent. Present also were twenty-three Vatican-delegated observers.

For the first time the theme focused on the Spirit: "Come, Holy Spirit—renew the whole creation" (Ryan 1991). This was also the first time the theme was formulated as a prayer.

The assembly was held while the Persian Gulf War was being waged and it affected the deliberations. For example, Emilio Castro, disappointed that all could not celebrate one Eucharist, hoped all the delegates would unite at the eucharistic table at the next assembly in 1998, the fiftieth anniversary of the founding of the WCC. He wanted to know how the presidents of warring countries could ever unite in peace if the churches could not unite around the Eucharist. This plea raised the perennial question: Is the Eucharist the expression of unity or a means to unity?

Some of the ecclesial questions that were debated included theological perspectives (particularly that of northern nations versus that of southern nations); the relation of men and women (and women's ordination); the cultural limitations of biblical language (particularly the dominance of male metaphors for God); and the inevitable tension between ecumenists and social activists. The former focus on the nature of God and church unity; the latter emphasize peace and justice. However, this tension reached a most critical point at Canberra because "it became apparent that the quest for Christian unity, and so issues of faith and order, were no longer the major concern of many of the delegates. If this is true as well of the churches they represented, then something significant has happened in the ecumenical movement" (Putney 1992, 633).

Orthodox participants were disturbed by some of the presentations that seemed to equate the presence and power of the Paraclete-Spirit in Jesus with the spirits of nature, of ancestors, or social movements. Specifically, they had in mind the provocative address of the Korean theologian Chung Huan-Kyung. She startled the assembly when she confessed that she no longer believed in an "omnipotent, macho warrior God who rescues all good guys and punishes all bad guys." The Orthodox delegation warned that they might withdraw from the organization if it deviated from basic Christian beliefs by accepting theological positions they considered "apostasy" and "syncretism."

Two important events took place in 1993. In January, Konrad Raiser assumed office as the fifth general secretary of the WCC. An ordained minister in the Evangelical Lutheran Church in Germany and a professor of ecumenical theology, Raiser had been deputy general secretary of the WCC from 1973 to 1983. The other event was the fifth world conference of the Faith and Order Commission at Santiago de Compostela, Spain, from August 3 to 14.

The Faith and Order Commission has two main goals: to promote the visible unity of Christians and to study the theological issues which continue to divide the churches. The first and second conferences were held at Lausanne, Switzerland in 1927, and at Edinburgh, Scotland in 1937, during the pontificate of Pius XI. The third was held at Lund, Sweden, in 1952, while Pius XII governed the Catholic church. The fourth was held in Montreal, Canada, in July 1963, five weeks after the death of John XXIII. Present representing 138 churches or communities were 207 official delegates and some 200 theologians, historians, church administrators, and laity. Several tributes were made to the late pope for convening Vatican II and for initiating "a repentance and a renewal" of all the Christian churches. Nonetheless, some honestly acknowledged that John XXIII never entertained another idea of Christian unity than the return of all Christian communities to the Catholic church.

The theme of the Santiago conference was "Towards Koinonia in Faith, Life, and Witness." The Catholic church had twenty-six official delegates, including Cardinal Edward Cassidy of the Pontifical Council for Promoting Christian Unity and the Dominican Jean-Marie Tillard, vice moderator of the Faith and Order Commission.

Two motifs dominated the conference. First, there were calls for repentance on the part of all the churches for their failure not only to do all that is ecumenically possible but also for their silence in the face of hatred or evil or, even worse, for their participation in them (Lefevere 1993). Second, there were calls for reinterpreting the goal of visible unity. Koinonia was the theme chosen for the conference precisely in the hope that it might be the focus for such a revisioning. The shift from the language of Christian "unity" or even "oneness" to "koinonia" is more than a stylistic change. "For some, 'unity' savors too much of uniformity, seems to privilege structures over action, and even raises echoes of concern about a superchurch. 'Koinonia,' a term taken from the New Testament, encompasses a wide variety of meanings and does not translate easily into any language. It can mean 'communion,' 'sharing,' or 'fellowship,' and projects an organic, participating image of unity. . . . [Also] this newer emphasis stresses the unity of the church as sign and instrument of a wider human unity within the whole creation" (Heim 1993).

In June 1994 John Paul II met with 114 cardinals. He gave them an essay of ten thousand words titled "Reflections on the Great Jubilee of the

Year 2000." This document included a section on ecumenism. The pope expressed the hope that in the year 2000 the Christian churches "would be—if not completely reconciled—at least less divided than we have been over the last 1,000 years." He proposed a pan-Christian reunion at Bethlehem and Jerusalem, to be realized in collaboration with the WCC and the Great Council of Orthodoxy. He even suggested a jubilee meeting of Christian, Jewish, and Muslim leaders atop Mount Sinai, where Moses received the Torah and where, according to the Koran, Allah spoke to Muhammad. Here the leaders of the "sons of Abraham" could affirm God and their common ancestry, renounce all violence, put aside antagonisms, and affirm the basic tenets of morality as given to Moses.

A Multifaceted Unresolved Issue

In terms of Von Hügel's triad, the Christian churches have a long way to go to solve the institutional, intellectual, and devotional problems that divide them. One significant issue—the way churches evaluate one another's ordained ministry—impinges on such debatable issues as the authority of the papacy, women priests, married clergy, and intercommunion. Thomas Rausch maintains that "while authority and ordained ministry are not synonymous, it is precisely the different understandings of the nature and authority of the ordained ministry which are at issue between the churches" (1989a, 74).

Paul VI remarked to the Secretariat for the Unity of Christians on April 28, 1967, that the papacy "is undoubtedly the greatest obstacle in the path of ecumenism." This sentence is often taken out of context. It was not intended to reflect the pope's own conviction, but was an observation. He was "entering sympathetically into the minds of other Christians" (Hebblethwaite 1980c).

The bishop of Rome has a special ministry: to serve and symbolize the unity of the church universal. At Vatican II, the bishops asserted that the bishop of Rome "presides over the entire assembly of charity and protects their legitimate variety while at the same time taking care that these differences do not diminish unity, but rather contribute to it" (LG 13). A restructured papacy that would provide more legitimate diversity, collegiality, and subsidiarity than presently exists would further the ecumenical movement. Furthermore, many voices urge the Catholic church to study other dimensions of ordained ministry. Presently the Vatican firmly rejects the idea of women priests and married clergy, and does not recognize the priestly ordination of most Protestant ministers.

Harvey Cox believes "the real ecumenical issue is the women's issue" (Rausch 1990). There is considerable evidence that women had public ecclesial roles in the early church. These roles were later subordinated in patristic teaching. Today, based on developments in the theology of charism and a concern for justice, several Protestant communities ordain women. The Catholic church supports full equality for women in the workplace and in political life, but not priesthood. But, it has to be noted, that even in those churches that ordain women, many problems remain. Some do not permit women priests into higher levels of ministry, allow them little decision-making power, and are still guilty of sexism in other ways (Goldman 1992c).

Efforts are underway to correct these injustices, especially sexism. Recently many Protestant churches adopted an inclusive language lectionary. Rosemary Ruether expressed the thought of many women (and men) when she wrote that "such a lectionary is needed because women in contemporary churches are suffering from linguistic deprivation.... They can no longer nurture their souls in alienating words that ignore or systematically deny their existence. They are starved for the words of life, for symbolic forms that fully and wholeheartedly affirm their personhood and speak truth about the evils of sexism and the possibilities of a future beyond patriarchy" (Ruether 1985, 4–5).

The acceptance of married clergy is another dividing concern. The issues of sexism, women priests, married clergy, and the mutual recognition of ordained ministry coalesced in a recent development in the Catholic church: the acceptance of married Anglican clergy into the Catholic church as married priests. When the CDF announced this process in March 1981, it made it very clear that "this exception to the norm of celibacy in favor of individuals should not be taken to imply a change in the thinking of the church about the value of priestly celibacy, which remains the norm even for future priestly candidates emerging from this group" (Hebblethwaite 1981a).

The history of this policy change has been clearly chronicled by such scholars as Joseph Fichter (1909–94), Jesuit sociologist (1988a, 1988b). In 1974 and 1975, female deacons in several Anglican communities in the United States were ordained to the priesthood, much to the distress of many Anglicans. Then in July 1976, the General Convention of the Episcopal Church ratified women's ordination to the priesthood. This move was protested by a large minority of laity and clerical ministers. In the fall of that year, a group of married Anglican priests opened discussions with Archbishop Jean Jadot, the Apostolic Delegate to the United States, about joining the Catholic priesthood. Jadot asked the United States bishops to discuss this request, which they did in 1978 and 1980. The bishops tentatively accepted the request and forwarded it to Rome, subject to the approval of the pope.

In June 1980, the CDF granted the request, with specific conditions for the married clergy. One limited the married clergy to educational ministries for the first five years of their Catholic ministry. Also included was the stipulation that if the priest's wife died, he could not remarry.

Rome's acceptance of married priests transferring from another Christian church is not without precedent. Pius XII accepted a number of married Lutheran clergy in Europe in the 1950s, and Paul VI allowed a married Anglican priest to carry on his priestly ministry in Australia in 1968 (Gaine 1991, 253).

By early 1990, approximately seventy Episcopal priests had become Catholic priests in the United States. The first Anglican priest was received into the Catholic church in September 1981 in New York. It was required that he receive the sacrament of orders at the hands of a Catholic bishop. This condition was a clear repudiation of the previous ordination by an Anglican bishop. It recalled the controversy in 1896 when Leo XIII declared Anglican orders "null and void." This reordination was perceived as a real threat to agreements reached in extensive ecumenical dialogues between Anglican and Catholic experts. For instance, in September 1981, the final report of the Windsor meeting of ARCIC I stated, "As God calls all the faithful to lifelong discipleship, so the gifts and calling of God to the ministers are irrevocable. For this reason ordination is unrepeatable in both our churches."

Intercommunion or eucharistic hospitality still fails to be an area of unity. As soon as Catholics and Protestants joined in social concerns, they discovered in such activities how much of the gospel they shared. Yet the Eucharist kept them apart. Robert McAfee Brown, a Presbyterian observer at the second and fourth sessions of Vatican II, expressed his dismay: "It seems a mockery to deny our oneness in Christ at the very point where he intended us to show it forth more clearly" (1972, 66).

Two extremes have to be avoided in practicing intercommunion: antidoctrinal carelessness which permits indiscriminate intercommunion; pre-ecumenical rigidity which denies any intercommunion.

Catholic and Protestant churches regard Eucharist differently. Catholics regard the Eucharist as a sign of an already existing unity in ecclesial life, apostolic tradition, and mission. For many Protestants, the Eucharist is a sign of a growing unity and a means to its fulfillment.

Vatican II set forth two principles for intercommunion. These principles are somewhat in conflict. First, since Eucharist is a sign of unity, then intercommunion is not recommended on a regular basis. Second, since Eucharist is a means of grace, then intercommunion is to be encouraged (UR 8). Intercommunion is appropriate on special occasions, for example, when friendship, cooperation, and ecumenical understanding will grow.

In May 1972, the Secretariat for Christian Unity published instructions concerning cases when other Christians may be admitted to the Eucharist. (Nothing was said about Catholics taking communion at a Protestant service.) The three conditions: they should be spiritually well-disposed and should ask for communion; they should share the eucharistic faith of the Catholic church; they should be allowed to receive only if there are no ministers of the would-be communicant's own church available. In short, only in cases of "urgent necessity" may Catholics share the Eucharist with others.

These Vatican directives do not rise above pre-ecumenical rigidity. Their inhospitality upset many committed ecumenists. Some, no doubt, were alienated further from the institutional church by its obviously ideological pronouncements. Gregory Baum explained: "A church that makes its institutional elements, even if divinely given, the sole norm of its practice and worship is in danger of becoming an obstacle, a wall, standing between men and women" (1972).

John Paul II: *Ut unum sint*

On May 25, 1995, John Paul issued his twelfth encyclical, *Ut unum sint* ("That They May Be One"). In this letter he reflected on three of the issues just discussed: intercommunion, priestly ordination, and the teaching authority of the Catholic church. He noted that these continue to be areas of serious division between the Catholic church and other Christians. In addition, he listed two other important areas of concern: the relationship of scripture and tradition and the place of Mary in ecclesial doctrine and devotion. He says all five issues require further study.

The letter may have been prompted by the imminence of the year 2000. John Paul wants the year 2000 to be the occasion to strengthen the faith and witness of Christians, a witness that is hobbled as long as the churches are divided. Consequently, the encyclical calls upon every Christian to work for unity by prayer, conversion, and "every possible form of practical cooperation at all levels."

John Paul discusses at length the teaching authority of the church, especially as this is manifested through papal primacy. He begins by reviewing points he has discussed on other occasions and in other documents. First, the pope as primate has a particular responsibility to promote unity among Christians. Second, he noted that it is widely acknowledged that the papacy "constitutes a difficulty for most other Christians, whose memory is marked by certain painful recollections." Third, he asks forgiveness for past sins and errors committed in the name of the church. Fourth, he reaffirms papal primacy. For John Paul, the authority of the bishop of Rome is not the real obstacle to reunion. The real problem is the manner in which papal authority has at times been exercised. The exercise of papal jurisdiction can be adjusted and changed because there is a real difference between the substance of the papal office and the historically conditioned forms it takes. John Paul acknowledges that there cannot be unity without a reform of the papacy. He asks—and here he breaks new ground—all the leaders of Christian churches and their theologians to engage with him "in a patient and fraternal dialogue on this subject." With this sentence John Paul extended an "unprecedented and revolutionary invitation" to other Christians "to a dialogue aimed at the reform of his own ministry" (Nilson 1995). Just as the Christian leaders invited to Vatican II had some influence on some of the conciliar documents, so the "separated brethren" can have input about papal reform.

The following points indicate that John Paul is serious about a reformed papacy: (1) In the encyclical John Paul refers to himself by such titles as the successor of Peter, bishop of Rome, and the "servant of the servants of God." The latter title, writes John Paul, "is the best possible safeguard against the risk of separating power (and in particular the primacy) from ministry." Titles that do not appear in the encyclical are Pope, Holy Father, Vicar of Christ, and Patriarch of the West. (2) He emphasizes the collegial dimension of his office. (3) He stresses his own conversion first and foremost. He asks all Christians to pray for his conversion so that he might carry out his ministry of service.

The encyclical received positive and negative reviews. Jon Nilson, a Catholic theologian and ecumenist, said, "The encyclical may mark the beginning of the end of Christianity's thousand-year division" (Nilson 1995). Georges Lemopoulos, executive secretary for church and ecumenical relations at the WCC, said that the encyclical presented a "powerful image of the pope's ecumenical commitment" (ibid.). The initial response of the Church of England was that there was "much in the encyclical with which Anglicans can agree wholeheartedly," and that "this urgent call by the pope to continue along a path which is difficult yet full of joy encourages us to continue with great determination" (ibid.). One of the negative responses came from Lukas Vischer, a Swiss Reformed theologian and a former director of the WCC's Faith and Order Commission. He questioned whether the tenure of John Paul offers a suitable model of service for the church. He asked, "Is it not in fact a much more authoritarian and centralizing model? The churches of the Reformation cannot in good conscience associate themselves with the vision of unity propagated by the Catholic church today" (ibid.).

Almost a year after the encyclical, John Quinn delivered a scholarly address at Oxford University on June 29, 1996, the solemn feast of the apostles Peter and Paul, in which he responded to the pope's request for "an honest and serious critique" of the way authority is exercised in the Catholic church and how it might be reformed in order to meet today's "new situation." Quinn, a theologian, retired archbishop of San Francisco, and former president for three years of the national episcopal conference, titled his lecture, "The Exercise of the Primacy: Facing the Cost of Christian Unity."

Claiming that during Vatican II "many cardinals and bishops said much of what I have said here today," Quinn proposed several ways the style of exercising papal jurisdiction can be changed. He declared that the centralization of power in the Roman curia should give way to the power of the bishops who are collectively responsible for governing the church in union with the pope. The pope needs his curia—an administrative network of cardinals and bishops who oversee church affairs worldwide—but it tends to become an independent force "exercising oversight and authority" over the bishops rather than serving as a supportive organization for them. In addition, the curia's concerns are less pastoral and more legalistic than are those of the bishops. It often does not have the ability to make judgments and advise the pope on matters that more properly belong to a local bishop or a national hierarchy. For example, the way the curia appoints bishops reduces the role of local bishops to an empty formula. Bishops and superiors of religious orders, Quinn said, have sometimes discovered, without prior knowledge or consultation, that a priest under their jurisdiction has been named a bishop. When this happens, "it obscures and diminishes both the doctrine and the reality of episcopal collegiality." He added that the same risk exists in regard to papal nuncios who "can easily assume too great a directive power" in regard to national church affairs. The archbishop also stated that the bishops have a limited role in church teaching. Many bishops feel that issues of major concern in the church—such as contraception, divorce and remarriage, general absolution, the ordination of women, the priest shortage, mandatory celibacy of the clergy—"are not open to free and collegial evaluation and discussion." Decisions are "imposed without consultation with the episcopate and without appropriate dialogue." He said the curia was impeding Christian unity "because of the way issues are dealt with by [it]."

Archbishop Quinn urged that several steps be taken to address and correct some fundamental issues of collegiality. First, he recommended that a commission be created (with a time line of not more than three years) that would consult experts in management, government, theology, canon law and other disciplines to offer reform proposals. These would be presented to the presidents of the episcopal conferences, meeting together for this specific purpose, and finally presented to the pope for approval and implementation. Second, Quinn stated that synods should have a deliberative and not merely a consultative vote on important subjects. The present procedures and structures of the international synods are "outdated and not conducive to collegiality." Third, Quinn said the church should heed the decree of the ecumenical Council of Constance (1415) which called for an ecumenical council every ten years. The regular convening of councils might also bring about a renewed sense of how the bishops and the pope in fact share in a single authority. In addition, there should be a special council "to mark the beginning of the new millennium." At this council bishops could discuss questions unresolved at Vatican II and those doctrinal and moral matters listed above inasmuch as they reflect "the new situation" John Paul spoke of. In short, what Archbishop Quinn said is that the papacy can become an effective sign and tool of Christian unity, if the legitimate authority of diocesan bishops and episcopal conferences is respected.

The archbishop's lecture evoked a wide spectrum of responses. He was denounced, defended, praised, and questioned. Some accused him of disloyalty to the pope for proposing that the local church play more of a role in the selection of bishops. Some defended Quinn by taking issue with those who seriously misrepresented his position (Untener 1996). Many congratulated the archbishop. They regarded his lecture as an enormous service to the church and ecumenism inasmuch as he offered a penetrating and nuanced analysis of the papal ministry today. Others questioned the archbishop's message. Some asked what took the archbishop so long to publicly state his vision. Would he have made the same speech if he were not retired? Why have other bishops not spoken up about the inadequate forms the papacy has taken since Vatican II? Is criticism of papal and curial procedures justified only when it is invited or is it justified whenever these procedures create obstacles to church identity and mission? If bishops can honestly and respectfully raise questions about women's ordination, contraceptives, and so forth, is it not equally true of theologians and other concerned Catholics? In fact, have not theologians already raised these very same issues in Europe through the "Cologne Declaration" of January 27, 1989, and in the United States through the CTSA's "Do Not Extinguish the Spirit" of December 8, 1990?

The exercise of papal power, authority, and jurisdiction continues to be a multifaceted unresolved ecumenical issue.

The Future of the One Church of Christ

In the preconciliar times the Catholic church urged (even demanded) that the other Christian churches return to the Catholic church. This perspective was dictated in good measure by the church's siege mentality and its ecclesiocentric theology. The Catholic church insisted that it was the one true church of Christ because it alone possessed the marks of the church as listed in the Nicene-Constantinopolitan Creed of 381: one, holy, catholic, and apostolic. At Vatican II there was a shift in perspective. The church acknowledged that the other Christian communities already belong to the one church of Christ. This view was based on historical consciousness and a christocentric theology. Nonetheless, the bishops declared that, since the church of Christ subsists in the Catholic church, other communities should be regrafted into the Catholic church.

In the postconciliar church ecumenical theology has taken a theocentric focus: the stress is on the threefold mission of the church to proclaim, manifest, and expand the kingdom of the Father of Jesus Christ.

This mission should be directed to all people, but especially the poor. The meaning of "true church" also shifted. It is now said that any church is true to the extent that it humanizes people's lives, and any church is false to the extent that it contributes to the dehumanization of its members and society. Accordingly, the Catholic church's claim to possess the four marks is relativized by its inner divisions, its sinful members, its overemphasis on its male and clerical members, and its concern at times for its own maintenance and development rather than its threefold mission.

As the churches work toward unity, they are asked to implement two principles. First, unity should be visible with the spiritual dimensions being incarnated in the forms and structures of the churches. This means that all the Christian churches should unite to manifest the holiness of the triune God and to worship this God. Unfortunately, the reports of too many ecumenical meetings read "like negotiations waiting for concessions rather than accounts of meetings seeking common worship" (Van Beeck 1985, 70). Second, visible unity should be such that each church can maintain its distinctive identity, and none would be absorbed by others or all leveled into a synthetic hybrid. When this happens, pluralism and diversity "will become synonymous with 'catholicity'" (Bühlmann 1986, 177). At Vatican II the bishops stated that "in order to restore communion and unity or preserve them, one must impose no burden beyond what is 'indispensable' (Acts 15:28)" (UR 18). Consequently, there is growing support for the model of church unity advocated by William Rusch (1985, 118), Cardinal Ratzinger (Hebblethewaite 1993c), and others: reconciled diversity.

Reconciled diversity protects and fosters the distinctive charisms, disciplines, and traditions of each church. Instances of such reconciled diversity exist. For example, in the Catholic church there are hundreds of religious orders of women and men. The Sisters of Mercy, the Sisters of Charity, Ursulines, Maryknoll Sisters, Carmelites, and the many other communities have their own charisms, traditions, style of dress, and constitutions, yet all work for the threefold mission of the church. Similarly, the communities of men (for example, the Christian Brothers, Benedictines, Jesuits, Dominicans, Franciscans, Holy Cross Brothers) have their own distinctive charisms and traditions, but all imitate Christ and are dedicated to fostering the identity and mission of the church.

Who or what can lead the churches to this reconciled diversity? Presently, this is not clear because the ecumenical movement is in such a serious state of instability that there is a strong call for "a new ecumenical movement" (Heim 1996). There are several reasons for this new situation and new call.

The first concerns the WCC itself. It presently faces two major problems, one financial and the other structural. Financially, the WCC does not have sufficient income to maintain its present level of activities.

There have been losses on investments and a steady decline of the WCC's total income. Some of the largest of the 330 member churches pay little or no dues.[14] Structurally, the WCC is not achieving its goals. As the only global ecumenical structure, it attempts to secure the participation of all the Christian churches. Its positive contributions to ecumenism since 1948 cannot be overestimated. But the WCC has actually failed to fulfill its purpose. Large communities such as the Catholic church, the Southern Baptists, many Pentecostals and other independent churches are not full participants. Furthermore, it is precisely these religious bodies that are experiencing a more dynamic growth than many who are full-fledged members of the WCC. This means that the percentage of Christians belonging to the WCC continues to decline. The WCC can no longer plausibly claim to be the primary, privileged vehicle of Christian unity. Consequently, it has been proposed that it be restructured. For example, Michael Nazir Ali, an Anglican bishop, urged that a new organization be planned to replace the WCC, one whose structures would allow a wider spectrum of Christians to come together.[15] Konrad Raiser proposed a new model for the WCC's identity and mission, what he calls "a new association of ecumenical organizations."[16] The WCC could become the "organizing agent" of a forum in which the WCC would be one member alongside other ecumenical organizations. Although the WCC is still the "most comprehensive" ecumenical body, it "cannot and should not pretend to be its main center." It is time to create "an inclusive framework" for dialogue among all ecumenical partners, including the Catholic church, other nonmember churches, and even international ecumenical organizations that are not actual churches. Examples of the latter include the Lutheran World Federation, the Anglican Communion, and the World Alliance of Reformed Churches. These three organizations often duplicate the work of the WCC. Although they have a close working relationship with the WCC, they are prohibited membership by the WCC constitution. Raiser believes it is time for these organizations to be given a place in the ecumenical movement in their own right.

Many of Raiser's proposals—particularly the replacement of the global assemblies by meetings of a new "global forum of churches and ecumenical organizations"[17]—were brought together for the first time at the end of 1996 in an official document, titled "Towards a Common Understanding and Vision of the World Council of Churches." This draft statement was discussed by the WCC's 156-member central committee in Geneva in September 1997.

A second reason the ecumenical movement is unstable is that "the ground under the movement has shifted" (Heim 1996a). The ecumenical movement emerged in 1910 out of the vitality of the missionary movement with its goal of unity for mission. The missionaries were acutely aware that they could not evangelize the world unless they were united and that they had to give up their "unseemly, wasteful competition" for their own quantitative development. Today, however, the question of mission itself has become one of the sharpest issues dividing the churches. We saw in the previous chapter that there are five distinct views of the universal mediatorship of Christ and that most churches officially limit themselves to one of these theologies. We also saw that evangelization can take place at a human or religious or Christian dimension. Should interreligious unity be primarily religious, "by this means transcending social differences, or should it be primarily a shared social commitment, by this means overcoming 'religious' differences" (ibid.)? Evangelization can hardly take place if the churches themselves are divided about the relationship of Christianity to the other religions.

A third reason the ecumenical movement is unstable is "the lack of a single burning cause that could pull Christians together across contemporary divisions the way that evangelization drew Christians together across denominational borders" in 1910 and 1948 (ibid.). However, it could well be that a "burning issue" came out of the meeting of the Faith and Order Commission in August 1996 in Moshi, Tanzania, namely, ecclesiology, the nature of the church. "The ferment around BEM pointed to a larger question: What is the nature of the church within which baptism, Eucharist and ministry are configured, the body of which they are living parts" (Heim 1996b)?

Conclusion

At the end of this review of the nature and history of ecumenism, several conclusions are in order. First, the Christian religion is composed of many vital communities around the world. However, in view of the deeply entrenched divisions of this religion into Protestant, Anglican, Orthodox, and Catholic branches, it is clear that the religion's principal elements—the institutional, intellectual, and mystical—need radical renewal and reform. This renewal and reform depend in great measure on the response of the churches to the Spirit. No one has addressed this point that ecumenism is both a gift and a task more pointedly than Raymond Brown (1984, 61–74).

In an explanation of Luke-Acts, Brown points out that "the distinguishing feature" of Luke's ecclesiology is "the overshadowing presence of the Spirit." For example, the Spirit directed Peter to the house of Cornelius, inspired Paul and Barnabas to seek out Gentile converts, and led Paul to decide he must go to Rome. But Brown wonders if this account of the many interventions of the Spirit leads easily "to a *deus ex machina* concept of the Spirit," especially with regard to ecumenism. He agrees that the ecumenical movement—from 1910 to 1948 to 1962 to 1982 to the present—is the work of the Spirit. But he points out that we cannot "assume that the Spirit will bring the work to a triumphal conclusion."

Brown shows that the Bible is filled with stories of how the people of God failed to respond to God and paid the price for their failures (e.g., the twelve tribes were reduced to two; religious institutions such as the monarchy and priesthood failed; and "Israel learned more about God in the ashes of the Temple destroyed by the Babylonians than in the elegant period of that Temple under Solomon"). He then concludes with this disturbing question: "If in the next two decades the churches do not seize the opportunity, if a union between two major churches does not take place as a sign of what may be possible, and if consequently Christianity enters the third millennium much more divided than it entered the second millennium, is it not possible, and even likely, that the opportunity will never come again?" (ibid., 72–73).

Second, since there is a scriptural and intrinsic mandate for Christian unity, ecumenism is more than a duty, it is a way of being Christian. A valid litmus test of a Christian's devotion to "the one and only church of Christ" is his or her involvement in ecumenism.

Third, the ecumenical movement has made great strides at the executive levels, especially through the many interchurch dialogues and such outstanding documents as BEM and those produced by ARCIC I. More work has to be done at the parish and congregational levels. For some ecumenists the parish level is "the most crucial area for future development of ecumenical life. . . . Ultimately it is here that Christian unity will or will not happen" (Horgan 1990).

Fourth, since there is only one prayer for Christians—the prayer of Christ as he gives himself to his Father—it is unfortunate that all Christians cannot join together with Christ at the Eucharist. More dialogue is needed about intercommunion. The next chapter will investigate the eucharistic life of the Catholic church and its bearing on the other Christian churches, other religions, and the world.

CHAPTER 8

The Church and Eucharistic Worship

Von Hügel wrote that a religion is as strong as its three principal elements: the institutional, the intellectual, and the mystical or devotional. This chapter and the one that follows explore the mystical or devotional dimension of the church's life, and the contributions of Vatican II, the popes, the people of God, and theologians to its development.

The official, public worship of the church is called liturgy. It is expressed in such rituals as the Mass, the seven ecclesial sacraments, and the divine office. This chapter will not cover the whole liturgical system but will be restricted to a study of the eucharistic liturgy, the heart of the whole liturgy.

Christian life begins for individuals when they are baptized into the life, death, and resurrection of Christ. In the Catholic tradition the seven ecclesial sacraments are celebrations of and participations in the baptismal faith. However, the sacrament most frequently celebrated in the world church is the Eucharist. It is the Eucharist that draws the disciples together for worship, providing nourishment, support, healing, and hope, and from which they go forth to their threefold mission. The bishops at Vatican II reiterated the church's ancient tradition that it is the Eucharist "by which the church continues to live and grow" (LG 26) and the eucharistic celebration is "the center and culmination of the entire life of the Christian community" (CD 30).

Distinctive Characteristics of Christian Worship

There is an ancient saying in the church that is attributed to Prosper of Aquitaine (c. 390–c. 463): *lex orandi, lex credendi*—the "law of worship is the law of belief," implying that worship shapes belief. This aphorism declares that correct belief follows the practice of correct worship, not vice versa. "The way people worship tells us more about their view of the sacred than any other activity. The prayers we use, the clothing we wear, the attitudes we adopt, the buildings we put up—all these are a living source of implicit theology" (Hebblethwaite 1975, 25).

211

First of all, Christian worship begins as a communal response to God's many initiatives. The Father of Jesus Christ creates, covenants, loves, and saves, and still speaks through the scriptures, the community, and the signs of the times. The community responds to the Father's unconditional love by praise, thanksgiving, and supplication with Jesus Christ in the power of the Spirit (Romans 8:26). There is an exchange of gifts: the Father gives us his Son and we in turn join with Christ, the only "holy and perfect sacrifice," as he gives himself back to his and our Father.

Second, Christian worship is sacramental. Just as the Word became flesh, so the word of God comes to us through bread, wine, words, oil, stone, and water, and so on. The word of God speaks to us through the interplay of all these symbols. We, in turn, use the symbols to communicate with God. The worship should reflect the lived and unique social experience of each community.

Third, in Christian worship the church most fully appears as a sacrament of Christ. Gathered around the altar, the community expresses and intensifies what God has done for all people in Jesus Christ. The celebration of the Eucharist is "the principal manifestation of the church" (SC 41). The community not only joins with Christ's commitment of his whole self to his Father but it also recommits itself to its vocation to promote and expand the saving presence of God in family, church, and society by promoting justice, mercy, and compassion.

The Tridentine Rite

The church made its official response to Luther's reformation through the ecumenical Council of Trent, shakily begun under Paul III in December 1545 and successfully concluded under Pius IV in December 1563. At the twenty-five sessions of Trent the bishops solidified the dogmas and disciplines of the church. In 1570, Pius V (1566–72) approved a Mass structured according to the aims of Trent (Jungmann 1951). Until this historic decision, the church knew sixteen centuries of distinct liturgies for different regions, dioceses, and religious orders, each without prejudice to any other. This one liturgy, which Pius V decreed should be prayed "in perpetuity," came to be called the Tridentine rite (also called the Roman Canon or the Missal of Pius V). It could be celebrated as "solemn" or "high" or "low." Nevertheless, there was little variation within each of these forms.

The Mass was said in Latin. The altar was in the very front of the church and there the priest (the celebrant) prayed the Mass with his back to the people. The priest followed detailed instructions (rubrics) about standing, genuflecting, and making innumerable signs of the cross over the objects on the altar. There was always the danger of ritualism, the mere continuation of the external actions without much internal faith.

The Mass had two kinds of prayers: the "ordinary," certain prayers repeated every day of the year; and the "proper," the prayers and readings which changed each day to observe particular feasts.

The scriptural readings played a secondary role. The three most important parts of the Mass began after the sermon: the offertory, consecration, and communion. All that went before these three was preliminary. The congregation received communion by approaching a rail that separated them from the altar. Here the people knelt and waited for the priest to place the consecrated bread on their tongues.

Aside from moving to and from the communion rail, the people were silent and passive spectators who either watched the sacred drama enacted at a distance or spent the time in personal prayer, often to Mary or a favorite saint.

The church buildings were, by today's standards, often gaudy. The altar was decorated with candles and flowers. Around the church were many side altars and statues where people could pray and light candles.

For those who attended with a prayerful attitude, there was a sense of mystery, wonder, and holiness created in part by the silence, the special language, and the decor. People knew they were on holy ground in the presence of the almighty triune God.

The Papacy and Eucharistic Worship: Leo XIII and Pius X

The twentieth century popes were devoted to the Eucharist. Each in his own way underscored the importance of Christian worship, especially attendance at the Sunday liturgy. Leo XIII wrote several encyclicals on the Eucharist. He also instituted a feast of the Holy Family in 1893 and consecrated the entire human community to the Sacred Heart of Jesus in 1900.

Pius X is hailed as a pioneer of the modern liturgical movement because his creative initiatives had far-reaching consequences for the rest of the century.

On November 22, 1903, scarcely four months in office, he issued an instruction on the "Restoration of Sacred Music." Pius, formerly a seminary choir director, offered Gregorian chant as the model for all worship and he used for the first time the liberating words "active participation of the faithful." He wrote that his concern was for "the holiness and dignity of the temple in which our people assemble for the purpose of acquiring that spirit from its first indispensable source, namely, their own active participation in the sacred mysteries and in the solemn public prayer of the church." In 1905, he issued numerous decrees enjoining frequent, even daily, reception of the Eucharist. He pleaded for people to shed their

Jansenist hesitations and scruples about worthiness. (Jansenism was a seventeenth and eigthteenth-century movement in Europe that discouraged frequent communion because its adherents believed only the very holy were worthy of the sacrament.) In 1910, he lowered the age for receiving one's first communion from twelve or thirteen to seven or eight, so that the young would have the benefit of receiving the grace of the Eucharist at an early age. Finally, in 1914, he initiated a revision of the Sunday liturgies so that they would have the precedence they deserved over the feasts of saints.

During Pius's pontificate, the liturgy was being studied intensely in Benedictine monasteries and in academic circles by theologians who investigated the scriptural, historical, and pastoral dimensions of the liturgy. The beginning of the modern liturgical movement is attributed to Lambert Beauduin (1873–1960), a Belgian Benedictine priest who specialized in ecclesiology and ecumenism. In 1909, he read a paper entitled "The Full Prayer of the Church" at a congress at Malines, Belgium, in which he pointed out that in the early church the Mass was the act of the whole Christian people. Active participation of the faithful, he said, was important for the vitality of the people and for the whole church (Sheppard 1967). Another theme of his writings was the unity of life and liturgy. He urged Catholics to bring their sacramental union with God to every action of daily life.

In addition to Beauduin, there were many liturgists and theologians active in the liturgical renewal in the preconciliar period.[1] These scholars contributed to several influential liturgical journals, such as *La Maison-Dieu, Irenikon,* and *Liturgie et Paroises.* The latter, for instance, was read at one time by one of four priests in France and Belgium (K. Hughes 1991, 149). These scholars also held study weeks to discuss liturgical matters. The First International Congress of Liturgical Studies was held in 1951 at Maria Laach, the famous Benedictine monastery in Germany. About forty-five scholars from Germany, France, and Belgium attended to discuss topics like the Easter vigil. In 1952 a congress was held at Strasbourg with nine nations represented. In 1953 a congress held at Lugano, Switzerland, included eight Americans in attendance. These meetings, as well as those held at Louvain (1954), Assisi (1956), Monserrat (1958), and Munich (1960), prepared the church for Vatican II.

In the United States, the liturgical movement was promoted by such pioneers as H. A. Reinhold (1897–1968), Michael Mathis (1885–1960), Gerald Ellard (1894–1963), Reynold Hillenbrand (1905–79), Martin Hellriegel (1890–1981), Godfrey Diekmann (1908–) and Virgil Michel (1890–1938). It is the Benedictine Virgil Michel who is credited with launching the liturgical reform in this country. He was sent to Rome and Louvain to study philosophy for two years (1924–25), but the liturgical movement sweeping across Europe captivated him and he brought the movement back to the United States.

Michel was troubled by the many problems wrought by industrial society and he sought to transform society through Christian values. He claimed that the roots of our social ills were found in individualism and a complacent bourgeois spirit. As a remedy, he proposed greater awareness of human solidarity, the retrieval of the image of the church as the people of God, and the practice of such Christian virtues as sacrifice, simplicity of life, and concern for others. For Michel, liturgy meant community and a concern for others. For him, "the labor encyclicals of Leo XIII and the liturgical reforms of Pius X did not just by accident happen within one generation, but were responses to cries of the masses for Christ who had power and gave good tidings. They belonged together."[2]

Michel considered the worldwide economic depression of the 1930s as a judgment on capitalism. He supported organized labor, the agrarian reform movements, and the opposition to racism. He insisted that the liturgy provided an instrument of social reform. Michel believed that the Mass could counteract the destructiveness of individualism by its communal emphasis. At the Mass, class barriers were transcended since all were admitted equally to the celebration, prayers were said that those in positions of power in society would act justly, and money and goods were collected for the needy and the sick. At the Mass, also, the faithful heard the biblical injunctions to live in solidarity with the poor and to shun a materialistic lifestyle. "But Michel also saw that to accomplish these, the liturgy had to be reformed. It would have to expel clericalism and promote active lay participation, symbolize an authentic community, and inspire service to the world at large" (K. Smith 1988).

To foster these ideas, Michel established The Liturgical Press in 1926 and published the influential journal *Orate Fratres*. He was assisted in 1933 by his pupil and fellow Benedictine, Godfrey Diekmann. When Michel died suddenly after a brief illness in 1938, Diekmann became editor-in-chief. As editor for twenty-five years (1938–63), he gave outstanding leadership to the movement. In 1951, when *Orate Fratres* was in its twenty-fifth year, Diekmann realized how incongruous it was for a journal in the forefront of promoting vernacular worship to have a Latin name. After wide consultation, the name *Worship* was selected.

The United States Benedictines also began a series of study weeks called The Liturgical Week. The inspiration to hold these meetings came from the very successful seminars conducted by their confreres in Belgium. The first was held in Chicago in 1940. Approximately 1,260 persons attended from across the country. These congresses continued until 1968. The impact of those held before Vatican II was uneven due to the war, to policy differences among the administrators, and to changing times. Nevertheless, they prepared many in the United States for the conciliar reforms.

Pius XI and Pius XII

Pius XI initiated the feast of Christ the King in 1925. Commentators see this move as an attempt to counter secularism. Pius believed that the church, the perfect society, should predominate in both the secular and religious spheres since it represented the kingdom of Christ on this earth. Secular society could not bring about the peace and prosperity required for the well-being of the world. Only the Catholic church could. Christ was the true sovereign over all people. Francis X. Murphy judged this thinking to be "a direct throwback to the absolutist claims of Gregory VII and Boniface VIII at the height of the Middle Ages" (1981, 44).

Pius XII published his encyclical *Mediator Dei* on November 20, 1947, the first encyclical ever to concern itself completely with Christian worship. He commended the "dialogue Mass" in which the faithful participated by making the oral responses that would otherwise have been made by the server. He issued two other encyclicals on liturgy: *Sacred Liturgy* (1947) and *On Sacred Music* (1955).

In 1951, Pius XII reformed the entire Holy Week liturgy, especially the Easter vigil. In 1957, he changed the rules of fasting before reception of the Eucharist. Instead of abstaining from food and drink from midnight, one had to fast only an hour before reception. He also allowed evening Mass on feastdays. It has been suggested that Pius's motive might have been to check the exodus from the church rather than to initiate the faithful more closely into liturgical life (Falconi 1967, 284).

In 1956, European liturgists organized the Assisi Congress as a tribute to Pius XII during his eightieth year. This congress gave the liturgical and pastoral leaders of the world the chance to express their gratitude to the pope for his leadership in making the liturgical movement "a *pastoral-liturgical apostolate*" (K. Hughes 1991, 161). Present were six cardinals, eighty bishops and twelve hundred participants from all over the world. Pius XII gave a closing address to the congress in which he referred to the liturgical movement as a sign of God's providential care of his church.

Diekmann and Mathis organized the large United States delegation. According to Diekmann, the real highlight of the meeting was a talk by Bishop Wilhelm van Bekkum, "The Liturgical Renewal in Service of the Missions." The bishop addressed the need of adapting the liturgy to the customs and cultures of peoples (ibid., 165). Since his thesis that the church act like a world church was advanced three years before the announcement of Vatican II, it caused a sensation. There is little doubt today that this talk paved the way for the council and its reforms, liturgical and otherwise.

Vatican II

John XXIII started some liturgical reforms before the council. Specifically, he approved a new code of rubrics on July 25, 1960, which greatly simplified the liturgical calendar, the breviary, and the celebration of the Mass. John said he made these changes because they "should no longer be put off" until the council. In 1962 the Tridentine Mass or Roman Canon was modified. In this Missal of 1962, the vernacular could be used, but the canon continued to be recited in Latin. The priest (the celebrant) and the people did not face each other during the celebration. There were two scriptural readings and only males could assist the priest at the altar.

When the council convened, Pope John selected liturgy as the first topic for major discussion. Vatican II was the "first council to try to think out the liturgy from basic principles" (Hebblethwaite 1975, 31). For many of the bishops it was clear that sacramental reform was indispensable to the renewal of the church.

Two Americans, Godfrey Diekmann and Fredrick McManus, professor of canon law at Catholic University, were invited as consultors to the liturgy committee and as *periti* to the council. They and fifty-three other international liturgists found themselves in the midst of Vatican politics and the tug of war between the traditionalist and the progressive viewpoints. It took the committee more than a year of discussion and debate to resolve such questions as the restoration of a deep love and reverence for the scripture, cultural adaptation of the liturgy, reform of the breviary, and the adoption of the vernacular. The most controversial of these issues was the proposal to permit the recitation of much of the Mass in the vernacular. The traditionalists favored the retention of Latin. They maintained "that Latin is the link that brings all men together in worship. It [was] their contention, too, that in continents with many languages, a babel would result from a vernacular Mass" (Dugan 1962a).

The Constitution on the Liturgy was the first text promulgated by the council. It was approved on November 22, 1963, by a vote of 2,158 to 19 (Jungmann 1969, 1). Of the sixteen documents, no other had such a direct and dramatic impact on the life of Catholics. The document incarnated the spirit of Vatican II, and its reforms enfleshed the council's dream of aggiornamento. It made Vatican II a part of the ordinary life of Christians. Liturgy, it declared, is "the summit toward which the activity of the church is directed; it is also the source from which all its power flows" (SC 10).

As can be seen from its many footnote references to Trent and Pius XII, the document is in continuity with the preconciliar teachings. The bishops wanted sound tradition retained and yet called for legitimate theological, historical, and pastoral progress. Its general objectives were to make the liturgy more dynamic, more simple, more intelligible, and more participatory.

To make the liturgy more dynamic, no "rigid uniformity" should be imposed. The bishops wanted to maintain "the substantial unity of the Roman rite" and yet provide for future "legitimate variations and adaptations to different groups." This formal embrace of the principle of cultural adaptation (and hence of cultural pluralism) was a major innovation within the church. Once the liturgy is based on community response rather than rubric, then certain ideas that Vatican II did not foresee surfaced. How far could cultural adaptation stretch? "It is perhaps the fundamental flaw of the Constitution on the Liturgy that it did not address this question in sufficient depth" (Keifer 1975).

To be more simple and more intelligible, the bishops said, the rites "should be short, clear, and free from useless repetitions. They should be within the people's powers of comprehension, and normally should not require much explanation" (SC 34). The bishops decided that the Latin language was to be preserved, but the competent, territorial ecclesiastical authorities could allow the use of the vernacular. During the council, the bishops of the English-speaking areas of the church organized the International Commission on English in the Liturgy (ICEL) and commissioned it to translate the Vatican's liturgical texts for its people.

In the preconciliar church, the priest and the bread and wine were the dominant symbols of the presence of Christ. The bishops said greater intelligibility would be achieved by rehabilitating the other sacred signs which symbolize the presence of the risen Christ, such as the assembly, the altar, and the scriptures. "Sacred scripture is of the greatest importance in the celebration of the liturgy" (SC 24). The biblical readings should be explained in the homily. "The homily is strongly recommended since it forms part of the liturgy itself. In fact, at those Masses which are celebrated on Sundays and holydays of obligation, with the people assisting, it should not be omitted except for a serious reason" (SC 52). In the preconciliar church the homilies were often topical sermons. Those who objected to the liturgical reforms sometimes called them "Protestant" because of the shift from Latin to the vernacular and because of the retrieval of the scriptures from a minor role to a place of importance.

The bishops agreed that the symbolism of Christ's death and resurrection would be more intelligible if the faithful receive the Lord's body under the bread and wine consecrated at the same sacrifice (SC 55). Communion can be received under both the bread and wine when the bishops think fit. Similarly, the two parts of the Mass, the Liturgy of the Word and the Liturgy of the Eucharist, "are so closely connected with each other that they form but one single act of worship" (SC 56). The faithful will have to be taught "to take their part in the entire Mass." Since every Mass celebrates the memory of Christ's death and resurrection, the feasts of the saints and even of Mary should not take precedence over the feasts which commemorate the very mysteries of salvation (SC 108).

The liturgy has to be more participatory. "In the restoration and development of the sacred liturgy the full and active participation by all the people is the paramount concern, for it is the primary, indeed the indispensable source from which the faithful are to derive the true Christian spirit" (SC 14). All the reforms calling for more dynamism, simplicity, and intelligibility have as their purpose more active participation.

More active participation can develop out of a renewed understanding of the role of the priest. Before Vatican II the priest was called the celebrant. The people "attended to hear" his Mass. After Vatican II, it was stressed that the people "assemble to participate" and the priest is the president of the assembly. Bernard Cooke explained that as presider the priest "has a distinctive and perhaps indispensable role: he voices the people's faith and prayer and symbolizes the link between a given community and the liturgy of the world-wide church. He does this as a member of the community and not as a mediator between the community and God. Christ himself is present as the mediator and member of the community" (1990).

The document said the people "should not be there as strangers or silent spectators" (SC 48). Some studies show, unfortunately, that most Catholics do not have living in the parish their five closest friends. Some have only one or two close friends there. What this means is that when people greet one another with the sign of peace, it is given to a virtual stranger (P. J. Palmer 1986). This puts a strain on participation.

Finally, there is another problem that affects participation. In fact, Joseph Champlin wrote in 1989 that the "most pressing and difficult issue facing pastoral leaders in the church today" is how to respond properly to those Catholics who rarely participate in liturgy yet want to do so on special occasions. He had in mind inactive engaged couples who desire marriage at a Mass and inactive Catholic parents who seek baptism for their child (1989a, 1989b).

Paul VI

Paul VI signed the Constitution on the Liturgy and then set about the task of implementing it. His numerous accomplishments were so outstanding that he will go down in history with Gregory the Great (590–604), Pius V, and Pius X, as one of the great reformers of the liturgy.

In 1964, Paul VI established a concilium (commission) to oversee the liturgical changes called for by Vatican II's Constitution on the Liturgy. In addition, he declared that the Tridentine Mass was no longer the official rite of the Catholic church. In 1966, priest and altar faced the people and churches were renovated. Most gaudy churches soon gave way to spare, uncluttered churches with the altar as the focus of attention. The removal of the altar rail allowed the people to move closer to the altar and their involvement increased when they helped plan the services, read aloud part of the service, and served as eucharistic ministers. In most parish churches communicants now receive the Eucharist standing and in their hands and feed themselves.

In 1965, Paul issued *Mysterium fidei,* an encyclical about liturgical reform and traditional eucharistic doctrine. He reiterated the teachings of Trent about the Eucharist as sacrifice and as the true substantial presence of Christ. Although his terminology is very different from the Constitution on the Liturgy, he made a good defense of the Eucharist as mystery. He urged that eucharistic worship continue "to be the point of convergence of all other forms of piety."

Other musical instruments besides the organ were officially approved in 1968. That year three new canons were introduced as alternatives to the Roman Canon (eucharistic prayer number one). On April 3, 1969, a new Mass order called the Missal of Paul VI was published. It incorporated many of the changes introduced since the council: the priest and people should face each other; there should be three scriptural readings instead of two; and communion can be received under both bread and wine. In addition, it introduced some important changes. It scraped off the stiff crust of rubrics. The 1570 Missal of Pius V had no directions for the people. This one did—the first time in the history of the church that the role of the congregation was spelled out. It also revised the liturgical year, placing emphasis on the central saving actions of Christ and tempering excessive attention to Mary and the saints. On May 8, 1969, the duties of the 1964 committee were subsumed by the newly-created Congregation for Divine Worship and the Sacraments (CDWS).

In March 1970, it was ruled that the Sunday Eucharist could be anticipated on Saturday evening. Also, the scriptural readings were updated. Instead of a one-year cycle of Sunday readings, the new lectionary contained a three-year cycle of readings. Priests were instructed to preach regularly on the biblical readings.

Finally, the council fathers, while in the process of retrieving the Catholic tradition, called for the restoration of two ancient traditions: the catechumenate for adults (SC 64) and the permanent diaconate (LG 29). Both were restored during the pontificate of Paul VI.

On January 6, 1972, in what "represents the most dramatic chapter in the liturgical revolution wrought by the council," the Rite of Christian Initiation of Adults (RCIA) was promulgated (Bokenkotter 1985, 169). One of those who had led the efforts to restore the catechumenate and to establish the RCIA was Christiane Brusselmans (1931–91), a Belgium liturgist and educator (Parker 1992).

The RCIA is the process by which people become members of the Catholic church. Since the process aims at the total formation of the person into the faith community, it covers doctrinal, liturgical, and apostolic matters. At Vatican II the bishops explained that the catechumenate should not consist in "merely an exposition of dogmatic truths and norms of morality, but [should be] a period of formation in the entire Christian life, an apprenticeship of suitable duration, during which the disciples will be joined to Christ their teacher. The catechumens should be properly initiated into the mystery of salvation and the practice of the evangelical virtues, and they should be introduced into the life of faith, liturgy and charity of the people of God by successive sacred rites" (AG 14). The RCIA culminates in the celebration at the Easter vigil of the sacraments of initiation—baptism, confirmation, and Eucharist (Mainelli 1986; Duffy 1987).

Two motives led the bishops to their decision to restore the permanent diaconate: to recover the full range of ordained ministries and to alleviate the priest shortage in mission territories. The bishops listed the pastoral, educational, and eucharistic responsibilities of deacons. Regarding the latter, they said a deacon's task is "to administer baptism solemnly, to reserve and distribute the Eucharist, to assist at and to bless marriages in the name of the church, to take Viaticum to the dying, to read the sacred scripture to the faithful, to instruct and exhort the people, to preside over the worship and the prayer of the faithful, to administer sacramentals, and to officiate at funeral and burial services" (LG 29).

Paul VI promulgated the norms for the restoration of the permanent diaconate in 1967. He stated that the diaconate "is not to be considered as a mere step toward the priesthood but is so adorned with its own indelible character and its special grace" that it is to be considered a "permanent" vocation. The United States bishops approved the restoration in 1968. In 1997 in the United States alone, there were more than eleven thousand deacons and nearly four thousand candidates for ordination.

The Liturgical Reforms Evaluated: 1975–90

Reforms such as the RCIA and the permanent diaconate have revitalized the intellectual and devotional life of the church, especially at the parish level. How effective have all the conciliar reforms been? Periodic evaluations have been made. Here are some examples.

Ten years after Vatican II, Ralph Keifer wrote that our liturgy is in a state of crisis. "The roots of our present crisis is a failure to put the gospel and conversion at the top of our list of liturgical priorities" (1975). According to Keifer, the major liturgical problem is one of spirituality and not the changes in ritual. "The most serious failure . . . has been the failure to develop, articulate, and make pastorally applicable the theology of the paschal mystery which animated liturgical reform in the first place, and which permeates the new rites." The new rites are built around the high Johannine and Pauline christology and ecclesiology, as well as Augustine's theology of grace. But our hymns and homilies, said Keifer, are pervaded with an optimistic humanism which depicts Jesus merely as an ethical example. "There is virtually no connection between the 'community celebration of life' almost totally at the mercy of the celebrant and the corporate Pauline proclaiming the death of the Lord until he comes or the Johannine entry into the liturgy of the heavenly court [see John 17]."

Twenty years after the Vatican II document, Patrick Collins wrote in an essay in 1984 that "No person or single group of persons has all the answers to the problems and questions of liturgical experience." Nevertheless, he went on to say that "what is still needed is a team effort by persons of several disciplines and skills, persons who are experienced in doing liturgy's most appropriate languages: image, symbol, story, and ritual action. Such persons are called artists."

Liturgy is an art. The Mass is a ritual, a dramatic symbolic action of Christ's death and resurrection specified by words. This ritual should be an aesthetic creation designed to set up the conditions for the possibility of religious experience. God is present in and through the people and materials (the sacramental principle). Christians are present at liturgy to encounter God through his Son and in the power of the Spirit. In the Eucharist God heals, teaches, and empowers, sending Christians back to their everyday life to transform the world into the kingdom of God. The Sunday Eucharist should not be an isolated entity, but a bridge to Christian worship and service throughout the week.

Today many complain that the liturgies lack a sense of mystery. Collins and others (see Dinter 1989) admit that the Tridentine rite evoked a sense of mystery—in part because of the special language, the silence, the decor, and the sense of a great distance between God and the people. On the other hand, these liturgists also believe there was a good measure of mystification and misunderstanding. Christ's presence was narrowed to the sacramentality of the priest and the eucharistic species. In the postconciliar church the sense of mystery can be retrieved without losing participation, simplicity, dynamism, and intelligibility by creating better rituals and by appreciating that the eucharistic mystery has been relocated: Christ is directly present in the midst of his people. At Vatican II "The liturgy became the immediate expression of the church as the gathered community" (Hebblethwaite 1975, 33). In other words, the experience of the sacred can be found in the community of disciples as they listen, forgive, celebrate, speak, sing, share the bread and cup, and then plan to share the gospel with the world, especially among the poor and where there are injustices.

Writing in 1988, Mark Searle explained at length that "the liturgical life of the American church is pretty much in the doldrums." He offers several reasons for his judgment. First, he cites symbolic minimalism. The Eucharist for communion is often taken from the tabernacle, the cup is not always available, gospel processions are rare, and the music, while singable, is not suited to the actual liturgy. Second, people still lack a sense of identity and purpose of parish or church. On the one hand, a significant number of parishioners do not know that the liturgy should promote an organic union among the community, and on the other hand, many still "thought that celebrating the liturgy was the most important thing their parish did." Third, in many places the liturgy is still too clerical. It is supposed to be the action of the whole community, but priests still dominate the scene. The community can become subject to his idiosyncrasies or to those of whoever else is in charge.

Mark Searle was convinced that the principal motive for the reform—active participation—was not understood and rarely done. Participation, he insisted, does not mean just "joining in." True participation has been overshadowed by trying to get people to sing. To take part by singing, listening, responding, and offering the sign of peace do not "of themselves constitute the 'active participation' the council had in mind." These activities are intended to "promote" participation. Active participation involves two things: sanctifying action and a social dimension (SC 59). Due to God's grace, the sanctifying action is a conscious and willed encounter with the risen Christ as he gives himself totally to his Father. The social dimension means that this act of worship should manifest itself in social justice. There is an intrinsic link between worship and justice. The liturgical spirit should radiate from the altar to all of life.

To help people participate, said Searle, we need better community and education. It is at the grassroots level that the renewal of liturgy must begin again. Surely, the time has come "to relaunch the liturgical movement." As of now, "there is nothing—or perhaps precious little—in the actual experience itself that suggests to the imagination fascination, wonder, surprise. In the absence of fascination, there is no illumination. . . . Liturgical renewal, I submit, has not even begun. Attempts to use the liturgy to educate, to indoctrinate, to transform character will only postpone the day of authentic renewal of the eucharistic story."

John Egan also evaluated Vatican II twenty years later. He contended in an essay in 1983 that the connection between liturgy and social justice "was entirely missed" by the bishops. He pointed out that *Gaudium et spes* "utterly omits any mention of the place of the liturgy of the church as source and summit of its mission for all humanity." According to Egan, then, the "relationship between liturgical celebration and the practice of justice is probably the most significant question calling for liturgists' attention today."

While both Egan and Searle agreed that the liturgy should radiate from the altar to all the world, especially where there is injustice, they differed about the link made by the council between liturgy and justice. In his presentation, Searle referred to paragraph fifty-nine of the liturgy constitution. However, paragraph fifty-nine does not use the word justice. It says the sacraments dispose the faithful "to practice charity."

Twenty-five years after the council, Andrew Greeley echoed the judgment of those liturgists who judged that the liturgical renewal has yet to begin. Greeley argued that the symbolism was wholly inadequate. For one thing, the eucharistic meal should resemble a common meal. Also, instead of a ritualized relic that needs constant explanation, the Mass had to become a fascinating story (1990b).

John Paul II

The pope is not unaware of the positive and negative results of the conciliar reforms. For example, he directed the Synod of 1983 to address the sacrament of reconciliation with the theme "Reconciliation and Penance in the Mission of the Church." This sacrament has many other names: the sacrament of penance, confession, sacrament of conversion, and the sacrament of forgiveness.

Since Vatican II there has been a noticeable abandoning of the sacrament of reconciliation, that is, one-to-one confession of sins. Several reasons are given for this decline: for many the Sunday Eucharist is a special moment of forgiveness and renewal at the deepest level of their lives; some experience reconciliation during spiritual direction; and some feel reconciled when they hear the good news of God's love and forgiveness in a homily. The synod addressed the ancient practice of individual confession and its infrequent use today, but with little success. There has been no noticeable increase in participation in this sacrament since the synod. Similarly, in an apostolic letter of thirty-seven pages addressed to the world's bishops and priests to mark the twenty-fifth anniversary of the liturgy constitution (May 13, 1989), John Paul insisted that the liturgical reforms must now concentrate on giving Catholics a "deeper grasp" of the meaning of the liturgy, and must now "root out" abuses and "outlandish innovations."[3] He insisted that it is wrong for priests to compose their own eucharistic prayers or to substitute "profane readings for texts from sacred scripture."

On March 15, 1994 (although not made public until a month later), the CDWS informed the national conferences of bishops around the world that girls may assist priests at Mass. The action approved a practice that had become increasingly common in many parishes, particularly in the United States, and which had stirred fierce emotions among many Catholics. The Vatican said each bishop was free to allow or disallow the practice in his diocese.

For those who fear departures from long-established traditions, the approval of altar girls was a bitter defeat. Arguing that the change in church law was misguided, one critic said, "It enshrines into law the principle of disobey and then get your disobedience ratified," while another critic declared that "an uninterrupted 2,000-year-old tradition" was being abolished "in the corridors of the Vatican, by nameless experts and bureaucrats" (D. Gonzalez 1994). Some felt the decision "was a 'loss of face' for priests who held out against altar girls on the grounds of fidelity to the church" (Malcolm 1996). For proponents of expanding women's roles in the church, the approval of altar girls was a small but symbolic victory. Some viewed the approval as a clarification of church law (see canon 230). Others considered it an example of inculturation, the attempt to integrate significant and acceptable cultural values and symbols within liturgical expression.

On March 29, 1994, the CDWS issued a thirty-page instruction, "The Roman Liturgy and Inculturation." This document, while it acknowledged that the liturgy can be enriched by local customs and culture, contains a new set of guidelines and urged caution in implementing changes. The Vatican emphasized that changes involving local languages, music, songs, gestures, art, and dance should "maintain the substantial unity of the Roman rite," and that all "radical" experimentation should be carefully limited and required Vatican approval.

This document appeared shortly before some 230 African bishops assembled on April 10 in Rome for a month-long synod (Henriot 1994; Hebblethwaite 1994a; Edwards 1994a). The official title of the episcopal conference is Symposium of the Episcopal Conference of Africa and Madagascar. (The acronym is SECAM.) Their theme was "The Church in Africa and Her Evangelizing Mission Towards the Year 2000." Hoping that their synod would be the foretaste of a "new Pentecost," the bishops had several agenda items, but the principal issue was inculturation, that is, making the church more genuinely African, especially with regard to such issues as liturgy, marriage, priestly celibacy, and reverence for ancestors (Edwards 1994b).

Some Africans viewed the Vatican document on liturgy and inculturation as a preemptive strike limiting the freedom of the synod. Others saw it as a stepping-stone to the emergence of new rites. African churches presently use several rites: the ancient Coptic rite is still used in Egypt and Ethiopia, and the Vatican approved a rite for Zaire in 1982.

The African synod discussed inculturation at length. The bishops agreed that hand in hand with the proclamation of Christ goes inculturation, for evangelization "is a dialogue of love of which the inculturation of the message is the necessary second moment." But, since Africa is a continent of fifty-three nations and numerous cultures, it was not possible for the synod to come up with practical answers on inculturation. The bishops did propose to set up commissions on inculturation in all their dioceses (Reese 1994a, 1994b).

When John Paul visited three African countries—Cameroon, South Africa, and Kenya—in September 1995, the focus was the pope's post-synodal document, *Ecclesia in Africa*, which summed up the themes of the

1994 synod. This 149-page text outlined a plan of evangelization "to the millions of people in Africa who are not yet evangelized." The pope noted that "inculturation is a difficult and delicate task, since it raises the question of the church's fidelity to the gospel and the apostolic tradition amidst the constant evolution of cultures." While in Cameroon, the pope said inculturation was essential to the church's future growth in Africa. "However, he stayed away from detailed discussion of specific liturgical and sacramental debates that arose at the synod" (Thavis 1995, 5).

To date, three serious problems have affected John Paul's pontificate: the priest shortage, the schism of Archbishop Marcel Lefèbvre in 1988, and the English translation of liturgical texts.

The Priest Shortage

Vatican II produced two decrees on the priesthood. These documents reflect the compromises discussed earlier. On the one hand, the bishops reiterated some preconciliar views of priesthood. The priest is one set apart to offer the eucharistic sacrifice in the name of the whole church (PO 3). This is the priest's "principal function" (PO 13). The priest is a delegate of the bishop (PO 5) and enjoys authority within the hierarchy of the church. On the other hand, the bishops described a different understanding of priesthood. They underscored the close union between bishops and priests, the pastoral (rather than cultic) roles of the priest, and the priest's participation in the office of Christ through the ministry of the gospel. The bishops wrote that "it is the first task of priests as co-workers of the bishops to preach the gospel of God to all" (PO 4). As pastor, the priest should be an enabler of the people, a servant of the needy, and a minister to the wider church and society. As celibates, priests are called to be models of abstinent chastity (PO 16). At the council there was no debate about priestly celibacy because Paul VI forbade it in a letter dated October 10, 1965. He wrote: "It is not opportune to debate publicly this topic which requires the greatest prudence and is so important. Our intention is not only to preserve this ancient law as far as possible, but to strengthen its observance." Neither did the bishops address the priest shortage. In fact, there is only a footnote reference to this issue in the decree on the formation of priests (OT 2).

The priest shortage is not that new. We have seen that the reason Pius XI called for the development of Catholic Action in 1922 was the priest shortage. Nevertheless, the current priest shortage in the global church is alarming. Between 1969 and 1985, as a result of retirements, withdrawals, and deaths, the number declined from 425,000 to 399,000 (Gaine 1991, 246–281). In the United States in 1966 there were 35,000 diocesan priests serving 45 million Catholics; it is estimated that in 2005 there will be 21,000 priests serving 74 million Catholics (Schoenherr 1995). Presently, about 10 percent of the parishes are priestless. The priest shortage might be the most serious problem facing the institutional and devotional church, and, given the steady decline in the number of seminarians, there is no solution in sight.

What are the reasons for the current priest shortage? The causes are many and are interrelated: the rejection by a large segment of the Catholic population of the image of the priest as one set apart to serve as the mediator between a transcendent God and humanity (Schmitz 1996); the development of an understanding of church that includes many paths to ministry and holiness; an increased awareness of the vocation of married and family life; the challenge of questions raised by a wholesome feminism; the tarnished image of priesthood due to criminal and sexual conduct on the part of some clergy; the toll taken by controversy and conflict within the church; and the requirement of celibacy.

At the international Synod of 1990 on the priesthood, the delegates discussed the formation of candidates for the priesthood, as well as the "identity crisis" and "burnout" said to be afflicting many priests. "But church leaders made it clear that a few fundamental aspects of the problem are not debatable, notably priestly celibacy and the prohibition against ordaining women and married men" (Haberman 1990b; see 1990c). Nevertheless, the possibility of ordaining women and married men continues to be discussed.

Edward Schillebeeckx addressed the priest shortage in a book which brought him into conflict with Rome (1981b). His principal contention—based on the fact that the right of the faithful to have the Eucharist is absolutely fundamental—was that local communities have both the ability and the responsibility to appoint their own presiders in cases where a serious lack of ministers occurs. The CDF directed the Dominicans to investigate the book. A group of Flemish and Dutch Dominicans found Schillebeeckx's thesis "dogmatically possible and pastorally necessary" (Willems 1987, 217). Rome was not satisfied, declaring that Schillebeeckx's conclusions were not in agreement with Vatican II.

At any rate, the problem persists, even intensifies. Some groups have boldly made public their solution: they have allowed nonordained to preside at a liturgy—not only Catholic men and women but even persons not Catholic (Timmerman, Zahn, and Baldovin 1988).

The growing phenomenon of a priest shortage and Sundays-without-Eucharist prompted several episcopal conferences to petition Rome for guidelines for communion services conducted by nonordained Catholics. Four guidelines were issued in the fall of 1988 by the CDWS. (1) Only one such service can be held each Sunday. The altar should be used only at the distribution of communion. (2) The service must be led by a deacon. If a deacon is not available, the service can be conducted by a lector or acolyte. (3) No Sunday communion service may be held if a Saturday vigil

Mass is celebrated. (4) Local episcopal conferences have the option to deviate from these standard procedures if local customs so require.

The Vatican document has temporarily alleviated the serious situation. Several issues, however, continue to receive discussion because, given the present low pool of priestly candidates, this is a problem that is going to get worse.

First, the relationship of the "ministerial or hierarchical priesthood" (based on ordination) to the "common priesthood of the faithful" (based on baptism) needs greater clarification. At Vatican II the bishops said both are interrelated, but "they differ essentially and not only in degree" (LG 10). This distinction is not easy to explain. Nonetheless, John Paul II continues to insist on it. He has warned of the dangers of "clericalizing the laity" and "laicizing the clergy" (Hebblethwaite 1994b). He stresses that the special mission of the laity is not in the church but in society. He cautions against the laity becoming too involved in inner church matters to the neglect of their involvements in family, work, and society. Although the laity derive their mission in society directly from Christ and his Spirit, when they perform ministries within the church they are assisting the priests in a sphere that is not properly their own. The laity's role is to help the priests do the work of the church. A pastoral view of priesthood claims the contrary: the priest's role is to help the laity do their work in society.

Second, many people often cannot tell the difference between a communion service (the reception of the Eucharist at a worship service) and the eucharistic celebration (when the bread and wine are consecrated at a Mass). Communion services are sacramental, but they are not eucharistic celebrations. At the Eucharist the fourfold action of taking, blessing, breaking, and sharing of the bread and wine is the symbolic representation of Christ's death. The distinctive dimension of eucharistic worship is to unite one's whole heart and being with the risen Christ who is forever fixed in the act of redeeming us. If the distinction between a communion service conducted by a deacon or nonordained minister and the eucharistic celebration presided over by a priest is not maintained, Catholics could very well assume a congregational character or hold worship services similar to those of evangelical Protestants. Their services are neither sacramental nor eucharistic. Rather, they focus on a very personal spirituality: a personal conversion to Jesus as savior, a personal but prayerful interpretation of the scripture, and group services of enthusiastic singing with fervent preaching.

Third, often (and unfortunately), some Sunday Eucharists at which priests preside actually move in the direction of communion services (Huck 1989). This occurs when the eucharistic prayer is not the central deed of assembly and presider together, and when the bread that some or all the people share in communion is previously consecrated bread taken from the tabernacle and not what the priest and people prayed over. Vatican II called this latter procedure "the more perfect form of participation in the Mass" (SC 55). In other words, individual reception of the Eucharist follows from the community action. It is the celebrating of Eucharist and not receiving communion that is the source and summit of the church's life (McClory 1995).

The priest shortage is a serious problem. However, Sunday-without-priests points to the deeper and more crucial issue: Sunday-without-Eucharist. Devoid of the eucharistic celebration, Christian community makes no sense. The conciliar bishops declared: "No Christian community is built up which does not grow from and hinge on the celebration of the most holy Eucharist. From this all education for community spirit must begin. This eucharistic celebration, to be full and sincere, ought to lead on the one hand to the various works of charity and mutual help, and on the other hand to missionary activity and the various forms of Christian witness" (PO 6).

Archbishop Marcel Lefèbvre

Lefèbvre (1905–91), a soft-spoken but stubborn Frenchman, became famous when he publicly denounced Vatican II, Paul VI, and John Paul II. He became a thorn in the side of Paul VI, accusing him of "philo-Lutheranism" and "Masonic behavior." In 1986, he charged John Paul with indifferentism for visiting the Roman synagogue on April 13 and for organizing the meeting on October 27 at Assisi with one hundred representatives of other religions (Hebblethwaite 1988b). John Paul was forced to announce his automatic excommunication in 1988.

The career and teachings of Lefèbvre are worth reviewing because they touch on every major issue in the previous chapters: modernity, tradition, Vatican II, the identity and mission of the church, papal and conciliar authority, religious freedom and pluralism, ecumenism, and liturgical inculturation.

Lefèbvre obtained doctorates in both theology and philosophy before his ordination in 1929 as a member of the community of the Holy Ghost Fathers. He served in French colonial Africa for thirty years, during which time he was consecrated the archbishop of Dakar, Senegal, in 1955. He resigned from the diocese in 1962 to become superior general of his religious community and, as such, participated in the four sessions of Vatican II. He refused to sign several conciliar documents: those on the church, the church in the modern world, and religious liberty.

His term as superior general concluded in 1968, when the general chapter of the Holy Ghost Fathers, embarrassed by his views about Vatican II, did not renew his mandate. He then began actively to oppose the reforms of the council, especially in liturgical and ecumenical questions, and in 1970, founded his own organization of priests, the Fraternity of St. Pius X, with its own seminary in Econe, Switzerland.

The Fraternity was given canonical approval on November 1, 1970, but this was withdrawn in May 1975 after Lefèbvre refused to obey Paul VI's request that he stop his bitter denunciations of Vatican II and stop advocating private celebrations of the Tridentine rite. In June 1977, he was suspended for unauthorized ordinations to the priesthood. Between 1974 and 1979, he illegally ordained some ninety priests.

In October 1984, the Vatican approved limited use of the Tridentine rite. This decision was seriously criticized by most liturgists and bishops because it both gave support to those who have resisted liturgical renewal and violated the collegial sense of the worldwide episcopate. At that time, 98 percent of the bishops had indicated that allowing the Tridentine rite was unnecessary (Hebblethwaite 1984d). For moderates, on the other hand, this approval was a timely concession designed to take the wind out of Lefèbvre's sails.

The pope's concession did not work. On June 30, 1988, without Vatican approval, Lefèbvre ordained four bishops at Econe. He was automatically excommunicated in accordance with church law (see canon 1382). His schism—a word that literally means "to set up a rival altar"—was the first since 1870, when the Old Catholics, many of them French, Dutch, and German, left the church after Vatican I had adopted the doctrine of papal infallibility. Lefèbvre said: "I prefer to be in the truth without the pope than to walk a false path with him." His reason for ordaining the four bishops was his fear of a communist takeover of Europe. Such an eventuality would cut Europe off from the rest of the world. Since one bishop was from Connecticut and another from Buenos Aires, they would be able to carry on the cause (Hebblethwaite 1988b).

The four bishops were also excommunicated, although they were legally bishops in the eyes of Rome. The other followers of Lefèbvre, including some 250 priests, were told they would be excommunicated only if they "knowingly" embraced the archbishop's schismatic practices. Since then, the Vatican policy of leniency and flexibility has led many of Lefèbvre's followers to return to Rome. In fact, the day after Lefèbvre's excommunication, John Paul issued *Ecclesia Dei*, a document that urged bishops to make the Tridentine rite available for those who wanted it. This was John Paul's way of reaching out to traditionalist Catholics who were alienated and/or withdrawing from the church. The pope encouraged the bishops to give "new awareness" to the Roman rite, noting its "richness," and he urged Catholics to see the revival of the Tridentine rite not as a challenge but rather as part of "that blended 'harmony' which the earthly Church raises up to heaven under the impulse of the Holy Spirit." A dozen priests and some seminarians subsequently withdrew from Lefèbvre's community and formed a new religious order, the Priestly Fraternity of St. Peter. With Vatican approval, the order trains men who prefer to offer Mass and the sacraments in the traditional Latin rite (Liberatore 1994). Their superior general is Joseph Bisig and their headquarters are in Germany. In 1994 they had enough candidates to open a seminary in Scranton, Pennsylvania.

We referred earlier to John Paul's apostolic letter of May 13, 1989, marking the twenty-fifth anniversary of the council's document on the liturgy in which he reprimanded those on the left who composed their own eucharistic prayers and introduced unauthorized readings. However, the real target of the letter was the right: Lefèbvre and his priests who regarded "religious practice as a private affair" and who rejected "fuller and more active participation" in the liturgy (Hebblethwaite 1989d). Lefèbvre and his followers promoted private celebration of the Tridentine rite. John Paul said "private" liturgical acts had no validity. The liturgy, he stated, belongs to the whole church and is regulated in its name by the hierarchical authority. John Paul declared that no one has permission to say the Tridentine Mass privately.

In general, Lefèbvre opposed the advances initiated by and following after Vatican II. As just discussed, Lefèbvre canonized the Tridentine Latin rite, insisting it is the one and only Mass for all times, in keeping with Pius V's decree that the rite must be maintained "in perpetuity." Lefèbvre called the Missal of 1962 "a bastard rite" and a "Protestant rite" that failed to convey the eucharistic doctrines of the church as formulated by the Council of Trent (Dinges 1988). The Tridentine rite leaves the Mass in the hands of the priest as the principal celebrant. It does not allow the laity to publicly read the scriptures, to administer communion, and, as the assembly, to be the celebrant.

It has been pointed out that the liturgy was "the medium, not the cause, of his ongoing conflict with Vatican authorities" (ibid.). Lefèbvre's real argument was not with the so-called abuses, distortions, or misrepresentation of Vatican II. Rather, it was the official church's acceptance of modernity.

Lefèbvre extolled not only a Counter-Reformation ecclesiology but also the political and social system of France before the Revolution of 1789. He believed all of France's problems, especially liberalism, socialism, communism, and modernism, originated with the French Revolution (Reese 1988). These three—religious liberty, ecumenism, and collegiality—were the religious equivalents of the French Revolution's tripartite slogan, "Liberty, equality, fraternity." Lefèbvre once said, "Vatican II is 1789 in the church" (P. Steinfels 1989). In addition to the French Revolution, Lefèbvre also repudiated the Protestant Reformation. He called both "the twin progenitors of secularization, pagan nationalism, scientific humanism and the apotheosis of the 'rights of man'" (Dinges 1988). According to Lefèbvre, the false principles—Protestantism, liberalism, and modernism—of these two revolutions were assimilated into the church at Vatican II. Lefèbvre asked a reporter: "Why should I submit to modernists and liberal-communist conciliar reforms?" (Hebblethwaite 1979a). Consequently, Lefèbvre opposed interreligious dialogue and ecumenism. He rejected universal religious liberty, since it denies a privileged position to the Catholic church. He declared that both the regular and wider ecumenisms lent credibility to "false" religions and churches.

Since 1965, Lefèbvre had repudiated Vatican II in lectures, sermons, and a 1976 book, *I Accuse the Council!* In a 1970 profession of faith, he declared: "We refuse, and have already refused, to follow the Rome of neo-modernists and neo-Protestant leanings. These are quite obvious in Vatican II and in the reforms that followed that council. . . . It comes from heresy and will finish in heresy, even if in all its stages it is not formally heretical" (Hebblethwaite 1987c).

Lefèbvre also questioned the identity of the postconciliar church, which he declared false. He claimed that his Fraternity was the true church, a faithful remnant holding fast to the church's true identity. The Roman church was rampant with error and heresy and made up of many of its enemies—such as the Freemasons, whom Lèfebvre believed were responsible for many of the conciliar reforms.

Authority was another issue that divided Lefèbvre from Rome. Being an integralist, he declared collegiality an error. He repudiated the exercise of papal authority in communion with all the bishops. He repudiated the exercise of authority by popes and a universal council. He taught that his view of the Catholic church was the only acceptable alternative to the church of Vatican II. In short, Lefèbvre created a sect. And, as in the case with all sectarian virtuosi, Lefèbvre presented his actions as something pristine and uncorruptible—proclaiming that he, and he alone, had continuity with the true church and the authenticity of the faith. Ostensibly, Lefèbvre challenged Vatican II's most visible reform, the new liturgy. Ultimately, his conflict with the Vatican was not first and foremost a battle over which rite is correct. The archbishop challenged "not the factual wisdom of Roman practice, but rather the very principle of whether Rome [had] the authority to legislate in liturgical and doctrinal matters."[4] Lefèbvre failed to realize that the church's tradition is not a set of answers found in books. Rather, it is an experience embodied in the living community of the church and in the bishops who, collegially, are entrusted with its oversight. He thought he was orthodox because he appealed to long-dead popes like Pius V against living ones, specifically Paul VI and John Paul II.

John Paul II was seriously disturbed by the public conflicts with Lefèbvre. In his traditional "state of the church" address at the end of 1988, John Paul listed the many good things that had happened during the year and then said there were "two shadows" which caused him "deep hurt."

The second was the weak resistance of the Anglican Archbishop Ronald Runcie to the ordination of women as priests and even bishops. The first was the schism of Lefèbvre (Hebblethwaite 1989a). When Lèfebvre died on March 25, 1991, John Paul prayed for his well-being, entrusting him "to the mercy of God" (Greenhouse 1991).

Gender-inclusive Language in the Liturgy

With the advent of the feminist movement many women and men have become sensitive to language in daily speech, liturgy, and official documents, especially the scriptures. It has become clear that "men and women hear the same words differently and process them differently" (Clifford 1995).

Language is described as inclusive and exclusive. Inclusive language incorporates all people without regard for race, creed, age, or gender; exclusive language omits some people for one or more of these aforementioned reasons, especially gender.

The English language has changed so much that words that once referred to all human beings are increasingly taken as gender-specific and consequently, exclusive. Nouns such as *men, sons, brothers, fraternity, brotherhood,* and pronouns and adjectives such as *he, his,* and *him,* which were once understood as inclusive, generic terms, today are often understood as referring only to males. This explains, for example, why Paul's words "For all who are led by the Spirit of God are sons of God" (Romans 8:14) can be translated in this way: "For those who are led by the Spirit of God are children of God."

Inclusive language that refers to human beings is called "horizontal inclusive language." To make exclusive language inclusive is often easy to do. For example, "Happy the man who follows not the council of the wicked" (Psalm 1:1) becomes inclusive when translated as "Happy those who do not follow the council of the wicked." On the other hand, if a text (a document or a period piece or a standard work) is so historically conditioned that it cannot be changed, it seems best to no longer use it. Many hymns, for instance, contain not only outdated or incorrect theology but also exclusive or obscure language. An instance of a hymn that fails on both these counts is the eighteenth-century English Christmas carol, "God Rest You Merry, Gentlemen." The words "rest you merry" in the opening clause mean "give or provide peace" and the address to "gentlemen" slights women.

Language that refers to God is called "vertical language." To make this language inclusive or neuter is very difficult for several reasons. First, the Bible was written within a patriarchal culture, one which fostered male superiority, grounded authority in physical power, and structured society hierarchically (Cooke 1983). As a result, male imagery has been used almost exclusively for God in theology and liturgy for the past two thousand years. God has been called king, judge, lord, warrior, and father (ibid.). It is not easy for many to get beyond these male metaphors. Second, Jesus called God "Father." This metaphor is used about 25 times in the Hebrew scriptures and occurs about 170 in the gospels, 109 of these in the gospel of John alone (Cort 1995). This makes it difficult for many to call God "Mother." Third, some recommend that God be worshiped by such gender-free terms as Creator, Holy One, Source of Being, Ground of Being, or Loving Being. Many find these metaphors hard to reconcile with the personal God of the Bible.

Aware of both the many linguistic, social, religious, and political problems involved in translating official texts into a modern idiom and the importance of inclusive language for the postconciliar church's intellectual, devotional, and institutional life, the United States bishops approved in November 1990 the final text of a document that explained the criteria for the use of gender-inclusive language in the liturgy (Jensen 1994). The document has a long title: *Criteria for the Evaluation of Inclusive Language Translations of Scripture Texts Proposed for Liturgical Use.* The bishops explained that the use of words that were once understood in inclusive, generic terms but are now understood as gender-specific terms "has become ambiguous and is increasingly seen to exclude women. Therefore, these terms should not be used when the reference is meant to be generic" (n. 18).

The New Revised Standard Version (NRSV) of the Bible is a translation that incorporates horizontal inclusive language. This translation is an ecumenical project inasmuch as the NCC owns the copyright and several Catholic scholars participated in its production. The NRSV has been widely accepted because of its fidelity to the meaning of the scriptural authors. It has also been used by Canadian Catholics in their liturgies since 1992.

The NRSV, a lectionary for Sundays and feast days that uses inclusive language, and the revised Psalter (a book containing the Book of Psalms) of the *New American Bible (NAB)* were approved for liturgical use by the National Council of Catholic Bishops (NCCB) in November 1991 by a vote of 192 to 24. The CDWS announced in May 1992 that the inclusive Psalter had been approved, but said nothing about the lectionary. In June 1992 the bishops approved an inclusive weekday lectionary and sent it to the CDWS. However, in June 1994, the CDWS revoked its approbation of the Psalter; nothing was said about the lectionaries. The CDWS later acknowledged that the revocation came from the CDF. The latter judged the Psalter, the NRSV, and the *NAB* unacceptable for liturgy (and catechetics) because some of their inclusive language was deemed incompatible with the Catholic theological tradition. It also declared that the approval given in 1992 by the CDWS had not been "definitive."

This decision of the CDF was welcomed by some and denounced by others. Each side had its arguments. First, the opponents of inclusive language declared that there is but a small number of "radical feminists" who insist on inclusive language. The proponents argue that virtually every publication in the English language now requires their contributors to employ inclusive language. In addition, Vatican II said the scriptures should have a paramount place in the liturgy. This cannot happen if many are turned off by exclusive language. Furthermore, the 1993 document from the PBC, *The Interpretation of the Bible in the Church*, regards biblical translations as an aspect of inculturation. The document declares that "the passage from one language to another necessarily involves a change of cultural context; concepts are not identical and symbols have a different meaning, for they come up against other traditions of thought and other ways of life" (IV.B). In short, inclusive language has become a necessity in today's American idiom.

Second, opponents maintain that inclusive language is a clear and present danger to the deposit of the faith and it leads to doctrinal deviations. They maintain that the CDWS and ICEL have gone beyond the true intentions of Vatican II. The Jesuit Joseph Fessio and his organization Adoremus (Adoremus: Society for the Renewal of the Sacred Liturgy) call for a complete rethinking and authentic renewal of the liturgical reforms. Their position is described as "reforming the reforms" (Mannion 1996). The proponents of inclusive language challenge their opponents to provide even one specific example of doctrinal deviation. They point out that the United States bishops have been waiting since May 1992 for a final approval from Rome of the translations. If these books contain doctrinal errors, these should certainly be clarified as soon as possible.

Third, opponents maintain that inclusive language is a ploy used by those who want to be politically correct, that is, they want to avoid language that would offend any and every class of people—women, minorities, the disabled, and so forth. The proponents insist that their translation not only follows the bishops' *Criteria*, but also "is only moderately inclusive, and in many ways returns to more traditional diction" (Jansen 1996).

Others were disappointed with the CDF decision for different reasons. Some pointed out that more fundamental than the inclusive-language question is the issue of collegial authority in the church. The decision of the CDF once again raised questions about the nature and exercise of episcopal authority. In practice, the CDF decision relegates the bishops to mere delegates of the pope (T. Fox 1994c). The Catholic Biblical Association (which has some eighteen hundred members) wrote the president of the NCCB saying they considered the treatment of the bishops in this matter "demeaning" because the action of the Vatican suggests that the episcopal conference is "not able to determine what is doctrinally sound and pastorally appropriate." But others went farther. They confronted the bishops themselves, challenging them to deal with their own exercise of teaching authority (Huck 1994). A full-page and hard-hitting editorial in the *National Catholic Reporter* declared that "As for the lay perception of the United States episcopacy, suspicion grows that for complex reasons involving in part a sense of loyalty, in part a lack of courage and in part ecclesial ambition, the church has been left largely shepherdless."[5]

In November 1994 the United States bishops accepted Rome's decision on the Psalter, but proposed a meeting with Vatican officials to clarify the reasons for the revocation and to learn the status of the lectionaries. A delegation of United States bishops had a "productive" meeting in Rome with Vatican officials and several scripture scholars but offered nothing substantive to report. In December 1996, seven United States cardinals went to Rome to urge the Vatican to conclude the process for confirmation of the lectionaries sent in 1991 and 1992. In February 1997, three American archbishops met in Rome with Vatican officials and announced an agreement in principle on a revision of the two lectionaries (McClory 1997). The new lectionaries will employ a "moderate degree of horizontal inclusive language." This means that gender neutral terms will be used for human beings (for example, *people* rather than *man; humans* instead of *man*). Rather than asking, "What does it profit a man to gain the whole world ?", Jesus asks "What does it profit a human being to gain the whole world?" (Mark 8:36). On the other hand, all vertical references—those to God and Christ—will be maintained unambiguously in male form (ibid.).

The CDWS's terms represent a compromise between the United States bishops and the Vatican. They also supersede the bishops' *Criteria* established in 1990. The head of the CDWS gave assurances that he would endorse the translations if the bishops accepted them.

In June 1997, the bishops debated the CDWS's compromise texts for about three hours. When the 120 bishops present voted on the resolution to accept the Vatican's versions of the lectionaries, they did not reach the minimum two-thirds required for the passage. They then moved to poll some fifty bishops who did not attend the meeting (Clark 1997).

Perhaps anticipating the outcome, the bishops made it clear that they regard the new lectionaries only as less-than-satisfactory interim texts to be used only until they can get a better translation. They also authorized that a full review of the lectionaries be made in five years with a view to their possible updating. In addition it was strongly recommended that a summary of the reasons for wanting the lectionaries to be improved again soon be forwarded to the CDWS.

During the debate several bishops urged rejection of the Vatican texts because they are not "pastorally helpful," i.e., they are "not inclusive enough," are not as "thoughtful and consistent" as the 1991 and 1992 lectionaries, are not in keeping with the advancements in scholarship and changes in the country's parishes," and are "out of touch with the pastoral reality we face" (ibid.).

In Von Hügel's terms, the debate about the use of gender-inclusive language in the scriptures and the lectionaries is more than a devotional or liturgical issue. It also involves such institutional and intellectual issues as collegiality, subsidiarity, ecclesiology, and inculturation.

The Liturgical Reforms Evaluated: 1991–97

M. Francis Mannion, priest-liturgist from Salt Lake City, Utah, outlined in a seminal essay in 1996 "five identifiable liturgical movements in the United States." He emphasized that the five liturgical agendas "are not entirely separate, free of overlap or mutually exclusive. While there exists a considerable variety of opinions and commitments in the perspectives I shall identify, it can be readily admitted that some elements of difference are more a matter of emphasis or of priority than of fundamental principle. At the same time the differences between the various agendas should not be underestimated."

Four of these movements have already been described in this chapter. The first is the official reforms of Vatican II promulgated through the CDWS. As we have seen, the CDWS's goals are the goals of the conciliar Constitution on the Liturgy, namely, the renewal of active participation and the reestablishment of diverse ministerial roles within the worshiping community. In addition, the CDWS attempts to ground liturgical life in trinitarian doctrine, christology, ecclesiology, and eschatology. Its efforts have taken concrete form in the nearly thirty liturgical books revised since Vatican II—and as these have been translated by ICEL.

The second liturgical movement is that of the "restorationists," that is, those who reject the reforms of Vatican II and the CDWS. Included in this group, but with each having its own agenda, are those who carry on Lefèbvre's Fraternity of Pius X, the Priestly Fraternity of St. Peter, and that "indeterminate body of Catholics who have learned to live with the Mass of 1969, but whose preference would be for the Tridentine Mass" (Mannion 1996).

The third group embraces the vision of Vatican II but claims that the reforms of the CDWS and ICEL have destroyed the Roman Canon. Joseph Fessio, and others, expecially members of Adoremus: Society for the Renewal of the Sacred Liturgy, maintain that the bishops have both abdicated their authority to specialists and scholars and have capitulated to the demands of radical feminists and others like them. The "reformers of the reform" call for a modification of the Missal of 1962 in light of the conciliar document on the liturgy. Their guiding principle comes from Vatican II: "There must be no innovations unless the goal of the church genuinely and certainly requires them, and care must be taken that only new forms adopted should in some way grow organically from forms already existing" (SC 23). Consequently, many in this group propose "the restoration of the recitation of the canon in Latin; exclusive use of the

Roman Canon; the restriction of communion to one species; priest and people facing in the same direction during the eucharistic liturgy; the use of two scripture readings instead of three; and the exclusive use of men in liturgical ministries" (ibid.).

The agenda of the fourth group calls for the continued inculturation of the liturgy by adapting the officially revised liturgical rites and texts to the various cultures of the world. The principal scholarly forum espousing the program of inculturation in the United States is the North American Academy of Liturgy. In the United States most parishes fall into this movement inasmuch as serious attempts are made to make the liturgy relevant to the community.

In 1995, Mannion founded the Society of Catholic Liturgy and inaugurated a fifth agenda. He accepts Vatican II and the work of the CDWS but advocates "recatholicizing the reform." He admits this term "is not a very elegant expression." But he uses it to invoke the understanding of "catholicity" found in such theologians as Henri de Lubac and Avery Dulles (1985a, 1988a). "Recatholicization means renewing the spiritual, mystical and devotional dimensions of the revised rites." It seeks to recover the sacred and the numinous in liturgical expression in order to correct "the sterility and rationalism of much modern liturgical experience." It desires to renew the praise-filled character of worship in order to correct present-day liturgies of their "excessively pragmatic, didactic and functional conceptions." In short, "spiritual rather than structural" reform is "the principal challenge of ongoing liturgical reform."

Mannion compares his agenda with the other four. He accepts the official reforms but believes they are "excessively academic in inspiration and in need of some correction." He is less concerned with further structural reform of texts, rites, and symbols than he is with spiritual reform. Mannion approves what the restorationists teach about the Catholic ethos of worship, but rejects their structural proposals. He endorses the warnings about the dangers of discontinuity in the postconciliar era coming from those who want to reform the reforms of the CDWS. He favors inculturation, especially the concern to engage the rich spirituality of other cultures, particularly the Hispanic, Native-American, Asian, and African-American cultures. He fears, however, that inculturating the reform can be inadequately attentive to the possibilities of cultural compromise of liturgical practice and spirituality. In short, "the recatholicizing agenda is primarily committed to a vital recreation of the ethos that has traditionally imbued Catholic liturgy at its best—an ethos of beauty, majesty, spiritual profundity and solemnity."

There is much to praise in Mannion's emphasis. It is rooted in an ancient tradition of the church: we attend liturgy not to learn something but to deepen our relationship with the triune God and his people. This deepening occurs when people have a religious experience. This entails getting beyond the public verbalization and explanation of the faith found in scripture and tradition to the spiritual meaning of the scripture and tradition. This meaning, since it can only be apprehended and expressed in symbolic form, can never be fully comprehended or be given complete intellectual expression. We are not able to express clearly and logically such religious concepts (or truths) as the Trinity, resurrection, and incarnation since these concepts refer to realities that lie beyond the reach of words. These transcendent realities can only be suggested in the symbolic gestures of the liturgy. Trinity, resurrection, and incarnation only make sense as spiritual experiences, that is, they have to be lived, not thought, because the life of God transcends human concepts. The revealed realities can only be grasped in the religious act of belief and trust and within a religious experience. "Taste and see how good the Lord is" (Psalm 33:9). Mannion wants liturgists to set up the conditions for the possibility of religious experience. He understands what the masters of the spiritual life tell us, namely, that if a mood or ethos of beauty and mystery is established, then the divine presence inherent in the revealed symbols "can be felt in one's bones and tasted in one's mouth."

On the other hand, since Mannion's essay is an outline of his position, there are questions for clarification. He makes a clear distinction between structural and spiritual reform. The others are structural whereas his is a spiritual reform. Can these two dimensions be separated? The "ethos of beauty, mystery, profundity and solemnity" he seeks seems more structural than spiritual. In the Tridentine rite much of the ethos depended on the silence and the use of Latin. In addition, Mannion makes only one mention of "active participation," the goal of the revised liturgy. The structural reform of texts, rites, and symbols is to provide the conditions for the possibility of active participation. Mannion does not explicitly relate his spiritual reform to the relationship between the liturgical celebration and the practice of justice. Moreover, Mannion does not discuss the relation of the priest to the people. In the past the priest alone controlled the ethos. How do you achieve a sense of mystery today when the postconciliar liturgy includes the people joining in as they hear the word, proclaim the acclamations, and sing hymns? The profundity of the liturgy consists in the presence of the triune God manifested through many symbols: the assembly, scriptures, altar, bread and wine, and the priest. It is very difficult to control the aesthetic dimensions of liturgy when there is no dress rehearsal. Obviously, we will need more information from Mannion about his positive proposals.

Conclusion

The Eucharist makes "the one and only church of Christ" visible and is the occasion for the community of disciples to celebrate its mission. The resurrected Christ, the source of the church, is present. Unfortunately, all Christians do not share the Eucharist at the same altar. Catholics, too, are divided in their appreciation of the Eucharist. On the one hand, many do not participate on a regular basis. Several opinion polls taken during the 1980s and 1990s indicated that only about 51 percent of Catholics attend Sunday Mass on a regular basis. Many of those who do attend are not pleased with the style of the ceremonies and the substance of the homilies, or they regret that women are excluded from ministry in the full sense. In a word, many agree that the liturgical reform "has yet to begin." On the other hand, many Catholics participate regularly and grow spiritually. The eucharistic liturgy grounds their lives and solidifies their connection to the community and its mission. The eucharistic celebration is their chief reason for being involved with the church, that is, at the Eucharist they experience great joy, love, peace, and healing, have a deeper sense of community, and attain a clearer understanding of their involvement in what contributes to a more just world.

Since the church is so divided over liturgical theory and practice, the task of fostering the liturgical life of Catholics in a world church will occupy the whole church for years to come. This task deserves priority because full, conscious participation in the liturgy "is the primary, indeed the indispensable source from which the faithful are to derive the true Christian spirit" (SC 14).

CHAPTER 9

The Church and Social Justice

In previous chapters we have seen that the identity of the institutional church is seriously marred if it does not provide its members the very same justice it teaches the world; that modern theology cannot afford to overlook the terrible injustices suffered by the Jews in the Holocaust; that action on behalf of justice is a constitutive dimension of the church's proclamation of the gospel; that interreligious dialogue is inseparable from cultural pluralism and global social justice; that ecumenists seek Christian unity within the struggle for justice; and that perceptive liturgists like Virgil Michel called for reform of the eucharistic celebration within the context of social justice. This chapter explores the intellectual, institutional, and devotional dimensions of social justice in the Catholic church of the twentieth century. It examines the contributions of the popes and bishops, theologians, clergy, and laity to the church's social teaching. As groups and individuals they are concerned with the progressive enhancement of human life by grounding the teaching in faith and revelation, by calling for a just use of the world's natural resources, by focusing on human reason, dignity, and equality, and by promoting a society marked by freedom, love, and respect for human rights.

Human Rights

The Catholic tradition, based on its sacramental consciousness, holds that God made a rational and ordered world, and that we humans are graced, moral agents responsible for the ethical character of our social, political, and economic existence. Unfortunately, from our very beginnings, we humans have been perverting our relationships and our world.

Human rights are usually coupled as civil-political and social-economic. The former include such rights as equality with no discrimination based on race, sex, religion; freedom of assembly, speech, and movement; and no arbitrary arrest, torture, or an unfair public trial; and the latter include such rights as food, shelter, basic health care, education, a living wage, private property, and the right to form labor unions.

241

Today, injustices abound as people's basic rights are violated. The gap between the poor and rich, both individuals and nations, continues to widen. Every minute the nations of the world spend millions on arms; every hour thousands of children die from hunger-related causes; every day a species becomes extinct; every month the world's economic system adds more billions of dollars to the unbearable debt burden already resting on third world shoulders.

These injustices fly in the face of the Christian belief that all people are equal in dignity because they are created by God, redeemed by Christ, and graced by the Spirit. The Creator gives all individuals both their essential dignity and their existential originality. The presence of the risen Christ to each person means that all persons are sacred. When Christians respect and serve others, especially the poor, imprisoned, and the hungry, they serve Christ himself (Matthew 25:40). It is disregard for human dignity that is the root of violence and injustice.

One reason there are so many problems related to human rights is that there is disagreement about their origin. Here are five theories.

First, some regard rights as God-given. The Declaration of Independence of 1776 asserted that the inalienable rights to life, liberty, and the pursuit of happiness are God-given. These rights are not "man-made" or created by humans. The first nine amendments to the Constitution—the Bill of Rights—were added to the Constitution on December 15, 1791, to provide adequate guarantees of individual liberties.

Today when we say "all men are created equal," we mean that all have God-given dignity and fundamental value. Both the Hebrew prophets and Jesus of Nazareth taught that each person is loved by God and of infinite worth. The Christian manifesto for the God-given dignity of the individual is contained in the parables of the one lost sheep (Luke 15:3–7) and the one lost coin (Luke 15:8–10). Many contemporary philosophers and jurists agree that human dignity is God-given, but they deny that human rights are God-given. They ask why is it that, if God is the source of rights, he arbitrarily allows impersonal nature (e.g., earthquakes and hurricanes) to rob some humans of their property, families, health, and even their lives. We do not claim that tornadoes or hurricanes (and other so-called "acts of God") do a person an injustice if they deprive a person of her home or family.

Second, totalitarian governments claim to be the source of rights. The state grants and denies them. Some socialist governments declare that the socioeconomic rights have priority over the civil-political rights, and that the state can restrict the latter to achieve the former. Under the infamous Nazi government of Adolf Hitler (1889–1945), those judged worthless (the disabled, homosexuals, the aged) were eliminated.

Those who argue against the government as the source of rights state that totalitarian governments actually limit and/or dispense rights based on their own ideological premises or agenda. Their decision as to who has rights or privileges is arbitrary (based on limited judgments) and totally subjective. The Nazis, for example, considered homosexuals to be abnormal because, by not having children, they did not advance the life of the nation. The trouble with totalitarian governments is that they "recognize no transcendent point of reference to which they are accountable and by which they are restrained. More specifically, they refuse to acknowledge the transcendent value embodied in each person" (Neuhaus 1978).

Third, humanists such as John Locke, Jean-Jacques Rousseau, as well as the twentieth-century philosopher John Rawls (1971), ground rights and justice in social contracts. According to this theory, persons exist primarily and most importantly as individuals, and persons have a domain within which they are sovereign. Human rights abide in the individual person. Individuals are self-enclosed, that is, they are already constituted with rights. Consequently, individuals can consent to share their rights with others when it is in their self-interest. Any forced sharing violates human rights. Followers of this theory concede that a society can have peace and order rather than suffering and disorder only if people opt for a system in which all citizens sacrifice some of their personal benefits at certain times in favor of others.

Many lawyers and jurists regard the contract theory (whereby justice and rights are based on grudging agreements entered into by self-interested parties) as wholly inadequate because it ultimately denies the inherent social nature of persons. It supposes that humans are social and political by choice and not by nature. Justice "is no longer a positive good but only a necessary evil" (Di Ianni 1989). The noted philosopher Robert O. Johann explains that we only have rights in the presence of others. I do not have rights if no other persons are present. "If I were the only person in the world it would not be the case that I *had* rights but no one was around to respect them. I would not have rights at all. Other persons are not therefore required simply to do justice to rights already constituted" (1967, 43).

Fourth, some persons and governments claim that rights are culturally conditioned and, therefore, the principles enunciated by some cultures conflict with the value systems of others. Consequently, some cultures uphold slavery, others female genital mutilation, others the death penalty, and some theocracies believe that those they label as heretics should be slain for their writings, as in the Salman Rushdie affair. In 1988 Rushdie published *The Satanic Verses*. This novel was denounced by many Muslims for portraying a character who resembles Muhammad in situations they deemed blasphemous. In February 1989, the authorities in Iran issued a decree calling upon the Islamic faithful to murder Rushdie, a British citizen. The bounty came to millions of dollars, and Rushdie has been in hiding ever since.

Those who dispute the claim that human rights are culturally conditioned do not deny that there is cultural variety in art, religion, manners, and politics (Schall 1978). Nonetheless, they deny that cultural pluralism is a satisfying answer to the issue of human rights. Their claim is that there are rights that transcend all cultures. Over the years the nations of the world have evolved international codes that express universal aspirations. The United Nations adopted the Universal Declaration of Human Rights on December 10, 1948, to enshrine universal concepts and to establish clear standards for the treatment of all citizens by their governments. In 1968 the United Nations sponsored in Teheran a World Conference on Human Rights to commemorate the twentieth anniversary of its 1948 landmark document. Another United Nations conference was held in Vienna for eleven days—June 14–25, 1993. Present were representatives of 168 nations as well as delegates from over one thousand nongovernmental advocacy groups, such as Amnesty International. Women formed "the strongest and most effective lobby." They "focused less on the struggle to end discrimination and more on the need to put an end to a series of acute human rights abuses suffered by women because they are women" (Riding 1993a). The Vatican sent delegates because it is an observer at the United Nations.

During the meeting there was discernible tension between those who hold that "human rights exist as a function of history, culture, value systems, geography and phases of development" (Riding 1993b) and those who hold that there are "knowable, universal principles of justice that ought to serve as a plumb line by which to measure various practices of peoples, government, cultures, societies, religions and traditions" (Stackhouse 1993). Nonetheless, the conference's conclusions showed conclusively that "the concept of human rights has global approval for the first time in history" (Drinan 1993). Those who opt for universal human rights consider slavery, sexual mutilation, the death penalty, and assassination edicts to be barbaric human rights crimes. Ironically, some communist countries that object to investigations into their human rights abuses as an intrusion into their national and cultural sovereignty preach the universal validity of Marxist principles. The lie is given to the cultural argument by such people as Aung San Suu Kyi of Burma (Myanmar), the 1991 Nobel Peace Prize laureate, and the Buddhist monks in Vietnam and Tibet. The former almost single-handedly has been sustaining Burmese hopes for democracy; the latter have bravely campaigned for cultural and religious freedom (Crossette 1996). Aung San Suu Kyi effectively makes her point about the rule of law and political accountability by citing the Buddhist view of kingship: "The Ten Duties of Kings are liberality, morality, self-sacrifice, integrity, kindness, austerity, non-anger, nonviolence, forbearance and non-opposition to the will of the people."[1]

Fifth, some contemporary philosophers (Johann 1968, 137–39) hold that human rights are grounded in our relationships to one another. They argue that the obligation to be just is identical with our nature as essentially relational beings. Human persons are rational agents who by nature respond to other beings in terms of what they are and do. In the presence of another person, a person is obliged to treat the other person as a person. Injustice is present when persons deliberately hurt others or are indifferent to their presence—that is, act in their presence as if they were not there. The injustice is not done by the mere fact that a person's reality as a person is ignored, or things are taken away from the person. Injustice is done primarily because a person refuses his or her obligation to be responsive to the personal character of the other person. In short, the foundation of human rights is our mutual obligation to be responsive to others as persons. Injustice is in the person who fails to be responsive to the personal character of others. This is the New Testament view of justice, as exemplified in Jesus' parable of the Good Samaritan (Allen 1989, 26–27). The kind-hearted Samaritan (Luke 10:30–37) treated the man who "fell victim to robbers" with compassion, a word accurately defined as "love-justice" by Matthew Fox (1979, 3).

Justice

The general description of justice is captured in the ancient Latin phrase *suum cuique*—to each what is due. Justice demands equality and fairness. There are three complementary forms of justice: commutative, distributive, and social. Commutative or individual justice concerns private claims which exist between individuals or groups. It entails such things as fidelity to agreements, contracts, and promises. Distributive justice specifies the claim which all persons have to some share in those goods which are essentially public or social, such as education, housing, health care, and the right to earn a living wage. Social justice concerns the realization of distributive justice. Both are based on the assumption that persons are social by nature. Social justice directs all citizens to aid "in the creation of patterns of societal organization and activity which are essential both for the protection of minimal human rights and for the creation of mutuality and participation by all in social life" (Hollenbach 1977, 220). For example, all citizens should contribute to the common good by paying taxes, performing jury duty, and by opposing structures that abet racism, classism, and sexism. In view of this description, social injustice is the structured exclusion of people from access to those things required by their dignity as human beings (Baum 1986a).

Liberal Capitalism

During the twentieth century, two visions of how society should be organized politically and economically have dominated: capitalism and Marxist socialism. Capitalism is characterized by the private ownership of both property and the means of production. It is based on individual initiative, competition, supply and demand, and a profit motive. We saw earlier in chapter 2 that Adam Smith believed that the free market, operating according to the law of supply and demand, can assure the well-being of society and raise the standard of living of the vast majority. Persons, then, function autonomously in their economic lives. Society and the privately controlled market are extensions of this private autonomy. Political, cultural, and market institutions do not function autonomously, but form one interlocking structure in the service of private capital accumulation. For example, the above named institutions depend upon the military, the secondary labor market, and race and gender role assignments.

Capitalism arose in the eighteenth century with the Industrial Revolution. At that time, the economic, cultural, and social structures of society moved from countryside farms to urban factories. It also began with some clear presuppositions: individuals are (and always will be) fundamentally selfish and destructive; there is conflict between the individual and society; this conflict can be moderated by individuals working to produce a healthy, harmonious social unit. The state is established by individuals out of enlightened self-interest because only institutional force can keep individuals from destroying one another. Otherwise, a political community is neither essential nor intrinsic to the human condition.

In theory, capitalism glorifies the freedom of the individual and views society not as organic or corporate, but as composed of atomistic individuals, who, as Adam Smith believed in the eighteenth century, are driven by self-love and self-interest. An example of this viewpoint is found in the thought of John Locke, a seventeenth century philosopher who set the stage for Adam Smith. Locke taught that humans are by nature aggressive competitors, each one a threat to all neighbors. Persons are essentially isolated and are selectively social in limited ways. Given this situation, individuals must protect themselves and their rights from the control of others. Rights in society belong to the individual. No one, including and especially government, can deny individuals their rights. Government is necessary to provide minimum security, but it is the people themselves who, by means of a formal contract, create a democratic state to protect their rights. Too much power should not be given to government.

The term *liberal capitalism* denotes a system wherein the free market is the one essential mechanism for regulating the production and distribution of goods (Baum 1989a, 77). At the end of the eighteenth century, those who advocated liberal capitalism argued that a free market would naturally increase economic development, generate enormous wealth, and eventually raise the material well-being of the entire society. Poverty and unemployment are basically individual social problems due to a temporary malfunctioning of the market, or to forces outside the economic system, such as ignorance, laziness, prejudice, and the disturbances of free exchange by labor unions or government interference (Hobgood 1989, 170).

There are many criticisms of liberal capitalism. Two interrelated ones are the following. First, liberal capitalism creates a wealthy class over against a large group that lacks access to the market or dignified participation in society. This extreme centralization of power in the hands of wealthy elite "is the fatal flaw of capitalist society" (Greeley 1981, 48). Second, liberal democracies pride themselves on fostering civil and political rights. However, they neglect the social and economic rights since explicit promotion of these rights seems to contradict the nature of capitalism. Communists judge capitalism's defense of civil rights as an ideological disguise of its refusal to honor the rights to life, adequate health care, a decent home, food, a job, and other needs.

At this point, a postscript about Protestantism and society is in order. In general, Protestant social theory, while based on the dialectical imagination, is similar to that of Locke and Marx insofar as it begins with the presupposition that the individual and society are in conflict or competition. They usually maintain that there is a dialectical relationship between the individual over and against the person as a social being. The individual strives for freedom and independence; society strives to constrain the independence of the individual for the common welfare.

Communist Socialism

Socialism advocates collective or government ownership and management of both the production and distribution of goods as the means to achieve those economic and social freedoms which cannot be guaranteed by a free-market economy. Karl Marx constructed his version of socialism as a reaction to some of the results of the Industrial Revolution and capitalism that deeply disturbed him. He was particulary disturbed by the struggle of the workers (proletariat) with the property-owning class (bourgeoisie or capitalist class). Marx was angry because the capitalist institutions—whether social, political, or economic—produced hierarchies of class (as well as the ancilliary divisions of race and sex) that enhanced the profit intake of corporate business. There is no way, Marx observed, that private profit can be made without exploiting the working people. Social solidarity, Marx maintained, is undermined as the people are pushed into individualism and competitiveness.

Like capitalism, socialism begins with some presuppositions: individuals tend to be selfish but they do not have to be this way; the individual and society are in conflict (as Marx found in capitalist society); and human nature can be changed so that the rational economic person can be produced, the person who not only contributes to society according to his or her means but also receives from society what he or she needs to live with dignity. This will happen once the constraints of the present economic and social class structures are eliminated.

In theory, communism glorifies the importance of the individual's obligations to society. Individuals are considered units isolated from a massive and perhaps highly structured society. This is the same kind of atomistic individualism we noted in capitalism. Society is not an organic or corporate body. Power is centralized in the party. Human rights originate from the state. "The inseparability of personal freedom and social solidarity is the cornerstone of Marxist social philosophy" (Hollenbach 1979, 21). The individual is essentially social. He or she gets individual meaning and rights from the people (or the nation or the state). An isolated individual can achieve only stunted growth.

Finally, communism claims to protect the social and economic rights of individuals. A major criticism of institutionalized communism over the years has been not only that its systems never really enhanced the social and economic right of its citizens but also that, for all practical purposes, it denied people their civil and political rights. The break-up of communist rule in eastern Europe in 1989 and of the USSR on December 21, 1991, when eleven of the twelve republics formed a commonwealth, was due in part to the wastefulness of the cold war arms race and to the demands of the people for social, economic, civil, and political rights. Soviet communism collapsed under the weight of its "inner contradictions": the collective ownership of the means of production and exchange proved to be not only a political tyranny but also an economic disaster.

Catholic Social Teaching

Despite the fact that the church has had to adjust to emperors, tribal chiefs, kings and queens, feudal systems, and democracies, it has fundamental social teaching. These teachings have developed in stages and, especially since 1968, have taken notably different directions, "not in [their] basic truths and values but in the practical implications for the life of the church" (Dorr 1983, 263). What concerns us here are these basic truths and values.

Catholic social teaching is based on "a pre-Protestant, pre-capitalistic, and pre-Marxist view of society" (Greeley 1981). It begins with two insights, one theological and the other political. First, God's presence to humans and their history as revealed in the human life of Jesus tells us human life is good and should be of quality for all. Second, self and society are not necessarily opposed but, rather, are interconnected. In fact, the formation of a state or a political community is a natural and necessary law of survival and maturation for humans (D. Maguire 1986, 20-21).

The most basic principle of Catholic social thought is the dignity, goodness, and inviolability of the individual. It opposes collectivist tendencies or systems that leave individuals, especially the poor, vulnerable to oppression of any kind. Its aim is the growth of a fully integrated human being.

Catholic social teaching places the dignity of the individual within the context of society, which is viewed as an organic, supportive network of overlapping and interlocking yet hierarchical relationships that work towards social well-being or "the common good." The common good is the result of reponsible citizens acting in a way that leads to mutual respect for rights and dignity. When the bishops at Vatican II discussed the common good, they declared that "Catholics should try to collaborate with all men and women of good will in the promotion of all that is true, just, and holy, all that is worthy of love (see Philippians 4:8)" (AA 14). "The common good, since it is founded on mutual dignity, is not in opposition to human rights, but rather their guarantee" (Hollenbach 1979, 61).

Traditional Catholic teaching reasoned that the common good of society encompassed more than the sum of the private goods of the individual persons. The common good embraces the institutions, laws, and values that regulate in terms of justice the interaction of individuals and groups in society and protect them from exploitation or oppression by the powerful and resourceful. In this perspective, the private good of individuals is subordinated to the good of the whole society. Personal freedoms have their clearly defined limits. The task of government is to enhance the common good by protecting the common values, institutions and laws, and by resisting any individualism that would elevate an individual's own private good over the common good (Baum 1979b).

This organic and supportive society is also decentralized. Healthy societies need to be built upon strong neighborhoods and local communities. Villages, towns, and cities have formal political and social power and authority. Since the principle of subsidiarity holds that choice is of the essence of human freedom, basic political choices must be left in the hands of those most affected by decisions.

This organic and decentralized society is also pluralistic. A plurality of cultures is necessary since there are many valid ways through which an individual can achieve wholeness.

Finally, the Catholic tradition is unwilling to separate civil and political rights from social and economic rights. It teaches that all four rights are indivisible and that violations of any of these rights are due to selfishness and greed. Right order and social justice can be reestablished in society if each and every person undergoes an intellectual and moral conversion to greater love, accepts the norms of justice, and strives to serve the common good.

At times the institutional church has not always been true to its own social teachings. For example, when the nineteenth-century popes condemned economic, religious, and political liberalism and, at the same time, denied civil rights, they were out of harmony with the Catholic tradition. Their justification was their belief that liberal political philosophy undermined the social cohesion of traditional society, total freedom of religion promoted indifferentism, and economic liberalism exploited the poor.

Vatican II did not endorse the unconditional rejection of modernity by the hierarchical church of the nineteenth century. Yet, there was some validity to the stance of the nineteenth-century popes. Classical liberalism did promote individualism and undermined social solidarity; it did relativize, even trivialize, the truth question of religion; and it did legitimate the free-market economy since it demanded that the government allow maximum freedom of production and trade.

Leo XIII

The future Leo XIII became an archbishop and nuncio to highly industrialized Belgium at the age of thirty-three. There he saw the smelting furnaces and the factories in the Meuse River valley. There he rode his first steam train and, in a letter home, wrote, "It is part of a miracle. We came from Brussels to Namur in three and a half hours, rushing over a distance of 64 miles."

He also saw the poverty and despair of the industrial workers. They lived in Dickensian slums and worked long hours while their children roamed the streets uncared for.

When he went to Perugia as bishop of the diocese at the age of thirty-six, he worked with the poor. He conducted schools, established orphanages, set up free kitchens—and even a savings bank (Lamboley 1979).

His predecessor, Pius IX, was preoccupied with church doctrine and the Papal States and so lost sight of the religious decline of the working class in the cities. Leo "fully grasped the importance of arresting this process, even if it was too late to reverse it" (Cheetham 1983, 272).

Leo was very aware of Catholic social theory and of his responsibility to promote and defend human rights and the common good in a world situation made more complex by the diversity of social, cultural, economic, and political styles and theories. This is not to say that he (or his successors) had any more competence than the economists and politicians to offer specific solutions and programs which would make the complex industrial economies of societies function equitably for individuals and the common good.

Leo inaugurated the modern church's struggle for social justice on May 15, 1891, with his famous, seventy-thousand-word encyclical *Rerum novarum* ("The Condition of Labor"). The historical setting for this encyclical was the Industrial Revolution in Europe and the United States. In 1891, approximately 77 percent of all Catholics lived in the industrialized world of the north and 23 percent in the countries now called the third world. Factory workers, many of them women and children, crowded into the cities where they either worked fifteen or more hours a day, seven days a week at less than subsistence pay, or were unemployed. Employers tolerated no interference in the way they operated their businesses. The law of supply and demand regulated hours, wages, and working conditions.

The official church's response to these intolerable conditions and slave-market practices was, in general, extremely conservative, even reactionary. One reason is that many feared socialism, particularly excessive government intervention in socioeconomic affairs. There were some outstanding exceptions. Some church officials tried to move the church towards the better aspects of socialism, especially its appreciation of the social nature of humankind. Among the church leaders were Félicité de Lamennais and Frederic Ozanam (1813–53) in France, Bishop Wilhelm von Kettler (1811–77) in Germany, and Bishop Gaspar Mermillod (1824–92), president of the so–called Fribourg Union.

At Fribourg, Switzerland, Catholic leaders from Germany, Austria, France, Belgium, and Italy, met annually for a week from 1885 to 1891 to study social problems. This group was open to progressive liberalism which faulted classical liberalism for its excessive individualism, its failure to understand the quasi-organic nature of society, and its inability to appreciate the radically social nature of human nature. One practical conclusion from these social-psychological premises was that government had the right and duty to intervene in the life of society, especially its educational and economic life. The Fribourg school favored the new democratic procedures over the prevailing Catholic paternalism and authoritarianism. For the workers, they advocated separate unions, instead of the joint unions of employers and workers favored by more conservative Catholics. They defended the right to work, to earn a living wage, and to have insurance against sickness, accidents, and unemployment. They also favored state intervention to protect the rights of workers. Their ideas and policies offered a powerful alternative to both liberal capitalism and Marxist socialism.

Lawrence Cunningham, professor of theology at the University of Notre Dame, proposed that *Rerum novarum* owed more to the social and economic developments in the United States than to Europe, especially because of the efforts of Cardinal James Gibbons (1834–1921), who worked closely with both the labor movement in this country and with curial officials in Rome (1986, 144–45). Gibbons was a bishop for fifty-three years, forty-four of them (1877–1921) as archbishop of Baltimore.

The liberal views of both the Fribourg Union and Gibbons were opposed by other Catholics who believed their policies, especially government intervention, would lead to socialism and other errors. For them, the remedy to the social problems was Christian charity.

Rerum novarum was intended to be a major intervention in defense of the poor and to correct the dehumanizing impact of industrialization on the dignity and rights of workers. Leo endorsed the Fribourg Union's arguments for government intervention, for the right of workers to organize unions of their own, and for the principle of a just wage. Against the socialist and Marxist idealization of the state, Leo defended the right to private property and insisted that the family is the basis of society and not the state. Leo had a "passionate concern for the plight of the working class" (Dorr 1983, 53). He did not mention liberal capitalism as such, but he did condemn abuses in the marketplace. For example, he complained that too few people controlled the production of goods and that the greedy laid on the poor "a yoke little better than that of slavery itself." He urged his readers to look on the whole of material existence from a Christian perspective, reminding all that "God himself seems to incline to those who suffer misfortune."

Rerum novarum is primarily moralistic in tone—it calls for a change of attitude rather than structural changes in society. Also, it focuses on the economic situation within the typical industrialized country of the West. Nevertheless, it represents a major achievement. "While rooted in tradition, it offers an opening to the new situation, including the emergence of democratic governments, the reality or threat of political revolution, and the development of an industrial proletariat ground down by poverty. It is not surprising, then, that Leo's teaching has remained the basis of the official Catholic position on social issues" (ibid., 51).

Leo's successors, Pius X and Benedict XV, made few notable advances in the understanding of Catholic social teaching. The former, the least socially enlightened of this century's popes, was preoccupied with Modernism; the latter with World War I and with a church still hobbled by a lingering anti-Modernism and suspicion of new thinking on social issues. Benedict addressed these issues in 1914 in his encyclical *Ad beatissimi* ("Appeal for Peace").

Pius XI

His pontificate was dominated by three social developments with extensive political consequences—the worldwide depression of the 1930s, the expansion of Soviet communism, and the emergence of fascism in Germany and Italy.

Fascism is a philosophy of government that opposes both democracy and socialism. It glorifies the nation-state at the expense of individual human dignity and rights, declaring that the state has control over the totality of a person's life. In 1931 Pius denounced the state absolutism of the Italian Fascists in an encyclical on Catholic Action in Italy titled *Non abbiamo bisogno* ("We Have No Need"). His response to the Nazis in Germany was very uneven. At first he negotiated a concordat with Hitler in 1933, moved, it seems, by a fear of communism and by trust in Hitler's assurances. The concordat temporarily enhanced the prestige of the Nazis. However, from 1933 to 1936, Pius frequently had to protest the Nazi oppression of the church. Finally, on March 14, 1937, he issued the encyclical *Mit brennender Sorge* ("With Burning Concern"), condemning the Nazis for violating the 1933 concordat by harassing church members and damaging church property.

Some commentators thought it deplorable that Pius never condemned the Nazis for their violations of the natural law (for example, their denial of the human dignity of Jews, homosexuals, and the mentally and physically disabled), their crimes against liberty, and their tyranny and oppression of every kind (Falconi 1967, 207). It has been reported that the German episcopate opposed Hitler from the beginning. When, on September 14, 1930, the National Socialist party secured sixteen million votes and 107 seats in the parliament, the bishops exhorted the faithful to examine their consciences (ibid., 193). But this is not the whole story of the German church's relationship with Hitler.

Concerning communism, the future Pius XI (Ratti) had first hand experience of it when he was nuncio to Poland for three years (1918–21). At that time the country was under the dictatorship of the socialist Marshal Josef Pilsudski. Ratti's tasks were to help rebuild the church in Poland, negotiate a concordat, and secure information about the thousands of Polish Catholics who had been deported to Siberia by the Russians. In the summer of 1920 the communist army laid siege to Warsaw. Ratti bravely remained in the city and saw with his own eyes the might of the Russian armies that enforced communism. On March 19, 1937—five days after the encyclical against Nazism—Pius declared in his encyclical *Divini Redemptoris* that communism was intrinsically wrong and the greatest of all evils (n. 58). He said no one should collaborate with communism in any way if Christian civilization would be saved, because it promotes atheism and class struggles and relies on the working class for leaders in its "dictatorship of the proletariat."

With regard to the problems of the working class, Pius, like Leo, had to evaluate two opposing schools of Catholic social thought. The *Sozialpolitik* school basically accepted the capitalist system but believed that its harsher features could be alleviated by various forms of social welfare, for example, by a strong social insurance system. Like Leo XIII, they advocated unions and insurance against sickness, unemployment, and old age.

The other group—the *Sozialreform* school—wanted to revamp capitalism. They denounced its many deviations from traditional Catholic social teaching, especially its exaggerated individualism which promoted both greed and an unjust distribution of wealth. They also urged harmony between the classes and denounced the call of the socialists for revolution. To achieve harmony between workers and management, they advocated industry councils on local and national levels in which employers and employees would determine local and general economic policy. They also advocated government intervention when the public good demanded it.

On May 15, 1931, the fortieth anniversary of *Rerum novarum*, Pius issued *Quadragesimo anno* ("On Reconstruction of the Social Order"). This major encyclical was written by Oswald von Nell-Breuning (1890–1991), a Jesuit theologian, economist, and social scientist (Murphy 1991). In this encyclical, Pius sided with the *Sozialreform* school and criticized the capitalist system not only as it had developed since the pontificate of Leo but in its essential nature. He wrote: "Free competition has destroyed itself; economic domination has taken the place of the open market." He rejected capitalism because its central principle—free competition—was affirmed as the determining factor in the economic order, regulating prices, profits, and wages. Furthermore, materialistic capitalism breeds greed and, in its single-minded quest for profits, pushes aside human compassion.

Some argued that Pius XI was proposing an alternative socioeconomic system, one that would replace socialism and capitalism. This is a debatable issue, but it does not seem to be the correct interpretation of his call for a reconstruction of the social order. *Reconstruction,* as Pius used the term, meant renovating old structures. Furthermore, what he was doing was laying down fundamental principles of social morality. On the basis of these principles, he ruled out "the acceptance of socialism in any form and of capitalism both in its basic ideological principle and in its actual historical development" (Dorr 1983, 63). Pius proposed "a free enterprise system which would be more or less equivalent to capitalism without its abuses and without its ideology" (ibid., 143). Finally, Pius declared that charity alone will not solve the problems of the poor. The economic structures that cause "the open violation of justice" have to be restructured. Perhaps we can say he advocated a limited free-market economy—capitalism with a human face.

Quadragesimo anno was a classic expression of Catholic social teaching, as described above. Its common themes were solidarity, smallness, cooperation, and subsidiarity, which entail both decentralization and respect for the existing networks of workers, families, and neighborhoods. The encyclical gave classic formulation to the principle of subsidiarity, some form of which "can be found in nearly every major social document of the tradition since *Rerum novarum*" (Hollenbach 1979, 157). Pius said it is "both a serious evil and a perturbation of right order to assign to a larger and higher society what can be performed successfully by smaller and lower communities" (n. 79). The basic reason for this principle was to prevent members of the social body from being destroyed or absorbed by society.

Thomas Bokenkotter said Pius XI's "prescriptions were so vague and indefinite that his plan was given a bewildering variety of interpretations" (1985, 362). Andrew Greeley, on the other hand, declared that the "Fundamental weakness of *Quadragesimo anno* and the Catholic social theory that it articulates formally is not that it has been tried and found wanting, but found hard and not tried" (1981).

During the first half of the twentieth century, many Catholics—liturgists, college professors, social activists, priests, and bishops—heeded the papal teachings on social justice and were concerned with the vast gulf separating the working class from the church. In Europe the so-called "worker-priests" in France evolved out of the Young Christian Workers founded in Belgium in 1912 by the renowned Joseph Cardijn (1882–1967). The worker-priests have had both positive and frustrating contacts with the Vatican from the time of Pius XI until today. Their story is too complex to tell here (see Willke 1984). In the United States, priests called "labor priests" served as chaplains to labor organizations, encouraged and supported the organizing efforts of workers, or ran "labor schools" to teach workers and union leaders both their rights under law and the official social teaching of the church, especially as enunciated in the social encyclicals (Higgins 1993).[2] In addition, there was the extraordinary contributions to the church's intellectual, institutional, and devotional life of John A. Ryan (1869–1945) and Dorothy Day (1897–1980).

Ryan, ordained a priest in Minnesota in 1898, was strongly influenced by the social concerns of his archbishop, John Ireland, by Cardinal James Gibbons's defense of the Knights of Labor in Rome in 1887, and by Leo XIII's *Rerum novarum*. After earning a doctorate in moral theology from Catholic University, he taught there from 1915 to 1939. He also served the bishops of the United States as director of the Social Action Department of the National Catholic Welfare Conference from 1920 to 1945. Ryan not only advised the bishops but also government officials on such issues as prohibition, women suffrage, labor unions, and child labor laws (Curran 1982, 26–91). He published *A Living Wage: Its Ethical and Economic Aspects* (1906), his doctoral dissertation, in which he emphasized the obligation of employers to pay wages sufficient to maintain a worker and his family in decent comfort. The source of his ideas was *Rerum novarum*. "Indeed, the whole book can be read as an application of that encyclical to the American situation" (Gustafson 1978, 24). Ryan later argued that *Quadragesimo anno* "supported the New Deal [of President Franklin Delano Roosevelt] in the United States" (ibid., 133).

Dorothy Day was probably the most influential Catholic of her time. Born in Brooklyn into a family affiliated with the Episcopal church, she grew up in Chicago, attended the University of Illinois for a short time, and then moved to New York City. Here she had a socialist interlude, several affairs, and an abortion. She later entered a common law relationship and gave birth to a daughter. Happy with her life as a mother, she turned to God in gratitude. She became a Catholic and had her daughter baptized.

Dorothy Day was prayerful and deeply devoted to the institutional church. She also had a lifelong love for the involuntary poor. In collaboration with Peter Maurin (1877–1949), a philosopher, poet, social visionary, and a former Christian Brother from France, she published the first issue of *The Catholic Worker* on May 1, 1933. Their paper was a direct challenge to the communist paper, *The Daily Worker* (Curran 1982, 130–34, 162–66).

Day and Maurin are credited with the first major expression of radical social criticism in United States Catholicism. They took literally the gospel challenge regarding peace, nonviolence, and voluntary poverty. Together they challenged the church's social conservatism which, with its focus on the hereafter, thwarted the development of a social conscience, especially when the church reinforced the conventional wisdom concerning such issues as war, civil disobedience, and taxes. Day and Maurin challenged the economic and political structures of the day, both national and international, because they wanted to make a world where "it is easier for people to be good." They condemned American capitalism, especially when it was abetted by the government, because, as a profit-driven system, it disregards the needs and dignity of working people and their families. One of their major efforts was to move society from the impersonalism of an urban-industrial society to the personalism of a rural-agrarian society. Their newspaper and houses of hospitality continue today.

Dorothy Day also influenced Vatican II. She went to Rome to lobby for her causes, especially nonviolence. She and nineteen other women convinced the bishops by word and action (a ten-day fast) to insert a paragraph (n. 80) in *Gaudium et spes* calling for the unequivocal condemnation of the indiscriminate destruction of cities (MacEoin 1991b).

Pius XII

Pius XII, whose motto was "Peace is the work of justice," and who wrote forty encyclicals, never produced a social encyclical equal in importance to those of Leo XIII and Pius XI. Nevertheless, his many pronouncements on social issues are similar to his predecessors'. In accordance with the Catholic tradition he condemned the omnipresent threats to the dignity of the person and families brought on by totalitarian governments, called for respect for basic human rights, and offered support for democratic political structures.

Concerning capitalism, his writings seem to accept it as the only feasible alternative to communism, nazism, and fascism.

During his pontificate the church gave strong religious and ideological support to those who opposed socialism and communism at all levels—international, national, and local. Pius was almost paranoid about communism in the Soviet Union, the first organized state in the history of the world to be openly atheistic. Inasmuch as he had joined the papal diplomatic service in 1914, Pius had intimate knowledge of the communist revolution in Russia on November 7, 1917, and the Soviet Union's relentless and ruthless rise to world dominance. The millions of Catholics in communist countries—some fifty million at the time of his death—were one of his main concerns. On June 30, 1949, he issued a decree denying the sacraments to those Italians who voted communist and excommunicating those who professed its "materialistic and antichristian" teachings.

Leo XIII and Pius XI had advocated economic justice within each nation. The teachings of Pius XII had a wider focus: he taught what would later be labeled "international social justice" (Hehir 1981). Pius was led to this level by at least four factors. First, before becoming pope, he had spent almost his entire career in the papal diplomatic service. He had been Pius XI's secretary of state from February 1930 until March 1939, when he was elected pope. In August 1944 he made himself secretary of state after the death of his secretary, Cardinal Luigi Maglione (1877–1944). Second, he was aware that around the globe people were subject to grave injustices not only from totalitarian governments but also from the development of large bureaucratic industries and governments. Third, six months after his election, the world suffered through its second world war, this one more tragic and disastrous than the first. That war came to a climactic end when the United States dropped atom bombs on Japan. Since then the world has lived under the menace of nuclear war. Pius eloquently warned about such a war: "There will be no song of victory, only the inconsolable weeping of humanity, which will gaze upon the catastrophe brought on by its own folly."[3] Fourth, after the war the nations of the world looked for international order, especially through the United Nations. In 1948, this body issued its Universal Declaration of Human Rights, a document that was not a binding treaty subject to the full strictures of international law, but, nevertheless, one that did serve as a "standard of achievement" for the nations of the world. Pius clearly understood the postwar changes in the social and economic spheres and the emergence of a truly global international system. In his addresses he focused on the political-legal meaning of international order (Hehir 1991). When Pius died on October 9, 1958, *The New York Times* report of his death was subtitled "All of world ills were his concern."

John XXIII

On May 15, 1961, John signed the encyclical *Mater et magistra* to honor the encyclicals of 1891 and 1931. This important letter was written with the assistance of Pietro Pavan (1903–94)—a scholar with degrees in economics and sociology who was made a cardinal in 1985 (Murphy 1996). John's encyclical was significantly different from those of his predecessors. In it he broke with the tradition of using rational arguments drawn from natural law. This tradition had been adopted in order to develop a public discourse of universal validity. Instead, John proposed and defended his social teachings with arguments drawn from scripture. Christians should be commited to justice and freedom in society because of Jesus and his gospel. Furthermore, a "natural" view of humans as a source for moral reasoning is inadequate. Christians should not view nature as "pure nature." Rather, since everyone always lives within the enduring offer of the grace of God, everyone has a supernatural origin and destiny.

Within this context, John adhered to the Catholic tradition of defending individual human dignity and integrating the individual and society.

However, John wrote to meet a new range of problems, especially the growing interdependence among nations. He lamented the widening gap between rich and poor nations, and asked for greater concern for the "international common good." While respecting the principle of subsidiarity, he believed that the common good actually required more government intervention. He even suggested greater need of government ownership, espousing a "welfare state model," which requires society and the state to assume responsibility for the public's well-being by remedying poverty and deprivation. He also stated that the right to private property was not an absolute, since God had given the world to everyone.

Regarding capitalism, John seemed to be optimistic about its future development. He never repudiated the condemnations of it made by Leo XIII and Pius XI, yet "he seemed to believe that before too long and without too much trouble the system could be effectively humanized" (Dorr 1983, 92).

Regarding communism, John mitigated his predecessors' hostility to it by arguing that, despite its false philosophy about the origins and purpose of human existence, it had good elements that could be used carefully in social analysis. The implications of this encyclical were so radical that the church came to have new allies and new opponents. For instance, conservative Catholics in the United States felt betrayed and cried, "Mater, si, magistra, no" (W. Buckley 1961).

Pacem in terris, drafted by Pietro Pavan and his colleagues, was signed on April 11, 1963, after Vatican II finished its first session and within the context of the nuclear arms race, the 1962 Cuban missile crisis, and the cold war. It marked the first time in history an encyclical was sent to "all men of good will" and not just to the Catholic bishops of the world. The document drew from specifically Catholic sources, yet appealed in its vision and sense of moral urgency to thoughtful men and women outside the Catholic community. Most thoughtful people agreed with its most quotable sentence: "It no longer makes sense to maintain that war is a fit instrument with which to repair the violation of justice." All did not agree, however, with John's call to ban nuclear weapons.

The encyclical was built on the Catholic vision of society: humans function best when there is order, solidarity, and peace on earth. Force, coercion, or fear destroy both individuals and society.

John addressed communism in this encyclical as well. He once more distinguished between a philosophy with false ideas about "the nature, origin and destiny of the universe and of man" and "the economic, social, cultural and political programs" which issued from it and which one had to contend with in the historical order because they "contain elements that are positive and deserving of approval" (n. 159). For some Catholics, these ideas were blatant heresy. Even Peter Hebblethwaite, that otherwise most liberal of interpreters, declared John was not that clear: "The link between theory and praxis in Marxism is allegedly such that one cannot drive a wedge between them, and this is one of the originalities of Marxism" (1975, 150).

David Hollenbach considered *Pacem in terris* "the most powerful and thorough statement of the Roman Catholic understanding of human rights in modern times" (1979, 41). In his encyclical John eradicated an argument about human rights that had befuddled the church's approach to human liberty for over a thousand years. The traditional axiom was "error has no rights." This proposition had been used by the Inquisition (1233) and other heresy-hunters. John insisted that only human persons have rights. Made in the image of God, every individual is entitled to live in peace and freedom for the pursuit of truth, justice, and love. This freedom had to be respected by church and state alike. In practical terms, John's teachings called for respect for the inviolability of the personhood of all, even those in error. He also said people are not to be forced to act in a fashion contrary to their beliefs, thus giving support to conscientious objectors to war. Finally, he condemned every type of discrimination, racial, sexual, national, and religious.

Vatican II

In a radio address on September 11, 1962, one month before the opening of Vatican II, Pope John said he hoped the council would present the church "in the underdeveloped countries as the church of all, and especially of the poor." In 1965, the bishops addressed social morality in two documents, the one on the church in the modern world *(Gaudium et spes)* and the other on religious liberty.

Gaudium et spes is by far the longest conciliar document. It is a synthesis of Catholic social teaching from Leo XIII to Paul VI, especially in sections 23 to 32 and 63 to 72. It declared that the church cannot stand by indifferent to the world and its changes. While the church has no mission in the political and economic world, its religious mission "can be the source of commitment, direction, and vigor to establish and consolidate the human community according to the law of God. In fact, the church is able, indeed it is obliged, if times and circumstances require it, to initiate action for the benefit of everyone, especially of those in need, such as works of mercy and the like" (GS 42). It also recommended that "some organization of the universal church" be established in order "to encourage the Catholic community to promote the progress in areas which are in want and to foster social justice between nations" (GS 90).

The bishops affirmed the dignity of the human person and acknowledged that the demands of human dignity are historically conditioned. It stated that the basis of the church's social ethics is personalism (the needs and rights of the person) rather than natural law (see GS 26). It also affirmed historical consciousness by acknowledging that people are more and more conscious of building "a better world in truth and justice. We are witnessing the birth of a new humanism, where people are defined before all else by their responsibility to their sisters and brothers and at the court of history" (GS 55). Finally, the bishops did make one condemnation, against "total warfare" (GS 80).

There have been many evaluations of *Gaudium et spes*—too many to synthesize here. A point made by Richard McBrien concerning the new understanding of social justice in the church deserves special attention, in part because it supplements the discussion on the proper mission of the church discussed in chapter 4. McBrien pointed out that before Vatican II the church's social teaching was regarded primarily as a subdivision within moral theology. With the council the focus shifted from moral theology to ecclesiology. Social justice activity was perceived by the council fathers not only as a way of practicing the virtue of justice, but also, and now primarily, as a way of fulfilling the mission of the church. The council taught that the demands of social justice are an obligation upon the whole church to serve the world based on truth and justice (1978b).

The Declaration on Religious Freedom was the most controversial of the sixteen conciliar documents, mainly because Gregory XVI had condemned Lamennais's teachings on religious freedom in 1832 and Pius IX had denounced religious freedom in his *Syllabus of Errors* in 1864. Paul VI described the document as "one of the major texts of the council" (Abbott 1966, 674). Mainly the work of John Courtney Murray,[4] in conjunction with many United States bishops, especially Albert G. Meyer (1903–65), Cardinal Archbishop of Chicago (Skerritt et al. 1993, 111–12), it was approved on December 7, 1965, by a vote of 2,308 to 70. The bishops grappled with this issue in order to "develop the teaching of recent popes on the inviolable rights of the human person and on the constitutional order of society" (DH 1). In the twentieth century, the rise of totalitarian governments prompted the popes to defend the dignity, freedom, and rights of the person. The conciliar bishops realized that since the historical circumstances of the nineteenth century had changed, the teaching on religious freedom had to change.

The conciliar document affirmed religious freedom as an inalienable human right (n. 2). It taught that all governments "must recognize and look with favor on the religious life of the citizens" (n. 3). It declared that "freedom of the church is a fundamental principle in what concerns the relation between the church and government and the whole civil order" (n. 4). Finally, it declared that since religious freedom is exercised in society, "civil society has the right to protect itself against possible abuses committed in the name of religious freedom. . . . However, this must not be done in an arbitrary manner or by the unfair practice of favoritism but in accordance with legal principles which are in conformity with the objective moral order. . . . [P]eople's freedom should be given the fullest possible recognition and should not be curtailed except when and in so far as is necessary" (n. 7).

This declaration—based as it is on the principles of historical consciousness—had many implications for church life. No more would the church seek to impose itself on any government or another religious body. This retreat from imperialism would improve ecumenical dialogues. Similarly, Rome would have trouble accusing any national local church of trying to be different from the rest of the church. An accusation, such as that of Americanism, for example, will not stand up because "the council recognized and called for the constitutional recognition and legal implementation of those fundamental human rights which validate all democratic governments" (Linnan 1986, 177). Finally, the bishops reaffirmed the most basic principle of Catholic social teaching: the dignity of the responsible person in society. It is this principle, declared David Hollenbach, that is "an important key to the problem of the foundation, interrelation and institutionalization of human rights" (Hollenbach 1979, 76).

Paul VI

During the pontificate of Paul VI, significant developments in the church's social teaching resulted from his writings, from the gathering of bishops at historic episcopal conferences and the Synod of 1971, and from the rise of political and liberation theologies.

In 1967, Paul published the encyclical *Populorum progressio* ("On the Development of Peoples"), building on John XXIII's theme of the international common good. Paul acknowledged that while there were many "situations whose injustice cries to heaven," nevertheless, he said he believed positive change was coming throughout the whole world and that a well-balanced society would soon break through. He urged the developed nations to achieve this social order by fostering the full self-development of the poor nations on every level—economic, social, political, personal, and spiritual. Development, he warned, cannot take place as long as liberal capitalists neglect their social obligations. Paul rejected liberal capitalism because it considers "profit as the key motive for economic progress, competition as the supreme law of economics, and private ownership of the means of production as an absolute right that has no limits and carries no corresponding social obligation" (n. 26). Is it any wonder that these strong words prompted the *Wall Street Journal* to call the encyclical "warmed over Marxism"?[5]

Philip Scharper was probably more on target when he said that the encyclical's "major flaw" was that, "although concerned for the poor, it was addressed to rich nations and persons, calling upon them to solve the problems of injustice and poverty." History seems to show, he said, that "effective altruism—rare enough in individuals—is seldom found in nations or groups possessing wealth and power" (1978).

In 1967 Paul VI established the Pontifical Commission on Justice and Peace because the conciliar bishops had recommended that there be an agency to assist in the establishment of international common good by promoting the social teaching of the church around the world (GS 90). This agency "is certainly the outstanding institutional consequence" of *Gaudium et spes* (E. McDonagh 1991, 109).

In 1968, the Vatican and the WCC jointly set up SODEPAX—the acronym for the Commission on Society, Development and Peace—to work on such thorny issues as international trade, human rights, and development in the underdeveloped countries. SODEPAX was formed from the Vatican's Commission on Justice and Peace and the WCC's International Action Commission.

This ecumenical organization took seriously its mandate to be a model of "practical ecumenism" and a "social witness." But eventually the two component bodies began to move in different directions. For example, at some international conferences Catholic speakers blasted Latin American regimes for human rights violations. Representatives of the governments so accused complained to the Vatican, suggesting that such attacks jeopardized diplomatic relations with the Vatican (McClory 1978b). Similarly, it became clear to the Catholic members of SODEPAX that there could be little development and peace as long as the Christian churches were divided. Consequently, they recommended that the Catholic church take a full part in the WCC. The Vatican rejected the suggestion in these words: "The confused situation in theology, the crisis of authority and certain attitudes to ecclesiastical discipline in individuals and whole groups make our hoped-for adhesion more difficult" (Bühlmann 1977, 218). These and other tensions made it inevitable that SODEPAX would disband. The WCC and the Vatican amicably terminated SODEPAX on December 31, 1980 (Hebblethwaite 1980d). The Vatican quickly noted that this ending did not mean the end of international ecumenical cooperation. Nonetheless, the dissolution of SODEPAX was a setback for the ecumenical movement.

Latin American Episcopal Conferences

Vatican II reinvigorated episcopal conferences; Paul VI ordered them to meet regularly in order that the decisions of the council would reach the local churches.

The Latin American bishops, at the initiative of Bishops Manuel Larrain of Chile and Helder Camara of Brazil, had held their first conference (CELAM is the acronym for *Conferencia Episcopal Latinoamericana*) in 1955 in Rio de Janeiro. Pius XII supported the conference and confirmed its constitutions. Inasmuch as CELAM I preceded Vatican II, it was ecclesiocentric. For example, it lamented the shortage of indigenous priests and condemned both Protestantism and communism. Vatican II rendered it obsolete.

On August 24, 1968, the bishops gathered for CELAM II at Medellín, Colombia, to discuss the role of the church in the actual transformation of Latin America in the light of Vatican II. Medellín had been approved by Paul VI in 1967, who even suggested that it take place when he could be present. Paul had already planned to be in Bogota for the International Eucharistic Congress. It worked out that Paul inaugurated CELAM II in Bogata and, thereafter, it met for two weeks in Medellín. Archbishop Helder Camara, the "architect of Medellín" (Wirpsa 1993b), was secretary general of the conference.

At Vatican II, the Latin American bishops (there were 531 present) introduced the term "church of the poor." This phrase denotes a church that denounces impoverishment caused by sin and injustice, yet preaches and commits itself to voluntary poverty. Not all 531 bishops were enthusiastic about the term and its consequences. For those who were, many of the questions so fiercely debated during the council—religious freedom, ecumenism, doctrinal development—seemed like "European" questions. For instance, Helder Camara declared that development was indeed the number one problem—but not doctrinal development. The development he was concerned with was "the social and economic development of peoples" (Hebblethwaite 1989c).

Medellín became the "new Pentecost" for the Latin American church. It was the bishops' opportunity to apply Vatican II to Latin America. It produced sixteen documents of uneven quality and without a unified conclusion. Nevertheless, the conference went beyond Vatican II in many respects. Summarized here are five of its principal themes.

First, the bishops agreed that, contrary to the view expressed earlier by Helder Camara and *Populorum progressio,* economic development was not the solution to their problems. The era of development was actually over because the attempt to make the undeveloped countries of the south like the developed nations of the north was impossible. Nothing had changed: the developed nations continued to prosper at the expense of the poorer ones. The organic networks of society had broken down. The rich and poor were in a serious conflict, and the bishops identified the main areas of oppression: "a situation of injustice that can be called institutionalized violence"; "internal colonialism" whereby a rich minority (oligarchy) dominate power; and an "external neocolonialism" of powerful, foreign nations. The true solution is liberation for the poor, the voiceless, and the oppressed.

The bishops also questioned the church's traditional alliance with wealthy, oligarchical establishments, and called for radical structural changes. Vatican II had declared a change of hearts (inner, personal transformation) as the way to achieve social justice. As people grow in virtue, political commitment would emerge and social justice would follow. The symbol for this stress on charity as the proper solution to social problems is the saintly Martin of Tours (316–97). According to legend, when Martin, a soldier, met a beggar who asked for shelter against the biting wind and snow, Martin cut his cloak with his sword and gave half to the desperate beggar. The bishops at Medellín had another solution. Beggars can obtain food, clothing, and shelter from the biting wind if they have education, work, and affordable housing. The bishops called for both a transformation of individuals and a transformation of the structures of society. Furthermore, some of the bishops insisted that the transformation of society must come first. Evil societies must be overcome first. Charity alone is inimical to change. In fact, they said, personal growth and holiness truly occur when people combat evil. Also, without the transformation of structures, the transformation of persons is extremely difficult. In the end the bishops compromised and called for both transformations because they were divided over which would be more appropriate for the different countries of the continent (Baum 1984a, 85).

Second, the bishops encouraged *conscientization*—helping people to understand that they become responsible for injustice if they remain passive. That is, if people out of fear of the personal risk involved do not take courageous and effective action to bring about necessary changes, they, by their passivity, perpetuate the injustices.

Third, the bishops declared that evangelization cannot take place except within the context of a commitment to the struggle against the systems of domination.

Fourth, Medellín condemned social sin, something never mentioned at Vatican II. The bishops reinterpreted the classic doctrine of sin by stating that persons need liberation not only from their personal sins but also from the social sin of oppressive social structures. Social sin has a powerful hold on people. It results from past personal choices for injustice that form into systematic institutions of socioeconomic and political oppression and deprivation. Social sin has to be identified and eliminated.

Fifth, the bishops declared that personnel and resources within the church must be redistributed so as to give effective "preference to the poorest and most needy sectors." This expression would be rephrased as the "preferential option for the poor" at CELAM III in 1979.

The preferential option for the poor is not exclusive, but it does require two things from the church: to look upon society in all its dimensions from the perspective of the poor, and to give public witness to the church's solidarity with the poor. It is through criticizing injustices that the church can express in a practical way this solidarity. This criticism should never be expressed through violence.

The phrase "preferential option for the poor" has evoked considerable controversy. Donal Dorr noted that it "became the most controversial religious term since the Reformers' cry, 'Salvation through faith alone'" (1983, 1).

The church has always taken care of the poor, particularly through almsgiving (see 1 Corinthians 16:1; Galatians 2:10) or through monks and nuns who commit themselves to serving the poor and sick. Also, concern for the involuntary poor pervades the Bible, which portrays God as being on the side of the oppressed and the outcasts. A paradigm of God's care for such people is the exodus of the Hebrew slaves from the clutches of the pharaohs, and God's electing them his chosen people. The Jewish prophets challenged kings, priests, and people to care for the sick, orphans, and widows; they also announced messianic promises. Jesus is also paradigmatic. He was voluntarily poor and fulfilled his mission among the marginalized, oppressed, and involuntary poor. His life as critic of injustices brought him persecution and death. However, his resurrection is a sign of God's promises of wholeness and life.

While the church always cared for the poor, it never proclaimed a preferential option for the poor. Why was this call not heard in the past—or why was it not heard in the same way as at Medellín (Baum 1986b)? There are two reasons. The first concerns the scriptural basis of this stand. The phrase "preferential option for the poor" is not found as such in the Bible. It is grounded in biblical teaching, but was formulated by interpreters who presuppose historical consciousness—that humans are the subject of their own history. In today's world there is massive suffering and oppression; many people do not have access to many of the basics of human life.

Modern hermeneutics proposes that written texts can be interpreted properly in two ways: the historical-critical method, which tries to discern the author's intended meaning, or with the critical method, which suggests the text's implications for today's world. The critical method, as David Tracy explained, is based on the belief that "once one has written a work, the work lives on its own. The author becomes another reader—with some privileged knowledge of what she or he once meant, but with no hermeneutical privilege at all in interpreting what the text really says. For that latter task, for better and for worse, the work alone speaks" (1990).

A second reason why the idea of a preferential option for the poor moved to the forefront is due to the way theology developed after Vatican II. Until the council, the church had a state-of-siege mentality. It withdrew from direct engagement with the social, economic, and political orders, viewing itself as separate from the world. The popes protested injustices, but the effect of their teachings often gave a measure of legitimation to the status quo. This defensive posture was captured in the phrase "in the world but not of it."

With Vatican II Christians found themselves "released from the world for the world" (Tracy 1981, 48). This perspective sees the church as part of the world but aware of its evils. The church must be released from the pretensions, delusions, and sin of the world, but at the same time it "should be released for the world as it really is: arbitrary, contingent, ambiguous, loved by God and by the Christian" (ibid.).

Involvement with the world, especially the world from which Christians must be released, entails interpretation. It is impossible to take a neutral position. Everyone views history, the historians inform us, from a particular value perspective. The Medellín bishops read history from the perspective of the involuntary poor. They wrote "people history." They realized that the conflict between the powerful rich and the powerless poor was one of the world's major problems, especially in Latin America. The bishops realized that their people had to be released from the deadly evil of the violence of poverty. The opponents of the bishops accused them of reading history with a Marxist perspective. But choosing for the poor is not Marxist. Marx promoted a preferential option for the workers, the industrial proletariat whose toil fueled the economy. Marx believed the unemployable had no destiny in society. He called them *Lumpen*, the German word for "hoodlum."

Gregory Baum maintains that the church's commitment to a preferential option for the poor is definitive and irreversible. This preference was adopted and developed by the Synod of 1971, by CELAM III and IV, by both Paul VI and John Paul II, and by national episcopal conferences, including the United States bishops in their pastoral letters of 1983 and 1986 (Murnion 1986, 203–37). Baum regards the turn to the poor begun at Medellín "as an extraordinary happening, possibly of world historical importance" (1986b). It has made a major impact on Catholic social teaching. Instead of viewing society as an organic network of interlocking relationships, Catholic social teaching now evaluates society from a critical, conflictive perspective. This perspective sees that society is divided by structures of oppression, and believes that the church should ally itself with the poor, workers, and the unemployable. By struggling together with the poor, the church can transform the social order (Baum 1984b). Eventually, and ultimately, the transformation sought would reflect the Catholic ideal: an organic, supportive, decentralized, and pluralistic society characterized by peace and freedom.

The Medellín documents represent compromise: not all the bishops favored the preferential option for the poor. One group that was fiercely anti-communist favored the establishment of a neo-Christendom, that is, a society and culture, aided by the moral and material support of the state, ruled by the Catholic Christian faith and tradition. These bishops insisted that society's principal enemy is the secularization of society encouraged by the growing industrial developments. Latin America is in danger of losing its soul and so must defend its homogeneous culture against secularization by becoming industrialized but without following the example of the West. These bishops maintained that the primary task of the church, therefore, is to promote a cohesive Latin American culture, adapted to the requirements of industrial society yet faithful to its original values, including the Roman Catholic faith. The primary thrust of the church's pastoral projects is religious. Concern for justice will follow from the transformation of persons.

The other group—the bishops who dominated at Medellín—viewed the Latin American scene differently. They believe injustice and oppression are the principal social evils in Latin America. Furthermore, they claim that a homogeneous Latin American culture has never existed and is an ideology that disguises the structural injustices in Latin American society (Baum 1983b).

Twenty-one years after Medellín, some seventy-five academics and social activists met at the University of Notre Dame in March 1989, to review the Medellín conference. They concluded that the church had made both advances and retreats since 1968. Among the advances was "the unravelling church-state entanglements when the church began to prefer the poor." One serious retreat: the appointment of "conservative bishops inclined more to pasteurizing doctrine and less to succoring those in desperate need" (Gibeau 1989).

Paul VI: *Octogesima adveniens*

In 1971 Paul published *Octogesima adveniens* ("Call to Action") to mark the eightieth anniversary of *Rerum novarum*. It also "may be understood at least partly as a response by Pope Paul to all that Medellín came to stand for" (Dorr 1983, 157).

This document was not an encyclical but an apostolic letter addressed to Cardinal Maurice Roy, then president of the Pontifical Commission on Justice and Peace. This important letter moved the church's socioeconomic concerns to another level, namely, from national and international issues to transnational issues (Hehir 1981). This is not to say that the national issues of economic justice (e.g., unionization of workers) or the international social questions (e.g., the disparity between rich and poor nations) had even approached resolution. However, by 1970 there emerged on the international scene in a qualitatively new way transnational actors (multinational corporations) and transnational problems (e.g., debt, environment, population, hunger) which placed new constraints on many nations, further complicating international relations.

Paul acknowledged the difficulties inherent in establishing a just social order and did not himself provide detailed moral norms for the transnational level such as Catholic thought had developed for national issues of social justice (Henriot 1988, 11). Nevertheless, he insisted that the complexity of our world makes the search for the common good even more important than in the past. He said that social justice problems "because of their urgency, extent and complexity, must, in the years to come, take first place among the preoccupations of Christians" (n. 7). Paul pointed to the role local Christian communities could play in this pursuit. At this level people could come together "to analyze with objectivity the situation which is proper to their own country," pray and reflect on their situation in the light of the gospel and the church's social teachings, and then take appropriate action. Moreover, local discernment of the signs of the times is important, said the pope, since "it is difficult to give one teaching to cover them all, or to offer a solution that has universal value. Such is not our ambition, nor is it our mission" (n. 4).

In addition to his critique of the new constraints and problems placed on the poorer nations by the transnational capitalists, Paul continued his warnings against Marxism. He admitted that Marxism has various elements—it is a philosophy of history, a political movement, and a form of social analysis. As "a rigorous method of examining social and political reality" it also attracts some adherents. He warned, however, that even revisionist statements of Marxism demand careful discernment. Ultimately, Paul rejected both Marxist socialism and liberal capitalism because they deny dimensions of personal and social development that are integral to human dignity.

Political Theology

This term is ambiguous. It goes back to the Stoics who used it "to justify theologically the primacy of politics and the absolute claims of the state" (Metz 1970). Actually, political theology is almost as old as recorded religious experience. For example, the Bible addresses the history and politics of ancient Israel, especially in the prophets' reproach of kings, priests, and people for their failures to fulfill the covenant and their warnings about Israel's precarious future as a political entity.

Johann Baptist Metz retrieved the term in an attempt to apply the gospel to today's society. Political theology is not a complete system. Rather, it is a critique of both modern society and modern theology that aims to correct them. Metz explained it as follows: "I understand political theology, first of all to be a critical correction of present-day theology inasmuch as this theology shows an extreme privatizing tendency (a tendency, that is, to center upon the private person rather than public, political society). At the same time I understand this political theology to be a positive attempt to formulate the eschatological message under the conditions of our present society" (1969, 107).

Political theology appeared in Germany and in other parts of the world in the late 1960s. Advocates of political theology included Metz, Jurgen Moltmann (1967) and Dorothee Sölle (1967). This account focuses on the writings of Metz, a priest-theologian and student of Karl Rahner.

The inspiration for this theology is threefold. First, it grew out of the Marxist-Christian dialogues during the years 1965 through 1967. In Roger Garaudy's famous phrase, the church moved "from anathema to dialogue" (1966). Marx had declared that the task of philosophy is not to interpret the world but to change it. Metz realized that this observation challenged Christian life and theology. Christian theology had to abandon its emphasis on the next life, an emphasis that had dominated Christian spirituality for centuries. Rather than staying aloof from society, Christians should commit themselves to changing it.

Second, political theology opposed the dominant spiritualities of pietism and existentialism. Pietism arose in the seventeenth and eighteenth centuries as a reaction to the cold objectivity of much of the prevailing theology, preaching, and prayer. In both Protestant and Catholic forms, pietism fostered a religion of the heart and feeling, and a deep and intimate relationship with God. It also stressed personal salvation and personal sins. Metz showed that this privatizing trend, once vital and imaginative, now left little room for the social dimension of the Christian message. Christianity in its privatized form had actually "been distorted by the modernity it claimed to be confronting since the Enlightenment" (McDade 1991, 432). Similarly, the existentialism of such influential biblical scholars as Rudolph Bultmann (1884–1976) underscored a personal relationship with God. The gospel, said Bultmann, is a daily call to individuals as they make important decisions about their individual lives. Existentialism had its roots in the Enlightenment, which shattered the unity of religion and society. Christianity was reduced to the status of one particular phenomenon in a pluralistic world. Once religion and society were separated, the social dimension of the Christian gospel descended to secondary importance (Fiorenza 1975, 8–9).

Metz opposed pietism and existentialism because they privatized the gospel message and limited Christian faith to individual decision, private virtue, and apolitical individual encounters with the Wholly Other. Religion and society, said Metz, must stand in tension. After all, the Bible promises liberty, peace, justice, and reconciliation—values that are necessarily social.

Third, Metz's theology developed in response to that of his mentor, Karl Rahner. Rahner's theology—called transcendental Thomism—highlighted the individual as a graced, self-transcendent subject. Rahner wanted to close the distance between grace and nature as set forth by the neo-Thomists. Humans, said Rahner, have a supernatural origin and destiny. God's grace is always present. It is not added to nature, or separate from it, or offered only intermittently in certain privileged times and circumstances. Based on this theological anthropology, Rahner insisted that the aim of theology is not to pump religion into people but "to find the art of drawing religion out of a person." Metz, while he found Rahner's focus significant, said it was individualistic, ahistorical, and ignored the sociopolitical, an essential dimension of human existence.

Political theology articulates a theocentric spirituality with a nuanced understanding of three central concerns of Christian theology: God, Christ, and church.

Christians have always acknowledged the transcendence of God. According to Metz, biblical faith points to a God who is oriented towards the future, a dimension that has been unduly separated from transcendence. Metz emphasized that God's transcendence is temporal. "God revealed himself to Moses more as the power of the future rather than a being dwelling beyond all history and experience. God is not 'above us' but 'before us'" (1969, 88). This orientation toward the future is also fundamental to the New Testament. The proclamation of the death and resurrection of Jesus "is essentially a proclamation of promise which initiates the Christian mission. This mission achieves its future insofar as the Christian alters and innovates the world toward that future of God which is definitely promised to us in the resurrection of Jesus Christ" (ibid., 89). To talk about God is to talk about his coming reign. Political theology is a theology of hope.

Metz emphasized Jesus' proclamation and manifestation of the reign of God—the liberating presence and power of God's unconditional love. Jesus' proclamation was not "strictly religious." Rather, Jesus fulfilled his mission among the oppressed and poor. His ministry was in the political, economic, and social order. For "inciting the people" (Luke 23:5) with his criticisms of the establishment and his association with sinners and the outcasts of society, Jesus was persecuted and crucified. But his resurrection anticipated the final promises of the kingdom: peace, justice, love, and life. Thus, Metz speaks of the disturbing and dangerous legacy of Jesus Christ, who summons people to greater love and holiness gained by working to promote and expand the kingdom of God (1980, 80–99, 200–4).

The preconciliar view of church and society set the church above and outside politics, angelically judging a sinful society for whose sins it shared no blame and for whose problems it had all the answers. Metz countered that if Christianity flees from the world and retreats into an isolated fortress, it will be condemned to the periphery of society because it ignores the hopes and needs of modern people. The justification for the church's mission to the world is the coming kingdom of God. To herald the advent of this kingdom, the church should be an institution of creative criticism of society. As such, it should also be the sacrament of hope; embodying, however imperfectly, people's aspirations towards greater freedom, peace, justice, and reconciliation. The task of political theology is to alert people to the structures of oppression and to prevent the political order from becoming a false absolute. The message the church offers in its creative criticism of society will be dangerous, subversive, disrupting, and disturbing.

By 1981, Metz had linked his political theology to Latin American liberation theology by endorsing the base-community churches as models of solidarity with the people, replacing the acculturated Christian churches of the West with their religious and economic individualism.

Liberation Theology

Political theology helped many Catholics move from a privatized to a political spirituality. Its direct political influence is not easy to gauge. Peter Hebblethwaite believes Metz's theology "remained rather notional. He gestures towards the marketplace without appearing to spend much time there" (Hebblethwaite 1975, 109). Metz and Moltmann are accused by liberation theologians "of writing endless prolegomena (introductions) to an action that never takes place. Their insistence that all political systems fall under the judgment of the gospel is dismissed as 'idealistic,' the strongest term of abuse in liberation vocabulary" (Hebblethwaite 1976). A similar criticism was made by John McDade, an English Jesuit theologian, when he wrote that political theology in Europe "still has the character of a university-based project, lacking real contact with a faith-community actively searching for a theological understanding of its social experience. It is overwhelmingly 'critical' in character, but it has been able to do little more than fulminate against the 'privatized' and 'bourgeois' character of contemporary Europe; this judgment is more a comment on the complexity of constructing a 'contextual' theology in capitalist Europe than on the inadequacies of its political theologians" (1991, 433).

These negative judgments do not seem to apply to Dorothee Sölle, a poet-theologian, who views herself as "living within the belly of the Beast." Instead of developing a theology of liberation, she speaks of "a theology of resistance." She uses the analogy of the resistance fighters (patriots who during World War II resisted the occupation of their country by foreign troops) to urge Christians to resist our all-encompassing and overwhelmingly unjust socioeconomic and political systems.

Liberation theology spends a lot of time in the marketplace, consciously attempting to change history through a struggle for justice because it originated, developed, and culminated in response to social, political, and economic injustices. Liberation theology began to emerge in Latin America, Africa, and Asia at the same time in the 1960s and for the same reasons—because liberation theologians wanted to live for, with, and as the poor, and Vatican II's concern for the poor had a positive influence on many bishops, priests, and nuns (Ferm 1986). The conciliar bishops taught that a free social order must be "founded in truth, built on justice, and enlivened by love; it should grow in freedom towards a more humane equilibrium" (GS 26). The following paragraphs highlight Latin-American liberationist thought.

Liberation Movements

Before liberation theology was written in the late 1960s, there were liberation movements. The most famous example is the case of Camilo Torres (1927–66), a young and charismatic Colombian priest and social activist.

He abandoned the clerical state and in early 1966 joined a guerrilla movement, only to be killed a few weeks later (February 15) in his very first skirmish with the army. His death had a profound symbolic impact. It was an unmistakable sign of a new mood in the Latin American church.

The cause of liberation has continued. Hundreds of thousands have been martyred as they struggled in the name of Christ against injustice. Most go unnamed and unnoticed. Nevertheless, some of the murders have been reported worldwide, drawing attention to the ruthlessness of the military rule in some nations. For example, El Salvador's 1979–1992 civil war took 70,000 lives. Included in this number were shocking assassinations of church people. For example, on March 24, 1980, Archbishop Oscar Romero (1917–80) was shot while presiding at the Eucharist. Four women missionaries from the United States were brutally raped and murdered on December 2, 1980: Jean Donovan and three nuns, Dorothy Kazel, an Ursuline; and Maura Clarke and Ita Ford, both of Maryknoll. On November 16, 1989, six Jesuit priests, their housekeeper, and her teenage daughter were ruthlessly tortured and executed. The two army officers responsible for this crime were sentenced to thirty years in prison on January 24, 1992. The civil war ended a week later on January 31, 1992.

Liberation Theology Is Pluralistic

Liberation theology is a term that covers, sometimes rather loosely, a variety of theologians and activists. What they share is a common starting point and an ultimate vision.

Vatican II replaced the official neoscholastic theology with the perspectives of the "new theologians." The point of departure of the conciliar theology was modernity and the social locus of the developing countries of the West. This theology directed the church into the modern world in order to connect with its scientific and technological enterprises for the promotion of human, political, social, and economic development. However, Leonardo Boff explained that the conciliar theology evaded "the basic question, the question of the profoundly unequal relationships that prevail among nations and between classes, and the price others have to pay for the benefits of accelerated development in the central countries" (1989, 54). Liberation theology's point of departure is "the people, the social locus of the popular, oppressed classes. It strives for the liberation of these classes and seeks to win them a voice in the historical process" (ibid.). Boff adds: "Liberation theology's starting point is ethical indignation in the face of the 'humiliating scourge' of poverty, together with an encounter with the Lord in the effort to search out, in company of the poor, the pathway of liberation" (ibid., 65). In other words, theology is understood as critical reflection on the life and actions of Christians committed to the struggle for the liberation of all humans, especially the poor (Nickoloff 1993, 514).

The ultimate vision shared by liberation theologians is of a salvation that achieves total liberation from both personal and social sin. Beyond this shared goal, there are many differences among liberationists, differences that are conceptual and strategic. For example, some denounce class conflict because it can lead to armed violence and guerrilla warfare.

Some of the male leaders include Gustavo Gutiérrez of Peru, Juan Luis Segundo (1925–95) of Uruguay, Hugo Assmann and Leonardo Boff of Brazil, Enrique Dussel and Jose Miguez-Bonino of Argentina, Segundo Galilea of Chile, Jose Miranda of Mexico, and Jon Sobrino of El Salvador. Some of the female leaders include Maria Pilar Aquino and Elza Tamez of Mexico, Ivone Gebara of Brazil, and Gladys Parentelli of Columbia.

The most famous of the group is Gutiérrez. This priest-theologian is often called the "intellectual father of liberation theology" (Lernoux 1989, 105) because he first proposed the term in July 1968 (Molineaux 1987) and because of his 1971 book, *A Theology of Liberation*.

Many regard Gutiérrez as a deeply spiritual man whose vision of the "church of the poor" teaches and inspires them as they face the overwhelming task of helping the poor. His critics attempt to portray him as a man who foments violence in society and infidelity to the church. There have been Vatican attempts to censure him, but to date he has not been silenced. He does not take this harassment that seriously, commenting wryly, "The Vatican has devised a new form of torture. They have made me defend what I have written. I have had to reread my writings three times!" (T. Fox 1988).

Liberation Theology Is New

The word that dominates liberation theology is the word *new*. This theology originates in a new experience of God that results in a new spirituality that is explained and guided by a new theology. It also offers a new self-understanding, new social structures, and a new future.

Liberation theology begins with a new experience of God, one which Gregory Baum believes "differs from other religious experiences which Christians have treasured over the centuries" (1983a).[6] The old experience was pietist, that is, one found his or her personal God primarily in prayer, while meditating on the scriptures, or in one's conscience. Those who have this new experience are either Christians "born into subjection" or Christians who recognize this struggle for freedom and self-determination as the significant sign of the times and believe they cannot grasp the Christian message apart from this. They see that the poor are "inhumanly poor precisely because the rich are so inhumanly rich" (Scharper 1978). They experienced God on their side in solidarity with them, summoning them to justice. Christ is not encountered as the sacrament of his Father or the servant of the world as highlighted at Vatican II, but as the divine liberator and protector of humanity who blessed "those who hunger and thirst after justice."

The new experience of God moved people beyond their privatized and pietist spirituality, a spirituality that had dominated the church during the nineteenth and twentieth centuries. Conversion took on new dimensions. A change of heart had to affect more than one's private relationship with God. It also should include an entry into a critical perception of society, especially an awareness of the structures of sin. The response to God requires a response to others.

Sorrow for sin encompasses more than repudiation of one's personal transgressions, according to liberation theology. What also must be taken into account is social sin, those structures of oppression that are the consequences of personal sins. Pietist spirituality taught salvation in terms overly individualistic and overly otherworldly. Liberationist spirituality revealed the illusion of individualism, created "a sense of solidarity with others, especially the poor, and [made] people aware that they [were] imbedded in a conflictual social matrix, the liberating movement of which is part of the mystery of divine redemption" (Baum 1987, 126).

Christian spirituality is built on faith. The new experience of God modifies the three traditional components of faith: conviction, commitment, and confidence (trust). Love and hope have always been acknowledged as dimensions of faith. Faith as commitment borders on love; faith as confidence borders on hope. But since love and hope have a justice dimension, the liberationists recognized that faith and justice are joined in an indissoluble way. The God who calls us to conviction, commitment, and confidence also calls us in the poor and their unjust situations. A "faith that does justice" not only makes people critics of the present order, but it also promotes the cause of liberation and justice. "Faith, therefore, is more than intellectual assent, more than hope in what God will do without us; it is also a present participation in the work that God is doing—that is to say, in the task of bringing forth justice to nations" (Baum 1984a, 77).

In many Latin American countries, but particularly in Brazil, this faith-justice spirituality is lived out in base communities *(comunidades eclesiais de base)* (Welsh 1986; Hewitt 1986). These communities actually grew out of the liberation movements in the 1960s and so they had a parallel but distinct history of development with liberation theology (McGovern 1989).

For Christians, the base-community churches are a new way of being church. As a matter of fact, such churches are as old as Christianity—the so-called "house-churches" of the primitive church (Acts 2:46, 5:42, 12:12). But they are a new structure in this era. These "popular" churches differ from the "hierarchical" churches or parishes, but like them they should serve as sacraments of the coming reign of God. In these base communities the gospel is proclaimed from the perspective of the poor in order to convert the rich and the powerful. The members, often with strong female leadership, serve the world by denouncing injustice and promoting social transformation. Together the members study the Bible and celebrate Eucharist. The Eucharist is "de-privatized" because it is no longer perceived simply as spiritual food for individual disciples on their journey. Rather, it creates community among the participants; it is a symbol of the banquet where all will have enough to eat; and it is the presence of Christ the liberator, himself oppressed and killed but now vindicated by God (Baum 1987, 115–16). Paul VI called the base communities "a real hope for the Church" in *Evangelii nuntiandi* (n. 58). Finally, the murder of Archbishop Romero and thousands of other Christians indicates that martyrdom is also new in Latin America. In the past when martyrs refused to renounce their faith in Christ, they were arrested, imprisoned, and publicly executed soon after; in Latin America men and women committed to the struggle for Christ's peace and justice face the threat of death at any moment from military death squads.

Liberation Theology and Marxism

The new experience of God, the new liberationist spirituality, and the new faith and justice movement have been explored and guided by a new theology, liberation theology.

Theology's primary task is to interpret "the Christ event in dialectical correlation to an interpretation of the situation" (Tracy 1981, 340). We have already seen that the liberation theologians read the Bible through the eyes of the poor. What was also new is that they critically used certain terms derived from Marxist or neo-Marxist social theory. Thus it is that liberation theology connects "the biblical idea of the deliverance of those who are in bondage or suffering and the Marxist hope for freedom from class oppression" (Kolden 1984, 123). But why the atheist Marx? When Gutiérrez was asked that question he promptly replied, "Because the people do." The Marxists had taught the people to demand their social and economic rights.

Some Marxist teachings are at odds with Christianity. For example, Marxism is atheistic, rejects humanity's spiritual destiny, and denies such economic rights as private property and such political rights as subsidiarity and the common good. It also encourages armed revolution, teaches the inevitability of class conflict, neglects the involuntarily poor, and singles out the economic conditions as the significant factor responsible for the transformation of society. Liberation theology not only rejects these teachings but it also ultimately (and ironically) attacks Marxism and any form of atheism "that perpetuates social structures which deform the image of God in human beings" (McDade 1991, 437).

On the other hand, Marxist social analysis also has several strengths. Marx explained the existence of ideologies. Liberation theology realized that traditional theology can be ideological. It can, for example, legitimize injustice and inaction. Hebrew prophets like Jeremiah (5:31) denounced the ways in which religion was used by some priests to support unjust kings.

Marx showed that evil is systemic. There can be no reform within an unjust system; the whole system has to be changed. For example, impoverished women are the most oppressed in society and the church. This situation will not change until the machismo ideology and the patriarchal structures that pervade both society and the church are transformed.

For Marx, humans are creative workers. He analyzed industrial or manual labor as the source of multiple alienations for workers and denounced it. He said labor caused a threefold alienation. First, it alienated a person from nature because the factory treated the worker like a machine, making the worker's own body feel like a stranger to him. Second, it alienated a person from himself because it removed the product of his hands from him. Third, it alienated the worker from his fellow workers because his relationship to others was completely determined by his place in the industrial process (Baum 1975, 21–39).

Finally, Marx had challenged the Aristotelian understanding of the process of gaining knowledge: first theory, then application. This is the order used in the physical sciences. First medicine is studied in a theoretic manner, then it is applied to the sick. According to Marx, the relation between theory and practice (praxis) is quite different for the human sciences. Marx believed that commitment and solidarity precede the true perception of reality and, in turn, this true perception of reality leads to action that transforms society (Baum 1976). Praxis is too often understood as mere practice. Actually, praxis is the critical relationship between theory and practice whereby each is dialectically influenced and transformed by the other. Furthermore, praxis reminds us that theoretical activity is itself a praxis—and one to be tested by the practice it serves (Tracy 1987b, 10).

The liberation theologians make praxis the touchstone of truth or authenticity. They say the Christian faith must be lived before it can make any kind of theological sense. Solidarity with the poor—living with, like, and for the poor—is the presupposition for the authentic grasp of the gospel. You know you are a disciple of Christ if you are in solidarity with the poor. This theory of knowledge is captured by the following paradox: we get our most objective knowledge by subjective participation.

Many critics of liberation theology focus on its use of Marxist ideas and its espousal of socialism (Novak 1975, 1987; Sigmund 1990). From the previous paragraphs it should be clear that many of the works written in the 1970s did indeed use Marxist social and economic-political analysis. Moreover, the fact that some liberationists did use Marxism imprudently made it easy for the critics of liberation theology to link them with the criticisms leveled at radical groups. For example, Helder Camara reported, "When I feed the poor, I am called a saint. When I ask why they are poor, I am called a communist." Similarly, it is true that the late 1960s and early 1970s were a time of great revolutionary ferment and some liberation theologians called for a revolutionary overthrow of the military dictators who kept themselves unjustly in power. For many of these theologians it seemed an obvious right and duty to rise up against them. However, books on liberation theology in the 1980s hardly contain any treatment of Marxist social analysis. This is not to imply, argue Arthur F. McGovern and Thomas L. Schubeck, two United States Jesuit priests, that the earlier writings can be labeled their "Marxist phase" (1988). Even in the early 1970s, Gutiérrez and others distanced themselves from Marxist options and warned against christianizing any revolutionary ideology (Kirk 1986). In February 1988, McGovern and Schubeck began a three-month study of liberation theology in Latin America which took them to eight countries. They found liberation theology working in a new context and taking new directions. There was some use of Marxist critique of capitalism "but liberation theologians used its concepts only at a very general level to describe exploitation by wealthy owners, the dominance of northern capitalist countries in the world economy, and the use of ideology to maintain and justify the tangentially status quo" (1988). In a two-week course in Peru under the direction of Gutiérrez, the two Jesuits said they heard no mention of Marxism in any of the talks they attended. Finally, McGovern and Schubeck report that the liberation theologians are quite aware that classic Marxist analysis does not adequately deal with the problems of indigenous peoples, racism, and the oppression of women.

The Effectiveness of Liberation Theology

Its results are mixed. On the negative side, its direct political significance remains small. Even in Brazil where its force seems greatest, its impact comes more from the strength and leadership of the episcopal conference which constitutes a strong voice in that country. Liberation theology enjoyed some influence early on. Now it seems that "the present historical situation in Latin America eliminates any hope for the success of liberation movements . . . [It may have to] moderate its aims and work together with the progressive sector of the bourgeoisie to stabilize civilian, democratic rule and assure the protection of civil liberties" (Baum 1989b, 123).

On the positive side, liberation theology has drawn the attention of the world to the plight of the poor, has drawn Christians to find in the Bible a God who favors the poor, and has drawn the institutional church to commit to a preferential option for the poor. Liberation theology has also contributed immeasurably to the one and only church of Christ in two interrelated ways: it has advanced the ecumenical movement and it has given theology a postmodern focus.

Liberation theology has advanced ecumenism even though not all Catholics and Protestants have accepted this theology. Nevertheless, it "is the first common theological movement of Catholics and Protestants since the sixteenth century Reformation . . . In a real sense, this marks the end of the Reformation and Counter-Reformation; and it is significant that it originated in and has taken deepest roots in Latin America, Asia and Africa, regions for which the Reformation as a European historical phenomenon was irrelevant" (MacEoin 1984). This means that liberation theology, which began as a movement in the church, is now almost a new movement *of* the church, albeit a minority movement.

Liberation theology has given theology—both Protestant and Catholic—a postmodern focus. Since we live in a world in which most people neither know Christ nor are Christian, traditionally theologians have written to and for these people. For example, in 1976, Hans Küng discussed the two great challenges for Christianity as he perceived them: the world religions and secular humanism (pp. 25–116). Küng's analysis is very helpful and accurate in many ways. In the past, theology has addressed three groups: those within the church, in order to help them clarify their faith; those who belong to other religions and churches, in order to dialogue with them about the God revealed in Jesus Christ; and those indifferent or antagonistic to religion, in order to dialogue with them about the ultimate meaning of life. Today, however, liberation theologians and theologians influenced by them—Harvey Cox (1980), Schubert Ogden (1980), Philip Scharper (1978) and Robert McAfee Brown (1978, 1980)—have gone beyond Küng.

These theologians do not deny the serious challenge from the world religions and secular humanism, but they argue that there is a more primary challenge, namely, the call of God to us through the poor, the oppressed, and the hungry. Millions of people live a life that is so minimally human that Gutiérrez referred to them as "nonpersons," that is, "people who are not considered human in our society" (Gibeau 1976b). Schubert Ogden explains the term more clearly: a nonperson is "one who, being excluded from the existing order in one or more respects, is to that extent unfree, a passive object of history instead of its active subject" (1980).

Why this shift from Küng's nonbelievers to liberation theology's nonpersons? The reason is that nonbelievers question our religious world but usually share our socioeconomic outlook. Like us they have a deep regard for human life and yet, at the same time, they contribute to the plight of the poor by being part of the power elites. Like us they foster the dominant, unchristian ideologies of our society. On the other hand, the poor and the oppressed challenge not only our religious world but our socioeconomic and political worlds as well. Their poverty and hunger challenge our consumerism, racial and sexual prejudices, and comfortable lifestyle. In short, liberation theology says there is a specifically Christian way to view society and to do theology—from the viewpoint of the nonpersons. The poor need a chance to live authentic and useful lives. At Vatican II the bishops reminded the faithful that the church community "is at once a sign and the safeguard of the transcendental dimension of the human person" (GS 76). Liberation theology defends the supernatural origin and destiny of all persons, especially the poor and marginalized.

Synod of 1971

In addition to the rise of political and liberation theologies and Paul VI's own encyclicals, the other important event that occurred during his pontificate was this synod. On September 30, 1971, the bishops met to discuss social justice. As we have already seen, Vatican II called for social justice. The bishops reminded the faithful that a free social order "must be founded in truth, built on justice, and enlivened by love; it should grow in freedom toward a more humane equilibrium" (GS 26). The bishops also observed that "Today, there is an inescapable duty to make ourselves the neighbor of every individual, without exception" (GS 27).

The bishops at the synod reiterated the conciliar teachings but, influenced by political and liberation theologies, did so more explicitly. The beginning of the most quoted sentence from its document, *Justice in the World*, insists that "action on behalf of justice and participation in the transformation of the world fully appear to us as a constitutive dimension of the preaching of the gospel" (n. 6).

This sentence evoked a great deal of discussion. The point of contention centered on the word *constitutive*. The bishops meant that social justice is neither incidental to the mission of the church nor does it take second place to more "spiritual" or "religious" matters. For example, some maintain that evangelization is primarily a spiritual enterprise. Those who question the word *constitutive* prefer the word *integral*, that is, something not absolutely essential to the church's mission but which pertains to its fullness (Dorr 1983, 188). But the writings of both Paul VI and John Paul II on evangelization and the "new evangelization" (as discussed in chapter 4) indicate that the church would fail to be true to its very identity if action on behalf of social justice was absent.

The 1971 Synod also went beyond Vatican II's analysis of social justice. The council fathers said justice would flow from a change of heart, a transformation of persons; the synod said justice would be achieved with the transformation of social structures. A conversion of heart is a great step but it does not change the context of people's lives. There are networks of domination and oppression which stifle freedom, truth, justice, and love, and prevent a greater part of humanity from sharing in the building up and enjoyment of a more just world. These sinful structures need to be eliminated. The church took this stand because it knew it had to be "the voice of those who have no voice."

John Paul II and CELAM III in 1979

John Paul II has been extremely active in the cause of social justice in society. Through his writings and charismatic presence he has forcefully denounced injustice and advocated justice around the globe. For example, during the Persian Gulf War in 1991 he made more than fifty appeals for peace. By June 1996, John Paul, a restless man, had made seventy-two visits to Catholic communities outside of Italy. In January 1979, the attention of the world was focused on Mexico for the pope's first overseas visit. There he toured the country for a week, delivering twenty-eight speeches. It is reported that he adjusted some of his prepared texts once he saw at first hand the massive poverty. But his main reason for the visit was to open CELAM III at Puebla (MacEoin and Riley 1980; Eagleson and Scharper 1979).

In his speech to the bishops on January 28, 1979, John Paul did not use the term liberation theology, but he did speak of liberation. "The church," he said, "feels the duty to proclaim the liberation of human beings; the duty to help this liberation become fully established; but she also feels the corresponding duty to proclaim liberation in its integral and profound meaning, as Jesus proclaimed and realized it." He reminded the bishops that Jesus "identified with the deserted," was committed "to the neediest," and was "never indifferent to the imperatives of social reality."

Commentators agreed that the address "was couched in abstract, traditional and highly nuanced language" (Brockman 1979). Reflecting on the pope's visit, the *New York Times* editorialized on January 30 that some of the pope's sentences about liberation and "political involvement" amounted to a rejection of liberation theology. However, most journalists believed he rejected extreme forms of liberation theology, particularly the kind that made "the gospel into political ideology" or which called for "all-out class warfare, and even [Fidel] Castro-style revolution, as the only way to achieve social justice" (Peerman 1979).

After his address, John Paul left the city, allowing the bishops to meet from January 28 to February 13, to make the pastoral decisions necessary for the good of the church in their region. Their theme—evangelization in the present and future of Latin America—had been proposed by Paul VI, who had planned to inaugurate the meeting just as he had done at Medellín.

The first thing the bishops reflected on was the socioeconomic conditions of their countries. However, there was a serious division among the bishops about the nature of their problem. Alfonso Lopez Trujillo, Archbishop of Bogotá and president of CELAM, led a group that insisted that secularization was their basic problem. The solution was "to evangelize the culture." Many bishops and theologians found this ill-defined phrase vague (MacEoin 1996). Other bishops insisted that the major problem continued to be the oppression of the poor and that what was needed was a radical change of the socioeconomic system. They reported that the social situation had severely deteriorated since Medellín in 1968. Most Latin American countries, they said, had become more impoverished, more debt-ridden, and more repressive. In addition, a surprising reversal had taken place between 1965 and 1990 in most of their countries. In 1965 most countries had a 70 percent rural population; in 1990, most were 70 percent urban (F. McDonagh 1990).

The bishops produced a lengthy final document with five major parts, each with chapters and subsections. This document, however, was a compromise document. On the one hand, the bishops insisted that the problem in Latin America was secularization which could be resolved by energetic evangelization. On the other hand, the bishops reaffirmed the direction set by Medellín. Four of their principal points were the following:

First, Medellín, they declared, "adopted a clear and prophetic option expressing preference for, and solidarity with, the poor." "Preferential option for the poor"—the title of one of the chapters in their document—became the catchword of Puebla and captured its spirit. The bishops expressed concern for many groups—the poor, youth, elderly, ill-housed city-dwellers; and those involved in liturgical, educational, and social services. All of these persons or groups are to be viewed in light of the option for the poor. This means the preferential option for the poor "is not itself optional—it is not one of several theological or pastoral tendencies among which Christian ministers or constitutions may pick or choose."

Second, the bishops expressed appreciation for the base communities and encouraged their growth (Hennelly 1979). In 1979 there were some forty-one thousand in Brazil alone.

Third, the bishops explained the crucial difference between evangelization and partisan politics, and they denounced violence of every kind.

Fourth, the bishops called attention to the problems of two exploited groups: the indigenous people and the women of Latin America. Medellín did not deal with either of these two groups (Ruether 1979). By focusing on them, the bishops indicated that gender and ethnic differences are aspects of the rampant poverty and oppression.

In March 1979, John Paul sent the Latin American bishops a letter with a ringing endorsement of their conference conclusions.

John Paul II's Prophetic Humanism

After studying the teachings of John Paul II as spiritual guide of the global church during the first fifteen years of his papacy, Avery Dulles explained in an essay in 1993 that the comprehensive theme of John Paul's teachings is "prophetic humanism." This term denotes that the primary concern of the pope is the "defense of the dignity of the human person and the promotion of human rights . . . The central and unifying task of the church, for John Paul II, is to rediscover and promote the inviolable dignity of every person." Clear examples of this prophetic humanism can be found in his two addresses to the United Nations and his three encyclicals on the social teaching of the church.

John Paul spoke at the United Nations on October 2, 1979 and on October 5, 1995. In 1979, the cold war dominated world politics. The pope addressed such topics as the possibilities of global conflict, the arms race, and the unjust distribution of resources. These issues prevented people from being free. He called the United Nations Universal Declaration on Human Rights, signed on December 10, 1948, the organization's "fundamental document" because its focus is "the rights of the human being as a concrete individual and of the human being in his universal value." This document, he declared, "is a milestone on the long and difficult path of the human race. The progress of humanity must be measured not only by the progress of science and technology, which shows man's uniqueness with regard to nature, but also and chiefly by the primacy given to spiritual values and by the progress of the moral life" (n. 7).

In 1995 the world was significantly freer because of the breakup of communist rule in eastern Europe in 1989 and the former USSR in 1991. John Paul reflected on "the extraordinary changes of the last few years" (n. 1). He observed that "the global acceleration of that quest for freedom" is one of the outstanding phenomena of our time. Since he had witnessed as a Polish citizen the depredations of nazism and communism, he is able to speak about individual and national freedom with authority and authenticity. He said that human beings have within them a capacity for wisdom and virtue so that they are able, with God's grace, "to build in the next century a civilization worthy of the human person, a true culture of freedom." He added that the countries of the world needed a declaration of national rights similar to the United Nations Universal Declaration of Human Rights because of cultural pluralism and because freedom is dependent on human solidarity and international cooperation. He called the United Nation's document "one of the highest expressions of the human conscience in our time."

At the center of the pope's address was the difference between a nationalism that fears the "other" and the "different," and "true patriotism," that is, a "proper love" of one's country that is shown by loyalty to, and respect for, one's country and taking pride in its traditions. He then discussed the abuses rising out of the freedoms people have achieved. He was concerned because some of the newly freed nations were losing their independence because the poor nations were increasingly dependent on rich nations. In short, the pope argued, in the words of Thomas Fox (1995a) that "Too little freedom or abuse of freedom separates humanity from authentic existence."

The theme of prophetic humanism pervades the three encyclicals John Paul has written about the church's social teaching.

Laborem exercens ("On Human Work") was written in 1981 to mark the ninetieth anniversary of *Rerum novarum*. John Paul's letter dealt with oppression and exploitation in the industrialized world of the North. In it he argued, as no other church document had ever done, that humans should be defined as workers, and that it is through labor (by which he means society-building) that people determine their world and in doing so, constitute themselves as persons (Baum 1986a). Humans differ from animals because they work. Only humans have to create the conditions of their survival by labor. Nature does not sustain human life unless it is transformed by work. The pope wrote: "Human work is a key, probably the essential key, to the whole social question, if we try to see that question really from the point of view of man's good."

Despite his Marxist language, what the pope did was develop a non-Marxist critique of liberal capitalism. He called for "the solidarity of labor and with labor." He offered the principle of "the priority of labor over capital" as central to a just society. Both communism and liberal capitalism operate out of the principle of the priority of capital over labor. Workers, the pope declared, are entitled to ownership and participation in decision making regarding the work process and the use of the capital they produce. Both liberal capitalism and communism exclude workers from this kind of participation. Both make labor alienating and the situation unjust because people are treated like cogs in a huge machine.

John Paul's encyclical differed from the style and substance of previous popes in that he called upon people to struggle for their own emancipation. His encyclical promoted the solidarity of workers and the poor in a joint struggle that included confrontation in order to ensure the common good. Leo XIII and other popes asked government officials to reform society and improve conditions of the poor and workers. John Paul called on all those who love justice—and he included the church—to be in solidarity with workers. Solidarity, explains Donal Dorr, "is an *attitude,* a commitment on the part of those who form community, to participate in the life of that community in a way that promotes the common good" (1989, 151).

In an extended and otherwise very favorable commentary on the encyclical, Gregory Baum pointed out two oversights in it. The pope was insensitive to the self-understanding of women, and he did not ask whether his principles that intended to protect "the subject character of human beings" were operative in "the Catholic ecclesiastical organization" (Baum 1982).

In *Sollicitudo rei socialis* ("Social Concerns"), an encyclical signed on December 30, 1987, John Paul commemorated the twentieth anniversary of Paul VI's *Populorum progressio.* In 1967 Paul VI had called for true development to occur in human terms, including the personal and spiritual dimensions of life, in order to close the gap between rich and poor nations. His best-remembered sentence was "Development is the new name for peace."

Asserting that little or no development had occurred since 1967, John Paul tried to impress upon the world how insufferable were its economic inequities. He identified the failure of development in global terms. He pointed out that in fact the gap between the developing North and the slowly developing South had widened. In this encyclical the pope examined the world from the perspective of the poor, particularly the third-world nations. He indicated that there were two principal causes for the ever-widening gap, one economic and the other political. The capitalist economic systems of global interdependence, he said, continued to allow the rich nations to reap the greater benefits. The political situation was dominated by the continuing rivalry between the two superpowers, the United States and the USSR, each claiming universal validity. The developing countries got caught between these two powers of the North. They were forced to choose one—so that their "development" got defined by either liberal capitalism or Marxist collectivism, two false economic understandings of development.

The world, the pope stated, was marked by hunger in the South, by arms production and sales in the North, and ecological damage on the entire globe. This encyclical marked the first time that the institutional church addressed the subject of ecology as a moral issue. The common good of the globe was so disregarded, declared the pope, that civilization was "oriented toward death rather than life." The way out of these crises situations was through interdependence and solidarity based on love and justice. "Peace is the fruit of solidarity."

John Paul repudiated both liberal capitalism and communism as ideologies and as economic systems. He placed both on the same level of iniquity: both are "imperialisms," one of power and the other of profit. Nevertheless, he never advocated their abolition. Rather, on the one hand, he asked capitalism to reconstruct its free-market inheritance into "some form or other of ethically-steered, mixed economy welfare capitalism;" on the other hand, he asked communism to transform its socialist heritage in order to "become more responsive to the economic initiative of individuals" (Baum 1989a, 87). John Paul offered no social theory or "third way" to which all must conform. His goal was to offer critical reflection in the name of the gospel so that the existing economic systems would take a more humane direction.

The encyclical received considerable praise. Yet there were some negative criticisms. First, "conservative" Catholics in the United States found it extremely radical. However, said Gregory Baum, both they and the pope needed a broader perspective. The encyclical did not convey "full realization that the capitalist economic system *has achieved global proportions,* that even the communist countries, including the Soviet Union, trade with the West and hence to a considerable extent depend on the global capitalist system, and that it is therefore the orientation of this global system that largely determines the economic well-being of the world population" (ibid., 75).

A second critique came from Maria Riley, a Dominican sister and social analyst. She said the encyclical was blind "to the essential contribution that feminists, both women and men, are making to the development debate. . . . It is becoming clearer that 'women's issues' are not marginal; they are central to the search for the kind of development in which people matter" (1989, 200).

In 1991, the centenary of *Rerum novarum*, John Paul published his third encyclical, which dealt with the topic of social justice. He commemorated Leo's landmark encyclical with his own, *Centesimus annus* ("The Hundredth Year"). This letter was signed on May 1, 1991, the feast of St. Joseph the Worker.

This encyclical of twenty-five thousand words celebrated one hundred years of Catholic social teaching in light of the collapse in 1989 of Marxism in the Soviet Union and Eastern Europe, and reaffirmed the option for the poor. John Paul insisted that major new efforts were required to meet the needs of the poor. For example, he argued that money and goods would be available if the huge military machines were dismantled.

The pope severely criticized Marxism for its economic inefficiency, for stifling the national rights of countries, and for its atheism which brings on a "spiritual void" in human affairs.

Capitalism (sometimes called "market," "free," or "business" economy by John Paul) received both positive and negative critiques in the encyclical. The collapse of communism prompted John Paul to ask whether capitalism should now be considered the model to be proposed both to European countries seeking to rebuild their economies and societies, and to the countries of the third world. His answer was yes, insofar as by capitalism was meant "an economic system which recognized the fundamental and positive role of business, the market, private property and the resulting responsibility for the means of production, as well as free human creativity in the economic sector." Capitalism, he agreed, has the potential for increasing freedom and dignity. The free market is the most efficient instrument for utilizing resources and for effectively responding to needs. However, capitalism must maintain a moral core by not exploiting the poor and by repairing injustices within its own system.

On the other hand, the pope warned that capitalism is not the best model for countries trying to rebuild and develop "if by capitalism is meant a system in which freedom in the economic sector is not circumscribed within a strong juridical framework which places it at the service of human freedom in its totality, and which sees it as a particular aspect of that freedom, the core of which is ethical and religious." Capitalism has its own inadequacies and these are especially visible in the "domination of things over people." The pope also warned against consumerism which leads nations and people to believe they can achieve material satisfaction without relying on spiritual values. Consumerism reduces humanity to the sphere of economics and the satisfaction of material needs.

Again, John Paul did not propose any specific "third way" between communism and capitalism. On the contrary, he warned that "the church has no models to present." In the end it is up to Christians, taking their cue from the social teaching of the church, to be creative and inventive in devising and introducing models that are ever more just and democratic.

There were many diverse reactions to the encyclical. Feminists were quick to point out that the document contains only one sentence referring to the special economic problems encountered by women. After noting that the elderly, the young, and those "part of the so-called Fourth World" can be marginalized if they do not keep up their skills in a rapidly changing, technological world, the encyclical simply states: "The situation of women too is far from easy in these conditions" (n. 33).

Two groups maintained that the encyclical reinforced their position: proponents of the free market and those who advocated more government control of the markets. The former overlooked or downplayed what John Paul said about the inadequacies of capitalism and the latter overlooked what was said about the excesses of the welfare state (Windsor 1991; Neuhaus 1992; McBrien 1992b, 1993a). Finally, others viewed the encyclical not only as a strong challenge to much recent United States economic and social policy but also as a call to "renew the effort to overcome the increasing marginalization and poverty of vast numbers of people who are left out of the market economies that are shaping the future of the globe" (Hollenbach 1991).

The social encyclicals of John Paul confirm Dulles's thesis: the pope stoutly defends the dignity of the human person. There is one very important reservation. Women have been quick to note that John Paul is insufficiently sensitive to the indignities and injustices suffered by women.

John Paul II and Liberation Theology

Catholics have different views of the interrelationship of church and society. Some believe that Christians, as individuals and together as church, must be involved in politics and economics if they are to fulfill their mission to be peacemakers who hunger and thirst after justice. Others find the church's involvement in economics and politics difficult to understand because their spirituality does not have a social dimension, one that demands that they go beyond personal piety to concern for the poor and oppressed. Others believe the church is "too political," meaning that the church is becoming primarily or even solely political.

John Paul has consistently warned Catholics that their commitment to liberation must not be understood in primarily political and economic terms. For example, in addressing priests in India in 1986, he said priests should give "humble service to all, including those who are not poor," and authentic love for the poor can only "spring from a deep experience of God."[7]

Listed in chronological order are some of the statements or actions of John Paul relative to liberation theology.

In September 1984, the CDF issued an "Instruction on Certain Aspects of the Theology of Liberation." It warned of dangerous trends in certain forms of liberation theology, particularly those which use Marxist concepts in "an insufficiently critical manner." This use can undermine the church's unity and the integrity of the Christian faith, the CDF warned. Specifically, the Vatican had in mind those who treat the Marxist method of social analysis as an "indisputable science," or who describe all social changes in terms of class struggle, or who reduce all opposing views to "bourgeois" ideology (Hebblethwaite 1984c).

Some commentators found difficulties with the CDF arguments. Arthur McGovern argued that just as Christian psychiatrists have learned to use Freud without approving his views on religion, so liberation theologians have learned to use Marx without accepting his atheism, materialism, or calls for violence (McGovern 1985, 259). The Jesuit Juan Luis Segundo, called "the Karl Rahner of liberation theology" because of his scholarship, wrote a sustained attack on the Vatican document in a book published in 1985: *Theology and the Church: A Response to Cardinal Ratzinger and a Warning to the Whole Church.* He argued that the Vatican instruction, while it aimed at muting liberation theology, had a hidden agenda, namely, the repudiation of Vatican II and the reintroduction of traditional dogmatic dualisms such as those that separated the spiritual and material order and personal and social sin (T. Fox 1996). Gregory Baum judged the instruction a caricature of Marxism and wrote it was based on an unbelievable thesis, namely, that those who accept certain aspects of Marxism inevitably assimilate, whether they like it or not, the entire Marxist system (Baum 1987, 104–5).

In February 1985, Leonardo Boff, a Brazilian Franciscan, was silenced. Cited in the notification that he was prohibited from teaching, speaking or writing, was his book, *Church: Charism and Power.* This book had been a best seller in Brazil when it was first published in 1981. Boff wrote about the church's abuse of power. He declared that the fundamental issue facing the church in the 1980s was human rights within the church. He argued that "to live power as service and as servant is the greatest challenge facing the institutional church." The overemphasis on hierarchy, he believed, should be balanced by a renewed awareness of charism and prophecy. He said the way of the future for the church was in the base communities, which he advocated as an alternative to the existing system of parishes and dioceses. The Vatican objected to his emphasis on charism and prophecy at the expense of hierarchy and authority (Lernoux 1989, 38–44; Doyle 1992).

Since Boff had wide personal support with the Brazilian episcopal conference, his punishment angered many Brazilians (Lernoux 1985). His case was followed with keen interest by some Protestant scholars in the United States, who found his ecclesiology very helpful (R. M. Brown 1986; Cox 1988a). Boff accepted the Vatican's "reservation" and voiced his intent "to walk with the church rather than walk alone with my theology." The censure was lifted eleven months later. However, in May 1991, Boff was forced to resign as editor of a Catholic magazine published in Brazil. His removal came after the publication of a series of articles that urged the Vatican to change its policies on several issues, such as its refusal to allow priests to marry. When John Paul II made his second visit to Brazil in October 1991, he admitted that the ratio of priests to people was low—one priest per 9,306—but said the ordination of married men was "not acceptable."

In July 1992, Boff resigned from the priesthood, complaining bitterly of the Vatican and Franciscan censorship and oppression he experienced over a twenty-year period. He blasted the Vatican as an "oppressive regime, which like a bat, fears the light." In choosing to leave the priesthood and his Franciscan community after twenty-seven years, Boff said his intent was "not to be free of the church, which I love and will never abandon, but to be free to continue working without impediments" (Hebblethwaite 1992a).

In April 1986, the CDF issued another instruction, this one titled "On Christian Freedom and Liberation." It never mentioned liberation theology or Marxism. Its five chapters covered the Western history of freedom and the church's understanding and practice of liberation.

The document had several controversial areas. It seemed to undercut the Puebla phrase "a preferential option for the poor" by substituting "a love of preference for the poor." The latter is an awkward phrase which has not caught on. Regarding the base communities, the instruction supported them as "a source of great hope" and "a real expression of communion." However, it warned that they only serve these purposes to the extent that "they really live in unity with the local church and the universal church." Those familiar with base communities and their attachment to the universal church thought this provision unnecessary.

Aside from these minor criticisms, the general reaction was that the instruction supported liberation theology in Latin America and elsewhere. Alfred Hennelly thought the instruction so profoundly integrated liberation themes into the mainstream of Catholic social teaching that it should have been written as a papal encyclical, "which would have given its teaching even greater weight on the world theological scene" (1986). Gutiérrez praised it as a "relaunching" of the liberation movement and insisted that "it closes a chapter; a new, more positive period is beginning" (ibid.).

In spring 1986, John Paul wrote the Brazilian bishops a letter in which he praised liberation theology. He wrote: "We are convinced, we and you, that the theology of liberation is opportune, useful and necessary." Not only did he take for granted the existence of base communities but he even praised them as the ordinary way of the church in that country. The letter brought great relief. The background for the letter goes back to July 1980, when John Paul made his first visit to Brazil. At that time he told the 372 assembled bishops, the largest episcopal conference in the world, that they should not substitute base-community churches for the parishes. But the bishops had built their entire pastoral policy on base communities. Why this change of mind between 1980 and 1986? The pope said he was now able to rectify the long and painful misunderstanding between himself and the bishops due to a "new and deeper form of collegiality, thanks to which the pope and his collaborators now know better the realities of the Brazilian church" (Hebblethwaite 1986b).

In the 1990s John Paul and the curia have given indications that there is no further need for liberation theology and they want to get rid of it. Gary MacEoin, who attended and reported on Vatican II and the three CELAM meetings since the council, explains why (1997). First, liberation theology offers strong challenges to socialism. But with the collapse of the Soviet Union in 1991, socialism has ceased to be a serious threat. Second, there is John Paul's "theological conservatism." The pope is faithful to the conciliar teachings. Those teachings, inspired by the "new theology," directed the church into the modern world as a servant and supporter of the efforts to promote human, political, and socioeconomic development. Liberation theology is a postconciliar movement that emerged because it became clear that the underdeveloped countries were paying for the accelerated development in the developing countries. This theology maintains that before the underdeveloped countries can be developed, they need liberation from "institutionalized injustice and violence." Liberation is based on justice. But John Paul downplays "the role of justice in the social order, stressing instead a solidarity that is defined as nothing more than charity" (ibid.). Once charity is substituted for justice as the basis of Catholic social teaching, then it is most difficult to insist that both individuals and nations have an obligation to provide for those with insufficient food, medicine, and education.

MacEoin fears that the Synod of Bishops for America scheduled to meet in Rome in November 1997 involves "a major dilution of the identity of the church in Latin America, as well as a major recentralization of decision making in Rome" (1996). The draft document for this special synod is entitled "Encounter with the Living Jesus Christ: The Way to Conversion, Communion and Solidarity in America." The document states that John Paul II proposes "the cultivation of the virtue of solidarity. Solidarity is understood to be a morally necessary reaction to the existence of injustice in social conditions which many individuals suffer today." MacEoin points out that this theology of solidarity would replace the theology of liberation because the injustice mentioned is "a problem affecting individuals, not groups or classes." In their CELAM meetings the bishops expressed their concern for their people suffering from institutionalized injustice and violence. The Vatican document calls for dedicated people to run centers of charity and assistance. "Solidarity would thus seem to be nothing more than another name for charity. Clearly it is quite different from justice, a word that is operationally absent from the document" (ibid.).

This 1997 synod was proposed by John Paul at CELAM IV in 1992. The pope said he believed that a meeting of representative bishops of the Americas would help "unite even more closely all the peoples that make up this great continent . . . to find ways to solve the dramatic situations of vast sectors of the population who aspire to legitimate overall progress and to more just and decent living conditions." This is a truly laudable objective. Many hope the synod will be fruitful.

John Paul II and CELAM IV in 1992

This meeting was held October 12–28, 1992, in Santo Domingo, Dominican Republic. The time was chosen to mark the fifth century of evangelization in the western hemisphere. The place was chosen because here the first Catholic diocese in the western hemisphere was established. In announcing the conference, John Paul declared that this meeting should pay particular attention "to a renewed evangelization of the continent, which will penetrate deeply into the hearts of individuals and into the culture of peoples." The theme of the conference was "New Evangelization, Human Advancement and Christian Culture."

During the preparations for the conference two interrelated concerns surfaced. First, active defenders of the option for the poor among Latin American bishops were now in a minority since many bishops appointed by John Paul since Puebla were chosen because of their fidelity to John Paul's ideological and ecclesiological guidelines. Those who had attended Puebla had fond memories of the successes achieved there but they were "not expecting great things" (MacEoin 1991a). While the Vatican still favored a preferential option for the poor, it claimed also that part of the problem in Latin America "is that the poor lack a work ethic" (MacEoin 1992a).

Second, there were rumors that there would be a shift in focus regarding the process of evangelization: from the poor to "the Catholic culture" of Latin America. This shift was deemed necessary, it was said, because in many Latin American countries, Pentecostal and evangelical churches had grown rapidly. For example, in Guatemala in 1991, the evangelical churches claimed 30 percent of the people in this traditionally Catholic country. In Brazil, 88 percent of the people identified themselves as Catholic in 1980, but in 1991 the number was less than 80 percent. When John Paul had visited Brazil in October 1991, the Brazilian bishops addressed these words to the pope: "We look forward to this conference in Santo Domingo and are glad to join with the church in this call to evangelization. But we would like to know who will be evangelized, how they will be evangelized and who will do the evangelizing" (Piccolino 1991). Many Latin American bishops feared that "Catholic culture" was simply a code word for the reimposition of a European model of church. These bishops insisted that the poverty of millions of their people should remain the starting point for their reflections on the theme of new evangelization.

John Paul was in Santo Domingo for six days, October 9–14. His schedule—which was originally planned to include stops in Jamaica, Nicaragua, and Mexico—was cut back to include only the Dominican Republic because he had undergone abdominal surgery in July. In his homilies and lectures he reiterated the preferential option for the poor: "We must feel other's poverty as our own and become convinced that the poor cannot wait." He praised the Latin American women for being "the guardian angels of Christianity" in their countries. Although he chided activist priests and nuns not to be blind to their primary religious role, he encouraged them to take up the program of Christ's beatitudes, especially as it affects the poor and the downtrodden. One of the key points made in his inaugural speech is that the evangelical churches were like "rapacious wolves . . . causing division and discord in our communities." Finally, despite the fact that he was aware of the bitter disputes over the legacy of Christopher Columbus, he thanked God for "the abundant fruits of the seeds planted over the last 500 years by [the] intrepid missionaries" (French 1992a; see also P. Steinfels 1992c; Stahel 1992a; Cleary 1992). During the pope's visit, protesters had called Columbus "the exterminator of a race" and they denounced the "500 years of hunger and massacre" (French 1992b).

John Paul inaugurated the episcopal conference attended by 307 voting bishops from 22 nations on October 12. In his lengthy address, he asked pardon for the church's offenses, past and present. Nevertheless, he stressed that the Catholic church had acted as the "untiring defender of the Indians, the protector of the values that existed in their cultures and supporter of their humanity in the face of the abuses committed at times unscrupulously by the colonizers." He also called for continuity with the Medellín and Puebla meetings, especially their preferential option for the poor (Wirpsa 1992a).

The sixteen-day conference was marked by serious debate about the future of the church (Wirpsa 1992b), and about the relationship of the bishops' "working document" (drafted over a three-year period) to the final document (Stahel 1992b). The two most important issues were poverty and the indigenous cultures. The bishops acknowledged that the major problem facing the Latin American church was the growing poverty and that in many of their countries "races and cultures [were] reasserting themselves—indigenous, blacks, mestizos—many of them impelled by spiritualities far older than Christianity that came to them across the water." The majority of the bishops believed that the gospel can flourish in a variety of cultures. Other bishops, however, talked about spreading and deepening the Christian culture, which they viewed "as a monoculture, European style" (Peerman 1993). The bishops who opposed this direction for evangelization did so "not only because of its recolonizing content, but also because it relativizes and reduces to a subordinate position the many cultures of the hemisphere, indigenous, African-American, mestizo, all of them with multiple variations" (MacEoin 1992b).

The bishops produced a sixty-one-page document, "Jesus Christ, Yesterday, Today and Tomorrow." It breaks very little new ground in its sections on such topics as human development, new evangelization, Christian culture, and neoliberal economic policies. It does contain a strong statement on ecology, an emphasis missing from the 1968 and 1979 documents. It reaffirmed both the Christian base communities as a new way of being church and the "irrevocable but not exclusive" option for the poor. The bishops emphasized the "new faces of poverty." Special attention, they maintained, must be paid when the rights of "children, women and the poorest groups in society—peasants, Indians and Afro-Americans—are violated." By linking these people to the ecological issues, the bishops manifested their sensitivity to the relationship between the oppression of the poor and the abuse of natural resources.

The impact of CELAM IV will probably not be realized for years to come, but it represented another major step by the institutional church to oppose, in the name of Christ the Liberator, the social, political, and economic forces that dehumanize everyone, especially the poor.

John Paul and Communism

Since John Paul spent most of his life under a communist government, he is knowledgeable of Marxism. Marxism has as one of its starting points the elimination of religion. Marx considered it a source of alienation. Vladimir Lenin (1870–1924), the major force behind the founding of the USSR, called religion "a sort of spiritual booze, in which the slaves of capital drown their human image, their demand for a life more or less worthy of man." Lenin supposed that communism would create a new species of human being—an atheistic, homogeneous Soviet man freed of religious, ethnic, or nationalist attachments. Lenin tried to suppress nationalism, believing that, since class struggle controlled political life, national sentiment was vain and illusory.

During the course of the twentieth century, the popes, *mutatis mutandis*, condemned communism in words that echoed Pius XI's declaration in 1937 that "Communism is intrinsically wrong and there can be no collaboration with it in any field on the part of those who want to save Christian civilization."

John Paul has written and spoken extensively against communism. He has done whatever he could to defeat it. For example, his visit to his native Poland in 1979 gave the people the self-confidence to found Solidarity and eventually defeat the communist regime by peaceful means.

Writing in 1992, Peter Hebblethwaite declared that "History will judge this [support] to have been John Paul's greatest achievement" (1992b). Francis X. Murphy added that John Paul "is likewise credited with the spread of the 'Polish contagion' to Hungary, Czechoslovakia, East Germany and eventually to all the Soviet satellite lands" (1990). Wilton Wynn believes John Paul was the catalyst for the fall of communism but not its cause. He suggests that "such other manifestations of Western culture as pop music had more to do with the fall of communism than the church" (Farrell 1995b). Wynn is not the first commentator to suggest that the spiritual aspirations expressed in popular culture (some of the music and some of the movies) have had genuine and compelling impact on non-democratic countries.

In June 1988 John Paul made contact with President Mikhail Gorbachev through a letter delivered by Cardinal Agostino Casaroli, his secretary of state from 1979–90, in which he expressed his concern for the welfare of Soviet Catholics. In January 1989, in his annual speech to the diplomatic corps attached to the Vatican, John Paul directly challenged the Soviets to follow up on their promises of greater religious freedom by taking some concrete steps. Beginning in February, the Soviets began to permit the restoration and appointment of bishops.

President Gorbachev traveled to Rome to see the pope on December 1, 1989—the first personal exchange between a Soviet president and a pope. Gorbachev acknowledged that Lenin was wrong, because even "after seven decades of Communist rule, the ties that bind religious faith to ethnic culture and nationalist sentiment [were] stronger than ever" (Murphy 1990). On the eve of the meeting, Gorbachev said that the Soviet Union had erred in long rejecting religion and now needed its moral force to help his plans for a restructured society to work *(perestroika)*. Gorbachev's words represent a major break with the Marxist-Leninist tradition: "We have changed our attitude on some matters, such as religion, for example, which admittedly we used to treat in a simplistic manner. Now we not only proceed from the assumption that no one should interfere in matters of the individual's conscience, we also say that the moral values that religion generated and embodied for centuries can help in the work of renewal in our country, too. In fact, this is already happening" (Haberman 1989).

At their ground-breaking meeting, Gorbachev promised full religious freedom in the Soviet Union and invited John Paul to visit Russia. John Paul agreed to resume official ties with Moscow, broken in 1917, and to support *perestroika*. John Paul concluded this historic summit by remarking that "Providence prepared the way for this meeting," one that put an end to decades of fear, anger, and oppression (Woodward, Nordland, and Coleman 1989, 11).

On September 26, 1990, the Soviet parliament decreed freedom of religion.

On September 4, 1993, John Paul launched the first papal visit to the former Soviet Union when he landed in Lithuania. This pilgrimage—his sixty-first overseas visit—was the start of a week-long tour of the Baltic states: Lithuania, Latvia, and Estonia, countries that were occupied by Soviet forces since 1940. Just five days before the pope's arrival, Moscow withdrew the last of its troops from Lithuania, removing a possible friction during the papal visit. The president of Lithuania called this departure of the troops "a very significant and symbolic coincidence." The opening sentence of an editiorial in the *New York Times* on September 11 stated: "The Pope has come and the Red Army has gone—two reasons for jubilation in Lithuania."

The mood of John Paul was singularly bereft of jubilation because the Baltic countries, like so many of the other countries in the former Soviet Union, are marked by ethnic, political, and religious strife. For varying reasons, John Paul views much of the world in the post-cold-war era as spiritually threatened. He said, "Tragically, the fall of the walls which separated East and West into two camps has made more evident the scandal of walls of poverty, violence and political oppression which still divide vast sectors of humanity." Consequently, he told the Baltic peoples that "there is need for a spiritual rebirth." He warned them that, although they had overcome communism and "left the tunnel of forced atheization," their next struggles would be with "the perils of indifference and secularism."

On November 19, 1996, John Paul welcomed Fidel Castro, President of Cuba since 1959, to the Vatican and accepted the communist leader's invitation to visit Cuba in 1997. John Paul set conditions: that he be allowed to travel and speak without restraint. Because of scheduling problems, the visit was postponed until January 1998.

Apparently, the exchange between these two strong, shrewd, and independent leaders who have often defied conventional wisdom was remarkable. By all reports, they did not discuss political differences but the problems that have hindered relations between Cuba and the Catholic church. John Paul has visited every country in Latin America except Cuba. This island country has an estimated population of 11 million, of whom 4.5 million are Catholic. The Vatican would like to get a solid foothold in Cuba so that the church could become a strong voice when Castro leaves power. Cuba has only one priest for every twenty thousand declared Catholics. But according to statistics, baptisms, Mass attendance, and church weddings and funerals are all increasing.[8] Both the church and Cuba can benefit from a papal visit. John Paul can proclaim once more respect for human dignity in the country's economic, political, and ecclesial systems.

Spirituality and Justice

With and since Vatican II the Catholic church's understanding of history and God's role in it has gone through some remarkable shifts and developments. How we respond to God's attempts to promote and expand his own presence in history is called spirituality.

The contemporary church is marked by three understandings of justice and spirituality.[9] The preconciliar is predominantly pietist or privatized: the church is a fortress that stands over against the world in an attitude of defense and offense. In this mindset there are two histories: sacred and secular. Christ is the light of a world steeped in darkness (John 12:46). God remains outside of secular history but will save the faithful in the next world. These Christians are otherworldly. God reigns in individual hearts. Sacred history operates through the church and this is a place of special encounter with God. The Bible is not central to this spirituality. Neither does this privatized spirituality evoke a keen sense of mission for all Christians.

All of this does not mean that these Catholics do not serve others. The spiritual and corporal works of mercy are encouraged. Much good is done through schools, orphanages, and hospitals. But changes in society, it is thought, will flow from personal transformation. A good example of this mindset was manifested at the time of the worldwide depression of the 1930s. The depression was considered to be the result of moral evil. Little consideration was given to ignorance about keeping an industrial economy functioning well.

"At its worst, this spirituality was ghetto-like, individualistic and escapist. But at its best it gave people a sense of God's transcendence . . . [and] a sense of security; there was little need for agonizing, since all knew their place and how they were expected to act" (Dorr 1984, 199). It is also important to add that it is just possible that the worst dimensions of this fortress spirituality "are just the fossilized relics" of a spirituality that at first challenged Christians—in a world where many were atheistic, materialistic, anti-Christian, and anti-church—to preserve not only God's transcendence and providence, but also the significance of baptism and a personal commitment to Christ.

At Vatican II there was a shift. The official church aimed at aggiornamento and a commitment to the world. It reversed one hundred years of teaching that began with the *Syllabus of Errors* (1864), whereby the church and world stood in opposition to one another. The council retrieved from the Bible a new dominant image, namely, the pilgrim people of God. The scriptures have an important place in this spirituality.

The great strength of this new model "is that it removes the traditional split between the sacred and the secular" (ibid., 201). There are not two histories but one, and this history has been redeemed in all its dimensions by Christ, the Lord of history. With his resurrection, Jesus made a real and powerful reentry into history. All the baptized should be involved in the church's mission to serve the world.

Instead of beginning with the church, this conciliar spirituality starts with the world redeemed by Christ, the servant of the world. At Vatican II the church applauded every human effort to build a better world. It encouraged Christians to transform their hearts. In this way the society would eventually change for the better. There is truth in this approach, namely, a person cannot be an instrument of peace if he or she is not at peace.

In the postconciliar church the shift from service of the church to service of the world was still operative, but with a major difference. The socioeconomic developments that the council fathers optimistically anticipated never materialized. This resulted in new questions: "When you set out to serve the world, whose world are you serving? Is it the world as structured by the rich and powerful, a world built on the dominant values of competition and success at all costs? Or is it the world as God wants it to be, one in which structural poverty and powerlessness are challenged, and the poor are privileged agents of God in bringing about the kingdom?" (ibid., 202).

The postconciliar church with its faith-justice spirituality is, in Leonardo Boff's apt phrase, a "church in the subworld" (Boff 1989, 12–13, 191–94). It underscores that we have a history marred by structural injustices and grinding poverty. God is on the side of the poor in their efforts at liberation. Christ's disciples serve Christ the liberator and the world by overcoming injustice. Full participation in the liturgy includes both celebrating God's saving interventions and answering his call to alleviate and eliminate injustices. The Bible is read and studied from the perspective of the poor. Structural transformation of society has been the message of Paul VI and John Paul II, Medellín, Puebla, Santo Domingo, and many other episcopal conferences.

This liberationist spirituality calls Christians to solidarity with the poor and to disentangle themselves from unjust structures. Such moves are not easy to make because our social, economic, and political lives are so interrelated that we are immersed in a huge interlocking system where almost all our actions play a part in maintaining structural injustice. We may be forced to make some compromises.

Compromises should not create guilt. There are reasons why it is necessary. First, although the Sermon on the Mount calls us to selfless love, it is not clear in our day-to-day living what this love requires of us. Compromise is possible because our vocation to be as holy as our heavenly Father cannot be identified with a clear and precise kind of moral perfection. Second, the proper spiritual response to our entrapment in structures of sin is mourning. The biblical word is *lamentation*. Mourning is part of the process of conversion. "Mourning unites those in the middle class with the victims of society who also mourn, even if for different reasons" (Baum 1989b, 119).

In addition to mourning, something can be done in small Christian communities, especially among the poor. Christians committed to the faith-justice spirituality will have to band together because they exist as a minority in the church. Nevertheless, they can be a countervailing current. Minorities sometimes find an appropriate strategy. Gregory Baum (1984a, 104) offered an imaginative and encouraging proposal:

> Imagine for a moment that in a city there were five just Christians in every parish, involved in local projects and joined in a lively network, what impact would such an active minority have on the church and on the city! The advantage of this minority strategy is that it does not depend on the cooperation of those in charge of the institutions, even though their cooperation is of great consequence. Thanks to such a minority strategy, moreover, there is always something we can do. We are not caught in total impotence. We can always find others with whom to promote the countervailing current of social justice, knowing that this is not a waste of time, but a contribution that in the long run prepares significant social changes.

Conclusion

In chapter 4, a sacramental consciousness was described as the single most powerful force holding the devotional life of the church together. In view of what has been presented in chapters 8 and 9, this point needs to be nuanced.

The sacramental consciousness of Catholics is most tangibly expressed at the Eucharist when the presence of the risen Christ is symbolized by the assembled community, the altar, the bread and wine, the scriptures, and the priest. The eucharistic celebration is indeed the most important thing a church community does and the Eucharist is the heart of the devotional life of the church—provided the celebration encompasses true, active participation. That is, the believing disciples not only participate in Christ's total surrender to his Father, but also bring this commitment to all facets of their lives, especially by participation in social justice.

This chapter reviewed the church's social teaching. From Leo XIII to the present, the popes have built on the teachings of their predecessors and, in view of the needs and signs of the times, offered guidance about justice and injustice to the Catholic church, other Christians, and the world. The bishops have joined in this teaching process at Vatican II, international synods, episcopal conferences, and as individuals. Theologians have illumined, explained, and guided this teaching. However, even though the teaching has been developing, not all members of the church have received and live the social teaching in the same way. Presently, there are in the Catholic church three very distinct mindsets or spiritualities—privatized, conciliar, and faith-justice. They are present at all levels of the global and world church. They have been (and are) manifested at synods and episcopal conferences, and in theology departments, parishes, and religious communities. These mindsets represent different views of how the church should take action against the powers of injustice. These powers, Gregory Baum maintains (1989b, 104), are presently so tenacious and demonic that only "a radical Catholicism renewed by the faith in Jesus Christ as the compassionate protector of humans on this earth" can challenge these destructive forces. Can a radical Catholicism emerge when the church has three different mindsets? Donal Dorr, for one, does not think so. "The different mindsets do not result in a healthy pluralism but rather in suspicion and intransigence" (Dorr 1984, 204).

The church can be the compassionate protector and liberator of the world and the sacrament of the reign of God if it follows the injunction of Paul to his church at Philippi (2:1–2): "If there is any encouragement in Christ, any solace in love, any participation in the Spirit, any compassion and mercy, complete my joy by being of the same mind, with the same love, united in heart, thinking one thing."

The Church and Sexual Ethics

All human affairs have moral dimensions. We have just reviewed the Catholic church's involvement with such radically important questions of national and international injustice as economic exploitation, political repression, the destruction of the environment, and the nuclear arms race. We turn now to sexual ethics. Although this topic was not given extensive pastoral investigation by Vatican II, there are several good reasons to single it out for a lengthy review.

First, in the 1960s and 1970s, the Western world went through a sexual revolution that had been spurred on by such factors as greater affluence, the contraceptive pill, the feminist movement, the destabilization of traditional values during the Vietnam War (1961–75), and by a new societal emphasis on self-fulfillment. On its negative side, the revolution trivialized sexuality. There was more tolerance of prostitution, divorce, cohabitation, and of nudity and pornography in the media and theater. The sexual exploitation of children and adolescents around the globe, but especially in Asia, became a big business, generating billions of dollars in income each year for traffickers, tourism promoters, and others (Smolenski 1995). Sexual activity among teenagers increased—a fact verified by the large number of out-of-wedlock births. People were exploited and many were seriously harmed by the epidemic spread of venereal diseases and HIV-AIDS.

On its positive side, the sexual revolution freed people to discuss sexual matters openly. In general, Victorian prudishness and its extremely damaging patriarchal notions about sexuality (e.g., the idea that women lacked sexual feelings altogether) were debunked. Some of the constructive power of sexuality was released and gains were made in sexual justice and equality. Most importantly, there was a significant shift in appreciation of marriage. Sexual intimacy and friendship were firmly combined. Previously, people tended to keep them separated. The purpose of sexual intercourse was procreation of children; friendships were often found elsewhere.

Second, from almost the beginning, much of the Catholic church's teachings on sexuality has been at odds with the Catholic sacramental

299

consciousness. Over the course of the church's history one can find not only popes and bishops but also outstanding theologians like Ambrose, Augustine, Albert the Great, and Aquinas fostering anti-sexual, misogynist theories. Is it any wonder that some declare that "the failure of the analogical imagination to subsume sexuality is the most grievous failure in the history of Catholic Christianity" (Greeley and Greeley Durkin 1984, 68)?

Third, since the council, the Vatican has issued many documents on sexual matters, spelling out what is right and what is wrong. Nevertheless, it is common knowledge that there is a sharp difference between the official hierarchical teachings and the practices of many faithful Catholics and the views of the majority of Catholic theologians. The Vatican teachings, no matter how vehemently repeated, have had little effect on the attitude and lifestyle of most United States Catholics. If these inconsistencies continue, there can only be grave harm to the church's relevance and credibility. For example, studies have shown that, in addition to the usual reasons why people do not participate in weekly Eucharist—laziness, work, lack of desire, an inability to get to church—many do not participate because of dissatisfaction with some of the church's official teachings, particularly the ban against contraceptive birth control and remarriage for the divorced (Winter 1975).

Fourth, chastity (the proper use of sex) is constitutive of the identity and mission of the church. The bishops at Vatican II reflected on this relationship when they reminded married persons that "Christ our Lord has abundantly blessed this [marital] love, which is rich in its various features, coming as it does from the spring of divine love and modeled on Christ's own union with the church. Just as of old God encountered his people in a covenant of love and fidelity, so our Savior, the spouse of the church, now encounters Christian spouses through the sacrament of marriage" (GS 48). Members of religious communities were reminded that their vow of chastity "is a special symbol of heavenly benefits, and for religious it is a most effective way of dedicating themselves wholeheartedly to the divine service and the works of the apostolate. Thus, for all Christ's faithful, religious recall that wonderful marriage made by God which will be made fully manifest in the age to come, and in which the church has Christ alone for her spouse" (PC 12).

Sexual misconduct, on the other hand, tarnishes the church's identity and mission. For instance, beginning in June 1985, the institutional church in the United States was rocked by national media attention given to numerous sexual scandals involving priests and bishops. Jason Berry, reporter and Catholic father of two children, spearheaded the reporting with an article in the *National Catholic Reporter* about the sexual abuse of children and adolescents by priests (1985; see also 1992, 1993). The fact that a Catholic publication reported the crimes defused potential public objections and freed the secular media to give full coverage to the issue. The number of priests in the United States involved was in the hundreds (approximately 1.7 percent of the priests) and the number of children molested was in the thousands. There were also reports about several bishops who had to resign their posts over reports of affairs with women.

The bishops had been quietly discussing cases of the sexual abuse of children and adolescents since 1985, but in 1993 reports of sexual misconduct by priests once again received such aggressive media attention and there was such a crisis of confidence in church leadership that in June the bishops formed a special national committee to deal with the problem (Reese 1993). Pope John Paul himself spoke out publicly in a letter to the bishops, dated June 11, 1993. He stated that out of concern "for the victims so seriously hurt by these misdeeds" he would help the bishops use church law to remove child molesters from the ranks of the priesthood. He established a committee "to study how the universal canonical norms can best be applied to the particular situation in the United States."

These scandals demoralized the community, especially the many bishops and priests faithful to their commitments, and they provoked investigations into the standards governing the recruitement and training of seminarians, men who should be models of justice and order.

Society and Order

To live a full human life we must live in a society marked by order, law, justice, and freedom. But society is often marked by disorder, lawlessness, injustice, and repression. Catholicism teaches that basic principles govern societies: (1) There exists an objective moral order in which some actions are good and others are bad. (2) Humans can know this objective order. (3) The objective moral order applies universally. Actions objectively morally evil are always objectively morally evil. (4) Individuals do not always realize their fundamental ability to know the objective order (Keane 1982).

If these principles are true, then the objective moral order cannot be achieved by either of the two extremes—legalism and relativism. Legalism is strict, literal adherence to law. Under this view morality becomes simply a matter of obedience to the law as promulgated by the authorities. One simply checks predetermined norms or commandments that establish which acts are good and which are evil. Legalism—justice without love—can subvert societies, especially religious communities. Both the Jewish prophets and Jesus condemned legalism because it changes radically the original purpose of the law, which is proper concern for and response to God's love. Legalism turns God into an exacting lawgiver and makes obedience to law the ultimate sign of faith and the principal means to holiness. In the preconciliar church, many Catholics showed legalistic leanings in their observance of Friday abstinence from meat, the eucharistic fast, and the avoidance of "servile work" on Sundays.

This critique of legalism does not mean societies and individuals do not need law. Since we are not completely free nor entirely conformed to the inspirations of the Spirit, laws instruct us about what is good for society and the individual, and they can correct our inconstancy in doing what is just and good. To deny the relevance of laws "would be to deny the continuity of human experience in history and all the wisdom laboriously acquired in the past" (Johann 1965).

The other extreme, relativism, is more a danger today than legalism. Alasdair MacIntyre argued in 1981 that with the Enlightenment, Western society lost Aristotelian principles and Judeo-Christian divine law tradition so that today we have no common moral philosophy other than relativism, which bases all judgments on individual preference or feeling. Relativism is the view that whatever the individual thinks is morally right is in fact objectively right or good and for that very reason. As such, relativism rules out interference—by the state or religion or anyone—in a person's private moral and religious conduct. It maintains that there is no moral good all can agree on (ethical agnosticism), and, therefore, everyone ought to have as much freedom as possible to pursue her or his notion of the good. This perspective assumes that each person is an autonomous source of value.

Relativism is expressed in such axioms as the following: I do what seems best for me and what does not hurt anyone; judge people only by their standards; any opinion seriously entertained is as correct as any other; all lifestyles are of equal value; and every culture has its own morality.

Relativism is based on certain truths. First, it is founded on an appreciation of the importance to morality of the subjective component, including individual free choice. Second, it is also true that we are always conditioned by cultural and historical circumstances, and some practices are culturally relative. But this does not make all practices relative. While it is true that certain values can be appreciated only by one culture, there are values that are valid for all cultures. For example, "the value of persons over things or the value of life over convenience are value-hierarchies that transcend culture" (Vacek 1984). Ultimately, relativism is unacceptable because it is individualistic and totally subjective. We are social beings: individualism is an inadequate account of human behavior and the means to an ordered society. Also, relativism is based on ethical agnosticism—a view incompatable with the Catholic notion that goodness and badness can be measured by objective reality.

In 1966, Joseph Fletcher (1905–1991), an Episcopal priest, professor of ethics and a founder of the field of biomedical ethics, developed a version of relativism which he popularized as "situation ethics." He was willing to call his theory "principled relativism" (Bennett 1966) and in 1978, he wrote, "If we were to choose the appropriate school term for it, situation ethics would be act-utilitarianism" (Fletcher 1978).

Fletcher did not coin the term *situation ethics*. The theory arose in Germany after World War II when there was serious questioning of why so many Germans had not protested the unjust Nazi rule and the morality that had permitted or at least tolerated the war with its atrocities and disregard for human dignity. In 1952, Pius XII delivered several addresses against situation ethics and those who based morality on circumstances rather than universal moral norms (Gallagher 1990, 225–35).

Fletcher rejected legalism and a morality based on abstract-universal norms. "The classic rule of moral theology has been to follow laws but do it *as much as possible* according to love and according to reason. Situation ethics, on the other hand, calls upon us to keep law in a subservient place, so that only love and reason really count when the chips are down!" (1966, 30).

Legalism subordinates the situation to predetermined general laws of morality and absolutizes these laws. Fletcher denied that human actions could be declared morally wrong in every circumstance. He did not totally eliminate objective laws of morality. He agreed that there are valid general moral rules that help people make moral judgments in particular cases. However, he argued that those general rules are not universal and absolute. To make them absolute is to advocate an excessive objectivism. The situationist, he wrote, "enters into every decision-making situation fully armed with the ethical maxims of his community and its heritage, and treats them with respect as illuminators of his problems. Just the same, he is prepared in any situation to compromise them or set them aside *in the situation* if love seems better served by doing so" (ibid., 26).

Fletcher forced Catholic moralists to reaffirm that "all morality, properly understood, is situational, is aware of the increasing importance placed upon circumstances, motives, historical evolution, the subjectivity of the moral agent" (Wassmer 1968, 191). In general, Fletcher's theory was roundly rejected. Karl Rahner, for example, wrote, "A situation ethic carried to its logical conclusion would become an ethical and metaphysical nominalism in which the universal could never actually bear upon the concrete with binding force" (1964a, 53). Other critics wondered what there was about the situation that suddenly enabled a person to choose wisely if no decision was valid outside the concrete situation. The experience of most people is that it is precisely in moments of crisis, when it is difficult to mobilize their powers of reflection to make a prudent choice, that they need guidelines, that is, values, ideals, aims, and purposes. Similarly, many thoughtful people believe that we would all be better off as citizens, parents, workers, and religious communities if we could live by the same basic moral guidelines.

Vatican II

In the period before Vatican II, moral theology was predominantly neoscholastic. It emphasized the sins of the individual; it was act-centered and law-oriented; and it was concerned primarily with human conduct in relation to the final destiny of humanity. In addition to emphasizing an objective moral order grounded in the natural law and divine revelation, it also stressed the preparation of seminarians for the proper administration of the sacrament of penance. Faith was declared the primordial Christian virtue, but Christ was not the center of morality.

Several theologians tried to renew moral theology. For example, Emile Mersch's studies on the church as the mystical body focused morality on Christ (1939), Gerard Gilleman put love at the center of the moral life (1952), and Fritz Tillman described morality as Christian discipleship (1960). Bernard Häring, whose *The Law of Christ* originally appeared in 1954, integrated moral principles and the great Christian mysteries by returning to the sources of the Christian faith, especially the scriptures (1961–66). Charles Curran (1996b) claims that "Bernard Häring has been the most significant figure in Catholic moral theology in the second half of the twentieth century."

The council fathers picked up these themes in their documents. In *Gaudium et spes* the bishops stated that moral matters should be studied in light of the gospel and human experience. They stated that "with the help of the holy Spirit, it is the task of the whole people of God, particularly of its pastors and theologians, to listen to and distinguish the many voices of our times and to interpret them in the light of God's word, in order that the revealed truth may be more deeply penetrated, better understood, and more suitably presented" (n. 44). In their decree on the formation of priests, the bishops wrote in a section written by Häring (1992, 60), that "special care is to be taken for the improvement of moral theology. Its scientific presentation, drawing more fully on the teaching of holy scripture, should highlight the lofty vocation of the Christian faithful and their obligation to bring forth fruit in charity for the life of the world" (OT 16).

Josef Fuchs of the Gregorian University in Rome commented on these conciliar directives. He said the bishops called for a moral theology that was biblical, christocentric, social, faith-centered, and scientific.

The scriptures, "the very soul of sacred theology" (DV 24), should have a central place in moral theology because they recount God's gracious calling of individuals to a life commensurate with their salvation in Christ. Contrary to the view of the rationalists of the Enlightenment period, Jesus was not primarily a moral teacher, one who designed a code of precepts and obligations for his followers. Rather, a christocentric morality should emphasize the full and rich relationship among the Father, Christ, and those "in Christ," his community. A morality of law is not ruled out, but law is only one element in the whole context of life in Christ. A biblical and christocentric morality should be social in contrast to the neo-Thomist view which was individualistic. Christian morality should also be faith-centered. The Christian mystery should be examined by reason enlightened by faith. Finally, moral theology should take account of psychology, anthropology, and history, as well as of ethics, dogmatic theology, and other Christian traditions (Fuchs 1970, 1–55).

Traditionalists vs. Revisionists

Right after Vatican II a revolution was set in motion in moral theology. It began with a seminal essay on the principle of double effect by the Jesuit Peter Knauer (McCormick 1989, 9; see Knauer 1979, 1–39). At the heart of his article was the question of whether some of the most important rules of morality, such as those forbidding masturbation, premarital sex, and contraceptive birth control, were to be considered absolute or whether exceptions were possible. Those who follow the church's traditional teaching on these matters are called traditionalists (or deontologists). Those who advocate another style of moral analysis, a relational-responsibility model, are called revisionists (or proportionalists or teleologists) (Spohn 1991).

The traditionalists maintain that morality is based on absolute moral norms and fear that the revisionists leave the door open for moral compromise and breakdown when they say there are few absolute norms and even these are not infallible. The revisionists argue that emphasis on absolute moral norms eliminates morally important elements from consideration such as circumstances, consequences, and motive. Revisionists accept formal norms, statements which inform us of values and of the kind of behavior that should be avoided. These values, say the revisionists, express the reflections and experiences of many people over many years. For example, the injunction not to kill recalls the value of life; and the commandment not to steal informs us about the right of private property.

Actually, revisionism and traditionalism are not two mutually exclusive models of moral theology, but are generic terms that indicate different forms of moral argumentation. Both models are committed to an objective moral order. However, the methodology of the traditionalists is deductive, comprehensive, and certain, whereas that of the revisionists is inductive, partial, and conditional (Cahill 1978). Revisionism is more of a loose tendency than a school of thought, and many of its proponents believe that the kind of weighing of circumstances and motives that traditionalists say is impossible, has in fact long been characteristic of Catholic moral analysis (Melchin 1990, 409).

The background of this debate is the clash between a classical and historical consciousness. Classical consciousness underscores the objective, the unchanging, the universal and abstract, and advocates a uniform approach to moral attitudes and principles. It regards the Bible as a moral code with ready-made normative laws and answers. Historical consciousness, on the other hand, looks to the subjective, changeable, particular, and practical. It accepts a certain pluralism in moral theology. The Bible is read in light of the historical-critical method, suggesting that what often seems like universal laws are actually conditional prohibitions.

Traditionalists

Traditionalists deplore both legalism and relativism. In the past, Catholic moral theology was often legalistic. It was "all too often one-sidedly confession-oriented, magisterium-dominated, canon law-related, sin-centered, and seminary-controlled" (McCormick 1989, 3). Law was stressed since morality was understood as a reflection of the eternal, divine, and natural law of God. Nevertheless, there were theologians and confessors who were "very pastoral and prudent, critically respectful, realistic, compassionate, open and charitable, well-informed" (ibid., 4). Theologians knew that legalism was an enemy of true religion and encouraged *epikeia* and casuistry. The former made allowances for human weakness by informing people that at times they should look to the meaning and intention of the lawmaker rather than the law; the latter affirmed absolutes in a rigorous fashion, yet permitted a wide range of exceptions.

Traditionalists counteract relativism by teaching a normative ethic based on absolutes and principles. The way absolutes are understood has bearing on four aspects of morality: acts as intrinsically evil, the principle of double effect, the natural law, and the ability of the church to teach morality.

The church has labeled certain acts as intrinsically evil and therefore forbidden without any possible exception. Some of these acts are abortion, contraceptive birth control, rape, bestiality, and incest. Other actions are ruled immoral or sinful (e.g., killing another person or an animal) because a person acts against a basic moral good. However, since these prohibitions are conditioned applications of general moral norms or rules for specific situations, exceptions are always permitted when proportionately greater goods or evils come into play (e.g., killing a person in self-defense or an animal for food).

Traditionalists also acknowledge the principle of double effect. It often happens that an intended action can have two effects, one good and one evil. For example, it is wrong to directly take the life of an innocent person even if doing so would save the lives of thousands. It might be permissable, however, to take innocent lives indirectly, as occurs when civilians are killed when bombs are dropped on military targets. The traditional formulation of the principle of double effect states that an evil effect could be permitted to follow from an action if four criteria were present: the action itself must be intrinsically good or indifferent; the good effect must be the intended effect; the evil effect must not follow directly from the action, only indirectly (the good effect cannot come about by means of the evil); and the good effect must proportionately outweigh the evil effect (T. O'Connell 1976, 170–73; Dwyer 1987, 152–61).

Natural law also plays a part in morality, traditionalists believe. Some mistakenly think the natural law involves the use of reason separated from faith and the believing community. On the contrary, "the basic thrust of the natural law was and still is that man's being is and must be the basis for his becoming" (McCormick 1968). There is a law implanted by God within every being; it is part of their very essence—this is what is meant by "natural law." The classical consciousness of the traditionalists, however, often reduces the natural law to the order of nature. They identify the demands of the moral law with biological and physical processes. Nature's norms are applicable always, everywhere, and for all. There is a blueprint in nature that needs to be uncovered and properly deciphered. The universe is a static structure reflecting the mind of God. All humans, despite variations of culture and history, are the same. There is an eternal law implanted in our rationality that is unchangeable. This law can be known by natural reason and it is often reinforced by revelation. Humans can rebel against this law, but it never changes.

Finally, traditionalists stress the teaching role of the official church. They uphold its ability to determine which actions are objectively wrong (Tripole 1996).

Revisionists

The revisionists also deplore legalism and relativism. They avoid both extremes by using a methodology that draws upon human experience and historical developments for their explanation of evil acts, the principle of double effect, natural law, and church teaching.

As for the idea of evil actions, the revisionists dislike labeling certain human acts as in themselves intrinsically immoral. Such an approach, they maintain, neglects morally significant factors such as motive and significant circumstances. They argue that a distinction must be drawn between the kind of evil that the act as such involves in its physiological structure and the kind of evil which the person intends without proportionate reason. Evil intrinsic to the action can only have a meaning in a premoral (or ontic or nonmoral or physical) sense.

Revisionists do not say that premoral evil is morally neutral. "To the contrary," as Lisa Sowle Cahill, professor of Christian ethics at Boston College, explains, "it is regarded as something generally not fulfilling for human nature, and indeed harmful to it. It always counts as a negative factor in a total moral evaluation. But taken by itself, it is not morally decisive" (McCormick 1985, 62–63). Moral evil occurs when the person intends the premoral evil without a proportionate reason.

Our human situation is filled with disvalues (premoral or ontic evil) that conflict with the values already there. Each person has essential dignity and existential originality. These basic values must always be protected. Formal moral norms and principles inform us about values; for example, "You shall not lie" tells us the importance of truth in relationships, personal and social. But disvalues such as error, fear, fatigue, boredom, ignorance, and violence are inevitable and unavoidable, due to the limitations built into our human situation. These we may cause but not intend while pursuing some course of action. These premoral qualities become moral evils against a person's essential dignity and originality when willed without proportionate reason. For example, basketball is a noncontact sport. However, when ten players scurry around the court to get position or the ball, accidents happen, sometimes even causing very serious physical harm to a player. Instinctively, the players, coaches, referees, and fans know when such a foul is accidental and when it is purposely intended to harm another. Similarly, premoral evil is present when a doctor amputates a limb, or a clerk mistakenly overcharges a customer, or a vacationer catches fish for his dinner. We know when these actions are maliciously intended and when they are necessary or normal to the situation.

The revisionists deny that acts in themselves can be labeled intrinsically evil, but they admit the existence of moral norms that are virtually exceptionless. That is, certain acts like cruelty to children, slavery, rape, direct killing of noncombatants in war, and not assisting persons in dire distress are clearly wrong. But it cannot be proven with the sharpness of syllogistic logic that no exceptions could ever occur.

The traditionalists argue that in relativizing the notion of acts as intrinsically immoral by subsuming them under the criteria of intention and proportionate reason, the revisionists have stripped the world of any distinctively moral character. If things cannot be known as morally good in themselves, then moral knowledge has been relativized. After all, one can easily marshall proportionate reasons to justify whatever one wishes.

Further, the revisionists reject the principle of double effect with its third condition that the good effect must not be produced by means of an evil effect. It is positive and proportionate consequences that justify the means used. We can judge whether an evil effect follows directly or indirectly from our formally willed actions, depending on the presence or absence of a proportionate (commensurate) reason. Revisonists actually reject the distinction between directly and indirectly intending the evil effect. They maintain that the key factor is the overall purpose in mind. In many cases the exceptions of the traditionalists are the result of involuted, unconvincing logic. For example, the traditionalists' description of an abortion to save the life of the mother as indirect killing does not seem consistent. In cases like this, actions are justified, based on an estimate of all the values and disvalues involved in the total consequences.

The revisionists also question the extent of the influence of the natural law. The relational-responsibility approach to morality is more dynamic than that of the traditionalists. The revisionists do not deny human continuity amid human change. But they insist that the abiding and unchangeable structures of the human person are fewer and more general than previous ages liked to believe. The revisionists root the natural law in the order of reason and discerning love. With the use of reason, humans subordinate and adapt the biological and physical facts of life to reach humane ends. Reason reflecting on the total human experience becomes the guide for human well-being, and not the order of nature. Biological processes become subservient to the total well-being of human life. This approach is in keeping with Vatican II, which marked a distinct turn in Catholic theology "from a cosmological orientation to one decidedly more personalist. There is a difference between seeing people as contingent beings and seeing them as personal participants in dialogue with a personal God" (Modras 1979).

Due to the findings of the human sciences, we have a better sense of the complexities of human nature. The structure of morality is not a static set of regulations constitutive of human nature. The natural law is "the cognitive realization of a pattern of dynamic norms generated by the human social experience of history" (Murphy 1978). Humans grow more truly as they assume more consciously their responsibility for the future of humankind and the world.

The revisionists' view of church teaching is less absolute than that of the traditionalists. The revisionists are accused by the traditionalists of dismantling the authority of the magisterium in moral matters. If there is no objectively definable set of evil actions and consequences, say the traditionalists, then the official magisterium is reduced to exhorting and counseling.

While not dismantling the magisterium's authority in moral matters, many theologians today give critical attention to Vatican documents. Several have warned that these documents should not be considered the final word, a view that would stifle further theological discussion and that would label those who questioned them as disloyal. To see the documents as unquestionable "would be theologically erroneous, pastorally tragic and practically harmful to both the theology of sexuality and the moral magisterium of the church" (McCormick 1976a). The revisionists might consider an example of this to be the CDF's "Declaration on Certain Questions Concerning Sexual Ethics" *(Persona humana)* issued on December 29, 1975. This document maintained that it is only in marriage that the full sense of mutual self-giving and procreation is preserved.

Based on this value judgment, premarital sex, homosexual relations, and masturbation fall short of this ideal.

This document had more critics than defenders, mainly because it so firmly represented the traditional arguments (McCormick 1981a, 668–82; D. Maguire 1976). Charles Curran criticized the document on the following five counts (1978, 30–52). First, it begins with immutable principles and a deductive approach, leaving little room for developing cultural and historical realities. This methodology stands in sharp contrast with Vatican II, which called attention to the signs of the times and to a much more inductive type of logic. Second, its conclusions are based on the finality of the physical act itself without reference to the personal dimension and the connection between love and sexuality. Third, it manifests a legalistic emphasis on principles, norms, and laws. Curran favored a relational-responsibility model that focuses on the values the laws are meant to safeguard. He argued that it is more difficult than is assumed to discover eternal and immutable laws. Over the years, moralists always recognized there was a place for exceptions. Fourth, the document pays insufficient attention to people's actual lives. It makes unsubstantiated assertions about what people think about such topics as masturbation and homosexuality. Fifth, it takes an unhistorical approach to scripture, treating the Bible as a moral code with ready-made answers.

The Vatican continues to monitor publications on morality and intervenes if it finds materials that deviate from the official teachings. For example, in 1977, two priest-theologians were censured for publishing books that taught sexual ethics from a revisionist viewpoint. Philip Keane's *Sexual Morality: A Catholic Perspective* had its imprimatur removed. Anthony Kosnik was removed from his teaching position in a Michigan seminary and told he could no longer teach sexual ethics. Kosnik edited *Human Sexuality: New Directions in American Catholic Thought*, a book that was the work of a five-member committee (two priests, two married men, and a nun) sponsored by the CTSA. This book proposed that Catholic sexual ethics return to a gospel ethic of love by not centering on procreation, natural law, and the physical contours of sexual acts but by focusing instead on creative growth toward personal integration. Such growth and integration, they suggested, would be promoted by sexual expressions that manifested these seven values: it should be honest, faithful, socially responsible, other-enriching, life-serving, joyous, and self-liberating.

The book received considerable support in some places. For example, Daniel Maguire, professor of moral theology at Marquette University, said the authors "dared to face issues which most Catholic moralists have not faced with candor. In so doing, they have smoked us all out and have guaranteed a more substantive and helpful discussion of human sexuality than we have had in years. Because of their work the debate they have stimulated also promises to be an event in theory. What committee of the CTSA has ever done more?" (1978, 46). On the other hand, Kosnik's book was criticized as a whole or in part by the Vatican, some United States bishops,[1] and some members of the CTSA (Winiarski 1977, 1979a). Some found the seven criteria for healthy sex unhelpful since they did not address what was specific to sex itself. The same criteria, it was said, could be applied to almost any human activity, such as athletics or a social club.

Revisionists and Relativism

Revisionists can seem like relativists, but there are several reasons why they are not. First, while revisionism seems to deny the existence of concrete universal norms, it does accept the principle of universality in moral theology. Once an action is understood to be objectively immoral, it will be so whenever and wherever it occurs. Some examples that are virtually exceptionless: deliberately calculated homicide, apostasy for socioeconomic advantages, perjury in order to ruin another, defrauding workers of their just wages, misusing funds given for the support of the helpless, such as orphans and widows.

Revisionism also seems to lead to consequentialism (i.e., the belief that actions are right or wrong depending solely on the consequences), especially since it rejects some of the language of double effect, particularly directly and indirectly intending the evil effect. The revisionists say they are not consequentialists because they ask if there is a proportionate reason for the action and proportionate reason includes more than weighing the good and bad results of an act. It also looks to norms and principles, as well as the values and disvalues in the total consequences.

Revisionism seems individualistic. However, the revisionists insist that an action does not become moral simply because someone thinks it is moral (Keane 1982, 266). Furthermore, as a person forms his or her conscience by weighing the values and disvalues involved in an action, the priority of the community and its objective moral judgments remains in place. As we saw in the chapter on authority, these include the judgments of popes, bishops, theologians, tradition, scripture, and the sense of the faithful. However, even here the revisionists remind the traditionalists that authoritative structures can never be final or absolute. "Not only must they continually recommend themselves by their reasonableness to the persons they are meant to serve, but, like all other human devices, they too stand in need of constant criticism and constant improvement" (Johann 1968, 66).

Revisionism seems to some to be chaotic and a cause of moral breakdown. The revisionists insist, however, that for all the vagueness of its objectives, which make it appear a threat to right order, there is an order to their method: our orientation to God and our abiding vocation to participate in God's work of promoting and expanding his reign. If relational responsibility means anything, "it means determining before God the appropriate response to a situation and acting accordingly" (ibid.). The touchstone for distinguishing better from worse is intelligent recognition. Since all of us are by nature open to God (that is, we are supernatural!), then "we all share a common light by which to judge whether steps proposed are really improvements, or not" and "we all share a common calling to move beyond where we are if we are going to be true to ourselves" (ibid., 67). We may not have metaphysical certitude about moral matters, but moral certitude is possible on specific moral matters, and on such matters, moral certitude is enough. To have moral certitude is to have a strong likelihood or a firm conviction, rather than actual evidence.

John Paul II: *Veritatis splendor*

The Vatican viewed the endless discussions about legalism, relativism, absolutes, traditionalism, and revisionism as "a genuine crisis." John Paul announced on August 1, 1987 that he would write an encyclical on "the very foundations of moral theology." That day was the 200th anniversary of the death of the saintly Alphonsus Liguori (1696–1787), founder of the Redemptorists in 1732 and patron of moral theologians and confessors. The proposed encyclical was in the making for six years. This document, titled *Veritatis splendor* ("The Splendor of Truth"), and subtitled "Regarding Certain Fundamental Questions of the Church's Moral Teachings," was signed by the pope on August 6, 1993, and released on October 5. It was written to the bishops but not in consultation with them.

Over the course of the six years the encyclical was being drafted, it was periodically the subject of many rumors (P. Steinfels 1990b). For example, some feared the letter would declare the church's teachings on contraceptive birth control to be infallible (Hebblethwaite 1993e). Others surmised that the Cologne Declaration of 1989 "was a preemptive strike against such a document" (McBrien 1993b). Earlier in this book (chapter 5) when the Cologne Declaration was discussed, it was pointed out that 163 German-speaking theologians complained about the way the pope connected the teachings about contraceptive birth control with the most fundamental teachings of the faith.

Before its publication, the encyclical was also the subject of important meetings. For example, in October 1990, the cardinals attended a three-day meeting in Rome to discuss the "defense of human life." When Cardinal Ratzinger discussed modern moral issues, he referred twice to "an eventual document on the defense of human life" (Hebblethwaite 1991b).

The encyclical, the tenth by John Paul, marked the first time the Vatican had set forth in detail the fundamental elements of moral theology (n. 115). The pope said the encyclical is especially needed today because new approaches to Catholic moral theology reject the traditional doctrine regarding natural law and the universality and permanent validity of its precepts (n. 4). Consequently, the church is facing "a genuine crisis," one which engenders difficulties that "have most serious implications for the moral life of the faithful and for communion in the Church, as well as for a just and fraternal social life" (n. 5).

The encyclical is often abstract and more philosophical than theological. Nevertheless, John Paul stated that the church "does not intend to impose upon the faithful any particular system, still less a philosophical one" (n. 29). Some commentators thought otherwise. They pointed out that the principal authors of the document were a group of like-minded theologians: Angelo Scola (bishop of Grosseto, Italy), Rocco Buttiglione (professor of moral theology), Georges Cottier (Swiss Dominican and theologian to the papal household), and two Polish theologians, Jozef Tichner and Tadeusz Styczen (Hebblethwaithe 1993b). Styczen was Karol Wojtyla's pupil at the Catholic University of Lublin. He also succeeded his teacher in the chair of ethics at Lublin. These advisors as well as the pope's philosophical and theological education help make sense of Richard McBrien's commentary on the encyclical. He wrote, "To anyone familiar with twentieth-century Catholic thought it is evident that . . . chapter [two of the encyclical] is written from a neoscholastic perspective lightly salted with the phenomenological-personalist philosophy of the so-called Lublin school" (McBrien 1993b).

The long encyclical of forty thousand words contains a brief introduction and three chapters. The introduction states the purposes of the letter: to set forth the foundations of Christian morality in the light of scripture and tradition, and "to shed light on the presuppositions and consequences of the dissent" which have often greeted the official teachings (n. 5). The pope lamented that dissent from the church's official teachings on moral issues was no longer "limited and occasional," but frequent, whereby these teachings were often called into question in an "overall and systematic" manner (n. 4).

The first chapter is a biblical meditation on Jesus' dialogue with a rich young man (Matthew 19:16–22). This section contains an inspiring Christ-centered morality. "Following Christ is . . . the essential and primordial foundation of Christian morality" (n. 19). The second chapter is the heart of the encyclical. In it the pope states that the church has the duty to voice those modern teachings which "are incompatible with revealed truth" (n. 29). Earlier, John Paul repudiated the notion that the magisterium can intervene only to "exhort consciences" or "propose values . . . in the light of which each individual will independently make up his or her decisions and life choices" (n. 4). In this chapter the pope challenges a series of false dichotomies (e.g., between freedom and law, between the fundamental option for God and particular moral acts) and he denounces individualism, subjectivism, relativism, consequentialism, and utilitarianism. John Paul insists on the existence of objective moral norms founded in natural law that are accessible to human reason in making moral judgments. The words "law" and "commandment" appear hundreds of times in this encyclical. The third chapter highlights the "central theme" of the encyclical, namely, "the reaffirmation of the universality and immutability of the moral commandments, particularly those which prohibit always and without exception intrinsically evil acts" (n. 115). The pope addresses the responsibility of bishops to teach Christian morality for the betterment of the church and the world (n. 116). The chapter also contains some biblically and historically based references to martyrdom—something that may be required today to directly and dramatically challenge false teachings. The conclusion entrusts the document to Mary, Mother of Mercy.

In the letter the pope accused some moral theologians (no names were given) of serious deviations from the Catholic tradition. Some are guilty of relativism, consequentialism, subjectivism, and individualism (nn. 32, 34, 75). Since in chapter 4 of this book it was shown that these perspectives are contrary to a Catholic sacramental consciousness, it is not surprising that Catholic moral theologians insisted that the encyclical misrepresented them because they neither hold nor teach these positions. The theologians said these perspectives are not "trends in moral theology today" (n. 115), but are instead the problems of modern secularized culture.

Since five of the pope's accusations relate to revisionism as discussed earlier, commentary is called for.

First, modern theologians are said to reject the notion of intrinsically moral acts (nn. 52, 81, 115). We have seen that revisionists do not deny that some acts are evil. But revisionists do not favor the use of the term "intrinsically" because too great an insistence on the intrinsic evil of a given act can obscure the effects of motive, circumstances, and consequences on the moral quality of the act. In other words, revisionists want to define the act more broadly. They do deny the supposition that an act can be intrinsically evil independently of other factors which determine its moral quality. They do maintain that it is never enough to look at the physical act alone. For example, killing another person is not evil when done in self-defense or in a just war. Also, the church permits a therapeutic abortion to save the life of the mother. What is intrinsically evil is murder, the killing of an innocent person.

Second, it is said that some moral theologians propose proportionalism. Proportionalism denotes the weighing of goods (or values) and evils (or disvalues) in morally ambiguous situations. Proportionalists maintain that just because a disvalue is involved in a person's decision does not by that very fact make the action morally wrong. As Richard McCormick explains: "The action becomes morally wrong when, all things considered, there is not a proportionate reason in the act justifying the disvalue" (1993b).

The encyclical claims that proportionalists advocate consequentialism and individualism. It says these theologians draw the criteria for the goodness of a given way of acting solely from a calculation of the foreseeable consequences of a moral choice and they attempt to justify morally wrong actions by a good intention (nn. 76, 80–81). But we have seen that proportionalists do not focus on any one premoral factor, such as consequences. Rather, they take into account all the factors, not only the intrinsic nature of the act, but also norms, motive, circumstances, and consequences. Richard McCormick explains: "When contemporary theologians say that certain disvalues in our actions can be justified by a proportionate reason, they are not saying that morally wrong actions *(ex objecto)* can be justified by the end. They are saying that an action cannot be qualified simply by looking at the material happening, or at its object in a very narrow and restricted sense" (McCormick 1993c). For example, most theologians—and here both John Paul II and the United States bishops concur—condemn the use of nuclear weapons, yet they give moral sanction to the building and stocking of these weapons for the sake of deterrence.

Third, the encyclical acknowledges that conscience is "the proximate norm of personal morality" (n. 60), but declares that the revisionists accord conscience "the status of a supreme tribunal" (n. 32), that is, complete autonomy in determining the criteria of good and evil. The revisionists do defend the supremacy of conscience, but they also insist that there are objective criteria of good and evil, of right and wrong. They also teach that there are six other complementary authorities (as explained in chapter 5). Furthermore, they remind their critics that several episcopal conferences have reiterated the teaching that conscience is the ultimate judge in decision making. For example, some bishops informed those who disagree with the official teachings on contraceptive birth control to "remain open-minded, continue to search and study, retain a basic respect for church teaching, and not try to persuade others away from the official line" (Doyle 1993).

Fourth, modern theologians are said to elevate a "fundamental option" above concrete moral choices (nn. 66, 70). The notion of a fundamental option was developed in the 1960s by Ladislas Boros, a Hungarian Jesuit. He argued that what mattered most in Christian life is the fundamental choice for God. If a person is genuinely turned toward God and trying to live a life of Christian discipleship in her or his relationships with neighbor, the world, and self, then individual acts cannot basically affect that orientation (Hebblethwaite 1993d).

John Paul rejects any understanding of fundamental option that "objectively changes or casts doubt upon the traditional concept of mortal sin" (n. 70). But McBrien stated that he knew no Catholic moral theologian "who argues that the fundamental option for God can never be reversed or changed by a particular moral action against God" (McBrien 1993b).

Fifth, the encyclical condemns those theologians who engage in public dissent "in the form of carefully orchestrated protests and polemics carried on in the media" (n. 113). This stance, says the encyclical, "is opposed to ecclesial communion and to a correct understanding of the hierarchical constitution of the people of God" (n. 113). The theologians counter with the argument that it is often public dissent from noninfallible teachings which has helped the official church clarify or modify or correct its teachings.

Veritatis splendor evoked many evaluations in the global church, some negative and others positive. Listed here are four positive evaluations of the papal letter. Joseph A. DiNoia, a Dominican priest and director of the United States bishops' Secretariat for Doctrine and Pastoral Research and Practices, said to those who considered the encyclical a witch hunt that it would be a "big mistake . . . to treat the encyclical as a catalog of errors" aimed at cracking down on certain theologians.[2]

Lisa Sowle Cahill stated that "the encouragement of humane and consensus-seeking public discourse about the relation of controverted ethical issues to the common good is one of the most important potential contributions of Catholic moral theology in today's culture. *Veritatis splendor* may give impetus to theologians who are renewing the natural law tradition in service of such discourse" (Cahill 1993).

Stanley Hauerwas, professor of theological ethics at the Divinity School of Duke University, noted that "As one often critical of those that would present the Christian moral life in terms of natural law, I found little reason to object to John Paul's account of natural law. That the moral law is 'in principle' accessible to human reason, as the pope maintains, I assume any Christian should believe" (Hauerwas 1993).

Cardinal Joseph Bernardin said he welcomed the encyclical at a time when people throughout the world seem to have "lost a sense of direction, a sense of purpose." He cited random killings in United States cities, political violence throughout the world, and moral failings within the Catholic community. The encyclical, he said, "calls individuals to rise above the limits of self-centered or self-defined morality and to live in accord with this objective order, which can be expressed in specific moral norms that have a universal and permanent character."[3]

There were some negative critiques. The editors of the *National Catholic Reporter* denounced the encyclical for being "a harsh, negative, rigid, authoritarian document."[4] Richard McBrien (1993b) noted that although the document invoked Paul VI's call for charity, tolerance, and patience towards those who differ in conscience from official teachings, nevertheless, "the spirit of enforcement" hangs heavy throughout the document. "Indeed the text is pockmarked with words like obedience, conformity, law, commandments and vigilance." Peter Hebblethwaite (1993f) was convinced that the encyclical's main purpose was disciplinary: bishops must be aware of the accuracy of moral teaching and take appropriate measures when they are not. Massimo Aprile, vice president of the

Italian Evangelical Baptist Union, declared that the encyclical shows the "antimodernist character of this pope" on sexual ethics. "It does not help the ecumenical dialogue of the church of Rome with the Protestant world."[5] Charles Curran (1993b) was disturbed because the encyclical said nothing "about how the papal teaching office learns the moral truth." The encyclical, he said "leaves the impression that the holy Spirit gives the knowledge and understanding directly to the pope. In reality the hierarchical teaching office enjoys the assistance of the holy Spirit, but it must use all the human ways of knowing the truth. *The Declaration on Religious Freedom* of Vatican II recognized that the hierarchical magisterium learned from the experience of people of good will." In a later essay (1996a), Curran carefully explained that, because John Paul uses two different methodologies in his moral teachings, they are marked by "problems of consistency and coherency." In his social teachings he employs "a more historically conscious approach than the teachings on sexual and personal morality, which employ a more classicist approach."

Ironically, the angriest comments were voiced by Bernard Häring, internationally-known Redemptorist moral theologian who taught for many years at the Lateran University in Rome. He wrote that "the whole document is directed above all towards one goal: to endorse total assent and submission to all utterance of the pope—and above all on the crucial point: that the use of any artifical means for regulating birth is intrinsically evil and sinful, without exception, even in circumstances where contraception would be a lesser evil." He said "the pope is confident that he has a binding duty to proclaim his teachings with no calculation whatsoever about the foreseeable practical consequences for the people concerned and for the whole church" (Häring 1993).

Sexual Ethics

Before turning to six specific questions of sexual morality, it is necessary to list the three characteristics or criteria on which sexual ethics depend for its integrity:

1. Sexual activity has the potential first and foremost of being linked with love in a relationship with another person.

2. Sexual activity has the capacity of procreation.

3. Sexual activity is accompanied by an intense pleasure which reaches its peak at orgasm.

These three—physical satisfaction, interpersonal intimacy and parenthood—"are not three separate 'variables,' or *possible* meanings of sex which we are morally free to combine or omit in different ways. Sex and love as fully *embodied* realities have an intrinsic moral connection to pro-creativity and to the shared creation and nurturing of new lives and loves" (Cahill 1990). Sexuality is a relational gift.

Masturbation

Masturbation is "the pursuit of induced sexual pleasure with or without orgasm, usually solitary but sometimes mutually, frequently involving the genitals but sometimes involving other orifices of the body" (Dominion and Montefiore 1989, 27).

Based on some sociological studies, the conventional wisdom holds that virtually all males and most females masturbate at some time during their lives and this action is not wrong. In fact, such studies conclude that masturbation is normal, not harmful, and relieves sexual tension. The Catholic church and most theologians teach otherwise.

The Congregation on Catholic Education issued an instruction in 1974 in which it called masturbation a youthful dysfunction but cautioned that "fears, threats, or spiritual intimidation are best avoided" when dealing with this conduct. The Vatican encouraged counselors to aim at helping young people form a balanced sexual attitude. Then, on December 29, 1975, the CDF published *Persona humana*, a document cited earlier and which will be cited several more times in this chapter. This document declared that masturbation is objectively a grave sin because it is "a deliberate use of the sexual faculty outside normal conjugal relations . . . that contradicts the finality of the faculty."

This 1975 document evoked considerable response from theologians and bishops (McCormick 1981a, 668–82). Many viewed it as theologically inaccurate, psychologically harmful, and pedagogically counterproductive. Bernard Häring, for example, granted that, on the one hand, some theologians had gone too far in reaction to an earlier rigorism concerning masturbation by simply dismissing it, but, on the other hand, he warned that a too facile judgment of mortal sin in sexual matters harms the faithful. "It must never for an instant be forgotten," he wrote, "that conversation about mortal sin, especially the mortal sins of children, is conversation about God" (see ibid., 676).

Charles Curran, who had previously written that masturbation is wrong because a person fails "to integrate sexuality in the service of love," (Curran 1970, 175–6), disagreed with the judgment that masturbation is an intrinsically and seriously disordered act. He said individual masturbatory acts, when judged in the context of the person and the meaning of sexuality, "do not constitute such important matter . . . providing the individual is truly growing in sexual maturity and integration" (McCormick 1981a, 677).

In the Catholic tradition what constitutes the heart of morality is the individual's relationship with God. "The moral life, therefore, consists of a deepening of our fundamental orientation. It consists of a growth process whereby we stabilize, deepen and render more dominant the love poured into our hearts by the Spirit" (McCormick 1968). Human or moral acts, say the revisionists, are a configuration of a person's multiple relationships with the triune God, neighbor, the world, and self (a person's fundamental option) rather than a single action. The single action must be seen against the developmental process and particular life-context. This is why it is wrong, wrote Bernard Häring, to propose that masturbation is always a mortal sin, and only then consider the difference between masturbation by adolescents, young adults, and a married person. Ethicists must "look first to the diversity of the phenomena" and "only then" ask about the moral meaning or possible sinfulness of the individual phenomenon (Häring 1979, 2:503, 560).

Jack Dominion, a British psychiatrist, noted that, according to sociologists, masturbation is very common among both males and females, especially during adolescence. He believes that although masturbation is narcissistic, it is a necessary part of growing up since it helps people discover new dimensions of their body and it prepares people for heterosexual relations. He does not believe it is a sin for adolescents. However, it lacks the three criteria for integral sexual activity listed above, since both interpersonal love and procreation are absent. When Dominion discusses other instances of masturbation such as that practiced by someone in prison or a widow, he insists that the three criteria must be used to judge the moral criterion of this behavior also.[6]

Philip Keane wrote that masturbation involved premoral evil, which had to be weighed against a variety of factors, depending on circumstances. He was hesitant to declare it a moral evil for adolescents, but he said people should move to a higher stage of sexual maturity. For adults, the premoral evil is more serious. Masturbation can signal a moral disorder. Individual evaluation is required and the person may need counseling if the masturbation is used compulsively as a substitute for more rewarding, interpersonal relationships. When Keane and other theologians discuss self-stimulation for sperm-testing for the treatment of infertility, they are inclined to accept it as a moral act that is quite different from masturbation as generally understood.

Richard McCormick, while he respects the sociological, psychological, and theological reasons for not attributing serious sin to adolescent masturbation, cautions that the young can stagnate their sexual development if, knowing the perspective of professionals, they decide to continue the habit of masturbation. For adolescents to simply indulge the habit is to feed and strengthen "the underlying causes of such symptomatic behavior" and to compromise their growth toward maturity. McCormick says he would tell adolescents two things: first, meet the challenge to become genuinely mature and free in sexual expression; second, the habit of masturbation is a serious challenge to growth that requires a serious response, a response that is "a resolute and adult attitude. As long as you maintain this, you are on the right path and responding properly to the challenge" (McCormick 1981a, 175).

Premarital Sex

In contemporary society premarital sex has become common. For many people and certainly in much of the media and the entertainment industry, premarital sex is regarded "as a sophisticated recreational activity for which the only moral criterion is mutual consent" (Cahill 1990). Most Catholics do not subscribe to this cavalier attitude, but Andrew Greeley reported in an essay in 1992 that there is a definite decline among Catholics in their acceptance of the institutional church's teaching on this topic. In his report he indicated that "only one of six American Catholics thinks that premarital sex is always wrong." Edward O. Laumann, a sociologist at the University of Chicago, reported in December 1994 that only 20 percent of Americans regard premarital sex as always wrong and 48 percent found it not wrong at all (McClory 1994).

Some religious leaders—Christian and Jewish—are also divided on this issue. For example, John S. Spong, an Episcopal bishop argued that "life-giving" premarital sex can be just as "holy" as marriage (1988). In April 1994 it was reported that a commission of rabbis of the conservative branch of Judaism proposed a set of ethical standards for unmarried Jews who were sexually active in "an ongoing, loving relationship." The rabbis condemned casual or promiscuous sex, and declared that teenagers "need to refrain from sexual intercourse, for they cannot honestly deal with its implications or results." As for sexual relations between unmarried partners, the rabbis said it should reflect an awareness of being persons created in God's image, should not be "simply pleasurable release," should not be manipulative, should be honest about the length and depth of the relationship, and should be faithful to one partner as long as the relationship lasts. If these standards are followed, then "committed loving relationships between mature people . . . can embody a measure of holiness, even if not the full portion available in marriage" (P. Steinfels 1994a).

The Catholic church has maintained that sexual intercourse should be limited to publicly committed married partners. Only then is it holy. But many ask this question: Is there any enduring and universal reason why this is so? Some note that moral theologians have yet to produce convincing proof why sexual intercourse must be matched in *every* case by a total covenant of love that can be expressed only in marriage (Kosnik 1977, 152–58; Cahill 1985a, 89–90; Mahoney 1990, 203).

The official church resolutely rejects premarital sex for two reasons. First, it claims that, since the partners have not committed themselves to one another in a stable and definitive way, their sexual intercourse is a lie. It does not express exclusive fidelity. In the Catholic tradition, passion and commitment go together: "commitment needs passion to sustain it over the long haul, and passion needs commitment if it is to keep its flame" (Greeley and Greeley Durkin 1984, 109). Second, it holds that the procreative character of sexual intercourse demands that the couple be ready and able to secure the education of the possible child. Premarital sex does not involve an adequate context for this value.

In order to give a solid reason why premarital sex is wrong, theologians like Richard McCormick begin by discussing the values found in a Christian marriage. Sexual intercourse is commonly called "the marital act." By so speaking, we indicate that sexual intercourse "has a sense and a meaning prior to the individual purpose of those who engage in it, a significance which is part of their situation whether or not the partners turn their minds to it" (McCormick 1981a, 365–67). The *sense* that is prior is that sex should be restricted to the marriage relationship; the *meaning* that is prior is that sex is the expression of love and friendship that is permanent and exclusive. Both the sense and meaning derive from centuries of human experience. Humans have learned that unless this type of intimacy is restricted to the marriage relationship, the integrity of sexual language is seriously threatened. Marriage is a covenant relationship built on friendship and it is friendship that generates fidelity, loyalty, and constancy (ibid., 447–62).

There are different patterns to premarital sex that occur between a client and a prostitute; during the one-night stand; in the temporary, semi-committed relationship; between cohabiting couples; and between the engaged. All of these are different human and moral situations. All have a premoral dimension; those involved in each of these situations will have to determine before God the extent of their immorality.

The status of those engaged to be married has received special attention because there is a pledge of permanence and, in a sense, the church's sacrament is involved. The sacrament of marriage has three distinct elements that normally take place in this order: the consent of the baptized partners, the consent of the church, and consummation. These three elements are not an instantaneous action, but a process that takes time. Engaged couples sometimes put the consummation before the consent of the church for different reasons. This is sometimes called "preceremonial intercourse." Some would argue this is not always immoral because the couple is in a state of committed love. Some ask about the relationship of the formal engagement to the sacrament itself. Are not catechumens who prepare for months for baptism to some extent already Christians before the actual baptism? Does marriage begin when the couple becomes formally engaged? Can the concept of "marriage" be so extended?

Despite these theoretical questions, premarital sex for the engaged has its own special, practical difficulties. For one thing, the intention to marry can be, and frequently is, revoked. If the engagement is broken, one of the partners can feel manipulated, used, abandoned, and dishonored. Second, McCormick observes that "the intention to marry is, indeed, part of the process leading to marriage. But the process leading to marriage cannot be converted that easily to read marriage-in-process" (ibid., 458). Third, the significance of the social and ecclesial dimensions of the marriage should not be disregarded. The "public ceremony seals a commitment in as full a human way as possible" (Dominion and Montefiore 1989, 34). The ceremony is meant to safeguard the commitment. "Treating the ceremony as if it were *merely* a ceremony . . . is an unhealthy symptom of an eventually destructive individualism" (McCormick 1981a, 458).

Finally, what Richard McCormick wrote about premarital sex in a brief essay in 1966 is worth citing at length today. He declared that in the Christian ethic it is always immoral to manipulate another person.

> That is why the cardinal rule of sexual conduct was and always will remain: physical expressions of intimacy express the person and therefore must correspond to the existing relationship of the persons. The unmarried are only preparing for the total relationship of marriage. They are learning, not chiefly but among other things, to fill their expressions of love with respect and protection, with more of the person; they are learning to drain off the elements that stifle personal communion. Since their love is protective, not possessive, they will give themselves to each other only to the extent that the person can be given at this point—in a limited way. Consequently, they will avoid those acts that of themselves signify total personal oblation, not out of blind servility to a negative 'thou shalt not,' but because, being in love, they will wish to speak a personal, and therefore a genuinely human language to each other.

Contraceptive Birth Control

The world is going through a population explosion. One pundit remarked that when God told Adam and Eve to increase and multiply "the population density was two persons per square world" (Wynn 1988, 107). Demographers indicate that at the time of Jesus the world population stood at some 250 million. Today the earth gains as many people in two years. In 1830, during the Industrial Revolution, the population reached one billion. By 1930 it reached two billion, and by 1975, four billion. By the year

2000 the population could be over six billion. No one with any sense is against birth control and responsible parenthood. No one wants human beings to be born into situations where they begin and end their lives as nonpersons. From the perspective of the Catholic church, the problem is contraceptive birth control. McCormick declared that he could "think of no moral issue or event in this century that impacted so profoundly on the discipline of moral theology" as did the 1968 encyclical *Humanae vitae* (1989, 12). Greeley judged the encyclical "the most important event of the last twenty-five years of Catholic history" (1990a, 91).

The church's first universal condemnation of contraception took place in December 1930 when Pius XI issued the encyclical *Casti connubii.* He wrote because earlier in the year, August 15, the Anglicans meeting for a Lambeth Conference approved contraceptives "in those cases where there is such a clearly felt moral obligation to limit or avoid parenthood."

From 1930 to 1960, no Catholic moral theologian openly espoused the position that contraceptives could be used in good conscience in some circumstances. But, in the late 1950s, the whole context of contraceptives changed when a Catholic doctor, John C. Rock (1890–1984) and his associates, developed, popularized, and championed the anovulant pill (Nyhan 1984; McLaughlin 1982). Rock and his supporters maintained that, in arresting the ovulation process, the pill does not violate the structure of the act of sexual intercourse. Use of contraceptives is an intervention into the marital act; the pill is an intervention into the generative system. Rock and others did not see it as any different from use of the infertile periods—those times when couples can engage in sexual intercourse without achieving conception.

Shortly before his death on June 3, 1963, John XXIII appointed a high-level, international committee of thirteen to investigate the threat of overpopulation and the morality of contraceptives. He acted on the advice of Cardinal Leo Suenens who feared that the church might have "another Galileo case" on its hands. By all reports, the group, which included Bernard Häring, was afraid at first to challenge the church's teachings that were firmly in place since 1930. Then, in fall 1964, at the second session of Vatican II, Cardinals Leo Suenens, Bernard Alfrink, Paul Léger, and Patriarch Maximos IV Saigh (1878–1967) spoke out for a study of the means of contraception other than total or periodic continence. Léger said, "We must affirm that the intimate union of the couple finds its legitimate end in itself, even when it is not directed toward procreation." These interventions were applauded by the majority of the bishops, but Paul VI, persuaded by Cardinal Ottaviani of the Holy Office, removed the issue from the council's agenda and assigned it to the commission previously set up by John XXIII. During the council, the bishops referred briefly to the church's teachings and simply reaffirmed them (GS 51).

In December 1964, Paul appointed forty more members to the commission of thirteen. Among the group was an American couple, Patrick and Patricia Crowley, cofounders of the Christian Family Movement (Crowley 1993; McClory 1988b). The committee of fifty-three met for the first time in March 1965. Although they quickly realized there were no easy answers, they did produce a large stack of documentation. In spring 1966 Paul further enlarged the committee by adding seven cardinals and nine bishops, bringing the group to sixty-nine. However, Karol Wojtyla, the future John Paul II, was involved but never attended any of the meetings. Robert Blair Kaiser said, "His absence was probably the most important no-show on record" (Kaiser 1986).

"A crucial turning-point was reached on April 23, 1966, when the four theologians on the commission who upheld the traditional opinion admitted that they could not show the intrinsic evil of contraception on the basis of the natural law alone" (Hebblethwaite 1975, 212). The four theologians were the Dutch Redemptorist Jan Visser, and three Jesuits, Marcellino Zalba of Rome, Stanley de Lestapis of France, and John C. Ford of the United States.

Another crucial point in this whole discussion was the role of the Spirit guiding the officeholders. Where was the Spirit in 1930? At Lambeth with the archbishop of Canterbury or in Rome with Pius XI? Could the church now reverse *Casti connubii*? Does the presence of the Spirit in the church guarantee lack of error or replace human analysis? Other problems surfaced: the encyclical may have indicated that the pope can choose the wrong advisers, that Rome should not be preoccupied with authority, that the church must be willing to examine its past formulations openly and critically, and that "honest theological input is called for both before and after official statements" (McCormick 1990).

In 1967, the committee voted to reformulate the church's teaching that all use of contraceptives is immoral. The vote was sixty-four to four. Despite the vote, Paul VI published his famous encyclical *Humanae vitae* on July 25, 1968. Fearing that contraceptives "could open the way to marital infidelity and a general lowering of standards" of chastity (n. 17), Paul reaffirmed the traditional teaching that contraceptive birth control was intrinsically disordered *(intrinsece inhonestum,* n. 14). "Intrinsically" means of its very nature, and permits no exceptions. The pope did not use *intrinsece malum,* which means intrinsically evil.

Reactions to the Encyclical

Humanae vitae "plays a role in [Paul's] pontificate comparable to the dropping of the atomic bomb in the presidency of Harry S. Truman. Taken alone, it can obscure many achievements; if one neglects it, one slights the seismic and epochal."[7]

Many bishops, priests, religious (Mother Teresa of Calcutta has spoken out frequently against contraceptive birth control), theologians, doctors, lawyers, and parents accepted the papal teaching. Organizations like Opus Dei and the Knights of Columbus accepted the encyclical in 1968 and do so now. John C. Ford and Germain Grisez, a professor of Christian ethics at Mount St. Mary's College in Maryland, have argued (1978) that the traditional Catholic teaching on birth regulation is infallibly taught.[8]

Paul VI was not ready for the vociferous dissent and the ferocious debates. "The incomprehension of the world was to be expected; the incomprehension of the church was his cross" (Hebblethwaite 1975, 209). After *Humanae vitae,* Paul never wrote another encyclical and stopped his overseas pilgimages. Were these decisions the result of the negative reaction to *Humanae vitae?* Did he retreat before the moral pressure or did he remain in Rome because his arthritic hip was a source of physical pain (Wynn 1988, 61)? No one really knows.

Several episcopal conferences issued statements that clearly modified the papal position. The Dutch bishops directed their people to form their consciences in light of the encyclical but also to consider such factors as "mutual love, family condition and social circumstances." They hoped that "the discussion of the papal letter [would] contribute to a better and better functioning of authority within the church" (Haughey 1968). The English bishops said they rejected a subjective conscience that will not accept ecclesial documents. Nevertheless, they stressed the primacy of conscience and insisted "neither the encyclical nor any other document of the church takes away from us our right and duty to follow our conscience" (ibid.). The United States bishops issued the statement "Human Life in Our Day" on November 15, 1968. They agreed with the pope that artificial contraception itself is an "objective evil," but they modified this by admitting that "circumstances may reduce moral guilt." In addition, they called on the priests and people "to form their consciences in [the encyclical's] light." Some people interpreted this general statement as a blank check to choose another course of action than that set down in the encyclical. But the bishops were quick to reply that whereas people form their own conscience, "they have the responsibility to form a correct conscience" (ibid.).

Charles Curran

Immediately after the publication of the 1968 encyclical, Curran, a priest and professor of moral theology at Catholic University since 1965, initiated a public dissent from the church's teaching that contraceptive birth control was intrinsically evil. Curran wrote that "spouses may responsibly decide according to their conscience that artificial contraception in some circumstances is permissible and indeed necessary to preserve and foster the values and sacredness of marriage." He was not alone. Over six hundred theologians, other academics (including twenty other professors at Catholic University), and priests signed Curran's statement of dissent (Häring 1987, 235–50; see also Baum 1968; McCormick 1973).

Many agreed with Curran because he argued that dissent from some authoritative but noninfallible teachings is legitimate inasmuch as these teachings have three characteristics: (1) They deal with matters remote from the core of the faith. (2) They are matters heavily dependent of support from human reason and the natural law. (3) They are so complex and yet so specific that logically it is not possible to claim absolute certitude in their regard (Curran 1986, 61).

Curran's position at Catholic University and the media coverage his dissent received brought on efforts to remove him from the university. Those moves were unsuccessful at that time. However, he came under investigation by the CDF in 1979 and, after a long, drawn-out process, he was informed in August 1986 that he was "neither suitable nor eligible to exercise the function of a professor of Catholic theology" (Curran 1986; see also May 1987). His struggles to return to his teaching position at Catholic University were of no avail. After one-year appointments at Cornell University, the University of Southern California, and Auburn University, he accepted a tenured position at Southern Methodist in the fall of 1991.

Curran has documented his case and his controversy with the Vatican. The questions evoked by the removal of Curran's canonical mission, particularly the issue of public dissent, prompted McCormick to rate the Curran affair "as among the most significant developments in moral theology in the past 50 years" (1989, 17).

Occasionally, Curran reiterates his belief that the Vatican teaching is wrong. For example, on October 23, 1994, he was invited to publicly debate Janet E. Smith, philosophy professor at the University of Dallas, a Catholic college. An overflow crowd of twelve hundred heard Smith emphasize the negative social consequences of contraceptive birth control. She argued that during the sexual revolution of the 1960s many expressed great confidence in the social promise of contraceptives. It was believed that they would improve marriage, reduce unwanted pregnancies and abortion, and free women from "enslavement to their reproductive capacities." But, Smith noted, statistics on divorce, illegitimate children, and abortion in the last thirty years reveal that the positive forecasts fall far short of the optimistic expectations. For his part, Curran affirmed that a Christian marriage is a "sacramental communion of life in the service of life" with "unitive and procreative aspects." Nonetheless, he insisted that "the individual sexual act must be seen in relationship to the person and in relationship to the marriage and the good of marriage. Therefore, within the context that will always be unitive and procreative, one can interfere with the individual act because this is necessary for the good of the marriage and the good of the persons" (Luker 1994).

The Birth Control Debate

There seem to be three major points of disagreement on this topic. First, those who are against the use of contraceptives say nothing should interfere with the biological integrity of sexual intercourse. This position is in accord with the understanding of natural law as an order of nature. The morally good must be in accord with nature. Contraceptives prevent the finality of the sexual act. Every conjugal act must be open to the transmission of life. Any interference in the nature of the act is intrinsically evil.

The counter argument questions why humans cannot intervene in human affairs. They acknowledge that contraceptives involve premoral evil since they preclude procreation. However, is it not true that humans often have to sacrifice one value for another? What is marriage for? "If excluding reproduction completely is in violation of the natural law, excluding healing and restorative powers of marital sex for a long period also would seem to be unnatural" (Greeley 1993). Furthermore, abstinence could endanger the unitive purpose of the marriage, that is, the couple's mutual and covenant love. Also, there are often other values to consider, for example, the couple may have too many children already.

Second, those against the use of contraceptives say the unitive and procreative goals of marriage are inseparable. The unitive cannot exist independently. One violates the unitive meaning of the sexual act whenever one violates the procreative meaning. To separate the two goals would leave no case against such actions as in vitro fertilization, anal intercourse, and bestiality.

The counter argument centers on the "Catholic method of birth control," namely, the rhythm method, or natural family planning. This method was forbidden until Pius XII announced in 1951 that it was permissible for a couple with "serious motives" to use natural family planning to limit births.

The rhythm method relies on the approximately six to nine days during the monthly cycle when the woman can conceive. During these times the couple practicing the rhythm method do not express love with sexual intercourse. But those who disagree argue that rhythm is not a perfect method. First, the method has its dark side (Finley 1991). It may work moderately well for some people, but it is not even an option for many others. It creates stress and is said to be psychologically harmful. Many couples say they cannot grow together when they have to structure their married lives around a method and a calendar. They argue that the rhythm method is impracticable because it fails to give a sufficiently secure foundation to their bodily rhythms and the regulation of birth. The uncertainties of the method create enormous fear. Second, this method is inconsistent with the church's principle that the conjugal act must always be open to procreation. What is the difference between using the "safe period" and using contraceptives? In actual practice, is the rhythm method not contraceptive?

Third, those against the use of contraceptives maintain that this is the infallible teaching of the church with a history going back to the third century. The church could not have erred for such a long time about so serious a matter. If the church admitted error on this point, it would irreparably damage its indefectibility, i.e., its belief that, due to the presence of the Spirit, the world church can never lose its fundamental grasp of the Christian gospel. Several arguments are offered to counter the infallibility argument. First, this teaching was never defined as infallible. Arthur Veermersch (1858–1936), the Jesuit theologian who drafted *Casti connubii* for Pius XI, insisted later that the teaching was infallible. However, it has been pointed out that the inclusion of the condemnation of contraceptive birth control was added to *Casti connubii* at the last moment. Veermersch believed the condemnation of contraceptives was necessary in view of the tolerance of contraceptive birth control by the Anglicans at their Lambeth Conference and "because he feared that many priests were not enforcing the doctrine in the confessional" (Greeley 1993). In 1968, when Monsignor Ferdinando Lambrushini, the official spokesman in Rome for *Humanae vitae,* presented the encyclical to the press, he said that Paul VI did not intend to make an irreformable statement (R. O'Connell 1968).

Second, the episcopal conferences were not consulted about the encyclical. Third, the church has made errors in the past and corrected them. This, they maintain, is the case here. Fourth, Catholics have much to learn from other Christian communities, some of whom permit contraceptive birth control to limit or avoid parenthood.

The Effects on the Church

Humanae vitae was rejected for many reasons: the pope had not consulted all the bishops, many of whom modified the pope's position for their people; papal teachings on sex had not developed since 1930 and yet there have been many advances in the sociological, biological, and physiological understanding of human sexuality; the pope rejected the majority vote of his commission; and many found the teachings unrealistic, for some of the reasons outlined above.

Many left the church in response. Others limited their involvement, especially their participation at Eucharist. Others questioned the ability of the church to instruct people about a correct conscience. The encyclical also created a crisis of authority (Komonchak 1978, 221–57). If the church is wrong about this important issue, where else is it in error? The result is that today many Catholics make their own decisions on moral and religious matters and yet continue to participate as active Catholics. But most of all, *Humanae vitae* constituted the first major test for the postconciliar church. "The encyclical was a catalyst which did most to bring about the crisis of identity within the church which had been imminent since the closing of the council" (Mahoney 1990, 300).

Synod of 1980

As bishop and cardinal of Krakow, the future John Paul II invested a significant amount of time on Christian ethics and morality, including sexuality. He wrote *Love and Responsibility* in 1960, a book which argues that contraceptive birth control degrades women. He inveighed in his sermons against artificial means of contraception. He established an Institute of the Family in Krakow to teach and advise people about moral matters such as atheism, abortion, and contraceptive birth control. In 1995 it was revealed in a biography of John Paul that while he was on the papal commission on birth control, he organized his own commission in Krakow. His commission prepared essays that were sent directly to Paul VI. During this period Wojtyla met frequently with Paul VI. A Polish theologian who worked on the Krakow commission said that "about sixty percent of our draft is contained in" *Humanae vitae* (Szulc 1995). This background explains in part why John Paul chose as the theme of his first synod the Christian family in the modern world.

In addition to the bishops, fifteen married couples were invited as resource persons, including John and Evelyn Billings, both medical doctors who specialized in natural family planning. The bishops did not want a change in the teachings found in *Humanae vitae,* but some bishops requested a clearer explanation of the encyclical since it was rejected by many Catholics whose faith, learning, and dedication to the church were beyond doubt. There was also a call for worldwide dialogue between the pope and theologians on the meaning of dissent.

In *Familiaris consortio,* the apostolic exhortation issued after the synod on November 22, 1981, John Paul II addressed the subject of contraception. He explained how, "in continuity with the living tradition of the ecclesial community throughout history," both Vatican II and *Humanae vitae* had "handed on to our times a truly prophetic proclamation, which reaffirms and reproposes with clarity the church's teaching and norm, always old yet always new, regarding marriage and regarding the transmission of life." It was this stance, he stated, that led the episcopal synod to reaffirm the teaching of Vatican II (GS 51) and *Humanae vitae,* "particularly that love between husband and wife must be fully human, exclusive, and open to new life" (n. 29).

John Paul then called on theologians to help the hierarchical magisterium make this teaching "truly accessible to all people of good will" by "illustrating even more clearly the biblical foundations, the ethical grounds and the personalist reasons behind this doctrine" (n. 31). The pope issued this call because he knows that a large number of Catholics simply ignore the official teachings. Italy, for example, has the lowest birth rate in Europe, yet 84 percent of the people profess to be Catholics (Bohlen 1995b).

Contraceptives: The Ongoing Controversy

Despite the exhortations of John Paul II, debate about the immorality of contraceptive birth control continued during the 1990s both within the church and among the churches. Here are several instances.

Two weeks before an informal meeting with John Paul II on May 12, 1992, George Carey, the 102nd archbishop of Canterbury, blasted the Catholic church's ban on contraceptive birth control, charging that *Humanae vitae* "actually stopped theological thinking."

The context of the archbishop's comments was the worldwide preparations for the United Nations Conference on Environment and Development to be held in Rio de Janeiro in early June. Carey said the church's teachings on contraceptives would inhibit discussion of population control. He was distressed because population control was not even on the conference's agenda. The archbishop said, "The moment the pope actually says this is a dogma, it creates a very big problem for the Church of Rome. That's their problem. It's also ours, in the sense that all of us are caught up in it."

In the summer of 1993, the twenty-fifth anniversary of the encyclical, numerous church leaders, theologians, and journalists commented on how much the 1968 encyclical continues to shape church life, authority, and discipline (Untener 1993; McCormick 1993a; Curran 1993a; Hebblethwaite 1993e). The encyclical has both defenders and critics. Defenders praised the encyclical's teachings that married love should be permanent and exclusive, and they offered fresh philosophical and theological defenses of the procreative teachings (Flannery and Koterski 1993). John Paul reaffirmed Paul VI's 1968 encyclical at the eighth World Youth Day in Denver in August 1993 and in *Veritatis splendor* (n. 80). Critics, on the other hand, remained unpersuaded by the encyclical's teaching that the dual meaning of sex—marital love and procreation—must be respected in the totality of a married life and in each act of intercourse. There is evidence that United States Catholics are as likely to use contraceptives as other Americans.

On September 6, 1994, a full-page advertisement about contraceptive birth control appeared in the *New York Times*. A group called Catholics Speak Out sponsored "An Open Letter to Pope John Paul II" that had been signed by thousands from this country and around the world. The sponsoring organization (and its fourteen co-sponsors) timed the letter of nine paragraphs for the beginning of the United Nations International Conference on Population and Development, held in Cairo, Egypt, from September 5 to 13. This was the third such conference. The first two were at Bucharest, Romania (1974), and Mexico City, Mexico (1984).

The nations of the world have become increasingly concerned about the number of people on the planet, development, hunger, pollution, and the depletion of the earth's resources. Whereas 136 and 147 nations attended the first two conferences, respectively, the Cairo conference attracted delegates from 170 nations. The theme of the conference was "Choices and Responsibilities." The purpose of the conference was to chart a plan to responsibly stabilize the growth of the world's population. The delegates proposed that the nations commit themselves to keep the world population under 7.8 billion by the year 2050.

The sponsors of the ad were upset because the Vatican had been waging an all-out campaign against the United Nations' plan, which included making available contraceptive family planning services. The ad declared that the church's teachings about contraceptives caused serious problems within the church and for the international community. The sponsors called for a serious new dialogue because, they declared quite bluntly, the Vatican's position is "wrong." Furthermore, the Vatican's stance "severely worsens our global crisis of population and resources." The ad called upon world leaders and the United Nations "to embrace as a worldwide goal the provision of voluntary contraceptive family planning services to every woman and man who wants them by the end of the decade." The ad declared the Vatican's position "a marginalized minority view in our church." They said that "couples have found that various forms of contraception enhance their mutual sanctification and caring in sexual love; Vatican opposition devalues this love." The sponsors stated that they shared the Vatican's concern for "responsible parenting," but find that its opposition to contraceptives "denies the moral adulthood of women in making reproductive decisions."

These well-publicized discrepancies between the official teaching and the beliefs and practices of Catholics are unhealthy for the church, its institutional, intellectual, and devotional life.

Contraceptives and AIDS

The first announcement of the existence of AIDS appeared in a medical journal on June 5, 1981. The medical world confessed it did not know what to make of this virus which suddenly showed up among a handful of homosexual men in New York City. But slowly and inexorably the virus spread due to such factors as sexual activity, unsanitary needles, and transfusions of contaminated blood. Within a short period of time the deadly virus became a worldwide epidemic. Anti-AIDS activists and health officials soon advocated several preventive measures: abstinence, marital fidelity, the prophylactic use of condoms, and needle-exchange programs.

In the late 1980s and 1990s emphasis was put on the distribution of condoms since many competent doctors affirmed that for those sexually active a condom of good quality is currently the only method of prevention. Education about condoms was deemed absolutely necessary. The nation's public schools were enlisted in the education program. Teachers were urged, in some places mandated, to provide information about HIV-AIDS, its causes, conditions, and consequences. Schools were even expected to provide condoms. Many social and religious groups objected to the involvement of the schools. They argued that providing condoms is not a proper means of education into marital sexuality. They offered several reasons. The distribution of condoms implicitly accepts nonmarital sexual activity, conveys a false sense of security, and fosters a mechanical device that is not perfectly reliable in preventing either conception or the transmission of viruses. If anything, it was argued, schools should advocate abstinence and provide moral instruction to create a stronger sense of moral responsibility.

During this discussion, the Catholic church continued to declare that any use of contraceptives was immoral, whether for family planning or for HIV-AIDS prevention. Nonetheless, since AIDS is lethal, moral theologians, clergy, and other concerned persons began to look beyond the Vatican's unqualified rejection of condoms for some qualified moral support for their use to prevent the spread of the deadly disease. They found an argument with an honored place in classic moral theology, namely, "the lesser of two evils." In order not to pass on the deadly virus, condoms can and should be used.

One official attempt to give qualified moral support to the use of condoms came from a committee of United States bishops in December 1987. They presented to all the bishops a document titled "The Many Faces of AIDS: A Gospel Response." The primary purpose of the document was to reassure those infected with HIV-AIDS of the church's unequivocal support against stereotyping, prejudice, rejection, or injustice. The document called for continuing concern, education, pastoral ministry and support for persons with HIV-AIDS, as well as for their families and friends. This document also endorsed the dissemination of accurate information about condoms to combat AIDS. The committee declared that, since some people will not act as they can and should, and since AIDS is a fatal disease, then public educational programs "could include accurate information about prophylactic devices or other practices proposed by some medical experts as potential means of preventing AIDS. We are not promoting the use of prophylactics, but merely providing information that is part of the factual picture."

These last sentences occasioned an unusual public dispute among the bishops (P. Steinfels 1988). Cardinals Bernard Law and John O'Connor pronounced the document "a grave mistake" and led a campaign to have any mention of condoms removed from the statement. Backed by other bishops, they took their grievance to Rome and prevailed in getting a new document issued in November 1989. In this document, titled "Called to Compassion and Responsibility," the bishops objected to programs that promote the use of condoms. In addition to a concern that this approach "means in effect promoting behavior that is morally unacceptable," the bishops were also concerned with the question of efficacy. They noted that the promotion of condoms is "poor and inadequate advice, given the failure rate of prophylactics and the high risk that an infected person who relies on them will eventually transmit the infection in this way."

This issue surfaced again in a dramatic way on February 12, 1996, when the French bishops issued a 235-page report called "AIDS: Society in Question" (Whitney 1996). The bishops declared that "condom use is understandable in the case where a pattern of sexual activity is established and in the interest of avoiding grave risk." In France health authorities had been endorsing the use of condoms to prevent AIDS and the young people were paying attention to them. Since the church was opposed to the use of condoms, it was "accused of promoting death." The bishops wrote in order to meet this very challenging teaching situation.

The bishops declared that they were opposed to advising adolescents to use condoms because such advice "far from helping them to understand their sexual identity, confines them to the power of their desires." On the other hand, they said the church's absolutist position—its unqualified rejection of the use of condoms for the prevention of AIDS—separated the church from its people. What the bishops had in mind were cases "where a pattern of sexual activity is already established," as in marriages where one partner has HIV or AIDS. In such situations married persons need to ask whether exposing the spouse to any risk of a lethal disease is tolerable. In this case, persons at risk should not add one evil to another evil. Condoms were necessary.

The bishops tried to make very clear that they were not defying Vatican teaching. Nor were they recommending or explicitly sanctioning the use of condoms. They were declaring that, under certain conditions, their use may be tolerated (Schaeffer 1996b). On moral grounds they themselves could not promote the use of condoms to prevent AIDS, but medical personnel and others might counsel their use to prevent the spread of AIDS.

Many bishops and theologians around the world, knowing full well that the position of the French bishops was a break from the official Catholic position, supported the French bishops.[9] The Vatican seems to recognize the complexity of the problem because no directives were given the French bishops either to change or reverse their teaching.

On October 22, 1996, Jon Fuller, a Jesuit physician who is assistant director of the clinical AIDS program at the Boston Medical Center and was founding president of the National AIDS Network, proposed that the official church reexamine its position on the use of condoms to prevent HIV-AIDS. He admitted that when the United States bishops rejected the use of condoms in their November 1989 document, "it was certainly reasonable to look to the available literature on contraception to determine how effective condoms might be in preventing HIV transmission. Since then, however, several sources of data have become available that more specifically assess the capacity of condoms to reduce HIV transmission in real-life situations." Furthermore, the epidemic has reached astronomical numbers. "Between 8,000 and 13,000 new infections are estimated to take place each day—up to 540 every hour." In the past the church has frequently reshaped its moral theology once novel and difficult cases strain the applicability of previously established principles. To make his case, Fuller uses an analogy. He points out that the development of nuclear weapons changed the context and meaning of waging war in such a way that it was impossible to apply the just war theory in a straightforward way. "Suddenly, critical elements of that theory were no longer applicable; concepts such as 'use of proportionate means' and 'protection of non-combatants' had become meaningless. This called for a reevaluation of moral maxims in the context of novel and problematic cases." The United States bishops noted this changed situation when they wrote their peace pastoral in 1983. Fuller argues that with the rise of the AIDS epidemic, the "moral implications of sexual intercourse and drug injection use have changed in as significant a fashion as did modern warfare" with the development of nuclear weapons in 1945. Something has to be done to slow down this epidemic now lethal to individuals and society in a way that has never been true before. Condoms are an effective means to prevent the spread of HIV-AIDS.

Abortion

Abortion is the removal or expulsion of a fetus from the uterus, deliberately procured or induced. There are three kinds: natural (when the fertilized egg does not get implanted in the uterus); therapeutic (when the fetus is removed for medical reasons); elective (when a person chooses to have the fetus removed).

In the United States elective abortion is a highly emotional and controversial topic that has been constantly in the headlines, especially since the Supreme Court decision that legalized it in Roe v. Wade of January 22, 1973. The court decreed that abortions are allowed up to the third trimester, except when it is necessary to preserve the life or health of the mother. The debate has reached a stalemate inasmuch as two values are locked in opposition: life and freedom. Prolife advocates argue for the rights of the unborn. Prochoice advocates argue for a woman's right to make her own decision about her own pregnancy. In the United States the number of abortions annually is approximately 1.5 million (or more than four thousand a day). Daniel Callahan wrote that the permissive abortion laws in our country and around the world "bring forward a whole class of women who would otherwise not have wanted an abortion or felt the need for one" (1973).

McCormick (1981a, 474) summarized the multiple problems raised by abortion:

> Abortion is a matter that is morally problematic, pastorally delicate, legislatively thorny, constitutionally insecure, ecumenically divisive, medically normless, humanly anguishing, racially provocative, journalistically abused, personally biased, and widely performed. It demands a most extraordinary discipline of moral thought, one that is penetrating without being impenetrable, humanly compassionate without being morally compromising, legally realistic without being legally positivistic, instructed by cognate disciplines without being determined by them, informed by tradition without being enslaved by it, etc. Abortion, therefore is a severe testing ground for moral reflection . . . and probably a paradigm of the way we will face other human problems of the future.

Church Teaching

The Bible never addresses the question of elective abortion. It does express great respect for the human being in the mother's womb. According to the Bible, all humans belong to God from their very beginnings. The church condemns abortion as the logical conclusion from the biblical condemnation of murder—the deliberate killing of an innocent human being. The magisterium teaches that human life begins at conception. Elective abortion, then, is alway immoral. Therapeutic abortion is allowed when killing the fetus is indirect and is done to save the life of the mother.

Abortion was not a major issue in the Catholic church until the 1970s. Pius XII rarely discussed it. John XXIII referred to it in *Mater et magistra* (n. 3). Vatican II gave it a firm but brief mention, describing both it and infanticide as "abominable crimes" (GS 51). Paul VI did not mention it in 1967 in his great moral statement, *Populorum progressio*. However, on November 18, 1974, the CDF published a "Declaration on Procured Abortion," the most detailed and authoritative utterance on abortion in years. It asserts that human life must be given equal protection at all stages from fertilization through adulthood. Speaking of the fertilized ovum, it states "it would never be made human if it were not human already" (n. 12).

John Paul II has condemned abortion firmly and frequently. For example, in June 1997 when he made his seventh visit as pope to his native Poland, he said, "A nation which kills its own children is a nation without a future." Although 90 percent of Poland's forty million people are Catholics, abortion has been part of the national debate since the collapse of communism. Consequently, John Paul called for a "general mobilization of consciences and a joint ethical effort in order to put into action a great strategy of the defense of life." He added, "A civilization which rejects the defenseless would deserve to be called a barbarian civilization even if it had great successes in the fields of economics, technology, art and sciences" (Perlez 1997).

The Catholic church considers abortion such a serious offense that it merits automatic excommunication (see canon 2350 in the Code of 1917 and canon 1398 in the Code of 1983). The latter states that "a person who procures a completed abortion incurs an automatic excommunication." In 1988 Vatican authorities clarified the legal definition of abortion to include new drugs and surgical procedures. They said that any method used to terminate a human life from the moment of conception until birth is an abortion. For an excommunication penalty to go into effect, one must know there is a pregnancy, and there must be a free choice to abort.

Reception of the Teaching

Despite the very clear teaching of the official church, the responses of Catholics to abortion are not radically different from those of other citizens. In general there have been three responses to the magisterium's absolute condemnation of all elective abortions: acceptance, a call for further dialogue, and rejection.

Nearly all Catholics view abortion as a grave moral evil—even those who consider themselves prochoice. Many express their opposition to abortion by participating in such organizations as the National Right to Life Committee (founded in 1973) and Operation Rescue (founded by Randall Terry in 1987), joining well-organized marches on Washington each January 22, and writing letters to government officials.

The United States bishops have spoken out on a number of occasions. Individual bishops have excommunicated Catholics who direct abortion clinics and some bishops have publicly criticized Catholics in political office who refuse to support antiabortion legislation. One bishop made national headlines in January 1990 when he suggested that Catholic politicians who vote to "facilitate" abortion risk hell if they die without repenting (Dicker 1990). In May 1990, the United States bishops hired a reputable and expensive public relations firm to spread the church's message that all abortions are wrong. Building on the prochoice theme, the bishops urged all citizens to "exercise the natural choice—choose life." Then in

January 1992, the bishops canceled their contract with the public relations firm for several reasons: there was criticism of the costs, questions arose about some of the controversial clients of the firm, and the bishops said they wanted to enter a new phase of their public education program.

Some Catholics think the question needs further dialogue since there are different views on abortion within the church. For example, a full-page advertisement with just that message appeared in the *New York Times* on October 7, 1984. The ad, titled "Catholic Statement on Pluralism and Abortion," asserted that there is a diversity of opinion among committed Catholics as to whether abortion is morally wrong in all instances and whether in certain circumstances "direct abortion, though tragic, can sometimes be a moral choice." They also asserted that the official church's position is not the only legitimate Catholic position on abortion. They declared that "it is necessary that the church community encourage candid and respectful discussion on this diversity of opinion within the church." Among the ninety-seven signees were twenty nuns. All the nuns were threatened with expulsion from their communities if they did not remove their names from the statement. On July 22, 1986, the Vatican announced that the nuns no longer faced disciplinary measures because they had made "public declarations of adherence to Catholic doctrine on abortion." Eleven nuns immediately denied the Vatican's claim.[10] They declared that they never recanted a syllable of the 1984 advertisement. They said they did issue clarifications in response to requests by the Vatican, but none of their statements supported church doctrine on abortion. They did support the church's respect for life.

Two Notre Dame sisters, Barbara Ferraro and Patricia Hussey, held out even with regard to the clarifications. Since 1981 they had been managing a home in West Virginia for poor women. From these women they heard pathetic accounts of rape, incest, battering, and abortion. They decided they could no longer accept the Vatican teaching that every abortion is an unspeakable crime. They continued to battle for their position. At first it seemed that they would be dismissed from their religious community because they received two official warnings in the first two months of 1988. But in June, the superiors of the Notre Dame sisters informed Ferraro and Hussey that they would not be dismissed. Dismissal, they said, would not be in the best interests of either the church or their own community. On July 13, 1988, still under considerable direct pressure from Rome, they withdrew from their community, vowing to continue "loyal, authentic dissent."[11] The leaders of the Notre Dame sisters said that "Sisters Pat and Barbara have done what the situation and their own integrity demanded. They know that the prayers of the Sisters of Notre Dame will follow them into the future" (Gramick 1988).

In the spring of 1990, the archbishop of Milwaukee, Rembert G. Weakland, held hearings with women in his diocese to gather their views on abortion, especially so he could understand the views of those who disagreed with the church's teaching. His report on the meetings was widely publicized. The archbishop upheld the church's teachings but warned that the antiabortion movement was driving away potential supporters, including Catholics, who viewed its focus as narrow, its tactics as aggressive, and some of its rhetoric as "ugly and demeaning." He also urged that politicians trying to face the abortion issue with respect for life should be given "as much latitude as reason permits." The frank discussions with the women affected Weakland so much that he declared he could never again be glib when talking about "the moment of conception" or talk glibly about bringing the baby to term and then "just give it up for adoption" (P. Steinfels 1990a; Martinez 1990).

A Vatican follow-up to Weakland's report came in November 1990 when it barred the theology faculty of the University of Fribourg from granting the archbishop an honorary degree. The awarding of the degree was meant to open the centennial celebration of Leo XIII's pioneering social encyclical, *Rerum novarum*. The archbishop was chosen primarily because of his central role in the drafting of the United States bishops' pastoral on the economy in 1986. The Vatican's reason for barring Archbishop Weakland from receiving the degree was that his statements on abortion had caused "a great deal of confusion among the faithful" (P. Steinfels 1990c; Windsor 1990b).

The church teaches that individual human life begins at the moment of conception, and that a fetus has the same rights and deserves the same legal protection as a child. These two points—when human life begins and when a human's full standing in the eyes of the law or as a member of the human moral community begins—are the kind of questions that many Catholics want discussed further since the medical, scientific, and legal communities continue to study and debate them.

Some Catholics reject the absolutism of official Catholic teaching that all abortions are immoral. A group called Catholics for a Free Choice (CFFC) endorses abortion rights. This organization, founded in 1970, was the force behind the *New York Times* ad of October 7, 1984 (Doerflinger 1985). Daniel Maguire, board member of CFFC and moral theologian at Marquette University, believes that some theologians and a majority of Catholics do not consider abortion immoral under a range of circumstances: rape, risk of health, genetically damaged fetus, physically handicapped woman, teenage pregnancy, a mother on public aid who cannot work, and a married woman who already has a large family (1983, 1984). However, the common opinion among moral theologians, including prominent scholars such as McCormick and Häring, is that abortion is allowed only to save the mother's life. "Beyond this case," wrote Häring, "I do not see any plausible reasons that could morally justify an interruption of pregnancy" (1981, 3:33).

The United States bishops emphatically distanced themselves from CFFC on November 4, 1993. They declared that "there is no room for dissent by a Catholic from the church's moral teaching that direct abortion is a grave wrong." The bishops stated that CFFC, a Washington-based, prochoice advocacy group, "has no affiliation, formal or otherwise, with the Catholic church." CFFC "can in no way speak for the Catholic church" and its millions of members in the United States. The bishops concluded: "Because of its opposition to the human rights of some of the most defenseless members of the human race, and because its purposes and activities deliberately contradict essential teachings of the Catholic faith, we state once again that Catholics for a Free Choice merits no recognition or support as a Catholic organization."

On March 15, 1995, the Vatican made a highly unusual diplomatic move when it requested that the CFFC—a non-governmental organization—be barred from attending the United Nations' Fourth World Conference on Women to be held in September in Beijing, China. About thirteen hundred non-governmental organizations, including CFFC, had earlier been approved for accreditation. The Vatican argued that because CFFC "publicly promotes some fundamental positions contrary to those held by the Catholic church, it cannot be recognized as Catholic." The Vatican's effort was strongly opposed by several governments, including the United States, in part because CFFC had been accredited to participate in four previous international United Nations' conferences without opposition from the Vatican (C. Collins 1995). In 1995 the CFFC launched a petition drive aimed at unseating the Vatican as a permanent observer to the United Nations.

The Prolife–Prochoice Debate

Here are the key points made by each side in the abortion debate. First, prolife proponents say that the fertilized egg has a right to life, which begins at conception and is paramount. However, not all Catholic theologians agree that individual human life begins with conception. McCormick describes the embryo during the first two weeks as "nascent human life," but he does not consider it an "individual human life" until later (1981a, 108–9). During the first two weeks, the new life does not exhibit the stable and determining character necessary for considering it a distinct individual or a person with human dignity. Others agree with this opinion, including Albert Di Ianni (1974), Karl Rahner (1972, 236), and Charles Curran (1973). The basis of their position is the scientific view that "hominization" cannot possibly be said to occur before fourteen to twenty-two days after conception (Diamond 1975). For example, twinning is no longer possible after the first fourteen days.

Prochoice adherents maintain that women have the right to decide whether and when to become mothers. Also, many persons believe human life begins at the time it can be sustained outside the womb.

Further, prolife proponents say abortion is murder; however, they make an exception for therapeutic abortions. Prochoice supporters maintain that stages in fetal life distinguish the fertilized egg from a human being and distinguish fetal rights from those of a human being. As we saw above, theologians agree there are different stages of human life, but they still claim that an abortion of this "nascent human life" is tragically justifiable only on very limited occasions.

Those who are prochoice accuse the prolifers of being inconsistent because they seem unconcerned about the extremely high natural abortion rate. The fact that half or more of fertilized eggs are lost after failing to implant themselves in the uterus raises many moral and theological issues. Are these fertilized eggs really images of God and our brothers and sisters?

Prolife supporters challenge the idea of choice pointing out that a woman and a man make a choice to have sexual intercourse knowing that pregnancy is a possible result. Prochoice proponents argue that contraceptive failures beyond a woman's control put her at risk of an unwanted pregnancy. The prolife view claims that women do not appreciate what an abortion is. The prochoice stand maintains that women know what abortion entails and to force on them information they do not require about the consequences of their actions is punitive.

Those who support prolife maintain that abortion can be an unsafe medical procedure; those who promote prochoice maintain that it is safe.

The prolife view maintains that adoption is a "loving alternative" to abortion and that there are many couples who wish to adopt children. The prochoice view says women are not obliged to provide babies for those who cannot conceive on their own.

Prolife adherents argue that the prochoice movement has made a woman's right to choose more important than the choice itself, which is wrongly portrayed as morally neutral. Abortion, they say, inflicts such harm on the fetus and its right to life that it cannot be considered a private issue but should be a matter of legitimate government regulation. Prochoice supporters maintain that abortion is a private issue best left to individual conscience and without the interference of law.

Abortion and Church-State Relations

Abortion is not a purely "sexual" issue; it has far-reaching social and political ramifications. For example, President Bill Clinton proposed a universal health care plan in early 1994. Since the plan would fund abortions, it came under attack from religious groups. The Christian Coalition, founded by Pat Robertson, promised to spend $1.4 million to defeat the president's bill. [12] The Catholic bishops also spoke out. They sent a letter to thirty Congressional leaders pledging their strong support for a major overhaul of health care that includes universal coverage. Nonetheless, they promised "vigorous opposition" to any plan that included a requirement of abortion coverage. They also warned that they were mobilizing millions of Catholics against any plan that required abortion coverage because such a plan "will force millions of employers, churches, and individuals to subsidize abortion in violation of their consciences." Furthermore, abortion coverage would "jeopardize the future of Catholic and other religious providers of health care" (P. Steinfels 1994b).

Also in early 1994, the Vatican attracted worldwide attention when it mounted a bold diplomatic campaign against the legitimization of abortion. The occasion was the United Nations' International Conference on Population and Development to be held in Cairo, Egypt, mentioned earlier in this chapter.

The global population is a complicated web that involves many interrelated factors such as women's rights, dignity, and equality with men, education, employment, ecology, poverty, development, and health care. To get at these issues the conference delegates had to discuss such issues as "reproductive rights," "reproductive health," "family planning," and "safe motherhood." The Vatican opposed these terms because they were evasive, called for the distribution of contraceptives, and could include abortion. Some radical Muslim states, Iran and Libya in particular, supported the Vatican's position. However, the word "abortion" appeared only once in the conference's sixteen-chapter draft document. All nations were urged "to deal openly and forthrightly with unsafe abortion as a major public health concern." Albert Gore, Vice-President of the United States, reported that more than two hundred thousand women worldwide die annually from medically unsafe abortions (Gore 1994).

The Vatican leveled bitter attacks on the Clinton-Gore administration before and during the conference for its role in shaping the United Nations' document. On June 14, 1994, an extraordinary gathering of 114 (of the 139) cardinals voted to oppose some of the policies of the Cairo meeting. They labeled as "cultural imperialism" proposals on women's rights and abortion sponsored by the United States (Cowell 1994b). Once the delegates assembled, "the Vatican consistently criticized the document for promoting an atmosphere of immoral sexual license, weakening the family and advocating homosexual relationships" (T. Fox 1994b). Pope John Paul attacked the United Nations' document not only because it lacked explanations of how developed nations could lower their consumer practices so that the poor could obtain life's necessities, but also because it tended to "promote an internationally recognized right to access to abortion on demand." The delegates from the United States argued that they did not advocate abortion. They contended that those that do occur "should be safe, legal, and rare." Based on this stance, the forty-five delegates from the United States walked a delicate line, resisting attempts to include language that specifically outlawed abortion but not endorsing it as a method of family planning either.

The Vatican underscored several points. First, it declared there is no such thing as a "safe abortion," since an abortion results in the death of human life. Second, it objected to all suggestions that abortion is a universal right or any implication that abortion has any role in the care of women, family planning, or the politics of population. Third, it rejected any view of sexuality that removed it from interpersonal responsibility, moral considerations, and communal contexts. After having argued forcefully for its principles, the Vatican delegate participated in the signing ceremony at the closing session on September 13, expressing reservations only about the fuzziness of such terms as "sexual and reproductive health" found in a couple of the chapters.

Some participants evaluated the Vatican's role at this important conference. Ellen Chesler, a director of the International Women's Health Coalition, a New York-based organization, was negative. She declared: "I think this conference can be seen as ending two thousand years of ecclesiastical authority or jurisdiction over marriage and women's lives. Medicine and science, not religion and belief, will govern family planning" (Crossette 1994). Daniel Maguire thought the Vatican delegates misread the positive thrust of the conference. He wrote: "In many ways the conference and its written product are a triumph for the values that define holiness in Judaism, Christianity and Islam as well as in other religions. Though the word religion seems not to have made it into the final document, the religiously championed values of compassion, social justice, and reverence for this generous host of an earth are enshrined in it. Religious representatives should have been celebrating, not bickering about disputable issues in reproductive ethics" (D. Maguire 1994).

On April 10, 1996, President Bill Clinton vetoed a bill—the Partial Birth Abortion Ban Act—which would have banned an abortion that doctors call "intact dilation and extraction." According to testimony given in graphic detail about the procedure before Congress, the fetus is partially extracted feet first, and the skull is collapsed by suctioning out the brain to make it easier for the fetus to pass through the birth canal. At that time it was reported that this procedure was rarely performed—only after twenty weeks of gestation (second trimester), in situations in which the life of the mother is threatened or the fetus is badly deformed and not expected to live. Of the 13,000 annual late-term abortions (third trimester), it is estimated that 450 to 2,000 use this method.

Anti-abortion forces called the procedure a "partial-birth abortion," and maintained that if Roe v. Wade were not in place, the procedure verged on infanticide. The bill had an amendment that would allow the procedure to save the life of a woman. Clinton vetoed the bill because the procedure was used rarely and because the bill did not allow the operation for "serious health consequences" for the woman or for "future fertility." Anti-abortion forces deemed these reasons notoriously slippery justifications that in practice amount to little more than abortion on demand.

The president's veto drew an angry protest from the nation's cardinals and Bishop Anthony Pilla of Cleveland, president of the National Conference of Catholic Bishops (Niebuhr 1996b). As far as the official church is concerned, all elective abortions are "partial birth abortions." Consequently, in a three-page letter dated April 16, the cardinals called the veto "beyond comprehension for those who hold human life sacred" and declared that his action "takes our nation to a critical turning point. . . . It moves our nation one step further toward acceptance of infanticide." Some of the cardinals' words translate into an undisguised political threat. "In the coming weeks and months, each of us, as well as our bishops' conference, will do all we can to educate people about partial-birth abortions."

On April 19, John Paul II sent a stinging rebuke to the president. He said the veto was "shameful," a "brutal act of aggression against innocent life," and an act that "morally and ethically imperils the future of a society which condones it."

On April 30, in an open letter to Congress and as a direct response to the cardinals, more than two dozen Protestant and Jewish leaders voiced support of the veto.[13] "We fully support the president's action in standing with women and families who face tragic, untenable pregnancies . . . We know that some religious leaders have criticized the president for that veto based on their sincere religious beliefs that human life is sacred. . . . [We,] too, hold human life sacred, yet we respectfully disagree with this legislation. In the case of severe fetal anomalies or threats to the life and health of the mother, people of faith are called to cherish the life of the mother and others who are affected—the husband or partner, the children already living, and others—and to have compassion for a fetus who, if born, would inevitably suffer or die."

On September 12, eight United States cardinals, more than sixty bishops, and about one thousand laity and clergy from a variety of denominations held a prayer vigil to protest Clinton's veto of the Partial-Birth Abortion Ban Act. This was the largest assemblage ever of United States bishops in a public demonstration on federal property. The vigil was organized to influence the vote on the override of the bill. The House voted by 285 to 137 to override the president's veto, but on September 26, the Senate sustained the president's veto by 57 to 41, well shy of the two-thirds needed to override a veto.

Shortly before the general election on November 5, 1996, some Catholic clergy made national headlines when they urged citizens not to vote for Clinton over the abortion issue. For example, Philip M. Hannan, retired archbishop of New Orleans, said in a televised news conference that "no Catholic should vote for any officeholder who believes in abortion. No Catholic should vote for the president."[14]

This issue resurfaced in March 1997, when it was learned that the debate in 1996 was less than honest (O'Brien 1997). No one had gathered the basic facts. The president, congressional officers, and the public were misled. Prolife groups had maintained that the procedure was used in the eighth and ninth months of pregnancy on healthy babies. Prochoice groups had responded by arguing that only a few hundred of these third-trimester abortions were done each year to protect the mother's health or because of fetal abnormalities. But they were silent on the thousands performed in the second trimester on healthy women with healthy fetuses.

The debate resumed. The two sides could not agree on what the procedure should be called, the reasons it is performed, when it is performed, and whether it should be performed (Seelye 1997). Prochoice groups said that all abortions performed in the second trimester are legal and constitutionally protected from undue state intervention. A ban on the procedure is an unacceptable political invasion of private medical decisions and an attempt to limit access to abortions (ibid.). Prolife groups said that if doctors are allowed to make decisions on their own, the country would abandon moral standards necessary in a civilized society. They also declared the procedure infanticide. The Catholic church and most other abortion opponents do not approve of the procedure to protect a woman's health or fertility. John O'Connor, cardinal-archbishop of New York, said at a Mass, "I plead with you to pray that this horror of infanticide will be once and for all banned from our land" (Petersen 1997).

It remains to be seen how this contentious issue will play out.

President Clinton has also been involved in the approval of RU-486, an abortion-inducing pill. Upon taking office in 1992, he directed the Department of Health and Human Services, the Food and Drug Administration's parent agency, to review ways to get RU-486 on the market. RU-486, whose generic name is mifepristone, provides a safe, private alternative to surgical abortion, allowing a woman to terminate a pregnancy in the privacy of a doctor's office or a clinic. The pill acts to counteract progesterone, a hormone needed to sustain pregnancy. A woman takes three RU-486 pills up to seven weeks after her last menstrual period. Then, in another 36 or 48 hours, she takes two tablets of another drug, misopristol, which causes the uterus to contract, thus expelling the fetus.

RU-486 has been available in France, Britain, and Sweden for more than a decade and with about 96 percent effectiveness. But fears about anti-abortion protests and boycotts of any company manufacturing or distributing the drug has kept it out of the United States. In September 1996, the pill was given provisional approval for marketing in this country sometime in late 1997. However, complicated manufacturing problems have delayed the availability of the pill until at least 1998.

A Sacramental Marriage

The Catholic church has always defended marriage. It teaches that there is a real difference between a civil and a sacramental marriage. The latter has three dimensions: the consent of two baptized persons to live together in love until death, the consent of the church through the witnessing priest, and consummation.

In a sacramental marriage the couple are baptized. This should not be understood in a juridical way. A sacramental marriage entails a commitment to be Christian disciples who publicly witness the covenant love of God through Jesus Christ and his Spirit. This is no easy commitment and some theologians wonder just how many couples are ready for it (Cahill 1987; Cooke 1987).

The priest witnesses the ceremony, symbolizing the ecclesial and social dimensions of a sacramental marriage. It is the couple, however, who function as ministers and recipients of the rite.

Consummation, too, must not be understood juridically, that is, occurring at least once after the church ceremony. Consummation involves more than this. It requires a lifelong commitment and struggle to deepen intimacy and love.

Annulments

The official church grants an annulment when it declares that the marriage was not a sacramental union in the first place. The church does this when, after examining the evidence, it has moral certitude there was no marriage. This annulment does not mean the couple were not legally married or that the children are illegitimate.

In the United States annulments have increased considerably. This increase is due in part to the latitude taken by judges in the marriage tribunals after Vatican II. For example, in 1967, John Catoir, a judge in a marriage tribunal, suggested that "even if the evidence does not convince the judges of moral certitude, if it enables them to arrive at a well-founded possibility that the [first] marriage was null, an annulment should be granted." By 1984 the annulments were so numerous that Pope John Paul II complained about the "alarming increase" (15,000 percent in fifteen years) and warned marriage tribunals about "easy and hasty" annulments (Farrell 1984). Annually, there have been approximately forty-five thousand to fifty thousand annulments in the United States from 1984 to 1994 (Edwards 1994c).

The large number of annulments has received two interpretations. Some say they indicate that the church's understanding of the indissolubility of marriage can change over time. Others hold that the annulment process is dishonest. They argue that while the church seems to offer a pastoral solution to divorced Catholics, annulment is in many cases simply "divorce, Catholic-style." They take this position because of the way the church evaluates the intention of the couple when they made their nuptial vows.

In church teaching an essential aspect of the sacramentality of a marriage is the quality of the consent at the time of the wedding. The consent must be free and discerning. Both persons must have the psychological and emotional maturity to establish and sustain a mutually supportive partnership with one another for their whole life (canon 1055). But most annulments are granted precisely because it is said the couple did not have the proper emotional and/or psychological intention when they exchanged their vows. The church has accepted the insights of modern psychology about states of mind or personality disorders that may prevent an individual from truly entering into a sacramental marriage. Because the church has embraced these perspectives, it is said to be dishonest, that is, because it reserves sacramentality only for marriages that meet all the mental and psychological criteria enumerated in the literature on annulment. It also requires the couple to have an intention not required for the reception of other sacraments. Infants are validly baptized even though they have no conscious intention to join themselves to Christ and his church. Teenagers are duly confirmed even if they go through the ceremony because their parents insisted on it. "Furthermore, if the only people who are validly, sacramentally married are those whose choice was perfectly free, who completely understood what marriage is and what it entails, then very few—if any—were sacramentally married at the time they exchanged nuptial vows" (Crowe 1996). Consequently, "the church must be more explicit and honest about the extent to which its annulment policy represents a change" or development (ibid.).

Vatican II and Marriage

The council did not change the traditional ideals and standards concerning the indissolubility of marriage (AA 11). It "did achieve a total turnabout in the church's appreciation of the physiological, psychological, and conjugal aspects of marriage that has resulted in a basic shift in its evaluation of mankind's sexual propensities" (Murphy 1978).

This change reflects the deeper understanding of human behavior achieved by the human sciences and the change in understanding of marriage in society. We witness today the change from a male-dominated, child-centered, ethnically defined marriage to one in which the man and woman are seen as equals, interdependent, growth-oriented, and open to many expanded relationships.

At Vatican II the bishops introduced two fundamental changes in the Catholic definition of marriage (see GS 47–52). First, they did not list two ends of marriage: primary (the procreation and education of children) and secondary (mutual love and assistance). This is how Augustine, Thomas Aquinas, and Pius XI had ranked them. Instead, love and procreation were joined equally as the purposes of marriage. The bishops spoke of marriage as "the intimate partnership of life. . . . [The] love which constitutes the married state has been established by the creator and endowed by him with its own proper laws. . . . The intimate union of marriage, as a mutual giving of two persons, and the good of the children demand total fidelity from the spouses and require an unbreakable unity between them" (GS 48). The bishops said that "marriage was not instituted solely for the procreation of children: its nature as an indissoluble covenant between two people and the good of the children demand that the mutual love of the partners be properly expressed, that it should grow and mature" (GS 50).

Second, the bishops did not refer to marriage as a contract but rather as a "community of love" (n. 47) and a "covenant of love and fidelity" (n. 48). As a contract, marriage gave the two partners the exclusive right to sexual intimacy for the sake of the children they would have. As a community of love and fidelity, marriage consists in the multiple relationships of the couple, whether interpersonal, sexual, social, or ecclesial. The bishops wrote that "The Lord, wishing to bestow special gifts of grace and divine love on married love, has restored, perfected, and elevated it. A love like that, bringing together the human and the divine, leads the partners to a free and mutual self-giving, experienced in tenderness and action, and permeating their lives; this love is actually developed and increased by its generous exercise" (GS 49).

Divorce

Divorce has been legal for some time in the Western world. Malta is the only European country where divorce is illegal. Irish voters, despite the vigorous opposition of the Catholic bishops and clergy, narrowly approved the removal of a 1937 constitutional ban on divorce in November 1995. The law took effect on February 27, 1997 (Clarity 1995, 1997). In the United States in the 1990s nearly half of all marriages end in divorce, compared with about a third in 1970. Catholics divorce as frequently as other citizens.

At the fourth session of Vatican II, Melchite Archbishop Elias Zoghbi proposed that the church consider a pastoral practice for the divorced-remarried that more closely resembled the discipline of the Eastern Catholics. Since that intervention, there has been a great deal of writing on divorce and remarriage, and Zoghbi's suggestion is often considered to be the stimulus for it (McCormick 1981a, 332–33).

One of the first questions asked concerns the indissolubility of marriage. Some, like canon lawyer Stephen J. Kelleher, say this is an ideal and a goal (1973; see also Brunsman 1985; Curran 1974a, 1974b); others, like Richard McCormick (1981a, 554–61) and P. F. Palmer 1975) that it is an absolute norm.

Those who believe marriage is an ideal accept divorce and remarriage. When Catholics get divorced and remarried, their first marriage is one of two kinds. It was a true sacramental marriage that failed or it was not truly a Christian marriage except in a canonical sense. For example, some of these marriages died because, right from the start, there was a radical incapacity to sustain the duties and obligations of marriage.

The questions of indissolubility and remarriage received national attention in 1968 through the writings of Stephen Kelleher, a Catholic priest with twenty-five years of active experience in church courts and, at that time, presiding judge of the marriage tribunal in New York City. Kelleher wrote that many marriages had become "intolerable," that is, "in which it cannot be realistically foreseen that the couple would be able to continue or to resume a common life" (1968, see also 1975, 1977, 1978).

He had three main contentions. First, he said that the church's marriage tribunals had no place in the life of the church. They are not a Christian structure. They produce very few annulments. "What they do produce is delayed justice (sometimes no justice), frustration, humiliation, distrust, suspicion and fear. They are as much the enemies of law as of freedom."

Second, he recommended that each person should decide "in his own conscience whether or not he is free before God from one marriage and free to enter another." The bond no longer exists when love, commitment, and other signs that visibly manifest a marital relationship have been irretrievably lost.

Third, Kelleher suggested that the church establish a system of marriage commissions (not courts) to assist individuals and the church to reach responsible decisions on marital status. Kelleher had always maintained that the church could not grant divorces but it could acknowledge that a marriage had dissolved.

Many viewed Kelleher's proposals as impractical, too subjective, and vague. By 1978, his solution to the intolerable marriage was deemed by James Young as "neither necessary nor desirable" (1978). He offered six reasons for his judgment. He pointed out that between 1968 and 1978 people became more tolerant of divorce among their loved ones. There was less stigmatization and ostracism and more support in putting together a new life, even when this entailed a second marriage without church approval. He also mentioned that the marriage tribunals had been reformed so that they were real instruments of pastoral healing; and that the church had developed a ministry to divorced Catholics in many parishes. Further, divorce and remarriage no longer resulted in automatic excommunication and its concomitant punishments: denial of a funeral Mass and Christian burial, and labeling the second marriage an "adulterous union." The United States bishops had made this a church law in 1884, but Paul VI removed all these penalties in 1977. And he added, there had emerged a new pastoral theology of the Eucharist as a meal of reconciliation. This made it possible for the authentic reunion of many divorced-remarried Catholics to full communion in parish communities. Finally, the Catholic church had learned from the experiences of Protestant and Orthodox churches. These churches had normally allowed second marriages, but they were infrequent. Now they were increasing dramatically. The other Christian churches feared their discipline was contributing to this increase.

Jesus and Divorce

In the Jewish scriptures there is only one text that authorizes divorce: Deuteronomy 24:1–4. Actually, it presupposes divorce rather than authorizes it.

In Jesus' day a man could divorce his wife, but not vice versa. The older Jewish tradition, based on Genesis 2:24, outlawed divorce. Jesus followed this tradition and forbade divorce for any cause (Luke 16:18). The constant teaching of the church has been that marriage is indissoluble.

Divorce is mentioned in five New Testament texts (see 1 Corinthians 7:10–16; Mark 10:1–12; Matthew 5:32 and 19:1–12; Luke 16:18). Jesus' divorce teachings always appear in the context of his proclamation of the kingdom and his radical call to conversion and discipleship. When modern scripture scholars examine the context of these passages, they ask if Jesus' most firm prohibition was an absolute law applicable to all times and all cases. Did Jesus teach that divorce was impossible—or that it was wrong? The opinion of many scripture scholars is that divorce is wrong (McKenzie 1980; 1985, 40–50; Fitzmyer 1981; Donahue 1981; R. Collins 1993). Jesus did not proclaim an absolute law, but, as a man of compassion, he spoke against divorce in order to protect women from being cast out of their families. The "prohibition of divorce may be rooted in a culture in which women, from birth to death, were secure only as long as they were the property of some man—father, husband, and in their old age, a son" (McKenzie 1980). Furthermore, the exegetes point out that the so-called Pauline privilege of 1 Corinthians 7:10–16, as well as the exceptive clauses in both Matthew texts, are exceptions made by the Pauline and Matthean churches to the prohibition. In other words, the fact that Jesus' sayings on divorce exist in so many different versions demonstrates that first-century Christians experienced a need not only to hand on Jesus' teaching on divorce but also to adapt it to ever new circumstances.

It is a fact that marriages fail for many reasons. Many biblical scholars suggest that Jesus in his wisdom and compassion would allow divorce in our context—although most reluctantly. Until now, the church has maintained an "inhumane rigidity" regarding divorce. The opposite extreme would be "amoral relaxation." Between these two extremes, argues John L. McKenzie (1980), there should be a position which would allow each individual case, as individual, to decide how best to live the life of peace to which God calls them (1 Corinthians 7:15).

The Divorced-Remarried and the Sacraments

Can the divorced-remarried ever receive the sacraments? At the end of the Synod of 1980 on marriage and in *Familiaris consortio* (1981), John Paul II reiterated not only that they may not, but that this is the church's "traditional practice" (Michaels 1980; Hebblethwaite 1980e). However, this teaching flies in the face of "a virtually unanimous theological opinion that some divorced-remarried may be admitted to the sacraments" (McCormick 1981a, 120). There is a traditionalist and revisionist understanding of this issue (ibid., 82–87, 332–47, 372–81, 544–61, 826–41).

The traditionalist position assumes the existence of a permanent bond of marriage, one that lasts until death. Since the bond is permanent, the traditionalists conclude that the remarried must either separate or live as brother-sister.

They have three reasons for this conclusion. First, the couple is living in sin or at least a proximate occasion of sin. They are not disposed for the sacraments of reconciliation or Eucharist because a firm purpose of amendment or change is required. The Italian episcopal conference stated in 1979 that this will to change "does not exist if the divorced-remarried remain in a condition of life that is contrary to the will of God. How is it possible at the same moment to choose the love of God and disobedience to his commandments" (ibid., 828–29)?

Second, the remarried couple is in a state of imperfect unity with Christ and not eligible to receive the Eucharist. The International Theological Commission said in 1978: "From the incompatibility of the state of the divorced-remarried with the command and mystery of the risen Lord, there follows the impossibility for these Christians of receiving the Eucharist, the sign of unity with Christ" (ibid., 838).

Third, scandal would result if the remarried were admitted to the sacraments. Others would conclude that it is not wrong to remarry after divorce and that the church approves second marriages.

The revisionists conclude that the divorced-remarried may be admitted to the Eucharist under certain conditions. Charles M. Whelan, Jesuit specialist in church-state relations, lists four: if the first marriage is irretrievably lost; if the circumstances that allow official reconciliation are not available, for example, an annulment or the death of a spouse; if the couple has indicated by their lives that they desire to participate fully in the life of the church; and if there are solid grounds for hope of stability in the second marriage that in all other respects is a Christian marriage (Whelan 1974).

The revisionists reject the traditionalists' arguments. They doubt that the bond of marriage perdures if the marriage is existentially and psychologically dead (McCormick 1981b). They think the traditionalists' view that the remarried can receive the sacraments as long as they live like celibates is absurd. How, they ask, is the principle of indissolubility not threatened by a second marriage without a sexual life but with sacramental participation, while it would be threatened by a second marriage with a sexual life and sacramental participation (McCormick 1981a, 550)?

The revisionists offer three reasons why some of the divorced-remarried may be admitted to the sacraments. First, the life of the couple often does not reflect a state of sin. Also, when children are involved, the church has frequently urged the remarried couple to remain together and to deepen their Christian life. Second, to exclude the divorced-remarried from the Eucharist on the basis of incompatibility with the unity between Christ and his church that the Eucharist signifies involves a static and "perfectionist" notion of the sacraments. Everyone who approaches the Eucharist admits unworthiness. Also, the Eucharist has another function: it is a means of grace. All Christians, including the divorced-remarried, need the grace of Christ. Third, if people are properly instructed, scandal need not follow from admitting the remarried to Eucharist. People should be able to weigh the premoral evil involved, namely, that remarriage undermines the stability of marriage, but understand that in this instance the Eucharist would be good for the Christian life of those involved.

The Vatican through the CDF had occasion to reaffirm its teaching that the divorced-remarried cannot receive the sacraments on October 14, 1994. In a letter addressed to all the bishops, it said that to allow the divorced-remarried to receive the Eucharist would be to lead them into "error and confusion regarding the church's teaching about the indissolubility of marriage." The CDF said the norm should not be viewed as "a punishment or discrimination against the divorced and remarried, but rather expresses an objective situation that of itself renders impossible the reception of Holy Communion." The context of the Vatican document was a joint pastoral letter on the issue of ministry to the divorced-remarried published by three German bishops on July 10, 1993.

The German bishops—Walter Kasper, Karl Lehmann, and Oskar Saier—called for exceptions to the church's thorny and painful law. They were not asking for blanket admission to the sacraments because this would be contrary to "Jesus' radical call to the indissolubility of marriage" and the order of the church. They had in mind the many persons who in good conscience believe their second marriage is valid because their first was not truly sacramental. Some persons "in this difficult situation" were unable to obtain an annulment, offering such reasons as the following: the length of time necessary to obtain an annulment appeared prohibitive given their emotional and/or economic situation; the annulment process seemed formidable, especially to those who could not face the pain involved in reviewing the history of their first marriage before a tribunal (Grabowski 1994).

The German bishops offered standard criteria to aid those involved to discern their case. They recommended an intensive pastoral dialogue between a priest and the person seeking admission to the sacraments. Some of the standard criteria include a determination that a return to the first partner is impossible; a demonstration of the permanent character of the second marriage over the course of time; real evidence of a Christian faith and witness on the part of the individual or couple; attention to the possibility of scandal in the community.

The Vatican had problems with the proposal of the German bishops because it had flaws and ambiguities. John Grabowski, theologian at the Catholic University of America, explained that important points were not clear: "the relationship of their proposal to the already established annulment procedure, the authority of individual conscience vis-à-vis the power of jurisdiction within the ecclesial community and the theological status of the second marriage" (ibid.).

The three German bishops dropped their policy after the CDF issued its statement in October. Nevertheless, they asked that the question remain open because this problem is so pervasive and the cause of a great deal of pain, injury, and guilt. The 1994 Vatican repudiation of the German pastoral aroused a chorus of protests. At least six European bishops publicly commented on it. One said the Vatican discriminated against divorced-remarried Catholics since members of Eastern and Orthodox churches were officially permitted to receive the Eucharist under certain conditions (Shafer 1995b).

The different approaches of the Vatican and German bishops to this issue highlights once again the tension among the institutional, intellectual, and devotional dimensions of the church. In this case, the theological problems have to be worked out. Because the German bishops did not eliminate the flaws and ambiguities in their explanation, neither they nor the Vatican are able to agree on the best way to meet the devotional needs of a large number of Christians.

Homosexuality

Homosexuality designates the psychosexual inclinations of the person who prefers sexual activity with persons of the same sex. Alfred Kinsey (1894–1956), a biologist at the University of Indiana, reported in 1948 in *Sexual Behavior of the Human Male* that 10 percent of the population is exclusively homosexual. This figure has been challenged in the 1990s. According to a 1994 study, *The Social Organization of Sexuality: Sexual Practices in the United States*, Edward Laumann and his associates found that about 2.8 percent of men identify themselves as gay and 1.4 percent of women identify themselves as lesbian. Kinsey's statistics, they maintain, are close to being accurate for gay males in the country's twelve largest urban areas, but not for the whole country. Laumann et al. added that their estimates may be lower than the actual numbers because many homosexuals were probably reluctant to talk about their sexual feelings and activities.[15]

In the United States especially, self-avowed homosexuals have become increasingly visible and even militant in their demand to be socially accepted as homosexuals and for freedom from discrimination. There is even a church that comprises mostly gay and lesbian members, the Universal Fellowship of Metropolitan Community Churches (UFMCC). Founded in 1968 by Troy Perry, this international denomination had thirty-two thousand participants in 264 congregations in the United States in 1996 and its worldwide membership was about forty-six thousand, with congregations in nineteen countries the same year. It is "the largest organization in the world touching the lives of gays and lesbians."[16]

Because there is widespread and deep-seated homophobia in our society, gays and lesbians face considerable social, legal, and religious discrimination (Nugent 1981; Boswell 1981). The emergence of AIDS has only heightened this fear.

At present there is no consensus among Christian churches or theologians regarding moral questions about homosexuality and homosexual behavior. For example, the UFMCC applied twice—in 1983 and 1992—for formal ties with the National Council of Churches, but its request for "observer status" was denied each time (Hevesi 1992). Nonetheless, it has official observer status at the WCC.

Four Interpretations of Homosexual Behavior

In society and the Catholic church there seems to be four views about homosexual activity: that it is a perversion, a disease, an irreversible orientation, or a normal alternative to heterosexuality.

Those who view homosexuality as a perversion condemn all homosexual activity as immoral, intrinsically evil, unnatural, and contrary to scripture. The Bible does indeed have strict and clear edicts against homosexual activity. The clearest condemnations are in two verses in Leviticus: "You shall not lie with a male as with a woman; such a thing is an abomination" (18:22) and "If a man lies with a male as with a woman, both of them shall be put to death for their abominable deed; they have forfeited their lives" (20:13).

Biblical scholars point out, however, that the scriptures are ambiguous. For instance, they have no doctrine on homosexuality and certainly do not address the question of an irreversible orientation. The concepts of "constitutionally homosexual" and "homosexuality" are unknown during the biblical periods. It is modern science that has proposed that some persons are not heterosexual by choice or preference. Throughout the Bible, the Genesis description of male-female relationships is taken for granted as the standard and, since all people are heterosexual by nature, their genital activity should reflect their nature. However, the inspired authors warn that whenever people turn from God and his created order, all kinds of disorders and depravities follow, not only homosexual actions by heterosexuals but also adultery and lying (see Jeremiah 23:14), and pride, gluttony, and arrogance (see Ezekiel 16:49–50).

There are five biblical references to homosexual activity (see Genesis 19:4–11; Leviticus 18:22 and 20:13; Romans 1:24–27; 1 Corinthians 6:9–10; and 1 Timothy 1:9–10). In some of these passages homosexuality is not condemned as such, but as a sin of idolatry (Romans 1), as a violation of the sacred duty of hospitality (Genesis 19), or as the dehumanizing pederasty that was widespread in the Greco-Roman culture of the first century (1 Corinthians 6).

In the days of the apostle Paul, homosexuality "was related to temple services and therefore adoration of false gods" (Nouwen 1967; see also R. Collins 1986, 172–74). This is the context of Leviticus 18 in which God commands the Israelites not to "behave as they do in Egypt where you once lived" or "as they do in Canaan where I am taking you." This concern for cultural purity suggests that homosexuality reflected the male and female prostitution common in mid-East religious cults (Wink 1979). This prohibition, as well as those in other passages (see Deuteronomy 23:18 and 1 Kings 14:24 and 15:12) suggests that homosexual activity was prohibited because of its intimate association with idolatry (G. Coleman 1987). Furthermore, passages such as Romans 1:24–31 cannot be used to establish that homosexual acts are intrinsically disordered and can in no case be approved. It is generally agreed that "Paul did not know homosexuality as a condition. He saw it as a human choice, and as such, a perversion which he condemned in general terms" (McCormick 1976a).

The second view of homosexual orientation and activity is that it is a disease. It results from a pathological constitution or is a psychological dysfunction caused by harmful behavioral patterns in the familial or immediate social environment. It can be cured by depth therapy, some believe (Socarides 1995).

Many modern scientists reject this view. The American Psychiatric Association moved in 1973 to drop its official diagnosis of homosexuality as a mental illness (Hansen 1986). The organization declared that homosexuality "implies no impairment in judgment, stability, reliability, or general social or vocational capabilities." Similarly, the World Health Organization did not list homosexuality in the 1993 edition of its International Classification of Diseases.

In 1980, at the invitation of Terence Cooke, Cardinal Archbishop of New York, John Harvey, a priest-theologian and an Oblate of St. Francis de Sales, formed Courage, an organization for Catholic homosexuals who fully accept the church's teachings on homosexual activity. By 1994 there were some seventeen chapters in the United States. Courage's basic approach to homosexuality is based on the spiritual principles of the Alcoholic Anonymous program, that is, it views homosexuality as a sickness. They offer as treatment a traditional regimen of prayer, direction, sacraments, spiritual reading, and acts of charity. In their view there is no difference between homosexual people and others struggling with sexual temptations (Harvey 1985).

Despite the fact that Courage has episcopal approbation, many priests are reluctant to work with the organization. They have several reasons, but the most important one is Courage's principal premise, namely, that "homosexual orientation is a psychological disorder" that usually "involves some neuroses or other emotional factors which tend to cripple" the relationships that gays have with others and themselves (see Nugent 1985).

The third view differentiates between homosexual activity and orientation. A person's sexual orientation is a given rather than a chosen or preferred condition. This distinction was popularized by Alfred Kinsey in 1948. What causes the orientation remains an unanswered question. Various explanations are offered: heredity or genetic factors; erratic behavior patterns in the family, or the social environment. A gay identity might be "adopted as a defense mechanism" (B. Williams 1987, 275).

One of the earliest statements on homosexuality as an orientation came from the United States bishops in 1973 in their document "Principles to Guide Confessors in Questions of Homosexuality." The principal author was John Harvey (Rashke 1976). The bishops acknowledged that people do not choose their sexual orientation. But they went on to say that "homosexual acts are a grave transgression of the goals of human sexuality and of human personality." Confessors were encouraged to help homosexuals work out an ascetical plan of life with a view to controlling their sexual activity.

On December 29, 1975, the CDF declaration *Persona humana* made the distinction between behavior and orientation. The document observed that some homosexuals are "innately" constituted as such and thus their "constitution" should not be thought "curable" (n. 8). Nonetheless, the document stated that homosexual acts necessarily involve objective moral evil inasmuch as they "lack an essential and indispensable finality" (n. 8). The United States bishops reiterated the distinction between orientation and behavior in their 1976 message "To Live in Jesus Christ." They condemned homosexual behavior but decried the prejudice against the basic human rights of homosexual people, especially friendship, respect, and justice.

In 1977 Robert Nugent, a Salvatorian priest, and Jeannine Gramick, a School Sister of Notre Dame, cofounded New Ways Ministry. Their organization offers compassion, understanding, and pastoral care to homosexuals who experience discrimination and homophobia within the church. They tell homosexuals that they must follow their conscience and do not have to make a choice between their faith and their sexuality. They have campaigned to convince heterosexual Catholics that the homosexuality issue does not involve only sexual behavior; it is also about human dignity and the respect owed to all persons.

Nugent and Gramick were ordered by the Vatican to end their association with New Ways Ministry in 1984. In 1994 the organization was still carrying on their work. With the support of their respective religious communities, Nugent and Gramick also continue to work for homosexuals. Consequently, in 1994 the Vatican conducted an investigation into their theological views and writings because of concerns that their ministry may have created "ambiguity" and "confusion in the minds of people" (Schaeffer 1996a). Conservative Catholics have criticized them as unorthodox, stating that the two have not adequately represented official church teaching; on the other hand, "radical gay" groups have chided them for not taking a strong stand against church teachings on homosexuality.

The 1983 statement from the Congregation for Catholic Education, "Educational Guidance in Human Love," encouraged sex education. However, it did not make the distinction between behavior and orientation in condemning homosexuality. It declared that homosexual activity "impedes the person's acquisition of sexual maturity." Without whitewashing this kind of sexual activity as a likely path to sexual integration, it did instruct educators not to disturb people who were troubled in these ways with accusations of guilt. Robert Nugent insisted in his commentary on the document that balance is needed in dealing with the question. "Homosexual *people* should not be reduced to their *orientation*; nor should the homosexual orientation be reduced to sexual *behavior*" (1984).

Disturbed by increasing challenges to the traditional teachings on homosexuality, the CDF published another document on homosexuality on October 1, 1986: "On the Pastoral Care of Homosexual Persons." In it they said too much had been made of the distinction between orientation and behavior. The orientation of the homosexual "is not a sin, it is a more or less strong tendency toward an intrinsic moral evil, and thus the inclination itself must be seen as an objective disorder" (n. 3). The document seemed to misunderstand homosexuality as an orientation. Ordinarily, the term refers to a psychosexual attraction toward one of the same sex, but the CDF document described it as a tendency toward evil acts. The document reiterates the teaching on the objective immorality of homosexual acts because they lack the complementarity and potential fruitfulness demanded by the nuptial truth of heterosexual marriages.

Commenting on the strong words in this analysis, an editorial in *America* said, "The letter explicitly aims at 'pastoral care' for homosexuals, but it is doubtful they will feel especially cared for."[17] The *Times* of London stated in its editorial on December 6, 1986, that the document's title is a misnomer, that its preoccupations "have more to do with the public, political dog-fight over sexual morality in the West than with the real pastoral needs of homosexuals" (B. Williams 1987, 271).

In 1990, the United States bishops again reiterated that "homosexual activity, as distinguished from homosexual orientation, is wrong." They added that homosexual orientation "in itself, because not freely chosen, is not sinful" (P. Steinfels 1990d).

Gregory Baum offered this advice to homosexuals: "If it is true that some people are constitutively homosexual and that homosexual relations allow for mutuality, then, from the viewpoint of Christian theology, it is the task of homosexuals to acknowledge themselves as such before God, accept their sexual orientation as their calling, and explore the meaning of this inclination for the Christian life" (1974). Baum does not say explicitly whether homosexual behavior between homosexual persons who were growing in friendship and covenant faithfulness was morally justifiable. Philip Keane took another perspective. He said homosexual acts always involve a significant degree of premoral evil since they are not open to procreation, the heterosexual ideal. Yet they are not necessarily an objective moral evil (1977, 87). For other commentators, both the homosexual orientation and overt acts are not in themselves good for people and therefore generally right, but they are not necessarily immoral in all cases, especially if the persons are in a stable, loving relationship and if neither celibacy nor marriage is a realistic alternative for them. For example, Curran offered a "theology of compromise": "One may reluctantly accept homosexual unions as the only way in which some people can find a satisfying degree of humanity in their lives" (1972, 217).

Finally, the fourth view of homosexuality is that it is a variation within the human condition and not something contrary to nature. As such, it is a fully normal alternative to heterosexuality. This group supports sexual expression by gay persons that is humane and humanizing, that is, it is "loving, life-giving and life-affirming." They also insist that their domestic partnerships are the equivalent of traditional marriages.

In the early 1970s, a group of Catholic homosexual men and women formed an association in Los Angeles to give witness to the church that it is possible to be both Catholic and gay. They said that, in imitation of Christ, they wanted to exercise their baptismal rights, to pray, and to live responsible, useful, and caring lives. They call themselves Dignity and held their first national meeting in Los Angeles on a weekend in September 1973. Their national headquarters are presently in Boston. By 1992 they had one hundred chapters throughout the United States and over four thousand members. In response to the CDF document of 1986, a number of United States bishops instructed the priests of their dioceses to withdraw support for Dignity and not to allow them to meet on church property. These actions only alienated and hurt a community already alienated and hurt (Opstrny 1988; McClory 1988a).

In a 1976 book *The Church and the Homosexual*, John McNeill, a charter member of Dignity, argued that homosexuality is part of God's plan for the world. Homosexual orientation in itself is a precondition of the affirmation of the homosexual Christian in her or his characteristic sexual lifestyle. For McNeill, gay love is morally good, even holy, when it is mutual, faithful, and unselfish, and so he objected to Curran's theology of compromise because for him the proposition that homosexual acts are permissible as the least offensive among objectively "evil" alternatives is demeaning. McNeill asked his readers to reconsider the condition of those homosexually-oriented individuals who regard themselves as Christians. These persons, he wrote, say they can express a relationship of shared love, fidelity, and responsibility. Together they can fulfill their identities as Christians-in-community and as persons-in-the-world, summoned to relate themselves in justice and love to all reality. John Giles Milhaven reviewed the book and asked the key question: "And how does one step from 'healthy and loving' to 'morally good'?" (1976).

When John McNeill wrote his book in 1976, he was a Jesuit priest. Without due process, he was given an ultimatum to keep silent on the question of the morality of homosexual activity or face dismissal from his community (Baum 1977; Berrigan 1977). In 1986, right after the publication of the CDF document "On the Pastoral Care of Homosexuals" and after thirty-eight years as a Jesuit, he withdrew from the Jesuits because he could no longer keep silent about the church's ministry to homosexuals (McNeill 1986). Since then he has continued to lecture, offer retreats, and write about homosexuality. In an essay in 1987, he argued that homosexual activity among committed lovers is an issue that challenges the Catholic church to grow. In 1988 he published *Taking a Chance on God* and in 1994, *Freedom, Glorious Freedom*. The latter has as its subtitle, *The Spiritual Journey to the Fulfillment of Life for Gays, Lesbians and Everybody Else*. Because so many homosexuals have a connection to a church community and trace their understanding of Catholicism and homosexuality to McNeill, one commentator judged that "it is fair to say he inspired an important theological movement that is now felt throughout the world" (Hunt 1996).

The gay and lesbian community in general and Dignity in particular were again deeply distressed when the CDF issued a twenty-five hundred-word statement on June 25, 1992, "Some Considerations Concerning the Catholic Response to Legislative Proposals on the Non-discrimination of Homosexual Persons." This document, "written in the United States by consultants to the CDF" (Vidulich 1992b), was offered as guidance for bishops in states considering gay-rights legislation (P. Steinfels 1992a; Vidulich 1992a). It contradicted its previous teaching that homosexual persons as people have the same human and civil rights as all citizens. Ultimately, the document was against those domestic partnership laws that would assure employment, housing, health benefits, credit, and other protections for homosexuals.

After repeating the 1986 description of homosexuality as "an objective disorder," the 1992 statement declared that gays and lesbians do not have the same rights to civil liberties that heterosexuals have and it urged the bishops to oppose civil-rights legislation for gays. Since a homosexual orientation "does not constitute a quality comparable to race" or ethnic background, there are "areas in which it is not unjust discrimination to take sexual orientation into account." Teaching, coaching, and military service are among the areas cited. The document also says that, while homosexuals have the same basic rights as anyone else, those rights "are not absolute" and they can be "legitimately limited for objectively disordered external conduct." This distinction is compared to the state's authority to restrict the exercise of rights "in the case of contagious or mentally ill persons, in order to protect the common good."

This Vatican document was judged by many to be not only pastorally insensitive but also uncatholic because there is nothing in the church's moral tradition that prevents gay and lesbian persons from participating fully in the social and economic life of society (Tuohey 1992). Many wondered how the bishops would handle the document because even before its publication a number of bishops, apparently believing that legislation to protect gay civil rights does not undermine family values, had taken steps to see that homosexuals do not suffer unjust discrimination in law and in life. In May 1995 Rhode Island became the ninth state to offer specific civil rights protections to homosexuals. Religious leaders were found on both sides of the issue. When the Catholic bishop of Providence, Louis E. Gelineau, was asked why he had not spoken out against the bill, he explained: "If proposed legislation attempts to condone or promote homosexual activity by equating morally all forms of sexual behavior, then it should be defeated. If it merely seeks to afford protection from unjust discrimination, which is not now afforded under our laws, then those laws should be changed" (Dunlap 1995).

Some Protestant churches have stirred up controversy by welcoming homosexuals to their community and/or by ordaining noncelibate ministers. Here are several examples that occurred in 1996. In January delegates to a special meeting of the American Baptist Church of the West expelled four San Francisco Bay Area congregations from their regional jurisdiction because they welcomed homosexuals as members without indicating that homosexual activity is sinful (Niebuhr 1996a). Also in January, two small Lutheran congregations in San Francisco that had hired homosexual pastors were expelled from the Evangelical Lutheran Church in America (Niebuhr 1996d). In April, the United Methodist church—the third largest religious body in the United States—sent 1,000 delegates to its General Conference. They voted to retain their declaration against homosexual behavior because it is "incompatible with Christian teaching." Their church law also bars "self-avowed, practicing homosexuals" from the ranks of the clergy. However, this decision did not deter fifteen bishops (out of a total of 130 bishops within the church) from declaring that it is "time to break the silence" and to ordain homosexuals to the ministry. The dissenting bishops did add their pledge to uphold current church law and not to commit ecclesiastical disobedience by ordaining gays (Niebuhr 1996c). Finally, on May 15, the Episcopal Church threw out a charge of heresy against Bishop Walter Righter, who was acting as Bishop John S. Spong's assistant and at his request ordained a noncelibate gay man as a deacon in 1990. The ecclesiastical court declared that the denomination had no "core doctrine" barring a bishop from ordaining as a deacon or priest a "noncelibate homosexual person living in faithful and committed sexual relationships with a person of the same sex" (Niebuhr 1996d). This decision not only cleared the way for individual bishops to ordain noncelibate gays and lesbians without fear that they would be breaking church law, but it also made the Episcopal Church the second mainline Protestant church to allow the ordination of noncelibate homosexuals. The first is the United Church of Christ (Niebuhr 1996e).

Same-Sex Marriages: A Social and Ecclesial Issue

The possibility of same-sex unions has been reported in the media since 1970.[18] In the 1990s the question of opening the institution of marriage to homosexuals has been the subject of an emotional debate within families, churches, state and federal legislatures, the courts, and in the press, not only in the United States but in other countries as well.

Gays argue that, since for the overwhelming majority of homosexual adults the condition of homosexuality is as involuntary as heterosexuality is for heterosexuals, they should be given not only equal economic treatment but also equal legal and moral status. Consequently, homosexuals want to break the age-old pattern of defining marriage as the union of one man and one woman. They advance two arguments. First, it is discriminatory to deny same-sex couples the marriage rights enjoyed by heterosexual persons. To do so is to impose an unjustified inequality. Second, it is senseless to deny legality to same-sex marriages since committed gays want to promote the very same values of heterosexual marriage, namely, emotional fulfillment, erotic intimacy, lifelong covenant, the creation of stable families, and, when feasible, the care of children.

Same-sex unions have been legalized in Europe. On February 8, 1994, the European Parliament meeting in Strasbourg passed a resolution that supported same-sex marriages and gave the same rights to homosexual couples as to heterosexual couples—including that of adopting children. On February 22, John Paul II published a long letter on family values. This letter, titled "Letter to Families," was drafted well before the European Parliament assembled, having been written to coincide with the United Nations Year of the Family. Since the pope ruled out homosexual unions, his letter attracted extra attention (Cowell 1994a). John Paul summarized the Catholic view of marriage: "Marriage, which undergirds the institution of the family, is constituted by the covenant whereby a man and woman establish between themselves a partnership for their whole life. Only such a union can be recognized and ratified as a marriage in society. Other interpersonal unions which do not fulfill the above conditions cannot be recognized, despite certain growing trends which represent a serious threat to the future of the family and society itself."

On April 16, 1996, the Dutch Parliament voted by an 81–60 vote to lift a ban on same-sex marriages and to extend to couples in long-term relationships all of the legal benefits of marriage. The Vatican newspaper condemned the Dutch Parliament, declaring that its law is "the victory of secularized man, of the rationalist man who substitutes God's ethical code with a code created by his own will and made absolute."[19]

On June 25, 1996, delegates to the Unitarian Universalist Association's annual convention voted to endorse the legalization of same-sex marriages—the first denomination in the United States to do so. They voted overwhelmingly to "proclaim the worth of marriage between any two committed persons." While the vote made same-sex marriages the official policy of the denomination, under church rules, each of the church's 1,040 congregations can decide for itself whether it will endorse the marriage of gay and lesbian couples.[20]

In the United States there are many who promote same-sex marriages. The movement to legalize them had picked up so much momentum in the beginning of 1996, that an editorial in the *New York Times* on April 7 on same-sex marriages opened with this sentence: "Chances are that Americans will look back 30 years from now and wonder what all the fuss was about." Nonetheless, most Americans reject equating homosexual unions with marriage. For example, fourteen thousand Southern Baptists present for their denomination's annual convention voted in June 1996, to censure the Walt Disney Company for having adopted a policy in 1995 that extended health insurance benefits to the same-sex partners of employees and for releasing movies that have homosexuality as a theme. Since the Southern Baptists are the second largest religious body after the Catholic church, they represent a politically and economically formidable group (Niebuhr 1996f). Later in the summer, several other churches accused Disney of "abandoning the commitment to strong moral values." In June 1997, the Southern Baptists focused on Disney once again, stating that the company had moved from wholesome entertainment and toward themes of sex, violence, and homosexuality. Initially the Baptists proposed a boycott of theme parks and stores but later extended the protest to the entire Walt Disney Company, including its movie, television, and publishing operations (Meyerson 1997).

In the summer of 1996, there was a firm possibility that the state of Hawaii would legalize same-sex marriages (Hawaii's state constitution does not define marriage). This possibility alarmed so many citizens in the continental United States that the matter was brought to Congress as the Defense of Marriage Act. Congress passed a bill which not only banned federal recognition of same-sex marriages but it also allowed each state to ignore such marriages performed in any other state. President Clinton signed the bill into law on September 22. The Vatican newspaper promptly hailed the law as common sense. In an editorial the paper said that "to pretend to raise a homosexual union to the level of matrimonial institution represents a challenge to good sense, reason and law."[21]

On December 3, 1996, a Circuit Court judge in Hawaii ruled that lawyers for the state had failed to show any compelling reason for the existing ban on same-sex marriages (Goldberg 1996). Calling the ban unconstitutional, the judge ordered the state to stop denying marriage licenses to same-sex couples. The judge's decision was immediately challenged and an appeal was made to Hawaii's Supreme Court. This appeal is expected to occupy the court for several years. Subsequently, on April 29, 1997, the Hawaii state legislature offered two compromises. It voted to grant gay couples the rights and benefits married couples receive (but stopped short of legalizing same-sex marriages) and agreed to put to the voters a constitutional amendment that would reserve marriage to heterosexual couples. Gay rights groups called these proposals a sellout and a retreat from the decision of December 3, 1996.

The social, economic, moral, and religious issues involved in same-sex marriages will challenge the government and the churches for many years to come.

Same-Sex Marriages: A Theological Issue

In the 1990s several prominent theologians examined the issue. Gregory Baum outlined the different directions the natural law tradition has taken within the Catholic community (1994). He noted that this tradition has relied frequently and heavily on rational arguments. He suggested, however, that today natural law theory also relies on "people's new ethical experiences and their historical struggle to transform the public consciousness." Baum explained how at one time the church defended its position on the morality of slavery, opposition to religious liberty, and acceptance of the inferiority of women by using philosophical arguments. However, these three positions were reversed once there arose a universal moral outrage against the inhumanity heaped upon slaves, members of other religions, and women. Baum believes the same reversal could be happening with the question of homosexual unions. He observed that, since "the meaning of human sexuality, while indeed rooted in human biology, cannot be defined apart from culture and people's historical experience," today many ethically-concerned people maintain that the violence and oppression heaped on homosexuals is so great that the churches need to reexamine their teaching, "listen to the Christian experience of homosexual men and women, and ask yourselves whether the dignity of homosexuals as human beings does not demand that their sexual orientation be respected."

Luke Timothy Johnson, professor of New Testament at the Candler School of Theology, Emory University, examined the challenge homosexuality places upon our understanding of the Bible and God's grace (1994). He insisted that as the church determines whether it "can recognize the possibility of homosexual committed and covenantal love in the way that it recognizes such sexual/personal love in the sacrament of marriage," it is incumbent on the church community to listen to "narratives of homosexual holiness." He suggested that this issue might be analogous to the one the first-century Jewish Christians faced after Gentiles started to accept the gospel. Peter, James, John, Paul, Barnabas, and others (see Acts 15:1–29) wondered whether Gentiles could be accepted into the church community just as they were, or must they first obey all the ritual demands of the Torah and be circumcised. Johnson pointed out how serious were the stakes at that point in time. The Gentiles "were 'by nature' unclean, and were 'by practice' polluted by idolatry." As such, they were unfit to participate in table fellowship. The decision of the church to let the Gentiles in "as is" and to establish a radically new form of table fellowship "came into direct conflict with the accepted interpretation of the Torah and what God wanted of humans." The right decision was not easy to reach. But Peter, Paul, and the others listened to the narratives of the Gentiles. According to Johnson, the contemporary church has to determine if homosexuality and holiness of life are compatible. The church must ask if homosexuals are "by nature" unclean and "by practice" polluted. "The church can discern this only on the basis of faithful witness. The burden of proof required to overturn scriptural precedents is heavy, but it is a burden that has been borne before."

Sidney Callahan wrote an essay in 1994 in which she argued that homosexuals who eschew promiscuity and desire to regularize and ritualize their loving commitment to one another "should be allowed to marry." She claimed that in Catholic sexual ethics there has been a "rigid overestimation of gender." She proposed that gender can often be a secondary consideration when a couple, struggling to achieve loving unity, realizes that there are so many other significant differences between them: "temperament, intelligence, taste, talents, and moral maturity." Her conclusion: since we must affirm embodiment and respect for the symbolic language of the body in our sexual relationships, "the rejection of loving gay erotic expression [is] a rejection of embodiment, and another form of resistance to the goodness of sexual desire and pleasure."

John Paul II: *Evangelium vitae*

On March 25, 1995, John Paul signed his eleventh and longest encyclical, *Evangelium vitae* ("The Gospel of Life"). The encyclical, requested by the cardinals at an extraordinary consistory in 1991 and written after canvassing the bishops of the world, expresses concern about the many threats to human life as the end of the twentieth century draws near. It carries forward several key themes developed in *Veritatis splendor* (1993), that is, it impugns individualism and ethical relativism (nn. 20, 70), regrets the loss of a sense of God (nn. 21–23), stigmatizes a "contraceptive mentality" (n. 13), and forcefully reaffirms the official church's teaching on murder, direct abortion, and euthanasia.

This very complex encyclical has four chapters. They cover, respectively, threats to life, the positive Christian vision of life, arguments for the defense of life in different circumstances, and building a culture of life. Commentators noted that the second and third chapters do not break new ground. The "power and value of the encyclical lie in its synthetic quality," that is, it projects "a definite viewpoint on a multiplicity of issues which are usually treated in isolation in our civil debates" (Hehir 1995).

The threats to life that the pope addresses can be classified as ancient, modern, and postmodern (ibid.). The ancient threats are hunger, poverty, war, genocide, and murder. The modern threats flow from the power over life which modern science and technology have placed in human hands. They involve medical intervention in all stages of life, especially the final stages. The pope's principal concern is the postmodern threats. These do not focus on what we can do but on how we think. He condemns the modern "Promethean attitude which leads people to think that they can control life and death by taking the decisions about them into their own hands" (n. 15). Specifically, the pope addresses the culture of advanced technological societies. He is concerned that crimes against life have a new and even more sinister character than they did in the past. He states: "Choices once unanimously considered criminal and rejected by the common moral sense are gradually becoming socially acceptable. . . . No less grave and disturbing is the fact that conscience itself, darkened as it were by such widespread conditioning, is finding it increasingly difficult to distinguish between good and evil in what concerns the basic value of human life" (n. 4).

The pope writes at length about murder, the unjust killing of the innocent—at any stage of life. He offers a long meditation on the first murder, the Cain and Abel story (nn. 7–10). Throughout the encyclical the pope argues against any legitimation of "crimes against life" at the cultural, social, and political level. He reaffirms the church's teachings on embryo and fetus experimentation. Euthanasia is also a major concern. It is analyzed and condemned in several sections (nn. 15, 46, 64–65, 73).

The encyclical also offers the Vatican's most explicit reservations about capital punishment. The pope indicates that God punished Cain for murdering his brother Abel, but did not execute him. Instead, God marked Cain with a distinctive sign to protect him from vengeance (n. 9). Several pages later the encyclical effectively rules out capital punishment. The pope says that, given the frame of mind of our times, the need for the death penalty is "very rare, if not practically non-existent." Nevertheless, it can be used "in cases of absolute necessity: in other words, when it is not possible otherwise to defend society" (n. 56). (This exception means some governments will continue to execute criminals, rationalizing that the executions are necessary for public safety.)

On the issue of capital punishment, the various voices of the magisterium have been uneven. The United States bishops have assailed the death penalty since 1980. Because they place high value on the human rights of life and dignity, they label the death penalty a retrograde measure that takes the easy way out of addressing the complex, pervasive, and expensive problems of society. On the other hand, the *Catechism of the Catholic Church* states that legitimate public authority has the right and duty to punish "malefactors by means of penalties commensurate with the gravity of the crime." In "cases of extreme gravity" the death penalty is acceptable (n. 2266). The pope's guidelines are much more restrictive than those of the *CCC* but not those of the United States bishops.

The encyclical reiterates the teaching that no exceptions are allowed for direct abortion since human life begins from the moment of conception (n. 60). This is the first time that the magisterium's opposition to abortion has been given the weight of an encyclical. The pope's words are most firm. They border on the language used in infallible statements. Richard McCormick believes "the papal language aims at making any dissent by Catholics as uncomfortable as possible" (1995). John Paul wrote: "Therefore, by the authority which Christ conferred upon Peter and his successors, in communion with the bishops . . . I declare that direct abortion, that is, abortion willed as an end or as a means, always constitutes a grave moral disorder, since it is the deliberate killing of an innocent human being. This doctrine is based upon the natural law and upon the written word of God, is transmitted by the church's tradition and taught by the ordinary and universal magisterium" (n. 62).

John Paul's theme—the gospel of life—is "at the heart of Jesus' message" and is "a single and indivisible gospel." It is offered to non-believers as well as believers (n. 101) because it includes "everything that human experience and reason tell us about the value of human life" (n. 30). Included are God's love for humankind; the dignity of the person; the proclamation of the person of Jesus; and even the raising of children by parents.

The encyclical is an exuberant exposition of life as a precious gift as found in the Hebrew and Christian scriptures. Many within and outside the church received the letter warmly because they agreed with the pope that today there are far too many assaults on the sacredness of life by what the pope calls a "culture of death" or a "conspiracy against life" (nn. 21, 24, 28).

On the other hand, some ideas received a cool reception. Many rejected two interrelated ideas that pervade the encyclical: a neo-Augustinian pessimism and a preconciliar dichotomy of church and society.

According to Augustine, human nature was so devastated by original sin that it could not handle God's revelation. Consequently, the revelation given through Christ was given over to the church. The church alone, especially through the papal office, possesses this gift of knowing and providing the truth. The encyclical maintains that the church has a hold on a "culture of life" whereas society is characterized by a "culture of death." Even though John Paul listed some encouraging signs of greater care of life within society, he unremittingly critiques modern society. He believes the forces of evil are strong and gaining ground.

This sharp, almost Manichean, struggle between a culture of life sponsored by the church and a culture of death at work in societies raises questions about how seriously the pope will be listened to and, therefore, how much he will get the "courageous cultural dialogue among all parties" he says he wants (n. 95). To declare that certain attitudes or actions contribute to a culture of life and others to a culture of death can be done at the expense of leaving out the complexities of circumstances and motives. As we have seen, even within the church there are some who accept abortion under certain circumstances and not the pope's absolute prohibition. These Catholics do not regard themselves as contributors to a culture of death. Rather, as much as they revere life, they question the official church's teaching that individual human life begins with conception. While it is true that the Catholic tradition has maintained that in practice one must act as if the human person is present from the moment of conception, this tradition, as Charles Curran noted, "is a prudential judgment that cannot claim an absolute certitude" (1995). This explains why some Catholics and other people of good will consider the frame of the pope's argument to be too narrow. For example, Konrad Raiser, secretary general of the WCC, remarked that the encyclical's teachings on abortion and other moral matters posed difficulties for ecumenical discussion, "making it nearly impossible to elaborate shared pastoral concerns and guidelines" (Lefevere 1995a).

Another problem with an absolute prohibition of abortion is that it fails to distinguish between general principles and their application or interpretation. All Catholic moral theologians accept the principle that human life may be taken only when such taking is, all things considered, the only life-serving and life-saving option available. The theologians might differ about the application of the principle. They will ask whether a particular abortion is, in the circumstances, the only life-serving and life-saving option available. They might disagree "whether a particular termination (e.g., of an anencephalic fetus) should be called an abortion in the moral sense" (McCormick 1995).

There will continue to be doubts and questions about the papal teaching on contraceptive birth control, euthanasia, abortion, and the death penalty. Nonetheless, what many Catholics take from this encyclical is a renewed determination to witness by word and deed to the value of human life, a life that has the triune God as its author, ground, and destiny.

Conclusion

The popes and bishops of the twentieth century consistently opposed dehumanizing and unchristian views of human sexuality—everything within the two poles of sexual repression and sexual license—by fostering the virtues of chastity and fidelity, the holiness of marriage, responsible parenthood, the sacredness of human life, and the profundity of conjugal friendship and love. Consistent, too, has been the hierarchical teachings on the six topics of sexual morality reviewed here.

Most preconciliar Catholics agreed with the Christian principles proclaimed by the hierarchy, and, in general, followed their specific directives. Although there were many instances of divorce, masturbation, premarital and extramarital sex, and so forth, Catholics were renowned for their strict moral standards. Today, and particularly since the so-called sexual revolution in the 1960s, many Catholics—priests, theologians, single and married persons—openly disagree with the official teachings about sexual morality. There is evidence that the number of Catholics involved in divorces, abortions, premarital sex, and so forth, is not much different from the rest of society. This striking reversal of "strict moral standards" has forced some to question just how well grounded preconciliar Catholic sexual morality was. For example, in a 1972 essay on the sexual revolution, the historian James Hitchcock argued that "emphasis on sexual purity was always, in a sense, a confession of failure on the part of Catholic educators, since they found it difficult to imbue their students with real piety and settled instead for morality. It was a morality that secular American culture also honored in theory, and hence it did not seriously estrange the young Catholic from society. He was distinguished, and heroic, for behaving in the way that other Americans secretly thought that they should behave in, too."

One of the themes of this book is that "real piety" must be grounded in a sacramental consciousness in imitation of Christ. But most Catholics would agree that our sexual morality has not been sufficiently shaped by faith in Jesus as God's *incarnate* self-gift. This failure can be illustrated by the way the sexuality of Jesus is often perceived.

In his elegant 1984 book *The Sexuality of Christ in Renaissance Art and in Modern Oblivion*, Leo Steinberg, a distinguished art historian, demonstrated that the early church focused on the divinity of Jesus and skirted the full reality of his bodiliness. The Renaissance artists, on the other hand, purposely exposed Jesus' genitals. Their art was "the first Christian art in a thousand years to confront the incarnation entire . . . not excluding even the body's sexual component." By this standard, the Renaissance also produced, said Steinberg, "the last phase of Christian art that can claim full Christian orthodoxy." Steinberg admitted he did not know precisely when or why post-Renaissance Christians decided that nudity and genital disclosure were shocking. His ultimate answer is theological: sometime after the Renaissance, the Christian West lost the "mythic roots" from which incarnational art drew its compelling power. Kenneth Woodward agreed and explained: "The living Christ disappeared, transformed into a tableau of tidy, rational propositions. Once that happened, the body of Christ no longer disclosed the meaning of his spirit because the faithful no longer had eyes to see" (Woodward and Moorman 1984).

There is some evidence that many Christians are now beginning to realize that sexuality and spirituality are part and parcel of each other, and that Jesus of Nazareth, the Word incarnate, continues to become flesh and dwell among us. For example, in his reflections on the sexual revolution, James Nelson reported that "The sexual revolution helped convince many Christians that an incarnationalist faith embraces the redemption of alienated sexuality as well as other estranged dimensions of our lives. *Justification by grace* signifies God's unconditional, unmerited, radical acceptance of the whole person: God, the Cosmic Lover, graciously embraces not just a person's disembodied spirit but the whole fleshly self—the meanings of which theology is only beginning to explore" (J. B. Nelson 1987).

The whole church—and particularly parents, the hierarchy, priests, theologians, and educators—has three interrelated areas to explore: the Christian understanding of what it means to be human and chaste, the official church's teachings, and the Catholic sacramental consciousness grounded in Christ Jesus, God's incarnate self-gift.

CHAPTER 11

The Church and Mary

Devotion to Mary the mother of Jesus has been a hallmark of the Catholic tradition. Over the centuries, millions of women and hundreds of churches, schools, and hospitals have been named for her. Theologians and popes have extolled her virtues, and the faithful, the saints, and the religious orders have often had a tenacious devotion to her. Vatican II opened and closed on one of her feast days. A chapter in *Lumen gentium* was devoted to her. In the postconciliar church devotion to Mary declined at first. Later interest in Marian history, symbolism, apparitions, and devotions intensified so much that Raymond Brown was able to observe that the theology of Mary (mariology) "is almost a bellwether [sic] indicating theological directions in the Roman Catholic church" (1985, 86). In addition, the December 1996 issue of *Life* magazine had a picture of a Marian statue on its cover with this commentary: "Two thousand years after the nativity, the mother of Jesus is more beloved, powerful and controversial than ever" (R. Sullivan 1996).

Brown's symbol *bellwether* suggests that this chapter should introduce this book. However, it is easier to place it here since it contains references to so many of the topics already covered: sacramental consciousness, the identity and mission of the church, tradition, historical consciousness, the popes, Vatican II, ecumenism, liturgy, spirituality, social justice, inculturation, and sexual morality.

Mary of History

Mary the mother of Jesus is probably the most influential woman in the history of the world. Yet, we know so little of her history and personality. As a member of the supporting cast in the gospels, Mary's appearances are seldom. It is actually more difficult to discern the Mary of history than the Jesus of history. No information is offered, for example, about her parents or where and when she was born. She married Joseph, a craftsman, and gave birth to a son, Jesus. We do not know how much she really knew about her son's uniqueness. That she had other children is a debatable issue and one that cannot be decided by trying to balance all the New Testament texts. For example, Matthew 1:18 is rather clear about the virginal conception of Jesus, but Matthew 13:56–57 refers to Jesus' sisters and four brothers, actually naming the brothers. We know little of Mary's relatives. Luke relates her to Elizabeth, the mother of John the Baptist. However, the Baptist said he did not know Jesus until he baptized him (John 1:31–33).

Mary appears only once during Jesus' public ministry in the first three gospels. Mark never mentions Joseph. Was this because he was dead by the time Jesus began to teach in the towns and cities? John's gospel places Mary at a wedding in Cana and at the cross when Jesus died. She is next mentioned praying with the community at Pentecost (Acts 1:14). There is not a single detail about Mary after Pentecost. We know nothing of her role in the community or of any personal contacts with such important disciples as Peter and Paul. Mary is never mentioned in Paul's epistles. Finally, there is no mention of when or where she died.

Mary in the Scriptures

The scriptures are not concerned with the Mary of history, but with mariology, the theology about Mary, a particular historical individual who has a definite, even unique, place in salvation history. In fact, there are more verses in the Quran naming Mary than there are in the Christian scriptures.

In 1979 a group of twelve Lutheran and Catholic biblical scholars issued a study titled *Mary in the New Testament* (R. E. Brown, Donfried, Fitzmyer, and Reumann). This book is a major accomplishment that has helped place ecumenical dialogues about mariology on a sound footing. In it, rigorous exegesis is applied to all the passages in the New Testament (and some other early Christian literature) where Mary is mentioned.

The earliest New Testament writings, the letters of Paul, mention that God sent his Son, "born of a woman, born under the law" (Galatians 4:4). The text is not a reflection on the mother of Jesus but, rather, on Jesus himself, a person truly human, truly Jewish, and truly the savior of all.

The only references to Mary by name in the New Testament are in the four gospels, plus one reference in Acts 1:14, the Pentecost story. Since we know so little of the Mary of history, what can we expect to learn about her by studying the gospels? Catholic and Protestant scholars agree that "Mary appears consistently as a symbolic character, and that therefore symbolism, not history, is the key to mariology" (Rausch 1982).

Turning to the gospels, we start with Mark, the earliest. The mother of Jesus appears in only one scene (3:31–35), in which Mark presents Mary in a poor light. He contrasts the natural family of Jesus who do not understand him with the family of disciples who do. Mary seems to be an outsider. A comparison of the words and the intrinsic staging of the same scene in Matthew 12:46–50 and Luke 8:19–21 indicates, say the Lutheran and Catholic scholars, that Mark's gospel offers a "negative portrait" of Mary. This judgment is reinforced by the one other allusion to Mary in Mark. When Jesus returns to Nazareth to preach in the synagogue the local people take offense and Jesus says, "A prophet is not without honor except in his native place and among his own kin and in his own house" (Mark 6:1–6). In the parallel scenes, Matthew 13:57–58 omits the phrase "among his own kin" and Luke 4:24 omits both phrases after the words "native place."

Compared with Mark, Matthew and Luke present Mary in a more favorable light. Why? Their theology of salvation history is more advanced. Both Matthew and Luke have infancy narratives. Although both these narratives differ quite a bit in details, each does say that Mary's child was conceived through the power of God. This fact made it impossible for them to portray Mary without an understanding of and honor for her son. Actually, Luke pictures Mary more positively than Matthew. In Matthew, Joseph is the main figure in the infancy narrative. In Luke, Mary is constantly center stage: the angel announces her child will be the Son of David and the Son of God; Mary visits Elizabeth and proclaims her famous prayer, the Magnificat (Luke 1:46–55); Mary presents the child in the temple where she encounters Simeon and Anna; and it is Mary who questions the twelve-year-old boy Jesus in the temple.

In Luke's gospel, Mary is presented as the first Christian and a model Christian. She accepts God's word with her *fiat*, which means "let it be to me." She proclaims that when God regarded her, a slave woman[1], he was showing his continued mercy to Israel, and also his dethronement of the proud and mighty. During Jesus' ministry, Mary is praised by Jesus for hearing and doing God's word. After the resurrection, she waits with the community for the Spirit at Pentecost. In Luke, says Raymond Brown, Mary "serves as the most consistent disciple in the whole gospel narrative" (1985, 94).

John's gospel does not add much to Luke's ideal picture of Mary as a model disciple. John never refers to her by name, only by title. The "mother of Jesus" appears in two scenes: Cana and Calvary. In the former she gives priority to what Jesus wills and in the latter she not only becomes the mother of the beloved disciple but with him witnesses her son's obedience to his Father's will on the cross (Grassi 1986). In John's gospel, Jesus leaves behind a community of disciples that includes his mother and the beloved disciple.

Mary and Feminism

During the 1960s and the 1970s, our society experienced several movements that were interrelated: civil rights, a crusade against the war in Vietnam, the sexual revolution, and the feminist movement. The next chapter will trace some of the complex changes and developments that have taken place within feminism, a movement that is pluralistic and multicultural. Here it is sufficient to relate Mary to the core feminist affirmation, namely, that our society is presently undergoing a major change "in the self-perception and self-definition of women, and consequently in the understanding of women's nature, capabilities, role, status and relationship to men and male-created structures" (E. Johnson 1985, 116–17). Women have been denied their full humanity in society and church because men alone have been considered the norm of authentic humanity. The image of Mary, too, has been limited by the androcentric presuppositions of society. As such, she has been presented as a passively obedient handmaid, a woman of unparalleled holiness and purity, a submissive and subjugated sorrowful mother, and the male projection of idealized femininity both as an asexual virgin and as a domestically all-absorbed mother in a patriarchal family.

Feminists (both women and men) reject the sexist dimensions of these perspectives, claiming that not only are they based on androcentric presuppositions but also that they have contributed to the perpetuation of patriarchal power. These images seem to benefit Mary. However, the actual outcome is a devaluation of both Mary and all women. Mary "is hailed for her virginity; however, her virginity is equated with biological impossibility. Mary is hailed for her sinless nature; however, sinlessness is equated with an acquiescent, submissive, nurturing woman. Mary is hailed as mediatrix, but her power is purely relational and subordinate. In each case, a potentially empowering image of Mary is appropriated by Catholicism into superficial exultation, only to mask an underlying devaluation of women. Whether the term is inversion or reversal, the result is a patriarchal definition of Mary, and, by implication, women, that maintains a system of domination and subordination" (Hamington 1995, 160).

Feminists seek to retrieve the Mary of history as a genuine woman. They acknowledge that Mary's actual life and culture are hidden in historical shadows and are quite removed from our own. Nevertheless, as Elizabeth Johnson, a Sister of St. Joseph of Carondolet and theologian at Fordham University, explains, "The very paucity of the historical record regarding her is a point of identification with all women, whose history has been largely hidden and unremarked" (1985, 130). Furthermore, some feminists regard Mary's life as a journey of faith marked by poverty, suffering and authenticity. Her *fiat* was the radical autonomous decision of a young woman willing "to risk her life on a messianic venture" (ibid., 126) and her Magnificat a prayer to a God of peace and justice.

Marian Dogmas

There are four Marian doctrines: immaculate conception, virginal conception, mother of God, and assumption.

Pius IX, after consulting all the bishops of the world, issued *Ineffabilis Deus* on December 8, 1854, declaring the immaculate conception a doctrine revealed by God, and, therefore, to be firmly and constantly held by all the faithful. The decree said, "We declare, pronounce and define: the doctrine that maintains that the most Blessed Virgin Mary in the first instant of her conception, by a unique grace and privilege of the omnipotent God and in consideration of the merits of Christ Jesus the Savior of the human race, was preserved free from all stain of original sin."

This teaching has an uneven history in the church. It is not found explicitly in the scriptures. It actually grew out of the conviction that, because Mary had a unique and intimate role in salvation history as the mother of the Son of God, it was only fitting and right that God should preserve her from sin. Augustine opposed the teaching because he held that original sin is transmitted by sexual intercourse, and Mary, unlike her son, was not the result of a virginal conception. The medieval scholars Bonaventure and Thomas Aquinas opposed it because of the church's fundamental conviction that all men and women—including Mary—are redeemed by Christ. It is hard to explain, they said, how someone free from sin from the moment of conception would be in need of redemption. But many others affirmed the teaching. John Duns Scotus (1266–1308) was the first major theologian to defend the belief. He explained that Mary, like all of us, is redeemed by Christ—although in her case, by way of an anticipation of Christ's grace. Accordingly, the institutional church fostered the doctrine. In 1476 the Immaculate Conception was made a feast day by Pope Sixtus IV; and in 1846, at the sixth provincial Council of Baltimore, the United States bishops proclaimed Mary the patroness of this country under this title.

What prompted Pius IX to proclaim this dogma? It seems he had a double motive: to crown his own lifelong and sincere Marian piety and to counteract the Enlightenment. The rationalists emphasized the goodness of human nature and the ability of humans to arrive at truth, progress, and success through human effort and universal consensus. The immaculate conception reminded the world that, since original sin wounds everyone's intellect, will, and affections, all people are sinners and need a divine savior (Hennesey 1989).

This doctrine, difficult as it is, has significance for Christian spirituality. While it first seems to set Mary apart from the rest of the human race, its true meaning is quite different, as Karl Rahner explained: "God did not will the difference between [Mary and] us principally because he loved us less, and therefore did not give us the gift of grace, which is himself, from the beginning, but rather so that through this difference, the full range of the significance of grace might find clear expression. . . . We who first come into existence graceless in soul, proclaim the truth that we are not the beloved children of God by our own powers" (1963, 49–50).

The virginal conception specifies that Mary conceived Jesus without a human father. The conception of Jesus was miraculous, and is attested independently by both Matthew (1:18) and Luke (1:34). Virginal conception differs from virgin birth. The latter (a second century concept) declared that Mary gave birth to Jesus in a miraculous way that preserved the integrity of her bodily organs.

The doctrine of the virginal conception of Jesus has never been given a solemn and extraordinary definition like the other three Marian teachings. Although the virginity of Mary is stated in the early creeds, these phrases are interpreted as statements "about Jesus' human reality without intending to define the historicity of the virginal conception as part of the teaching" (Tambasco 1984, 19). Nevertheless, the virginal conception is considered infallible because it has been the constant, ordinary teaching of the Catholic church.

This doctrine, while not an "open question" for Catholics, has, nevertheless, become very problematic in the modern church for several reasons. First, the infancy narratives seem highly symbolic. Some maintain that Matthew and Luke intended to make christological statements by proclaiming that God had intervened in history with a new creation. Furthermore, it is presumed that the evangelists took over the concept of the virginal conception from their sources and simply presumed it was true. Second, this extraordinary event is not mentioned elsewhere in the New Testament. Third, there is no evidence that it was held from the beginning as a universal teaching in all the New Testament churches. Fourth, the two infancy narratives disagree on some points and contain some inaccuracies (e.g., Luke records a Roman census at the time of Jesus' birth but Matthew does not).

The historicity of the virginal conception came into postconciliar discussion through the publication of the New Dutch Catechism in 1966. This textbook, published in 1967 in the United States as *A New Catechism, Catholic Faith for Adults,* avoided the doctrine in its traditional meaning. It stated that Jesus is "God's gift" and "the son of promise, like none other." Some Dutch Catholics complained to Rome that "the book does not affirm [Mary's] biological virginity prior and subsequent to the birth of Jesus. Its use of ambiguous expressions seems to deny her virginity."

The Vatican wrote on October 15, 1968, that "it must be openly professed in the Catechism that the holy mother of the incarnate Word remained always adorned with the honor of virginity. It must teach equally clearly the doctrine of the virginal birth of Jesus, which is so supremely in accord with the mystery of the incarnation" (see Dhanis and Visser 1973, 538).

The Vatican directives to the authors of the Dutch Catechism did not faze Hans Küng, who unequivocally asserted in 1976 that "the virgin birth cannot be understood as a historical-biological event," but should be interpreted as "a meaningful symbol at least for that time." As a symbol, the virginal conception signaled a new beginning for the human race brought about by God in Christ. According to Küng, there are several other ways in which this new beginning was given expression in the New Testament. For example, in Luke's gospel the genealogy of Jesus traces him all the way back through Adam to God. Küng believes this new beginning by God can still be proclaimed today, but "without the aid of the legend of a virgin birth" (1976, 456–57).

Between the evasive interpretation of the Dutch Catechism and the outright denial of its historicity by Küng stands the interpretation of Raymond Brown—one in keeping with the Catholic tradition. In his research (and that of others, for example, Fitzmyer 1973) Brown found that the story of Jesus' conception is in a form for which there are no exact parallels or antecedents in the material available to the Christians of the first century. For example, in non-Jewish literature there are stories of women giving birth to deities, but none of them are like the nonsexual virginal conception found in Matthew and Luke. In the non-Jewish literature the deity either has normal sexual intercourse or there is some other form of penetration. In the New Testament there is no male deity or element to impregnate Mary. Similarly, in Jewish literature miraculous births such as that of Isaac are the result of God's blessing on the normal intercourse of a man and a woman. Brown's conclusion: "No search for parallels has given us a truly satisfactory explanation of how early Christians happened upon the idea of a virginal conception—unless, of course, that is what really took place" (R. E. Brown 1972, 33; see also R. E. Brown 1986a and 1986b).

The theology of Mary as mother of God received special debate in the fifth century. Bishop Nestorius (428–31), a theologian of the Antioch school, posited a double personality in Christ, one human and one divine. Cyril of Alexandria (412–44) opposed this teaching at the ecumenical Council of Ephesus in 431. Ephesus taught that since Jesus, the God-man, was one divine person, then his mother could rightly be called the mother of God. The Greek term used was *theotokos,* which literally means "she who gives birth to God." The bishops used this term to honor Mary. More importantly, they wanted to guard the belief that the Word of God took flesh from Mary and became fully human also.

Mary's title Mother of God holds a preeminent place in all the churches of the East. In the West, Mary is honored with this title in the liturgical calendar on January 1. Pius XI commemorated the 1500th anniversary of the Council of Ephesus in 1931.

Hans Küng found this title problematic for several reasons, four of which are listed here. First, the title Mother of God has no biblical basis. In the scriptures Mary is called the mother of Jesus. Second, Cyril of Alexandria manipulated the bishops at Ephesus to accept "his definition of 'God-bearer' before the arrival of the other, Antiochene party at the council." Third, as Mother of God, Mary was a replacement by the Ephesians, albeit an enthusiastic replacement, for their ancient "Great Mother," who was originally the virgin goddess Artemis or Diana. Finally, the title Mother of God "might imply a Monophysite conception of divine sonship and incarnation, hypostasizing God (as if God could be born and not a man in whom as God's *son* God himself is *evident* to faith)" (Küng 1976, 459–60). Monophysites divide the humanity of Jesus from his divinity.

On November 1, 1950, and after extensive consultation with the bishops through an encyclical, *Deiparae virginis Mariae* (1946), Pius XII defined the assumption of Mary into heaven a dogma of faith. This doctrine had been celebrated liturgically by the beginning of the sixth century. It has no biblical or patristic warrant, but it is the conclusion of an argument from fittingness, that is, it was "fitting" that the body-person that conceived Jesus should be "preserved from the corruption of the tomb."

Pius said, "We do pronounce, declare and define as a divinely revealed dogma: The Immaculate Mother of God, Mary ever Virgin, after her life on earth, was assumed, body and soul, to the glory of heaven." Nothing was said about the manner or time of Mary's assumption, and it is not clear whether the pope intended to teach that Mary died at all.

Robert Kress offered two reflections on the meaning of this doctrine (1977). First, this teaching "reminds us that God's original plan to give us the gifts of life and being has not been undone by sin and the obscurity of life and death caused by sin." Second, this is a feast especially for women. The sexist society in which Mary lived designated a low status to women. "In the kingdom of God there is no sexist subordination of women." Others welcomed the doctrine as a positive response to World War II when millions of body-persons were mutilated, gassed, or destroyed by chemicals, guns, and bombs, including nuclear bombs. The assumption of Mary affirmed the dignity of the human body and rekindled faith in the resurrection of the body.

Marian Titles

In addition to the four just discussed, Mary has hundreds of titles. Some have been linked together in litanies. Often the titles are culturally and socially conditioned. For example, Mary, a poor, Jewish, Palestinian mother and wife became "Our Lady" in feudal times, "Queen of Heaven" in the age of monarchies, and "Mother of the Liberator" in liberation theology.

Some of the titles involve complicated theological and ecumenical matters. Two that became very controversial in the twentieth-century church and were discussed at length at Vatican II are coredemptrix, meaning Mary merited our salvation, and mediatrix, meaning Mary obtains grace for sinners. These titles go back to the medieval period when Mary was given divine prerogatives as a result of the parallels in grace, virtue, and dignity that were drawn between her and her son, Jesus Christ.

Apparitions of Mary

Hundreds of apparitions of Mary have been reported. Three that have had significant influence on the twentieth-century church and popes are those at Guadalupe (1531), Lourdes (1858) and Fatima (1917).

Spanish explorers and missionaries arrived in Mexico around 1500. In their ethnocentricism, they systematically enslaved the Aztec Indians and tried to root out their language, religion, and culture. On Saturday morning, December 9, 1531, an Aztec peasant named Juan Diego (an imposed Spanish name) was on his way to church. On the hill of Tepeyac, just outside of Mexico City, Mary appeared to him for the first of four times. Tepeyac was the site of an ancient temple dedicated to Tonantzin, Aztec virgin mother of the deities.

Mary appeared as a short, swarthy Aztec woman, apparently pregnant. She identified herself in the Aztec language: "Know and understand that I am the ever-virgin Holy Mary, mother of the true God, from whom one lives; the Creator, the Lord of Near and Togetherness, the Lord of Heaven and Earth." Later it was to Juan Diego's uncle that she gave the name Our Lady of Guadalupe.

Juan Diego was commissioned to deliver a message to the bishop: "I ardently desire that a shrine may be built on this site, so that in it I can give all my love, compassion, help and protection; for I am your most holy mother, ready to hear all your laments and to alleviate all your miseries, pains and sufferings."

As a sign of her authenticity, her picture was imprinted on Juan Diego's tunic. This garment was woven from cactus, material which normally would disintegrate in about twenty years. This relic is on display today in the cathedral built at Guadalupe in 1533. The picture has been studied by scientists using the latest technology. They have discovered in it some intricate symbols, many not visible to the naked eye.

The apparitions at Guadalupe have bearing on inculturation and liberation theology. Mary appeared as an Aztec woman. She did not come as someone foreign, nor as one identified with the dominating, albeit Catholic, Spanish culture. "She came as one of their women, clothed as they would be clothed, adorned not only with the cross of her Son but also with the symbols sacred to their nation and culture. She came to a place sacred to their goddess, a goddess of fertility . . . inviting all the symbolism that surrounded that goddess to . . . find its place within a true, enriched understanding and experience of Mary and of her Son" (Pennington 1975, 68).

In representing the righteous poor, Mary gave millions of Indians their dignity. Mary's desire to give "love, compassion, help and protection" was not the image of God conveyed by the Spaniards. Their God, while he could inspire courage, was also a judge who punished sinners with eternal hell. He showed little compassion and understanding.

John Paul II visited Mexico in 1979 and in 1990, his first and forty-eighth overseas trips as pope. On May 6, 1990, he affirmed liberation theology by beatifying Juan Diego (Hebblethwaite 1990b), and by making such points as the following: "We cannot live and sleep tranquilly while millions of our brothers, very close to us, lack that which is most indispensable to conduct a worthy human life" (Haberman 1990a). On May 12, 1992, John Paul opened a chapel in honor of Our Lady of Guadalupe in the Vatican grottoes. He said the chapel witnesses not only the "Marian vocation" of the Mexican people, "but also [their] historical roots and the unifying strength of [their] culture which enriches the entire church."

Between February 11 and July 16, 1858, Mary appeared eighteen times to a peasant girl of fourteen named Bernadette Soubirous (1844–79) at Lourdes, a town in southwestern France. Bernadette was a shy girl, naturally laconic but not neurotically introverted. Mary appeared to Bernadette as a beautiful French woman. She announced that she was the Immaculate Conception and asked that a chapel be built where a miraculous stream had appeared. Since that time, millions of pilgrims have gone to Lourdes annually. Countless miracles, both physical and spiritual healings, have taken place there.

At the age of twenty-two, Bernadette joined the Sisters of Charity at Nevers and died at the age of thirty-five, after enduring years of pain from asthma and tuberculosis. She was canonized by Pius XI in 1933. During the canonization process, Bernadette's body was exhumed three times. Each time her body was found to be preserved. Today her body rests in a bronze and crystal coffin in the convent at Nevers. Her body remains intact.

During the pontificate of Benedict XV, in a period from May until October 1917, Mary appeared six times on the 13th of each month to three Portugese children in their village, Fatima. The children's names were Lucia Santos and Francisco and Jacinta Marto.

In her conversations with the children, Mary declared that her immaculate heart would triumph. She asked that the faithful recite the rosary daily, wear the scapular of Mount Carmel, and make daily sacrifices in reparation for sins that offended her immaculate heart. She also showed the children a terrifying vision of hell.

On July 13, Mary revealed three secrets to the children. The first was that two of the children would die young. The Marto children, brother and sister, died during a flu epidemic in 1919 and 1920, respectively. Lucia went on to become a Carmelite nun and, in 1991, at the age of eighty-four, joined John Paul II on his second visit to Fatima to venerate Mary. The second secret concerned Russia. Mary predicted that this country would spread errors throughout the world but would eventually be converted and an era of peace would follow. The Russian Revolution did occur on November 7, 1917. Many viewed this event as a confirmation of Mary's prediction of imminent catastrophe for the world. The third secret has never been revealed. By all reports it was delivered to the pope. It has been the subject of endless speculation centered around some dreadful cataclysm. Cardinal Joseph Ratzinger said the secret has not been made public in order "to avoid confusing religious prophecy and sensationalism" (Riding 1991).

On October 13, 1917, the sixth and last appearance, a miracle of great magnitude occurred, one witnessed by over 700,000 people. It is reported that the unrelenting rain that had greeted the crowd suddenly ceased. The sun came out, began to "dance in the sky," and then plunged toward earth. The terrified pilgrims began crying out to God for mercy and the sun retreated to its place in the sky. All the rain-soaked pilgrims were suddenly comfortably dry.

These three apparitions, while officially approved by the church, remain within the realm of private revelation and are valid only to the extent that they repeat public revelation. Since they do not rank as sources of faith, Catholics are not obliged to believe them. Church approval does not guarantee their historical truth or authenticity. What the institutional church reports is that it has sufficient evidence, especially the miracles, to allow veneration of Mary at these sites. Also, the shrines are a sign of the nearness of the triune God who always invites everyone to a personal relationship.

Many people question the validity and/or value of the apparitions. Stafford Poole, an accomplished historian of colonial Mexico, has argued at length (1995) that there is no objective historical basis for the existence of a poor indigenous man named Juan Diego and the story of the Guadalupan apparitions. Other critics indicate that there is often a curious resemblance of many details in the visions to prior experiences of those involved. For example, Bernadette was naturally laconic and her vision of Mary was not talkative either. Also, the doctrine of the immaculate conception had been infallibly defined four years before. Bernadette said she had never heard the term. Some suggest she heard it at school or in church or at home. An objection to the value of the apparitions is that the mariology involved is often what many Catholics reject and Protestants scorn. For example, Mary is too condemnatory and threatening in these images. The Fatima children were shown a terrifying vision of hell and Mary's account of the number of damned souls is distressing. In addition, the semi-apocalyptic tone of the apparitions has given a militant tone to Marian devotions. The Legion of Mary, founded in 1921, and the Blue Army of Mary, founded in 1950, promote a church engaged in a mighty struggle with evil forces on behalf of the world. The evil forces have been discrepantly identified as Adolf Hitler, or the Red Army of communism, or cold-war communism, or the "modern world."

On the other hand, it is not easy to dismiss the impressive portrait of Mary imprinted on Juan Diego's cloak, the miraculous spring at Lourdes which still supplies more than 44,000 quarts of water daily, and the powerful development of communist Russia hardly a month after the Fatima apparitions ceased. Catholics continue to flock to these Marian centers.

For example, in 1991 Lourdes "had a record 5.5 million visitors—1.5 million more than in 1983" (Simons 1993). Each December 12, the feast of Our Lady of Guadalupe, as many as 3 million pilgrims crowd the site of the apparitions.

Finally, the apparitions at Medjugorje (fifty miles south of Sarajevo in what was Yugoslavia) deserve a brief mention, especially since between 1981 and 1991 some seventeen million pilgrims had visited the site. On June 24, 1981, six Croatian children, ranging in age from ten to sixteen, claimed that Mary appeared to them as a young Croatian woman with black hair, blue eyes, and pink cheeks. She emphasized worldwide conversion, asking for more involvement in prayer, fasting, confession, and the Eucharist. She told the children that these apparitions would be her last appearances in our time and she warned of worldwide cataclysms. Some of the visionaries claimed to have had visions for years, for some as late as 1988.

True to its policy of caution in these matters, the official church often takes a wait-and-see attitude. In March 1984, the local bishop judged the apparitions fraudulent and accused the alleged visionaries and the Franciscan priests who supported them of lies, manipulation, and "fabricated miracles." In January 1991, the episcopal conference of Yugoslavia approved this statement by a vote of 19 to 1: "On the basis of studies conducted so far, it is not possible to affirm that supernatural apparitions are occurring" in Medjugorje. In the summer of 1996, the Vatican forbade "official" pilgrimages to Medjugorje, stating that there was no proof that supernatural apparitions had occurred there (Spear 1996). When John Paul visited Sarajevo in April 1997, he made no references to the apparitions at Medjugorje.

Mary and Protestant Christians

Martin Luther and Ulrich Zwingli (1484–1531) regularly observed and preached on the Marian feasts. Both accepted Mary's virginal conception and perpetual virginity as well as her immaculate conception and total sinlessness. Mary was upheld as a paramount model of faith and humility.

If this is true, why do few Protestants have a devotion to Mary? Why is Mary an ecumenical liability? Several reasons are given. First, John H. Elliott, Lutheran biblical scholar, explained in an essay in 1982 that in the seventeenth century when the two churches became more entrenched in their theologies and disciplines, Mary "became a pawn in a deadly game of ecclesiastical polemics and apologetics." Whereas for Catholics, devotion to Mary became a mark of orthodoxy and fidelity to Rome, for the Reformation churches Mary's role was deemphasized and devotion neglected. In the eighteenth and nineteenth centuries when pietism arose "in reaction to the sterile intellectualism of the Counter-Reformation and

Lutheran orthodoxy," Catholics stressed the loving and motherly care of Mary, and Lutherans sought the same qualities in Jesus and invested him "with feminine qualities of compassion, tenderness and care" (ibid.).

Second, Protestants found that Mary had been so elevated to a semi-divine status that either she was given titles that parallel those given to Christ or she functioned like the Paraclete-Spirit. This excessive veneration of Mary is called mariolatry.

Third, some of the Marian doctrines have a scriptural base and others do not. Protestants who accept Jesus' divinity call Mary the mother of God. The virginal conception is generally accepted because it is scriptural. But even here there are differences. Karl Barth defended this teaching for the sake of Jesus' divinity. For him, just as the spirit of God moved over the waters at creation (Genesis 1:1–2), so the Spirit overshadowed Mary to place within her God's own Son. Human initiative, particularly that of the male, is excluded. Paul Tillich, on the other hand, denied the virginal conception in order to preserve the humanity of Jesus.

The two doctrines that most Protestants say are not sufficiently supported by scripture are the immaculate conception and the assumption. John McHugh, an English Catholic professor, wrote a book in 1975 to show that these doctrines "are either plainly expressed or necessarily implied in Holy Scripture."

Raymond Brown gave this book a negative review (1975b), pointing out that "McHugh's solution is both unnecessary and impossible." Why? "There is only one source of our knowledge of Christian revelation, namely, the divinely guided reflection of the Christian community on the mystery of Jesus, a reflection that is articulated in church tradition of all ages—and the New Testament is the tradition of only the first-century church. All dogma must be expressed or implied in the revelation that is Jesus Christ, but not necessarily in the New Testament, which is a witness to the first-century understanding of Jesus Christ."

By 1979 Lutheran and Catholic biblical scholars had reached a new plateau in their appreciation of the scriptures and how they contributed to Marian doctrines. We have already seen that in their book *Mary in the New Testament*, the scholars found a definite line of development in mariology in the New Testament. Mark's rather ambiguous portrait of Mary as one who did not understand her son was followed by Matthew's assertion of the virginal conception, by Luke's portrayal of Mary as the first Christian disciple, and by John's depiction of her symbolic role in Jesus' new community as the mother of the beloved disciple.

It is precisely Mary's discipleship that is acknowledged as the key to later developments in Marian doctrine and devotion. While it is true that the immaculate conception and assumption are not explicitly in the scriptures, as doctrines they are fitting because they are in line with the New Testament development of mariology. Disciples are freed from sin through the grace of Christ. Mary, as the first disciple, was given this grace at conception. Furthermore, disciples are called to God's eternal life as body-persons. What awaits all disciples already happened to Mary.

If Protestants accepted the immaculate conception and assumption as teachings in line with the total scriptural witness to Mary, then Mary would cease being an ecumenical liability. She could even become an asset to Protestant spirituality because they would recognize that "veneration of Mary is deeply rooted in the Christian tradition and is a practice of piety with great spiritual potential" (Bokenkotter 1985, 140).

Marian Devotion in the Eighteenth and Nineteenth Centuries

In the first half of the eighteenth century there was intense devotion to Mary as mediatrix and coredemptrix in such writings as *True Devotion to the Blessed Virgin* by Louis-Marie Grignion de Montfort (1673–1716) and *The Glories of Mary* by Alphonsus Maria Liguori (1696–1787), the Italian Redemptorist. De Montfort went so far as to say that the devil feared Mary more than God himself.

In the second half of the eighteenth century, under the impact of the rationalism of the Enlightenment, devotion to Mary appeared to be a medieval relic and greatly declined.

In the nineteenth century, rationalism was succeeded by romanticism. This movement was spurred on in part by the libertarian and egalitarian ideals of the French Revolution. The romantics stressed, among other things, a return to nature, the innate goodness of people, the exaltation of the senses and emotions, and a keen interest in the medieval period. In harmony with this mood, devotion to Mary took on a new life, especially as it was reenforced by a series of remarkable apparitions in France. There were apparitions in Paris to Catherine Labouré (1830), at La Salette to two young illiterate children (1846), at Lourdes to Bernadette Soubirous (1858).

The attacks on Christianity by atheists, socialists, and positivists were certainly deflected by these unusual interventions of the sacred into human history. Pius IX contributed immensely to the church's triumphalism by defining the doctrine of the immaculate conception in 1854.

The Preconciliar Popes and Marian Devotion

Leo XIII wrote sixty encyclicals during his long pontificate of twenty-five years. Eleven of these were on devotion to Mary and the rosary. He built a replica of the Lourdes grotto in the Vatican gardens. Leo emphasized Mary's roles as mediatrix and coredemptrix. The same themes are found in the encyclicals of Pius X, Benedict XV, and Pius XI.

Compared to his four predecessors, Pius XII's devotion to Mary was intense, even though he tempered the titles of mediatrix and core-demptrix. Pius "was obsessed with Fatima" (Hebblethwaite 1984b). The first appearance at Fatima, on May 13, 1917, was also the day Pius was installed as an archbishop. He subsequently consecrated the world to the Immaculate Heart of Mary in 1944 and again in 1954. Also, Mary's prediction about the rise of communist Russia associated Fatima with anti-communism, a comfort to Pius's own virulent anti-communism.

Pius XII defined the assumption on November 1, 1950. In 1954, he instituted a special year of devotion to Mary, the one hundredth anniversary of the declaration of the immaculate conception. This was the first time in the history of the church that such a year of devotion had been instituted. On October 11 of that year he also instituted the feast of the Queenship of Mary. The announcement was greeted with some ambivalence. Some regarded it as an instance of triumphalism because the church found itself "politically beleaguered, in danger of losing its power on earth" (Gordon 1982). Others were more favorable. For them it was fitting to imagine "choirs of angels and the mother of God enthroned, not above her children, but in the midst of them, their voices raised in a harmony impossible to them in their life on earth."

The preconciliar mariology had its negative and positive sides. On the negative side, Mary was given a semidivine status. The devil feared her more than God, as De Montfort remarked. She was mediatrix, core-demptrix, queen of heaven and earth, "uncorrupted by childbearing, sin or death." She became a model of Christ. This theology—called christo-typical—had Mary and Jesus side by side facing the church and world in the work of redemption (Tambasco 1984, 10–11). To a certain extent Mary was kept distinct from the church and other Christians. It is no wonder that some Protestant Christians believed Catholics gave Mary the very same worship given to God.

Mary also played a negative part in sexual and spiritual development. Andrew Greeley (1974) wrote:

> In my adolescence, our teachers converted the gentle lady into a stern, negative sex goddess who banned 'dirty thoughts' and presided over the depth of necklines and the length of hemlines. Like most other young men who aspired to the priesthood, I said the rosary every day and would have claimed a 'strong devotion' to Mary. But in my seminary years she became identified with the sweet, sickly, sentimental piety preached by the spiritual directors—long, flowery, elaborate prayers which said nothing. She was used to reinforce a religious viewpoint in which obedience had become more

important than charity, chastity more important than dedication, and prudence more important than commitment. The people who claimed to be her devoted followers were creeps lugging statues about, preaching secret revelations rather than the gospel, and substituting ethereal pieties for both social concern and personal involvement. I turned the whole thing off.

On the positive side, Mary was a model of purity and fidelity. She was the one who helped Catholics respect women and children. Many people "experienced the love of God and the saving mystery of divine reality in the figure of a woman" (E. Johnson 1989, 513). Devotion to Mary helped overcome exclusively masculine symbolization of God. She was the one to whom people entrusted their needs through novenas and other devotions. Even Andrew Greeley admits (1974) that when his generation was starting out in the parochial schools in the 1930s, "the Mary myth was for the most part benign and tender . . . a soft, gentle, reassuring aspect of religion."

Vatican Council II

During the preconciliar period when mariology was christotypical, there was also considerable thought and writing about Mary within the mystery of the church—labeled ecclesiotypical—due in large measure to the developments in scripture, patristics, liturgy, and ecumenism. A good example is found in the only systematic treatise on ecclesiology in the twentieth century, *The Church of the Word Incarnate* by Charles Journet (1891–1975). This three-volume work, published in 1940, 1962, and 1969, was judged by Yves Congar as "the most profound dogmatic work to have been written on the church in our century" (De Fiores 1988, 481). Journet wrote that "mariology and ecclesiology can be seen as two parallel treatises." The church "finds in the Virgin its highest success." "Mary is mother, bride and virgin *before* the church and *for* the church; *in* her above all and *through* her, the church is mother, bride and virgin."

When Vatican II began, some bishops had a christotypical mariology, others an ecclesiotypical one. In the latter, there is greater recognition of Mary's identity with the rest of humanity, her need for redemption, and her development in faith and discipleship. Mary joins the church as it faces Christ, its redeemer and the only mediator of salvation. Mary and the church are part of the history of salvation and the wonderful works of God.

When the bishops took up the document on Mary there was a major disagreement about where it should be placed. Some wanted a separate document on Mary lest some Catholics deduce that Mary had been neglected. Others insisted that her chapter be restored to "the place in the schema on the church that was intended for it at the beginning of the preparatory period" (Semmelroth 1969, 285). This group argued that Mary should not be isolated from Christ and his church, and they feared that a separate document would not sit well with many Protestant communities.

The English-speaking bishops were as divided on this question as the other bishops. On the eve of the vote to resolve the issue, about 250 bishops assembled to hear a panel of experts on mariology. Barnabas Ahern (1915–95), William Coyle, Godfrey Diekmann, and Eugene Maly provided theological background so the bishops could make an informed decision. On October 29, 1963, it was decided by one of the closest votes in the whole council, 1,114 to 1,074, to include the schema on Mary in the church document. It became the last chapter, number eight, in the Constitution on the Church *(Lumen gentium)*. Diekmann regarded the vote as a personal triumph. From the positive response of many of the bishops to the panel discussion, he was convinced the four experts had made a difference in the extremely close vote (K. Hughes 1991, 238–40).

During the council the Marian chapter (nn. 52–69) had several titles. At one point it was "On the Blessed Virgin Mary, Mother of the Church." Most of the bishops voted against this title—though not against the teaching that Mary is the mother of the faithful. The negative vote reflected concern for sound theological terminology. Those with an ecclesiotypical mariology believed that the connection between mariology and ecclesiology ought to appear in the very title. On the other hand, these same bishops viewed the title as christotypical, with the risk that Mary would be outside, over, and above the church as mother rather than inside as member and disciple. Finally, those with an eye to the Protestant communities were cautious about using titles not found in the scripture.

The final title given the Marian chapter was "The Role of the Blessed Virgin Mary, Mother of God in the Mystery of Christ and the Church." This title satisfied both mariologies, the ecclesiotypical and the christotypical. It also showed that they need not be in complete conflict. From one point of view, they do complement one another: Christ can no more be separated from either his mother or the church any more than Mary can be separated from her Son and his community.

The final version received almost unanimous approval by a vote of 2,080 to 10, on November 21, 1964. It was not intended to be "a complete doctrine on Mary" or "to decide those questions which the work of theologians has not yet fully clarified" (LG 54). Like most of the conciliar documents, it represented a compromise whereby the different theologies of the various bishops could be represented.

In the christotypical sections, Mary is glorious and triumphant and receives special cult. Yet even here the Marian privileges are toned down and Mary's cooperation with Jesus in the redemptive process is not defined. The document says that her union "with the Son in the work of salvation is made manifest from the time of Christ's virginal conception up to his death" (LG 57). Because of her role as mother of the Son of God, Mary is "the beloved daughter of the Father and the temple of the holy Spirit. Because of this gift of sublime grace she far surpasses all creatures, both in heaven and on earth" (LG 53). In the ecclesiotypical sections, Mary is described as "being of the race of Adam." As such, she is "united to all those who are to be saved" (LG 53). She can be invoked "under the titles of advocate, helper, benefactress, and mediatrix. This, however, is understood in such a way that it neither takes away anything from, nor adds anything to, the dignity and efficacy of Christ the one Mediator" (LG 62). Mary "is hailed as pre-eminent and as a wholly unique member of the church, and as its exemplar and out-standing model in faith and charity" (LG 53). Finally, she is "a type of the church in the order of faith, charity, and perfect union with Christ" (LG 63).

The final document has several strengths. Underlying the chapter and unifying it is the perspective of salvation history. Mary does have a part in saving history. For example, as a result of an accommodated and symbolic reading of Old Testament texts (n. 55), Mary is seen foreshadowed in Genesis 3:15 and Isaiah 7:14. Yet there is a movement away from a mariology that would feature Mary's privileges and obstruct ecumenical efforts. In particular, Mary is not called Mother of the Church or coredemptrix, two titles susceptible to dangerous misunderstanding.

The document has some weaknesses. It does not relate Mary to the Spirit in a clear way. Second, "the most glaring omission is of an anthropological and cultural nature" (De Fiores 1988, 474). Mary is not connected to the pastoral thrust of the council—there are no references to the problems of daily life, to people's legitimate aspirations, and to Mary's place within the various cultures of the church. It is this point that helps explain in part the tremendous decline in Marian devotion in many parts of the global church. Certainly in the United States many forms of Marian piety disappeared. Rosaries, medals, and scapulars have been discarded; statues of Mary have been shunted off to the side in many parish churches; fewer Marian hymns are sung; and hardly any attention is paid to devotions on Saturdays and in the month of May.

Paul VI

Paul VI had a traditional devotion to Mary. On December 8, 1965, at the Eucharist closing the council, he said in his homily that was heard by one hundred thousand people: "We are honoring Mary most holy, the immaculate one, therefore innocent, stupendous, perfect. She is the woman, the true woman who is both ideal and real, the creature in whom the image of God is reflected with absolute clarity, without any disturbance as happens in every other human creature" (Doty 1965).

Paul is remembered for three honors he bestowed on Mary: he reactivated her title Mother of the Church in 1964, visited Fatima in 1967, and wrote *Marialis cultus* in 1974.

In his discourse on November 21, 1964, the closing date of the third council session, Paul said the Marian chapter in the Constitution on the

Church "is the first time . . . that an ecumenical council has presented such a broad-ranging synthesis of Catholic doctrine on the place that the Blessed Virgin Mary holds in the mystery of the Christ and of the Church." Later in the homily, Paul referred to Mary as Mother of the Church. When he did so, there was applause, "principally from other than bishops in the audience. [Paul] paused and beamed broadly" (Doty 1964).

Mother of the Church is not an ancient title. The earliest known reference occurs about the beginning of the twelfth century (Semmelroth 1969, 292). The council, as we have seen, had deliberately avoided this title because its meaning is not so clear as one might at first suppose. So why did Paul VI return to this title? It could have been a gesture of reassurance to those who wanted the title and to those who wanted more doctrinal declarations about Mary.

It is interesting to note that at Puebla in 1979, the Latin American bishops accepted Mary as "mother and model of the church." They were able to sponsor these prerogatives once they were placed within the sociocultural circumstances of Latin America. For the people of Latin America, the church is always a family. They recognize the church "as the family whose mother is the Mother of God." It is Mary who creates the family atmosphere, including such natural qualities as "receptivity, love and respect for life" (De Fiores 1988, 511–12).

Paul VI was the first pope to make overseas visits to the global church. He made nine. His third was to Fatima on May 13, 1967, the fiftieth anniversary of the first apparition there. For the liberals, this was generally regarded as a setback and a disappointment because Paul was setting the seal of pontifical approval on a secondary devotion that some Catholics mistrusted and many Protestants scorned. Many have difficulty with reports of the sun falling from the sky and a mysterious revelation about communist Russia.

In February 1974 Paul issued an apostolic exhortation, *Marialis cultis,* offering criteria to update Marian devotion and to solve the serious neglect of Marian devotions since the council. He taught that Marian devotion should be biblical; be imbued with the great christological themes; be in harmony with the liturgy; reflect ecclesial and ecumenical concerns; be attentive to contemporary social conditions; and eliminate exaggerations, sentimentalism, and legendary elements.

Paul's theology of Mary was biblical and very much in line with the latest biblical scholarship. He said Mary had always been proposed as an example for Christians to imitate. However, since her specific sociocultural situation was long past, Christians today cannot imitate precisely the type of life she lived. What should be imitated is her full and responsible acceptance of the will of God. She heard the word of God and lived a life of charity and service. "She is worthy of imitation," he concluded, "because she was the first and most perfect of Christ's disciples" (n. 35).

John Paul II

John Paul, the first Polish pope, has a great devotion to the Virgin of Czestochowa at Jasna Gora. He has made it known that he believes his call to the papacy is connected to his devotion to the shrine. When he first moved into his Vatican apartment, he added only one item: a replica of the Virgin of Czestochowa (Wynn 1988, 171).

The shrine is a focal point of Polish nationalism. It dates back to 1656 when King John Kasimir proclaimed Mary the Queen of Poland after a victory over the Swedes (L. Cunningham 1986, 27). Mary's statue is black and called the Black Madonna. Ancient black stones are connected "with the fertility power of maternal deities, black being the beneficient color of subterranean and uterine fecundity" (E. Johnson 1989, 506).

Like Paul VI, John Paul accepts fully the Marian chapter of Vatican II. At a general audience in Rome in May 1972, he said the Marian chapter is "in a certain sense a *magna charta* of the mariology of our era." Like Paul VI, he went to Fatima. His first visit on May 13, 1982, was to thank Our Lady of Fatima for saving his life exactly one year before when an assassin's bullets almost killed him. One of the bullets extracted from the pope's body has been set alongside diamonds in a golden crown that is placed on a statue of Mary on special occasions. His second visit on May 13, 1991, was to express thanks to Mary for saving his life in 1981 and for interceding to free Eastern Europe from communism. On that day the pope also entrusted the entire world to Our Lady of Fatima.

John Paul asked all the world's bishops on March 25, 1984, to "renew the consecration of the world to the Immaculate Heart of Mary" made by Pius XII. Like Pius XII, he called for a Marian year on January 1, 1987. The "year" lasted for fourteen months, June 7, 1987, the feast of Pentecost, until August 15, 1988. The reason he gave for the year was that he was anticipating the year 2000. Just as Mary prepared for Jesus while he was in her womb, so now she waits with us as we look forward to the 2,000th anniversary of her son's birth. Mary not only watches with us but she also accompanies and assists us, her fellow pilgrims, towards a new start in the year 2000.

On March 25, 1987, John Paul issued *Redemptoris mater*, an encyclical to mark the Marian year. In the letter he took up the themes of the Marian year just outlined. Also, with his global consciousness, he added that the purpose of the Marian year was to celebrate the anniversary of the church's seventh ecumenical council, Nicea II in 787. That council, by putting an end to iconoclasm, promoted a flourishing and artistic devotion to Mary. Furthermore, the Marian year commemorated the arrival of Christianity in Russia in 988, a thousand years before.

The Marian year supported the concerns of liberation theology (Hebblethwaite 1987a). John Paul declared that Mary exemplified the truth that the God who saves us is the God who has a preferential option for the poor. Her Magnificat "truly proclaims the coming of the 'Messiah of the poor.'"

John Paul also used the encyclical to treat ecumenical matters. Marian devotion in the Orthodox churches is a source of unity between the East and Rome. Mary, "our common mother," should be a sign of unity among all Christians instead of division. The encyclical did not dwell on such devotions as the rosary. Instead it sought to find in Mary as presented in the scriptures a common ground that Christians can (and should) accept. This mariology, in which care of the poor and ecumenism were linked together, was welcomed in some Protestant circles. For example, Robert McAfee Brown said (1987b) that "the Mary of the Magnificat is already becoming increasingly important to us as a beacon for illuminating the difficult path of being a Christian in a world of oppression."

Not all were enthusiastic about all parts of the encyclical. It has one paragraph (n. 46) on feminism. In this paragraph the pope lists as Marian virtues "limitless fidelity" and "tireless devotion to work." These are desirable virtues for all people. In their context in the encyclical, feminists balked.

In September 1990, John Paul went to the Ivory Coast, a very poor country that he had already visited in 1980 and 1985. Here he dedicated the largest church in the world, the cathedral of Our Lady of Peace in Yamoussoukra. At 489 feet, it is thirty-seven feet higher than St. Peter's in Rome, which it resembles. It cost 150 million dollars and was a personal gift to the institutional church from the president of the country. It was earlier rumored that the Vatican might turn down the gift because of its cost and questions about its funding.

On November 19, 1994, Pope John Paul published an apostolic letter on the approaching millennium, *Terti millennio adveniente.* He set forth a theological theme for each of the years—1997 to 1999—constituting the period of proximate preparation for the event. Each year has a Marian dimension. The year 1997 is to be a year of faith, especially in Jesus as Son of God. Mary the mother of Jesus will be invoked as a model of faith. In 1998 attention will shift to the sanctifying presence of the Paraclete-Spirit as a source of hope. Mary, "the spouse of the Spirit," will be presented as an exemplar of hope. The year 1999 will focus on God the Father's unconditional love and the part the people of God play in building a civilization of love. Mary, the beloved daughter of the Father, will be honored for her love for God and all his children.

Finally, we saw in chapter 6 that Tissa Balasuriya, a seventy-two-year old Oblate priest-theologian, was excommunicated on January 2, 1997, for his teachings on missiology. The notification of his dismissal actually fixed on his book, *Mary and Human Liberation,* published in his native Sri Lanka in 1990. Balasuriya was accused of teaching that Mary's motherhood, immaculate conception, virginity, and her "bodily assumption into heaven" were not "truths belonging to the Word of God." The CDF stated that "Wanting to present a vision of Mary free from 'theological elaborations, which are derived from a particular interpretation of one sentence or other of the scriptures,' Father Balasuriya, in fact, deprives the dogmatic doctrine concerning the Blessed Virgin of every revealed character, thus denying the authority of tradition as a mediation of revealed truth."

Mariology in the Postconciliar Church

Marian devotion declined drastically in many areas of the world church after Vatican II. Several reasons are offered. First, the increased appreciation of the presence of the resurrected Christ as mediator, teacher, and liberator leaves little place for Mary as a "relay station" or "bridge" on the way to Jesus. Second, many Marian devotions are not related to the liturgical year. At the council the bishops urged that popular devotions "be so drawn up that they harmonize with the liturgical seasons, accord with the sacred liturgy, are in some way derived from it, and lead the people to it, since in fact the liturgy by its very nature is far superior to any of them" (SC 13). Furthermore, once the people could participate in the Mass by vocal prayers, hymns, and responses in the vernacular, there was little need for paraliturgies in the vernacular, such as novenas, praying the rosary, and observance of first Saturdays. Third, new ecumenical relations with Protestants tempered Marian devotions. As we have seen, Protestants have been critical of the modern Marian doctrines (immaculate conception and assumption) and mariolatry. Ecumenical Catholicism, while not repudiating Mary's role in the Catholic tradition, has tempered devotion to her. Fourth, Catholics cannot agree on the role of women in the modern church. Traditional approaches to Mary as virgin and mother emphasized fulfillment in the home and family to the exclusion of all else. Also, women had been taught to interpret Mary's humility as submissiveness and her obedience as docility.

These perspectives do not sit well with women who want more involvement and decision-making power in the church. Writing in 1976, Marina Warner asserted in a scholarly yet tendentious book that, despite the beauty inspired by veneration of Mary—superb churches and cathedrals, poetry and paintings—such veneration has led to a denigration of women. Mary's exaltation and uniqueness not only separate her from other women but also damages the identity and standing of the majority of women who cannot measure up to Mary.

Rosemary Ruether took up the same theme, but much more forcefully. She says that the image of Mary as faithfully receptive to God and morally perfect has generally been used to heighten the disparity between her and all other women. Other women "are simultaneously disparaged and called to an impossible ethic of sexual repression and total submission to male authority. Thus Mary does not become a model of woman as autonomous person, but rather appears as a fantasy by which celibate males sublimate their sexuality into an ideal relationship with a virgin mother, while projecting the hostility caused by this sexual repression into misogynist feelings towards real women" (1987, 282).

Lisa Sowle Cahill (1985b) and others think that Mary Magdalene fills the disciple and servant role model better than Mary. All four gospels attest that Magdalene was a major first witness to the resurrection of Jesus and had "the primary role" among women recipients of the appearances (O'Collins and Kendall 1987). She became "the apostle to the apostles," one entrusted with authority to teach and preach.

On the other hand, some deny that Marian devotion has been that counterproductive for women's authenticity. Sidney Callahan, for example, argues quite impressively that Marian devotion now and always enhances "the well-being of women and the good of the church" (1993). She explains that Marian devotion has always served a twofold function. First, in each age it seems to witness to those gospel values and truths that the official church is either ignoring or distorting. Mary's role as mediatrix, for instance, flowered because the presence and work of the Paraclete-Spirit was slighted. Second, Marian devotion seems to anticipate "what is coming next in the church's pilgrimage." Today, for example, "Feminist concerns for peace, nurturing power, and new movements of ecological feminism bent on mothering the earth" find a prayerful expression within Marian devotions. In places where people experience intense political, social, economic and religious oppression, Mary is often invoked as "woman of the poor, unwed mother, widowed mother, political refugee, seeker of sanctuary, sign of contradiction, mother of the homeless, mother of the nonviolent, mother of the executed criminal, model of risk, trust, courage, patience, perseverance, and wellspring of peace." Callahan even predicts that when the ordination of women takes place in the Catholic church, Mary "will be cited as the model of women's equality and emancipation within the church." While gender is an important dimension of human identity, doing God's will and deeds of justice and compassion are more important. Consequently, Marian images will be used not only in the official documents that announce priestly ordination for women but also in the ordination ceremonies themselves.

Writing in 1995, Rosemary Ruether was not equally sanguine about either a renewed Marian spirituality or a more inclusive church. While she expressed sincere appreciation for the reclamations of the image of Mary in the postconciliar church—a woman of the poor, our sister in the struggle for survival, a woman of faith—she said these images

> have not given birth to effective new movements of Marian spirituality in the Catholic church. The key reason for this is that the Catholic church continues to present a regressive and

negative face toward women's hopes for inclusive ministry and full human development. Thus any effort to elaborate a mariology that celebrates such liberated female humanness and mutuality in ministry falls upon a contradiction, arousing disbelief rather than creative elan. Without a real praxis of solidarity with women and inclusion of women in ministry, a mariology that seeks to express such a vision falls fruitless on stony ground.

Mary and Language about God

At Vatican II the bishops acknowledged the existence of the feminist movement when they wrote that "women claim parity with men in fact as well as of right, where they have not already attained it" (GS 9). In the 1970s Christian feminists such as Mary Daly (1973), Rosemary Ruether (1977), and Mary Buckley (1978) explained that at the heart of Christianity as a patriarchal religion is the heretical identification of God as a male and the worship of God as "Father." The effect of this androcentric tradition has been to deify male experiences and concepts and depreciate the role and experience of God among all persons, male and female. Consequently, there was a call to refer to God with feminine symbols. First, it was pointed out that there are several scriptural texts in which God acts in feminine or maternal ways or has feminine qualities and emotions. For example, God creates both Adam and Eve in his image (Genesis 1:26–27); Yahweh is likened to a midwife (Psalm 22:9-10); Moses reminds the Israelites that God gave them birth (Deuteronomy 32:18; Numbers 11:12); Isaiah writes that even if a mother forgets her baby, God will not forget the nation (42:14); and God brings Jerusalem to birth and comforts the city as a mother comforts her child (66:9). Second, it was noted that the experiences of women indicate that God-language "in female symbol emerges gracefully, powerfully, and necessarily from women's encounter with divine presence in the depths of their blessed selves. Women's reality forms part of the treasury of created excellences that can be used to refer to God" (E. Johnson 1993b; see also 1993a).

At this point, other authors suggested that Mary reveals the feminine dimension of God. For example, Andrew Greeley wrote that Mary helps us see God as "passionately tender, seductively attractive, irresistibly inspiring, and graciously healing" (1977, 13). He also argued that, despite the doctrinal and ecumenical difficulties raised by a christotypical view of Mary, she is "a sacrament of God's life-giving, nurturing, healing, maternal love" (Greeley and Greeley Durkin 1984, 54). Mary, it was said, keeps alive the feminine dimension of God because she remains the "defining image" for a Catholic sacramental consciousness. "Mary is essential to Catholicism, not perhaps at the level of doctrine but surely on the level of imagination because she more than any other image blatantly confirms the sacramental instinct: the whole creation and all its processes, especially its life-giving and life-nurturing processes, reveals the lurking and passionate love of God" (Greeley 1990a, 253).

Those who prefer to speak of "God Mother" object to the view that Mary reminds us of the female element in God. This, they maintain, is a misuse of Mary. God the Father of Jesus Christ can also be called Mother if we break out of purely patriarchal imagery. Once God is fully envisioned as also having a female face and as a loving mother who creates, nurtures, loves and saves, then Mary will no longer have to bear the burden of keeping alive the female imagery of the divine (E. Johnson 1989, 524).

Conclusion

On the threshold of the third millennium, devotion to Mary in the institutional church and among the people is sporadic, its vitality depending in great measure on culture and local conditions. All persons and nations do not spend a great deal of time calling her blessed (Luke 1:47). Devotion to Mary will not return to its fitting and proper place within the Catholic tradition and the world church until the institutional and intellectual dimensions are clarified. There is as yet no coherent renewed mariology in the postconciliar church—even though Mary is, as Raymond Brown observed, "almost a bellwether of theological direction in the Roman Catholic church," as cited earlier. In order to revive a vibrant and sound devotion to Mary, at least these two conditions will have to be met. First, the church must become more inclusive of women in ministry, service, and administration. Second, Mary will have to be retrieved as a woman, virgin, wife, mother, and disciple in nonsexist terms, and in view of the fact that most of the world's poor are mothers and women of color. Such a renewed mariology would contribute immensely not only to the essential dignity of all women (and men) but also to the development of the church as a community of disciples with a threefold mission to promote and expand the reign of God, especially through a preferential option for the poor.

CHAPTER 12

Women in the Postconciliar Church

The term *feminism* denotes the theory or doctrine of those who advocate or demand such legal and social changes as will establish political, economic, social, and religious equality of the sexes. The modern feminist movement is not merely a present-day issue. The liberation of women has been a passionate concern for over two centuries. Its beginnings are traced to England where the founding document of feminism was published in 1792: *A Vindication of the Rights of Women* by Mary Wollstonecraft (1759–97). In the nineteenth century English women agitated for the right to vote, but in 1867 the British Parliament voted against this civil right. Despite this setback, the crusade continued, sometimes with the strong support of men. For example, John Stuart Mill (1806–73), philosopher, economist, and member of Parliament in 1867, was an energetic advocate of women's rights. In his 1869 book, *The Subjection of Women,* he argued that the equality of women is essential if the interests of the family as such are to be served. Women's suffrage, he wrote, is needed precisely to check the pursuit of male self-interest and because it is an essential step toward the moral improvement of humankind. Women were not fully enfranchised in Britain until 1928.

In the United States, Elizabeth Cady Stanton (1815–1902) and Lucretia Mott (1793–1880) organized the first women's rights convention in 1848 in Seneca Falls, New York. Stanton, a housewife and mother living in Rochester, New York, came out of the evangelical reform movement; Mott was a Quaker minister from Philadelphia. Later, Stanton and Susan B. Anthony (1820–1906), a Quaker and school teacher, led the fight for full political, social, and educational equality with that of men. Women obtained the right to vote with the passage of the Nineteenth Amendment to the Constitution in 1920. In 1963, Betty Friedan published her landmark book, *The Feminine Mystique,* which played an important part in the resurgence of feminism. She argued that the roles of wife and mother (for white, middle-class housewives) were not the only ones in which women could hope to be happy. In 1966 she and her friends and colleagues founded the National Organization of Women (NOW), an organization that seeks to end discrimination, sexual harassment, and sex stereotyping.

Not all efforts at liberation have been successful. Powerful social and religious forces have been marshalled against women. For instance, spurred on by NOW, women campaigned for an Equal Rights Amendment, one which called for the prohibition of discrimination on the grounds of sex. In 1972 Congress approved such an amendment but it failed to become law because it did not secure ratification by thirty-eight states within ten years of its passage.

A social and religious organization that seems to oppose the feminist movement is Promise Keepers. Founded in 1990 by Bill McCartney, a former Catholic who was the football coach at the University of Colorado from 1981 to 1994, this all-male, all-Christian movement is "possibly the fastest growing spiritual phenomenon in America" (Rich 1996). In 1996 almost one million men attended its rallies held in sports stadiums across the country (Spalding 1996). These impressive rallies are a combination of "religious revival, inspirational pep talks and spiritual support groups (Niebuhr 1995). The assemblies of tens of thousands of men are marked by racial diversity, exhuberant singing, and outstanding preaching (De-Celle 1996).

This nondenominational organization, which established international affiliates in February 1997, declares that it aspires to bring men to God and to help them "honor" Jesus Christ. "Jesus, the movement insists, is a man's man. He is not the androgynous Christ of sentimental Protestant iconography, but a mighty king and warrior, a leader of men and a willing Savior, a wild man with a redeeming purpose—and also the best buddy a guy could ever have" (Woodward 1996).

Promise Keepers also aspires to make men better husbands and fathers. It "never tires of reminding men that male friendship, mutual accountability and mutual support are crucial for male spiritual direction" (DeCelle 1996). Similarly, it strives to further racial reconciliation. Its official magazine, *New Man,* contains numerous articles "focusing on the plight of immigrants, advocating on behalf of poor people, editorializing against injustices in American courts" (Tapia 1996). However, its agenda also calls for demonizing homosexuals, bringing prayer and the teaching of creationism to public schools, and "taking back" power from women. Many women fear that Promise Keepers is striving to roll back their hard won progress over the past two hundred years. They regard Promise Keepers as a backlash against feminism because it offers man "reassurance in a time of dramatic social change, when traditional gender lines have become blurred at work and at home" (Niebuhr 1995). Many women and feminists are disturbed when they learn that one of the organization's favorite chants is "Thank God I'm a man" (Rich 1996).

Feminism is a complicated human issue, and like other complex human issues, it accommodates a diversity of ideas, concerns, and goals.

Historians suggest that it has moved from one set of goals to another set. Until after World War II, the goal of many women was to get into male society and to achieve the same political, social, and economic rights as men. Since then, there has been a major transformation in the lives of women brought on by such factors as education, by having fewer children, by a longer life expectancy, and by the expansion of women's roles throughout the world in education, politics, economics, medicine, the sciences, and religion. Concomitantly, the feminist movement has taken a radical turn: many women reject our androcentric society and aspire towards another society in which women and men would be partners. In other words, the aim of the Christian feminist movement is the reformation of both society and church. As defined earlier, reformation means "reform by transformation or by revolution," whereby society or an organization is given a new identity, new structures, and new goals.

Many feminist issues have already been addressed in this book. Many women believe that, in the spirit of Mary Ward in the seventeenth century, they have an apostolic mission in society (chapter 2). Pope John XXIII noted that the quest by women for equality in domestic and public life was one of the signs and needs of the times (chapter 3). Many women are involved in the ecumenical movement because they desire to see all Christians united in Christ (chapter 7). Feminists (men and women) know that words both shape and limit our concepts and attitudes. Consequently, they understand the importance of gender-inclusive language in scriptural and liturgical texts (chapter 8). Many women want empowerment, integration into public life, and economic equality. They are deeply disturbed because hundreds of thousands of women (and their children) live in involuntary poverty. Many women, like the late Dorothy Day, are firmly committed to the church, but have no fear about opposing some of its policies and practices deemed unchristian. Many women are also uneasy because scant attention has been given to their socioeconomic concerns in most papal social encyclicals (chapter 9). Women want respect as body-persons. They look to the church to support them with an enlightened sexual ethic for themselves, their families, and society (chapter 10). Many women seek recognition of their gifts, talents, and needs. They want a renewed mariology: one which presents Mary the mother of Jesus as a model for a life of discipleship, liberation, and faith-justice. Mary, many women maintain, can be an inspiration for living in the modern world because she was open, adventurous, and willing to tolerate uncertainty (chapter 11).

This chapter follows the same format as the previous chapters: it provides a summary of the preconciliar, conciliar, and postconciliar aspects of the women's movement in light of Von Hügel's triad. Unfortunately it is beyond the scope of this book to address feminism in the other Christian communities, the Jewish tradition, and the feminist spirituality movement.

Women and Vatican Council II

The preconciliar church promoted a long litany of dualisms: grace and nature, church and world, tradition and scripture, clergy and laity, Western and Eastern culture, Christianity and the other religions, Catholic Christianity and the other Christian churches, and so forth. In each instance the first component of the dyad was more valuable and more significant than the second. This was especially true of two dualisms—male and female, private and public—that the church inherited from the Greco-Roman culture. These dualisms ran so deep in Christian theology and spirituality that they permeated every aspect of the faith and life of the Christian churches.

The role of women in society and church during the preconciliar times is not easy to capture in a few paragraphs. On the one hand, women were in fact an equal of men in many familial and social situations. Spiritually they were equal to men since they were created in the image of God. On the other hand, it appears from a multitude of historical and sociological studies that women had a subordinate, marginal, and somewhat invisible place in society and the church. Men were taught to define themselves as superior to women, intellectually, socially, and politically. Women were excluded from important roles in the public sphere. Men worked in the public realm while women, because they were ordained by God and nature for motherhood were *house*wives. Men were the providers of the family and held authority over their economically and socially dependent wives.

Women also had subordinate roles at all levels of the church's institutional, intellectual, and devotional life. They were not officeholders or administrators in the ecclesial structures. Their connection to the institution, especially for religious sisters, was through Catholic primary schools, orphanages, and hospitals. There they worked zealously but received minimal wages and had little or no power or autonomy. Even principals of parochial schools had to clear important decisions with pastors or diocesan administrators. There were few women in higher education. Women receiving degrees in religious studies and theology was unheard of. However, women were deeply involved in the church's devotional life. Their attendance at liturgical and paraliturgical services far exceeded that of the men. Women were idealized as more religious and moral than men. Mothers taught their children their prayers and provided informal religious instruction and education by word and example. The official church fiercely defended the family because it underpinned the stability and determined the character of society.

Given this context, it is not surprising that when the twenty-seven hundred council fathers assembled on October 11, 1962, there were no women present in an official capacity. However, at the end of the second session, December 4, 1963, Cardinal Leo Suenens asked his fellow bishops: "Why are we even discussing the reality of the church when half of the church is not even represented here?" This provocative question midway through the council was a breakthrough that prodded Paul VI and the bishops to invite women to the ensuing sessions. At the opening of the third session on September 14, 1964, Paul VI welcomed women as auditors. As auditors they could watch and listen to the assembly proceedings, but they could not speak or vote.

The story of the twenty-three women from fourteen countries officially invited as auditors has been documented by Carmel McEnroy, a Sister of Mercy and theologian, in a 1996 book she titled *Guests in Their Own House*. This book provides information about the women: their backgrounds, their participation at the council, and their subsequent implementation of the council. For example, nineteen were single (eleven were sisters), three were widows, and one was married.

All twenty-three "council mothers" did not show up at St. Peter's on the same day. They arrived over several months, depending on where they were when they received their invitation. The first to arrive was Marie-Louise Monnet of France, a long-time worker with youth in her native land and president of the International Federation of the Independent Social Welfare Organization. She was first because she was already in Rome. She was there to monitor the council, especially its concerns with the lay apostolate. She entered the council for the first time on September 25, 1964, her sixty-second birthday (McElroy 1996, 47). This date is rarely noted in histories of the council, yet its significance for church history cannot be underestimated. Never before in the history of the church have women been present at one of its ecumenical councils.

Representing the United States were Claudia Feddish, Catherine McCarthy, and Mary Luke Tobin. Feddish was a Sister of St. Basil the Great, a congregation of Slavonic-speaking sisters of the Ukrainian Byzantine rite. Her community, founded in 359 by St. Basil, established missions in the United States in 1911. Before becoming the superior general of her community in 1963, she taught in several schools in Pennsylvania and New Jersey and had administrative posts in New York. "She took her appointment as a recognition of the Eastern rites" (ibid., 74). In 1969, she presided at her community's renewal chapter. When her term as superior general ended in 1971, she worked in Rome. Here she was seriously injured in a bus accident and died from complications on January 1, 1978 (ibid., 251).

Catherine McCarthy was a married woman from Boston whose husband had died in 1949. She had a long and successful record of service to the church through Catholic Action. In 1964 she was president of the National Council of Catholic Women. This organization, founded in 1920, is a federation of thousands of organizations of Catholic women in the

United States. It provides a medium through which women, as organizations and individuals, may speak and act upon matters of common interest. After the council, McCarthy toured the country, spreading the message of Vatican II and inviting the laity, and especially women, to be involved in strengthening the church and its mission.

In 1964, Mary Luke Tobin was superior general of the Sisters of Loretto and the newly elected president of the Conference of Major Superiors of Women, a post she held until 1970. Tobin reported in 1986 that Bernard Häring urged that women have a place in the commissions formulating the documents. Accordingly, Mary Luke Tobin served on two commissions: ecumenism and the church in the modern world. On the commissions the women could speak as freely as they wished—and they did so.

The presence of the twenty-three women did not create a countervailing current toward turning around the patriarchal attitude of the official church toward women. This is clear from the fact that in the sixteen conciliar documents there are very few references to women and the contributions they could make to the renewal and reform of the church. In the index to the 1966 Abbott edition of the conciliar documents, there are only five entries about women, not counting those under nuns, consecrated virgins, widows, and laity. Nonetheless, the five brief statements when taken together are significant—and I have taken the liberty of putting them in one paragraph.

The bishops declared that all persons "have the same nature and origin and, being redeemed by Christ, they enjoy the same divine calling and destiny; there is here a basic equality between all and it must be accorded even greater recognition . . . [Consequently], any kind of social or cultural discrimination in basic personal rights on the grounds of sex, race, color, social conditions, language or religion, must be curbed and eradicated as incompatible with God's design" (GS 29). The bishops acknowledged that women opposed discrimination and claimed "parity with men in fact as well as of right, where they have not already attained it" (GS 9). Because of this demand for equality, "women are now involved in nearly all spheres of life: they ought to be permitted to play their part fully in ways suited to their nature. It is up to everyone to see to it that women's specific and necessary participation in cultural life be acknowledged and developed" (GS 60). Their domestic role as nurturers of children "must be safeguarded without, however, underrating [their] legitimate social advancement" (GS 52). Finally, the bishops stated that "since in our days women are taking an increasingly active share in the entire life of society, it is very important that their participation in the various sectors of the church's apostolate should likewise develop" (AA 9).

On December 8, 1965, at the close of the solemn ceremonies marking the end of the council, six messages were read to various groups of people, such as workers, youth, and women (Abbott 1966, 729–37). The message to women stated that over the course of history the church had "brought into relief [woman's] basic equality with man" (ibid., 733). The bishops urged women "to save the peace of the world" and noted women's perennial contribution to society, mainly through the family. The message also struck a prophetic note: "But the hour is coming, in fact has come, when the vocation of woman is being achieved in its fullness, the hour in which woman acquires in the world an influence, an effect, and a power never hitherto achieved. That is why, at this moment when the human race is undergoing so deep a transformation, women impregnated with the spirit of the gospel can do much to aid mankind in not falling" (ibid.).

Conciliar Teaching Evaluated: 1980–90

We saw in chapter 3 that one of the major results of Vatican II is that the global church became, in Rahner's famous term, a world church. The preconciliar church's mission was to export to India, Africa, and East Asia a superior culture and religion. John Glaser, priest-theologian, explains that the Christianity exported was not only European but also male (1983). Implicit in Rahner's major thesis, claims Glaser, is that the church must be de-masculinized. To become a world church, "it must become a church of both sexes, female as well as male. It cannot become world church without expanding beyond two boundaries: horizontally beyond the boundary of European culture; vertically beyond the boundary of male culture." Women need to be freed to be themselves and to be equal partners with men in the intellectual, devotional, and institutional church. This can occur if all centers of power and influence in the church "dedicate energy and imagination to mechanisms of communication with and inclusive of women." Unless the church is de-masculinized, grave injustices will continue, the meaning of Vatican II will be betrayed, and the church will lose immense wisdom and humanity. Women have the possibility of bringing to the world church "an experience significantly different from men, at least in areas such as: community, ambiguity, body, power, symbol, violence, time, nurturance, sex, space, law, impotence, service."

We also saw in chapter 3 that, following the lead of John XXIII, the bishops wanted to update the church in relation to the modern world. Aggiornamento entails a spirituality that eliminates the many dualisms: the social and domestic, the public and private spheres, the world of work and home, people's social and religious lives. The bishops wrote this striking passage:

> Let there, then, be no such pernicious opposition between professional and social activity on the one hand, and religious life on the other. Christians who shirk their temporal duties shirk

their duties toward their neighbor, neglect God himself, and endanger their eternal salvation. Let Christians follow the example of Christ who worked as a craftsman; let them be proud of the opportunity to carry out their earthly activity in such a way as to integrate human, domestic, professional, scientific and technical enterprises with religious values, under whose supreme direction all things are ordered to the glory of God (GS 43).

This integral spirituality was hardly actualized. Compartmentalization continued; the dualisms remained. Many well-meaning Catholics clung to a privatized spirituality. On the other hand, feminists like Christine Gudorf indicated that there was a way out of these dualisms and privatization (1983, 231–51). The phrase that succinctly summarizes their major focus is "the personal is the political." Through the use of history, psychology, economics, and sociology, feminist scholarship discovered that the political world has always influenced the structures of personal life. What most people and the institutional church took for granted as natural—such concepts as the social institution of childhood, the nuclear family, an androcentric view of women—were actually the result of widespread social patterns in the economic and political areas (ibid., 245). In other words, the social and domestic are inseparable, with the political as the dominant factor. The home cannot be isolated from the currents sweeping society. Family or "personal" problems are manifestations of social problems. "Social problems are echoed in family problems" (ibid.).

Feminist scholars became convinced that if the church is to succeed in serving the modern world, it must address and eliminate the many dualisms that undergirded society and church, especially the social-private dualism. The institutional church was itself at fault. It was sometimes inconsistent. For example, its public messages stress autonomy, responsibility, community, conscience, openness to the Spirit, and relational responsibility as the appropriate moral methodology; its internal messages impose an absolutist moral code (especially in sexual ethics and canon law), and a method of decision making that is hierarchical and authoritarian. In this method people are asked to listen to the Spirit manifested in the tradition of the church as explained by the magisterium and clergy (ibid., 247). Similarly, the church cannot evangelize the world by relegating some Christian virtues (e.g., compassion, forgiveness, love) to the home while relegating others to society (e.g., honesty, justice, tolerance). All these virtues should be practiced in all areas of life.

Feminists propose that the institutional church take steps to eliminate the public-private dualism. Summarized here are six of them: (1) Ordain women, make celibacy voluntary, and open some governance positions (at synods, councils, and in the curia) to male and female laity.

"This would separate the clerical/lay division from the male/female division, from the celibate/sexually active division, as well as prevent these three from coinciding with the powerful/powerless division" (ibid., 248). (2) The magisterium should intensify and broaden its consultation before it teaches through letters and encyclicals. (3) The church should foster democratic processes that will enable local communities to recapture their original role relative to calling priests to ordination and opening up the relationship between parish and pastor, and parish and bishop. Each parish should not be an end in itself. Liturgy should lead out to the needs of the world. Each parish should become more other-oriented, that is, have a mission. (4) The institutional church should eliminate its moral dualism. The same ethical method should be used in both the private and public spheres. The relational responsibility model should replace the traditional method's absolutist propensities. The seven complementary voices of authority should be consulted. Giving priority to the authority of the magisterium only "makes any form of authentic communal responsibility impossible" (ibid., 249). "The laity cannot be expected both to function in the public world of critical rationality and autonomy and to uncritically follow the dictates of the hierarchy" (ibid., 244). (5) The church should use inclusive language in scripture, liturgy, and official documents. (6) The church must cease teaching traditional sex roles in sermons, schools, and official documents. For example, it is wrong to say that mothers are the primary nurturers of their children. Rather, both parents are fully responsible for the care of their children and the establishment and maintenance of domestic life.

We also saw that Pope John Paul assembled the Synod of 1985 to evaluate the effects of Vatican II on the church's institutional, devotional, and intellectual life. When it was clear that only men would be present and that women would have no voice in the assessment of the council at the synod, some women expressed in print their evaluation of Vatican II. For example, Elisabeth Schüssler Fiorenza of Harvard University wrote a seminal essay in 1985 in which she outlined the theology of Vatican II, placing special emphasis on the five conciliar statements about women cited above. Her thesis was that "while the council taught us to value our human and Christian dignity and rights, the women's liberation movement enabled us to act upon them." She judged that many women had indeed put into practice the spirit of the council for the past twenty years for the benefit of the global church, but "this would not have happpened if the women's liberation movement and if the conciliar movement for the renewal of the church had not coincided."

Her evaluation of what had happened to women in the church between 1965 and 1985 had both negative and positive aspects. On the negative side, she regretted the silent "exodus" of so many women from active participation in the church. They left because, in Glaser's term, the church had not de-masculinized. Schüssler Fiorenza reported that many women say that their "human and ecclesial dignity and rights are violated by institutionalized sexism." She upbraided the official church for maintaining an "ecclesiastical patriarchy" that excluded "women from sacramental, doctrinal, and governing power on the basis of sex."

On the positive side, she praised Vatican II for its emphasis on the church as the people of God. This symbol, she contended, evokes "a participatory model of church that is not an end in itself, but serves the realization of God's intention in creation and redemption." She also praised the council's stress on collegiality because it engenders "a transformation of the monarchical pyramid into a circle of the discipleship of equals." She further praised Vatican II for its stress on freedom of conscience, the rights and dignity of the human person, and social responsibility because these values "envisioned a dialogical community of adult Christians with different gifts and vocations but with a common commitment."

Schüssler Fiorenza concluded by giving women high grades for bringing the spirit of Vatican II into all levels of church ministry: for living the gospel among the poor; for seeking to create institutional forms that respect and foster the dignity of women and those marginalized in the church; for actualizing the participatory model of the church; and for living as disciples who advance "God's reign of justice and love in all human dimensions of life."

In 1986 Mary Luke Tobin reviewed some of the effects of Vatican II on women in the church. She stated that "For me, Vatican II was an opening, although just a tiny crack in the door, to a recognition of the vast indifference toward women and the ignoring of their potential within the whole body of the church."

She outlined some positive developments and some negative factors. On the positive side, she noted that the women's movement had grown and shows no sign of slowing down. Religious orders of women had developed collegial and personalist insights and practices. Laywomen's groups, such as the World Union of Catholic Women's Organizations, had become articulate about "painful, conflict-generating topics and situations." And many outstanding women theologians and biblical scholars have emerged. On the negative side, she regretted that "on the part of the Vatican, understanding of the evolution of United States women religious has been terribly lacking." She also regretted that many women continue to leave the church because the official church remains insensitive to their desire to "participate fully" in its life and mission.

Like Schüssler Fiorenza, Tobin ended on an optimistic note. Presuming on the good will already evident among some male officeholders and noting that it was becoming more obvious to everyone that women have a minimal role in the church, she stated that "women can have a more secure hope that perhaps a new day of mutuality, equality and sharing may be on its way."

On December 7, 1990, in commemoration of the twenty-fifth anniversary of *Gaudium et spes,* the Quixote Center of Hyattsville, Maryland, sponsored a four-page advertisement in the *National Catholic Reporter* that declared that a new day of equality and mutuality was not yet here. The ad, which contained more than three pages of names by people from practically every state in the continental United States, called for "new and prophetic initiatives to eliminate sexism from the life of the church." It accused church leaders of mocking the teachings of the council, calling their disobedience to church teaching "grave scandal and social sin." Some of their complaints were the following: (1) "Discrimination based on sex remains deeply imbedded in the structures of ministry and decision making in our church." (2) "Communities starve for Eucharist in our church that refuses to ordain women." (3) "Issues of sexuality and reproduction are excluded from serious dialogue." (4) Men "consult with other men about women rather than initiating a dialogue with women as peers to talk about the real problem, sexism."

The advertisement called upon "the church community to confess our shared responsibility for the sin of sexism"; "to join in a serious, prayerful planning process for fundamental reform to eradicate sexism from all church structures"; "to use inclusive language for God and humanity in all readings, preaching and music"; and "to inaugurate serious dialogue on issues of sexuality, reproduction, shared decision making and women's ordination." In short, they declared that "It is time to heal the sin of sexism so that the Good News will go forth throughout the land that Christ's love is born anew in the hearts of the Catholic people."

Paul VI

Pope Paul VI announced in two separate ceremonies in 1970 that two saintly women, Teresa of Avila (1515–82), a Carmelite nun, and Catherine of Siena (1347–80), a celibate laywoman, were to be honored as "doctors" of the church. They are the only two women so honored. Doctors of the church are those who have contributed to the church by their outstanding holiness and distinguished doctrinal teachings. Until these announcements in 1970 all doctors of the church were clerics (Weaver 1985, 190–97).

Many viewed these honors as a way of enhancing the role of women as teachers in the church. Others viewed the honors as a way of demonstrating the compatibility of feminist psychology and Christian spirituality. First, both Teresa and Catherine were mystics who stressed the primacy of self-understanding for a person's spiritual growth (Conn 1986, 177–200). Contemporary feminists maintain that feminist psychology is an essential resource for this self-knowledge. Some questioned this connection because feminism promotes self-fulfillment whereas Christian spirituality fosters self-denial. But Christian feminists indicated that there was no need to assume conflicting goals. Both feminist psychology and Christian spiritual development have a common goal: maturity. Both emphasize the balance needed between autonomy (independence or self-direction) and relationships (interdependence or self-surrender). In the past men were said to strive for autonomy and women for relationships. Today, most psychologists emphasize that both autonomy and relationships should be the focus of every person at every stage of their development. Spiritual directors teach that the Paraclete-Spirit affirms each person's self-direction as well as their self-surrender. "What is essential for mature spirituality is the conviction that only an independent self can achieve authentic religious surrender" (Conn 1987, 257). Teresa of Avila thought that relationships in community were often a greater indication of one's relationship to God than the heights of mystical prayer.

Second, Teresa and Catherine advocated a process of self-knowledge compatible with modern feminists. Feminists encourage women to critically examine the ways in which enculturation in a patriarchal culture affects their self-understanding. Once they understand how this process works, then they can become the authors of their own destiny. Teresa and Catherine advocated a parallel process, namely, discernment. They recommended "a process in which one examines one's feelings and thoughts, one's assumptions and actions in order to distinguish authentic religious experience from false projections, to separate illusion from honest self-assessment, to relinquish blind fear and egoism in favor of courageous adherence to truth and free commitment to love" (ibid., 255).

On September 14, 1972, the Vatican promulgated *Ministeria quaedam,* a document that reformed priestly orders. It eliminated the subdiaconate and made lector (reader) and acolyte (attendant to the priest) "lay ministries." Women were excluded from these ministries or offices in keeping with "sacred tradition." However, since it was quite common for women in the United States to serve as acolytes and lectors, some argued that the document excluded women only from official installation into these offices but not from the liturgical functions as such. Sandra Schneiders, an Immaculate Heart of Mary Sister and professor of spirituality and scripture, pointed out that this interpretation actually resulted in unfortunate consequences, what she called an "alternate Christianity" for women. Women, she explained, were still not the equals of the male disciples. They performed an alternate form of service but not an official one. For example, deacons can give homilies but women cannot, even though many of them are more professionally trained in theology and scripture. An "alternate" form of preaching was developed for women. They cannot give a homily but they can give "reflections." The latter are not given after the reading of the gospel but at some other time before or after the liturgy. In a word, the reflections of a woman at liturgy are not part of the official service (see Conn 1987, 248).

On September 14, 1975, Paul canonized Elizabeth Ann Bailey Seton (1774–1821). She was born in New York City of a wealthy and distinguished

Episcopalian family. In 1794 she married William Seton, a wealthy young merchant. When he lost his fortune in 1803, the family (they had five children) travelled to Italy to see friends. There her husband died. Elizabeth remained in Italy where she came in close contact with the Catholic church. She developed a respect for the church and its teachings. Upon returning to New York, she was baptized there in 1805. Soon she became interested in educating girls. Bishop John Carroll directed her to found a community to do the work. He later presided over her vow ceremony, permitted her and her companions to adopt a religious habit, and gave her the title of Mother. In 1809 Elizabeth moved to Emmitsburg, Maryland, where she adopted a modified rule of the Sisters of Charity composed in 1633 by Vincent de Paul and Louise de Marillac. She died at Emmitsburg on January 4, 1821.

Elizabeth Seton is the first American-born saint and foundress of the first American religious community for women. Historians acknowledge that she laid the foundation of the very successful American parochial school system. Her Daughters of Charity of St. Vincent de Paul continue to carry out her work and charism today.

On October 15, 1976, Pope Paul reiterated the church's traditional teaching prohibiting the ordination of women. His document will be discussed later in this chapter.

John Paul II

In contemporary discussions of the interdependence of men and women, two models are proposed.[1] The "one nature" model holds that there are no rigidly defined roles for women and men other than biological. Women and men are complete and integral wholes capable of complementary relationships through being alike and different at the same time. All women and men are androgynous. Each sex can and should develop those qualities traditionally associated with the other. They base their approach in part on the words of the apostle Paul: "There is neither Jew nor Greek, there is neither slave nor free person, there is not male and female; for you are all one in Christ Jesus" (Galatians 3:28; see also 1 Corinthians 12:13).

The other model, the "two natures" model, claims that women's nature is equal to, but distinct from, that of men. Their natures are complementary. This model also has roots in scripture. Ephesians 5:23 states: "For the husband is head of his wife just as Christ is head of the church, he himself the savior of the body." Similarly, 1 Peter 3:7 declares: "Likewise, you husbands should live with your wives in understanding, showing honor to the weaker female sex, since we are joint heirs of the gift of life, so that your prayers may not be hindered." Thomas Aquinas argued, following Aristotle, that the nature of men and women differed because their biological nature differed. Women were "defective" and "misbegotten" (*Summa theologiae* 1, 92, 1). Papal teachings from Leo XIII to the present use the two natures model.

Those who follow the one nature anthropology regret the nuances given to the word *complementary* by those who hold the two natures anthropology. For the latter "complementary" involves patterns of domination and subordination (e.g., women should keep to their traditional roles as wives and mothers) or of superiority and inferiority (e.g., women are inferior; women are incapable of representing the male Christ at the altar). In short, the term "complementary" refers to women "completing" men by serving their needs and interests.

In 1960, when he was the auxiliary bishop of Krakow, Karol Wojtyla, the future John Paul II, published an important book, *Love and Responsibility*. In this book about marriage, the roles of men and women, and contraception, John Paul adheres to the two natures model. Knowing this fact helps the reader understand the pope's many messages to the church and society. For example, in *Familiaris consortio*, the apostolic exhortation issued to report on the Synod of 1980 on the family, it states that, although all women have a "right of access to public functions," it urges that society be "structured in such a way that wives and mothers are not in practice compelled to work outside the home." To this is added the statement: "true advancement of women requires that clear recognition be given to the value of their maternal and family role, by comparison with all other public roles and all other professions." The Vatican tends to see women's work outside the home as an unfortunate economic necessity. Feminists view such work as potentially a vocation in society.

On September 30, 1988, the pope released a 120-page apostolic letter entitled *Mulieris dignitatem* ("On the Dignity and Vocation of Women"). The pope made several points. First, his letter represents the strongest papal affirmation of women's moral equality. It called for the end to all discrimination against women in marriage and in the "different spheres of social life," going so far as to link prejudicial attitudes against women to sin. However, it warned women that their struggle for equality "must not under any condition lead to the masculinization of women." By this term the pope meant that "in the name of liberation from male domination, women must not appropriate to themselves male characteristics contrary to their own feminine 'originality'." According to John Paul and the two natures anthropology, women's resources are different from men. Women, he says, are more prophetic, sensitive, and loving than men. The pope fears that if women copy men, "they will not 'reach fulfillment' but instead will deform and lose what constitutes their essential richness."

Second, John Paul insisted that men and women are equal religiously because they are both created in the image of God. Both receive the "outpouring of divine truth and love in the holy Spirit." Christ, he said, consistently protested against whatever offended the dignity of women. Third, the pope urged women to accept Mary the mother of Jesus as their basic role model because her union with God is the definitive measure of every person's dignity and vocation. Mary is also the "eminent and singular exemplar of both virginity and motherhood." The latter are the "two dimensions of the female vocation." Fourth, John Paul reiterated the church's ban against women priests. He argued that Jesus' decision to choose male disciples was not, as some have held, the product of the social conditioning of his times but a freely-made decision. Consequently, at the Eucharist only a male priest can act in the person of Christ.

Many commentators praised the pope's strong affirmation of women's equality. Others faulted the letter's emphasis on the two dimensions of the female vocation as mother and consecrated virgins in imitation of Mary. This emphasis, they maintained, not only makes Mary so unique that she ceases to be an exemplar of Christian discipleship, but it also leaves out many women, including childless wives and single women. Some felt that the use of the two natures model tended toward sexual stereotypes by stressing traditional feminine qualities as exclusive to women. Others complained that the pope's explanation why Jesus decided to choose only male disciples as his priests disregards current biblical scholarship.

On July 10, 1995, John Paul released a "Letter to Women," a document that contains some positive comments about the feminist movement. He wrote the letter to "the heart and mind of every woman . . . as a sign of solidarity and gratitude on the eve of the [United Nations] Fourth World Conference on Women to be held in Beijing this coming September."

The pope paid tribute to women's often hidden role in making history, past and present. He began by profusely thanking women "present in every area of life" for their "contribution to the growth of a culture that unites reason and feeling." He affirmed the Genesis theme that men and women share equally in the task of responsibly transforming the earth. In this regard, he noted the specific "genius of women" not only in the spiritual and cultural sphere (called "primary" for women), but in the sociopolitical and socioeconomic spheres as well. He asks what can be done about "the obstacles which in so many parts of the world still keep women from being fully integrated into social, political and economic life. As far as personal rights are concerned, there is an urgent need to achieve real equality in every area: equal pay for equal work, protection for working mothers, fairness in career advancements, equality of spouses with regard to family rights and the recognition of everything that is part of the rights and duties of citizens in a democratic state."

The pope's letter was unprecedented in two ways (Redmont 1995). First, he acknowledged the sin of sexism and apologized to women for the church's historical complicity in denigrating and dehumanizing women. He wrote: "Unfortunately, we are heirs to a history which has conditioned us to a remarkable extent. In every time and place, this conditioning has been an obstacle to the progress of women. Women's dignity has often been unacknowledged and their prerogatives misrepresented; they have often been relegated to the margins of society and even reduced to servitude. This has prevented women from truly being themselves and it has resulted in a spiritual impoverishment of humanity."

Second, the pope recognized in the women's movement a positive contribution to human and social well-being. He expressed his personal "admiration for those women of good will who have devoted their lives to defending the dignity of womanhood by fighting for their basic social, economic and political rights, demonstrating courageous initiative at a time when this was considered extremely inappropriate, the sign of a lack of femininity, a manifestation of exhibitionism, and even a sin." He acknowledged that their journey "has been a difficult and complicated one . . . but it has been substantially a positive one, even if it is still unfinished . . . The journey must go on!"

In his letter the pope continued to use the two natures model of male and female relationships by insisting on a "complementary" diversity of roles for men and women that can never change. "Womanhood expresses the 'human' as much as manhood does, but in a different way . . . The presence of a certain diversity of roles is in no way prejudicial to women, provided that this is not the result of an arbitrary imposition, but is rather an expression of what is specific to being male and female." The pope's position aims at valuing women and securing special protections for them.

Those who favor the one nature model ask what are the roles specific to the "genius of women" and who defines them? Are not women kept subordinate and powerless by the roles society has determined for them. In Jane Redmont's commentary on John Paul's letter (1995), she states that it is "risky to base our theories and policies on 'the special gifts of women' or even 'the genius of women'. Better to follow John Paul's language on dignity. The rest, as the rabbis say, is commentary."

The United Nations Fourth World Conference on Women met in Beijing, September 4–15, 1995. Its theme was action for equality, development, and peace. More than forty thousand people—delegates, non-governmental organizations, and observers—from 189 nations assembled for the largest international conference in the history of the world.

The Vatican chose Mary Ann Glendon, a Harvard law professor, to lead its twenty-member delegation. This marked the first time that a woman was selected to head an official Vatican delegation. Glendon, a strong opponent of abortion, champions the rights of women and children involved in a divorce and also supports economic measures to help third world countries (Tagliabue 1995).

Before the conference, the Vatican attacked positions taken in preparatory meetings that promoted abortion, undermined the central place of the family, and ignored the God-given differences between women and men. According to the two natures model, the differences between men and women are natural and are not socially constructed. During the conference the Vatican took a less contentious approach to issues than it did at Cairo in 1994, when it dominated the talks. For example, the Vatican delegates dropped their active opposition to the use of condoms for the prevention of AIDS, knowing they could not fight a battle in which they were badly outnumbered (Faison 1995). Nonetheless, the Vatican was able to exert influence in three areas, namely, human rights, the family, and motherhood.

The conference's final document improved on Cairo by guaranteeing the same rights for women that have long been enjoyed by men. The key sentence in the final document states: "The human rights of women include their right to have control over and decide freely and responsibly on matters related to their sexuality, including sexual and reproductive health, free of coercion, discrimination and violence." The sentence originally began with the term "sexual rights," but was replaced with "human rights" because some delegates were uncomfortable with the term. The Vatican, for example, opposed the term "sexual rights" because it is an undefined term that could be read as including the right to be homosexual (Wooden 1995).

Regarding the family and motherhood, the Vatican delegates objected to the use of the word "families" in places where it could imply that any group of two or more individuals constitute a family, including a gay couple. They also complained that the document focused on the family only when it discussed situations that lead to the oppression of women, violence against them, and factors preventing their full involvement in political and economic activities. They urged that something be said about the positive role of families in the life of women. They argued that some militant feminists regard the family and motherhood as repressive, as an impediment to women's self-realization. The final document stated: "Women play a critical role in the family. The family is the basic unit of society and, as such, should be strengthened. It is entitled to receive comprehensive protection and support."

Regarding motherhood, the document declared: "Maternity, motherhood, parenting and the role of women in procreation must not be a basis for discrimination nor restrict the full participation of women in society." The document added that the media should depict women as "leaders who bring to their positions of leadership many different life experiences, including but not limited to their experiences of balancing work and family responsibilities, as mothers, as professionals, as managers and entrepreneurs, to provide role models, particularly to young women."

Laywomen, Ministry, and the Devotional Life of the Church

In the preconciliar period, ministry and the devotional life of the church were understood to be the exclusive preserve of the clergy. They were responsible for teaching, governing, and sanctifying the laity who accepted the ministrations of their priests in a spirit of obedience and resignation. In a word, ministry was synonymous with clerical power and authority. The ordained clergy and the baptized laity were quite distinct. The proper sphere of a priest's ministry was the church; the laity ministered to the world.

At Vatican II the bishops retrieved the church's biblical roots. They viewed ministry more in keeping with the New Testament understanding of service inasmuch as Jesus came to serve rather than to be served. In addition, a renewed theology of baptism led the bishops to teach that the laity had a legitimate responsibility for church ministry. Ministry is what ordinary Christians daily do in and for both the material and spiritual needs of society and the church. The laity were not to be ecclesial outsiders. The dualism of church and world was rejected. The ministry of both the clergy and the laity is in the church and in the world. The vocation of all Christians is to be *the* church *in* the world.

Because of the persistent pervasive presence of patriarchalism and sexism in society and the church, a spectrum of responses to the conciliar theology developed. Some women still felt so alienated that they no longer participated in the sacramental life of the church. Others lost hope in the institutional church and sadly walked away. Others, like the National Council of Catholic Women, rejected the presuppositions and goals of the Catholic feminists. A significant number chose a stance of loyal opposition, steadfastly maintaining active membership while demanding to be equal partners with the men in the church's ministry. We will see later that the United States bishops spent ten years—1982 to 1992—writing a pastoral letter to meet the institutional, intellectual, and devotional concerns of women. The project ended in failure. The bishops voted not to release their letter because they could not agree about what constitutes equality and full membership in the church's ministerial and devotional life. They could not articulate how baptism gives women a full share in Christ's threefold office of priest, prophet, and servant-king. Specifically, the bishops were not ready to address Catholic feminism because "Feminism may well be the most radical challenge ever to arise within the church. For while previous challenges pronounced judgment upon doctrines or practices by recourse to the original tradition, many feminists pronounce judgment upon the tradition itself" (Oliver 1985). Feminists reexamine every aspect of the church's life and faith, and reclaim their rightful place within this tradition.

The first public "shaking of the foundations" by Catholic feminists probably began with the first Women's Ordination Conference (WOC) held in Detroit, November 18–20, 1975. WOC was formed by Mary B. Lynch, a Catholic laywoman, who asked thirty-one of her friends in a 1974 Christmas message if the United Nations 1975 International Year of the Woman would be an appropriate time to discuss women's ordination. What was intended to be a one-time conference became a movement (Whelan 1985, 112).

When WOC met in Detroit, Elizabeth Carroll, a former mother general of the Religious Sister of Mercy, said in an address titled "'The Proper Place' of Women in the Church": "We are not the whole church nor do we claim to speak for the whole church. Some may even dispute our right to meet as a church at all, for we have not been called together by any official or our hierarchy. We would have welcomed such an invitation, but none has been forthcoming. Therefore, we speak our part of the dialogue publicly, unofficially, but nonetheless as church" (cited in M. Riley 1984).

The import and the theological significance of that insight has grown through the intervening years. It was raised again at the second meeting of WOC in Baltimore in November 1978. But perhaps the clearest expression of Catholic feminists' understanding of themselves as church and of their call to mission as church came at a conference held in Chicago, November 11–13, 1983. The full title of the conference was "From Generation to Generation Woman-Church Speaks." The conference was sponsored by eight member groups of the Women of the Church Coalition, a network of organizations working for the advancement of women in both church and society. Some of the participants were from WOC, NARW, and WATER (the Women's Alliance for Theology, Ethics and Ritual). The conference's title illustrated the theological development of the claim of Catholic feminists to be equally church, that is to say, a community redeemed from sin and death by Christ. The women gathered to identify their particular mission as church, a mission shaped by their particular experience of being women. Priestly ordination, while it remains, according to Maria Riley, a Dominican Sister, "the core symbol of exclusion of women at the heart of the church," was not the central issue for most of the women at the conference. "The central issue was patriarchal structures both in the church and in society and their legitimization by religious language, symbol, theology and institutions" (ibid.). Maureen Fiedler addressed this issue in her keynote address: "Authentic spirituality today calls us to work toward a world and a church where power is shared, not oppressive. That is *political and spiritual* work: these are not and cannot be separate spheres of life for Womanchurch" (cited in Weaver 1985, 187).

The conference attracted about fourteen hundred women, almost all Roman Catholic. Laywomen outnumbered the religious sisters, 59 percent to 41 percent. All present wanted to eliminate the dualism of lay and religious and to recognize their common call. "The women gathered represented women in ministry in diocesan and parish situations as well as women who no longer maintain clear links with the institutional church.

They were Hispanic, black and white, single, divorced, lesbian and community women. Some came with their children" (Riley 1984).

The term *Woman-Church* (which is also written as *Womenchurch* or *Women-Church*) calls for further explanation. It is a renewal group which organizes forums for exchanging stories of women's experiences, sharing spiritualities, celebrating liturgies, and identifying issues and resources for future empowerment. Rosemary Ruether explains that its source is the deep alienation many Christian women feel toward Christianity as a religion that fails to affirm them as women. The Christian churches do not allow women to use their leadership talents and do not respect their female humanity made in the image of God (1993).

It is not the intention of Womenchurch to cut themselves off from men or historical Christianity in order to form a distinct church. Their exodus is from patriarchy and not from the church. The church must be inclusive of men and women, for it points to the new humanity of men and women in the risen Christ. Womenchurch is a renewal group. They want historical Christianity to renounce its patriarchal ways and to include women (and other oppressed people) as equal partners. Women are leaving the church in growing numbers because it has become irrelevant to their lives. Consequently, equal partners, explains Ruether (1984), does not mean a token integration of women into a patriarchal church "nor a new appropriation of the traditional symbolism of the church as bride and mother." When men are called "sons of God," says Ruether, they relate to God as the ruling patriarch and "then think of the church collectively as like a dependent spouse in relationship to this great divine patriarch." Consequently, "the female symbolization of the church as bride and mother does not elevate women but rather enforces their dependency and subordination to males in the human counterpart of this divine-human patriarchal marriage." Womenchurch wants men to cease patronizing women by "including them in ministry only in token ways even as they maintain patriarchal institutions" (ibid.). Womenchurch, then, is not to be understood in exclusive, sectarian terms. "Rather, it is a hermeneutical feminist perspective and linguistic consciousness-raising tool that seeks to define theologically what church is all about" (Schüssler Fiorenza 1990).

The next Womenchurch conference was held in Cincinnati, October 9–11, 1987, the same month that the Synod of 1987 on the laity met in Rome. Sponsored by Women-Church Convergence, a coalition of twenty-six United States Catholic women's groups, it attracted almost three thousand Roman Catholics and dozens of Anglican, Protestant, and Jewish women from across the United States and from more than twenty countries around the world. Their theme was "Claiming Our Power." Speakers explained that women must take charge of their destinies by reclaiming their political, economic, spiritual, and sexual power.

The Synod of 1987 spoke of expanding the roles women have in the church. Womenchurch members signaled to a male church that they intended to "be" church their way and to "be" Catholic, too. They would not wait patiently while the hierarchy decides their roles. They spoke of reclaiming the best of the Catholic tradition, forging links with women of other faiths and nations, and building a new social order. In other words, their first priority is not to reform the patriarchal institution, but to be church, like the earliest Christian communities (Hansen 1987). In addition, they made it clear that the only one with power over them is God. From God came their authority, their vision which "is the sacramental equality within human relationships," and the courage and peace to focus their vision (K. Smith 1987).

By 1989 there were over one hundred liturgical Womenchurch communities in the United States alone. They meet in homes and on college campuses for regular worship, rituals, a meal, and to plan works of justice. They aim to keep alive the memory of the Christian church with which they exist in continuity (Ziegenhals 1989).

The third meeting of WOC was held in Arlington, Virginia, November 10–12, 1995. About one thousand participants, overwhelmingly females and most in their 50s and 60s, gathered to explore the agenda of the conference, "Discipleship of Equals: Breaking Bread, Doing Justice." This meeting marked the twentieth anniversary of WOC. It was filled with conflicting visions and goals. On one side, Womenchurch members, led by Elisabeth Schüssler Fiorenza, Krister Stendhal of Harvard Divinity School, and Diana Hayes of Georgetown University, presented a vision of church as a "discipleship of equals." In this church they declared there would be no priesthood and no hierarchy. They argued that feminism and Catholic priesthood are incompatible. Their goal is major deconstruction of clericalism, partriarchy, and hierarchy. They are wary of women seeking ordination within the present system without seeking significant structural changes in the way ministry is understood and practiced. According to Schüssler Fiorenza, "Ordination means subordination" as long as the Catholic church remains "an elite, male-dominated, sacred pyramidal order of domination" based on structures inherited from Roman imperialism (P. Steinfels 1995a).

On the other side, those led by Maureen Fiedler and Jeannine Gramick still envision the ordination of women—but their goal is an "ordination to a renewed priestly ministry" and not priesthood as we presently know it (Schaeffer 1995a). For them, securing the ordination of woman is the most revolutionary act they could do because "the celebration of the eucharistic sacrifice is the center and culmination of the entire life of the Christian community" (CD 30). This contingent also felt that Womenchurch had coopted WOC in three ways. First, they argued that, while the model of church as discipleship of equals reflects the Pauline churches, it is associated more with the radical wing of the Protestant Reformation and with movements like the Quakers rather than with Catholicism. Second, they noted that the structures of the discipleship model were ill-defined. It was also unclear how such a church could be achieved. Third, while they agreed with Womenchurch that women need to develop feminist symbols and rituals, they said that since Womenchurch often drawns its rituals and symbols from interdenominational and interfaith sources, they are often neither christocentric nor eucharistic.

This was not the first time Gramick and others challenged Womenchurch's christological and eucharistic spirituality. In 1993, just before the third Womenchurch Convergence Conference set for April 16–18 in Albuquerque, New Mexico, they objected to the conferences agenda because of its lack of christology and because a eucharistic liturgy celebrated by a male priest was not scheduled. Mary E. Hunt, cofounder with Diann Neu of WATER, gave this response about the Christian focus of the conference: "There is no question but that many women are not only dubious about christocentric theology, but there are also many who are bored by it. I would not discount the boredom factor" (Martinez 1993). During the conference she added: "We cannot back away from the relation between the [Womenchurch] movement and the Catholic or Christian tradition. . . . This weekend we have begged the question of Jesus. . . . It is premature to say whether Womenchurch will remain Christian in focus, but it is important to name its roots as such" (P. Steinfels 1993). Regarding the availability of Catholic Eucharist, Ruth Fitzpatrick, national coordinator of WOC, said the value of conferences such as Womenchurch is that women can experience women-led Eucharists. But, "if women want to go to churches, there are plenty of them" (ibid.).

Despite the major different approaches to spirituality, the mood of 1995 WOC meeting was festive. Many participants seemed content with the affirmation that each woman was free to follow her own convictions, and that WOC would support both ordination and a discipleship of equals.

Not all women's groups advocate a discipleship of equals or ordination of women. The National Council of Catholic Women, for example, often reflects the views of the American bishops. In their defense against the Equal Rights Amendment and against the ordination of women, they maintain the two natures model of human nature. Women are different from and complementary to men, that is, women are best suited to roles which serve and support men. Mothers are the primary parent and the support for male leadership (Conn 1987, 246).

Eileen Egan

Many intelligent and courageous women have worked for the mission of the church, ultimately becoming role models in their families, their parish, and among their friends. None of them are national figures. Nonetheless, there are some women with national stature, but they are only known to those who keep up with Catholic journals. One such woman is Eileen Egan. In 1996 the Catholic Relief Services established the Eileen Egan Journalism Award for Catholic newspapers that have educated "the people of the United States to fulfill their moral responsibilities in alleviating human suffering, removing its causes and promoting social justice in developing countries."

Eileen Egan was born the eldest of six children to an Irish couple in Wales in 1912. Her father was a timber man who propped up coal mines; her mother taught her ecumenism and nonviolence. The family emigrated to the United States in 1926, when Eileen was fourteen. She graduated from Cathedral High School and Hunter College in New York City. After both her parents died in the 1930s, she assumed responsibility for her brothers and sisters. She found work at the Catholic Relief Services in 1943, becoming the first layperson and the first woman on the staff. She labored for the next thirty-five years assisting projects or helping to develop new ones that sent non-sectarian humanitarian aid to needy parts of the globe.

In the 1960s she cofounded the American Pax Association, which became Pax Christi USA in 1972, a branch of the international peace organization. With Dorothy Day and nineteen other women, she lobbied bishops during the final session of Vatican II over peace and war concerns. They were able to get the bishops to condemn the indiscriminate bombing of civilians (GS 80). Later Egan worked closely with Mother Teresa of Calcutta, even writing her biography in 1985.

In summary, it is clear that women in many parts of the world have assumed many new pastoral roles in the postconciliar church: preaching, baptizing, officiating at weddings, attending the pastoral needs of the sick, distributing Eucharist, directing parish liturgy and social justice committees, and serving as associate pastors and administrators of priestless parishes. In the United States about 10 percent of the parishes are priestless. With the inevitable decline in the number of priests, many laywomen will continue to be deeply involved in the church's ministerial and devotional life.

Sisters in the Postconciliar Church

Technically speaking, *sisters* refers to women in active orders and *nuns* designates those in contemplative communities, perpetually enclosed. Here the words are used interchangeably because both the popular media and the sisters themselves use them as synonyms.

In the preconciliar church many sisters served overseas as missionaries. Most served at home through the education of children in Catholic parish schools, and in such social services as orphanages and hospitals. Whether abroad or at home, their lifestyle was monastic. When not directly working at their apostolate, they were separated from the world behind their convent walls (cloisters) where they were dependant upon and subordinate to the hierarchical and patriarchal church. For example, they imported their liturgists, spiritual directors, confessors, retreat masters, and in some cases their rule of life from the male church. Many had masculine names, such as Sister Mary Paul or Sister Mary Jeremy. Their clothing was distinctive. Originally, their "religious habit" reflected the ordinary style of clothing worn by women at the time their community came into existence. With the passage of time and styles, their habits became their distinctive uniform. Their one uniform habit served as their communal, social, professional, and recreational attire. Their rule of life involved silence, study, and prayer. All were expected to obey the orders of the superior of the house.

Not all the sisters were happy with these conditions. For instance, in 1956, six years before Vatican II, the superiors of women's religious communities in the United States formed the Conference of Major Superiors of Women. Their goals were to articulate a theology of religious life, to educate themselves and others for justice, to study, pray, and act on behalf of women, to develop leadership, and to meet with other groups who could assist them in their mission.

Vatican II treated the theology of the religious life in *Lumen gentium* (nn. 31, 43–47) and produced a separate document titled "Decree on the Appropriate Renewal of Religious Life" *(Perfectae caritatis)*. This decree of twenty-five articles underwent five revisions before being finally approved on October 28, 1965 (Vorgrimler 1969, 2:301–32). None of the eleven sisters present as official auditors were on the commission, "and they were the superiors who were expected to implement the changes being legislated" (McEnroy 1996, 169).

The conciliar discussions focused on two polarized positions. One side, represented by Roman bishops and leaders of religious communities opposed to changing their longstanding and clearly defined lifestyle, understood religious life in traditional and clearly articulated terms as a "state of perfection." This view, found in the ascetical theology of Thomas Aquinas and the 1917 Code of Canon Law, holds that religious are called to a life of asceticism and the strict observance of juridically defined vows of poverty, chastity, and obedience. The other side represented the ideas of progressive bishops and leaders of religious congregations who were feeling their way toward a way of life "which stressed freedom, diversity and effective service to the contemporary world" (Schneiders 1991, 157). *Perfectae caritatis* did not elaborate on these different theologies. Rather, it concentrated on the basic principles of appropriate renewal. The bishops instructed all religious communities of women and men to renew their communities in two interrelated ways: by returning to the gospel and the original inspiration (charism) behind their community and by adjusting their community's lifestyle to the changed conditions of the times (PC 2). Consequently, religious communities rewrote their constitutions (the rules by which the community is governed) through delegates elected to a general chapter, the highest decision-making level of the community. Once the general chapter approved the constitutions, they were submitted for approval to the Vatican curial office titled the Sacred Congregation for Religious and Secular Institutes (SCRIS).

Before rewriting their constitutions, women religious spent years discerning new responses to the needs and signs of the times. They revised their constitutions only after testing and evaluating their postconciliar experiences within their own membership and after consulting with such resource persons as theologians, canon lawyers, and those they served. While going through the renewal and reform process, the sisters took more control over their lives. They began to stress democracy, femininity, and shared power and experience.

Many were in the forefront of both the feminist and the ordination movements. While many personally recommitted themselves to their community's life and mission, many others withdrew for a combination of institutional, theological, social, and political reasons. Some withdrew en masse. For example, in 1965, one hundred Glenmary Sisters in Cincinnati and in 1968, four hundred Immaculate Heart of Mary Sisters in Los Angeles chose to redefine themselves as noncanonical communities of laywomen. They made these daring, radical, yet painful decisions because their archbishops ordered them to retract the reforms approved by their general chapters and to return to some of their preconciliar religious practices (Whelan 1985, 92–94). This change of status gave them, they said, "the freedom to be self-determining and to make moral choices on the basis of conscience without leaning on the authority of others" (McEnroy 1996, 250). When John XXIII opened Vatican II in 1962, there were approximately 173,000 sisters in the United States; in 1996 there were approximately 89,000 (Tripole 1996). In 1982 the median age of the nuns was fifty-nine; in 1996, it was sixty-eight.

For many sisters, religion became embodied in the struggles and opportunities of life in society. Many communities modified their religious habit. (Mary Luke Tobin was hissed by some Italian nuns when she walked into the conciliar assembly for the first time in a modern, short-skirted habit). Others opted to dress in contemporary clothing because they considered their religious habit an anachronism and an impediment to their work in today's society. Many left the schools. In 1966, 64 percent of sisters were in school education; in 1982 only 29 percent served in schools. They left the schools for a couple of reasons. Some believed that since the education of the poor was being handled by the public school system, they were no longer needed; others withdrew because they no longer viewed themselves as agents of the institutional church but persons dedicated to serving the Catholic faithful and to changing the structures of society. Many sisters placed themselves on the margins of society in order to challenge its limitations and deficiences, and to serve at the most critical points where justice, love, and truth are threatened. Accordingly, many took up nontraditional work like prison ministry, associate pastor of parishes, lobbyists for the poor, and in the political arena as mayors and state congresspersons.

For some the experience of getting SCRIS's approval of their renewed constitutions worked out smoothly; for others it was painful and full of anguish. Some religious communities could document the long history of violence, nonsupport, unfounded accusations and attacks, and unilateral decisions imposed. One sister who had served as head of her international community compared herself in a long essay to a battered woman. And, as is frequently the case with battered wives, the author asked for anonymity. Her opening paragraph states: "An important fact unknown to many within the church is that superiors of religious orders in the United States are, in many cases, battered women in the church. The form of violence is not as blatant as it is in some marriages, but the physical and mental anguish is strikingly similar. The parallels to domestic violence are unmistakable; the reasons for the silence are identical. But the silence must be broken so all in the church can participate in the ministry of justice, reconciliation and conversion" (Anonymous 1984).

Religious sisters encountered these difficulties because SCRIS made it clear that its view of religious life is quite different from that of the new nuns. In a document titled "Essential Elements in the Church's Teaching on Religious Life," issued on May 31, 1983, SCRIS returned to a preconciliar view of religious life. The document declared that "religious life" is set apart from the world, lived in "canonically erected" communities, distinguished by "religious garb" and presided over by a superior. Woven through the document were the themes of dependence, authority, obedience, and surrender. For SCRIS, religious life cannot be lived "in the world."

Some communities welcomed the Vatican's intervention but others were not convinced. For them religion is embodied precisely in the tensions and opportunities of daily existence in society. Consequently, they rejected the Vatican's claim to ultimate power over them and to its efforts to curtail their new identity and their new apostolic works.

On May 11, 1983, twenty days before the SCRIS document was promulgated, Agnes Mary Mansour, a Religious Sister of Mercy for thirty years, resigned from her community. Her story exemplifies the conflict between SCRIS and many American sisters. Her case—too complicated to detail here—raised many questions not only about religious life but also about such issues as due process, justice, theology, collegiality, subsidiarity, and abortion (Kolbenschlag 1983).

Mansour was appointed in December 1982 to head the Michigan Department of Social Services. She had the approval of her community and the archbishop of Detroit. However, since her position involved providing funds for abortions for poor women who qualified under Medicaid, anti-abortion groups bombarded Mansour and the archbishop with letters and threatened boycotts. On February 23, 1983, the archbishop suddenly announced his objection to Mansour's appointment and called for her resignation.

Mansour's views on abortion and state aid were well known long before her appointment. She had clearly stated her personal opposition to abortion but added that as long as abortion remains legal, she had no right to cut off Medicaid funding for abortions.

Mansour, her community, government officials, the archbishop, and the Vatican were soon entangled in a series of letters and phone conversations. In April Mansour attempted to ameliorate the situation by requesting a leave of absence from her community. The community granted her request, but it was denied by the Vatican. On May 9, Mansour was faced with an ultimatum directly from the pope: resign her political post or be dismissed from her religious community. So far as Rome was concerned, the crux of this case was that Mansour was a woman religious. She was told that her "ecclesial identity" required that she adhere strictly to magisterial teaching. Mary Jo Weaver (1985, 98) pointed out that what rankled the Vatican "was the fact that the position was taken publicly by a woman." Mansour's predecessor in the Michigan post, a Catholic layman, was never harassed regarding his appointment and policies.

On October 7, 1979, during the first visit of John Paul II to the United States, Theresa Kane, administrator general of the Sisters of Mercy of the Union in the United States, president of the LCWR, and later a firm defender of Agnes Mary Mansour, respectfully addressed the pope before his speech to five thousand women religious assembled at the National Shrine of the Immaculate Conception in Washington, D.C. She said, in part: "As women we have heard the powerful message of our church addressing the dignity and reverence for all persons. As women we have pondered these words. Our contemplation leads us to state that the church in its struggle to be faithful to its call for reverence and dignity for all persons must respond by providing the possibility of women as persons being included in all ministries of the church."

The applause for these words was thunderous. The pope did not respond to Theresa Kane's challenging words even when she went to him, kneeled and kissed his ring as a sign of her deep loyalty in spite of their differences. Within a few days Theresa Kane received many letters of support. One commentator said, "The incident with Sister Kane was so important because it was the only time he heard anything other than adulation" (Hyer 1979, 7). On the other hand, other sisters, believing that Sister Kane had overstepped her boundaries, disavowed any connection with "the public rudeness" shown the pope (Weaver 1985, 86).

During October 2–29, 1994, 224 bishops and other delegates assembled in Rome for the eleventh international synod, the Synod of 1994 on the consecrated life. The full title was "The Consecrated Life and Its Role in the Church and the World." The bishops discussed many aspects of the religious life such as the directions it had taken since Vatican II, the radical decline in membership, the impact of religious orders on culture, the continued importance of contemplative and monastic life for the identity and mission of the church, and even the term "consecrated life." Some commentators stated that "consecrated life" links "the religious life to a kind of sacramental order rather than to baptism and the role of the laity. The problem is also that the phrase seems not to include the central aspect of mission" (Torrens 1994).

During the synod, women religious received lavish praise from many speakers. The women, however, were not pleased with either their assigned role during the synod or some of its conclusions. Although three-quarters of the religious in the global church are women, only fifty-nine women attended in an official capacity—but only as auditors or consulting members. On the other hand, twenty religious priests attended as voting members. The women religious appealed to the bishops for greater participation in administrative roles in the church. The bishops agreed, but at the end of the synod excluded them from the highest ranks of decision making. The bishops declared that "consecrated women should participate more in the church's consultations and decision making, as situations require" (Cowell 1994c). In protest, several nuns representing the National Coalition of American Nuns demonstrated in St. Peter's square. They carried banners with these words: "They are talking about us without us" and "Women want to be a part, not apart" (Drozdiak 1994; Vidulich 1994). The bishops and the sisters were following two distinctly different and opposing models of authority based on different ecclesiologies: one is hierarchical, the other is the discipleship of equals.

On March 25, 1996, the pope issued *Vita consecrata*, a 208-page apostolic exhortation in response to the Synod of 1994. The document highlighted the power of the vows of poverty, chastity, and obedience to challenge modern forms of selfishness and materialism. Knowing that two-thirds of the church's estimated one million consecrated members are women, John Paul expressed "the gratitude and admiration of the whole church" for their dedicated lives, prayer, and work. He acknowledged that the equality and rights of women are not fully recognized in the church and society. He called for greater involvement of religious women in decision making, "above all in matters that concern women themselves." The pope also "strongly recommended" that women and men religious "wear their proper habit, suitably adapted to the conditions of time and place" (Wooden 1996).

Mother Teresa of Calcutta (1910-97)

The most famous nun in the postconciliar church was Mother Teresa, a simple Christian woman with common sense and uncommon faith. One reason she became a symbol of devotion to the sick, dying, and the poor is that she had received several prestigious awards. For example, in 1972 John M. Templeton, a Tennessee-born multimillionaire who became a British citizen, decided to create a monetary award equivalent in the field of religion to the Nobel prizes for peace, science, and literature. Mother Teresa was the first recipient of the Templeton Prize for Progress in Religion. In 1979, she was awarded the Nobel Peace Prize. People wondered why a woman who took care of the sick and dying should receive this prize. The Nobel committee declared that, in an age capable of nuclear destruction, Mother Teresa manifested that true peace rests on the utter inviolability of all human life and the need to nurture it by works of mercy. In awarding the prize the committee asserted that they had posed a focal question that humans encounter as they attempt to build bridges across the great gulfs that separate parts of the human family. They asked: "Can any political, social or intellectual feat of engineering, on the international or on the national plane, however effective and rational, however idealistic and principled its protagonists may be, give us anything but a house built on a foundation of sand, unless the spirit of Mother Teresa inspires the builders and takes its dwelling in their building?" (cited in Egan 1980). On October 1, 1996, President Bill Clinton signed a resolution conferring honorary citizenship on Mother Teresa as "a special expression of love and respect and appreciation for contributions to this country." This honor has been granted only three other times.

Mother Teresa was born Agnes Gonxha Bojaxhiu, daughter of an Albanian grocer, at Skopje, in the former Yugoslavia, on August 27, 1910. She joined the Loretto Sisters of Ireland at the age of seventeen, studied in England, and, as Sister Teresa, was assigned in 1929 to a convent school in Calcutta. There she taught with energy and dedication for seventeen years. But everything changed on September 10, 1946. On that day she felt a powerful "call within a call," as she put it, to serve the poor and the dying in the city's slums while living among them. She realized that God no longer wanted her "in her Loretto convent with its pleasant garden, eager schoolgirls, congenial colleagues and rewarding work" (Muggeridge 1971, 19). With permission from Rome, she withdrew from her community and made India her adopted land. Her work with the poor, sick, and dying soon attracted other women to her side. They formed the Missionaries of Charity in 1950.

Teresa and her sisters wear the white cotton sari of the poor Indian women, but with a distinctive blue trim. They take the traditional three vows of voluntary poverty, chastity, and obedience. In addition, they take a vow to provide "wholehearted, free service to the poorest of the poor." Since they live like and with the poor, their lifestyle is quite ascetical. They strive to create and maintain a pleasant community life. They have a lot of togetherness, but their "community is not based on togetherness.

It is based on rule. The ideals of the Missionaries of Charity are set forth in a clearly worded rule, and this rule is proposed for unqualified acceptance to any would-be member" (Swetnam 1979).

Since 1950 the Missionaries of Charity have had a worldwide growth, something astonishing at a time when most communities of sisters are declining in numbers, have a limited number of new recruits, are aging, have financial problems, and are unable to fulfill their mission. In 1997, Mother Teresa's community had over four thousand sisters and four hundred brothers serving in more than one hundred countries (Burns 1997). They go where there is the greatest need and the greatest suffering. They care for lepers, the poor, the sick, including patients with AIDS, the elderly, and the dying. They opened their first foundation in the United States in 1971 in the Bronx in New York City.

Mother Teresa was very attached to the official church's doctrinal teachings and devotional practices. She was most firm in her opposition to women priests, abortion, sterilization, and contraceptive birth control. The only family-planning program she accepted was the rhythm method. From time to time she represented the Vatican. For example, she was a delegate to the Congress of the International Women's Year in Mexico City in 1975.

One criticism of Mother Teresa is that she was not involved with the structures that cause poverty (Jennings 1981). She alleviated suffering but was not concerned with the long-range correction and elimination of the causes of social injustice, disease, and death. Her approach was quite different from her very good friend, Dorothy Day, who combined works of mercy with very strong challenges to the social and political structures of society. She was also very different from many American sisters who are involved in support of such causes as civil rights and women's rights, reform of the judicial system, and protests against defense spending, the death penalty, and third world dictatorships. When Mother Teresa was asked if she ever sought government intervention to help her with her work with the outcasts of society, she firmly replied: "I am not a social worker. I am called to help the individual, to love each person—not to deal with institutions" (ibid.). Similarly, when asked why she did not seek to change the structures of society, she stated: "If there are people who feel God wants them to change the structures of society, that is something between them and their God. We must serve him in whatever way we are called. I am called to help the individual; to love each poor person, not to deal with institutions" (Egan 1990).

Mother Teresa was commended because she had completely enculturated herself in her adopted country: she took Indian citizenship in 1950 and spoke Bengali and Hindu fluently. In India she was called Ma Teresa. "Ma," meaning mother, is a reminder of the way the goddess Kali is addressed, "Kali Ma" or "Mother Kali." "From the beginning of her work with the destitute dying, Mother Teresa has been connected in the public mind with Mother Kali, goddess of death, destruction and purification, from whom Calcutta (Kalikata) takes its name. By a strange providence, the city fathers of Calcutta gave the Missionaries of Charity the Pilgrim's Hostel adjoining Kali's shrine as a shelter for those found dying in gutters and alleyways" (ibid.).

Mother Teresa was also countercultural. From time to time she was dragged into the tensions between Hindus and Christians sparked by allegations that Christians have desecrated Hindu shrines or by charges that Christians attempted to convert Hindus. One of India's highest-ranking Hindu priests publicly charged that Mother Teresa was "cleverly converting Hindus" to Christianity.[2] There is no evidence that Mother Teresa tried to convert or surreptitiously baptize those who were dying. She did explain the differences between Hinduism and Christianity. For example, for Hindus the undergirding of living, suffering, and death is karma, the law of cause and effect in the moral world. Mother Teresa challenged karma. She taught that the suffering and dying are not living out their karma. Rather, they need loving care because they are other Christs. For Hindus death is a time of pollution. Mother Teresa surrounded death with dignity, that is, her patients were treated as human persons and not as detritus. When the people heard of Christ's cruel death, they wondered what awful thing he had done. She explained that Christ's death is part of the incarnation and a model of innocent suffering. Is there any wonder why this plainspoken and humble woman became an icon of Christianity throughout the world?

Due to health problems, Mother Teresa stepped down at the age of eighty-six as head of her community on March 13, 1997. She was succeeded by Sister Nirmala Joshi, a member of the Brahmin class who converted to Christ and his church at the age of twenty-four. Sister Nirmala earned a master's degree in political science and studied law before opening a mission in Panama, her community's first mission outside India. In view of her age, piety, education, and international experience, Sister Nirmala appears eminently suited to lead her community.

Mother Teresa died on September 5, 1997. Many, many tributes of love, appreciation, and respect were paid to this honest, faithful, and prayerful woman.

A fitting conclusion to this section on women religious is found in the writings of Sandra Schneiders, author of many articles and books on the religious life. She believes (1986, 11) that as a group, women religious (and those assimilated to them educationally and culturally) are the most creative element in the Catholic church today. They are theologically educated, have a variety of professional skills, have a wide experience of ministry in the global and world church, and have been the most enthusiatic about implementing the reforms of Vatican II in daily life.

According to Schneiders (1991, 161), religious communities of women offer their members "a challenging invitation to follow Christ in evangelical solidarity with the poor and in the company of companions who, in response to a personal call to consecrated celibacy, are committed to the evangelical transformation of the world through prophetic witness and action."

Women, Theology, and the Intellectual Life of the Church

In the preconciliar church many sisters' communities administered and staffed colleges for women. These sisters, if not the forerunners of the feminist movement in the church, served as models for those women who wanted intellectual freedom, independence, and a chance to achieve equal status in the church and society. In 1997 almost 100 of the nation's 237 four-year Catholic colleges and universities are administered by sisters.

In the preconciliar church theologians were with very few exceptions clerics. There were no women in theology. In the postconciliar church women theologians abound. Why this dramatic change? There are several interrelated reasons. First, the conciliar bishops declared that "it is very important that [women's] participation in the various sectors of the church's apostolate should develop" (AA 9). Second, Vatican II's sixteen documents called for radical changes in the church's institutional, devotional, and intellectual life. Faithful Catholics wanted to know the basis for this renewal and reform. Third, since all Catholics had been brought up in the neoscholastic theology and spirituality of the preconciliar church, many realized that they were spiritually unformed and theologically undereducated for the new tasks at hand. To meet these apostolic, intellectual, and spiritual needs, new graduate programs in theology and religious education sprang up in colleges and universities, and almost all admitted women. Within a few years even some seminaries began to admit laypersons, men and women, motivated in part by the desire to stay open, as the number of candidates for the priesthood dwindled.

Today women theologians work in Catholic seminaries, colleges, and universities, in parishes and dioceses. They work also in ecumenical and Protestant seminaries and universities, publishing houses, and elsewhere. Many have published. In March 1971, Josephine Massingberd Ford, professor at the University of Notre Dame, was the first woman to publish in *Theological Studies*, an influential theological journal founded in 1940. Her article on the biblical understanding of speaking in tongues was followed the next year by an essay by Rosemary Ruether (1972) titled, "Paradoxes of Human Hope: The Messianic Horizon of Church and Society." Today the books and research by women theologians enhance every respectable theological library. In 1965 women theologians started joining the Catholic Theological Society of America, which was founded in 1946. The first woman to address the convention was Agnes Cunningham, a Sister of Saints Cyril and Methodius, who lectured in 1969 on "The Role of Women in Church and Society." Six women have served as presidents of that society: Agnes Cunningham in 1977, Monika Hellwig in 1986, Ann E. Patrick in 1989, Lisa Sowle Cahill in 1992, Elizabeth Johnson in 1996, and Mary Ann Donovan in 1997.

In the United States most of the women theologians are white. In the past two decades some tensions have developed between some white and black theologians because some black theologians questioned giving priority to women's rights when racism, classism, and sexism are so inseparable from issues of human rights (Conn 1991). The black theologians use the term *womanist* to denote a black Christian feminist or feminist of color. The term is borrowed from the writings of the noted novelist, Alice Walker. She uses the term *womanish* to refer to "a black feminist or feminist of color." Womanish also means to act like a woman, as opposed to girlish, that is to act in a frivolous and irresponsible manner. As used by Catholic African-American women scholars, womanists try to achieve three goals: to identify a critical posture toward sexism and the dominant patriarchal culture, to call attention to the abuse of black women in the family, academy, and church, and to signal to other theologians the ways in which black women's experience has been ignored or rendered invisible in other theologies (D. Williams 1996).

Theology is faith or religious experience seeking understanding. When theologians use "the method of correlation," they critically connect or correlate the basic Christian experience of the life, death, and resurrection of Jesus found in the Christian scriptures with contemporary human experience and language. Once women studied theology, they raised new questions, questions that threatened the existing theological horizons. For example, how can the Bible function normatively for Christians, especially women, once its patriarchal and androcentric content has been identified?

Theology from the perspective of women is called feminist theology. It is participation in and critical reflection upon the Christian faith by persons (women and men) who are aware of the historical, political, and cultural restriction of women and who intend to retrieve the Christian faith in such a way that it promotes mutuality and equality. Feminist theology is a liberation theology. According to Joann Wolski Conn, it offers a radical critique of traditional Christian perspectives. "Christian feminist theologians admit from the outset that their tradition is relentlessly patriarchal in language, custom, practice, symbolism, memory, history, theological articulation, and ritual" (1987, 249). "It is this experience of a patriarchal religious world that feminist theologians evaluate in a comprehensive project that calls for a complete transformation of theology from within. What feminist theology wants is a total conversion of theology" (Conn 1991).

While most feminist theologians would accept the description of feminist theology just outlined, they approach the tradition from quite different perspectives. In a seminal essay in 1991, M. Francis Mannion identified "five types of church-related feminism operating" in the Catholic church.[3] He acknowledges that "as with all such schemes, it is necessary to keep in mind their limitations and conceptual impairments. The five types of feminism are best understood as colors in a rainbow. It is clear that the types overlap and flow into each other at the edges and that there is considerable diversity within each type."

First, some feminists are "separatists." They judge the tradition to be so intrinsically sexist that it cannot be reformed. Mary Daly, a pioneer feminist theologian who teaches at Boston College, took this approach in her first book, *The Church and the Second Sex* (1968), a book that marked the beginning of modern Catholic feminism. In her second book, *Beyond God the Father: Toward a Philosophy of Women's Liberation* (1973), she connected to the tradition by offering theological arguments for a process God, for dynamic revelation, and for non-patriarchal language about God. According to Daly, the male symbols of God, Savior, and Trinity, and the "procession of a divine son from a divine father" are not adequate symbols for women (Carr 1982, 279–82). Since the publication of those two books, Daly's subsequent works have challenged her readers to choose between a radical feminism that creates an all-feminine Utopia and the Christian community. Daly clearly continues to be connected to and concerned with Christian ideas, institutions, and influences, even if in a fundamentally negative way.

Other feminists believe that Daly's radical approach only reinstates the divisive dualisms they have been attempting to overcome. Schüssler Fiorenza wrote that in the late 1970s she was searching for a positive alternative to the exodus image found in the writings of Mary Daly and others. This "image tends to engender the illusion that women can move out of the bondage of patriarchy into a 'promised land' or feminist 'other world.' Yet no space exists—not even in our own minds—that is a 'liberated zone' to which we could move. Whereas some privileged women could move out of patriarchal institutions, most of us could not." Rather than engage in the illusion of exodus, Schüssler Fiorenza (1990) believes that feminist theologians need to struggle in the church as church to make the church a community of disciples equal in dignity and mission. Similarly, other Catholic feminists argue that both historically and in the present, the Christian symbols of God, Jesus, sin, salvation, the church, and the Paraclete-Spirit have been life-giving and liberating for women (Ruether and McLaughlin 1979).

A second type of Christian feminism is "reconstructive." Their position is exemplified by Schüssler Fiorenza and Ruether. They want to reconstruct the tradition in order to change its direction and open it to the influence of women's experience (Conn 1987, 250). They want to dismantle and restructure the church in order to recreate new religious communities that are egalitarian and non-hierarchical. They believe the church can only be redeemed from its sexist, racist, and classist thinking by something approaching a revolution.

Rosemary Ruether, a specialist in the classics of early Christian writers, is the most prolific writer in the Catholic feminist movement. Her work is wide-ranging. She has written about abortion, birth control, christology, Jewish-Christian dialogues, Vatican II and its aftermath, liberation theology, and many other issues. Social sin "has been a catalyst for her thinking and writing" (Conn 1987, 251). She believes that feminism, like biblical prophecy, is based on conversion and repentance as well as a commitment to both justice and authentic human life. In *The Radical Kingdom* in 1970 she raises critical questions on the very first page that she continues to grapple with in later books and articles. She wanted to know "in what sense does Christianity have a gospel of revolution, a gospel of radical reform of the human community in history? What is really meant by the suggestion that the gospel is a sociopolitical message?" In *Religion and Sexism* in 1974 she summarized feminist issues at a time when very few people understood the dimensions of the problem of women in the church. She explained how the sources of Christianity are characterized by hostility, denigration, and even romantic mystification of women (Conn 1991). In *New Women New Earth: Sexist Ideologies and Human Liberation* in 1975, she shows the pervasiveness of sexism infecting issues such as racism, anti-Semitism, religion, and even psychoanalysis and ecology. *Sexism and God-Talk: Toward a Feminist Theology* is a work of systematic theology. In this 1983 book, she deconstructs traditional categories such as sin and redemption and reconstructs theology from a feminist perspective. She begins with women's experiences. Her thesis is that "the critical principle of feminist theology is the promotion of the full humanity of women. Whatever denies, diminishes, or distorts the full humanity is, therefore, apprised as not redemptive (1983, 18).

Elizabeth Schüssler Fiorenza, a specialist in New Testament studies, made her mark in 1983 with *In Memory of Her: A Feminist Theological Reconstruction of Christian Origins*. The subtitle accurately describes the purpose and scope of her book. She argues that a radically egalitarian interpretative framework is the only one that can do justice to the scriptural portrayal of Jesus' life, teachings, and the early Christian missionary movement. She traces and makes historically visible the visions and countercultural struggles of the early Christian women and men in a patriarchal world. She seeks to reconstruct the points of tension between the patriarchal Greco-Roman society and the Christian community. She explains historically and theologically how and why both the discipleship of equals and the patriarchal male pyramid of subordination had become constitutive of Christian identity throughout the centuries. She not only demonstrates how God is on the side of the oppressed but she also insists that the Christian tradition is not inherently or necessarily sexist. Patriarchy did not originate with Christianity but has been mediated by it. A new interpretive paradigm (i.e., that men and women are equal) can be used, she argues, to reconstruct the ancient traditions and contemporary church life and practice. Consequently, she resists two groups: those who reject the biblical tradition and those who judge a feminist reconstruction of the New Testament churches to be eccentric or marginal.

Mannion also includes in this group Sandra Schneiders, the Womenchurch movement, WATER, the National Coalition of American Nuns, and NARW.

The third type of feminists Mannion calls "affirmative." He relates them to the conservative varieties of feminism in American society. He has in mind people like Phyllis Schlafly, one of the leaders who campaigned against the Equal Rights Amendment in the 1970s. This group—and many question whether their view can be called feminism—is for the most part skeptical of the modern women's movement. They regard it as harmful to the traditional understanding of women, marriage, the family and motherhood. Women, they say, should not be forced into employment outside the home. Some Catholic feminists espouse these views, especially since their position is quite similar to the official church's traditional view of women. Like the official church, they affirm the complementarity of men and women in church and in society. For example, during the debates over the ERA, some women lamented "the striking absence of the American bishops from the growing coalition of those who recognized the justice of the woman's cause and urge the ratification of the ERA" (Burke 1975). "Affirmative feminism" opposes women's ordination, is strongly anti-abortion, is not enthusiastic about altar girls, recoils at the entry of women into traditional male leadership roles, prefers that married women commit themselves primarily to the home and to the church in an auxiliary way, and holds that religious women should restrict their roles to the traditional ones of teaching, nursing, and service of the poor. Janet E. Smith, the Catholic Daughters of America, and the Institute on Religious Life would be representative of this group.

Fourth, some feminists are "corrective." They espouse a deep respect for the Catholic tradition, Catholic culture, and family life, but they want things changed and corrected. They criticize the abuses heaped on women throughout history. In keeping with the directions set forth by Vatican II, they want women to exercise their role in the modern world and to be included more fully in the life and leadership of the church. They favor ecclesiastical roles for women as long as these do not entail any major changes in the fundamental institutions and doctrines of the church, such as the ordination of women as priests. They welcome women in other liturgical ministries, as theologians, and in leadership roles in diocesan administration and parish ministry. Some feminist theologians who reflect these corrective ideas are Sara Butler of Mundelein Seminary in Illinois and Agnes Cunningham. Mannion also includes the National Council of Catholic Women, many American bishops, and Raymond Brown. The latter "seems cautiously open to women's ordination," but, in general, is "of a corrective outlook on matters of church and ministry" (Mannion 1991).

The fifth group is "reformist." They are "very much a product of the mainstream American feminism . . . that developed in the 1960s" (ibid.). These feminists focus on gaining equal rights and gender-uninhibited status for women within the sociopolitical and socioeconomic spheres. They aspire to secure for women the ideals of historical consciousness: freedom, autonomy, and self-determination. This group attracts very many United States Catholics. They see "the need to reshape the fundamental structures and doctrines of the church to allow for the participation of women in all ecclesiastical roles, including ordained ministry. While there remains a strong commitment to the traditional strengths of Catholicism, particularly its sacramental, communitarian and incarnational characteristics, there is also an emphasis on the need for a less hierarchical and more democratic ecclesial style, a less centralized and authoritarian organization and a greater acceptance of pluralism and local autonomy. Gender-inclusive 'vertical' God-language is freely used and encouraged in this approach" (ibid.).

Among Catholic women scholars, the following exemplify this outlook: Denise Carmody, Dolores Leckey, and Monika Hellwig. Male scholars who explicitly support this agenda include Karl Rahner (1977), Leonard Swidler (1979) and Richard McBrien (1992, 113–35). They also receive support from the CTSA, the National Federation of Priests' Councils, some American bishops, and the LCWR, which represents more than 90 percent of the country's religious sisters.

Catholic women theologians have won respect in every branch of theology: in biblical studies, dogmatics, morality, spirituality, church history, canon law, and so forth. It is not possible to identify all of them here or to compare them to their mainstream and evangelical Protestant counterparts. But it needs to be pointed out that not all of them sailed smoothly into their academic and ecclesial careers. For example, Mary Daly faced a lot of opposition after she became the first woman to join the theology faculty at Boston College in 1966. In 1969 she was given a terminal contract, but following protests from both students and faculty, the university changed its mind and granted her tenure. Her first bid for full professorship was denied without explanation in 1975, and the university later denied her second request for such status, which brings with it a greater salary and increased academic prestige. Ultimately, she became a full professor. Another theologian, Marjorie Reiley Maguire, related in 1982 her struggles to be hired by Marquette University. Reluctantly, she went so far as to file federal discrimination complaints and legal suits to achieve her goal.

Back in 1982, Ann Carr, a Blessed Virgin Mary sister, wrote an essay titled "Is a Christian Feminist Theology Possible?" She finished with a comprehensive conclusion that still makes sense of our situation in the late 1990s:

> Women's religious protest and affirmation is a grace for our times. In its protest about the clear and real issues of women, it raises to view the scandal of the past and its confident, even idolatrous assertions about God and Christ and human persons. In its courageous iconoclasm and its symbolic association with the other 'others' of history and the present, it exposes and denies the splits, dichotomies, manipulation, and exploitation— the sin of our times from a particular and practical perspective. In its new apprehension of God and of Christ, it affirms a vision of human wholeness, integrity, and community, a genuinely new Christian consciousness that extends inclusion, mutuality, reciprocity, and service beyond its own causes. In so doing, Christian feminism transcends itself and enables the tradition to transcend itself, to become the hope, the future, that is promised (Carr 1982, 296–97).

Women and Jurisdiction in the Institutional Church

Before Vatican II a well-worn cynical expression described the functions of the laity: "to pray, pay, and obey." The proper ministry of the clergy was within the church; the ministry of the laity in society. Vatican II did away with this defective theology by highlighting that all Catholics were responsible for both the life and mission of the church and the common good of society. The bishops wrote that "Priests are to be sincere in their appreciation and promotion of lay people's dignity and of the special role the laity have to play in the church's mission. . . . Priests should confidently entrust to the laity duties in the service of the church, giving them freedom and opportunity for activity and even inviting them, when opportunity offers, to undertake projects on their own initiative" (PO 9). In addition, "Bishops, parish priests and other priests . . . will remember that the right and duty of exercising the apostolate are common to all the faithful, whether clerics or lay; and that in the building up of the church the laity too have parts of their own to play" (AA 25).

Despite these conciliar statements, intense discussions continued in the postconciliar church about the roles of the laity and clergy. In the 1970s, the United States bishops warned about the clericalization of the laity and the secularizing of the clergy and the sisters. These warnings occurred because shortly after Vatican II, priests and sisters suddenly began becoming community leaders, running for political office, and directly confronting the country's economic, political, and military systems in the name of social justice. Consequently, many laity thought that priests and nuns were neglecting their roles within the church by doing what the laity should do. On the other hand, thousands of the laity were becoming part of the formal ministry of the church. Many parishes had lay people and sisters in paid pastoral positions, e.g. youth ministers, directors of the RCIA, and directors of religious education. In addition, the laity served on parish councils, finance and building committees, and other parish and church-based activities. Thousands of lay persons had replaced sisters in parochial schools as teachers and administrators. Many others served in Catholic colleges and universities and diocesan offices and institutions. Many Catholics thought that some bishops, pastors, and leaders of religious orders were so preoccupied with lay ministry in the church that they were neglecting the laity's task of sanctifying secular society.

On December 12, 1977, forty-seven Catholic lay and religious leaders from Chicago issued a document titled *A Chicago Declaration of Christian Concern* (McClory 1977). They expressed concern that the laity were losing confidence in the church's social teaching and mission. They charged that the church was "becoming turned in on itself," was "devaluing the unique ministry of lay men and women," and was "facing the threat of a revived clericalism." They regretted the decline, and in some instances the demise, of those preconciliar organizations and networks "whose task it was to inspire and support the laity in their vocation to the world through their professional and occupational lives." They had in mind such organizations as the National Catholic Social Action Conference, the Association of Catholic Trade Unionists, Young Christian Workers, the National Council of Catholic Nurses, and the Catholic Council on Working Life (McClory 1978a).

The changes in work and lifestyle of priests, sisters, and the laity created false divisions in the mind of many people. Many believed that there were laity and priests who "work for the church" and laity and priests who "work in the world." However, these false notions were slowly corrected through discussions created by such documents as the Chicago Declaration. Those who disagreed with the Chicago group said they detected a note of nostalgia in their document and wondered if its signers had given sufficient attention to the complex social factors which led to the demise of the preconciliar lay organizations. More to the point, critics of the document pointed out that it made too sharp a distinction between the respective roles of the laity and the clergy in the social ministry of the church. Instead, they emphasized that all baptized Catholics are responsible for the renewal and reform of both the church and society.[4] The United States bishops would later exemplify this perspective when they delved deeply into this country's sociopolitical and socioeconomic interests in their pastorals on peace (1983) and the economy (1986).

In Protestant and evangelical churches women had been brought into the hierarchical church through ordination. Some of these churches had ordained women as priests or ministers since 1944 and as bishops since 1980. For example, on September 24, 1987, the first woman was elected bishop in the worldwide Anglican communion. Barbara C. Harris, a black woman and a native of Philadelphia, served the church in that city since her ordination to the priesthood in 1980. In 1987, at the age of fifty-eight, she was elected suffragan (assistant) for the Episcopal Diocese of Massachusetts, an appointment scheduled to take place in 1989. Her election caused considerable concern, even outrage, among the Anglican communion around the world, most of which did not ordain women. They were outraged because bishops are considered successors of Jesus' male disciples and are a divinely ordained element of church structure (Burkholder 1987). Many Catholic women were pleased with Harris's election because it gave them reason to hope for their own cause.

On the other hand, many feminists oppose the incorporation of women into the hierarchical institutional church through priestly ordination. They believe this move could only lead to further clericalization of the church—and not to changing it. Furthermore, since many experienced a bureacratic powerlessness and encountered a sharp dichotomy between the theory fostered by Vatican II and the kind of church those in hierarchical power actually nurture, they wanted to move the discussion to a different level. They asked if the power to govern is restricted to the clergy or can it be exercised by the laity, including women. In 1996 Aurelie Hagstrom, a Catholic theologian, not only asked this question but she also asked that the discussion of this question be reopened because "the precise relationship between sacred orders and the exercise of the power of jurisdiction or governance is by no means a closed issue." She argued that there is a school of thought in the church that holds "that baptism engenders in the laity the capacity, in certain circumstances, to receive and exercise the jurisdictional aspects of sacred power in the church."

Ladislas Orsy quickly took up her challenge (1996). He pointed out that there is overwhelming historical evidence of lay persons participating in decision-making processes in the church "from at least the fourth century well into the 20th." Even the first Code of Canon Law (1917) did not require priestly ordination for the exercise of jurisdiction, "but only tonsure, which was no more than a commitment to receive ordination." But, shortly before Vatican II, Klaus Mörsdorf, a canon lawyer from Munich, proposed a new theory intended to uphold and honor the episcopal office. He correctly argued that bishops are not the delegates of the pope but receive the power to consecrate and to govern through their ordination. But in order to further uphold the episcopal office, he excluded the laity from all participation in church government and restricted jurisdiction to the clergy: bishops, priests, and deacons. Orsy judged Mörsdorf's theory "a novelty and an unwarranted ideology," because he not only left out the sacred power given by the Spirit at baptism to all Christians, but he also "introduced a new rule: no sacred power outside sacred orders." In addition, Mörsdorf's theory had three other results: it sharply divided clergy and laity, laid the foundation for a clerical church, and it denied the historical tradition of laypersons participating in decision-making processes that are an integral part of the governance of the church. Orsy noted that, while the Canon Law of 1983 did not take a formal position on Mörsdorf's theory, it "in fact left no opening for the laity to participate effectively in decision-making processes."

For his part, Orsy offered five simple suggestions which, if put in place, would allow the whole church to discover the directions it should take. All five have roots in the sacred power given to every man and woman through baptism. (1) Creative theologians and canon lawyers, while revering the unique character of the episcopal power, should study the sacred power granted all Christians by baptism. (2) Lay persons should be made voting members of extraordinary decision-making bodies such as synods and councils. (3) Lay persons should be made members of decision-making bodies in the ordinary administration of the church, such as the curia. (4) Lay persons should administer the financial assets of the church. (5) Qualified lay persons should be officially designated as homilists.

The Ordination of Women: 1963–1976

In his 1963 encyclical *Pacem in terris,* Pope John XXIII asserted that the changing status of women in contemporary society was one of the signs of the times. He wrote: "Since women are becoming even more conscious of their human dignity, they will not tolerate being treated as mere material instruments, but demand rights befitting a human person both in domestic and public life" (n. 41). That year Betty Friedan summoned white, middle-class women to a new level of consciousness beyond the male-female and private-public dualisms with her book *The Feminine Mystique.* Many women soon assumed equal roles with men in business, higher education, government, labor, law, medicine, and the ordained ministry in many Christian churches.[5]

Feminism is another example of historical consciousness in action. Within classical consciousness, women were subject to the authority of men inasmuch as they were controlled by a patriarchal tradition. With the rise of historical consciousness, many women around the globe sought a life marked by freedom, sharing, community, dialogue, and democracy. It is important to note that feminism is not a middle-class American aberration. It is a worldwide phenomenon, as manifested at the United Nations' meetings in Cairo in 1994 and in Beijing in 1995.

In the 1960s Catholic women did not advocate for priestly ministry as one of their rights and an aspect of their dignity. But in the 1970s the ordination of Catholic women received considerable attention. Some of the factors that accelerated this interest were social and others were ecclesial. The social influences included the feminist movement and the civil rights movement. The ecclesial factors involved both the Catholic and Episcopal churches.

In 1972 the United States bishops issued a report titled, "Theological Reflections on the Ordination of Women." That report states in part: "The constant tradition and practice of the Catholic church against the ordination of women, interpreted (whenever interpreted) as of divine law, is of such a nature as to constitute a clear teaching of the ordinary magisterium (teaching authority) of the church. Though not formally defined, this is Catholic doctrine." The bishops offered several other reasons why women should not be ordained, e.g., since Jesus is a male, only men can represent him; Jesus did not make his mother a priest.

The bishops' report was challenged by several theologians (G. O'Collins 1973; Stuhlmueller 1974). Josephine Massingberd Ford argued that Jesus may have chosen male disciples, but "the best priests are the most human, not the most masculine." In response to the argument that Jesus did not make even his mother Mary a priest, Ford stated that, if a woman could give birth to the incarnate Word of God, then a woman should be able to celebrate the eucharistic mysteries of his body and blood (J. M. Ford 1973, 692–93).

Gregory Baum wrote an essay in 1973 in which he maintained that ministry in the church has a twofold prophetic function: It reveals the oppressive character of worldly authority and it presents an ideal of leadership that serves the true needs of the people. The ordination of women would restore a prophetic quality to the church's ministry because it would educate people to discern the injustices to women in present society and it would present our society with an ideal for the participation of women in the life of society.

On July 29, 1974, four Episcopal bishops ordained eleven women as priests in Philadelphia (Carroll 1974; Lyle 1974). This action was widely publicized and created considerable controversy. At no time were the

bishops accused of breaking with the church. No excommunication procedures were inaugurated against them. The 220-member House of Bishops mildly rebuked them for their action on the grounds that they lacked
jurisdiction, since the ordinations were authorized by neither the bishops
nor the people of a diocesan community. Although the eleven women
were never rebuked, their ordination was declared irregular (against
church law) and invalid (non-sacramental). Some Episcopalians argued
that, because any ordination by validly ordained bishops is valid, the ordinations were valid but irregular. Franz Josef van Beeck offered a different reason why the ordinations were valid but irregular. He argued that
canonical disobedience "*need* not result in invalidity of sacraments, although it *may*" (1974, 392). The canonical provision that prohibits the ordination of women, he said, is a prohibiting impediment. He argued that
there is growing consensus that being a woman is not a diriment or nul-
lifying impediment to ordination because women, like men, have an essential capacity to be ordained to the priesthood and the episcopate. A
diriment impediment renders something totally void. Even in Catholic
statements that forbid the ordination of women, the primary argument is
based on tradition and not a woman's innate incapacity of receiving the
sacrament.

In 1975 the Women's Ordination Conference was organized and held
its first meeting in Detroit.[6] Its theme was "Women in Future Priesthood
Now: A Call for Action." They declared that their conference "focuses on
the ordination of women to priesthood as epitomizing a long prevailing
inequity. So long as women are excluded from ordination, their participation in the sacramental life and ministry of the church can only be secondary and auxiliary, reflecting a theological view of them as diminished
persons, deficient recipients of the sacraments of initiation." Fourteen
hundred attended and 600 were turned away for lack of space. In 1975
about 30 percent of United States Catholics favored women priests
(Fiedler and Pomerleau 1978).

In April 1976, a report on the ordination of women by the nineteen-
member Pontifical Biblical Commission was leaked to the press
(Fitzmyer 1996). The PBC stated that "the first [Christian] communities
were always directed by men exercising the apostolic power." Consequently, "the masculine character of the hierarchical order which has
structured the church since its beginning thus seems attested to by scripture in an undeniable way." Nonetheless, they concluded their study
with this sentence: "It does not seem that the New Testament by itself
alone will permit us to settle in a clear way and once and for all the problem of the possible accession of women to the presbyterate." Although
the PBC text was never officially published, it reinforced the thinking of
those in the women's ordination movement. It is even reported that when
the Episcopal church officially approved of women's ordination in 1976,
they cited the PBC document. David Stanley (1914-96), a Canadian Jesuit

and scripture scholar, resigned from the PBC because Paul VI ignored the commission's findings.

Paul VI and the Ordination of Women

In October 1976, Pope Paul VI, with encouragement from the United States bishops, moved to the center of the discussion of women's ordination. He simply reiterated the church's traditional teaching prohibiting the ordination of women in *Inter insigniores,* the "Declaration on the Question of the Admission of Women to the Ministerial Priesthood." This document was issued by the CDF on October 15, 1976, and promulgated on January 27, 1977.

This document did not claim to break new ground, but was issued merely to sum up and repeat the longstanding tradition of the church. The CDF judged "it necessary to recall that the church, in fidelity to the example of the Lord, does not consider herself authorized to admit women to priestly ordination . . . [T]hat by calling only men to the priestly order and ministry in its true sense, the church intends to remain faithful to the type of ordained ministry willed by the Lord Jesus and carefully maintained by the apostles" (n. 1).

This papal document was welcomed by some and questioned by others. Some who questioned it considered it "ecumenically offensive, political in intent, dishonest and faulty in scholarship and so regressive it threatens the credibility of the church" (Rashke 1977). In 1978, Leonard and Arlene Swidler edited *Women Priests: A Catholic Commentary on the Vatican Document,* a book containing forty essays by well-known Catholics. Many of these essayists were disturbed not only because the CDF never cited the findings of the Pontifical Biblical Commission, but also because by March 1977 almost 41 percent of United States Catholics favored the ordination of women, according to a Gallup poll (Fiedler and Pomerleau 1978).

The CDF based its arguments on scripture, tradition, and the theological argument "from fittingness." Biblical passages were cited to show that it was the intention of Jesus to preclude women from the priesthood. Out of fidelity to Jesus' practice, the twelve apostles and Paul did not confer ordination on women. Scripture scholars analyzed the declaration's exegesis of scripture and found it wanting.

The Vatican declaration states that Jesus' "attitude toward women was quite different from his milieu, and he deliberately and courageously broke from it." When Jesus excluded women from the inner twelve disciples, "it was not to conform to the custom of his time." The exclusion of women was due to conscious intent.

Those who questioned the papal teaching admitted that there are indeed several passages where Jesus is pictured as a "cultural nonconformist": his association with tax collectors (Luke 15:1–2), his sabbath healings (Mark 3:2), and his opposition to the established religion (Matthew 23:1–36). However, overemphasis on these passages can disguise the essential Jewishness of Jesus. He faithfully attended synagogue, prayed before meals, invoked the teachings of Moses, and observed the Passover. Matthew's theology presents a Jesus who did not come to abolish the law or the prophets but to fulfill them (Matthew 5:17–18).

John Donahue, a Jesuit scripture scholar, concluded in an essay he wrote in 1977 that the CDF "moves too quickly, it seems, from the fact that Jesus *sometimes* broke with his cultural milieu to the conclusion that he never accommodated his words and actions to the milieu. It is therefore questionable whether in the exclusion of women from the Twelve, Jesus can be said to be free of that law and custom which so determined his life in other areas."

The argument from tradition stated that the ordination of women has not been done before: "The church has always acknowledged as a perennial norm her Lord's way of acting in choosing the twelve men whom he made the foundations of his church." There are three counter arguments to the Vatican's appeal to an unchanging tradition. First, since the church's two-thousand-year history of an exclusively male priesthood developed out of a patriarchal culture to further support this culture would tie the church's understanding of Christ and his church to one time and culture. Second, several Protestant churches have been ordaining women as priests since 1944. Third, to appeal to an unchanging tradition is clearly opposed "to the notion of a living, developing tradition that theologians have had to produce when speaking about Mary's immaculate conception or assumption, or when defending the definitions concerning the papacy" (Principe 1988, 28).

The theological argument from fittingness stated that the priest representing Christ to the community must be male. The CDF maintained that there would not be a "'natural resemblance' which must exist between Christ and his minister if the role of Christ were not taken by a man." Women were particularly hurt because this notion attacked their self-concept as human beings and as women of faith. They argued that through baptism all Christians are other Christs. Furthermore, the Vatican placed heavy emphasis on the fact that the Word of God became male, rather than that he became human.

The Ordination of Women: 1978–94

Despite the papal teachings, the debate about women's ordination continued. It was kept alive by meetings and through documents. WOC held its second meeting in 1978 in Baltimore, and organized twenty-eight local and regional meetings during 1982–83 (M. Riley 1984). The CTSA issued a research report on "Women in Church and Society" in 1978. It concluded with this statement: "The task force does not, in sum, find that

the arguments adduced on the question present any serious ground to justify the exclusion of women from ordination to the pastoral office in the
Catholic Church." In 1979 the Catholic Biblical Association of America
issued a report titled "Women and Priestly Ministry: The New Testament
Evidence." Their concluding paragraph stated: "An examination of the
biblical evidence shows the following: that there is positive evidence in
the New Testament that ministries were shared by various groups and
that women did in fact exercise roles and functions later associated with
priestly ministry; that the arguments against the admission of women to
priestly ministry based on the praxis of Jesus and the apostles, disciplinary
regulations, and the created order cannot be sustained. The conclusion we
draw then is that the New Testament evidence, while not decisive by itself, points toward the admission of women to priestly ministry."

Because the debate would not go away, the United States bishops
scheduled several meetings with WOC and other organizations between
1979 and 1983. One which had long-lasting consequences was held in
Washington, D.C., November 11–13, 1983. Some one hundred bishops
met with fifty women representing thirteen Catholic women's organizations, such as the Catholic Daughters of America, the NARW, Las Her-
manas, and WOC. Their theme was "Women in the Church." The bishops
were so impressed with the dialogue that they believed it was fitting for
them to write a pastoral on women's issues. The women advised against
it. They wondered if an all-male organization could make a credible pronouncement on women in either the church or society. Nonetheless, later
that month when the entire body of bishops convened for their semian-
nual meeting they voted unanimously to write a pastoral. They gave
themselves four years to complete it, appointing Bishop Joseph L. Imesch
of Joliet, Illinois, the chairperson of the drafting committee.

The bishops met with groups of women from time to time to hear
their ideas. During 1985–1986, an estimated seventy-five thousand
women participated in consultations sponsored by the bishops in dioceses, on college campuses, with women's organizations, and even on military bases. The bishops found that the women themselves were divided
over the pastoral because they had a great range of concerns. For example,
a bishops' committee, composed of six bishops and five women consultants, listened to spokeswomen from nine invited Catholic women's
groups in Washington, D.C., in March 1985. Some women suggested that
the bishops should not be writing the pastoral. Others recommended post-
ponement until women had more opportunities to explore their concerns.
Still others said the letter's focus should be the sin of sexism inasmuch as
this is the real problem (Beifuss and Bourgoin 1985).

The first draft, issued in April 1988 and titled "Partners in the Mystery of Redemption," had 164 pages. It discussed sexism as a moral and social evil, the family, hiring practices of church-related employers, and the

feasibility of the ordination of women to the diaconate. It did not consider ordination to the priesthood.

The document was distributed nationwide for evaluation. It was well received by most women. They acknowledged its strengths, especially the selected quotations from some of the thousands of women who testified before diocesan commissions and national organizations, and in hearings organized by the drafting committee. These hearings allowed women to describe their experiences with men, with society, and with the church. Negative responses were also recorded. Conservative women's groups faulted the bishops for buying into what they called feminist themes and rhetoric. Catholic feminists were even more vocal in their criticism, contending that the bishops had caved into the Vatican's hard line against women's ordination to priesthood.

The second draft, titled "One in Christ Jesus: A Pastoral Response to Women's Concerns," was ninety-nine pages in length and was issued in April 1990. This document affirmed the equality of women, condemned discrimination and sexual harassment as moral and social evils, endorsed equal opportunity and equal pay for women, called for greater sensitivity to women by the clergy, questioned the Vatican ban on altar girls, and asked that a Vatican study on the admission of women to the permanent diaconate "be undertaken and brought to completion soon." Although the bishops spoke of "the value of further study" of the issue of women priests, they emphasized the church's traditional teaching that only men can serve as priests.

The strengths of the draft were clear. It declared the equality of women as persons in every aspect of their lives. The bishops stated that "Boys and men must be educated to respect the personal integrity of women, to recognize how sinful violence and every form of sexual exploitation really are." The draft also received many very negative reviews—too many to cite here. I do cite a scathing letter by Rosemary Ruether (1990) not only because it had the support of thirteen women's organizations, such as WOC and NARW, but also because her response to the first draft had been so very positive. While she agreed with some of those who pointed out the flaws in the first draft, she argued that "it is important that the practical, pastoral possibilities of the document not be lost" (1988). Ruether's essay on the second draft began with this paragraph: "In the new draft . . . you call on the world to repent of sexism and to give to women that full equality of personhood which is their God-given nature. Yet, your pastoral reaffirms every aspect of the patriarchal system that is the basis of sexism. Dear bishops, you embarrass us. You insult our intelligence." She then explains several points that support her position and then says, "Finally, and most incredibly, you claim to affirm the equality of women with men in the image of God, yet you deny to women equality in Christ, who is, for Christians, the veritable image of God."

Even some bishops publicly denounced the draft—something highly unusual on their part. For example, Rembert Weakland, Archbishop of Milwaukee, found the letter "preachy." He stated that "A strident, negative, judgmental tone seemed to dominate. Apparently the authors felt that to persuade their readers, vinegar was better than honey. I felt wrung out after reading it." He advised the bishops to drop the pastoral because it failed to add anything to what has been said in papal documents like *Inter insigniores* (1976) and *Mulieres dignitatem* (1988). Weakland said, "It would be wiser to permit them to stand as is" (Windsor 1990a).

On May 28–29, 1991, five Vatican officials and bishops from twelve countries met with six United States bishops in Rome for a conference called by John Paul II to review the pastoral. The United States bishops were praised for their "pastoral solicitude" in undertaking the project. But the seventeen Vatican consultants suggested that the bishops downgrade the pastoral letter to a statement, add more mariology, and emphasize women's "complementarity" with men rather than their equality. The United States bishops did not want to downgrade their letter. Since they had already produced pastorals on peace (1983) and economic justice (1986), the bishops felt that to downgrade the pastoral carried with it the very real danger of some people thinking that women's concerns were not as important as those presented in the earlier pastorals.

The third draft was issued in April 1992. The eighty-one-page pastoral was titled "Called to Be One in Christ." The bishops condemned the "sin of sexism" in both church and society. On the question of women's ordination to the priesthood, the bishops affirmed the teaching of John Paul II that Christ called men only to the priesthood. Concerning the ordination of women as deacons, the new draft simply called for "continued dialogue and reflection" on various ministries such as the diaconate (Goldman 1992b; P. Steinfels 1992b).

In June 1992, when the bishops met to discuss the third draft, they were so divided over its contents that they put off a vote until their November 1992 meeting. The fourth draft, titled "One in Christ Jesus," was released on September 2, 1992. This draft was based largely on the criticisms raised at the June meeting. This final version differed significantly from the third draft in several ways: (1) Whereas the third draft focused on sexism as a sin, the fourth took a broader look at evils harming women. It eliminated any reference to the "sin of sexism" within the church. The bishops warned that "to identify sexism as the principal evil" harming women socially would be "to analyze the underlying problem too superficially." (2) Whereas the third contained a short, simple affirmation of the teaching of the church on women's ordination, the fourth offered an extended defense of that teaching and rebuttal of counterarguments. (3) Whereas the third highlighted the dialogue and shared examination of the issues by both women and the bishops, the fourth emphasized the bishops' responsibility to teach "fundamental truths about the human person and . . . applications of these truths" (Vidulich and Fox 1992). Opposition to the fourth draft was especially high among the women most involved in the institutional structures, including nuns, theologians, religious educators, and employees in diocesan and parish offices (Reese 1992).

On November 18, the 247 bishops present voted not to issue the pastoral. The vote of 137 for to 110 against marked the first time since the modern bishops' conference was formed in 1966 that the bishops failed to reach a required two-thirds majority consensus on a proposed pastoral letter (Vidulich 1992c).

Many bishops found the document incomplete and likely to alienate many women. It is reported that very few of the bishops who voted against the document wanted to see women ordained as priests. Nonetheless, "the letter could not be read apart from its own history. Under Vatican prodding, later drafts adopted an increasingly guarded tone" (P. Steinfels 1992d). The bishops' vote became a referendum on women's ordination and the teaching office of the bishops rather than the content of the letter. There is little doubt that the Vatican's insistence that women could not be ordained became the governing principle and major premise of the pastoral. But what ultimately divided the bishops was their own teaching role. When should they stand firm and draw sharp boundaries and when reach out and advocate change? Many of those who voted against the document "concluded that a letter subordinating the new concerns of women to laying down sharp limits to the examination of church teachings would not only forestall dialogue but provoke a backlash against church teachings as well" (P. Steinfels 1992e).

Margaret O'Brien Steinfels (1992) expressed the disappointment of many Catholics after the pastoral was scrapped: "The church's response to the rapidly altered status of women may be as fateful for its future as were its tragically insufficient response to the intellectual rebellions of the eighteenth century and to the working class movements of the nineteenth."

Many Catholics were disappointed that the bishops did not resist the Vatican pressure about priestly ordination. A Gallup poll reported in June 1992 that two-thirds of American Catholics favored opening the priesthood to women (Goldman 1992a). Many Catholics believe that the movement to ordain women as priests is one of Christianity's great and historic transformations. Sandra Schneiders declared that "the last time there was such a ground swell that was not heeded was the Protestant Reformation" (Ostling 1992, 53).

Meanwhile, the discussion of ordination intensified in part because of developments within the Church of England. On November 11, 1992, the General Synod of the Anglican Church voted (384 to 169) to ordain women as priests. One of the strongest arguments of the opposition was that their church would be departing from the tradition still upheld by the Roman Catholic and Orthodox churches. The Vatican immediately declared the decision a "new and grave obstacle to the entire process of reconciliation" among the Christian communities.

Opposition to women priests continued to mount within the Church of England (Hebblethwaite 1993g). Nonetheless, on March 12, 1994, thirty-two female deacons were ordained as priests at the Bristol Cathedral. This ordination had the approval of the archbishops of Canterbury and York, and, according to one poll, 90 percent of Britons. Once again the Vatican reacted sharply to the ordinations, declaring them a setback for eventual reunion (Darnton 1994).

John Paul II and the Ordination of Women

On May 22, 1994, John Paul II issued a brief apostolic letter, *Ordinatio sacerdotalis* ("Priestly Ordination Reserved to Men Alone"). Avery Dulles regarded the letter as the pope's formal response to the many ordinations in the Church of England. The pope wrote the letter "to prevent the Catholic church from being torn apart by this issue as the Anglican communion had been" (Dulles 1994). John Paul wrote: "Wherefore, in order that all doubt may be removed regarding a matter of great importance, a matter which pertains to the church's divine constitution itself, in virtue of my ministry of confirming the brethren (Luke 22:32), I declare that the church has no authority whatsoever to confer priestly ordination on women and this judgment is to be definitively held by all the church's faithful" (n. 4).

Reactions to the Vatican letter were both affirmative and negative. Some thought the letter would allow the church to get on with more important issues such as combating poverty and promoting religious education for adults. Others reacted in anger and pain, labeling the papal letter arrogant, condescending, and patronizing (A. Jones 1994). For many, the document came at the wrong time in view of the fact that more women than ever have assumed pastoral, liturgical, and administrative responsibilities in parishes and dioceses. Women are the primary strength of the church in the United States and in other parts of the world church. The United States bishops, conscious of the tremendous role of women in the church, promised to enhance "the participation of women in every possible aspect of church life," short of priestly ordination. In November 1994, they approved a document, "Toward Strengthening the Bonds of Peace, A Reflection on Women in the Church occasioned by Pope John Paul's Letter on Priestly Ordination," by a vote of 228 to 10. The bishops agreed "to look at alternative ways in which women can exercise leadership in the church." They encouraged women to pursue studies in canon law, biblical studies, and theology. They also called for the end of authoritarian conduct and sexism in church teaching and practice. They declared: "We commit ourselves to make sure that our words and actions express our belief in the equality of all women and men."

John Paul's letter did not advance any new arguments for the church's firm stance for not ordaining women. What is new are the two words *definitively held*. Both words create new theological problems. It has been consistently taught that when the pope teaches noninfallibly, he does so authoritatively—but in a non-definitive way. The term *definitively* seems to create a new category of teaching. It seems to mean that this apostolic letter has presented the absolutely last word on the topic. The word *held* also raises problems. There is a distinction between declaring that something is to be believed (for then one is in the realm of divine revelation) and something is to be held. It appears that *held* means that the pope is not "proposing something as a doctrine of faith, or expecting a response of faith to a dogma divinely revealed. Is that the loophole?" (Hebblethwaite 1994c; see also Gaillardetz 1994).

The CDF responded to these questions in a brief "Response" that was signed on October 28, 1995, but released on November 18, 1995 (P. Steinfels 1995b). The words "definitively held" mean two things: the church cannot ordain women priests because this teaching is part of the deposit of faith and this teaching has always been infallibly taught by the ordinary and universal magisterium. Specifically, the CDF stated: "This teaching requires definitive assent, since, founded on the written word of God, and from the beginning constantly preserved and applied in the tradition of the church, it has been set forth infallibly by the ordinary and universal magisterium. . . . Thus, in the present circumstances, the Roman Pontiff, exercising his proper office of confirming his brethren (Luke 22:32), has handed on this same teaching by a formal declaration, explicitly stating what is to be held always, everywhere, and by all, as belonging to the deposit of the faith."

This supplementary teaching had supporters and opponents. Some supporters insisted that, since the pope had declared authoritatively that the traditional teaching is infallible and had demanded definitive assent, further discussion of the authority of tradition in this question is forbidden. Hence, any attempts to keep the door open for responsible discussion are illegitimate. Furthermore, since the discussion of women's ordination is so recent and the church has endeavored through the ages to be faithful to the practice of Jesus, "the pope is fully justified in saying that he has no authority to change the tradition on his own initiative. Claiming such authority would be papalism of the most extreme kind. The proper forum for a decision in a matter of this kind is a council" (Pottmeyer 1996).

The staunchest supporter of the Vatican teachings was Avery Dulles. He urged the faithful, especially women (1994), and theologians at a meeting of the CTSA (Roberts 1996) to accept the Vatican teachings. He even exhorted the bishops to line up behind the Vatican teaching by issuing an unambiguous statement of their support (ibid.). Dulles argued that the papal teaching is not based on any antipathy toward women, "but on fidelity to immemorial tradition and deep insight into the meaning of revelation." He warned the bishops to move against those holding a "radical position," a position that "is gaining ground at an alarming rate." He explained that there is "a progressive wing that seeks to correct what it regards as an obsolete, distorted, culture-bound tradition." He mentioned by name WOC, Call to Action, CORPUS (the association for a married priesthood) and "some gay and lesbian groups." Dulles indicated that there are four classical fonts for determining church teaching: scripture, tradition, the magisterium, and theological reasoning. No one of the four is "to be taken in isolation." Concerning the ordination of women, all four are "manifestly opposed" to it.

Dulles acknowledged that the New Testament does not discuss the ordination of women as such. He explained that, when the magisterium declares that "the doctrine 'pertains' to the deposit of faith, they do not necessarily mean that it is divinely revealed." In this instance, "the doctrine is a deduction or inference from the word of God and is not itself a revealed truth." The tradition barring women from priesthood "is ancient, universal and constant." While it is true that some women had a prominent place in the early churches, "they are not described as holding apostolic or priestly office." Past attempts to ordain women "were branded as heretical." Concerning theology, he states that major theologians of both medieval (1200–1550) and baroque scholasticism (1550–1750) "were unanimously opposed to the possibility, principally because of the authority of Christ and the apostles." Dulles added that some theologians have argued "that women could not suitably represent Christ in his spousal relationship to the church as bride, which the priest must represent." Finally, the magisterium has made pronouncements on this matter "beginning with the popes and bishops of the patristic period and continuing through Innocent III [1198–1216] in the thirteenth century." The doctrine has been firmly taught by the magisterium in recent documents, specifically, *Inter insigniores* in 1976 and *Ordinatio sacerdotalis* in 1994. The doctrine has not been formally declared *de fide,* but it has been infallibly taught.

Those who disagreed with the pope and the CDF also addressed "the four classical fonts" cited by Dulles. First, with regard to scripture, they pointed out that the CDF has never addressed the 1976 PBC statement that the Bible by itself alone will not permit a clear answer about the accession of women to the priesthood. Second, with regard to the CDF's desire to hand on "the constant and universal tradition of the church" that goes back to Jesus, Hermann Pottmeyer, German priest-theologian and member of the Pontifical International Theological Commission, asked a series of questions in a provocative 1996 essay about Jesus choosing and commissioning only men as members of the Twelve. "Did the church in past centuries really ask whether faithfulness to Jesus required that only men be ordained?" Given the social and cultural situations in which the church has lived hitherto, could this question have been asked? If the church did not ask this question, how can we claim that the impossibility of women's ordination is "a teaching to be held definitively and absolutely"? Is it not true that Jesus' free, independent, and crucial decision to call only men to the Twelve could not have been understood as symbolizing Israel (see Matthew 19:28) had he included women? If Jesus acted freely in accord with the culture of his day, then does not our faithfulness to him require us to do the same? If we are to be true to his example, must we not take account of the changed role of women today? "Is it not possible that tradition actually compels us not to limit ordination to men but rather to follow Jesus' example in taking seriously the culture of his time?" Pottmeyer calls the last question "the decisive question before the church today."

Joseph Fitzmyer, a scripture scholar, responded to Pottmeyer, a dogmatic theologian, by pointing out that there are scriptural problems Pottmeyer glossed over. Pottmeyer wants the church to be "faithful to Jesus," but, says Fitzmyer, he never describes what "faithful to Jesus" means. Fitzmyer points out that the only Jesus to which the Christian church in the twentieth century can be faithful is "the different portraits of Jesus painted for us by the four inspired Evangelists and the interpretations of him and the tradition associated with him in the rest of New Testament writings" (1996). We do not know whether Jesus of Nazareth even ever thought of the question of women's ordination. In addition, Fitzmyer says Pottmeyer presumes that Jesus ordained (imposed hands) on the twelve disciples. But there is no evidence in the New Testament that Jesus ordained the twelve (Mark 3:14) or the seventy-two (Luke 10:1) he commissioned to preach the reign of God. Neither is there New Testament evidence that the twelve disciples were regarded as priests, or even as bishops. While it is true that the ordination of men is mentioned in several texts (1 Timothy 4:14, 5:22; 2 Timothy 1:6), the Christian scriptures do not tell us when ordination began in the early church and we "have no idea when the early Christians began to distinguish ordination to diaconate, priesthood or bishopric." Fitzmyer concludes that the ordination of men has little to do with the ordination of women and that the question of the ordination of women does not involve "fidelity to Jesus; but fidelity to the tradition of the church."

Third, with regard to theological reasoning and fidelity to the tradition of the church, the opponents of the Vatican position point out that the question of ordaining women only arose in the 1970s, mainly because the historical context has changed dramatically. The question is actually a new question because for the first time in human history it is being discussed in the context of the equality of women. In the past women were not ordained because they were considered inferior, or in Thomas Aquinas's term, "defective males." Today, it is said, the Paraclete-Spirit is leading the church to ordain women because "Woman is not independent of man or man of women in the Lord" (1 Corinthians 11:11). In addition, opponents argue that just as the church grounded the ordination of men in

Jesus' commissioning of his male disciples (Mark 3:12, Luke 10:1), so the teaching church should ground the ordination of women in Jesus' commission to Mary Magdalene and the other women to witness to his resurrection (Matthew 28:9–10, John 20:17–18). Church history shows that the tradition develops under the guidance of the Spirit. Elizabeth Johnson reminded her readers (1996) that "history is replete with examples of unbroken tradition-breaking due to the moral sensibilities of believers, the insights of critical thinkers, and careful searching on the part of the teaching office, all converging in the context of cultural change. [For example,] at one time it was official church teaching that it was unlawful for married couples to take pleasure in the marital act."

Fourth, concerning the magisterium, critics of the Vatican document pointed out that there are two ways the magisterium exercises infallibility and neither one applies to the Vatican document. According to Vatican I's *Pastor aeternus*, the pope can exercise under certain specific conditions "that infallibility which the Divine Redeemer willed to bestow on his church." While not personally infallible, the pope can exercise infallibility when he "speaks *ex cathedra* as pastor and teacher of all Christians." This involves a formal presentation with the evident intention of binding all Christians. In addition, canon 749 states that "No doctrine is understood to be infallibly defined unless it is clearly established as such." Furthermore, the pope can never make an infallible statement unilaterally. He must act with the bishops assembled at an ecumenical council (as at Vatican I in 1870) or he must consult all the bishops (as in the Marian doctrines of 1854 and 1950). In this instance the bishops of the world were not consulted (Schaeffer 1995b). *Ordinatio sacerdotalis* did not explicitly claim infallibility. It was not an infallible exercise of the papal office. The response of the CDF is not an infallible text—nor does it even claim to be. The CDF does not possess such authority. Ladislas Orsy argued (1995) that the addition of the term "infallible" to explain the pope's apostolic letter does not redefine that letter. "It conveys the interpretation of the [CDF]." The CDF's response to questions about the pope's letter is precisely an authoritative but noninfallible interpretation of the letter. Both the pope and the CDF maintain that the prohibition against the ordination of women in *Ordinatio sacerdotalis* reiterates the infallible teaching of the ordinary magisterium.

The second way infallibility can be exercised is by the college of bishops in communion with the pope. At Vatican II the bishops explained the prerequisite for the infallible exercise of the ordinary magisterium of the universal episcopate. They wrote: "Although individual bishops do not enjoy the prerogative of infallibility, they do, however, proclaim infallibly the doctrine of Christ when, even though dispersed throughout the world but maintaining among themselves and with Peter's successor, the bond of communion, in authoritatively teaching matters to do with faith and morals, they are in agreement that a particular teaching is to be held definitively" (LG 25).

Theologians maintain that it is hardly possible to find a basis for the CDF's judgment that all the bishops of the world agree with John Paul's teaching (Roberts 1996b). For example, Francis Sullivan, a Jesuit who taught ecclesiology for thirty-six years at the Pontifical Gregorian University in Rome, said, "I think it is a fair question to ask how they know this is a clearly established fact. . . . Unless this is manifestly the case, I do not see how it can be certain that this doctrine is taught infallibly by the ordinary and universal magisterium" (1995). Richard McBrien concurred, stating that "There is no evidence of such unanimity in this instance. On the contrary, a minority of Catholic bishops in the United States alone have been positively disposed to the ordination of women; a larger minority regard it as an open question that should continue to be studied and discussed; and a still larger number, perphaps even a majority, would not have regarded the teaching—even if they agree with it—as part of the deposit of faith, equivalent to the teaching that Jesus Christ is divine as well as human, that he redeemed us by his death . . . and so forth" (1995d; see Roberts 1996b).

There have been serious consequences following the Vatican documents in 1994 and 1995. Individuals have been affected in different ways. Some simply withdrew from the church; others were punished by the institutional church. For example, Carmel McEnroy, a Religious Sister of Mercy and theologian, was dismissed without due process or warning on April 26, 1995, from her teaching position at St. Meinrad's Seminary in Indiana, where she had taught for fourteen years (McEnroy 1996, 273–79). She was dismissed for signing an advertisement endorsing women's ordination. Her name appeared with about two thousand others under a statement titled "An Open Letter to Pope John Paul II and the U.S. Conference of Catholic Bishops." This statement, sponsored by WOC, was published as an ad in the *National Catholic Reporter* on November 4, 1994. Authorities at the seminary stated that "For their students' sake and for the good of the whole church, it is essential that seminary faculty members fully support our church's teachings both in the classroom and in the public forum."

The dismissal of McEnroy was denounced by the CTSA at its annual meeting in 1995[7] and by the American Association of University Professors in 1996. The latter denounced the administration of the school, charging that the school violated its adopted principles of academic freedom and its own faculty constitution. The seminary administrators responded that McEnroy's dismissal was not an academic matter at all. Rather, it was a church matter and thus the provisions for due process in both the school's adopted statement of principles and in its faculty constitutions did not apply (Schaeffer 1996d). In September 1996, the

National Coalition of American Nuns called for a letter-writing campaign to urge a boycott of St. Meinrad's theology, retreat, and sabbatical programs, and of Abbey Press, its publishing outlet. In May 1996 McEnroy filed a federal suit, accusing the school of sexual discrimination and breach of contract in her termination. When this effort failed, she filed a suit in May 1997 in state court against the school and the Benedictines involved in her firing.[8]

In addition to the aforementioned advertisement, there were many other evaluations of the Vatican edicts on women's ordination. Here are four that highlight the far-reaching consequences of the Vatican's teachings. First, Thomas Fox acknowledged that the Vatican's definitive stance on the ordination of women marked a defeat for reform-minded Catholics. "But in the long term it may have the opposite effect: if there is a schism in the church in the next century, its source may well turn out to be the unyielding right" (1995). If down the line a different pope allows the ordination of women, it will be the traditionalists citing the pronouncements of John Paul II who will have the most difficulty accepting the change.

Second, Hermann Pottmeyer and Hans Küng indicated some of the ecumenical ramifications of the pope's decision. Pottmeyer (1996) said it will strengthen Catholic-Orthodox dialogues because both churches reject women priests. Also, the Orthodox would not look kindly on a resolution of the question by papal fiat. For them, the proper forum for a decision in a matter of this kind is an ecumenical council. Küng stated that the decision would harm Protestant-Catholic dialogues because practically all the Reformation churches have women priests and ministers. In effect, the pope has condemned a practice that they have long tried and tested. Küng concluded that "it is hardly possible to kick our ecumenical brothers and sisters in the teeth more roughly than this pope has done" (1995).

Third, at its national convention in June 1996, the CTSA presented to its members a draft paper titled "Tradition and the Ordination of Women: A Question of Criteria."[9] This document, written by a six-member task force, does not argue for or against the priestly ordination of women. It does examine the reasons cited by the CDF for not permitting the ordination of women. The theologians contend that they have "serious doubts regarding the nature of the authority of this teaching and its grounds in tradition."

In June 1997 the CTSA concluded its year-long study of the extensively revised draft. By a vote of 216 to 22, with 10 abstentions, the group endorsed the final document (P. Steinfels 1997, Schaeffer 1997b). At issue was the CDF teaching that the restriction of the priesthood to males has been "set forth infallibly" and is therefore beyond reconsideration. The CTSA study declares respectfully that there are "serious doubts" about the reasons given by the CDF that the teaching on priestly ordination is both infallible and part of the deposit of faith. The Vatican argues that its teaching is based on scripture, has been constantly upheld in Catholic tradition, and has been taught universally by the bishops. The CTSA study argues that "legitimate questions can be raised about each of these reasons, and their probative force." After presenting their arguments, the CTSA called for "further study, discussion and prayer regarding this question."

Finally, the purpose of the "Response" by the CDF was to silence the faithful, clergy, and laity on the question of women priests. Far from laying the question to rest, the CDF's explanation has escalated the discussion. For example, in July 1996, members of WOC joined fifty other women from ten countries to form an international coalition to work for the ordination of women in the Catholic church. They call themselves Women's Ordination Worldwide (WOW). They plan to expand their network and to hold a strategy convocation in 1997 or 1998 (Fiedler 1996). Members (and supporters) of WOC and WOW think it is merely a matter of time until the institutional church catches up with the intellectual dimension (the theology supporting women's ordination) and the devotional dimension (the widespread involvement of so many women in so many pastoral ministries).

Conclusion

In this thematic history of the Catholic church we have seen that the church has lost one social group after another in the Western world, not as a whole, but certainly close to a majority in each group. Beginning in the sixteenth century the church lost many intellectuals because it would not accept the autonomy of science, first the physical sciences and later the social sciences. Due to the Industrial Revolution the church lost many workers because it did not take their socioeconomic problems seriously enough. Due to the Enlightenment, the church lost many men because they refused to be treated like children. Now, as a result of such factors as the feminist movement, the sexual revolution, increased educational opportunities, the call for gender-inclusive language and the desire for priestly ordination, the church is losing many women, the ones who "form the main contingent at the basis of the church but have no voice at the top" (Bühlmann 1986, 133). The commentary of Gary MacEoin right after Vatican II is still true today: "The emancipation of women is . . . a triumph of the secular world, one that the [official] church is still far from accepting emotionally or implementing institutionally" (1966, 174–75).

This chapter has reviewed the institutional church's postconciliar teachings on women. It seems that many feminists do not stay on top of these church pronouncements because they are skeptical, and in some cases resentful, of statements made by male church leaders about them. Not only do many Catholic women not heed the official church teachings about their role as women, but many devote their theological energies to the exploration of other issues that concern women directly—issues which are certainly related to questions of faith, but which lie beyond the traditional scope of official church discussion and attention, for example, feminist theological treatment of violence against women, poverty, racism, and other allied issues. In other words, some feminist theologians have expanded the definition of what constitutes a "religious" or "spiritual" issue, and, in doing so, they have made it possible to work for change in church and society beyond institutional avenues, and despite the traditional obstacles to such work.

On the other hand, many women are deeply involved in the institutional, devotional, and intellectual life of the church. For example, there is in the United States a coalition of some thirty-five groups known as the Catholic Organization for Renewal. The latter is not an autonomous organization, but "a forum, a table" where Christians can talk. Included are such groups as Call to Action, WOC, Dignity, Future Church, and the Association for the Rights of Catholics in the Church. Women belong to most of these groups. Their participation and leadership in these significant organizations insures a vital role for women in the future for the Catholic church. In addition, many women foster the devotional life of the church by planning parish liturgies, caring pastorally for the sick and dying, working on social justice committees, and serving as pastoral associates. Many dedicate themselves to these concerns because they know that a "Christian feminist spirituality relies on contemplation in action for justice as its only hope for the future" (Conn 1987, 233). The number of women theologians and religious educators continues to grow. They already have a great effect on the renewal and reform of both the church and society. In short, women are manifesting in a variety of ways their devotion to Christ, his church, and the Catholic tradition, and as such, they are a significant part of that vanguard that is promoting and expanding the new Pentecost.

Postscript: Identity
and Mission for the Future

Christians are disciples of Jesus Christ who respond to his call to participate in God's own work in expanding and promoting his reign among all people. Fulfilling this mission on all six continents has not been easy during the twentieth century for several reasons: Christians themselves are divided into hundreds of churches; many Christians have given up their faith; Christianity exists side by side with other vibrant religions; many people profess atheism and an absence of the experience of God; many, many people struggle against structural poverty and injustice.

Within the Catholic church, the obstacles to mission are further compounded today because the church is facing perhaps its greatest crisis since the Reformation. There is a hydra-like crisis in its institutional, intellectual, and devotional dimensions. The institution faces a crisis of authority, community, freedom, finances, identity, and mission. The intellectual is struggling to learn how best to hand on the tradition, with religious illiteracy, with interreligious dialogue and ecumenism, and with what it means to be a world church. The devotional dimension is hobbled by a serious decline in sacramental faith and a shortage of priests. There are also serious disagreements over ministries for women, sexual ethics, participation in the liturgy, and the spirituality that is fitting and proper for the postconciliar church. Presently, the major spiritualities are the neo-Augustinian, communitarian, and liberationist. In an age of pluralism it seems tolerant to allow these to exist side by side. On paper this is possible. But bring an ecclesial body together (an international synod, an episcopal conference, a diocesan synod, a parish council, a religious community) to discuss sensitive issues like liturgical changes, interreligious dialogue, the disposition of funds to the homeless or victims of AIDS, school curricula, euthanasia, or the death penalty and see how little consensus and mutual respect exist and how quickly and violently tempers fly.

Liberationist spirituality is new in the church. Many believe it represents a paradigmatic shift in theology comparable to what occurred with Augustine in the fifth century and Thomas Aquinas in the thirteenth. It

453

has growing support from recent popes, many bishops, and many of the faithful, clergy, and theologians because the gap between the rich and the poor continues to widen. For example, on June 24, 1996, the World Bank reported that more than one-fifth of the world's population lives on less than one dollar a day.[1] This startling statistic lends increased credibility to the words of Paul VI in *Octogesima adveniens* in 1971 when he wrote that social justice questions, "because of their urgency, extent and complexity, must, in the years to come, take first place among the preoccupations of Christians" (n. 7).

This liberationist spirituality is history and community-centered (and not ahistorical), justice and freedom centered (and not pietist or privatized), and grace and kingdom-centered (and not self-centered). It takes these perspectives because modernity was not only too optimistic about human advancement but also self-centered. Its goal or ideal was individual autonomy through rational self-fulfillment. According to David Tracy (1975, 11), the postmodern and postconciliar ideal is self-transcendence, that is, "a radical commitment to the struggle to transcend our present individual and societal states in favor of a continuous examination of those illusions which cloud our real and more limited possibilities for knowledge and action." And Bernard Lonergan counsels (1972, 55) that it is only "a religion that promotes self-transcendence to the point, not merely of justice, but of a self-sacrificing love, which will have a redemptive role in human society inasmuch as such love can undo the mischief of decline and restore the cumulative process of progress." In short, the church needs a spirituality that fosters a sacramental consciousness and that focuses on the massive social evil in which we live our history and from which God promises to redeem us.

It seems that some moments in history call for a particular theology and spirituality in preference to others, and even to the exclusion of others. Many believe a liberationist spirituality is what will best enable the devotional, intellectual, and institutional church to meet the challenges it faces as it moves into the twenty-first century.

Endnotes

CHAPTER 1.

1. For a summary of Von Hügel, see Dulles 1988a, 63–64. See also, Imbelli 1986; Tracy 1987b, 268–72; 1989b, 548–52; 1994, 85–93; 1995. For an extensive examination of Von Hügel's triad, see Lash 1988, 141–77. Lash indicates that, since for Von Hügel each of the elements takes an active and/or passive form, his final name for them was historical-institutional, critical-speculative, and mystical-operative. Lash also explains that, with reference to the mystical-operative, Von Hügel stressed the pervasive sense of God experienced by all and that, while he was aware that religion has social dimensions, unfortunately he never developed the relation of religion to the social and political problems of his day. In this book the mystical or devotional will denote not only religious experience, prayer, and a sacramental life, but also involvement in deeds of justice and mercy.

2. A news notice, "Housekeeper Breaks Long Silence on Pius XII's View of the Nazis," *National Catholic Reporter* 19 (4 March 1983): 2. For more details on Sister Pascalina Lehnert, see Paul I. Murphy and René R. Arlington, *La Popessa* (New York: Warner Books, 1983). This book, tainted with sensationalism and inaccuracy about the close relationship between Pius XII and this sister, was given a long, decisive rebuttal by Andrew Greeley (1983).

3. Editorial, *New York Journal American*, 29 October 1958.

4. Editorial, *National Catholic Reporter* 14 (18 August 1978): 8.

5. When Marcinkus was director of the Vatican Bank, it lost more than $1.2 billion in 1982 in doubtful transactions with Italy's failed Banco Ambrosiano.

6. A news notice, "The September Pope," *Time* (9 October 1978): 79.

7. Editorial, "After Two Conclaves, A Polish Pope," *New York Times*, 6 November 1978.

8. It is estimated that thirty-three popes died by violence since Peter was crucified near the Vatican in 67: "12 martyrs; 8 sure, or relatively sure, assassinations; and 13 quite possible assassinations" (McGinn 1985).

9. A news notice, "Why Did He Shoot?" *National Catholic Reporter* 30 (27 May 1994): 6.

CHAPTER 2

1. Historicism is the theory that all history is an account of what actually happened so that there is no room for the subjective or reflective view(s) of the historian. In other words it is "the view that all thought is essentially related to and cannot transcend its own time" (Bloom 1987, 40).

2. Gilhooley (1984) provides an interesting account of the effect of the condemnation of Modernism on the career of Father Francis Patrick Duffy (1871–1932), professor of philosophy at the New York diocesan seminary for fourteen years and the most celebrated chaplain of World War I.

3. This passage is from a 1916 work, *Escrits du temps de la guerre,* and found in Mooney 1967, 485.

4. For appreciative tributes to Henri de Lubac see Komonchak 1990c, 1992a; Dulles 1991.

CHAPTER 3

1. Hebblethwaite (1993a, 688) judged the Synod of 1977 on catechetics "the most modest, unadventurous, unnoticed, unnewsworthy, invisible and ignored synod there had so far been."

2. See Greeley 1971, 1973, and 1977. *The Cardinal Sins* was his first novel (1981). His novels are usually about priests and their involvement with sex, power, and corruption in the church. Asked why he writes these novels, Greeley has one consistent answer: "Religion has been passed along through stories since it began, and *The Cardinal Sins,* which is really about the power of God's love, carries on the tradition. It's as appropriate for a priest to be a novelist today as it was for priests in medieval times to make stained-glass windows" (*Wall Street Journal,* 20 April 1982).

3. Editorial, "Vatican II: 25 Years," *Commonweal* 117 (7 December 1990): 707–8.

4. A news notice, "Catholic Theologians Accuse Vatican of Resisting Change," *New York Times,* 14 December 1990. See also Windsor 1990c.

CHAPTER 4

1. Quoted in footnote 192 in Abbott 1966, 264.

2. Dulles (1988b) renamed the servant model, calling it "a secular-dialogic theology."

3. See P. Steinfels 1985; Imbelli 1986; Lamb 1986; Hebblethwaite 1986a; Dulles 1988a, 184–206; Murphy 1986.

Chapter 5

1. The older tradition was revived during Vatican II and placed in the Constitution on the Church (LG 22). A special postscript, dated November 16, 1964, and signed by Cardinal Pericle Felici, Secretary General of the council, was added to the document to explain the nature of the bishopric and its relationship to the papacy.

2. A news notice, "Vatican Document on Collegiality Draws Both Rejection, Support," *National Catholic Reporter* 25 (9 December 1988): 25. See *America* 158 (19 March 1988): 65–72 for four articles on the theological and juridical status of episcopal conferences.

3. Editorial, "Refusing the Draft," *Commonweal* 115 (2 December 1988): 644–45.

4. "The Cologne Declaration," *Commonweal* 116 (24 February 1989): 102–4.

5. A news notice, "Ousted French Bishop Meets with the Pope," *Christian Century* 113 (28 February 1996): 224.

6. A news notice, "Ratzinger Criticizes Postconciliar Changes," *National Catholic Reporter* 21 (21 June 1985): 26.

7. Dulles is quoted in an editorial, "Vatican Limits Dissent," *Christian Century* 107 (11 July 1990): 665.

8. Editorial, "Dangerous Opinions," *Commonweal* 117 (10 August 1990): 435–36.

9. Gregory Baum is quoted in an editorial, "Gorbachev and John Paul Must Face Contradictions," *National Catholic Reporter* 26 (19 January 1990): 32.

10. A news notice, "Dutch Start Petition," *National Catholic Reporter* 32 (19 April 1996): 8.

11. Quoted by John Tracy Ellis in a letter to the editor, *Commonweal* 117 (9 February 1990): 66, 94.

12. A news notice, "Dialogue Calls Mislead, [Dulles] Says," *National Catholic Reporter* 33 (6 December 1996): 10.

13. Editorial, "Cooling the Family Fight," *America* 175 (9 November 1996): 3.

Chapter 6

1. Schineller presents four views. There are actually more. The three outlined here are those most Catholics would accept and understand because all three are found in the church.

2. See Hebblethwaite 1987b, 1989f, 1994e. At the time of the fiftieth anniversary of the Warsaw uprising, Pope John Paul told fourteen Carmelite nuns to move from their convent at the Auschwitz death camp. Some Jews viewed

the presence of a Catholic convent at the place where 1.5 million Jews perished an affront to Jewish sensibilities. See Perlez 1993.

3. A news notice, "A Papal First," *Christian Century* 103 (30 April 1986): 432.

CHAPTER 7

1. A news notice, "Orthodox Numbers Are Increasing," *Christian Century* 113 (24 January 1996): 71–72.

2. A news notice, "No Forgiveness for Luther," *Christian Century* 97 (27 February 1980): 223.

3. A news notice, "Lutheran–Vatican Declaration Delayed," *Christian Century* 113 (23 October 1996): 1003–4.

4. A news notice, "Paisley vs. the Pope," *Christian Century* 105 (2 November 1988): 978.

5. A news notice, "Protesters Denounce Anglican Archbishop over Ecumenism," *National Catholic Reporter* 26 (2 February 1990): 9.

6. A news notice, "Black Baptist Rejects Apology by SBC," *Christian Century* 113 (27 September 1996): 879–80.

7. A news notice, "Disciples Vote in Favor of COCU," *Christian Century* 113 (22 November 1996): 1110.

8. A news notice, "Cardinal Questions Church's Ecumenical Stance," *National Catholic Reporter* 23 (29 May 1987): 24.

9. A news notice, "Pope and Patriarch Offer Joint Blessing," *Christian Century* 112 (19 July 1995): 705–6.

10. A news notice, "Pope, Orthodox Leader Seek to Heal Old Wounds," *Los Angeles Times,* 1 August 1995.

11. A news notice, "Orthodox–Catholic Communion Still Distant," *Christian Century* 112 (13 December 1995): 1210.

12. A news notice, "Pope and Archbishop of Canterbury Conduct 'Joyful' Meeting in Africa," *New York Times,* 10 May 1980.

13. "Baptism, Eucharist and Ministry: An Appraisal [by the Vatican]," *Origins* 17:23 (19 November 1987): 401–16.

14. A news notice, "'Radical Changes' for WCC," *Christian Century* 113 (25 September 1996): 885–87.

15. A news notice, "Scrap WCC for Greater Unity, Urges Bishop," *Christian Century* 113 (20 March 1996): 321–22.

16. A news notice, "Roman Catholics and the WCC," *Christian Century* 112 (27 September 1995): 882.

17. A news notice, "WCC Faces Major Structural Changes," *Christian Century* 113 (18 December 1996): 1247–48.

CHAPTER 8

1. There are too many to list here. Some of the more prominent scholars were Karl Adam, Louis Bouyer, Odo Casel, Romano Guardini, Pierre-Marie Guy, Johannes Hofinger, Robert Hovda, Clifford Howell, Josef Jungmann, A. Martimort, Pius Parsch, A. Roguet and Gerald Vann.

2. This is part of H. A. Reinhold's tribute to Virgil Michel after his death as reported in K. Hughes 1991, 18.

3. A news notice, "Pope Urges End to Abuse of Liturgy Changes," *National Catholic Reporter* 25 (26 May 1989): 15.

4. Editorial, "Lefèbvre Knows How to Hurt Rome," *National Catholic Reporter* 13 (26 August 1977): 10.

5. Editorial, "Catholics Want Solidarity with Their Bishops," *National Catholic Reporter* 31 (11 November 1994): 24.

CHAPTER 9

1. Editorial, "The New Attack on Human Rights," *New York Times*, 10 December 1995.

2. Some of the labor priests include Leo Brown, S.J., of St. Louis, Eugene Boyle of San Francisco; Philip Carey, S.J., of New York; Raymond Clancy of Detroit; John Corridan of New York; Mortimer Gavin of Boston; Francis Gilligan of St. Paul-Minneapolis; John Monaghan of New York; Charles Owen Rice of Pittsburgh; William Smith, S.J., of New Jersey; Louis Toomey, S.J., of New Orleans; and Monsignor George Higgins of Chicago (McBrien 1995c). Higgins is the most famous of this distinuished group, in part because he served in the Social Action Department of the National Catholic Welfare Conference in Washington from 1944 to 1972. He later taught at the University of Notre Dame and the Catholic University of America. In 1993 a Center for Labor and Economics was established at the University of Notre Dame and named the Higgins Labor Studies Center.

3. This quote from Pius XII on nuclear war and the headline that follows were taken from an unsigned article in the *New York Times* on the day of his death, 9 October 1958.

4. Murray also wrote the sixty-two footnotes to the text. For a detailed history, see Linnan 1986 and Pavan 1969. For an appreciative review of Murray's career, his education in Europe in the mid-1930s, his conflicts with the Vatican in the 1950s, and his contribution to Vatican II, see Komonchak 1992b.

5. *Wall Street Journal*, 30 March 1967.

6. For a moving, first-person account of this experience, see Sobrino 1991.

7. A news notice, "Pope, in India, Prays for the Bhopal Victims," *New York Times*, 6 February 1986.

8. A news notice, "Pope Meets with Castro, Plans to Visit Cuba," *Christian Century* 113 (4 December 1996): 1191.

9. Dorr (1984) speaks of four spiritualities or mindsets: fortress, pilgrim, people of God, and power pyramid. The fourth is complicated and is explained at pages 55–56 and 202–4. While I do not accept his four divisions nor do I use all of his "models," I do find some of his explanations of the spiritualities presently operative in the church helpful and insightful.

CHAPTER 10

1. A news notice, "Sex Book Provokes Critical Statements from Bishops," *National Catholic Reporter* 15 (29 July 1977): 8.

2. A news notice, "*Veritatis Splendor* Draws Cheers and Jeers," *National Catholic Reporter* 29 (15 October 1993): 15.

3. Ibid.

4. Editorial, "John Paul II's Truths Sacrifice Tradition of Pastoral Concern," *National Catholic Reporter* 29 (15 October 1993): 17.

5. A news notice, "*Veritatis Splendor* Draws Cheers and Jeers," *National Catholic Reporter* 29 (15 October 1993): 15.

6. Dominion and Montefiore 1989, 27–29. They add a fourth criterion: sexual activity relieves sexual tension.

7. Editorial, "The Pilgrimage of Pope Paul," *Christian Century* 95 (30 August 1978): 779–80.

8. A response was made to Grisez by Hallett (1982); Grisez followed (1986). See also Hallett 1988; Hebblethwaite 1990a.

9. A news notice, "Church Leaders Mix Condoms and Caveats," *National Catholic Reporter* 32 (15 March 1996): 8.

10. A news notice, "Nuns Deny Vatican Claim," *Christian Century* 103 (13 August 1986): 704.

11. A news notice, "Former Nuns Vow to Keep Dissenting," *National Catholic Reporter* 26 (12 October 1990): 15. See Ferraro and Hussey, *No Turning Back* (1990).

12. A news notice, "Health Care Reform and Neighbor Love," *Christian Century* 111 (23 March 1994): 305–6.

13. A news notice, "Protestant and Jewish Leaders Back Veto," *Christian Century* 113 (15 May 1996): 537–38.

14. A news notice, "Election Comments Stir Controversy," *National Catholic Reporter* 33 (15 November 1996): 6.

15. A news notice, "Study Details Sexuality in America," *Christian Century* 111 (2 November 1994): 1008.

16. A news notice, "Gays and the Gospel: An Interview with Troy Perry," *Christian Century* 113 (25 September 1996): 896–901.

17. Editorial, "Consulting Stephen's Experience: Pastoral Care of Homosexuals," *America* 155 (23 November 1986): 313–14. See also McManus 1986; Quinn 1987.

18. Editorial, "Homosexual Marriages," *America* 123 (30 December 1970): 621; "For Same-sex Marriage," San Francisco Chronicle, 16 December 1990; Dean 1991; Hartinger 1991.

19. A news notice, "Dutch to Lift Ban on Gay Marriages," *National Catholic Reporter* 32 (3 May 1996): 10.

20. A news notice, "Unitarians Endorse Same-Sex Marriages," *Christian Century* 113 (28 August 1996): 807.

21. A news notice, "Vatican Hails Marriage Law," *National Catholic Reporter* 32 (27 September 1996): 6.

CHAPTER 11

1. Brown (1985, 99) indicates that the translation of Luke 1:48 as "handmaiden" does not do justice to the fact that Mary is speaking from within the stratified society of the Roman Empire where slave women were among the lowest of peoples.

CHAPTER 12

1. Mary Buckley (1979) proposes a third model, "a transformative person-centered model." But other feminists believe her method is but a variation on the two natures model (M. Donovan 1987, 290–91). Buckley's contribution is her criticism of the one nature model: it needs to be joined to a critique of social structures if it is to be future-oriented rather than past-confirming.

2. A news notice, "Hindu-Christian Tensions Mount in India," *Christian Century* 113 (17 January 1996): 42.

3. Glendon (1996) refers to "five dogmatic extremes that have shed more heat than light on women's issues": "sameness" feminism that states there is no significant difference between women and men; "difference" feminism that regards women and men as virtually different species; "dominance" feminism that advocates female superiority; "gender" feminism that regards the categories of male and female as mere social constructs; and "rigid biological determinism" that wants no part with feminism because it prefers the traditional roles women had in past centuries.

4. A symposium that included the full text and responses to it by four individuals representing various theological and social-political experiences (Robert Hoyt, Rosemary Ruether, John Garvey, and John Coleman) was offered by *Commonweal* 105 (17 February 1978): 108–16.

5. In 1989 the National Council of Churches issued a report, "Women Ministers in 1986 and 1977: A Ten Year View." In 1977 it was estimated that 76 out of 163 reporting denominations ordained women to the full ministry. See "Women in Ministry," *Christian Century* 106 (20 March 1989): 280.

6. John C. Haughey invited six participants at the Detroit WOC to report their impressions of the conference: "Impressions from Detroit," *America* 134 (17 January 1976): 26–31.

7. "A Statement of the CTSA on the Dismissal of Sister M. Carmel McEnroy, RSM, Ph.D.," in *Catholic Theological Society of America Proceedings* 50 (1995): 326–29.

8. A news notice, "McEnroy Files New Suit," *National Catholic Reporter* 33 (30 May 1997): 6.

9. Appendix B: "Tradition and the Ordination of Woman: A Question of Criteria," *Proceedings of the Catholic Theological Society of America* 51 (1996): 333–41.

POSTSCRIPT

1. A news notice, "20% of World's Population Live on a Dollar a Day," *New York Times*, 24 June 1996.

Bibliography

Abbott, Walter M., ed. 1966. *The Documents of Vatican II*. New York: America Press.

Allen, Diogenes. 1989. "Christian Values in a Post-Christian Context" In *Postmodern Theology: Christian Faith in a Pluralistic World*, edited by Frederic B. Burnham, 20–36. New York: Harper and Row.

———. 1990. "The End of the Modern World: A New Openness to Faith." *The Princeton Seminary Bulletin* 11.1 (Supplement): 11–31.

Anonymous. 1984. "Nuns: The Battered Women in the Church?" *National Catholic Reporter* 21 (21 December): 25.

Anton, Angel. 1988. "Postconciliar Ecclesiology." In vol. 1 of *Vatican II*, 407–38. See Latourelle 1988.

Aubert, Roger. 1978. *The Church in a Secularized Society*. New York: Paulist Press.

Azevedo, Marcello de C. 1984. "Inculturation and the World Church." *Catholic Theological Society of America Proceedings* 39: 122–27.

Balasuriya, Tissa. 1976. "Women in the Church." *Commonweal* 103 (16 January): 39–42.

———. 1991. "Mission Encyclical's Dubious Claim of Church Monopoly." *National Catholic Reporter* 28 (25 October): 22

Baum, Gregory. 1968. "The Encyclical: The Right to Dissent." *Commonweal* 95 (23 August): 553–54.

———. 1970a. *Man Becoming*. New York: Herder and Herder.

———. 1970b. "Vatican II and the Reinterpretation of Doctrine." *The Ecumenist* 9 (November): 1–4.

———. 1972. "Eucharistic Hospitality." *The Ecumenist* 11 (November): 11–16.

———. 1973. "Ministry in the Church." *The Ecumenist* 12 (July): 76–80.

———. 1974. "Catholic Homosexuals." *Commonweal* 100 (15 February): 479–82.

————. 1975. Religion and Alienation: *A Theological Reading of Sociology.* New York: Paulist Press.

————. 1976. "Liberation Theology: First the Theory." *National Catholic Reporter* 12 (8 October): 8–9.

————. 1977. "Documentation: A Letter Demanding Due Process," *The Ecumenist* 16 (November): 9.

————. 1979a. "The First Papal Encyclical [of John Paul II]." *The Ecumenist* 17 (May): 55–59.

————. 1979b. "Catholic Foundations of Human Rights." *The Ecumenist* 18 (November): 6–12.

————. 1982. *The Priority of Labor: A Commentary on Laborem Exercens.* New York: Paulist.

————. 1983a. "After Twenty Years." *The Ecumenist* 21 (January): 17–19.

————. 1983b. "Gutierrez and the Catholic Tradition." *The Ecumenist* 21 (September): 81–84.

————. 1984a. "Faith and Liberation: Development Since Vatican II." In *Vatican II: Open Questions and New Horizons,* edited by Gerald M. Fagin, 75–104. Wilmington, Del.: Michael Glazier.

————. 1984b. "Class Struggle and the Magisterium: A New Note." *Theological Studies* 45 (December): 690–701.

————. 1985. "After Liberal Optimism, What?" *Commonweal* 112 (21 June): 368–70.

————. 1986a. "The Theology of the American Pastoral." *The Ecumenist* 24 (January): 17–22.

————. 1986b. "Catholic Inconsistencies." *The Ecumenist* 24 (January): 23–30.

————. 1987. *Theology and Society.* New York: Paulist Press.

————. 1988. "The Churches, Israel and the Palestinians." *The Ecumenist* 27 (November): 1–6.

————. 1989a. "Liberal Capitalism." In *The Logic of Solidarity,* 75–89. See Baum and Ellsberg 1989.

————. 1989b. "Structures of Sin" In *The Logic of Solidarity,* 110–126. See Baum and Ellsberg 1989.

————. 1989c. "Sociology and Salvation: Do We Need a Catholic Sociology?" *Theological Studies* 50 (December): 718–43.

————. 1994. "Homosexuality and the Natural Law." *The Ecumenist* 1:2 (January): 33–36.

Baum, Gregory, and Robert Ellsberg, eds. 1989. *The Logic of Solidarity.* New York: Orbis Books.

Beauchesne, Richard J. 1995. "Yves Congar Leaves Rich Legacy." *National Catholic Reporter* 31 (14 July): 2.

Beifuss, Joan Turner, and Mary Fay Bourgoin. 1985. "Catholic Women Voice Divergent Views, Concerns at D.C. Hearings." *National Catholic Reporter* 21 (15 March): 1, 35–36.

Bellah, Robert, Richard Madsen, William M. Sullivan, Ann Swidler, and Stephen M. Tipton. 1985. *Habits of the Heart: Individualism and Commitment in American Life.* Berkeley, Ca.: University of California Press.

Bennett, John C. 1966. Review of *Situation Ethics,* by Joseph Fletcher. *Religious Education Review* 61 (November): 482–83.

Bernardin, Joseph. 1996a. "Called to Be Catholic: Church in a Time of Peril." *America* 175 (13 August): 5–8.

———. 1996b. "Bernardin Answers Common Ground Critics." *National Catholic Reporter* 32 (6 September): 9.

Berrigan, Daniel. 1977. "The Leveling of John McNeill." *Commonweal* 104 (9 December): 778–83.

Berry, Jason. 1985. "Pedophile Priest: Study in Inept Church Response." *National Catholic Reporter* 21 (7 June): 6, 19–21.

———. 1992. *Lead Us Not into Temptation.* New York: Doubleday.

———. 1993. "Listening to the Survivors: Voices of the People." *America* 169 (13 November): 4–9.

Bishop, Katherine. 1988. "Father Serra, a California Friar, to Be Beatified." *New York Times,* 3 May.

Bloom, Allan. 1987. *The Closing of the American Mind.* New York: Simon and Schuster.

Bohlen, Celestine. 1995a. "Pope, Noting Liberation of Auschwitz, Denounces Anti-Semitism." *New York Times,* 30 January.

———. 1995b. "Catholics Defy an Infallible Church." *New York Times,* 26 November.

———. 1996. "Pope Talks with Anglican Leader Appears to Stall." *New York Times,* 6 December.

———. 1997a. "A Sri Lankan Priest Is Excommunicated for His 'Relativism'." *New York Times,* 7 January.

———. 1997b. "Discordant But Quiet Sarajevo Gets Papal Visit." *New York Times,* 13 April.

———. 1997c. "Pope, in Sarajevo, Calls for Forgiveness." *New York Times,* 14 April.

———. 1997d. "Pope in Beirut Urges Healing Muslims' Ties to Christians." *New York Times,* 11 May.

———. 1997e. "Pope Calls Upon Lebanese to Put Strife Behind Them." *New York Times,* 12 May.

Bokenkotter, Thomas. 1977. *A Concise History of the Catholic Church.* New York: Doubleday.

———. 1985. *Essential Catholicism.* New York: Doubleday.

Boff, Leonardo. 1985. *Church: Charism and Power. Liberation Theology and the Institutional Church.* New York: Crossroads.

———. 1989. *Faith on the Edge: Religion and Marginalized Existence.* New York: Harper and Row.

Bono, Agostino. 1995. "Pope Accepts Groer's Resignation." *National Catholic Reporter* 31 (22 September): 7.

Boswell, John. 1981. *Christianity, Social Tolerance and Homosexuality.* Chicago: University of Chicago Press.

Boys, Mary C. 1994. "Answers and Questions: The New Catholic Catechism." *Christian Century* 111 (23 November): 1115–19.

Braaten, Carl E. 1992. *No Other Gospel! Christianity among the World's Religions.* Minneapolis, Minn.: Fortress Press.

Briggs, David. 1993. "Spiritual Leaders Gather to Counter Religious Violence." *Los Angeles Times.* August 28.

Brockman, James R. 1979. "Seventeen Days in Puebla." *America* 140 (10 March): 180–83.

Brouwer, Arie R. 1986. "The Steps of Ecumenical Formation." *Christian Century* 103 (24 September): 803–5.

Brown, Raymond E. 1970. *Priest and Bishop: Biblical Reflections.* New York: Paulist Press.

———. 1972. "The Problem of the Virginal Conception of Jesus." *Theological Studies* 33 (March): 3–34.

———. 1975a. *Biblical Reflections on Crises Facing the Church.* New York: Paulist Press.

———. 1975b. Review of *The Mother of Jesus in the New Testament,* by John McHugh. *America* 133 (25 October): 260–63.

———. 1981. "'And the Lord Said'? Biblical Reflections on Scripture as the Word of God." *Theological Studies* 42 (March): 3–19.

———. 1984. *The Churches the Apostles Left Behind.* New York: Paulist Press.

———. 1985. *Biblical Exegesis and Church Doctrine.* New York: Paulist Press.

———. 1986a. "Gospel Infancy Narrative Research from 1976 to 1986: Part I (Matthew)." *Catholic Biblical Quarterly* 48 (July): 468–83.

———. 1986b. "Gospel Infancy Narrative Research from 1976 to 1986: Part II (Luke)." *Catholic Biblical Quarterly* 48 (October): 660–80.

Brown, Raymond, Karl P. Donfried, and John Reumann. 1973. *Peter in the New Testament.* New York: Paulist Press.

Brown, Raymond, Karl P. Donfried, Joseph A. Fitzmyer, and John Reumann. 1979. *Mary in the New Testament.* New York: Paulist Press.

Brown, Robert McAfee et al. 1972. "A Round Table: Where Are We in Ecumenism?" *America* 126 (22 January): 50–66.

———. 1978. *Theology in a New Key.* Philadelphia: Westminster.

———. 1980. "Starting Over: New Beginning Points for Theology." *Christian Century* 97 (14 May): 545–49.

———. 1986. "Leonardo Boff: Theologian for All Christians." *Christian Century* 10 (2 July): 615–18.

———. 1987a. "A Protestant Looks at an Aggressive Papacy." In *The Church in Anguish,* 177–85. See Küng and Swidler 1987.

———. 1987b. "Protestants and the Marian Year." *Christian Century* 104 (3 June): 520–21.

Brunsman, Barry. 1985. *New Hope for Divorced Catholics.* New York: Harper and Row.

Buckley, Mary. 1978. "Rediscovering the Christian God: A Feminist Reflection." *Catholic Theological Society of America Proceedings* 33: 148–54.

———. 1979. "The Rising of the Woman Is the Rising of the Race." *Catholic Theological Society of America Proceedings* 34: 48–63.

Buckley, William F. 1961. "This Week." *National Review* 11 (12 August): 88.

Bühlmann, Walbert. 1977. *The Coming of the Third Church.* New York: Orbis Books.

———. 1986. *The Church of the Future.* New York: Orbis Books.

Burke, Mary. 1975. "The Church and the Equal Rights Amendment." *America* 132 (17 May): 374–78.

Burkholder, Steve. 1987. "First Woman Elected Bishop in Anglican Church." *National Catholic Reporter* 24 (7 October): 12.

Burns, John F. 1997. "Followers Struggle to Fill Mother Teresa's Sandals." *New York Times,* 9 March.

Butterfield, Herbert. 1966. *The Origins of Modern Science, 1300–1800.* New York: Macmillan.

Cahill, Lisa Sowle. 1978. "Sexual Ethics in Christian Theological Ethics: A Review of Recent Studies." *Religious Studies Review* 4 (January): 1–14.

———. 1985a. "Humanity as Female and Male: The Ethics of Sexuality." In *Called to Love: Towards a Contemporary Christian Ethic,* edited by Francis A. Eigo, 79–95. Pennsylvania: Villanova University Press.

———. 1985b. "Morality: The Deepening Crisis." *Commonweal* 112 (20 September): 496–99.

———. 1987. "Divorced from Experience: Rethinking the Theology of Marriage." *Commonweal* 114 (27 March): 171–76.

————. 1990. "Can We Get Real about Sex?" *America* 117 (14 September): 497–99, 502–3.

————. 1993. "Veritatis Splendor." *Commonweal* 120 (22 October): 15–16.

Callahan, Daniel. 1973. "Abortion: Thinking and Experience." *Christianity and Crisis* 32 (8 January): 295–98.

Callahan, Sidney. 1986. "Conscience Reconsidered." *America* 155 (1 November): 251–53.

————. 1993. "Mary and the Challenge of the Feminist Movement." *America* 169 (18 December): 6–11, 14.

————. 1994. "Thinking about Gay Marriage." *Commonweal* 121 (22 April): 6–8.

————. 1996. "Let's Talk: The Search for Common Ground." *Commonweal* 123 (27 September): 8–9.

Carmody, Denise Lardner, and John Tully Carmody. 1983. *Christianity: An Introduction.* Philadelphia: Westminster Press.

Carr, Anne. 1982. "Is a Christian Feminist Theology Possible?" *Theological Studies* 43 (June): 279–97.

Carroll, James. 1974. "The Philadelphia Ordination." *National Catholic Reporter* 11 (16 August): 14.

Castel, Pol. 1994. "Looking for the Way Together in Jewish-Christian Dialogue." *America* 171 (17 December): 12–15.

Catoir, John T. 1967. "The Church and Second Marriage." *Commonweal* 94 (14 April): 13–14.

Chadwick, Owen. 1987. *Britain and the Vatican During the Second World War.* New York: Cambridge University Press.

Champlin, Joseph M. 1989a. *The Marginal Catholic.* Notre Dame, Ind.: Ave Maria Press.

————. 1989b. "Barriers to the Sacraments." *Commonweal* 116 (20 October): 559–61.

Cheetham, Nicholas. 1983. *Keepers of the Keys.* New York: Charles Scribner's Sons.

Clarity, James F. 1995. "Irish Vote to End the Divorce Ban by a Tiny Margin." *New York Times,* 26 November.

————. 1997. "Irish Greet First Day of Divorce Cautiously." *New York Times,* 28 February.

Clark, Monica. 1997. "U.S. Bishops Debate Mass Text Revisions, Await Vote Results." *The Catholic Voice* 35 (30 June): 1, 7.

Cleary, Edward L. 1992. "John Paul Cries 'Wolf': Misreading the Pentecostals." *Commonweal* 120 (20 November): 7–8.

Clebsch, William A. 1979. *Christianity in European History.* New York: Oxford University Press.

Clifford, Richard J. 1995. "The Bishops, the Bible and Liturgical Language." *America* 172 (27 May): 12–16.

Clooney, Francis X. 1997. "Relativism in Perspective: Rereading Ratzinger." *Commonweal* 124 (31 January): 9–10.

Cohen, Roger. 1994a. "In Croatia, a Frail Pope John Paul II Calls for a 'Culture of Peace'." *New York Times,* 11 September.

———. 1994b. "Pope Urges Croats to Renew 'Unbreakable' Slavic Ties." *New York Times,* 12 September.

Coleman, John A. 1981. "The Future of Ministry." *America* 144 (28 March): 243–49.

———. 1989. "Who Are the Catholic 'Fundamentalists'?" *Commonweal* 116 (27 January): 42–47.

Coleman, Gerald D. 1987. "The Vatican Statement on Homosexuality." *Theological Studies* 48 (December): 727–34.

Collinge, William, and Daniel Sheridan, Denise Lardner Carmody, William P. Lowe, and Willaim Cenkner. 1986. A review symposium of *No Other Name?: A Critical Survey of Christian Attitudes toward the World Religions,* by Paul Knitter. *Horizons* 13 (Spring): 116–30.

Collins, Carole. 1995. "Vatican Applies Muscle at U.N." *National Catholic Reporter* 31 (31 March): 7.

Collins, Patrick W. 1984. "Liturgical Renewal, Twenty Years Later." *Commonweal* 111 (1 June): 330–34.

Collins, Raymond F. 1986. *Christian Morality: Biblical Foundations.* Notre Dame, Ind.: University of Notre Dame.

———. 1993. *Divorce in the New Testament.* Collegeville, Minn.: Liturgical Press.

Congar, Yves. 1966. *Tradition and Traditions: An Historical and Theological Essay.* New York: Macmillan Co.

———. 1968. *A History of Theology.* New York: Doubleday.

Conn, Joann Wolski, ed. 1986. *Women's Spirituality: Resources for Christian Development.* New York: Paulist Press.

———. 1987. "A Discipleship of Equals: Past, Present, Future." *Horizons* 14 (February): 231–61.

———. 1991. "New Vitality: The Challenge from Feminist Theology." *America* 165 (5 October): 217–19.

Cooke, Bernard. 1977. *Ministry to Word and Sacrament.* Philadelphia: Fortress Press.

———. 1983. "Non-patriarchal Salvation." *Horizons* 10 (Spring): 22–31.

———. 1985. "U.S. Lay Ministry Bouncing Over Old Boundaries." *National Catholic Reporter* 21 (15 March): 17.

———. 1987. "What God Has Joined Together." *Commonweal* 114 (27 March): 178–82.

———. ed. 1989. *The Papacy and the Church in the United States.* New York: Paulist Press.

———. 1990. "Entire Faith Community Performs Eucharist." *National Catholic Reporter* 26 (14 May): 14.

Cornwell, John. 1989. *A Thief in the Night: The Death of John Paul I.* New York: Simon and Schuster.

Cort, John C. 1995. "God Is Not an It." *Commonweal* 122 (17 November): 17–19.

Cortesi, Arnaldo. 1962. "Pomp and Prayer Reign on Sunny Day at Vatican." *New York Times,* 11 October.

Cowell, Alan. 1991. "Europe's Bishops Unable to Heal Rifts." *New York Times,* 15 December.

———. 1992. "After 350 Years, Vatican Says Galileo Was Right: It Moves." *New York Times,* 31 October.

———. 1994a. "Pope Calls Gay Marriage Threat to Family." *New York Times,* 23 February.

———. 1994b. "Vatican Fights Plan to Bolster Role of Women." *New York Times,* 15 June.

———. 1994c. "Catholic Synod Keeps Top Jobs for Men Only." *New York Times,* 29 October.

———. 1995a. "Pope, in Sri Lanka, Seeks to Soothe Buddhist Critics." *New York Times,* 21 January.

———. 1995b. "Buddhist Monks in Sri Lanka Boycott Meeting with Pope." *New York Times,* 22 January.

———. 1996. "Files Suggest British Knew Early of Nazi Atrocities against Jews." *New York Times,* 19 November.

Cox, Harvey. 1980. "Theology: What Is It? Who Does It? How Is It Done?" *Christian Century* 97 (24 September): 874–79.

———. 1988a. *The Silencing of Leonardo Boff: The Vatican and the Future of World Christianity.* Oak Park, Ill.: Meyer Stone.

———. 1988b. "Many Mansions for One Way? The Crisis in Interfaith Dialogue." *Christian Century* 105 (17 August): 731–35.

Crossette, Barbara. 1994. "Population Debate: The Premises Are Changed." *New York Times,* 14 September.

———. 1996. "Snubbing Human Rights." *New York Times,* 28 April.

Crow, Paul A. 1986. "Assisi's Day of Prayer for Peace." *Christian Century* 103 (3 December): 1084–85.

Crowe, Marian E. 1996. "The Annulment Game." *Commonweal* 123 (13 September): 13–15.

Crowley, Patricia. 1993. "Confessions of a Birth Control Commission Catholic." *National Catholic Reporter* 30 (17 December): 19.

Cuddy, Edward. 1979. "The Rebel Function in Catholicism." *Commonweal* 106 (14 September): 495–97.

Cunningham, Agnes. 1986. "Decree on Ecumenism." In *Vatican II and Its Documents*, 62–77. See O'Connell. 1986.

Cunningham, Lawrence S. 1986. *The Catholic Experience*. New York: Crossroad.

———. 1993. "The New Catechism: A First Reading." *Commonweal* 120 (12 March): 8–12.

Curran, Charles E. 1970. *Contemporary Problems in Moral Theology*. Notre Dame, Ind.: Fides Publishers.

———. 1972. *Catholic Moral Theology in Dialogue*. Notre Dame, Ind.: University of Notre Dame Press.

———. 1973. "Abortion: Law and Morality in Contemporary Catholic Theology." *Jurist* 33 (Spring): 180.

———. 1974a. "Divorce: Catholic Theory and Practice in the United States." *American Ecclesiastical Review* 168 (January): 3–34; 168 (February): 75–79.

———. 1974b. "Two Signs of the Times." *National Catholic Reporter* 10 (18 October): 7–8.

———. 1978. *Issues in Sexual and Medical Ethics*. Notre Dame, Ind.: University of Notre Dame Press.

———. 1982. *American Catholic Social Ethics*. Notre Dame, Ind.: University of Notre Dame Press.

———. 1986. *Faithful Dissent*. New York: Sheed and Ward.

———. 1993a. "Encyclical Left Church Credibility Stillborn." *National Catholic Reporter* 29 (16 July): 14–15.

———. 1993b. "*Veritatis Splendor.*" *Commonweal* 120 (22 October): 14–15.

———. 1995. "Encyclical Is Positive, Problematic." *National Catholic Reporter* 31 (14 April): 4–5.

———. 1996a. "Two Traditions: Historical Consciousness Meets the Immutable." *Commonweal* 123 (11 October): 11–13.

———. 1996b. "Häring Reflects on Ministry in Priesthood Imperiled." *National Catholic Reporter* 33 (8 November): 21–22.

———. 1997. "Open Letter to Tissa Balasuriya." *National Catholic Reporter* 33 (7 February): 5–7.

Daly, Gabriel. 1980. *Transcendence and Immanence*. Oxford: Clarendon Press.

———. 1985. "Catholicism and Modernity." *Journal of the American Academy of Religion* 53 (December): 773–96.

Daly, Mary. 1968. *The Church and the Second Sex*. New York: Harper and Row.

———. 1973. *Beyond God the Father*. Boston: Beacon Press.

Darnton, John. 1994. "Church of England Ordains 32 Women to Join Priesthood." *New York Times*, 13 March.

D'Costa, Gavin. 1984. "John Hick's Copernican Revolution Ten Years After." *New Blackfriars* 65 (July): 323–30.

———. 1986. *Theology and Religious Pluralism: The Challenge of Other Religions*. Oxford: Basil Blackwell.

———. 1990. *Christian Uniqueness Reconsidered*. New York: Orbis Books.

Dean, Craig R. 1991. "Legalize Gay Marriage." *New York Times*, 28 September.

De Celle, Douglas. 1996. "Among the Promise Keepers: A Pastor's Reflection." *Christian Century* 113 (3 July): 695–97.

De Fiores, Stephano. 1988. "Mary in Postconciliar Theology." In vol. 1 of *Vatican II*, 469–539. See Latourelle. 1988.

De Nevi, Don, and Noel Francis Moholy. 1985. *Junipero Serra*. San Francisco: Harper and Row.

Deschner, John. 1986. "What To Do with a 'Convergence'." *Commonweal* 113 (31 January): 50–52.

Desseux, Jacques. 1983. *Twenty Centuries of Ecumenism*. New York: Paulist Press.

Dhanis, Edouard, and Jan Visser. 1973. "The Supplement to A New Catechism" in *A New Catechism: Catholic Faith for Adults*, 511–74. New York: Seabury Press.

Diamond, James J. 1975. "Abortion, Animation and Biological Hominization." *Theological Studies* 36 (June): 305–24.

Dicker, Fred. 1990. "Judgment by a Higher Authority." *New York Post*, 23 January.

Di Ianni, Albert. 1974. "Is the Fetus a Person?" *American Ecclesiastical Review* 168 (May): 323–24.

———. 1989. "Faith and Justice: A Delicate Balance." *America* 161 (22 July): 32–36.

Dinges, William D. 1988. "Quo Vadis, Lefèbvre?" *America* 158 (18 June): 602–6.

Dinter, Paul E. 1989. "Standing in the Way of Worship." *Commonweal* 116 (16 June): 367–70.

Dionne, E. J. 1985. "Pope and Jews: Strain Amid Celebration." *New York Times*, 29 October.

Doerflinger, Richard. 1985. "Who Are Catholics for a Free Choice?" *America* 153 (16 November): 312–17.

Dolan, Jay P. 1975. *The Immigrant Church*. Baltimore: Johns Hopkins University Press.

———. 1978a. *Catholic Revivalism: The American Experience: 1830–1900*. Notre Dame, Ind.: University of Notre Dame Press.

———. 1978b. Review of *A Concise History of the Catholic Church,* by Thomas Bokenkotter. *Critic* 36 (Spring): 75–77.

———. 1985. *The American Catholic Experience: A History from Colonial Times to the Present.* New York: Doubleday.

Dominion, Jack, and Hugh Montefiore. 1989. *God, Sex and Love.* Philadelphia: Trinity Press International.

Donahue, John R. 1977. "Women, Priesthood and the Vatican." *America* 136 (2 April): 285– 89.

———. 1981. "Divorce: New Testament Perspectives." *The Month* 242 (April):113–20.

———. 1993. "A Journey Remembered: Catholic Biblical Scholarship 50 Years After *Divino Afflante Spiritu.*" *America* 169 (18 September): 6–11.

Donders, Joseph G. 1990. "Inculturation and Catholicity in Relation to the Worldwide Church." *Catholic Theological Society of America Proceedings* 45: 30–40.

Donohue, John W. 1981. "The Centennial of John XXIII." *America* 145 (22 November): 314.

Donovan, Daniel L. 1985. "Church and Theology in the Modernist Crisis." *Catholic Theological Society of America Proceedings* 40: 145–59.

Donovan, Mary Ann. 1987. "Women's Issues: An Agenda for the Church?" *Horizons* 14 (Fall): 283–95.

Dorr, Donal. 1983. *Option for the Poor: A Hundred Years of Vatican Social Teaching.* New York: Paulist Press.

———. 1984. *Spirituality and Justice.* New York: Orbis Books.

———. 1989. "Solidarity and Integral Human Development." In *The Logic of Solidarity,* 143– 54. See Baum and Ellsberg 1989.

Doty, Robert C. 1964. "Pontiff Adjourns Council and Honors Mary." *New York Times,* 22 November.

———. 1965. "Pope Paul Closes Vatican Council Amid Pagentry." *New York Times,* 9 December.

Doyle, Dennis M. 1992. "Communion Ecclesiology and the Silencing of Boff." *America* 167 (12 September): 139–43.

———. 1993. "*Veritatis Splendor.*" *Commonweal* 120 (22 October): 12–14.

Drinan, Robert F. 1993. "World Conference on Human Rights." *America* 168 (5 June): 15–16.

Drozdiak, William. 1994. "U.S. Nuns Challenge Vatican over Role of Women in Church." *Washington Post,* 27 October.

Duffy, Regis. 1987. "The RCIA Misunderstood." *America* 156 (9 May): 385–86.

Dugan, George. 1962a. "Study of Liturgy Begun at Council." *New York Times,* 23 October.

————. 1962b. "2nd Rome Session Will Open May 12." *New York Times*, 13 November.

————. 1962c. "Vatican Council to Reopen September 8." *New York Times*, 28 November.

Dulles, Avery. 1974. *Models of the Church.* New York: Doubleday.

————. 1980. "The Symbolic Structure of Revelation." *Theological Studies* 41 (March): 51–73.

————. 1981. "Imaging the Church in the 1980's." *Thought* 56 (Spring): 121–38.

————. 1982. "Toward a Christian Consensus: The Lima Meeting." *America* 146 (20 February): 126–29.

————. 1983. "The Teaching Authority of Bishops' Conferences." *America* 148 (11 June): 453–55.

————. 1984. "The Emerging World Church: A Theological Reflection." *Catholic Theological Society of America Proceedings* 39: 1–12.

————. 1985a. *The Catholicity of the Church.* Oxford: Clarendon Press.

————. 1985b. "Authority: The Divided Legacy." *Commonweal* 112 (12 July): 400–3.

————. 1986a. "Paths to Doctrinal Agreement: Ten Theses." *Theological Studies* 47 (March): 32–47.

————. 1986b. "Sensus Fidelium." *America* 155 (1 November): 240–42.

————. 1988a. *The Reshaping of Catholicism: Current Challenges in the Theology of the Church.* New York: Harper and Row.

————. 1988b. "Vatican II and Communications." In vol. 3 of *Vatican II*, 528–47. See Latourelle 1980.

————. 1989. "A Half Century of Ecclesiology." *Theological Studies* 50 (September): 419–42.

————. 1990. "Episcopal Conferences: Their Teaching Authority." *America* 162 (13 January): 7–9.

————. 1991. "Henri de Lubac: In Appreciation." *America* 165 (28 September): 180–82.

————. 1992a. *The Craft of Theology: From Symbol to System.* New York: Crossroad.

————. 1992b. "John Paul II and the New Evangelization." *America* 166 (1 February): 52–59; 69–72.

————. 1993. "The Prophetic Humanism of John Paul II." *America* 169 (23 October): 6–11.

————. 1994. "Women's Ordination." *Commonweal* 121 (15 July): 10–11.

————. 1995. "John Paul II and the Advent of the New Millennium." *America* 173 (9 December): 9–15.

Dunlap, David W. 1995. "Rhode Island Senate Vote Sends Gay-Rights Bill to Governor." *New York Times,* 20 May.

Dwyer, John C. 1987. *Foundations of Christian Ethics.* New York: Paulist Press.

Eagleson, John, and Philip Scharper, eds. 1979. *Puebla and Beyond.* New York: Orbis Books.

Eck, Diana. 1993. "In the Name of Religions." *The Wilson Quarterly* (Autumn): 90–100.

Edwards, Robin T. 1994a. "African Bishops Offer Wish Lists to Synod." *National Catholic Reporter* 30 (29 April): 7.

———. 1994b. "Inculturation Is Africa's Ecclesial Crux." *National Catholic Reporter* 30 (29 April): 8–9.

———. 1994c. "'No' Again to the Divorced and Remarried." *National Catholic Reporter* 31 (28 October): 10–11.

Egan, Eileen. 1980. "Mother Teresa, the Myth and the Person." *America* 142 (22 March): 239– 43.

———. 1985. *Such a Vision of the Street.* New York: Doubleday and Company.

Egan, John J. 1983. "Getting Liturgy and Justice to Merge." *National Catholic Reporter* 19 (30 September): 9, 16–17.

Elliott, John H. 1982. "The Image of Mary: A Lutheran View." *America* 146 (27 March): 226– 29.

Englund, Steven. 1995. "Provocateur or Prophet? The French Church and Bishop Gaillot." *Commonweal* 122 (6 October): 12–18.

Fahey, Michael A., ed. 1986. *Catholic Perspectives on Baptism, Eucharist and Ministry.* Lanham, Md.: University Press of America.

Faison, Seth. 1995. "Women's Meeting Agrees on Right to Say No to Sex." *New York Times,* 11 September.

Falconi, Carlo. 1967. *The Popes of the Twentieth Century.* London: Weidenfelf and Nicolson.

Farrell, Michael J. 1984. "Annulments: 15,000% Increase in 15 Years." *National Catholic Reporter* 21 (16 November): 1, 9.

———. 1995a. "Bishop Moved from Highways to Byways." *National Catholic Reporter* 31 (14 July): 9–11.

———. 1995b. "Rome, Where the Pontiff Is Supreme." *National Catholic Reporter* 31 (11 August): 14–16.

Fauss, Jose I. Gonzalez. 1989. *Where the Spirit Breathes: Prophetic Dissent in the Church.* New York: Orbis Books.

Ferm, Deane William. 1986. *Third World Liberation Theologies: An Introductory Survey.* New York: Orbis Books.

Ferraro, Barbara, and Patricia Hussey. 1990. *No Turning Back.* New York: Poseidon Press.

Feuerherd, Joseph. 1990. "Theologians Tossing Vatican's Latest Hot Potato." *National Catholic Reporter* 26 (13 July): 10.

Fichter, Joseph H. 1988a. "Married Priests and Ecumenism". *The Ecumenist* 26 (January): 26–30.

———. 1988b. "The Ordination of Episcopal Priests." *America* 159 (24 September): 157–61.

Fiedler, Maureen. 1996. "WOW! Women's Ordination Network Now Worldwide." *National Catholic Reporter* 32 (13 September): 15.

Fiedler, Maureen, and Dolly Pomerleau. 1978. "American Catholics and the Ordination of Women." *America* 138 (14 January): 11–14.

Filteau, Jerry. 1996. "Reformers Launch U.S. Signature Drive." *National Catholic Reporter* 32 (31 May): 5.

Finley, Mitch. 1991. "The Dark Side of Natural Family Planning." *America* 164 (23 February): 206–7.

Fiorenza, Francis Schussler. 1975. "Political Theology and Liberation Theology: An Inquiry into Their Fundamental Meaning." In *Liberation, Revolution and Freedom: Theological Perspectives*, edited by Thomas M. McFadden, 3–26. New York: Seabury.

———. 1982. "The Church's Religious Identity and Its Social and Political Mission." *Theological Studies* 43 (June): 197–225.

———. 1984. *Foundational Theology: Jesus and the Church*. New York: Crossroad.

Fitzmyer, Joseph A. 1973. "Virginal Conception in the New Testament." *Theological Studies* 34 (December): 541–75.

———. 1981. *To Advance the Gospel: New Testament Studies*. New York: Crossroad.

———. 1994. *Scripture: The Soul of Theology*. New York: Paulist Press.

Fitzpatrick, Joseph P. 1978. "Justice as a Problem of Culture." *Catholic Mind* 76 (January): 10–26.

Flannery, Austin, ed. 1996. *The Basic Sixteen Documents: Vatican Council II*. New York: Costello Publishing Company.

Flannery, Kevin, and Joseph Koterski. 1993. "Paul VI Was Right." *America* 169 (25 September): 7–11.

Fletcher, Joseph. 1966. *Situation Ethics*. Philadelphia: Westminster Press.

———. 1978. "Love and Utility." *Christian Century* 95 (31 May): 692–94.

Ford, John C., and Germain Grisez. 1978. "Contraception and the Infallibility of the Ordinary Magisterium." *Theological Studies* 39 (June): 258–312.

Ford, Josephine Massingberd. 1973. "Biblical Material Relevant to the Ordination of Women." *Journal of Ecumenical Studies* 10 (Fall): 685–96.

Fox, Matthew. 1979. *A Spirituality Named Compassion.* New York: Winston Press.

Fox, Thomas C. 1988. "Inside NCR." *National Catholic Reporter* 24 (29 July): 2.

———. 1994a. "Cardinals To Ponder Millennium." *National Catholic Reporter* 30 (17 June): 2.

———. 1994b. "Vatican OKs Most of U.N. Document after Cairo Tactics Stir Bitterness." *National Catholic Reporter* 30 (23 September): 8–9.

———. 1994c. "Vatican Veto." *National Catholic Reporter* 31 (11 November): 1, 12.

———. 1995a. "Papal Challenges Replace Condemnations." *National Catholic Reporter* 31 (20 October): 3.

———. 1995b. "Can the Pope Be Wrong?" *New York Times,* 25 November.

———. 1996. "Liberation Theology Founder Dead at 70." *National Catholic Reporter* 32 (2 February): 2.

French, Howard W. 1992a. "Pope Arrives in Dominican Republic." *New York Times,* 10 October.

———. 1992b. "Protests Follow the Pope on Santo Domingo Visit." *New York Times,* 14 October.

Friedan, Betty. 1963. *The Feminine Mystique.* New York: W. W. Norton.

Fuchs, Josef. 1970. *Human Values and Christian Morality.* Dublin: McGill and Macmillan.

Fuller, Jon. 1996. "AIDS Prevention: A Challenge to the Catholic Moral Tradition." *America* 175 (28 December): 13–20.

Gaffney, James. 1986. "From Models of the Church to Models of the Model." *America* 155 (13 December): 377–80.

Gaillardetz, Richard R. 1994. "An Exercise of the Hierarchical Magisterium." *America* 171 (30 July): 19–22.

Gaine, Michael. 1991. "The State of the Priesthood" In *Modern Catholicism,* 246–55. See Hastings 1991.

Gallagher, John. 1990. *Times Past, Time Future: An Historical Study of Catholic Moral Theology.* New York: Paulist Press.

Garaudy, Roger. 1966. *From Anathema to Dialogue: A Marxist Challenge to the Christian Church.* New York: Herder and Herder.

Geffre, Claude. 1989. "The Political Dimensions of a New Theological Paradigm." In *Paradigm Change in Theology,* 390–96. See Küng and Tracy 1989.

Geyer, Alan. 1983. "The Pains of Peace at Vancouver." *Christian Century* 100 (31 August): 765–67.

Gibeau, Dawn. 1976a. "WCC Finale Mood: Sense of Struggle, Spirit of Unity." *National Catholic Reporter* 12 (9 January): 4.

————. 1976b. "God Puts His Foot in History." *National Catholic Reporter* 12 (15 September): 7–9.

————. 1989. "Advances, Retreats Since Medellín." *National Catholic Reporter* 25 (31 March): 3–4.

————. 1994. "New Catechism Designed for Bishops, Educators." *National Catholic Reporter* 30 (17 June): 14–15.

Gilhooley, James. 1984. "Father Duffy: Priest with a Tin Hat." *America* 150 (24 March): 204– 7.

Gilkey, Langdon. 1975. *Catholicism Confronts Modernity*. New York: Seabury Press.

————. 1989. "The Paradigm Shift in Theology." In *Paradigm Change in Theology*, 367–83. See Küng and Tracy 1989.

Gilleman, Gerard. 1959. *The Primacy of Charity in the Moral Life*. Westminster, Md: Newman Press.

Glaser, John W. 1983. "Epoch III: The Church Feminized." *Commonweal* 110 (28 January): 44–45.

Glendon, Mary Ann. 1996. "A Glimpse of the New Feminism." *America* 175 (6 July): 10–15.

Goldberg, Carey. 1996. "Judge in Hawaii Says the State Cannot Prohibit Gay Marriages." *New York Times*, 4 December.

Goldman, Ari L. 1992a. "Catholics Are at Odds with Bishops." *New York Times*, 19 June.

————. 1992b. "Support Fading for Document about Women." *New York Times*, 19 June.

————. 1992c. "Even for Ordained Women, Church Can Be a Cold Place." *New York Times*, 29 November.

Gonzalez, David. 1994. "Endorsing Growing Practice, Vatican Approves of Altar Girls." *New York Times*, 15 April.

Gonzalez, Justo L. 1984. *The Story of Christianity, The Reformation to the Present*. Vol. 2. New York: Harper and Row.

Gorday, Peter. 1989. "Raimundo Panikkar: Pluralism without Relativism." *Christian Century* 106 (6 December): 1147–50.

Gordon, Mary. 1982. "Coming to Terms with Mary." *Commonweal* 109 (15 January): 11–13.

Gore, Albert. 1994. "What We Really Want: Less Need for Abortion." *Los Angeles Times*, 2 September.

Goslin, Tom. 1988. "New Struggles for Spanish Catholics." *Christian Century* 105 (31 August): 759–60.

Grabowski, John. 1994. "Divorce, Remarriage and Reception of the Sacraments." *America* 171 (8 October): 20–24.

Graham, Robert A. 1966. "Non–Christians." In *The Documents of Vatican II*, 656–59. See Abbott 1966.

Gramick, Jeannine. 1988. "Catholic Nuns and the Need for Responsible Dissent." *Christian Century* 105 (7 December): 1122–25.

Granfield, Patrick. 1985. "The Uncertain Future of Collegiality." *Catholic Theological Society of America Proceedings* 40: 95–106.

———. 1987. *The Limits of the Papacy*. New York: Crossroad.

Grassi, Joseph A. 1986. "The Role of Jesus' Mother in John's Gospel: A Reappraisal." *Catholic Biblical Quarterly* 48 (January): 67–80.

Gray, Paul. 1994. "Man of the Year: Empire of the Spirit." *Time* 144:26 (26 December): 53.

Greeley, Andrew M. 1970. "Myths, Meaning and Vatican III." *America* 123 (19 December): 538–42.

———. 1971. *The Jesus Myth*. New York: Doubleday.

———. 1973. *The New Agenda*. New York: Doubleday.

———. 1974. "Hail Mary." *New York Times Magazine*, 15 December.

———. 1977. *The Mary Myth: On the Feminity of God*. New York: Seabury.

———. 1980. "Mary Survives." *America* 142 (23 February): 135–37.

———. 1981. "*Quadragesimo Anno* after Fifty Years." *America* 145 (8 August): 46–49.

———. 1982a. "The Failures of Vatican II After Twenty Years." *America* 146 (6 February): 86–89.

———. 1982b. "Going Their Own Way." *New York Times Magazine*, 10 October.

———. 1983. Review of *La Popessa* by Paul I. Murphy and R. René Arlington. *National Catholic Reporter* 19 (6 May): 22–23.

———. 1990a. *The Catholic Myth*. New York: Charles Scribner's Sons.

———. 1990b. "Good Liturgy Is Little More Than a Good Weave." *National Catholic Reporter* 26 (16 March): 12–13.

———. 1992. "Sex and the Single Catholic: The Decline of an Ethic." *America* 167 (7 November): 342–47, 358–59.

———. 1993. "Contraception: A Baby among Catholic Sins." *National Catholic Reporter* 29 (15 October): 18–21.

———. 1997. "Polarized Catholics? Don't Believe Your Mail!" *America* 176 (22 February): 11–15.

Greeley, Andrew M., and Mary Greeley Durkin. 1984. *How To Save the Catholic Church*. New York: Viking Press.

Greene, Jack P. 1975. "The 'New History': From Top to Bottom." *New York Times*, 8 January.

Greenhouse, Steven. 1991. "Archbishop Lefèbvre Dies; Traditionalist Defied the Vatican." *New York Times*, 26 March.

Grisez, Germain. 1986. "Infallibility and Contraception: A Reply to Garth Hallett." *Theological Studies* 47 (March): 134–45.

Gros, Jeffrey. 1990. "Discerning the Gospel: Dialogue in the Catholic Church." *Christian Century* 107 (2 May): 460–63.

Gudorf, Christine E. 1983. "Renewal or Repatriarchalization? Responses of the Roman Catholic Church to the Feminization of Religion." *Horizons* 10 (Fall): 231–51.

Gustafson, James M. 1978. *Protestant and Catholic Ethics*. Chicago: University of Chicago Press.

Haberman, Clyde. 1989. "Gorbachev Lauds Religion on Eve of Meeting Pope." *New York Times*, 1 December.

———. 1990a. "Pope, Amid Mexico's Poor, Laments." *New York Times*, 8 May.

———. 1990b. "Vatican Synod Studies 'Burnout' and 'Identity Crisis' among Priests." *New York Times*, 1 October.

———. 1990c. "Synod in Vatican Bars Change in Celibacy Rule." *New York Times*, 28 October.

———. 1993. "Israel and Vatican Sign Their Accord on Diplomatic Ties." *New York Times*, 31 December.

———. 1994. "Full Relations for Israelis and Vatican." *New York Times*, 16 June.

Hagstrom, Aurelie A. 1996. "Can Lay Catholics Govern the Church?" *America* 172 (17 February): 20–21.

Haight, Roger. 1990. "Modernism: Vatican Had to Create It to Condemn It." *National Catholic Reporter* 26 (27 July): 14–15.

Hallett, Garth L. 1982. "Contraception and Prescriptive Infallibility." *Theological Studies* 43 (December): 629–50.

———. 1988. "Infallibility and Contraception: The Debate Continues." *Theological Studies* 49 (September): 517–28.

Hamington, Maurice. 1995. *Hail Mary? The Struggle for Ultimate Womanhood in Catholicism*. New York: Routledge.

Hansen, Susan. 1986. "Vatican's Homosexual Letter Disputed." *National Catholic Reporter* 23 (26 December): 5.

———. 1987. "Woman-Church Sounds Radical Call." *National Catholic Reporter* 24 (23 October): 1, 4.

Hanson, Eric O. 1987. *The Catholic Church in World Politics*. Princeton: Princeton University Press.

Happel, Stephen, and David Tracy. 1984. *A Catholic Vision*. Minneapolis, Minn.: Fortress Press.

Häring, Bernard. 1961–66. *The Law of Christ*. 3 vols. Westminster, Md.: Newman Press.

———. 1978–1981. *Free and Faithful in Christ*. 3 vols. New York: Crossroad.

———. 1987. "The Curran Case." In *The Church in Anguish*, 235–50. See Küng and Swidler 1987.

———. 1992. *My Witness for the Church*. New York: Paulist Press.

———. 1993. "Encyclical's One Aim: Assent and Submission." *National Catholic Reporter* 30 (5 November): 14–15.

Hartinger, Brent. 1991. "A Case for Gay Marriage." *Commonweal* 118 (22 November): 681–83.

Harvey, John. 1985. "Courage Encourages Gays." *National Catholic Reporter* 21 (18 January): 11.

Hastings, Adrian, ed. 1991. *Modern Catholicism: Vatican II and After*. New York: Oxford University Press.

Hauerwas, Stanley. 1993. *"Veritatis Splendor."* *Commonweal* 120 (22 October): 16–18.

Haughey, John C. 1968. "Conscience and the Bishops." *America* 119 (12 October): 322, 324.

———. ed. 1977. *The Faith That Does Justice*. New York: Paulist Press.

Hebblethwaite, Peter. 1975. *The Runaway Church: Postconciliar Growth or Decline*. New York: Seabury.

———. 1976. "Not about But for Liberation." *National Catholic Reporter* 13 (12 November): 11, 13.

———. 1978a. *The Year of Three Popes*. Cleveland, Ohio: Collins.

———. 1978b. "Pope John Paul, the Smiling Pope, Dead at 65." *National Catholic Reporter* 14 (6 October): 1–5.

———. 1979a. "Was Archbishop Lured into Candid Comments?" *National Catholic Reporter* 15 (2 March): 19.

———. 1979b. "Pope Unveils His Papacy: 'Restoration' Era Begins." *National Catholic Reporter* 15 (19 October): 1, 18.

———. 1979c. "John Paul's Renewal Engulfs Aggiornamento." *National Catholic Reporter* 16 (16 November): 1, 4.

———. 1979d. "John Paul Welcomes Galileo Back." *National Catholic Reporter* 16 (23 November): 3, 20.

———. 1980a. "Orthodox Dialogue Continues." *National Catholic Reporter* 16 (28 March): 7.

———. 1980b. "Orthodox-Roman Meeting 'Troubled'." *National Catholic Reporter* 16 (6 June): 16.

———. 1980c. "Is the Pope Committed to Ecumenism?" *National Catholic Reporter* 16 (4 July): 14–15.

———. 1980d. "SODEPAX's Justice Work to End." *National Catholic Reporter* 16 (3 October): 3.

———. 1980e. "Synod Ending 'Anticlimactic'; Some Bishops 'Disappointed.'" *National Catholic Reporter* 7 (7 December): 1, 18.

———. 1981a. "Bishops Will Aid Converts." *National Catholic Reporter* 17 (12 April): 18.

———. 1981b. "What John Thought of the Popes He Knew." *National Catholic Reporter* 18 (27 November): 13–14.

———. 1982. "The Council Opens." *National Catholic Reporter* 18 (8 October): 34.

———. 1983. "Why John XXIII Wrote *Pacem in Terris*." *National Catholic Reporter* 19 (8 April): 9, 20–21.

———. 1984a. "New Concordat." *National Catholic Reporter* 20 (2 March): 5.

———. 1984b. "Consecration to Mary a Loyalty Test." *National Catholic Reporter* 20 (3 April): 10.

———. 1984c. "Document Warns about Liberation Theology 'Abuses', Does Not Condemn." *National Catholic Reporter* 20 (7 September): 1–2.

———. 1984d. "Tridentine Decision a Slap at Collegiality." *National Catholic Reporter* 21 (21 December): 5.

———. 1986a. *Synod Extraordinary*. New York: Doubleday.

———. 1986b. "Letter to Brazilian Bishops Termed Papal Turning Point." *National Catholic Reporter* 22 (2 May): 4.

———. 1986c. "Encyclical on Holy Spirit Judged Pessimistic." *National Catholic Reporter* 22 (20 June): 8.

———. 1987a. "Marian Year Shores Up Liberation Theology." *National Catholic Reporter* 23 (5 June): 4.

———. 1987b. "Vatican Seems to Lack 'Prudence' over Waldheim." *National Catholic Reporter* 23 (23 July): 4.

———. 1987c. "Lefèbvre 'Dialogue' His Vindication?" *National Catholic Reporter* 24 (13 November): 1, 16.

———. 1988a. "A Private Note and What It Wrought." *America* 158 (18 June): 598–601, 614.

———. 1988b. "Lefèbvre Moves Out of Church." *National Catholic Reporter* 25 (1 July): 4.

———. 1989a. "Pope Lists Two 'Shadows' in State of Church Speech." *National Catholic Reporter* 25 (27 January): 4.

———. 1989b. "Häring on *Humanae Vitae*." *National Catholic Reporter* 25 (10 February): 7.

———. 1989c. "Hope, Anguish of the People of Our Time." *National Catholic Reporter* 25 (17 March): 15–17.

———. 1989d. "Apostolic Letter Throws 'Dynamite' into Lefèbvre Camp." *National Catholic Reporter* 25 (26 May): 15.

———. 1989e. "Papal Style at Issue Between Rome, Canterbury." *National Catholic Reporter* 25 (2 June): 15.

———. 1989f. "Auschwitz Legacy an 'Unholy Mess.'" *National Catholic Reporter* 25 (25 August): 8.

———. 1989g. "Runcie Leaves Hardly a Ripple in Rome." *National Catholic Reporter* 25 (13 October): 8–9.

———. 1989h. "Australian to Head Vatican Unity Council." *National Catholic Reporter* 26 (29 December): 4.

———. 1990a. "Excavating for Foundation of Infallible *Humanae Vitae.*" *National Catholic Reporter* 25 (4 May): 16.

———. 1990b. "Beatification of Juan Diego Affirms Liberation Theology." *National Catholic Reporter* 26 (11 May): 8.

———. 1990c. "Alternative of Cowed Silence Strange Way to Defend Faith." *National Catholic Reporter* 26 (13 July): 28.

———. 1991a. "John Paul I." In *Modern Catholicism,* 444–46. See Hastings 1991.

———. 1991b. "Theological Squabbles Stall Pope's Human-life Encyclical." *National Catholic Reporter* 27 (19 March): 7.

———. 1992a. "Boff Leaves Priesthood and Order for 'Periphery.'" *National Catholic Reporter* 28 (17 July): 12–13.

———. 1992b. "From John Paul II Superstar to a Super Surprise?" *National Catholic Reporter* 28 (11 September): 5-7.

———. 1992c. "A Few 'Thou Shalt' and 'Shalt Nots' for Our Day." *National Catholic Reporter* 29 (4 December): 14.

———. 1993a. *Paul VI: The First Modern Pope.* New York: Paulist Press.

———. 1993b. "Final Report: 'Small But Substantial Changes'." *National Catholic Reporter* 29 (22 January): 12.

———. 1993c. "Ratzinger Comments on Changing Papacy." *National Catholic Reporter* 29 (26 February): 10.

———. 1993d. "Encyclical Insists Intercourse Is Language of Love." *National Catholic Reporter* 29 (16 July): 15–16.

———. 1993e. "Infallibility Boosted in Leaked Encyclical." *National Catholic Reporter* 29 (13 August): 20.

———. 1993f. "Discipline, Not Doctrine Is Nub of Pope's New Encyclical." *National Catholic Reporter* 29 (1 October): 9.

———. 1993g. "Anglicans Backpedal on Ordaining Women." *National Catholic Reporter* 30 (3 December): 13.

———. 1994a. "A Synod 'of Africa,' 'for Africa,' or 'New Pentecost'?" *National Catholic Reporter* 30 (22 April): 6–7.

———. 1994b. "Pope Draws Sharp Distinction Between Priests, Lay Ministers." *National Catholic Reporter* 30 (6 May): 10.

———. 1994c. "Catholics Try To Digest Papal Bombshell." *National Catholic Reporter* 30 (1 July): 6.

———. 1994d. "Rome Manhandled Catechism's Language." *National Catholic Reporter* 30 (1 July): 16.

———. 1994e. "Waldheim, John Paul Cultural Links Go Way Back." *National Catholic Reporter* 30 (29 July): 11.

———. 1994f. "Lamenting a Hope for Peace Now Gone By." *National Catholic Reporter* 30 (16 September): 10.

Hehir, J. Bryan. 1981. "A New Era of Social Teaching." *Commonweal* 108 (23 October): 585, 607.

———. 1991. "From Leo XIII to John Paul II: The Evolution of Catholic Social Teaching." *Commonweal* 118 (3 May): 281–82.

———. 1995. "Get a (Culture of) Life." *Commonweal* 122 (19 May): 8–9.

Heim, Mark S. 1986. "BEM Finds Favor with American Churches." *Christian Century* 103 (14 May): 476–77.

———. 1993. "Ecumenical Pilgrims Taking Stock in Santiago." *Christian Century* 110 (23 November): 1086–92.

———. 1996a. "The Next Ecumenical Movement." *Christian Century* 113 (14 August): 780–83.

———. 1996b. "What Is the Church?" *Christian Century* 113 (23 October): 1000–2.

Hennelly, Alfred T. 1979. "The Grassroots Church." *Catholic Theological Society of America Proceedings* 34: 183–88.

———. 1986. "The Red Hot Issue: Liberation Theology." *America* 154 (24 May): 425–28.

Hennesey, James. 1971. "The Two Vatican Councils: The Church Becomes Universal." *The Catholic Mind* 69 (June): 22–31.

———. 1989. "Catholicism in an American Environment: The Early Years." *Theological Studies* 50 (December): 657–75.

Henriot, Peter J., ed. 1988. *Catholic Social Teaching.* New York: Orbis Books.

———. 1994. "Hopes for the African Synod." *America* 170 (9 April): 12–14.

Hevesi, Dennis. 1992. "Gay Church Again Rejected by National Council Group." *New York Times*, 15 November.

Hewitt, W. E. 1986. "Basic Christian Communities in Brazil." *The Ecumenist* 24 (September): 81–86.

Hick, John. 1973. *God and the Universe of Faiths.* New York: St. Martin's Press.

Hick, John, and Paul Knitter, eds. 1988. *The Myth of Christian Uniqueness: Toward a Pluralistic Theology of Religion.* New York: Orbis Books.

Higgins, George. 1993. *Organized Labor and the Church: Reflections of a 'Labor Priest.'* New York: Paulist Press.

Hillman, Eugene. 1980. "From Tribal Religion to a Catholic Church." *America* 143 (15 November): 303–5.

———. 1989. *Many Paths: A Catholic Approach to Religious Pluralism.* New York: Orbis Books.

Hitchcock, James. 1972. "The Church and the Sexual Revolution." *America* 127 (23 September): 197–201.

Hobgood, Mary E. 1989. "Conflicting Paradigms in Social Analysis." In *The Logic of Solidarity,* 167–85. See Baum and Ellsberg 1989.

Hollenbach, David. 1977. "Modern Catholic Teaching Concerning Justice." In *The Faith That Does Justice,* 207–32. See Haughey 1977.

———. 1979. *Claims in Conflict: Retrieving and Renewing the Catholic Human Rights Tradition.* New York: Paulist Press.

———. 1989. "The Common Good Revisited." *Theological Studies* 50 (March): 70–94.

———. 1991. "The Pope and Capitalism." *America* 164 (1 June): 590–91.

Holmes, J. Derek. 1981. *The Papacy in the Modern World 1914–1978.* New York: Crossroad.

Horgan, Thaddeus D. 1990. "The Second Vatican Council's Decree on Ecumenism." *America* 162 (2 June): 548–52.

Howell, Leon. 1984. "Emilio Castro's Election as WCC Secretary." *Christian Century* 101 (1 August): 732–34.

Huck, Gabe. 1989. "Why Settle for Communion?" *Commonweal* 116 (27 January): 37–39.

———. 1994. "Rome Speaks: Inclusive Language Verboten." *Commonweal* 121 (18 November): 4–5.

Hughes, John Jay. 1971. "Infallible? An Inquiry Considered." *Theological Studies* 32 (June): 183–207.

———. 1980a. "Hans Küng and the Magisterium." *Theological Studies* 41 (June): 368–89.

———. 1980b. "Episcopalians and Rome." *America* 143 (13 September): 111–12.

Hughes, Kathleen. 1991. *The Monk's Tale: A Biography of Godfrey Diekmann, OSB.* Collegeville, Minn.: The Liturgical Press.

Hunt, Mary E. 1996. "A Pioneering Trilogy on Being Gay and Catholic." *National Catholic Reporter* 32 (17 May): 16.

Hyer, Marjorie. 1979. "Papal Trip [to the United States]." *National Catholic Reporter* 15 (19 October): 7.

Imbelli, Robert P. 1982. "Vatican II: Twenty Years Later." *Commonweal* 109 (8 October): 522–26.

———. 1986. "Theology after the Synod: Boundaries." *Commonweal* 113 (31 January): 41–44.

Jay, Eric G. 1978. *The Church: Its Changing Image Through Twenty Centuries.* Atlanta: John Knox Press.

Jehl, Douglas. 1997. "Troubled Christian Minority Awaits Pope in Lebanon." *New York Times,* 9 May.

Jennings, Jack A. 1981. "A Reluctant Demurrer on Mother Teresa." *Christian Century* 98 (11 March): 258–60.

Jensen, Joseph. 1994. "Inclusive Language and the Bible." *America* 171 (5 November): 14–18.

———. 1996. "Watch Your Language! Of Princes and Music Directors." *America* 174 (8 June): 7–11.

Johann, Robert O. 1965. "Responsible Parenthood: A Philosophical View." *Catholic Theological Society of America Proceedings* 20: 115–28.

———. 1967. "Love and Justice." In *Ethics and Society,* edited by Robert T. George, 25–47. New York: Doubleday.

———. 1968. *Building the Human.* New York: Herder and Herder.

John Paul II. 1994. *Crossing the Threshold of Hope.* New York: Afred A. Knopf Publishers.

———. 1996. *Gift and Mystery.* New York: Doubleday and Company.

Johnson, Elizabeth A. 1985. "The Marian Tradition and the Reality of Women." *Horizons* 12 (Spring): 116–35.

———. 1989. "Mary and the Female Face of God." *Theological Studies* 50 (September): 500–26.

———. 1993a. *She Who Is: The Mystery of God in Feminist Theological Discourse.* New York: Crossroad.

———. 1993b. "A Theological Case for God-She: Expanding the Treasury of Metaphor." *Commonweal* 120 (29 January): 9–14.

———. 1996. "Disputed Questions: Authority, Priesthood, Women." *Commonweal* 123 (26 January): 11–12.

Johnson, Luke Timothy. 1994. "Debate and Discernment: Scripture and the Spirit." *Commonweal* 121 (28 January): 11–13.

Jones, Alfred H. 1985. "Edinburgh 1985." *Christian Century* 102 (17 July): 671–72.

Jones, Arthur. 1987. "Pope's South Carolina Stop Is a Major Move to Ecumenism for Evangelicals." *National Catholic Reporter* 23 (11 September): 1, 25.

———. 1992. "Apostolic Delegate Left Seal on U.S. Church." *National Catholic Reporter* 28 (25 September): 5–8.

———. 1994. "Women React in Anger and Pain." *National Catholic Reporter* 30 (17 June): 3–4.

———. 1996. "Conversations Led to Common Ground." *National Catholic Reporter* 33 (10 October): 9.

Jossua, Jean-Pierre. 1987. "Jacques Pohier: A Theologian Destroyed." In *The Church in Anguish*, 205–11. See Küng and Swidler 1987.

Jungmann, Joseph Andreas. 1951. *The Mass of the Roman Rite: Its Origins and Development*. New York: Benzinger.

———. 1969. "Constitution on the Sacred Liturgy." In vol. 1 of *Commentary on the Documents of Vatican II*, 1–87. See Vorgrimler 1969.

Kaiser, Robert Blair. 1986. *The Politics of Sex and Religion*. Kansas City, Mo.: Leaven Press.

Kasper, Walter. 1989. *Theology of the Church*. New York: Crossroad.

Keane, Philip S. 1977. *Sexual Morality: A Catholic Perspective*. New York: Paulist Press.

———. 1982. "The Objective Moral Order: Reflections on Recent Research." *Theological Studies* 43 (June): 260–78.

Keifer, Ralph A. 1975. "Rite or Wrong: Ten Years after the Constitution on the Liturgy." *Commonweal* 102 (15 August): 328–30.

Kelleher, Stephen J. 1968. "The Problem of the Intolerable Marriage." *America* 119 (14 September): 178–82.

———. 1973. *Divorce and Remarriage for Catholics?* New York: Doubleday.

———. 1975. "The Laity, Divorce and Remarriage." *Commonweal* 102 (7 November): 521–24.

———. 1977. "Catholic Annulments: A Dehumanizing Process." *Commonweal* 104 (10 June): 363–68.

———. 1978. "Looking Back, Looking Ahead." *America* 139 (18 November): 355–57.

Kelly, George A. 1976. "An Uncertain Church: The New Catholic Problem." *Critic* 35 (Fall): 14–26.

———. 1979. *The Battle for the American Church*. New York: Doubleday.

———. 1982. *The Crisis of Authority*. Chicago: Regnery Gateway.

Kelly, J. N. D. 1986. *The Oxford Dictionary of the Popes*. New York: Oxford University Press.

Kennedy, Eugene C. 1976a. "Insufficient Guilt in the Room." *America* 134 (27 March): 244–51.

———. 1976b. "A Myth for Ministers." *America* 134 (12 June): 509–12.

———. 1988a. *Tommorow's Catholics, Yesterday's Church*. San Francisco: Harper and Row.

———. 1988b. "The Problem with No Name." *America* 158 (23 April): 423–25.

Kerlin, Michael. 1973. "A New Modernist Crisis? Hardly." *America* 129 (6 October): 239–42.

Kilmartin, Edward. 1979. *Toward Reunion: The Orthodox and Roman Catholic Churches.* New York: Paulist Press.

King, Thomas M. 1985. "The Milieu Teilhard Left Behind." *America* 152 (30 March): 249–53.

Kinsey, Alfred Charles. 1948. *Sexual Behavior in the Human Male.* Philadelphia: W. B. Saunders Co.

Kinzer, Stephen. 1995. "German Bishops Cite Catholic 'Denial and Guilt' at Holocaust." *New York Times,* 27 January.

Kirk, Robin. 1986. "Gustavo Gutierrez's New Way to Be a Christian." *National Catholic Reporter* 23 (31 October): 7–8.

Knauer, Peter. 1979. "The Hermeneutical Function of the Principle of Double Effect." In *Moral Norms and the Catholic Tradition,* 1–39. No. 1 of *Readings in Moral Theology,* edited by Charles Curran and Richard McCormick. New York: Paulist Press.

Knitter, Paul F. 1985. *No Other Name?: A Critical Survey of Christian Attitudes toward the World Religions.* New York: Orbis Books.

———. 1986. Knitter's response to a review symposium of his *No Other Name? Horizons* 13 (Spring): 130–35.

———. 1990. "Key Questions for a Theology of Religions." *Horizons* 17 (Spring): 92–102.

Kolbenschlag, Madonna. 1983. "Sister Mansour Is Not Alone." *Commonweal* 110 (17 June): 359–64.

Kolden, Mark. 1984. "Marxism and Latin American Liberation Theology." In *Christians and the Many Faces of Marxism,* edited by Wayne Stumme, 123–31. Minneapolis, Minn.: Augsburg Press.

Komonchak, Joseph A. 1978. "*Humanae Vitae* and Its Reception: Ecclesiological Reflections." *Theological Studies* 39 (June): 221–57.

———. 1983. "The Return of Yves Congar." *Commonweal* 110 (15 July): 402–5.

———. 1985a. "The Ecclesial and Cultural Roles of Theology." *Catholic Theological Society of America Proceedings* 40: 15–32.

———. 1985b. "What's Happening to Doctrine?" *Commonweal* 112 (6 September): 456–59.

———. 1987. "Issues Behind the Curran Case." *Commonweal* 114 (23 January): 43–47.

———. 1990a. "Marie-Dominique Chenu: A Tribute." *Commonweal* 117 (20 April): 252–54.

———. 1990b. "What They Said Before the Council." *Commonweal* 117 (7 December): 714–17.

———. 1990c. "Theology and Culture at Mid-Century: The Example of Henri de Lubac." *Theological Studies* 51(December): 579–602.

————. 1992a. "Recapturing the Great Tradition." *Commonweal* 119 (31 January): 14–17.

————. 1992b. "The Coldness of Clarity, the Warmth of Love: The Measure of John Courtney Murray." *Commonweal* 119 (14 August): 16–17.

————. 1995. "A Hero of Vatican II." *Commonweal* 122 (1 December): 15–17.

Kosnik, Anthony, William Carroll, Agnes Cunningham, Ronald Modras, and James Schulte. 1977. *Human Sexuality: New Directions in American Catholic Thought.* New York: Paulist Press.

Kress, Robert. 1977. "Mary's Assumption, God's Promise Fulfilled." *America* 137 (30 August): 71–74.

Küng, Hans. 1967. "The World Religions in God's Plan of Salvation." In *Christian Revelation and World Religions,* edited by Joseph Neuner, 25–66. London: Burns and Oates.

————. 1976. *On Being a Christian.* New York: Doubleday.

————. 1992. *Judaism: Between Yesterday and Tomorrow.* New York: Crossroad.

————. 1995. "Theologians Now Face Either-Or Situation." *National Catholic Reporter* 32 (15 December): 6–7.

Küng, Hans, and Karl-Joseph Kuschel, eds. 1994. *A Global Ethic: The Declaration of the Parliament of the World's Religions.* New York: Continuum Publishing Group.

Küng, Hans, and Leonard Swidler, eds. 1987. *The Church in Anguish.* New York: Harper and Row.

Küng, Hans, and David Tracy, eds. 1989. *Paradigm Change in Theology.* New York: Crossroad.

Lamb, Matthew L. 1986. "Theology after the Synod: Beyond Culture." *Commonweal* 113 (31 January): 46–49.

Lamboley, Kathryn. 1979. "Leo XIII, 'The Workers' Pope,' Favored Unions." *National Catholic Reporter* 15 (7 September): 37.

Lapomarda, Vincent A. 1986. "Some Reflections on Catholics and the Holocaust." *America* 155 (27 December): 424–27.

Lash, Nicholas. 1988. *Easter Is Ordinary.* Charlottesville, Va.: University Press of Virginia.

————. 1992. "Theology on the Way to Stuttgart." *America* 166 (4 April): 266–68.

Latourelle, Rene, ed. 1988a. *Vatican II: Assessment and Perspectives.* 3 vols. New York: Paulist Press.

————. 1988b. "Absence and Presence of Fundamental Theology at Vatican II." In vol. 3 of *Vatican II,* 378–415. See Latourelle 1988a.

Laumann, Edward O. 1994. *The Social Organization of Sexuality: Sexual Practices in the United States.* Chicago: University of Chicago Press.

Lauret, Bernard, ed. 1988. *Fifty Years of Catholic Theology: Conversations with Yves Congar.* Minneapolis, Minn.: Fortress Press.

Lavin, Henry St. C. 1984. "A View from Rome: The Concordat." *America* 150 (5 May): 340– 41.

Lefevere, Patricia. 1993. "Christian Unity: No Deadline, But a Boost in Spain." *National Catholic Reporter* 29 (27 August): 13.

———. 1995a. "WCC Head Sees Pothole in Rome Road." *National Catholic Reporter* 31 (28 April): 8.

———. 1995b. "Anglicans, Catholics Discuss Holy Orders." *National Catholic Reporter* 31 (12 May): 7.

———. 1996. "Ecumenism Is Slow But Steady, Cardinal Says." *National Catholic Reporter* 32 (13 September): 5.

Lernoux, Penny. 1985. "Act 'Shocks' Brazilians United With Theologians." *National Catholic Reporter* 21 (24 May): 1, 23.

———. 1989. *People of God: The Struggle for World Catholicism.* New York: Penguin Press.

Liberatore, Alfred M. 1994. "Beyond Nightmares and Dreams: Trent and Vatican II." *America* 170 (16 April): 16–17.

Lindbeck, George A., Monika Hellwig and George Higgins. 1985. "The Ratzinger File." *Commonweal* 112 (15 November): 635–42.

Linnan, John E. 1986. "Declaration on Religious Liberty." In *Vatican II and Its Documents,* 167–79. See O'Connell 1986.

Lonergan, Bernard. 1972. *Method in Theology.* New York: Seabury.

———. 1974. *A Second Collection.* Edited by William Ryan and Bernard Tyrrell. Philadelphia: Westminster Press.

———. 1985. *A Third Collection.* Edited by Frederick E. Crowe. New York: Paulist Press.

Luker, Carol. 1994. "Curran, Smith Update Birth-Control Debate." *National Catholic Reporter* 31 (11 November): 7.

Lyles, Jean Caffey. 1974. "Episcopal Agony over Ecclesiastical Disobedience." *Christian Century* 91 (4 September): 812–14.

———. 1983. "Unity and Diversity at Vancouver." *Christian Century* 100 (28 September): 836–37.

MacEoin, Gary, and Nivita Riley. 1980. *Puebla: A Church Being Born.* New York: Paulist Press.

MacEoin, Gary. 1966. *What Happened at Rome?* New York: Holt, Rinehart and Winston.

———. 1973. "Maryknoll Adopts New Mission Concept." *National Catholic Reporter* 10 (6 April): 1, 20.

―――. 1984. "Liberation Theology under Fire." *The Witness* 67 (December): 12–14.

―――. 1991a. "Struggle for Latin American Soul Quickens." *National Catholic Reporter* 27 (22 January): 15–19.

―――. 1991b. "Lay Movements in the United States before Vatican II." *America* 165 (10 April): 61–65.

―――. 1992a. "View of Rome Neocolonialism Issue Clearer." *National Catholic Reporter* 28 (28 August): 10.

―――. 1992b. "Curia Faction Goes for Total Control over CELAM IV." *National Catholic Reporter* 29 (6 November): 14–15.

―――. 1996. "American Synod, Rome Agenda." *National Catholic Reporter* 33 (25 October): 4–5.

―――. 1997. "Papal Doubts about Unbridled Capitalism." *National Catholic Reporter* 33 (31 January): 12.

MacIntyre, Alasdair. 1981. *After Virtue: A Study in Moral Theory.* Notre Dame, Ind.: University of Notre Dame Press.

Madges, William. 1986. "Authority and Persuasion: Ignaz von Dollinger." 61–77. In *Raising the Torch of Good News.* Edited by Bernard P. Prusak. Lanham, Md.: University Press of America.

Maguire, Daniel C. 1976. "The Vatican on Sex." *Commonweal* 103 (27 February): 137–40.

―――. 1978. "Human Sexuality: The Book and the Epiphenomenon." *Catholic Theological Society of America Proceedings* 37: 38–49.

―――. 1983. "Abortion: A Question of Catholic Honesty." *Christian Century* 100 (14 September): 803–7.

―――. 1984. "Visit to an Abortion Clinic." *National Catholic Reporter* 20 (5 October): 9, 14.

―――. 1986. *The Moral Revolution.* New York: Harper and Row.

―――. 1994. "Cairo Consensus." *Christian Century* 111 (12 October): 916–17.

Maguire, Marjorie Reiley. 1982. "Catholic Women and the Theological Enclave." *Christian Century* 99 (3 February): 109–111.

Mahoney, John. 1990. *The Making of Moral Theology.* New York: Clarendon Press.

Mainelli, Vincent P. 1986. "RCIA: Option or Panacea?" *America* 154 (5 April): 279–80.

Malcolm, Teresa. 1996. "Conservative Priests Let Down by Vatican." *National Catholic Reporter* 32 (19 January): 6.

Maloney, Donald. 1970. "Rahner and the 'Anonymous Christian.'" *America* 123 (31 October): 348–50.

Mannion, M. Francis. 1991. "The Church and the Voices of Feminism." *America* 165 (5 October): 212–16, 228–30.

———. 1996. "Agendas for Liturgical Reform." *America* 175 (30 November): 9–16.

Martin, James. 1995. "Opus Dei in the United States." *America* 172 (25 February): 8–15, 26–27.

Martinez, Demetria. 1990. "Weakland on Abortion: Who's Confusing Whom?" *National Catholic Reporter* 27 (23 November): 7.

———. 1993. "Women-Church: 'Adrift' from Catholicism." *National Catholic Reporter* 29 (16 April): 3–4.

Marty, Martin E. 1988. "The State of the Disunion." *Commonweal* 115 (29 January): 43–46.

May, William W., ed. 1987. *Vatican Authority and American Catholic Dissent: The Curran Case and Its Consequences.* New York: Crossroad.

McBrien, Richard P. 1973. *The Remaking of the Church.* San Francisco: Harper and Row.

———. 1978a. "Who Is a Catholic?" *National Catholic Reporter* 14 (February): 7, 9.

———. 1978b. "Catholic Social Action." *National Catholic Reporter* 14 (3 March): 7–8.

———. 1979. "The Roman Catholic Church: Can It Transcend the Crisis?" *Christian Century* 96 (17 January): 42–45.

———. 1981. *Catholicism.* Minneapolis, Minn.: Winston Press.

———. 1992a. *Report on the Church: Catholicism after Vatican II.* San Francisco: HarperSanFrancisco.

———. 1992b. "Capitalists Should Worry about Pope." *National Catholic Reporter* 28 (18 December): 2.

———. 1993a. "Social Justice the Conservative's Achilles' Heel." *National Catholic Reporter* 29 (5 February): 2.

———. 1993b. "Teaching the Truth." *Christian Century* 110 (20 October): 1004–5.

———. 1994a. *Catholicism: New Edition.* New York: Harper and Row.

———. 1994b. "No Pope Moved Closer to Jews than John Paul II." *National Catholic Reporter* 30 (24 April): 14.

———. 1995a. "Gaillot Dismissal Defies Logic, Reason." *National Catholic Reporter* 31 (10 February): 2.

———. 1995b. "Red Hat Did Not Undo Vatican Harm." *National Catholic Reporter* 31 (8 September): 2.

———. 1995c. "Labor Priests Now Management Priests." *National Catholic Reporter* 32 (1 November): 13.

———. 1995d. "Focus Shifts from Ordination to Infallibility." *National Catholic Reporter* 32 (15 December): 9.

————. 1996. "The Bernardin Unity Initiative Fails to Deal with Key Issues." *National Catholic Reporter* 32 (20 September): 8.

McCarthy, Timothy G. 1996. *Christianity and Humanism: From Their Biblical Foundations into the Third Millennium.* Chicago: Loyola Press.

McClory, Robert J. 1977. "Lay Role Regressing, 47 Catholics Charge." *National Catholic Reporter* 14 (23 December): 16.

————. 1978a. "'Concern' Signers Speak Out." *National Catholic Reporter* 14 (6 January): 1, 4.

————. 1978b. "SODEPAX No Longer in Limbo." *National Catholic Reporter* 14 (10 March): 8.

————. 1988a. "Archdiocesan Mass for Gays Ruptures Catholic Dignity." *National Catholic Reporter* 24 (1 August): 4.

————. 1988b. "Patty Crowley, at 75, Bruised But Unbowed." *National Catholic Reporter* 24 (12 August): 5–6.

————. 1994. "Catholics' Sex Practices Follow U.S. Norms." *National Catholic Reporter* 31 (16 December): 6.

————. 1995. "Holy Orders Surrounded by Controversy." *National Catholic Reporter* 32 (20 October): 15–16.

————. 1996a. "Conservative Group Seeks 'Kinder' Image." *National Catholic Reporter* 32 (12 April): 8.

————. 1996b. "The Path to Common Ground Is a Rocky Road." *National Catholic Reporter* 33 (8 November): 5.

————. 1997. "Vatican Agreement 'Moderately' Inclusive." *National Catholic Reporter* 33 (9 May): 3–4.

McCormick, Richard A. 1966. "Modern Morals in a Muddle." *America* 115 (30 July): 116.

————. 1968. "The New Morality." *America* 119 (15 June): 769–72.

————. 1973. "The Silence Since *Humanae Vitae*." *America* 129 (21 July): 30–33.

————. 1976a. "Sexual Ethics: An Opinion." *National Catholic Reporter* 12 (30 January): 9.

————. 1976b. "Human Rights and the Mission of the Church." *Theological Studies* 37 (March): 107–19.

————. 1981a. *Notes on Moral Theology 1965 through 1980.* Lanham, Md.: University Press of America.

————. 1981b. "Notes on Moral Theology." *Theological Studies* 42 (March): 119–24.

————. 1984. "The Chill Factor: Recent Roman Interventions." *America* 150 (30 June): 475–81.

————. 1985. "Notes on Moral Theology." *Theological Studies* 46 (March): 50–64.

———. 1986a. "Dissent in Moral Theology and Its Implications." *Theological Studies* 48 (March): 87–105.

———. 1986b. "The Search for Truth in the Catholic Context." *America* 155 (8 November): 276–81.

———. 1989. "Moral Theology 1940–1989: An Overview." *Theological Studies* 50 (March): 3– 24.

———. 1990. "Changing My Mind about the Changeable Church." *Christian Century* 107 (8 August): 732–36.

———. 1993a. "*Humanae Vitae* 25 Years Later." *America* 169 (17 July): 6–12.

———. 1993b. "Document Begs Many Legitimate Moral Questions." *National Catholic Reporter* 29 (15 October): 17.

———. 1993c. "*Veritatis Splendor* and Moral Theology." *America* 169 (30 October): 8–11.

———. 1995. "The Gospel of Life." *America* 172 (29 April): 10–17.

———. 1996. "Authority and Leadership: The Moral Challenge." *America* 175 (20 July): 12–17.

McCormick, Richard A., and Richard P. McBrien. 1991. "Theology as a Public Responsibility." *America* 165 (28 September): 184–89, 203–6.

McDade, John. 1991. "Catholic Theology in the Postconciliar Period." In *Modern Catholicism*, 422–43. See Hastings 1991.

McDonagh, Enda. 1991. "The Church in the Modern World." In *Modern Catholicism*, 96–112. See Hastings 1991.

McDonagh, Francis. 1990. "With Eyes to CELAM IV." *National Catholic Reporter* 27 (16 November): 10.

McDonnell, Kilian. 1982. "Anglicans and Catholics: Where We Stand." *America* 147 (27 November): 326–30.

McEnroy, Carmel. 1996. *Guests in Their Own Home: The Women at Vatican II.* New York: Crossroad Publishing Company.

McGinn, Bernard. 1985. "Papal Assassinations: An Historical View." *Criterion* 24 (Winter): 13–18.

McGovern, Arthur F. 1985. "Liberation Theology and the Vatican: An Assessment." In *Religion and Economic Ethics*, edited by Joseph F. Gower, 251–62. Lanham, Md.: University Press of America.

———. 1989. "Liberation Theology Adapts and Endures." *America* 161 (3 November): 587–90.

McGovern, Arthur F., and Thomas L. Schubeck. 1988. "Updating Liberation Theology." *America* 159 (16 July): 32–35.

McHugh, John. 1975. *The Mother of Jesus in the New Testament.* New York: Doubleday.

McKenzie, John L. 1980. "A Bill of Divorce." *Commonweal* 107 (30 May): 301–5.

———. 1985. *Source.* Chicago: Thomas More.

McLaughlin, Loretta. 1982. *The Pill, John Rock and the Church: A Biography of a Revolution.* New York: Little, Brown.

McManus, Jim. 1986. "New Homosexuality Guidelines Seen as a Step Back." *National Catholic Reporter* 23 (7 November): 7.

McNeill, John J. 1976. *The Church and the Homosexual.* Kansas City, Mo.: Sheed Andrews and McMeel.

———. 1986. "No Time for Silence." *Commonweal* 113 (5 December): 647.

———. 1987. "Homosexuality: Challenging the Church to Grow." *Christian Century* 104 (11 March): 242–46.

———. 1988. *Taking a Chance on God.* Boston: Beacon Press.

———. 1994. *Freedom, Glorious Freedom.* Boston: Beacon Press.

Mecklenburger, Ralph D. 1979. "Are Christians 'Honorary Jews'?" *Christian Century* 96 (21 March): 302–3.

Melchin, Kenneth R. 1990. "Revisionists, Deontologists, and the Structure of Moral Understanding." *Theological Studies* 51 (September): 389–416.

Mersch, Emile. 1939. *Morality and the Mystical Body.* New York: P. J. Kenedy and Sons.

Metz, Johann Baptist. 1969. *Theology of the World.* New York: Herder and Herder.

———. 1970. "Political Theology." In vol. 5 of *Sacramentum Mundi: An Encyclopedial of Theology,* 34–38. New York: Herder and Herder.

———. 1980. *Faith in History and Society.* New York: Crossroad.

———. 1981. *The Emergent Church: The Future of Christianity in a Postbourgeois World.* New York: Crossroad.

———. 1985. "Theology Today: New Crises and New Visions." *Catholic Theological Society of America Proceedings* 40: 1–14.

———. 1989. "Theology in a New Paradigm: Political Theology." In *Paradigm Change in Theology,* 355–66. See Küng and Tracy 1989.

Michaels, James W. 1980. "U.S. Theologians' Hopes 'Dashed' by Synod Results." *National Catholic Reporter* 17 (7 December): 1, 19.

Milhaven, John Giles. 1970. "The Abortion Debate: An Epistemological Interpretation." *Theological Studies* 31 (March): 106–24.

———. 1976. Review of *The Church and the Homosexual,* by John J. McNeill. *National Catholic Reporter* 14 (8 October): 12.

Miller, J. Michael. 1983. *What Are They Saying about Papal Primacy?* New York: Paulist Press.

Misner, Paul. 1983. "Vancouver 1983: A Catholic View." *The Ecumenist* 22 (November): 1–4.

Modras, Ronald. 1979. "Solidarity and Opposition in a Pluralistic Church." *Commonweal* 106 (14 September): 493–95.

Molineaux, David. 1987. "Gustavo Gutierrez: Historical Origins." *The Ecumenist* 25 (July): 65–69.

———. 1995. "Rome Moves to Silence Brazil's Gebara." *National Catholic Reporter* 31 (26 May): 5.

Moltmann, Jurgen. 1967. *Theology of Hope*. New York: Harper and Row.

Mooney, Christopher F. 1967. "Teilhard de Chardin and Christian Spirituality." *Thought* 42 (September): 483–502.

Moore, Arthur J. 1983. "More Than Politics [at Vancouver]." *Commonweal* 100 (9 September): 452, 454–55.

Moran, Gabriel. 1966a. *Catechesis of Revelation*. New York: Herder and Herder.

———. 1966b. *Theology of Revelation*. New York: Herder and Herder.

———. 1972. *The Present Revelation*. New York: Herder and Herder.

Muggeridge, Malcolm. 1971. *Something Beautiful for God*. San Francisco: Harper and Row.

Murnion, William E. 1986. "The 'Preferential Option for the Poor' in *Economic Justice for All*: Theology or Ideology?" In *Raising the Torch of Good News*, edited by Bernard P. Prusak, 203–37. Lanham, Md.: University Press of America.

Murphy, Francis X. 1978. "Christianity, Marriage and Sex." *Commonweal* 105 (16 June): 380– 86.

———. 1981. *The Papacy Today*. New York: Macmillan.

———. 1986. "The Politique of the Synod." *America* 154 (25 January): 49–51.

———. 1990. "Aggiornamento to Perestroika: Vatican Ostpolitik." *America* 162 (19 May): 494–98.

———. 1991. "Oswald von Nell-Breuning: Papal Surrogate." *America* 165 (26 October): 293– 95.

———. 1992. "John's Council as Catholic Camelot." *National Catholic Reporter* 28 (2 October): 2.

———. 1996. "Cardinal Pietro Pavan: Inveterate Optimist." *America* 174 (10 February): 23– 24.

Murray, John Courtney. 1966a. "Religious Freedom." In *The Documents of Vatican II*, 672–74. See Abbott 1966.

———. 1966b. "Freedom, Authority and Community." *America* 115 (14 September): 734–37, 740–41.

Myerson, Allen R. 1996. "For the First Time in 151 Years, Baylor Puts a Bounce in Its Step." *New York Times*, 30 January.

———. 1997. "Southern Baptist Convention Calls for Boycott of Disney." *New York Times*, 19 June.

Nelson, James B. 1987. "Reuniting Sexuality and Spirituality." *Christian Century* 104 (25 February): 187–90.

Nelson, J. Robert. 1976. "The World Council's Second Generation Takes Over." *Christian Century* 93 (18 February): 144–47.

Neuhaus, Richard John. 1978. "What We Mean by Human Rights, and Why." *Christian Century* 95 (6 December): 1177–80.

———. 1992. *Doing Well and Doing Good: The Challenge of the Christian Capitalist.* New York: Doubleday.

Nichols, Aidan. 1989. *Yves Congar.* Wilton, Conn.: Morehouse-Barlow.

———. 1990. *From Newman to Congar.* Edinburgh: T. and T. Clark.

Nickoloff, James B. 1993. "Church of the Poor: The Ecclesiology of Gustavo Gutierrez." *Theological Studies* 54 (September): 512–35.

Niebuhr, Gustav. 1995. "Men Crowd Stadiums to Fulfill Their Souls." *New York Times,* 6 August.

———. 1996a. "Open Attitude on Homosexuality Makes Pariahs of Some Churches." *New York Times,* 8 February.

———. 1996b. "Cardinals Condemn President's Veto of Ban on an Abortion Procedure." *New York Times,* 17 April.

———. 1996c. "Methodists Rule Against Homosexuality." *New York Times,* 25 April.

———. 1996d. "Episcopal Bishop Absolved in Gay Ordination." *New York Times,* 16 May.

———. 1996e. "Episcopal Bishop Hails Victory on Gay Priests." *New York Times,* 28 May.

———. 1996f. "Baptists Censure Disney on Gay-Spouse Benefits." *New York Times,* 13 June.

———. 1996g. "Cardinal Aims for New Unity for Catholics." *New York Times,* 13 August.

———. 1996h. "Cardinal Opposed in Effort to Find 'Common Ground'." *New York Times,* 24 August.

———. 1996i. "A Cardinal Defends Plan to Open Up Discussions." *New York Times,* 1 September.

Nilson, Jon. 1995. "John Paul II, Ecumenist." *Commonweal* 122 (14 July): 5–7.

Norman, Edward. 1991. "An Outsider's Evaluation." In *Modern Catholicism,* 457–62. See Hastings 1991.

Nouwen, Henri J. M. 1967. "Homosexuality: Prejudice or Mental Illness?" *National Catholic Reporter* 4 (29 November): 8.

Novak, Michael. 1975. "Theology of Liberation." *National Catholic Reporter* 11 (21 November): 12.

———. 1987. *Will It Liberate?* New York: Paulist Press.

———. 1993. *The Catholic Ethic and the Spirit of Capitalism.* New York: Free Press.

Nugent, Robert. 1981. "Homosexuality and the Hurting Family." *America* 144 (28 February): 154–57.

———. 1984. "Homosexuality and the Vatican." *Christian Century* 101 (9 May): 487–89.

———. 1985. "Courage Curbs Gays." *National Catholic Reporter* 21 (18 January): 10.

Nyhan, David. 1984. "The (Catholic) Father of the Pill." *National Catholic Reporter* 21 (28 December): 7.

O'Brien, Nancy Frazer. 1997. "Abortion Debate Tainted by 'Half-truth, Lies'." *National Catholic Reporter* 33 (14 March): 10.

O'Collins, Gerald and Daniel Kendall. 1987. "Mary Magdalene As Major Witness to Jesus' Resurrection." *Theological Studies* 48 (December): 631–46.

O'Collins, Gerald. 1973. "An Argument for Women Priests." *America* 129 (1 September):122– 23.

———. 1990. "Catholic Theology (1965–1990)." *America* 162 (3 February): 86–87, 104–5.

O'Connell, Gerald. 1996. "Italians Join the Trend: Petitions Support Reform." *National Catholic Reporter* 32 (26 January): 9.

O'Connell, Robert J. 1968. "A Discussion of 'Human Life'." *America* 119 (17 August): 96–98.

O'Connell, Timothy, 1976. *Principles for a Catholic Morality.* New York: Seabury.

———. 1986. ed. *Vatican II and Its Documents: An American Reappraisal.* Wilmington, Del.: Michael Glazier.

Oesterreicher, John M. 1969. "Declaration on the Non-Christian Religions." In vol. 3 of *Commentary on the Documents of Vatican II*, 1–136. See Vorgrimler 1969.

O'Grady, Desmond. 1977. "Reassessing the Missioner's Role." *National Catholic Reporter* 13 (15 April): 3.

Ogden, Schubert M. 1980. "Faith and Freedom." *Christian Century* 97 (17 December): 1241–44.

Oliver, Harold H. 1985. "Beyond the Feminist Critique: A Shaking of the Foundations." *Christian Century* 102 (1 May): 446–47.

O'Malley, John. 1989. *Tradition and Transition: Historical Perspectives on Vatican II.* Willmington, Del.: Michael Glazier.

Ong, Walter J. 1996. "Do We Live in a Post-Christian Age?" *America* 174 (3 Februrary): 16–18, 29–34.

Opstrny, David J. 1988. "Gay Catholics Evicted from San Francisco Church." *San Francisco Examiner*, 20 November.

Orsy, Ladislas. 1987. "Magisterium: Assent and Dissent." *Theological Studies* 48 (September): 473–97.

———. 1989. "The New Profession of Faith and Oath of Fidelity." *America* 160 (15 April): 345–60.

———. 1990. "Magisterium and Theologians: A Vatican Document." *America* 163 (21 July): 30–32.

———. 1995. "The Congregations Response: Its Authority and Meaning." *America* 173 (9 December): 4–5.

———. 1996. "Lay Persons in Church Governance? A Disputed Question." *America* 174 (6 April): 10–13.

———. 1997. "A Profession of Faith and an Excommunication in Ecumenical Perspective." *America* 176 (22 February): 6–9.

Osborne, Kenan B. 1993. *Ministry: Lay Ministry in the Roman Catholic Church.* New York: Paulist Press.

Ostling, Richard. 1992. "The Second Reformation." *Time*, 14 November.

Outler, Albert C. 1982. "Protestants Found Three Councils." *National Catholic Reporter* 18 (8 October): 4, 37–38.

Palmer, Paul F. 1975. "When a Marriage Dies." *America* 133 (22 February): 126–28.

Palmer, Parker J. 1986. *The Company of Strangers.* New York: Crossroad.

Papa, Mary. 1978. "Women Mix Social Change, Ordination Aims." *National Catholic Reporter* 15 (24 November): 1, 12.

Parker, James. 1992. "The Mother of Christian Initiation." *Commonweal* 119 (31 January): 19–21.

Pavan, Pietro. 1969. "Declaration on Religious Freedom." In vol. 3 of *Commentary on the Documents of Vatican II*, 49–63. See Vorgrimler 1969.

Pawlikowski, John T. 1982a. *Christ in Light of the Christian-Jewish Dialogue.* New York: Paulist Press.

———. 1982b. *The Challenge of the Holocaust for Christian Theology.* New York: Anti-Defamation League.

———. 1988. "Christian Ethics and the Holocaust: A Dialogue with Post-Auschwitz Judaism." *Theological Studies* 49 (December): 649–69.

Peerman, Dean. 1979. "Did the Pope Apply the Brakes at Puebla?" *Christian Century* 96 (28 February): 203–4.

———. 1993. "CELAM IV: Maneuvering and Marking Time in Santo Domingo." *Christian Century* 110 (17 February): 180–85.

Pelikan, Jaroslav. 1971–1989. *The Christian Tradition: A History of the Development of Doctrine.* 5 vols. Chicago: University of Chicago Press.

Penfield, Janet Harbison. 1980. "COCU at 20: An Anniversary Waltz." *Christian Century* 97 (3 December): 1186–91.

Pennington, M. Basil. 1975. *Mary Today*. New York: Doubleday.

Perlez, Jane. 1993. "Pope Orders Nuns Out of Auschwitz." *New York Times*, 15 April.

———. 1997. "Pope Renews Call for Poles to Fight Abortion." *New York Times*, 5 June.

Petersen, Melody. 1997. "Cardinal Calls on President to Shift View." *New York Times*, 10 March.

Piccolino, Alberta. 1991. "Pope Confronts a Different 'Less Catholic' Brazil." *National Catholic Reporter* 28 (1 November): 12.

Poole, Stafford. 1995. *Our Lady of Guadaloupe: The Origins and Sources of a Mexican National Symbol, 1531–1797*. Arizona: University of Arizona Press.

Portier, William L. 1983. "Catholic Theology in the U.S., 1840–1907: Recovering a Forgotten Tradition." *Horizon* 10 (Fall): 317–33.

Pottmeyer, Hermann Josef. 1992. "The Traditionalist Temptation of the Contemporary Church." *America* 167 (5 September): 100–4.

———. 1996. "Refining the Question about Women's Ordination." *America* 175 (26 October): 16–18.

Principe, Walter H. 1988. "The History of Theology: Fortress or Launching Pad?" *Catholic Theological Society of America Proceedings* 43: 19–40.

Provost, James H. 1989. "The Papacy: Power, Authority and Leadership." In *The Papacy and the Church in the United States*, 189–215. See Cooke 1989.

Putney, Michael E. 1992. "Come, Holy Spirit, Renew the Whole Creation: Seventh Assembly of the World Council of Churches." *Theological Studies* 52 (December): 607–35.

Quinn, John R. 1987. "Towards an Understanding of the Letter on the Pastoral Care of Homosexual Persons." *America* 156 (7 February): 92–95.

———. 1996. "The Exercise of the Primacy: Facing the Cost of Christian Unity." *Commonweal* 123 (12 July): 11–20.

Rahner, Karl. 1963. *Mary, Mother of the Lord*. New York: Herder and Herder.

———. 1964a. *Nature and Grace*. New York: Sheed and Ward.

———. 1964b. "On the Question of a Formal Existential Ethics." In vol. 2 of *Theological Investigations, Man in the Church*, 217–34. Baltimore: Helicon Press.

———. 1966. "Christianity and the Non-Christian Religions." In vol. 5 of *Theological Investigations, Later Writings*, 115–34. New York: Herder and Herder.

———. 1969. *Grace in Freedom*. New York: Herder and Herder.

———. 1972. "The Problem of Genetic Manipulation." In vol. 9 of *Theological Investigations, Writings of 1965–67*, 225–52. New York: Herder and Herder.

———. 1974. "Anonymous Christianity and the Missionary Task of the Church." In vol. 12 of *Theological Investigations*, 164–78. New York: Seabury Press.

———. 1977. "Women Priests." *National Catholic Reporter* 13 (7 October): 7, 14.

———. 1979. "Towards a Fundamental Theological Interpretation of Vatican II." *Theological Studies* 40 (December): 716–27.

Ranly, Ernest W. 1977. "Constructing Local Theologies." *Commonweal* 104 (11 November): 716–19.

Rashke, Richard. 1976. "Homosexuality and the Church Today." *National Catholic Reporter* 12 (26 March): 1, 4.

———. 1977. "Coalition: Ordination Paper 'Political, Dishonest, Faulty'." *National Catholic Reporter* 13 (11 February): 1.

Ratzinger, Joseph Cardinal with Vittorio Messori. 1985. *The Ratzinger Report.* San Francisco: Ignatius Press.

Rausch, Thomas P. 1982. "The Image of Mary: A Catholic Response." *America* 146 (27 March): 231–34.

———. 1984. "An Ecumenical Eucharist for a World Assembly. *America* 150 (21 January): 25–29.

———. 1985. "Rome and Geneva: The Experience of Ecumenism." *America* 152 (19 January): 41–45.

———. 1986. *The Roots of the Catholic Tradition.* Wilmington, Del.: Michael Glazier.

———. 1989a. *Authority and Leadership in the Church.* Wilmington, Del.: Michael Glazier.

———. 1989b. "Ethical Issues and Ecumenism." *America* 160 (21 January): 30–33.

———. 1990. "The Ecumenical Movement in the 1990's: Is It Still Moving?" *America* 163 (3 November): 218–22.

Rawls, John. 1971. *A Theory of Justice.* Cambridge, Mass.: Harvard University Press.

Redington, James D. 1983. "The Hindu-Christian Dialogue and the Interior Dialogue." *Theological Studies* 44 (December): 587–603.

Redmont, Jane. 1995. "'Letter to Women' Bares John Paul's Isolation." *National Catholic Reporter* 31 (28 July): 11.

Reese, Thomas J. 1984. "The Selection of Bishops." *America* 151 (24 August): 65–72.

———. 1988. "Archbishop Lefèbvre: Moving Toward Schism." *America* 158 (4 June): 573–74.

———. 1992. "Women's Pastoral Fails." *America* 167 (5 December): 443–44.

———. 1993. "Bishops Speak in Public Session of Sexual Abuse." *America* 169 (3 July): 4–6.

———. 1994a. "The Synod on the Church in Africa." *America* 170 (14 May): 4–6.

———. 1994b. "The African Synod: You Had to Be There." *America* 170 (4 June): 8–9.

———. 1996. "Digging into 'Common Ground'." *America* 175 (21 September): 6–7.

Rhodes, Anthony. 1983. *The Power of Rome.* New York: Franklin Watts.

Rich, Frank. 1996. "Thank God I'm a Man!" *New York Times,* 25 September.

Richard, Lucien. 1981. *What Are They Saying about Christ and World Religions?* New York: Paulist Press.

Riding, Alan. 1991. "Pope Visits Fatima to Tender Thanks." *New York Times,* 14 May.

———. 1992. "New Catechism for Catholics Defines Sins of Modern World." *New York Times,* 17 November.

———. 1993a. "Women Seize Focus at Rights Forum." *New York Times,* 16 June.

———. 1993b. "Human Rights. The West Gets Some Tough Questions." *New York Times,* 20 June.

Riley, Maria. 1984. "Women, Church and Patriarchy." *America* 150 (5 May): 333–38.

———. 1989. "Feminist Analysis: A Missing Perspective." In *The Logic of Solidarity,* 186–201. See Baum and Ellsberg 1989.

Riley, Michael C. 1978. "Teaching All Nations . . . and Learning." *America* 138 (18 March): 202–6.

———. 1979. "Cross-cultural Evangelization." *America* 141 (22 December): 409–11.

Roberts, Tom. 1994. "Eyes on Accord, Jews Shrug Off Pope's Affront." *National Catholic Reporter* 30 (29 July): 11.

———. 1996a. "Dulles Urges Bishops to Enforce Papal 'No'." *National Catholic Reporter* 32 (26 July): 6.

———. 1996b. "Unanimous Voice Is Recommended, But Bishops Divided on Women's Issues." *National Catholic Reporter* 32 (26 July): 7.

Rohter, Larry. 1990. "Pope, in Mexico, Faces Rising Protestant Tide." *New York Times,* 12 May.

Rosato, Philip J. 1992. "The Church of United Europe: Reflections on the Recent Special Synod." *America* 166 (11 January): 4–7.

Ruether, Rosemary Radford. 1970. *The Radical Kingdom.* New York: Paulist Press.

———. 1972. "Paradoxes of Human Hope: The Messianic Horizon of Church and Society." *Theological Studies* 33 (June): 235–52.

———. 1974. *Religion and Sexism.* New York: Simon and Schuster.

———. 1975. *New Heaven New Earth: Sexist Ideologies and Human Liberation.* New York: Seabury Press.

———. 1977. *The Feminine Face of the Church.* Philadelphia: Westminster Press.

———. 1979. "Consciousness-Raising at Puebla: The Women's Project at CELAM III." *Catholic Theological Society of America Proceedings* 34: 176–82.

———. 1983. *Sexism and God-Talk: Toward a Feminist Theology*. Boston: Beacon Press.

———. 1984. "Women-Church Calls Men to Exodus from Patriarchy." *National Catholic Reporter* 20 (23 March): 16.

———. 1985. *Women-Church*. San Francisco: Harper and Row.

———. 1987. "John Paul II and the Growing Alienation of Women from the Church." In *The Church in Anguish*, 279–83. See Küng and Swidler 1987.

———. 1988. "Bishops' Pastoral Flawed But Important." *National Catholic Reporter* 25 (23 December): 13.

———. 1990. "Dear U.S. Bishops, You Insult Our Intelligence." *National Catholic Reporter* 26 (18 May): 16.

———. 1993. "Women-Church: A Way to Stay While Patriarchy Wears Away." *National Catholic Reporter* 29 (13 August): 22.

———. 1995. "Mary in U. S. Catholic Culture." *National Catholic Reporter* 31 (10 February): 15–17.

Ruether, Rosemary, and Eleanor McLaughlin, eds. 1979. *Women of Spirit: Female Leadership in the Jewish and Christian Traditions*. New York: Simon and Schuster.

Rusch, William G. 1985. *Ecumenism*. Philadelphia: Fortress Press.

Ryan, Thomas. 1991. "Report on the World Council of Churches General Assembly." *America* 164 (25 May): 566–71.

Schaeffer, Pamela. 1995a. "WOC Gathers to Promote Women's Ordination Amid Conflicting Visions, Goals." *National Catholic Reporter* 32 (1 December): 9–11.

———. 1995b. "Assessing Ambiguous Infallibility Factor." *National Catholic Reporter* 32 (8 December): 3–6.

———. 1996a. "Vatican Has More Questions for Priest, Nun." *National Catholic Reporter* 32 (16 February): 10.

———. 1996b. "Condoms Tolerated to Avoid AIDS, French Bishops Say." *National Catholic Reporter* 32 (23 February): 9.

———. 1996c. "Vatican Threatens Sri Lankan Who Linked Mary, Liberation." *National Catholic Reporter* 32 (14 June): 13.

———. 1996d. "AAUP Denounces Meinrad Officials." *National Catholic Reporter* 32 (9 August): 5.

———. 1996e. "Initiative Seeks 'Catholic Common Ground'." *National Catholic Reporter* 32 (23 August): 3.

———. 1996f. "Theologian, Under Heavy Fire, Appeals to Pope." *National Catholic Reporter* 33 (27 December): 5.

———. 1997a. "Vatican Excommunicates Balasuriya." *National Catholic Reporter* 33 (17 January): 3.

———. 1997b. "Theologians Opt for Diplomacy in Dispute." *National Catholic Reporter* 33 (22 June): 3.

Schall, James V. 1978. "Culture and Human Rights." *America* 138 (14 January): 14–17.

Scharper, Philip. 1978. "Toward a Politicized Christianity." *Commonweal* 105 (16 June): 392–99.

Schillebeeckx, Edward. 1981a. *Interim Report on the Books Jesus and Christ.* New York: Crossroad.

———. 1981b. *Ministry.* New York: Crossroad.

Schineller, Peter J. 1976. "Christ and Church: A Spectrum of Views." *Theological Studies* 37 (December): 545–66.

Schlette, Heinz Robert. 1966. *Toward a Theological of Religions.* New York: Herder and Herder.

———. 1976. "Anonymous Christianity: A Disputed Question." *Theology Digest* 24 (Summer): 125–31.

Schmitz, Robert E. 1996. "Of Dinosaurs, Carrier Pigeons and Disappearing Priests." *America* 175 (12 October): 7–11.

Schneiders, Sandra M. 1986. *New Wineskins.* New York: Paulist Press.

———. 1991. "Religious Life *(Perfectae Caritatis)*." In *Modern Catholicism: Vatican II and After,* edited by Adrian Hastings, 157–62. New York: Oxford University Press.

Schoenherr, Richard A. 1995. "Numbers Don't Lie: A Priesthood in Irreversible Decline." *Commonweal* 122 (7 April): 11–14.

Schoof, Mark T. 1970. *A Survey of Catholic Theology: 1800–1970.* New York: Paulist, Newman Press.

Schüssler Fiorenza, Elisabeth. 1983. *In Memory of Her: A Feminist Reconstruction of Christian Origins.* New York: Crossroads.

———. 1985. "The Discipleship of Equals." *Commonweal* 112 (9 August): 432–37.

———. 1986. "Theology after the Synod: Acknowledging Women." *Commonweal* 113 (31 January): 44–46.

———. 1990. "Changing the Paradigm." *Christian Century* 107 (5 September): 796–800.

Searle, Mark. 1988. "Renewing the Liturgy—Again." *Commonweal* 115 (18 November): 617–22.

Seelye, Katherine Q. 1997. "Hearing Displays Chasm on Abortion Method." *New York Times,* 12 March.

Semmelroth, Otto. 1969. "The Role of the Blessed Virgin Mother." In vol. 1 of *Commentary on the Documents of Vatican II,* 285–96. See Vorgrimler 1969.

Shafer, Ingrid. 1995a. "500,000 Petition for Church Tolerance." *National Catholic Reporter* 31 (14 August): 8.

———. 1995b. "Petition Drive Moves to Germany." *National Catholic Reporter* 31 (25 August): 11.

Sheppard, L. C. 1967. "Catholic Liturgical Movements." In *New Catholic Encyclopedia,* vol. 8, 900–4. New York: McGraw-Hill.

Sigmund, Paul E. 1990. *Liberation Theology at the Crossroads: Democracy or Revolution?* New York: Oxford University Press.

Simons, Marlise. 1991. "Italy Reopens Investigation into the 1981 Shooting of the Pope." *New York Times,* 19 May.

———. 1993. "Pilgrims Crowding Europe's Catholic Shrines." *New York Times,* 12 October.

Skerrett, Ellen, Edward R. Kantowicz, and Steven M. Avella. 1993. *Catholicism, Chicago Style.* Chicago: Loyola University Press.

Smith, Huston. 1991. *The World's Religions.* San Francisco: HarperSanFrancisco.

Smith, Karen Sue. 1987. "'Claiming Our Power': Dialogue, Worship and Development." *Commonweal* 114 (6 November): 613–15.

———. 1988. "Michel Blows His Horn: Social Justice and Liturgy." *Commonweal* 115 (9 September): 456–57.

Smolenski, Carol. 1995. "Sex Tourism and the Sexual Exploitation of Children." *Christian Century* 112 (15 November): 1079–81.

Sobrino, Jon. 1991. "Awakening from the Sleep of Inhumanity." *Christian Century* 108 (30 April): 364–70.

Socarides, Charles W. 1995. "How America Went Gay." *America* 173 (18 November): 20–22.

Sölle, Dorothee. 1967. *Christ the Representative: An Essay in Theology after the 'Death of God'.* London: SCM.

Spaeth, Robert L. 1993. "The Galileo File: Still Open." *Commonweal* 120 (26 March): 6–7.

Spalding, John D. 1996. "Bonding in the Bleachers: A Visit to the Promise Keepers." *Christian Century* 113 (6 March): 260–65.

Spear, Lois. 1996. "Marian Apparitions Meet Ancient Need." *National Catholic Reporter* 32 (6 September): 14.

Spohn, William C. 1991. "Forum: Proportionalism: Method or Menace?" *Catholic Theological Society of America Proceedings* 46: 158–60.

Spong, John Shelby. 1988. *Living in Sin? A Bishop Rethinks Human Sexuality.* San Francisco: Harper and Row.

Stahel, Thomas H. 1992a. "The Cry from Santo Domingo." *America* 167 (31 October): 315–17.

————. 1992b. "A Tale of Two Cities: Rome and Santo Domingo." *America* 167 (28 November): 419.

Stackhouse, Max L. 1993. "Multiculturism in Vienna: The Future of Human Rights." *Christian Century* 110 (30 June): 660–62.

Stammer, Larry B. 1993. "Meeting of World Religions Leads to Ethics Rules." *Los Angeles Times*, 5 September.

Steinberg, Leo. 1984. *The Sexuality of Christ in Renaissance Art and in Modern Oblivion.* New York: Pantheon.

Steinfels, Margaret O'Brien. 1992. "The Unholy Alliance Between the Right and the Left in the Catholic Church." *America* 166 (2 May): 376–82.

Steinfels, Peter. 1985. "Conflicts and Code Words: A Sober Look at the Synod." *Commonweal* 112 (20 December): 698–700.

————. 1988. "Catholic Bishops Vote to Retain Controversial Statement on AIDS." *New York Times*, 28 June.

————. 1989. "[Archbishop Lefèbvre] A Champion of Tradition." *New York Times*, 30 June.

————. 1990a. "Flexibility Urged on Abortion Issue." *New York Times*, 21 May.

————. 1990b. "Theology Awaits the Vatican's Word on Evils Lesser and Greater." *New York Times*, 2 September.

————. 1990c. "Vatican Bars Swiss University from Honoring Archbishop of Milwaukee." *New York Times*, 11 November.

————. 1990d. "Bishops Issue Warning on Birth Control." *New York Times*, 15 November.

————. 1990e. "Pope Endorses Prague Statement on Anti-Semitism." *New York Times*, 7 December.

————. 1991. "Papal Letter Spreads the Faith and the Debate." *New York Times*, 29 January.

————. 1992a. "Vatican Urges Restrictions on Homosexual Rights." *New York Times*, 18 July.

————. 1992b. "Struggling for Unity." *New York Times*, 6 September.

————. 1992c. "A Pivotal Conference Is Begun by Latin Bishops." *New York Times*, 13 October.

————. 1992d. "Pastoral Letter on Women's Role Fails in Vote of Catholic Bishops." *New York Times*, 19 November.

————. 1992e. "Why Did God Make These Debates So Hard?" *New York Times*, 22 November.

————. 1993a. "Women's Group Recasts Religion in Its Own Image." *New York Times*, 21 April.

————. 1993b. "More Diversity Than Harmony." *New York Times*, 7 September.

———. 1994a. "Rabbis Draw Up Ethics of Nonmarital Sex." *New York Times,* 30 April.

———. 1994b. "Bishops Mobilize Against Abortion in Health Plans." *New York Times,* 13 July.

———. 1995a. "Woman Wary about Aiming to Be Priests." *New York Times,* 14 November.

———. 1995b. "Vatican Says the Ban on Women as Priests Is 'Infallible' Doctrine." *New York Times,* 19 November.

———. 1996. "Russian Church Breaks Off from Its Historic Center." *New York Times,* 28 February.

———. 1997. "Catholic Theologians Urge More Discussion of Female Priests." *New York Times,* 8 June.

Stransky, Thomas F. 1986a. "Surprises and Fears of Ecumenism: Twenty Years after Vatican II." *America* 154 (25 January): 44–48.

———. 1986b. "The Catholic-Jewish Dialogue: Twenty Years after *Nostra Aetate.*" *America* 154 (8 February): 92–97.

———. 1993. "Vatican-Israel Diplomatic Relations." *America* 169 (6 November): 4–9.

Stuhlmueller, Carroll. 1974. "Women Priests: Today's Theology and Yesterday's Sociology." *America* 131 (14 December): 385–87.

Sullivan, Francis A. 1995. "Guideposts for Catholic Tradition." *America* 173 (9 December): 5–6.

Sullivan, Robert. 1996. "The Mystery of Mary." *Life* 19:14 (December): 244–50, 54–60.

Suro, Roberto. 1988. "An Assailed Missionary to America Is Beatified." *New York Times,* 25 September.

Swetnam, James. 1979. "A Midrash on Some Sisters." *America* 140 (3 March): 156–58.

Swidler, Leonard, and Arlene Swidler, eds. 1978. *Women Priests: A Catholic Commentary on the Vatican Declaration.* New York: Paulist Press.

Swidler, Leonard. 1979. *Biblical Affirmations of Women.* Philadelphia: Westminster Press.

———. 1987. "A Continuing Controversy: Küng in Conflict." In *The Church in Anguish,* 193–204. See Küng and Swidler 1987.

Szulc, Tad. 1995. *Pope John Paul II.* New York: Scribner.

Tagliabue, John. 1994. "Holocaust Lamentations Echo at Vatican." *New York Times,* 8 April.

———. 1995. "Vatican Attacks U.S.-Backed Draft for U.N. Women's Conference in China." *New York Times,* 26 August.

————. 1996. "Pope Bolsters Church's Support for Scientific View of Evolution." *New York Times*, 25 October.

Tambasco, Anthony J. 1984. *What Are They Saying about Mary?* New York: Paulist Press.

Tapia, Andres. 1996. "Promise Keepers Hear Minority Message." *National Catholic Reporter* 33 (25 October): 15.

Tavard, George H. 1960. *Two Centuries of Ecumenism.* Notre Dame, Ind.: Fides Publications.

Teasdale, Wayne. 1995. "Bede Griffiths As Mystic and Icon of Reversal." *America* 173 (30 September): 22–23.

Thavis, John. 1995. "Pope Closed Synod, Urges Justice in Africa." *National Catholic Reporter* 31 (29 September): 5.

————. 1996. "The New Danger, Ratzinger Says, Is Relativism." *National Catholic Reporter* 32 (18 October): 12.

Thompson, Betty. 1985a. "W. A. Visser't Hooft: Mover and Shaker." *Christian Century* 102 (17 July): 668–70.

————. 1985b. "Eugene Carson Blake: A Noble Prophet." *Christian Century* 102 (28 August): 756–57.

Tierney, Brian. 1988. "Pope and Bishop: A Historical Survey." *America* 158 (5 March): 230–37.

Tillard, J. M. R. 1983. *The Bishop of Rome.* Wilmington, Del.: Michael Glazier.

Tillman, Fritz. 1960. *The Master Calls.* Baltimore: Helicon Press.

Timmerman, Don, Gordan Zahn, and John F. Baldovin. 1988. "The Eucharist: Who May Preside?" *Commonweal* 115 (9 September): 460–63, 466.

Tobin, Mary Luke. 1986. "Women in the Church since Vatican II." *America* 155 (1 November): 243–46.

Toolan, David. 1982. "Is There Life after Ecumenism?" *Commonweal* 109 (29 January): 43–46.

————. 1993. "The Other Half of Our Soul: Dom Bede Griffiths." *America* 168 (5 June): 3–4.

————. 1997. "Heresy or Hokum in Sri Lanka?" *America* 176 (8 February): 4–5.

Torrens, James S. 1994. "Synod on 'The Consecrated Life'." *America* 171 (26 November): 3–4.

Tracy, David. 1975. *Blessed Rage for Order.* New York: Seabury.

————. 1977. "The Catholic Analogical Imagination." *Catholic Theological Society of America Proceedings* 32: 234–44.

————. 1981. *The Analogical Imagination.* New York: Crossroad.

————. 1987a. "On Hope as a Theological Virtue." In *The Church in Anguish*, 268–72. See Küng and Swidler 1987.

———. 1987b. *Plurality and Ambiguity*. New York: Harper and Row.

———. 1989a. "Hermeneutical Reflections in the New Paradigm." In *Paradigm Changes*, 34–62. In Küng and Tracy 1989.

———. 1989b. "The Uneasy Alliance Reconceived: Catholic Theological Method, Modernity and Postmodernity." *Theological Studies* 50 (September): 548–70.

———. 1990. "God, Dialogue and Solidarity: A Theological Refrain." *Christian Century* 107 (10 October): 900–4.

———. 1991. *Dialogue with the Other: The Interreligious Dialogue*. Grand Rapids, Mich.: William Eerdmans Publishing Co.

———. 1994. *On Naming the Present: God, Hermeneutics and Church*. New York: Orbis Books.

———. 1995. "Reasons to Hope for Reform." *America* 173 (14 October): 12–18.

Tripole, Martin R. 1996. "The American Church in Jeopardy." *America* 175 (28 September): 9–15.

Tuohey, John F. 1992. "The CDF and Homosexuals: Rewriting Moral Tradition." *America* 167 (12 September): 136–38.

Tyrrell, George. 1910. *Christianity at the Crossroads*. London: Longmans, Green.

Untener, Kenneth E. 1984. "Local Churches and Universal Church." *America* 151 (13 October): 201–5.

———. 1993. "*Humanae Vitae:* What Has It Done to Us?" *Commonweal* 120 (18 June): 12–14.

———. 1996. "How Bishops Talk." *America* 175 (19 October): 9–15.

Vacek, Edward. 1983. "Authority and the Peace Pastoral." *America* 149 (22 October): 227.

———. 1984. "Popular Ethical Subjectivism: Four Preludes to Objectivity." *Horizons* 11 (Spring): 42–60.

Van Beeck, Franz Josef. 1974. "Invalid or Merely Irregular? Comments by a Reluctant Witness." *Journal of Ecumenical Studies* 11 (Summer): 381–99.

———. 1985. *Catholic Identity after Vatican II*. Chicago: Loyola University Press.

Vidulich, Dorothy. 1990. "Weakland: Vatican II Spirit Has 'Spun Itself Out'." *National Catholic Reporter* 26 (12 October): 7.

———. 1992a. "Vatican Strikes at Legal Protection for Gays." *National Catholic Reporter* 28 (31 July): 9.

———. 1992b. "Gay Groups Say 'Outing' Bishops Is Out of Bounds." *National Catholic Reporter* 28 (14 August): 3.

———. 1992c. "Women's Pastoral Buried after 10 Years." *National Catholic Reporter* 29 (4 December): 3–5.

———. 1994. "Nuns Keep Tabs on Synod and Talk Back." *National Catholic Reporter* 31 (4 November): 7.

Vidulich, Dorothy, and Thomas Fox. 1992. "Women's Letter Draft Moves Sharply Right." *National Catholic Reporter* 28 (11 September): 3.

Visser't Hooft, Willem A. 1982. *The Genesis and Formation of the World Council of Churches.* Geneva: World Council of Churches.

Voegelin, Eric. 1956–1987. *Order and History.* 5 vols. Baton Rouge: Louisiana State University.

Von Hügel, Friedrich. 1908. *The Mystical Element in Religion as Studied in St. Catherine of Genoa and Her Friends.* 2 vols. London: J. M. Dent and Sons; New York: E. P. Dutton, 1921, 1926.

Vorgrimler, Herbert. 1969. ed. *Commentary on the Documents of Vatican II.* 3 vols. New York: Herder and Herder.

Warner, Marina. 1976. *Alone of All Her Sex: The Myth and Cult of the Virgin Mary.* New York: Alfred A. Knopf.

Wassmer, Thomas A. 1968. "The New Morality." *America* 117 (10 February): 190–92.

Watson, Russell. 1978. "A Death in Rome." *Newsweek,* 9 October.

Watts, A. M. 1989. "Christian Claims in a Pluralistic Society." *Christian Century* 106 (1 March): 222–23.

Weakland, Rembert G. 1992. "Crisis in Orthodox-Catholic Relations: Challenge to Hopes." *America* 166 (25 January): 30–35.

Weaver, Mary Jo. 1985. *New Catholic Women.* San Francisco: Harper and Row.

Webster, Alexander F. C. 1996. "Split Decision: The Orthodox Clash over Estonia." *Christian Century* 113 (5 June): 614–23.

Welsh, John R. 1986. "Comunidades Eclesiais de Base: A New Way To Be Church." *America* 154 (8 February): 85–88.

Whelan, Charles M. 1974. "Divorced Catholics: A Proposal." *America* 131 (7 December): 363–65.

Whitney, Craig R. 1995. "Thousands in France Protest Dismissal of Leftist Bishop." *New York Times,* 23 January.

———. 1996. "French Bishop Supports Some Use of Condoms to Prevent AIDS." *New York Times,* 13 February.

Wilkinson, Tracy, and Richard Boudreaux, "Pope Ignores Evidence of Assassination Plot in Bosnia." *Los Angeles Times,* 13 April.

Willems, Ad. 1987. "The Endless Case of Edward Schillebeeckx." In *The Church in Anguish,* 212–22. See Küng and Swidler 1987.

Williams, Bruce. 1987. "Homosexuality: The New Vatican Statement." *Theological Studies* 48 (June): 259–77.

Williams, Dolores S. 1996. *Sisters in the Wilderness: The Challenge of Womanist God-Talk.* New York: Orbis Books.

Willke, Joseph J. 1984. "The Worker-Priest Experiment in France." *America* 150 (3 April): 253–257.

Windsor, Pat. 1989. "Häring Fears 'Psychological Exodus' from Church." *National Catholic Reporter* 25 (28 April): 5.

———. 1990a. "Weakland Advises U.S. Bishops to Drop Women's Pastoral." *National Catholic Reporter* 26 (18 May): 3.

———. 1990b. "Vatican Vetoes Doctorate for Weakland." *National Catholic Reporter* 27 (16 November): 1, 8.

———. 1990c. "Theologians' Statement Benign Yet Critical of Vatican." *National Catholic Reporter* 27 (21 December): 9.

———. 1991. "Neoconservatives Capitalize on Papal Encyclical." *National Catholic Reporter* 27 (17 May): 3.

Winiarski, Mark. 1977. "Theologians Debate Resolutions on Sex Report." *National Catholic Reporter* 13 (1 July): 1, 6.

———. 1979a. "Vatican Chides 'Human Sexuality' Authors." *National Catholic Reporter* 15 (29 July): 4, 20.

———. 1979b. "Pope Didn't Boost, Harm Ecumenism." *National Catholic Reporter* 15 (19 October): 15.

Wink, Walter. 1979. "Biblical Perspectives on Homosexuality." *Christian Century* 96 (7 November): 1082–86.

Winter, Art. 1975. "Doctrinal Stands Lurk Below 'Usual Reasons' for Mass-going Dropoff." *National Catholic Reporter* 12 (31 October): 4.

Wirpsa, Leslie. 1992a. "Rome Sails into Carribbean against the Wind." *National Catholic Reporter* 29 (23 October): 11–14.

———. 1992b. "Curia Ignites Angry Protest at CELAM IV." *National Catholic Reporter* 29 (6 November): 12–13.

———. 1993a. "Hints of Ecclesial Self-Criticism Disappear." *National Catholic Reporter* 29 (22 January): 13.

———. 1993b. "After 25 Years Medellín Spirit Lives, No Thanks to Vatican." *National Catholic Reporter* 29 (15 October): 11–13.

Wojtyla, Karol. 1981. *Love and Responsibility.* New York: Farrar, Straus, Giroux.

Wooden, Cindy. 1995. "Vatican Quiet on Final Document in Beijing." *National Catholic Reporter* 31 (22 September): 13.

———. 1996. "Pope Issues Document on Religious Life." *National Catholic Reporter* 32 (12 April): 7.

Woodward, Kenneth. 1983. "Luther in Excelsis." *Notre Dame Magazine* 12 (October): 11–15.

———. 1996. "Gender and Religion." *Commonweal* 123 (22 November): 9–14.

Woodward, Kenneth, and Margaret Moorman. 1984. "The Sexuality of Christ." *Newsweek,* 23 April.

Woodward, Kenneth, Rod Nordland, and Fred Coleman. 1989. "The Highest Summit." *Newsweek*, 11 December.

World Council of Churches. 1982. *Baptism, Eucharist and Ministry.* Geneva: WCC.

Wynn, Wilton. 1988. *Keepers of the Keys.* New York: Random House.

Yallop, David A. 1984. *In God's Name.* New York: Bantam Books.

Young, James J. 1978. "Six Factors in a Climate of Change." *America* 139 (18 November): 347–51.

Ziengenhals, Gretchen E. 1989. "Meeting the Women of Women-Church." *Christian Century* 106 (10 May): 492–94.

Index of Subjects

Index of Personal Names

Abbott, Walter M., ix, 77
Ahern, Barnabas, 385
Alexsie II, Patriarch,188, 190
Alfrink, Bernard, 323
Ali Agca, Mehmet, 19
Anselm of Canterbury, 120
Anthony, Susan B., 395
Aquinas, Thomas, 23, 43, 49, 300, 346, 373, 407, 418, 448, 453
Aristotle, 23, 29, 31, 46, 276, 302, 407
Arrupe, Pedro, 107
Athenagoras, Patriarch, 60, 186
Augustine of Hippo, 96, 169, 221, 300, 346, 366, 373

de Balaguer, Josemaría Escrivá, 115
Balasuriya, Tissa, 163-64, 389-90
Barth, Karl, 124, 381
Bartholomeos I, Patriarch, 189
Baum, Gregory, 71-72, 127, 162, 184, 202, 266, 273, 285, 287, 297, 298, 357, 362-63, 436
Bea, Augustin, 50, 181, 183
Beauduin, Lambert, 214
Bellah, Robert, 36
Bellarmine, Robert, 87
Belloc, Hilaire, 82
Bernardin, Joseph, 133-38, 316
Berry, Jason, 300-1
Billings, John and Evelyn, 329
Blake, Eugene Carson, 182, 186
Boff, Leonardo, 137, 273, 287-88, 296
Bokenkotter, Thomas, 2, 254
Bonaventure, 50, 104, 122, 373
Boniface VIII (1294-1303 papacy), 216